DECISIVE ENCOUNTERS

DECISIVE ENCOUNTERS

THE CHINESE CIVIL WAR,

1946-1950

Odd Arne Westad

Stanford University Press, Stanford, California   2003

951.042
W522d
2003

Stanford University Press
Stanford, California
© 2003 by the Board of Trustees of the
Leland Stanford Junior University

Printed in the United States of America

Westad, Odd Arne.
  Decisive encounters : the Chinese civil war, 1946-1950 /
Odd Arne Westad.
    p. cm.
  Includes bibliographical references and index.
  ISBN 0-8047-4478-5 (cloth : alk. paper) —
  ISBN 0-8047-4484-X (pbk. : alk. paper)
    1. China—History—Civil War, 1945–1949. 2. China—Politics and
government—1945–1949. I. Title: Chinese civil war, 1946–1950. II. Title
  DS777.54.W463   2003
  951.04'2—dc21   2003000527

Typeset at Stanford University Press in 10/13 Sabon

Original printing 2003

Last figure below indicates the year of this printing:
12 11 10 09 08 07 06 05 04 03

Frontispiece: Ren Han, "Assault Section"

This is Jenny's book

Acknowledgments

This book started out as a series of lectures that I gave in Oslo and in Hong Kong in 1993–94, and it was first written up as a text during a sabbatical in Cambridge in 1997. Since then, it has been revised (and revised again) with the inclusion of much new Chinese and Russian source material, and has—by the help of a number of better craftsmen—found its present form.

First and foremost I am grateful to my students in Oslo, Hong Kong, and now in London for asking the questions that set someone who regards himself primarily as an historian of international affairs on the track of exploring a Chinese revolution. By forcing me to reflect on connections between the domestic and the international, and by asking questions about motives and causes that I found hard to answer, my students in a very direct way got this book started.

Another primary debt of gratitude is to those many scholars in the field of Chinese history on whose work this book is based. Without the numerous studies that have appeared over the last decade, detailing the most diverse aspects of life in China in the late 1940s, it would have been impossible for anyone even to attempt writing a new survey history of the civil war era. I am particularly thrilled, and at times even slightly overwhelmed, by the blossoming of studies on this period in China itself, on both sides of the Taiwan Strait. As should be obvious to the reader, these new works from China have influenced my understanding of the period to a very large degree.

There is a very long list of institutions and individuals who have, at different stages, helped get this book off the ground. I am especially grateful to the staff of the Norwegian Nobel Institute, and its director, Geir Lundestad, for assisting me in multiple ways during my time in Oslo. The Nobel Institute Library and its head librarian, Anne Cecilie

Kjelling, provided me—and I think everyone who has worked there—with a pattern of what the services of a good research library should be. In Hong Kong, the Centre of Asian Studies at Hong Kong University and Lingnan College both provided excellent working facilities. My colleagues at the London School of Economics have been very supportive in the latter phases of the work. And in Cambridge, then as now, the Master and Fellows of Corpus Christi College offered their hospitality when most needed.

In Oslo, Yao Xiaoling and Liao Ran provided research assistance well beyond the call of duty.

I have also been fortunate enough to have been helped, at various stages of this work, by the staffs of Peking University Library, National Beijing Library, the Institutes of American Studies and of Modern History at the Chinese Academy of Social Sciences (Beijing), the Institute of Modern History at Academia Sinica (Taibei), the Guomindang Party Archives (Taibei), the Foreign Ministry Archives (Taibei), the Number Two (Republican Era) Archives (Nanjing), the Universities Service Centre (Hong Kong), the Hong Kong Municipal Library, the Fairbank Center Library at Harvard University, the Harvard-Yenching Library, the Library of Congress, the Foreign Policy Archives of the Russian Federation (Moscow), the Russian State Archive of Social and Political History (Moscow), the British Library, Cambridge University Library, and the Library of the School of Oriental and African Studies at the University of London.

A number of friends and colleagues have generously set off time to share their knowledge with me as I was working on this project. They include Jung Chang, Chen Yung-fa, Sergei Goncharenko, Jon Halliday, Nancy Hearst, Dieter Heinzig, Jing Huang, Michael Hunt, Jin Chongji, William Kirby, Li Haiwen, Li Danhui, Liu Hsiang-wang, Vladimir Miasnikov, Shen Zhihua, Michael Sheng, Shi Yinhong, the late R. B. Smith, Tao Wenzhao, Frederick Teiwes, Sergei Tikhvinsky, Haruki Wada, David Wolff, Xu Yan, Yang Kuisong, Joseph Yick, Zhang Baijia. and Shu Guang Zhang.

I am particularly grateful to Lucien Bianco, Chen Jian, Niu Jun, Hans van de Ven, and Wang Chaoguang, who altruistically agreed to read and comment on all or parts of the manuscript before publication. Their friendly and incisive advice was crucial to the book (though not on all occasions in a form they would recognize).

As always, Ingunn, Anders, and Jenny have assisted in ways more numerous than I can tell—and this *is* Jenny's book.

Contents

A Note on Transliteration and Usage xi

Introduction 1

1. East Asian Cockpit: The Aftermath of World War II 17

2. Two Bridges: The Outbreak of Civil War 35

3. Takeovers: Resurrecting the Guomindang State 69

4. Adjusting Heaven: Communist Rule in the Provinces 107

5. Into the Cauldron: The Guomindang
Offensives 147

6. The Turn: Battlefields of the North 181

7. The Chase: Crossing the Yangzi 215

8. To Tian'anmen: Constructing New China 259

9. To the Yalu River: New China and the World 297

Postscript: The Chinese Civil War Today 327

Notes 333

Studying the Chinese Civil War: A Brief Bibliography 383

Index 403

Maps

1. Areas of Communist Control, 1945 37

2. Manchuria, 1945–47 156

3. North China, 1948 200

4. South China, 1949 283

5. East China and the Taiwan Strait, 1949–50 298

6. Western China, 1949–51 300

A Note on Transliteration and Usage

This book uses *hanyu pinyin* (Chinese phonetic alphabet) throughout for romanizing Chinese names, terms, and expressions, since it is felt that consistency will be of help to the reader who is not familiar with Chinese script. While not necessarily linguistically superior to other systems, *pinyin* has become the standard for the transliteration of Chinese into English and other languages written in the Roman alphabet, and it is gradually being introduced in reference works and library catalogs everywhere. The use of *pinyin* means that a few personal names more well known to Western readers in various other transcriptions may look slightly unfamiliar when first encountered here. To help in identification, such names are always introduced with older transliterations in brackets, and the index includes alternative spellings for the names of all non-Communists from the Republican era.

To assist Western readers, the book also uses contemporary identifications for place names and provinces in China. For example, Beijing (Northern Capital) keeps its name throughout, even though it was officially renamed Beiping (Northern Peace) during the Republican Era in China.

DECISIVE ENCOUNTERS

INTRODUCTION

The Chinese civil war was one of the key conflicts of the twentieth century. Its Communist victory determined the framework of Chinese history for several generations, and defined international affairs in East Asia during the Cold War and afterward. Its battles were the largest military engagements following World War II, with profound effects on the societies that suffered through them. For good reason, memories of the war strongly influenced the thinking and behavior of most Chinese who experienced it, and helped to frame the mindsets of their children, who encountered these memories as myth or as political coda. Thus, the encounters of the civil war—between armies, classes, and nations—decided a course for the future.

The purpose of this volume is to summarize what we know about the history of the civil war, half a century after its end. The main emphasis is on the political and military history of the war, but there are also excursions into the social and cultural aspects of the period in which it was fought. The late 1940s was a period of great transformation in China, not just in terms of changing political power but also through more subtle changes in the way people perceived their own roles in society, in public forums, at work, or in the family. The present survey tries to integrate accounts of these rearrangements with presentations of high politics and warfare.

The international history of the Chinese civil war plays an important role in this book. Civil wars are almost never purely domestic; they influence and are influenced by foreign states and societies, as well as participants coming in from the outside, often to such an extent that the borders between the internal and the external blur and fade away. This account attempts to see the Chinese civil war in such a larger perspective, telling its history both as Chinese experience and as a narrative of revolution with participants from many countries and continents.

Chinese Revolution and Other Revolutions

As a survey history of the Chinese civil war, this book builds on several noteworthy predecessors. The English-language historiography of the war goes back to eyewitness accounts and contemporary war histories of the late 1940s and early 1950s, by intrepid reporters such as Anna Louise Strong, Jack Belden, Harrison Forman, Freda Utley, Annalee Jacoby, and Theodore White.[1] It was in the 1960s, however, that the civil war got its first major chroniclers, with Tang Tsou's history of U.S. involvement with the warring Chinese factions (1963) and with the 1965 translation into English of Lionel Chassin's military history of the war, originally published in French in 1952.[2] Lucien Bianco's interpretative history of the whole span of the Chinese revolution, published in English translation in 1971, remains even today the benchmark study of the historical causes of the Communist victory.[3]

Much in response to the U.S. war in Indochina, the trickle of interest in the Chinese revolution in the 1960s became a flood in the 1970s. A substantial part of this literature explored the growth in popular support for the Chinese Communist Party (CCP) during and immediately prior to the 1937–45 war against Japan. The debates connected to this issue—on the relative importance of land reform and nationalism; on the role of the United Front as a temporary alliance between the Nationalists (the Guomindang, or GMD) and the CCP; and on CCP military strategies—remain important today. Often, however, these historians avoided covering the post-1945 civil war directly, believing that the main explanations for why the Guomindang lost were to be found in earlier periods. Lloyd Eastman, who in his own work did link pre- and postwar events, confirmed the general trend by calling the second volume of his GMD history *The Seeds of Destruction*. Suzanne Pepper, the author of what is certainly still the best political history of the civil war in English, was one of the few dissenting voices, stressing the importance of GMD failures in 1946 and 1947 to the final outcome.[4]

In the 1980s and 1990s, work on the history of the Chinese revolution became both deeper and broader. The political conclusion of the revolutionary phase in the People's Republic of China and the end of the GMD dictatorship on Taiwan started making archival sources available, while a rapidly increasing number of Western scholars trained in the Chinese language and culture could join Chinese scholars freed from dictatorial controls to explore the period. The new sources created an explosion of work on local and regional aspects of the revolution and the history of the CCP. Suddenly, almost every town and valley seemed to have their own very diverse revolutionary histories, as Chinese local historians passed from a hagiographic to a critical stage of scholarship.[5]

These changes to the circumstances of the study of the Chinese revolution also influenced the way we came to see the events themselves. The history of the revolution became more China-centered, with less emphasis on foreign influences and more on locally determined conditions, making it possible to see its various societal or ecological connections. It also became more comparative with regard to other periods of Chinese history, with several scholars attempting to look at differences and similarities between the CCP revolution and peasant-based rebellions against the Qing Dynasty, or even at how community-based memories of these failed uprisings may have inspired allegiance to the CCP cause. In the 1990s, as debates emerging from historical literature written in Chinese began blending with those from literature in English to—for the first time—form one field of study, the history of the revolution seemed set to gain both methodologically and interpretatively.[6]

Another avenue through which the study of the Chinese revolution has gained new vistas is created by recent theoretical advances. As a historian, I am a firm believer in the adage, often attributed to E. H. Carr, that theory without history is barren, and history without theory is blind. The causes of events are found in their specific circumstances, and the job of the historian is to discover links between events and to unravel the webs that tie them together. But theoretical explanations of general trends help historians to ask questions that can put them on the right track to new discoveries. The new sociological and anthropological literature on revolutions counts among the most substantial advances in these fields over the past generation, with fieldwork in the most unlikely of locales opening up possibilities for useful comparisons and general insights. I have benefited much from this still emerging literature in framing my key questions.

Works on relative state weakness as a cause of revolutionary change have been particularly important in informing the background for my conclusions. Structuralist approaches—such as those by Theda Skocpol or Jack Goldstone—view the recognized purposes of the state, and its degree of success in representing key elites, as its main weapons in defending itself against enemies. If the state lacks flexibility in creating internal and external alliances, it will gradually lose out, because the existence of the state becomes less relevant for the groups in society that clothe its soldiers and feed its bureaucrats. Increasingly, it will be unable to defend itself against pressures from either abroad or within.

As shown in recent literature—for instance on the Iranian revolution—a Third World state that has embarked on a project of extending its role in society may be particularly vulnerable to this form of weakening support and the resulting loss of legitimacy. If the leadership is not able to create domestic or comprehensive foreign alliances supportive of its project, then local or class-based resistance to the encroachments of the state may overwhelm it and stimulate its organized opponents. The reason for this dilemma is that most Third World states lack both a skilled administrative apparatus and a commonly accepted framework of duties and contributions by its citizens. It therefore does not take much attempted expansion to get the state into trouble, and its servants are often too few, too ideologically divided, too badly trained, or too corrupt to protect it.

Another reason why general explanations of state weakness as structural causes of revolution are particularly relevant for the late twentieth century is the peculiar shape of the Cold War international system. Unlike periods with a multipolar international scene, in which several great powers vie for influence abroad, the sharp bipolarity and the ideological character of the Cold War made it difficult for weak regimes to profit from making arrangements with both superpowers simultaneously. To make things worse for the state, the late-twentieth-century international system enabled revolutionary parties to find international alliances of their own, based on ideological commitment or simply through offering their services to the superpower with which the government they fought was not in alliance. An internationally recognized status could therefore be of scant use to a regime in fighting its enemies.[7]

Other general insights of relevance to the theme of this volume can be had from the sociological literature on war. The organizational and perceptual changes that accompany large-scale warfare tend to favor those institutions that are highly centralized—if they are also flexible and able to learn through absorbing the experience of individual units. The issue of how to feed an army's soldiers is a case in point: In a society of peasants, how to procure essential supplies can be learned only from below, at the unit level, and as a result of grasping the individual political and economic circumstances of a particular region. A state or a movement may, over time, learn general principles of procurement, but the lessons are learned locally. And in the fluid world of domestic warfare, rapid learning becomes essential, since civil wars always polarize society and may quickly negate set patterns of behavior. Lenin, for instance, argued that civil wars in themselves may be a revolutionary experience.

The debate on so-called peasant consciousness—an issue of great importance in the disputes of the 1960s and 1970s over the character of the Chinese revolution—took on a new character as it came under the influence of general theoretical and comparative scholarship on revolutions. Instead of debating anti-Japanese nationalism contra antielite land reform as the main causes of peasant support for revolution in China, more recent studies have tended to underline a mix of negative and positive factors, both push and pull, so to speak, often linked to the physical and ideological havoc of war, the manipulation of local peasant politics, or the absence of state power.[8] Several scholars, both Chinese and foreign, have recently negated the nationalism versus socialism debate by describing the purpose of the great majority of peasants as reactive—that is, as aiming at avoiding warfare and surviving its immediate consequences, rather than consciously committing themselves to the revolutionary cause.[9] What is certain is that, as in the French or Russian cases, the Chinese revolution operated within a wide and diverse range of consciousnesses. And instead of one main cause for changes in consciousness there were many, varying in importance geographically and chronologically across the whole spectrum of Chinese society and the timeline of the Chinese revolution.

The move away from monocausal explanations with regard to consciousness has led to renewed interest in the qualities of the revolutionary movement itself. What was it that preserved the unity of the Communist leadership (even when hard pressed militarily), developed the intense dedication of numerous cadres to the cause, and made a great many party members into effective propagandists? Inspired by research into the anthropology of leadership, some scholars now underline the charismatic character of Mao Zedong's political style as an important element in the party's successes. What happened during the ten years that the party's headquarters were based in remote parts of Shaanxi province—the Yan'an period, from 1936 to 1947—was a transformation from a Leninist to a charismatic style of leadership in which the cult of Mao's personality, the ideal of complete adherence to his instructions, and the belief in the myths and visions he developed gradually became the center of the party's existence. Although real disagreements existed—and were allowed to exist—among the party's top leaders, they successfully transmitted the image of the Chairman's attainments to the party faithful and to everyone with a need for something to believe in during troubled times.[10]

Viewing the CCP as a charismatic movement has created new questions about how the tools that welded the party together were honed during the Yan'an period and during the civil war. This has led to a re-examination of key party documents as pedagogic texts and of key party practices—for instance, rectification and self-criticism as devotional social rituals, or "exegetical bonding," to use David Apter's term. At the center of both texts and practices was Mao's extraordinary capacity as creator of myths about the party's past and visions of its future. By firmly fixing the party's mission within a larger teleological framework of China's "fall" and "resurrection," Mao created an effective rewriting of the party's troubled past and a powerful call to action on behalf of its future, which was said to be China's future. But his teleology also justified brutal sanctions against those within the movement who did not, or could not, adhere to all the truths validated by the Chairman.[11]

Compared with other twentieth-century revolutions outside Europe, the Chinese revolution is primarily distinguished by the ideological cohesion of the revolutionary leadership and by the size of its final military engagements. As one of only two Third World countries in which a Communist party by itself has won complete control through a military campaign—Cambodia being the other—China was influenced by an extraordinary set of domestic and international conditions that weakened the existing regime and gave advantages to a revolutionary party. The devastating effects of war, the state's limited capabilities, the localized resistance to state power, and the Cold War pattern of alliances are all features of twentieth-century revolutions that ought to be studied in a comparative perspective to the benefit of historians as well as social scientists.

Understanding the Communist Victory

Although I hope that this book and its findings will be used by theorists and those interested in comparative studies, it is not my purpose to test general theories, nor indeed to answer questions pertaining to the overall character of the Chinese revolution. Rather, the aim of this volume is to look at the rather neglected history of the 1946–50 civil war and attempt to understand why the CCP came out victorious. In order to do so, it is first of all necessary to grasp the fundamentals of the situation in China at the end of World War II. As will be seen from Chapter 1, I find that the state of affairs in China (and East Asia) in 1945 explains some of the general trends that in the end defeated Jiang Jieshi's (Chiang Kai-shek's) dictatorship, although it does not provide sufficient explanations to understand the 1949 debacle. Those explanations must primarily be sought in the 1946–50 civil war and the events that accompanied it.

The wartime causes that conditioned the outcome of the post-1945 civil war are mainly three, all linked to the effects of the Japanese attack: the accentuation of rural poverty, the crisis of massive collaboration, and the weakening of Guomindang state and party institutions. The impoverishment of rural societies in parts of China as a result of wartime dislocation and destruction provided the Communists with a social laboratory for land reform. The high level of collaboration with Japanese authorities, especially in the coastal cities, effectively split the prewar Chinese elites. And the onslaught of the Japanese army, against which it formed the main, but generally unsuccessful, resistance, reduced the GMD regime's reserves of military power, economic resources, and morale.[12]

The China and the Chinese government that was rescued from collapse by the U.S. defeat of Japan in the Pacific were very different from what they had been in 1937. Although there is no doubt that some of the Guomindang's postwar troubles—factionalism and corruption among them—had prewar roots, it was during the last phase of the world war that these ills reached crisis proportions. Faced with the last Japanese offensives and the Communist insurgency, the GMD leaders had neither the will nor the means to eradicate the rot within their own party. In terms of morale and organizational strength, the GMD was therefore ill prepared to take on the massive challenge of postwar reconstruction.[13]

But in spite of the Guomindang's weaknesses, the outcome of the postwar conflict with the Communists was in no way predetermined in 1945. On the contrary, the GMD possessed considerable advantages over all domestic challengers as the war with Japan ended. It was in control of the state, with its powers to tax, to conscript, and to appoint. Its government's legitimacy was widely recognized, both at home and abroad, mainly because of the stature that Jiang Jieshi had as the leader of the resistance against Japan. Its formal international position was strong, with comprehensive treaties with both the United States and the Soviet Union. Helped by the United States, the GMD armies had fanned out after VJ-Day in August 1945 to take control of all of the major regions in China south of the Great Wall, much to the disappointment of its domestic enemies and to the surprise of many foreign observers.[14]

The CCP, meanwhile, had major problems as well as successes coming out of World War II. Although its membership and the areas under its control had increased significantly during the war, the party's main forces were still located in northwest China, at the country's periphery. Its troops could in no way match the government's elite forces in terms of training and equipment, and although the main part of the GMD armies was not well equipped, their sheer numbers meant that the Communists could be outgunned and outmaneuvered in all major regions of the country. The failure to get Soviet support and the botched attempts at grabbing new territories after Japan's collapse disappointed many party members. In the cities, from which the industrial power of the country sprang, the Communist Party was barely represented at all.[15]

The story of the Chinese civil war is therefore not just a tale of the Guomindang's terminal decline and the CCP's irresistible rise. While structural causes help us to understand the framework within which decisions were made, it is on these decisions themselves that we must center in order to explain the outcome of the civil war. As told here, the civil war is first of all the story of how the GMD leaders, by their decisions, squandered most of the relative advantages they had in 1945, while Mao Zedong and his colleagues gained the minimum support needed first to survive Jiang's offensives against them and then, as the GMD weakened, to launch military strikes of their own.

The GMD made five major mistakes in the period from 1945 to 1948 that together explain the collapse of their state. Instead of repairing the cohesion among Chinese elites broken by the long Japanese occupation of key regions, the GMD leaders when returning to the coastal areas ostracized many businessmen, intellectuals, and civic spokesmen who had stayed on under foreign rule. By doing so, the GMD added vitally to the distrust against it in regional terms. But the party also alienated local elites in regions on the periphery, such as Manchuria, southwest China, and Xinjiang, by attempting to make them subservient to officials from the central government. Instead of strengthening the ties between these provinces and the center, the GMD policies probably weakened them, and made them more vulnerable.[16]

Jiang Jieshi's insistence on solving the conflict with the CCP through a military offensive in the late spring of 1946 was another mistake. Although the Communists' behavior in Manchuria was a major provocation to Jiang's ideals of national unity, his decision to use force put strains on government finances and on his system of international alliances that neither of them in the long run could bear. Having started the offensive, Jiang and his advisers also made several crucial errors in military strategy, the most important of which were not to pause to consolidate their gains in late 1946 and early 1947, and to insist on continuing to fight in Manchuria, even after the Communists there had gained the upper hand in the spring of 1948. Together with the tactical mistakes made in the decisive HuaiHai battles in late 1948, these strategic errors probably lost the war for the Guomindang.

Finally, the GMD dramatically weakened its cause by its inability to explore domestic and international alliances that could have strengthened its position, particularly during the crucial year of 1947. Instead of trying to broaden its appeal to urban elites or local strongmen, the GMD regime tried—unsuccessfully, as it were—to terrorize them into subjugation. Internationally, instead of making use of Stalin's uncertainties about the Chinese Communists, the GMD increasingly placed itself into a Cold War framework, in which, through allying itself with the United States, it would benefit from a U.S. victory in the coming war with the Soviet Union, just as it had benefited from the American defeat of Japan. But the substantial U.S. assistance for the GMD came too late to change its fortunes; by refusing to give in to U.S. pressure for negotiations in 1946, the GMD scuttled its vital alliance at the point when it was most needed.

If these were the main GMD losses, which were the CCP's key gains? Its main advantage was the extraordinary cohesion within the top leadership, which not only secured it from defections in difficult times but also greatly facilitated communications and top-level debates over tactics. Primarily a product of the charismatic style of leadership within the party, the identification with Mao Zedong among the top leaders helped preserve a unity of purpose and a unity of command that all the Communist Party's Chinese opponents sorely lacked. It was this cohesion, and the reliance on orders transmitted secretly, that gave many lower-level Communist organizations the flexibility they needed to successfully create temporary alliances and to manipulate local politics. By fitting into local struggles for power, land, and money—when needed, to the point of being all things to all men—the CCP managed to gain a following, build up influence, and survive through difficult times. Their local successes were also, however, dependent on their propaganda skills. By portraying their opponents as enemies of all groups of Chinese—poor and rich, peasant and bourgeois, man and woman—and itself as defender of the nation, the CCP skillfully managed to increase its support. It also—vitally—avoided having most groups draw specific links between the party's long-term ideological aims, its present practices, and their own aspirations. Lastly, the party was helped by its Soviet alliance, without which the crucial CCP counteroffensives in Manchuria in late 1947 and early 1948 would have been very difficult to carry out.[17]

But the history of the civil war is much more than just a unilinear timeline setting out the stages of the GMD debacle and the construction of the new CCP state. Until the CCP armies won the decisive encounters in the HuaiHai campaign in late 1948, the final outcome of the war was in no way certain. In military terms, the Communists as well as the Nationalists made grievous mistakes along the way, and, in spite of later myths, it would be true to say that the CCP's political subversion of the Guomindang did as much to uphold its victories on the battlefield as the military efforts of the CCP forces, the People's Liberation Army (PLA). During phases of all three major campaigns that the GMD lost—the battles in central Manchuria, the Liaoxi-Shenyang campaign, and the Huai-Hai campaign—the Nationalist armies could have seriously weakened the PLA had their leadership not committed crucial tactical mistakes, often the result of lack of coordination, regional political considerations, or rivalries between commanders. On the other hand, the CCP's own weaknesses—Mao's rashness and interference, their armies' lack of standardization, their generals' unfamiliarity with air and sea operations, and the limited tactical register of their troops—could have deprived them of victory even when the GMD had already been substantially weakened and demoralized.

The much-expounded land reform campaigns that the Communists carried out in the countryside also must be re-evaluated based on new evidence. There were areas and periods during the civil war when propagating radical land reform did help the party survive the onslaught of its enemies—for instance in parts of North China in 1946 and early 1947. But, on balance, its dedication to redressing the gross inequalities in land distribution in rural areas probably did the party as much harm as good in its military and political struggle to defeat the Guomindang. For the purposes of the war, what mattered in the villages was who supported and who opposed the PLA, and unless the local elites actively allied themselves with the Guomindang (which they rarely had any reason to do), the redistribution of land would be destabilizing and counterproductive. One of the reasons the CCP won was that Mao Zedong was brought to realize early enough—by 1947—that in the new areas the party controlled, the wartime policy of rent reductions and debt settlements was the maximum social program that could be introduced. Without this correction, the takeover of central and southern China—where rural social conflict was much less prevalent than in the north—would have been made much more difficult.

In spite of the party's "Mao-centeredness," it would be wrong to believe that, throughout the civil war, the CCP's leadership was always inwardly united on strategy and political aims. New materials show that the Communist leaders differed substantially among themselves on issues of how to conduct the struggle against their opponents and how to organize a CCP-led China. Mao's impatience with social transformation and his belief in the potential for short-term change in Chinese society strengthened his dedication to "sweeping the house clean": that is, to decisively defeat his enemies and to keep party ideals pure. More traditional Marxists within the leadership, such as Liu Shaoqi and Ren Bishi, underlined the limited nature of the national-democratic stage of the revolution, as well as the need for the Communists to show tangible results, to improve the lot of China's people, in order to win the war and successfully reconstruct postwar China. Throughout the civil war, men like Liu and Ren—firm believers in the need to improve the party's Marxist foundations and learn from Soviet models—were in the ascendance within the party, although always within the limits of Mao's supremacy.

An issue that takes on less significance in my interpretation than it generally has done is GMD economic mismanagement as a direct cause of its collapse. Granted, in part as a result of the wars it fought, the GMD government was unable to control inflation, which by mid-1948 had reached record levels. But very few Third World states embarked on projects of aggrandizement—which the GMD project might be called—have historically been able to avoid high levels of inflation, and most of these regimes have survived. Likewise, official corruption has (rightly) played a significant part in the public indictment of the GMD regime. But in terms of the regime's survival, it is uncertain how much harm corruption did. After all, most parts of the GMD government were not much more corrupt than significant sectors of today's mainland regime, which, although challenged, has so far been able to resist its challengers. Also, in the late 1940s neither increased inflation nor corruption had immediate significance in many of the rural areas where the war was fought, since these areas were still on the fringes of the market economy.

What lost the GMD government adherents in the cities and among elites elsewhere was not so much accusations of mismanagement as claims of injustice in terms of the established order. It was the aggressive GMD policies—administrative and fiscal—to exploit all classes of citizens for its own purposes that led to the breakdown of trust between Jiang's regime and those it had been seen to represent. When the government attempted to add taxes, monopolies, and levies to the burdens of elites already hard hit by the effects of war, while showing no sensitivity to their needs—for instance, in terms of local administration, communications, and credit—it liquidated the legitimacy it had gained through wartime resistance and prewar achievements. If the GMD regime had been a fully developed modern state, it might have been able to withstand this loss of legitimacy. But as it were, the regime attempted to lay claim to the prerequisites of a modern state without having developed the ideological or administrative framework for giving in return even the most essential services that modern elites need. It should not be surprising, then, that even among its former supporters the GMD state at the end of its existence came to be viewed as a brigand, next to which virtually any alternative focus of power would be preferable.

What the GMD attempted to do—facing the worst possible circumstances—was to extend the role of the state. The attempts were met by common resistance, both in the cities and in the countryside. As Ralph Thaxton has shown in his study of the local salt trade in western Shandong, at least some of the groups that in the end supported the CCP did so because it seemed the only way that their businesses could be protected against an increasingly predatory government. The Communists were very good at making themselves fit into the niches of legitimacy vacated by the GMD. The CCP's political strategy aimed at accumulating legitimacy in areas where it had had little or none. By the end of the 1940s, this strategy had done much to give it victory.

But even on this issue one should be careful about viewing the process as simple or straightforward. To a larger extent than most historians have noted, the CCP had rivals for the new positions it attempted to occupy. Even if the Communists' political strategy was their major asset, they could not alone control China's political agenda until they had taken power by military means. Right up to the very end of the GMD regime, there were other groups with alternative visions of China's future that commanded substantial support. These included liberal groups, factions of the student movement, regional organizations, secret societies, religious sects, and even factions in the ruling Nationalist Party itself. All of these third parties need to have their place in the history of the civil war.

In China's twentieth century there seem to have been two broad ideological trends at work—one localist and traditional, another centralist and modernizing. The Guomindang, while on the mainland, managed in the end to antagonize both, while the third parties were spread all over the spectrum between the two. The CCP, on the other hand, seemingly transformed itself from a Leninist party, via a charismatic sect, to a solidly centralist and modernizing national movement. It was the latter image that maximized its support in the late 1940s, although, as fifty years of CCP rule would testify, the party carried with it important aspects of its past. The irony of the civil war era is that the Chinese, instead of using successful resistance against state power to create more influence for themselves within the state, ended up supporting an alternative regime that was, if anything, more brutal and exploitative than the GMD had been.

1

EAST-ASIAN COCKPIT

The Aftermath of World War II

Hang Shangyi, "Ploughing in a Ricefield"

For the villagers of Siping County, some four hundred miles northeast of Beijing, the first months of 1946 had brought little good. "Year One of the reconstruction of China"—as the head of government Jiang Jieshi had dubbed it—had seen little but a succession of outside troops move through the area. The villagers viewed these soldiers as intruders, and whether they owed their allegiance to the Soviet Union, the Chinese government, the Communists, or no one but themselves was of little significance to the inhabitants of the Siping area. Many villagers had already started to look back to the time before the collapse of Japan with a certain nostalgia. In spite of their brutality, the Japanese officers had at least provided some stability to the area and prevented the constant requisitioning of the villagers' scarce supplies.[1]

For the peasants around the town of Siping, however, the spring of 1946 was to be the beginning of the most turbulent years of the century. As they attempted to plant their fields that spring, the first battle of the civil war was being fought right at their doorstep. Then, a year later, the Communists came back and turned the patterns of power and income in the villages upside down through land reform. More fighting followed in late 1947 as the CCP defended the area against the final GMD attempts to win it back. And then, after the new Red government had been set up in Beijing and the villagers prepared for their first normal harvest in years, the authorities marched off a large group of young men to join the army during the war in Korea. It was a time of hardships and terror, of surprise and almost disbelief in events as they unfolded. Most of all it was a time of profound and lasting change.

China and East Asia at Midcentury

At the end of World War II, all regions of Asia outside Japan were still predominantly agricultural. The great majority of people were peasants who practiced various forms of low-level farming, relatively untouched by capitalist markets. Very few of them had ever left their own district, or even their village, and their views of the world were dominated by local traditions and customs. Only a small percentage—in China less than a fifth of the population—could read, and a written culture played only a limited part in their daily lives. Their main social identifications were with family or clan, with village and local community, with religious congregation, and, in most parts of China, with ethnic group. In those areas where it did exist, this sense of ethnic cohesion was broad and usually comprised a vague definition of self as opposed to a more sharply defined other. In those few cases where a state based on ethnic foundations existed—such as in China or Thailand—very few of the inhabitants whose allegiance was claimed viewed the existence of the state as key to their self-definitions.[2]

In much of Asia, foreign colonial domination was a main reason why the state was only of remote concern to most people. Large areas—such as India, Indochina, and what is today Indonesia—had for a century or more been under the direct control of European powers that governed their politics and managed their economies. These appropriations during the eighteenth and nineteenth centuries had prevented indigenous states from developing, and created sharp divisions in status, income, and world view between small, urbanized elites that had become an active part of the colonial system and the masses of peasants that had not. The elites were trained to join in different forms of interaction with the foreign presence, but their access to foreign education also meant that they encountered ideas of emancipation and nationality emerging from the European revolutions of previous centuries. In many cases it was the younger members of these elites who formed the core of anticolonial movements in Asia.[3]

By the 1930s colonialism as an idea was in decline, both because of challenges from the colonized and because of problems within the system. The Depression had meant declining prices for the raw materials that Asia supplied to Europe and North America, and had therefore made direct foreign control less relevant in economic terms. Advances in technology had firmly anchored the more profitable production in the modern cities of the West, and made it more difficult to develop local industries. Finally, the confrontation in Europe between the main powers with dependencies in Asia—Britain, France, and the United States—and the authoritarian regimes in Germany, Italy, and the Soviet Union made colonialism less attractive as an idea. If London or Paris claimed to stand for freedom and liberalism on their own continent, how could they be seen to perpetuate a system of blatant bondage in Asia?[4]

Ironically, the last nail in the coffin of colonialism in East Asia came neither from anticolonial protesters nor from the European powers, but from Japan's attempts at creating a new empire for itself in the region. At the beginning of the century, many educated East Asians had seen the rapidly industrializing Japan as a model for how to transform their own countries. Some of these even remained to cheer as the imperial Japanese

armies attacked and crushed the power of Britain, France, and the Netherlands in Southeast Asia in the early 1940s. But for most East Asians any
identification with what Japan stood for had been demolished by the Japanese themselves decades before, as a result of their brutal colonization of
Korea and their increasing attempts at dominating China. And as Japanese imperialist dreams came to a halt with Tokyo's disastrous military
campaign against the most powerful of the Western countries, the United
States, during World War II, all over Asia indigenous elites hoped to fill
the power vacuum that a Japanese defeat would create.[5]

China had avoided being directly colonized by outside powers during
the nineteenth century, but in less than two generations it had nevertheless moved from being the center of an East Asian system of states to becoming an object of foreign domination. Beginning with China's defeat in
the Opium Wars of the 1840s, foreign powers had grabbed parts of Chinese territory for themselves. Along the coast and on the great rivers, a
number of cities had had foreign enclaves carved out of them: the so-
called concessions, in which foreigners could trade and run businesses
without regard for China's benefit or law. Foreign powers had repeatedly
intervened to enforce their interests or to influence Chinese politics: In
1900 foreign troops had sacked the imperial capital Beijing, and in the
decade following 1911 and into the 1920s, as China seemed to fragment
into warring factions after the fall of the Qing empire, foreign support
had time and again tipped the domestic balance of power.[6]

While the immediate effects of the weak Chinese state were mainly of
concern to urban elites competing for profit or power, the long-term consequences gradually became a problem for a much larger part of the population. As the Chinese state disintegrated, wars and armed conflicts occurred with frightening regularity on a national or regional scale.
Between the time of the civil wars of the 1850s and 1860s—the so-called
Taiping rebellion—and 1945, China had seen seven major wars and numerous lesser conflicts. Contenders for power had ravaged the countryside, especially in North and Central China, in search of resources—food,
manpower, recruits, animals—anything that could give them the upper
hand, or deny it to their enemies.[7] In the later decades, as the cumulative
effects of these campaigns became visible, observers reported that parts
of the country looked as if they had been repeatedly visited by swarms of
human locusts that descended on the villages and took away everything
on which the peasants depended—their tools, their seed, their crops, their
children.[8]

What made the effects of war catastrophic for peasants in some parts of North and Central China was the endemic rural poverty of those regions. While most Chinese peasants who escaped the repeated effects of war were neither better nor worse off than the majority in other parts of Asia—or, for that matter, than their forebears had been in previous generations—some areas suffered from a near social and economic breakdown as a result of being repeatedly deprived of the meager resources that in the past had kept them afloat. When war and banditry were added to the pressures already imposed on a fragile ecology by population growth, primitive technology, and soil erosion, the results were hunger and mass migrations—that is, the destruction of the world the villagers knew. In a country in which the average life expectancy was less than forty years for men, the wars and their effects could make off with the surplus on which organized society depends.[9]

In the areas hardest hit by successive wars, social exploitation intensified. In a political climate of chronic uncertainty—the army that commanded an area today could be replaced by another army tomorrow, or next week, or next month—the landlords and rich farmers found it increasingly difficult to retain their status. With their own position in danger, the rural upper class was often unwilling to reduce rents and interest rates to help the peasants who depended on them. On the contrary, in some areas of North China landlords attempted to increase the burden on the already impoverished peasantry.[10] These landlords had often already moved to the cities to be safer from the endemic warfare. Their links to their home villages made more tenuous, these landlords came to depend more on the capitalist market, and their expenses became increasingly influenced by inflation and scarcity. The traditional bonds of reciprocal loyalties between gentry and peasants that had mitigated social exploitation in the past dissipated, with cruel results for those at the bottom of the social ladder.[11]

Such increasing burdens fell upon a peasantry among whom oppressive social practices, inherited from the past, were still widespread. Debts could reduce poor peasants to slavery, sometimes for generations. Those who lost their plots of land or could not live off the land they had became laborers for others during the short periods of sowing and harvesting. During the rest of the year, they and their families were lucky not to starve. Some sold their children to work for others. Girls—always the most exposed in Chinese society—could be left to die right after birth, or could be sold to a brothel in a nearby town at the age of eight or nine. In such a society, the misery brought about in those regions hardest hit by the effects of war and instability was immense.[12]

This book will deal primarily with political, military, and diplomatic events going on far from the villages. Still, in order to understand these events it is necessary to understand the setting that made them possible. For China—and indeed for all of Asia—this setting was primarily villages and small towns serving as focus points for agricultural societies in different stages of penetration by the capitalist market. War was the agent that set off the economic depression and social instability that affected many of these areas at various times during the hundred years from the Opium Wars to World War II. In militarily contested areas, the different layers of society gave political allegiance to those they saw as their best bet for replacing depression with betterment, instability with social justice, and, most of all, war with peace. In the post-1945 civil war, which decided the outcome of a century of conflict, these issues would be of crucial importance.

Contending Nationalisms

If the setting for the decisive part of the Chinese revolution was the hundreds of thousands of villages on the North China plains, then the origins of its main contenders for power were in the big cities on the coast and along the rivers—in Shanghai, Tianjin, Guangzhou, and Wuhan—where foreign and Chinese influences had interacted for generations. Because of their semicolonial character, these bustling centers of trade and industry both attracted and repelled young educated Chinese; they were the symbols of their country's disgrace as well as the focal points for the ideas, the technologies, and the modernity that could save China.

In China, as in the rest of Asia, the ideologies of resistance to foreign domination and domestic chaos were formed in the colonial centers—and, by extension, in the faraway cities in Europe, Japan, and North America that they were linked to. The key ideas of the revolutionaries were often imports from abroad, filtered through images of one's country's past and one's personal experiences. At the beginning of this century, in the years immediately before and after the fall of the Qing, these ideas centered on some of the main themes of late-nineteenth-century nationalism in Europe: mass organization, regimentalization, and violent action. The production ideals of the factory and the machine were transferred onto human society in the form of a modern state. In Asia, the aim of many revolutionaries—and of quite a few of those who believed in gradual evolution toward independence—was to build a state as powerful as (or more powerful than) the imperialist states. Only through state construction could the Asian peoples show the potential of their nations.

Not many of the new generation of Asian leaders had much direct experience with the countryside in which the great majority of their countrymen lived. Their nationalism was filtered through what they had observed in the cities—the enormous productive potential of modern industry and technology, and the human suffering that followed from the capitalist system of production in the form it had taken in Asian cities. There was a striking contrast between the value of the goods produced and the fortunes made by foreign or local businessmen on the one hand, and, on the other, the hundreds of thousands of workers who labored ten to twelve hours a day for less than three dollars a month, and who often lived in squalid, company-run dormitories with dozens of men, women, and children to a room. The need for social justice inspired most Asian anticolonial elites, whatever their political orientation.

After the 1917 Russian revolution, Marxism in its Leninist form became one of the main ideological inspirations for Asian revolutionaries. Marxism promised independence, social justice, and modernity—the state and the factory in one package, so to speak—and held out the potential for an alliance with a powerful Western state: the new Soviet Union. The international organization of Communist parties—the Third International, or Comintern—put a high priority on Asia in its activities; the new Soviet leader, Lenin, famously said that "the destiny of all Western civilization now largely depends on drawing the masses of the East into political activities."[13]

However, only in one Asian country, Vietnam, were the Communists the leading party in the break from colonial rule or foreign domination. Numerically speaking, the great majority of Asian revolutionaries or reformers of the pre–World War II era were inspired by ideals other than Marxism. Leaders such as Mahatma Gandhi in India, Sukarno in Indonesia, or even Korea's Syngman Rhee—however different their ideologies—represented the broad mainstream of Asian nationalism, which combined modern ideals of state-building and nationhood with indigenous practices and rhetoric. Their ability to mitigate the harsh demands of the struggle for independence and social change with ideas that were immediately recognizable in a cultural sense to local elites, gave them tremendous advantages over those who were seen as purveyors of imported political or religious ideologies.

In China, the interplay between authoritarian nationalism and Marxism became a main element of the political struggle from the early 1920s on. In the Chinese intellectual flourishing that is often symbolized by the events of 4 May 1919, when Beijing students protested against the Versailles Treaty awarding former German concessions in Shandong to Japan, there was initially no sharp distinction between the two. The CCP, which was founded by Marxist intellectuals and Comintern agents in 1921, soon joined the main nationalist party, the Guomindang, as the minority partner in a revolutionary alliance directed against military power-holders accused of selling out to the imperialists. Only gradually did it become clear to the Chinese elites that the main struggle for power in the future would not be between the Chinese revolutionary parties and imperialism but between the revolutionary parties themselves.[14]

The Guomindang was founded by the nationalist leader Sun Yixian (Sun Yat-sen) in 1912, soon after the fall of the Qing empire, as a successor to revolutionary organizations he had directed from exile in Japan. Although it won the first national election in China, the Guomindang was soon shunted aside by military leaders from the former Qing armies, who themselves took power both in the capital, Beijing, and in the provinces. After the May Fourth protests, Sun saw his chance to return to the center stage of Chinese politics at the head of a militarized and radicalized Guomindang. In 1923 he set up a new government in Guangzhou, with a radical anti-imperialist program of national reunification. Sun, too, sought and got support from the Soviet Union, which supplied his government with weapons and money, and he coaxed the CCP into joining in a United Front with the GMD. Lenin and Joseph Stalin, his main successor, believed that the Guomindang leadership represented the "national bourgeoisie," and that their revolution had to precede any attempts to move China toward socialism.[15]

In 1925, just before his long-promised march on the North to reunify the country was to have begun, Sun Yixian died. His place as paramount leader of the party was soon taken by Jiang Jieshi (Chiang Kai-shek, in his own idiosyncratic spelling), the young military commander who headed the GMD forces already advancing toward the North. In part because of Jiang's talents as a military leader and the fierce loyalty he commanded among his officers, the campaign turned out a success. Against all predictions by foreign observers, who were used to writing Sun and his party off as revolutionary dreamers, by 1927 the GMD was in control of the rich coastal provinces, as well as the important cities of Wuhan, Nanjing, and Shanghai. Along the way, warlord armies—and their commanders—flocked to the victorious forces, and the Soviets, crucially, continued to provide advisers, weapons, and money.[16]

Jiang Jieshi, the commander who had given GMD victory, was born in 1887 to a merchant family in Zhejiang province near the port of Ningbo, a city that had had a British concession since the 1840s. As a young man, Jiang had studied in Japan, returning to serve in the anti-Qing revolution as a regimental officer. At thirty-five, after being sent by Sun Yixian to study military organization in Moscow, he was appointed head of the GMD military academy at Huangpu, near Guangzhou, from where he had planned the Northern Expedition, as the campaign to take control of China came to be called. As Sun Yixian's brother-in-law—in 1927, Jiang married the U.S.-educated Song Meiling, sister of Sun's widow Song Qingling—the young general felt a particularly strong personal attachment to the nationalist leader and believed that after Sun's untimely death he needed to take responsibility for the whole party, and not just its military affairs.[17]

As a leader, Jiang Jieshi has been aptly described, by the Indian diplomat K. M. Panikkar, as "a mass of contradictions—a Christian who believed in Confucianism, a democratic president who believed in military dictatorship, a scrupulously honest man who tolerated large-scale corruption among the people who surrounded him."[18] In his worldview, Jiang combined a strong attachment to modern ideals about the state and the army with an affinity to Chinese traditions. His aim was to unify China, rid it of foreign control, and help its economy advance to the level of the industrialized states through the benevolent guidance of the Guomindang. By nature a retiring and aloof man, Jiang, with the success of the Northern Expedition, formed a strong belief that he himself was the ultimate carrier of China's fate—that he could not fail, for if he did, China would fail. Always a ruthless political infighter, he now embarked on a program of introspection and the creation of rigid rules of self-control that he believed would give him the moral rectitude he needed to defend the revolution and defeat its enemies. For Jiang, these enemies were anyone who threatened the supremacy of the GMD or his own supremacy within the party. The outcome for China, the General believed, would depend on his abilities and his courage.[19]

The conquest of Shanghai in 1927 strained to the breaking point the

---

Jiang Jieshi and Song Meiling Meet Foreign Diplomats

At five the next afternoon, the President's secretary escorted us to the residence. We passed several sets of guards and were asked to be seated on the shaded porch so that our arrival could be announced. In a few moments, we were taken into the main reception room. The Generalissimo was in his uniform. He stood to greet us and shake hands. He looked young and alert but seemed definitely nervous. When he listens to what is being said, he keeps up a continuous "Hm, hm, hm, ha, ha, ah." He hesitates frequently, as if searching for the right term. He has a pleasant, winning smile.

Suddenly Mme. Chiang walked in. We stood up. The Generalissimo was called away on some urgent matter, and she took his place, the conversation continuing in English. She is a very impressive woman. She speaks English with an Eastern American accent. When the Generalissimo returned, she acted as interpreter, speaking to him with a Shanghai accent, although her Mandarin is perfect. She is quite bitter about the Communists, and her eyes flashed when she denounced them.

From Chester Ronning's autobiography. Ronning grew up in China and later served there as a Canadian diplomat. Chester Ronning, *A Memoir of China in Revolution: From the Boxer Rebellion to the People's Republic* (New York: Pantheon Books, 1974), pp. 113–14.

---

relationship between Jiang Jieshi, his supporters, and the Communists. In spite of his grudging respect for the Soviet Union, Jiang had always been suspicious of the CCP, forming, as it did, a party within the GMD. Before marching on Shanghai, the General had had a falling out with the GMD government, now at Wuhan, which Jiang accused of being too subservient to the Communists. In Shanghai itself, the leftists and Communists had mobilized some of the newly formed trade unions ahead of the arrival of the GMD troops, and while having given substantial aid to the military takeover, the trade unions and the CCP formed an immediate threat to Jiang's power as soon as the military conquest was completed. In April 1927, after negotiating temporary alliances with the city's foreign concession-holders and the main secret societies, Jiang turned on the Communists. Thousands were killed in Shanghai and in other cities as the conflict intensified. In the end the Communists and their Wuhan allies were no match for Jiang's troops. By the end of 1928, North China and Manchuria had joined the GMD bandwagon, and Jiang Jieshi had set up his capital in Nanjing, making himself Chairman of the State Council of an internationally recognized Republic of China.[20]

The so-called Nanjing decade, the ten years of Guomindang rule that followed Jiang's victory in Shanghai, was the first period of relative peace China had known for almost a century. While politics were kept in tight rein by Jiang and his associates, the urban economy slowly began picking up, helped by foreign investments. In the countryside, while little was done to solve the long-term problems of the peasants, most regions could at least sow and harvest unhindered by war. But the potential of both the urban and the rural economies was held back by Jiang's almost unlimited need for revenue to run the state and fight his enemies: former warlords, GMD rivals, Communists. The Nanjing decade was a period of slow and sporadic progress, in which Jiang's stature as the leader of China was enhanced by his abilities to outmaneuver and stalemate his opponents.[21]

For the Chinese Communists, the Shanghai massacres and the repression that followed had been a disaster. Having accepted the advice of the Soviets—in some cases Stalin's personal advice—they had not only been driven out of the cities but had also lost many of their best leaders. By 1930, Communist power in the country was limited to a few small bases in rural regions of South-Central China, the biggest of which was in the mountainous area between Jiangxi and Fujian provinces, where Mao Zedong at first headed a force of about fifteen hundred soldiers. Constantly harassed by superior GMD forces, the CCP in Jiangxi banked their survival on finding ways of redistributing land and lowering rents and interest, in return for manpower and supplies from local peasants. Still, by 1934 luck had run out for the Jiangxi Communists, and, fleeing from Jiang's military encirclement, they began the one-year, six-thousand-mile Long March across China that ended in a new base in Shaanxi province, ultimately centered on the town of Yan'an. Of the eighty thousand who originally set out—along with the many CCP followers who joined them during the first part of the march—fewer than ten thousand made it to the new base.[22]

It was during the Long March that Mao Zedong began to emerge as the leader of the Communist movement throughout China. Born in 1893 on a farm in Hunan province, Mao had run away from home to join the anti-Qing army in 1911, spending some time as an agitator for Hunanese independence before participating in the founding of the Communist Party. With little formal education, the young Mao had joined radical groups in Beijing and Shanghai before ending up as a propagandist for Sun Yixian's new government in Guangzhou. When the United Front drowned in blood in Shanghai and other cities in 1927, Mao was in the

---

Meeting Mao

Mao seemed to me a very interesting and complex man. He had the simplicity and naturalness of the Chinese peasant, with a lively sense of humor and a love of rustic laughter. His laughter was even active on the subject of himself and the shortcomings of the soviets—a boyish sort of laughter which never in the least shook his inner faith in his purpose. He was plain-speaking and plain-living, and some people might have considered him rather coarse and vulgar. Yet he combined curious qualities of naivete with incisive wit and worldly sophistication. . . . He had a deep sense of personal dignity, and something about him suggested a power of ruthless decision when he deemed it necessary. I never saw him angry, but I heard from others that on occasions he had been roused to an intense and withering fury. At such times his command of irony and invective was said to be classic and lethal.

From Edgar Snow's account of his first meeting with Mao. Snow, an American journalist, traveled to Shaanxi in 1936, where he interviewed Mao at length and spent four months with the CCP forces. Edgar Snow, *Red Star over China* (London: Victor Gollancz, 1968 [1937]), pp. 93–94.

---

countryside, doing Marxist analysis of the rural class structure. His rump CCP in Jiangxi was first laughed at and then ignored by many leading Communists and by the Comintern, but by 1930 he had become a leader by default as the urban CCP slid into terminal decline.

Mao's view of the world was influenced by his prodigal reading, his enthusiastic temperament, and his strong hatred for everything that in his view kept China down—imperialism, ancient traditions, and an oppressive class structure. In Marxism the young Mao found a tool to destroy all these ills and to create a just and modern society. While heading the Jiangxi Soviet, as the Communists called their meager base, Mao concentrated his studies on two issues: military tactics and strategy, which he learned from old warlord soldiers who had joined his forces and from Chinese military classics, and the transformation of peasant discontent into class warfare, which he learned by testing out different approaches on villages under his control. It was these lessons that helped the Communists survive on the Long March and in their new base area in remote Shaanxi, and which convinced most rank-and-file Communists that Mao was the only leader who had anything to offer besides repeated defeats.[23]

The Anti-Japanese War and Its Effects

The factor that prepared and conditioned the culmination of the GMD-CCP conflict was the Japanese attack on China in 1937. While Jiang Jieshi's regime had been quite successful in maneuvering between the Western powers and exploiting to his advantage their wishes for commercial opportunities in China, Jiang had much more trouble dealing with Japan—ironically, the only foreign country that he really admired. In 1931 the Japanese military had completely taken over Manchuria— China's Northeast—where Japan had had a strong influence since its war with Russia in 1904–5. In the following years there was fighting between GMD forces and the Japanese in Shanghai and in various areas of North China. Jiang came under increasing criticism—even within his own party—for not being robust enough in his defense of the country.[24]

For the GMD leader, the issue was not that he was unwilling to fight the Japanese, but that he wanted to buy time to create a more unified and better prepared China for a future all-out war. However time ran out for Jiang at the end of 1936, when he was kidnapped at Xi'an by his own officers, who demanded that he form a new United Front with the CCP and all other forces willing to confront Tokyo. Jiang, unwilling to bow to his captors, would probably have been killed if it had not been for the Soviet Union's asking the CCP to request his release. Stalin still believed that Jiang, as head of the GMD and symbol of the national revolution, was the only leader who could successfully spearhead Chinese resistance against Japan. By New Year 1937, Jiang was back in Nanjing, formally at the head of a new United Front but with few intentions of letting the Communists or his other rivals into the government.[25]

Then, in July, the Japanese launched a large-scale attack on North China, taking control of the entire Beijing-Tianjin region. In many ways this was the outbreak of World War II, and Jiang had no longer any choice but to resist. His armies fought with great tenacity both in North China and around Shanghai, but they were driven onto the defensive. In December 1937, Nanjing fell, and its civilian population, in one of the worst crimes of World War II, was made to feel the rage of the Japanese army. By the end of 1938 almost all of coastal China, north to south, was under Tokyo's control, along with all of its main cities. Jiang fought on from Chongqing in Sichuan province, convinced of the need to hold out until a war between Japan and the Western powers, including the Soviet Union, would save his country and his regime.[26]

The costs for China of this, its last war on its soil against foreign imperialism, were immense. Over the eight years that the war lasted, between fifteen and twenty million Chinese died as a direct result of warfare, and millions more were made homeless or had their livelihoods destroyed. In Shanghai, 50 percent of all industries were destroyed; in the state sector, which the GMD had wanted to make the mainstay of economic development, a national total of 55 percent of industry and mining, 72 percent of shipping, and 96 percent of the railroad lines were wrecked. In rural areas almost all regions were affected by the fighting, and the problems in agriculture intensified. The state was constantly short on revenue, and in spite of new taxes and levies, widespread requisitioning, and more than $1.5 billion in grants and credits from the United States, its income could not keep up with the turns of the money presses. In the gradually diminishing territories under GMD control, inflation rose to an annual average of about 230 percent.[27]

The Guomindang as a party was seriously weakened by the Japanese onslaught. Because of the war, Generalissimo Jiang—as he was now styled—concentrated his attention on the state and the conduct of military affairs, and had less time for the party and its organization. The attempts at forming the GMD into an elite party with a strictly hierarchical organization—on the model of the German National Socialists or the Soviet Communists—were dropped, and the party's policies suffered under the thousands of big and small compromises it had to strike with local power-holders. Corruption inside and outside the party became a major problem as inflation rose and central control weakened. The final Japanese offensives in 1944—code-named *Ichigo* ("Number One")—pushed Jiang's regime almost to the edge, depleting its resources and crippling its leadership.

The Communist Party was also profoundly changed by the war. From its main bases in Shaanxi, it made use of the collapse of GMD power to expand into other parts of North China, giving Mao Zedong—from 1943 chairman of the CCP Politburo—the opportunity of practicing his version of rural revolution in some of the poorest and most deprived areas of the country. Translating the Comintern's United Front policies into practice, Mao no longer redistributed land outright, but emphasized rent reduction and progressive taxation, which still benefited the poorer peasants immensely. The party set up local governments with a substantial participation by rich farmers and even landlords. By 1940 the party had about 800,000 members, and by 1945 more than 1.2 million. The war, and Mao's United Front policies, had saved the party from oblivion and made it a force to be reckoned with.[28]

But while the outward appearance of the Communist Party made it into more of a mainstream political organization, the inner life of the party, as it developed in Yan'an and other isolated strongholds, became increasingly oriented toward new political practices. The recently recruited cadres, mostly from peasant backgrounds, were instilled with a new version of party history that extolled the virtues of Chairman Mao and made the Long March and Mao's rise to power the parables through which the truths of Communism and the objectives of the party could be explained. The chanting of slogans and the public declamation of key texts were essential parts of membership inductions. All party leaders had to go through intense sessions of criticism and self-criticism, during which their previous "mistakes" were exposed and their loyalties to the party line and the Chairman were assessed. During the Yan'an period, in the words of one scholar, the CCP moved from being a Leninist to being a charismatic group, with Mao Zedong as the master narrator of the past, the present, and the future. For the party faithful, there was no alternative but to conform.[29]

In his efforts at securing the party's influence, Mao emphasized the role of propaganda above all else. Applying Comintern instructions to present its own version of the United Front as the true national resistance against aggression, the Chairman's aim was to portray the Communists as the real heroes in the war with Japan. The Communists persistently claimed that they bore the main brunt of the fighting, while, in reality, the one major CCP campaign against the Japanese, the so-called Hundred Regiments Offensive in 1940, was at least as unsuccessful as the GMD's many offensives. Communist guerillas did create difficulties for the Imperial Army in some areas, but the CCP did not come close to challenging Japanese power in the key regions of China. Still, in part because of the very visible failures of the GMD, Communist propaganda was quite successful. Many Chinese who saw the CCP from the outside during the war came to view the party leaders primarily as agrarian reformers and patriots—a completely new image for a party that in the past had been mostly known for its sectarian infighting and for butchering the rich.

In August 1945, as the CCP was planning how best to make use of the results of the *Ichigo* offensive for its purposes, Japan collapsed, broken by U.S. bombing. The suddenness of the collapse came as a near disaster for the CCP, as Jiang Jieshi used his international stature and close relations with the Americans to demand that the areas held by the Japanese be transferred to his forces only. Freighted by U.S. ships and planes, and assisted by Japanese officers, GMD soldiers fanned out to take control of most of China. The only glimmer of hope for Mao was in Manchuria, where Soviet troops had taken control after a brief war. But Stalin had little use for CCP forces in the Northeast, inasmuch as he had already secured an agreement with Jiang that gave the Soviet Union military and economic rights in the region. Still, after some hesitation, the Soviet leader permitted CCP troops to cross into Manchuria, primarily as a guarantee in case Jiang should renege on his promises.[30]

While strongly critical of the CCP's inability to exploit the collapse of Japan for its advantage—especially in the cities—Stalin told the Chinese Communists that their best hope for the future was through negotiations for a continuation of the United Front with the GMD. In spite of his doubts, Mao went to Chongqing for talks with Jiang Jieshi in late August, while the GMD, with U.S. logistical assistance, intensified its military pressure on the Communists both north and south of the Yangzi. By early November the fighting was spreading, and the CCP was desperately short of options. In October, Stalin had agreed to supply the Communist forces in Manchuria with Japanese weapons and limited amounts of Soviet supplies, but he had no intention of extending his support. On 10 November the Soviet leader instructed his assistants that "all our liaison officers and other people should be removed from Yan'an and the operation zones of Mao Zedong's troops as soon as possible. The civil war in China is taking a serious turn, and I am worried that our enemies would later blame our people in these regions, who are not controlling anything, as the organizers of the civil war in China. The sooner we remove them from there the better."[31]

In December, in a dramatic move to prevent a full-scale civil war and the increased Soviet influence he expected such a conflict to lead to, U.S. president Harry Truman sent General George C. Marshall, the wartime head of the U.S. Joint Chiefs of Staff, to China to act as mediator. Marshall's mission took both the GMD and the CCP by surprise. While Jiang feared that the U.S. envoy would prevent him from defeating the Communist challenge by force if necessary, Mao—told by Stalin that Marshall was in China to carry out a Soviet-American compromise over China— welcomed what he saw as a change in U.S. policy supporting the Guomindang.[32]

For a few weeks in the spring of 1946, after George Marshall had secured a cease-fire and a preliminary agreement on a coalition government, the question of war or peace hung in the balance. Jiang Jieshi was impatiently waiting for the CCP to give up their arms as part of a negotiated agreement; when the Communists stalled, he was held back from taking military action against them only by his U.S. allies. Mao and the Communist leaders were uncertain, unable to trust theory or previous experience in predicting the future and in deciding what actions to take. For a while in January and February 1946, they clung to their Moscow-inspired definition of the postwar era's being "a new stage of peace and democracy," in which "progressive forces" would gradually overcome "reactionaries" by peaceful means. But could the Communists put faith in their GMD opponents not to wipe them out while they were preaching peace? Their decision would be taken in Manchuria—the region in which the question of war or peace had been decided in the 1930s, and which in 1945 was under Soviet control.

In the spring of 1946, GMD foreign minister Wang Shijie thought that there were two bridges that separated peace from war in China. The first crossed the divide between foreign and Chinese perceptions of events in the country since the end of World War II, wherein Washington's and Moscow's view of China as part of a global power game was split from Nanjing's and Yan'an's prospect of their parties' positioning for national influence. The other was the bridge at Siping, the most important strategic crossing between GMD-held North China and the Communist-controlled parts of Manchuria.[33] At Siping—as elsewhere along the CCP-GMD divide—both parties were busy preparing for war, bringing in men and stocking up weapons and supplies in expectation of an all-out conflict that could come any day. The only barrier that protected these bridges was the fragile negotiations between the party leaders, and that obstacle would be in place only as long as the Generalissimo feared the international repercussions of attacking and the CCP believed that there was any peace in China worth rescuing.

2

TWO BRIDGES
The Outbreak of Civil War

Unknown artist, "Terror"

It was Stalin's policy that finally shattered the fragile peace General Marshall had set up. This happened not, as some scholars have argued, as part of a larger Soviet-CCP plan to bring down the Guomindang regime, but because of the timing of the Soviet military withdrawal from China's Northeastern provinces. The withdrawal, which was the Soviet leader's response to the stalled Sino-Soviet economic talks, was intended to destroy the possibility of a U.S.-led comprehensive peace settlement and to leave the CCP in control of as much of Manchuria as they could grab by their own force. Stalin's aims were to force the GMD to make economic concessions, to prevent a united China from allying with the United States, and to placate Washington on the international arena by giving in to American demands for withdrawal.[1]

Instead of achieving any of these aims, Stalin inadvertently set off a civil war that would last for four years and have consequences beyond what the Soviet dictator had thought possible. The problem was that Stalin's action made available to the Chinese the last, and possibly largest, prize in the contest for formerly Japanese-held territory just at the time when the peace negotiations had reached a critical stage. Jiang Jieshi's government was committed to taking control of Manchuria as part of its program of national unification, and Jiang viewed the Soviet withdrawal as his chance of achieving that aim. The withdrawal would also help him break away from the political straitjacket that Jiang felt the Americans had placed him in through Marshall's peace initiative. Jiang wanted the Communists to defer to his regime. If they would not do so peacefully, then he felt he would have to use military force, especially when a vital area like Manchuria was in the balance.[2]

For the Communists, their control of parts of Manchuria—and in particular of the Manchurian cities—was the main prize gained after the end of the war with Japan. Elsewhere the party had failed; only in Manchuria, with the GMD-government obstructed by the Soviet occupation, had the CCP gained substantial new territories. As GMD troops started advancing on these territories, Mao did not dare to place his trust in negotiations. In ordering the CCP armies to counterattack, the CCP leader knew that he was burying the chance for peace, even though some of his associates, like Zhou Enlai, continued for some time to hold to the illusion that civil war could be contained in Manchuria. "Everything is decided by victory or defeat on the battlefield[;] do not put any hope on negotiations," Mao told his Manchurian commander Lin Biao in late April.[3] As the British observer Michael Lindsey, who had served with the

CCP troops against Japan, put it during the postwar mediation: "The Communists were first rigidly conciliatory and later rigidly intransigent, and in both cases the rigidity was almost certainly contrary to Communist interests."[4]

The Soviet final withdrawal started in southern Manchuria on 13 March 1946. With both Chinese parties in doubt about the future of the peace negotiations, conflict was certain to ensue. On 31 March, GMD forces attacked Communist units at Siping in Jilin province in an attempt to break through to the provincial capital, Changchun. Mao responded by ordering Lin Biao, the commander of the CCP Manchurian forces, to counterattack at Siping and occupy Changchun and Harbin as soon as Soviet forces had left the two cities. Changchun fell to the CCP on 18 April, and Harbin, the industrial powerhouse of northern Manchuria, was taken by the Communists a week later. The Chinese government had had only a token military presence in the two cities, and most GMD officials chose to leave with the Soviets when they withdrew.[5]

Guns and Land: The CCP Strategy

The cheap victories in the very first weeks of the civil war convinced Mao that there was no need to return to the negotiating table—at least not yet. Instead he prepared for new but limited offensives in the North, especially in Manchuria. Mao and Lin Biao believed that the timing and sequence of the Soviet withdrawal from the Northeast had given the CCP critical strategic advantages over their opponents in this area: The Communists controlled the main routes into Manchuria; the main cities and county seats in central and northern Manchuria were in their hands; and—especially important—their supply routes were far better developed than anything the GMD could come up with during an invasion of the Northeast. Mao felt that the CCP was going from strength to strength in Manchuria, and that Lin's military achievements there were gradually dispelling the gloom that had spread among the party's military cadres since the defeats of the previous winter.[6]

Lin Biao, born in 1907 in Hubei province to a landowning family, had graduated from Jiang Jieshi's Huangpu military academy at the age of eighteen. During the CCP's Long March from Jiangxi to Shaanxi in 1934 and 1935 he came to prominence as commander of one of the two main military columns. Wounded in a battle with Japanese troops, Lin had lived between 1938 and 1942 in the Soviet Union, where he went

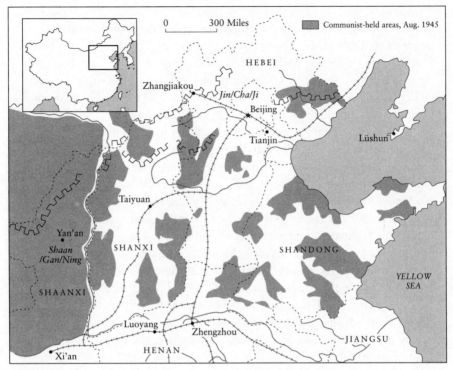

Map 1. Areas of Communist Control, 1945

through additional military training at staff level. A man of fragile temperament, Lin early showed signs of the depressions that would return to haunt him in later life. But during the civil war these weaknesses were more than compensated for by his remarkable gifts as a military leader—first and foremost his ability to quickly grasp the strategic dispositions of his enemies and to mislead them with regard to his own. Perhaps the peculiarities of Lin's mind—the sudden shifts from inertia to explosions of activity—helped him to take opposing forces by surprise when the strike came. Because Mao recognized Lin's brilliance—even when he was exasperated with his commander's occasional doubts and hesitations—Lin Biao was closer to the Chairman, in personal terms, than any of his other generals.[7]

In the rest of the country—except some areas of North China—the CCP held its forces in abeyance, still concentrating on propaganda work and attempts to expand its political control. Yan'an believed that the civil war would stay concentrated in the Northeast for some time, and therefore saw no need to develop a comprehensive defensive plan for the territories it held outside that region. In spite of his offensive moves in Manchuria, Mao still had one leg in the camp of the peacemakers: He would not completely let go of the framework for negotiations set up in early 1946, and ordered CCP units to complain to the U.S.-led truce teams when attacked.[8]

If Yan'an's military strategy did not change much in mid-1946, one of its political pillars did. The party's policy on land reform, which during the war against Japan had been a moderate one, emphasizing reductions in rents and interest rates, now changed into a policy of distributing land to landless peasants. The change in policy had three main reasons: First, the peasants' courage to take over land had increased, and the landlords' ability to resist such takeovers had diminished in many areas at the end of the anti-Japanese war. Second, there was a significant degree of expectation among party activists, particularly those recruited during the war, that Yan'an would initiate a more radical land policy as soon as the war was over. And third, the party leaders—and Mao in particular—realized the tactical advantage that a policy of land redistribution would give the party in case of an all-out civil war—not least in the areas the CCP had just taken over.[9]

Still, the party leadership had not forgotten the lessons learned from the failure of radical land reform in party-held areas before the war. It is telling that the CCP Center chose Ren Bishi—one of the main Marxist theoreticians in the party—to present the new policy. Ren was born in 1904 in Mao's home province of Hunan, in a well-to-do peasant family. He had studied in the Soviet Union between 1921 and 1924, was elected to the CCP Politburo by 1931, and had been the party's top representative in Moscow in the late 1930s. On several occasions during the party rectification campaign in the early 1940s, Ren had criticized the party cadres for not paying enough attention to Marxist-Leninist principles, although at the same time making sure to praise Mao's leadership. Ren was a close ally of Liu Shaoqi, and together these two leaders worked out the details of what became known as the Central Committees May Fourth 1946 Directive on land reform.[10]

The May Fourth Directive told the CCP cadres that they "should understand that a solution to the land question in the liberated areas is the basic historic task confronting the party and the main element in our work at present." Yan'an exhorted local leaders to "solve" the land ques-

---

Settling Scores: CCP-led Struggle Meeting
in Shanxi Province, 1946

At this critical meeting, Fu-yuan, the village head, was the first to speak. Because he was a cousin of Ch'ung-wang, his words carried extra weight with the rest of the village. When a man was moved to accuse his own cousin, the provocation had to be serious.

"In the famine year," Fu-yuan began, talking directly to Ch'ung-wang, "my brother worked for your family. We were all hungry. We had nothing to eat. But you had no thought for us. Several times we tried to borrow grain from you. But it was all in vain. You watched us starve without pity."

Then Ho-pang, a militiaman, spoke up. His voice shook as he told how he had rented land from Ch'ung-wang. "One year I could not pay the rent. You took the whole harvest. You took my clothes. You took everything." He broke down sobbing as a dozen others jumped up shouting. "What was in your mind?" "You took everything. Miao-le and his brother died." "Yes, what were your thoughts? You had no pity. Didn't you hound P'ei Mang-wen's mother to her death?" "Speak." "Yes, speak. Make him talk. Let's hear his answers!"

But Ch'ung-wang had no answers. He could not utter a word. When the peasants saw that he could not answer them, they realized that they had him cornered, that they had already won a victory. Many who had been afraid to open their mouths found themselves shouting in anger without thought of the consequences.

From William Hinton's account of land reform in China in the late 1940s. Hinton, an American sympathetic to the aims of the CCP, spent several months in one of the Communist base areas. William Hinton, *Fanshen: A Documentary of Revolution in a Chinese Village* (New York: Monthly Review Press, 1966), p. 134.

---

tion as soon as possible through transfer of land from landlords and, in some cases, from rich peasants to peasants who did not own land. It was important that the landless peasants themselves redistribute the land after holding mass meetings to criticize the landlords and deprive them of their political power. To the party leaders, the social and political disempowerment of the landholding class was as critical as the egalitarian principle of land redistribution: It was an act of creating allies (and enemies) in the social landscape of the Chinese countryside that, over time, tied some groups of peasants to the Communist cause.[11]

But the Central Committee's May Fourth directive was double-edged. While emphasizing the need for a revolutionary transfer of land controlled by the party, the directive also stressed that one should avoid the radical excesses of the early 1930s. In principle no land should be confiscated without compensation to the owner; industry and commerce should be "protected"; and the landownership of the middle peasants should not be violated. Even among big landowners the CCP cadres should distinguish between "despotic" and "nondespotic" landlords and local officials, and always make sure that the latter group was shielded from attack.[12]

The issue here, as CCP party leaders saw it, was the United Front—the strategy for gaining acceptance for party rule among landowners and bourgeoisie that Mao had developed from the Comintern model of the 1930s. Mao's model stressed the long-term advantages of cooperation between the CCP and "progressive elements" among the nonproletarian classes and their political representatives, while also underlining the tactical advantages the party got from such cooperation. Mao believed that the successes of the United Front strategy were a main reason for the party's expansion during the anti-Japanese war. Since the GMD had been as important a target for this strategy as the Japanese, it was a given that the Chairman wanted to continue to use the United Front as a powerful weapon in the new conflict with Jiang Jieshi.[13]

In the spring of 1946, both the United Front policy and the version of land reform that emanated from it were rather uncontroversial among CCP cadres. Most leaders saw these policies as continuations of the principles that had worked well during the war of resistance. In addition, they were backed up by Mao's prestige and by the political decisions the party had made during the negotiations with the GMD. But over the ensuing twelve months both moderate land reform and the United Front came under pressure. Some groups among the party rank-and-file grew impatient and pushed for a more radical land policy, especially in the newly occupied areas. Mao Zedong himself gradually changed his views, and—in contrast to leaders like Liu Shaoqi and, especially, Ren Bishi—increasingly began viewing the United Front as a mainly tactical instrument. And behind both these developments was the development of the war, which, by mid-1946, was not going well for the Communists.[14]

CCP Defeats and the Second Cease-fire

Some CCP leaders, Mao among them, had viewed the successful defense of Siping and the occupation of Harbin and Changchun as a stage-setter for further CCP expansion in the Northeast. This soon turned out to be a dramatic miscalculation: Reinforced by two GMD armies that the Americans had transported to the Liaoning coast, Jiang's forces attacked again at Siping in mid-May. The town and the strategic area surrounding it fell to the government on May 19. The CCP then quickly evacuated Changchun and Jilin, which both were taken over by Jiang's forces in late May.[15]

In Nanjing, the Generalissimo himself pretended to be above the fighting. On the evening of 22 May, as GMD forces were entering Changchun, Jiang told the U.S. mediator, General Marshall, that "he had not heard from his military leaders in Manchuria for three days."[16] He was worried, Jiang said, that his generals would widen their offensive in the Northeast, and he asked Marshall for an American plane to take him to Shenyang. From there he would be able to "get control of the situation."[17]

The Communist delegation in Nanjing, headed by Zhou Enlai, was getting alarming reports about the military intentions of the GMD in the Northeast. On 24 May, Zhou asked Mao for permission to make a new offer to General Marshall and the GMD, accepting a cease-fire based on the status quo in Manchuria and North China as well as a future military reorganization that would give the GMD control over all areas in the Northeast except Heilongjiang province. Zhou thought that Marshall was closer on many of these matters to the CCP positions than to those of the Generalissimo and predicted that the U.S. envoy would intensify pressure on the GMD to stop its advances in Manchuria. Mao accepted Zhou's recommendations.[18]

Zhou Enlai was one of the urban, Comintern-connected, CCP top cadres who had joined Mao's leadership group during the late 1930s and early 1940s. Skilled at negotiations and with a sure eye for public image and perceptions, Zhou became the main external conveyor of CCP policy during the civil war. Politically he was a moderate and a pragmatic—concerned not only with winning the war but also with postwar reconstruction. During the late 1940s he was never a main political decision-maker in his own right, and, although his views often coincided with those of Ren Bishi and Liu Shaoqi, he rarely voiced his own opinions on issues other than political tactics and always supported Mao's positions on matters of doctrine. Foreigners often found Zhou both agreeable as a person and reasonable as a negotiator—images that Zhou knew how to manipulate to his and his party's advantage.[19]

This time Zhou was right in judging Marshall's mood. The General was getting increasingly upset with Jiang's actions, which he regarded both as a violation of the truce and as a personal affront. With his acute

Jiang Jieshi on Mediation, April 1946

Now is the time to tell Marshall that the Americans should reconsider their policy on the Northeast and on the CCP and make a quick decision whether they would like to play an active role in East Asia or just a passive [role]. They should not repeat their mistake from 18 September [1937]—at that time, if the Americans and the British would have exerted some pressure on the Japanese, then the Japanese would not have been so rampant in their aggression. Now the situation is the same. The CCP could be scared by empty words. The Americans should help us prepare for war, if they really wanted to stop the Russians' ambition of expansion.

Entry for 29 April 1946, *Jiang chugao*, vol. 6, book 1, p. 126.

notion of military honor, Marshall understood that the Generalissimo made a mockery of his efforts at mediation when using a U.S. plane to go to Shenyang to direct the advance of his armies. He also realized what effect that and similar actions would have on Yan'an's trust in American motives. On 29 May, before he had received any new offers from the Communists, Marshall telegraphed Jiang, saying that "the continued advances of the Government troops in Manchuria in the absence of any action by you to terminate the fighting . . . are making my services as possible mediator extremely difficult and may soon make them virtually impossible."[20] It was Marshall's sharpest attack on the GMD to date, being intended to force Jiang back to Nanjing.

But Jiang had no immediate plans to give up his offensives against the Communists. The summer of 1946 saw the Chinese leader at the height of his power—Japan defeated, the Soviet Union out of Manchuria, and an alliance with Washington that solidified with every new twist in the tightening of the Cold War. On the home front his position seemed secure. He had forced his regionalist opponents to seek accommodations with the Guomindang, and he had balanced the influence of the party's own factions in ways that made any challenge from within seem futile. And most important, the Communists were on the run, as they had been before Japan interfered with his anti-Communist campaigns in 1937. As Jiang himself observed, by mid-1946 he was accorded respect as the national leader in a way he had never been before.[21]

Jiang did not intend his war with the Communists to continue beyond the destruction of their main military forces. He expected that after having understood the military power of the government and the earnestness of his own commitment to being accepted as the leader of the nation by all Chinese parties, the Communists would fold up their insurgency and seek accommodation with the GMD, as had insurgent parties before them. Jiang's long-term thinking on this, as on most other political issues, was determined by his odd mixture of Confucian attitudes and nontraditional political aims. The Generalissimo wanted to set up a new type of political organization of Chinese society, patterned to some extent on the Western ideologies of Fascism and Stalinism, with one political leader, a powerful, select elite, and a mass-party that could carry out the leader's commands in making the country rich and strong. But at the same time Jiang kept some of the Confucian ideals of his youth in his political practice: the belief in hierarchical and horizontal loyalties, and in the usefulness of compromise between men of sincere convictions.[22]

Jiang had not realized how harshly Marshall had reacted to his personal involvement in the GMD's Manchurian offensives. When the Generalissimo finally returned to Nanjing on 3 June, the U.S. mediator lambasted him for breaking not only previous agreements but also Marshall's personal trust. Jiang, on his side, termed the situation "a misunderstanding" and agreed to a two-week cease-fire to facilitate new negotiations. But he also made clear to Marshall that he expected the Communists to agree to his terms and that "this would be his final effort at doing business" with them. Upon returning to his residence later that night, Jiang conceded to his diary that he worried how much damage the wrongheadedness of the U.S. representative could cause to the Chinese government. Although increasingly confident that he had President Truman's support, Jiang believed that Marshall was a holdover from Franklin Roosevelt's administration and—like the late president—was someone who was quite willing to put the GMD at risk in order to reach a compromise with the Communists.[23]

When he met with his commanders the next morning, Jiang made it clear that he did not expect the cease-fire to last, unless Mao decided that his party had already taken enough of a beating. The preparations for war should continue, and although his generals should avoid direct clashes with the enemy for the time being, Jiang ordered the GMD forces in southern Manchuria and in Shandong province to improve their strategic positions. He did not believe that the Americans would put too much pressure on the Guomindang if only the generals did not behave stupidly or were seen to engage in too many antirebel operations within a short period of time.[24]

General Marshall was surprised and delighted that he had been able to force the Guomindang leaders to accept a truce. He had by now learned enough about the situation in China to realize that many obstacles remained on the way to peace, but at the beginning of June, for the first time in several months, Marshall felt that there were grounds for optimism. "This is a hell of a problem," he told his subordinates, "but we will lick it yet, pessimists to the contrary notwithstanding."[25]

What Marshall did not fully realize, however, was how the political ambiguity of the U.S. presence in China contributed to the "problem." Jiang and his generals expected to build on the anti-Soviet and anti-Communist rationale of the Marshall mission, and they could not understand that Marshall increasingly had come to view himself as a true mediator. The Communists hoped to use Marshall's mediation to get a break in a war that was going badly for them. But they also observed how the Americans continued their financial and military support of the Guomindang, and, in the minds of most Communist leaders, that fact combined with the fear of imperialism, Soviet allegations, and past experience to make them distrust U.S. motives.

Borrowing Marshall's personal plane, Zhou Enlai flew to Yan'an on 7 June, the day the cease-fire took effect, for the first in a series of summer meetings that would determine CCP political and military strategy. The meetings were often informal sessions of the Politburo, taking place in the front room of Mao's cave dwelling or in one of the makeshift assembly halls erected in the area where the CCP leaders lived. The debates were lively, and although Mao chaired most of these sessions, at least some of the other participants voiced opinions that differed substantially from the Chairman's own.[26]

The main division within the party leadership was on the prospects for peace. Ren Bishi and Liu Shaoqi held that the CCP should make further concessions in the Northeast in order to avoid an all-out confrontation with the Guomindang. Mao, supported by several of the military commanders, felt that nothing could be accomplished by yielding to GMD pressure. Zhou Enlai, as usual, took a centrist position, claiming that resistance in Dongbei (Northeast China, or Manchuria) would not mean countrywide civil war. It all depended on the attitude of the Americans, Zhou believed. In the end, Mao instructed him to fly back to Nanjing and test how far Marshall was willing to go in pressuring Jiang to continue the cease-fire. While preparing for a war that he did not want, the Chairman was willing to give Marshall one final chance to secure the peace.[27]

When meeting with the U.S. general on 10 June, Zhou Enlai emphasized the role of the United States in preventing the outbreak of large-scale fighting. "In order to eventually secure cooperation in certain things between the Kuomintang and the Communist Party," Zhou told Marshall, "it would be desirable to first secure cooperation between the Chinese Communist Party and the United States as a bridge."[28] During the crucial negotiations from 10 June to 26 June, Marshall could not build that bridge, because he was not willing to back up his threats to cut future U.S. assistance to the Nationalist government with promises to continue working with the Chinese Communists. Zhou reported back to Yan'an that the Americans had lost faith in their mediation and that not much could be expected from the negotiations.[29]

With the breakdown of negotiations in late June, Jiang Jieshi had once more avoided an American attempt to hem in his policy of confrontation with the Communists. The decision by the U.S. Congress to extend the lend-lease agreements with his government, of which Jiang was informed in mid-June, convinced him that the Americans would continue their economic and military support for the GMD. His most immediate challenges, besides planning the war, were to prevent Washington and Moscow from moving closer together on the China issue as a result of his intransigence and to prevent public criticism of his war policy within China, particularly in the cities.[30]

On the diplomatic front Jiang's tactics were twofold. First, he let his intelligence agencies provide the Americans with numerous reports about Soviet shipment of supplies to the CCP and Moscow's intentions to set up an independent state in North China. Second, he informed the Soviets that the GMD did not plan to undertake any major offensives in Manchuria for the time being—with the obvious intention of quieting Soviet concerns over their position in the Northeast.[31] In the cities, Jiang settled for a policy of intimidation against his opponents. The murders in Kunming of two prominent leaders of the Democratic League, Li Gongpu and Wen Yiduo, who had argued for closer relations between the League and the CCP, were turned into national causes celebres by Zhou Enlai's propaganda apparatus.[32]

First Months of War

As he often did when encountering opposition within his own ranks, Mao moved to the left during the discussions in Yan'an in June and July. From mid-June onward, the planning of war, not the bargaining for

---

Jiang Jieshi on Guomindang Aims, August 1946

We knew that the Communist Party was not an ordinary party with a democratic structure. It is a party with an independent military force, an independent administration. It taxes the people it controls and remains outside the authority of the National Government. . . . We must not permit another state to exist within our state, nor permit a private army to operate on the side of the national army. . . . We must have a deep understanding of the issues confronting our country and realize our responsibilities. We must put down rebellions, and make China a peaceful, democratic, unified, and strong country.

Jiang Jieshi's speech on the anniversary of the Japanese surrender, 13 August 1946, in *Zongtong Jiang gong sixiang yanlun zongji.*

---

peace, was what preoccupied him. On 19 June he argued to Liu Bocheng and Deng Xiaoping that "Jiang has made up his mind to conduct a total war; it is difficult to stop it. If we win big victories after the war breaks out, then we will be able to bargain for peace. If our victories equal our losses, [it is] still possible to bargain for peace. But if they [the GMD] win, there will be no hope for peace."[33]

While claiming that some form of political compromise was still his ultimate aim, the chairman spent the late summer of 1946 working out the CCP's battle plans in close cooperation with Lin Biao, Chen Yi, He Long, and other military leaders. The purpose of this strategy, which was formally adopted by the Politburo in late July, was to extend the CCP strongholds in Manchuria, defend the party's positions in North China, and withdraw from indefensible areas in Central and South China. The Politburo's directive drew on the party's experiences in the war against Japan, emphasizing mobile warfare and rural bases. It also underlined the need to isolate and defeat GMD forces in exposed areas, such as in parts of Shandong and Shanxi.[34]

On the Guomindang side, with plans for offensives already drawn up and with increasing support within the party for Jiang's hard line, July and August was spent implementing its military plans, while stalling the negotiations in Nanjing. Whenever meeting with his advisers, Jiang Jieshi admonished them that to "use force first" was the only way to overcome the Communist challenge.[35] His armies attacked Communist units in Central China and along the coast, with the hardest clashes on the Central Plains north of the Yangzi, in Jiangsu, and in Shandong.

The attack on the roughly forty thousand CCP troops in the Dabie mountains between Hubei and Anhui in late June was particularly worrying to Yan'an. The mountain region had been a Communist stronghold for years, and the CCP's local commander, Li Xiannian, had succeeded in generating much local support, as well as posing a permanent threat to GMD communication lines and to the city of Wuhan. Li, a forty-year-old former carpenter who grew up in Hubei, first tried to hang on, but Mao ordered him to withdraw. In July and early August, under constant attack by GMD air and ground forces, the remnants of Li's army slowly made their way westward, toward Yan'an. Less than half of them arrived safely at the central base. GMD losses were negligible.[36]

In a style reminiscent of his strategy during the Northern Expedition of 1926–27, after defeating Li, Jiang immediately struck in the other direction, toward the east. There, in northern Jiangsu, CCP general Chen Yi's forces had expanded considerably in the countryside since the Japanese capitulation. The forty-five-year-old Chen, a short, stocky man, the eldest son from a family of officials and scholars who wrote poetry in his spare time, was supremely self-confident and therefore often controversial among his own, but he was one of Mao's favorite commanders. Faced with strong but badly coordinated GMD attacks from three directions, Chen chose to divide his 100,000-man force in two, ordering his deputy Zhang Dingcheng to move to the North, while he himself confronted GMD general Li Mi's forces in the South. For three weeks Chen held back, lulling Li's forces into a false sense of security. Then he struck furiously into southern Jiangsu, broke through the Nationalist lines, and inflicted heavy casualties on the GMD units.[37]

Although Mao felt that the victories in the south ought to be pursued, he agreed to Chen's request to move northward to relieve Zhang's troops, which were losing out to superior, U.S.-trained Nationalist divisions. But Chen came too late. In August and early September, Zhang's forces were crushed and their headquarters at Huai'an conquered. More than thirty thousand Communist soldiers died or were wounded. Almost ten thousand surrendered. These were the worst weeks of his life, Chen later admitted.[38]

In the fall of 1946, Chen Yi was on the run, as were many Communist commanders all over China. Chen was lucky; he and the remnant of his troops escaped across northeastern Jiangsu into southern Shandong province, where they could join small groups of local guerrillas. In other areas of Central and Northern China, Communist units were not that fortunate. Along the Grand Canal most CCP groups ceased to exist, and in Henan and northern Anhui provinces the Guomindang took almost complete control, even in the countryside. Worst of all for Yan'an, Nie Rongzhen's forces did not succeed in protecting the valleys leading into Manchuria from the Southwest through the north of Shanxi and Hebei provinces. Nie, an intelligent but prudent military commander, educated in France and the Soviet Union, was criticized by Mao for failing to hold the Manchurian corridor and especially the city of Zhangjiakou, the last major city in China controlled by the Communists. Zhangjiakou fell to Fu Zuoyi's troops on 10 October.[39]

Raymond de Jaeger, a foreign observer sympathetic to the Guomindang, commented that "the Communists lost prestige when they lost Kalgan [Zhangjiakou], which even the most experienced and seasoned United States correspondents who had talked with me earlier had predicted could never be taken by Nationalist troops. During my short stay in Kalgan I saw General Fu Tso-yi quite often and I admired his calmness and modesty in victory. The Communists had fired Kalgan as they retreated, and General Fu set about restoring and rebuilding the city at once, and his efficiency promised a minimum of hardship for the people there."[40] The fifty-year-old Fu, who had never been close to the Generalissimo in spite of a distinguished military record against the Japanese, in late 1946 earned much praise in Nanjing for his strategic and political skills.[41]

Inside Manchuria, things were not going much better for the Communists. Lin Biao had told Mao in early summer that his troops would be able to hold their own against Jiang's onslaught, but Lin was wrong. In mid-October the forty-two-year-old General Du Yuming, who commanded more than 200,000 men in southern Manchuria, struck against CCP defenses in the East. The Communist resistance collapsed after just a few days of fighting. Several CCP companies rebelled and crossed over to the enemy. For the first time during the fighting in the Northeast, which had gone on intermittently since the Japanese capitulation, CCP forces turned and fled, and the National Army pursued them all the way to the Korean border. The Communist forces in southeastern Manchuria dispersed in November; some set up local guerrilla groups in the mountains, and others crossed into Soviet-held North Korea or traveled up along the border to join the main CCP forces in the North.[42]

The International Scene

Most people who read newspapers or followed reports from the war in the North early during the fall of 1946 believed that Jiang was winning. Not only in China but also in foreign capitals—Washington, Moscow, and London—the clear sense was that the Guomindang armies had the Communists on the run, and that the best the CCP could hope for was a return to the negotiating table. The *Times* wrote in September 1946 that "General Chiang Kai-shek has replied to the Communist attacks . . . and the Communists have been unable to resist the Government troops, which enjoy the advantage of American training and American equipment. If the present advance on the important Communist centre of Kalgan succeeds, the entire position of the Yenan [Yan'an] administration in northern China will be undermined."[43]

For President Truman, the focus of his concerns over China during the course of the summer shifted from Communist collusion with the Soviets in Manchuria to Jiang's opposition to the U.S. vision for China's peace and democracy. Advised that Jiang's government had the upper hand in the fighting, the president agreed to withhold further military support for the GMD until peace had been restored. Like General Marshall, the president felt that the longer the war continued, the better were Moscow's chances of ultimately gaining influence in China. Truman, a proud and stubborn man, was angry that Jiang Jieshi would not listen to U.S. advice and reform his government in line with what the United States had hoped for. Through the embargo, effective in mid-September and lasting for eight months, the Truman administration in a not too subtle way expressed its displeasure with the Guomindang regime. In military terms, however, the embargo's effect was limited, since the Nationalist forces had already been well equipped with surplus materiel from U.S. bases in the Pacific.[44]

In Moscow, concerns also shifted as Jiang's troops made their way to the North. By September 1946, Stalin worried that the CCP would not be able to survive under what he saw as the combined onslaught of the GMD and the Americans. To his advisers, he recalled the disasters of 1927, when the supporters of Jiang Jieshi and his allies had turned on the Communists and their Soviet advisers at the end of Jiang's successful march to the North. The Kremlin welcomed the CCP's statements of adherence to Moscow's increasingly bipolar view of the world, but in spite

President Truman on the United States and China, December 1946

At peak strength a year ago we had some 113,000 soldiers, sailors and marines in China. Today this number is being reduced to less than 12,000. . . . Thus during the past year we have successfully assisted in the repatriation of the Japanese, and have subsequently been able to bring most of our own troops home. We have afforded appropriate assistance in the reoccupation of the country from the Japanese. We have undertaken some emergency measures of economic assistance to prevent the collapse of China's economy and have liquidated our own wartime financial account with China.

It is a matter of deep regret that China has not yet been able to achieve unity by peaceful methods. . . . The views expressed a year ago by this government are valid today. The plan for political unification agreed to last February has been made difficult of implementation because of the fighting since last April, but the general principles involved are fundamentally sound.

China is a sovereign nation. We recognize that fact and we recognize the National Government of China. We continue to hope that the Government will find a peaceful solution. We are pledged not to intervene in the internal affairs of China. Our position is clear. While avoiding involvement in their civil strife, we will persevere with our policy of helping the Chinese people to bring about peace and economic recovery in their country.

President's Statement on China, 18 December 1946, *Public Papers of the Presidents: Harry S. Truman, 1946* (Washington, DC: U.S. Government Printing Office, 1962), pp. 499–505.

of sanctioning further limited assistance to the Chinese party, Stalin was not about to get ensnared in a new imbroglio in China.[45]

As war flared up, in Nanjing General Marshall sought desperately for ways to quell its fires. Aided by newly arrived U.S. ambassador John Leighton Stuart, Marshall's main strategy was to push the Generalissimo to halt his offensives by threats of ending all U.S. aid to his regime. An all-out civil war "would lead to Communistic control in China," Marshall warned Jiang on 8 August. By implication, Jiang did not understand what was in his own best interest.[46]

But General Marshall's problem was that, however clearly he claimed to have understood Jiang Jieshi's interests, he did not have the leverage to force the Generalissimo to promote them. The only way in which Marshall's leverage could have improved was if Jiang perceived Washington as drawing closer to the CCP or to the Soviet Union. As long as Jiang believed that the United States, ultimately, would have no choice but to help his government win its battle against the Communists, Jiang would not be moved by the General's entreaties.[47]

It did not help Marshall's efforts that his government in late August had signed an agreement on the transfer to Jiang's regime of substantial amounts of so-called civilian surplus property—including machinery, motor vehicles, communications equipment, rations, and medical supplies—from U.S. bases. The Communists quite naturally saw the transfers as belying the arms embargo, and they used the agreement copiously in their propaganda, accusing the United States of "meddling" in the conflict in China. For Jiang Jieshi, however, the agreement was just a token sign of U.S. good-will, following after the arms embargo that he had seen as yet another insult by Marshall. He noted in his diary that "even when we offer to pay cash for American weapons, their State Department still refuses to issue an export licence. This was obviously further pressure from Marshall. America's China policy is changing after the failure of Marshall's mediation."[48]

Jiang had long been skeptical of the U.S. wish for his government to sign a new commercial agreement with the United States, although his main foreign policy advisers all favored it. The Generalissimo feared that Washington would make use of his requests for American aid to force through trade concessions. The text of the Treaty of Friendship, Commerce, and Navigation between the United States and China, which Jiang did sign on 2 November, gave the United States free access to most Chinese markets and opened all Chinese ports for U.S. merchant vessels, although based on the same reciprocal most-favored-nation treatment that would soon be embodied in the General Agreement on Tariffs and Trade (GATT), of which China was a founding member. In spite of Jiang's reluctant agreement to sign, the treaty was furiously opposed by many conservative GMD leaders, and the Communists had a field day in their propaganda, claiming that Jiang's "bureaucrat-comprador capital has become linked with U.S. imperialist capital through the notorious and treasonable Sino-U.S. Treaty of Commerce."[49]

If Jiang was disappointed with his U.S. allies, many of the Communist leaders were furious over what they saw as Washington's double-dealing. The cease-fire, Mao suspected, had served only as a cover for the United States to resupply Guomindang forces. The propagandistic vehemence with which Mao turned on Marshall and Washington from the hot month of July on was considerably fiercer than any Communist statements against the Americans since World War II began in Asia. The U.S. government was "attempting to take over Japan's position in this country and to transform China into a colony of American imperialism," charged Yan'an on 7 July. "The aid given by the American reactionaries [is intended] to encourage dictatorship and civil war in China."[50]

But besides showing Chinese, Russians, and Americans that Yan'an had seen through U.S. perfidy, Mao also styled the CCP missives so as to widen the split that the Chairman had long detected in U.S. public opinion on China. "American media in China has started to criticize the GMD and oppose a civil war in China," Mao told Zhou in late June. "You must . . . persist in our policy to win over the Americans and isolate the reactionaries." As had been the case during the CCP's last anti-U.S. propaganda offensive, in late fall and winter 1945, Mao still insisted that the people of the United States could be won over and, in turn, push the government to cut its aid to the Guomindang.[51]

Although he knew that Stalin agreed with this analysis, Mao still expected his harsh attacks on U.S. policies to work to his party's advantage in Moscow. The global rivalry between the Soviet Union and the United States had intensified in mid-1946. Mao had hoped for increased Soviet military supplies after the breakdown of negotiations, but he got little from Stalin except promises of political support. The Soviet military assistance to the CCP in the Northeast did continue, however, and sometime during the summer or early fall of 1946, Moscow agreed to accept several hundred Communist cadres for military training in the Soviet Union. But alongside his belief in a basic community of interest between the Soviet Union and the Chinese party, Mao was always aware of the need to cater to Stalin's tastes in terms of the rhetoric and timing of CCP statements.[52]

The Opposition to the War

With the enormous prestige that the United States had in China at the end of World War II, most Chinese who followed events in Nanjing had expected Marshall's mediation to succeed in some form. Even the head of the conservative CC-Clique, the authoritarian Confucian Chen Lifu, one of Jiang Jieshi's most hard line advisers, had conceded, at the start of the U.S. mission, that "Marshall is too big. He will force a solution."[53] When fighting started again in late spring, most Chinese still did not believe that a full civil war would ensue. But as the war intensified during the summer and early fall, the question of the day became whom to blame.

As could be expected, Chinese opinion was divided on who had destroyed the search for peace. The CCP came under attack from a number of important leaders in the cities, including some who had few, if any, links to the GMD establishment. The main charge against the Communists was their intransigence on the Manchurian question, and especially the claim that the CCP was setting up a separate state in the Northeast in alliance with the Soviets. For almost a generation, Manchuria under Japanese domination had been a symbol of foreign encroachments on Chinese territory, and the CCP's new bases, with their Soviet links, reminded many Chinese uncomfortably of the past. Many of the refugees who came from the Northeast could tell stories about atrocities committed by Red Army soldiers.[54]

In line with traditional Chinese views of the state, a number of opinion leaders also believed that the government had the right to attack and punish rebel groups. In the summer of 1946, the Communist Party, to most Chinese, was still little but another band of rebels who challenged centralized rule by Jiang Jieshi and his government. The slogan "Beat the rebels—make China strong" had considerable legitimacy all over the country, and particularly in those regions in which Mao's troops had not operated.

But it was still Jiang and the Guomindang leaders who—in the eyes of the informed public—came to bear most of the blame for the new instability that civil war caused. Jiang could have avoided war, many voices claimed, if only he had been willing to leave the CCP and its bases alone. The perception of the GMD as the instigator of conflict was helped along both by bellicose statements from Jiang's generals and by the commonly held view that the Communists—given their relative weakness—never would have provoked clashes with the government.[55]

Jiang's main problem in terms of public perceptions was his own unwillingness to speak out on the need for peace and cooperation between all Chinese. The Generalissimo's phrases about order and sacrifice badly fitted the public mood just a year after the end of the decade-long life or death struggle with Japan. Many commentators, even on the conservative side, felt that Jiang's calls for sacrifice did not square well with the obvious lust for material benefits that his cadres had shown upon taking over the cities from the Japanese.[56]

Jiang's relations with the Americans also created trouble. In spite of urgings even from his liberal-minded advisers, Jiang did not think it "proper" to go public with any of his differences with Marshall. There-

The Poet Wen Yiduo Blames Jiang Jieshi
for the Civil War, July 1946

A few days ago, as we are all aware, one of the most despicable and shameful events of history occurred here in Kunming. What crime did Mr Li Gongpu commit that would cause him to be murdered in such a vicious way? He merely used his pen to write a few articles, he used his mouth to speak out, and what he said and wrote was nothing more than what any Chinese with a conscience would say. We all have pens and mouths. . . .

The reactionaries believe that they can reduce the number of people participating in the democratic movement and destroy its power through the terror of assassination. . . . Throughout history, all who have opposed the people have been destroyed by the people! Didn't Hitler and Mussolini fall before the people? Chiang Kai-shek, you are so rabid, so reactionary, turn the pages of history, how many days do you think that you have left? You're finished! It is over for you! [Enthusiastic applause]

Bright days are coming for us. Look, the light is before us. Just as Mr Li said as he was dying: "Daybreak is coming!" Now is the darkest moment before dawn. We have the power to break through this darkness and attain the light! The coming of our light marks the final moment for the reactionaries.

This an extract from Wen Yiduo's speech at the memorial service for Li Gongpu. Li was shot by members of Jiang's secret police on 9 July 1946. After giving the speech, Wen—one of the major poets of the era—was himself assassinated on his way home from the memorial service. The extract is from Pei-kai Cheng and Michael Lestz, with Jonathan Spence, *The Search for Modern China: A Documentary Collection* (New York: Norton, 1999), pp. 337–38; original in Wang Kang, *Wen Yiduo zhuan* (Hong Kong: Sanlian, 1979), pp. 434–37.

fore, most of those who viewed the relationship from the outside—often spurred on by Communist propaganda—believed the Nanjing-Washington axis to be much stronger than it actually was. The charges that Jiang took orders from foreigners—unfair as they were—hurt the Generalissimo's reputation at a time when many Chinese cherished the return of a "nationalist" government.

But the GMD's worst mistake in terms of public relations in the summer of 1946 was the murders and intimidations that its thugs committed in the cities in response to the emerging criticism of Jiang's policies. Strong-arm methods by GMD cadres against their opponents were certainly nothing new, and had—just like CCP violence against its real or perceived enemies in Communist-held areas—been going on for decades. During the winter of 1945–46 a local mob inspired by GMD leaders had killed a number of antiwar demonstrators in Kunming. From April on, different groups—including Communists—put on several rallies against civil war in other Chinese cities, in part in response to the killings in Kunming. The activities of the government's critics peaked in the summer of 1946, after the murders of Li and Wen in Kunming and the increasing use of violence by GMD supporters against their opponents.[57]

At the center of antigovernment protest in 1946 were the leaders of the Democratic League and the nascent student movement. The campaigns, rallies, and public meetings held to protest civil war and GMD brutality throughout the summer and fall were most often decided on by supporters of the League or others among the liberal intelligentsia. In spite of both contemporary GMD and subsequent CCP claims, Communist cells seem to have played a very limited role in planning and executing these early protests against state violence. To the astonishment of many observers—including foreigners, Communist agents, and the GMD secret police—the protests against civil war and foreign domination were organized by new organizations and by individuals who had no allegiance to the Communist Party or to traditional centers of power.

The Democratic League had been formed in 1941 as an umbrella movement for several radical and reformist groups. Although infiltrated from the very beginning by small numbers of GMD and CCP supporters, the DL became an increasingly vocal force in Chinese politics after the end of the anti-Japanese war. Benefiting from Marshall's mediation and from the lack of both GMD and CCP party structures in the newly liberated cities, the DL gained large numbers of adherents among urban intellectuals, students, and small businessmen. It also got some support from skilled workers and employees, especially in foreign-owned companies.[58]

The leadership of the Democratic League was a patchwork of differences in attitudes and backgrounds. Zhang Junmai was a humanist Confucian and a moderate socialist, educated in Japan and Germany. With his curious mixture of vision and pragmatism, Zhang became the best known of the DL leaders. Other DL front figures, such as the agrarian reformer Liang Shuming, rejected Zhang's emphasis on elections and parliamentary control. Liang emphasized China's special "national character" and argued for a political system based on the role of meritocracies, economic equality, and decentralized politics. What united these leaders were a common opposition to dictatorial rule of both the right and the left, and a dedication to constitutional government and the rule of law. In

1945–46, these values seemed considerably more attractive to many Chinese than the Nationalist or Communist revolutions.

In terms of organizing the ordinary Chinese against civil war and foreign intervention and in favor of democratic and social reforms, the student movement probably played a more important role than the Democratic League. While the leaders of the League debated and wrote declarations, the students marched in the streets, set up action committees, and arranged protest meetings. In making their voices heard, the activists in schools and universities linked up to a long tradition of student protest in China, going back to the radical movements of the beginning of the century. Although four-fifths of the population were illiterate and the number of college students was small compared with the general numbers of the population—no more than 100,000 students in all of GMD-held China—the student movement against the war became a vital part of the opposition to Jiang Jieshi's policies.

There were two main reasons for the importance of the student movement. To many Chinese, the students were carriers of the national consciousness, a role inherited both from earlier movements and from the special position that examination candidates, as aspiring members of the elite, had had in Confucian ideology. As had been the case before, and would be the case later, teachers, employees, and workers often identified with the lofty ideals of the students, even though they did not always share or even understand their political demands. And the student radicals had perfect stages for their roles. Their small numbers were concentrated in China's main cities, in which onlookers, the press, and foreign observers could pick up their message and spread it.[59]

In spite of government attempts to limit its influence, the student movement became an important voice in Chinese politics from the summer of 1946 on. Its inventive methods—posters, chanting, street theater—always secured the students an audience. During its early phase, in 1946 and early 1947, the movement was a local, mostly spontaneous, and loosely organized nationalist force that raised slogans against war and foreign domination of China. Even though the Communists spent much time discussing how best to gain influence among the students, they could still not set the political agenda of the movement. They were rudely reminded of the limits to their influence in the spring of 1946, when Nanjing and Shanghai students, who had demonstrated against U.S. policies, suddenly went out in protest against the continued Soviet occupation of Manchuria.[60]

Jiang's National Assembly and the End of Mediation

Zhou Enlai and Ren Bishi spent much time in the fall of 1946 reflecting on how the alliance policies of the CCP could be used to offset some of the party's military setbacks. Zhou's considerations were mainly tactical—he attempted to devise ways in which the Communists could influence the opposition parties, the student movement, and factions within the Guomindang in line with CCP positions. The party's United Front department, which Zhou headed, consisted of a group of very talented young intellectuals, educated in GMD areas and steeped in Comintern techniques of gaining influence and achieving control. The department spanned a wide array of activities—propaganda, undercover work, and different forms of intelligence activities—and was increasingly successful as the urban public's disenchantment with GMD rule grew.[61]

While Zhou attempted to get CCP members in the cities to "appear as ordinary people to actively influence the protests against the government," Ren Bishi was mainly preoccupied with the long-term implications of gaining and keeping allies outside the party.[62] More than anybody within the party leadership, Ren viewed the civil war as a defensive battle that some day would have to be replaced by political activities, both in the cities and especially in the countryside. Ren worried that radical land reform, while an excellent defensive weapon in times of crisis, did not prepare the CCP well for the political contest that would have to come in rural areas. The excessive delineation between poor peasants, who stood to gain from CCP policies, and everyone else, the potential victims of confiscations and random violence, made the Communists too many enemies and too few friends, he complained.[63]

What would decide the long-term prospects for peace, Zhou and Ren agreed, was the issue of the national assembly that Jiang Jieshi was determined to call by mid-November. If Jiang could be pressured to halt the military offensives and include CCP members in the parliament, the Communists could gradually turn the political game to their advantage, while getting the respite from fighting they badly needed. Two meetings of the Politburo in early October concluded that there was no hope of returning to the framework for a National Assembly worked out through negotiations that past spring. But there could still be a chance that the victorious Generalissimo, pressured by the Americans and the Chinese liberals, would ask the CCP to come to Nanjing for the assembly. The Soviets advised Yan'an to do whatever it could to be represented in the new assembly.[64]

Mao disagreed with this perspective. The Chairman thought that the National Assembly was a sham that Jiang had constructed to crown his military victories against the Communists. "Over the past eight months," he wrote to Zhou on 24 August, "we have too many times been cheated by the GMD and the Americans; we should be more alert now."[65] Almost alone among the central party leadership, Mao believed in military victory, that the tide would turn, and that Jiang's divisions would be forced back. Gradually, during October, Mao's views on the National Assembly won out. The main point for the CCP became to prevent the liberal groups from participating and to delay and, if possible, postpone the opening of the meeting.

Jiang Jieshi in October thought it quite likely that the CCP would in the end accept his conditions for participating in the assembly, if only the GMD itself did not waver. He agreed to meet the leaders of the Democratic League and promised them to issue an immediate cease-fire order if they and the Communists decided to attend. But by early November, Jiang had lost hope. He told his advisers that "the Third Party is controlled by the CCP and [neither of them] will join the National Assembly."[66] The Generalissimo's declaration of a unilateral cease-fire a few days before the assembly met, and a last-minute delay by three days until November 15, were not intended to bring the Communists on board, but aimed at splitting the DL leadership, who did not agree among themselves on the conditions for participating.[67]

The opening of the National Assembly should have been Jiang's moment of crowning glory. His forces controlled almost all of China. The Japanese were gone, the Soviets had withdrawn, and the Communists were on the run. He had defied the U.S. "FDR party," broken with the mediation straitjacket, and called a National Assembly of his own choice. The National Assembly would ratify his constitution for China, extending the people's rights while giving his party and himself the decisive voice in public affairs. Still, Jiang's worries about the future of China and about his own position in its past and present marred his speech and made it less of an event than it should have been. It was as if he could never be quite satisfied, as if his fear of not being understood by his people shone through even in celebration.[68]

Two weeks before the Assembly met, Jiang and his family had been touring Taiwan. The recovery of the island for China, after fifty years of Japanese occupation, was one of his proudest achievements. He had high hopes for the territory. It was, he wrote in his diary, "the last piece of

*The Democratic League Majority Boycotts
the National Assembly*

As far as we know, the sole purpose of the convocation of the N.P.A. [National People's Assembly] is to enact the Constitution. This important task can only be accomplished after the unity of the people and of all the parties and groups in the country has been achieved. At present the Kuomintang and the Communist Party are engaged in the greatest civil war in the history of China. It would be a mere illusion to think that under these circumstances, the representatives of the two parties could calmly sit down in the same room and discuss the basic law of the nation. . . . Furthermore, if the situation develops to a stage where all parties will convoke their own assemblies, enact their own Constitutions, set up their own governments, and organize their own nations, the N.P.A., if convoked on 12 November, will cause a permanent split in the nation. This is a situation which we dread most and we would rather die than see it. We feel that under the present circumstances, China must immediately stop her civil war and restore peace. Then, an N.P.A. supported by the entire nation should be held and a truly democratic constitution should be enacted, thereby achieving peace, unity and democracy in the country.

Statement signed by Zhang Lan, Shen Junru, Huang Yanpei, Zhang Junmai, Zhang Dongsun, Zhang Shanfu, Zhang Bochun, Liang Zouming, Luo Rongji, 30 September 1946. *Da gong bao*, 1 October 1946, trans. in American Consulate General, Shanghai, *Chinese Press Review*.

clean land that had not been polluted by Communism." If his enemies continued to persecute him, "what could they hope to achieve here?"[69]

As agreed by the Politburo some weeks before, just as the National Assembly got underway in Nanjing, Mao sent a telegram recalling Zhou Enlai to Yan'an. He left on 19 November. Although few thought so at the time, it was to be the end of Zhou's longest stay behind enemy lines. It was also perhaps the end of the period of his best service to his party. Zhou's tactical skills, the attractiveness of his personality, and his tremendous ability for deception contributed much toward the blossoming of interest in the CCP in the cities during his twelve months in the GMD capitals. While many urban Chinese had, until Zhou's arrival, viewed the Communists as a sect of rural fanatics, in 1946 they had been charmed by the energetic propagandist and his young assistants into giving the CCP the benefit of the doubt. As the civil war progressed, these changes were to have great significance.[70]

But Zhou's services did not enhance his status when he returned to the guerrilla capital. In Yan'an the military commanders were in ascendance, and it was they who had Mao's ear. Two days after Zhou's return, Mao lectured him and Liu Shaoqi on the global situation: "The postwar world has been turned into a state in which American reactionaries are antagonistic to the world's people. In China this is the same. Thus, our struggle in China is closely connected with the political struggle in the world. Among the Chinese people, as well as inside our party, there was uncertainty whether or not we should fight the war. Now, this uncertainty has been cleared up. Another suspicion was whether we could win or not. . . . . The world is developing and the Soviet Union is progressing whereas the United States is facing crises. The conflict between America and the capitalist states will become the main conflict of the world."[71]

Mao's understanding of how this world of conflict looked was deeply influenced by Stalin and by Soviet perceptions. In spite of Moscow's advising caution in terms of Communist prospects in China, Mao found justification for his own prognosis for the civil war in Soviet theory. The world was divided into a conflict between the United States and its many enemies. The Soviet Union was the rising power. Reactionaries everywhere were losing. The gun ruled. It would perhaps take a year, perhaps a little more, before the CCP could go on the offensive against Jiang's troops, Mao told Zhou and Liu. It would be a long war, but in the end the CCP would win.[72]

In Nanjing, General Marshall and his staff were finally preparing to put an end to their Chinese ordeal and return to Washington. The only reason why the General had stayed as long as he did was his loyalty to the president and his orders. Marshall had been a hero of World War II, and he felt that he had wasted his time in China: Instead of serving his country in an important position at home, he would have to return, unsuccessful, from a mission to an area of limited strategic significance to the United States. President Truman's almost immediate appointment of Marshall as his new Secretary of State after his return to Washington in January 1947 may have alleviated the General's sense of failure. It certainly, as far as China was concerned, placed an avowed noninterventionist at the head of the main U.S. foreign policy–making body.[73]

In China, only the liberals regretted Marshall's departure. The CCP stepped up its propaganda offensive, accusing the U.S. mediator of having attempted to trick the CCP and having aimed at U.S. control of China through the traitorous GMD regime. Jiang wrote in his diary after his last meeting with the American envoy: "From what Marshall said, it was not difficult to sense that he felt more than a little bit guilty about his past at-

A Peasant Remembers the Guomindang Counterattack, 1946

In late 1946 the Guomindang did return. . . . A lot of irregular troops, bandits really, and a landlord army called the Homecoming regiment came with the Guomindang. They killed a number of Communist Party members and cadres. No one was killed in Houhua, but thirteen new Communist Party members capitulated to the enemy and renounced their Communist affiliation. All of them had joined the party in 1946. At that time anyone who wanted to could join, without even waiting for the usual one-year probation period. When those new members saw the New Fifth Army and the Homecoming regiment return, they became frightened and left the Communist Party. . . . I didn't dare to speak at that time. I was not a cadre, but I was an activist in the land reform movement, so I kept quiet for two months until the bad people left.

Wang Fucheng, a peasant leader from northern Henan, interviewed by Peter Seybolt. Seybolt, *Throwing the Emperor from His Horse: Portrait of a Village Leader in China, 1923–1995* (Boulder, CO: Westview, 1996), p. 34.

titude toward us, and [that he] worried whether it would have a negative impact on cooperation between us in the future." "He must," Jiang added, "be moved by our sincerity."[74]

Mao on the Defensive

During the last six months of 1946, the CCP lost 174,000 square kilometers of territory and 165 towns. Government forces drove the Communist armies out of the defensive positions that they had created during the first part of the year and forced them into retreat. In the villages that the Communists left, the traditional order returned with a vengeance. Those peasants who had taken advantage of the land confiscations were punished and sometimes killed by the returning landlords. The local cadres were caught, ran away, or renounced the CCP.[75]

The defections were particularly troubling to the CCP leadership. They testified in an all too obvious way to the fickleness of its position in the countryside. As long as the Communist armies were there, local cadres would carry out land reform and instigate political campaigns. But with military protection gone, the new adherents to the cause in the villages—those who had been recruited during the last phase of the war against Japan and during the postwar years—often switched allegiance. While in most cases cadres in the "old" Communist areas—base areas set up during the first years of the anti-Japanese war—escaped into the mountains or marches when their areas were overrun by the GMD, the CCP organizations in the "new" areas were simply wiped out. It is not surprising that some CCP leaders came to see the defections as a political deficiency. The architect of radical land reform, Ren Bishi, complained in January 1947 that the party was making too few friends and far too many enemies in the countryside.[76]

While telling everyone about his firm belief in military victory, Mao was also groping for policy changes that could underpin the CCP war effort. They key to the problem was land reform, Mao kept repeating. He often called for greater flexibility in carrying out social change in the countryside, reminding his audiences of past mistakes of excessive radicalism and of the variations in the existing social situation in the different parts of the Chinese countryside where the Communists operated. But Mao refused to turn land reform into merely an issue of political tactics: "The battle for China," he reminded the Politburo, "is a battle for the hearts and minds of the peasants."[77]

In part in response to the need to keep the leadership united through difficult times, Mao's role within the Party Center went through a gradual transformation from late 1946 on. Although reserving the privilege of intervening whenever he saw fit, Mao left day-to-day policy-making for the Communist-held areas and long-term political planning to his chief lieutenants, Liu Shaoqi and Ren Bishi, while himself concentrating on the conduct of the war. Sometimes, as in the early fall of 1947, Mao would turn his attention back to policy issues, and then almost always to give those issues a radical twist. But most of the time his vast energies were squarely focused on the war.[78]

Increasingly, in the late 1940s, this meant that Liu Shaoqi became the first among equals in the group around Mao Zedong. A Hunanese like Mao and Ren Bishi, Liu was born in 1898 in a rich peasant family and educated in the Soviet Union. In 1922 he had returned to China to become a Communist trade union organizer. From the late 1920s on—after the CCP had been decimated in the cities by Guomindang terror—Liu was the most successful organizer to stay on behind enemy lines, setting up the underground movement in Wuhan and Shanghai. Since arriving in Yan'an in early 1942, Liu had made a name for himself as a dour but respected supporter of Mao's policies, with party organization and doctrine as his specialities. In 1945, at the 7th CCP Congress, he had been elected the second man in the party, to serve as Mao's deputy when the Chairman was ill or absent.[79]

Mao Zedong on the Military Situation, October 1946

The Chinese and American reactionaries will not change their policy of wiping out our liberated areas. The comrades in our party cannot indulge in fantasies about a bestowed peace. Temporary cease-fires are possible only when the enemy's military attacks are repeatedly shattered and their most effective [forces] are annihilated on a large scale. Now, both in the country at large and in the Northeast, the situation is still that the enemy is powerful and we are weak. To change this, we have to prepare for a long and hard struggle.

Mao to the Central Committee Northeast Bureau, 25 October 1946, *Mao Zedong junshi wenji*, vol. 3, p. 529.

The core of Mao's military strategy was the Northeast—it was the battles for Manchuria, he kept telling his colleagues, that would decide the fate of the Chinese revolution. There were both tactical and ideological reasons why Mao concentrated on the Northeast. This was the only area in China in which the Communists could have any hope of doing an equal battle with the GMD—their forces were of similar size, the Nationalists had trouble with their supply lines, and Soviet aid was available to boost the CCP's fighting skills. But Mao also concentrated on Manchuria for different reasons. Because of the Japanese colonization, the Northeast had developed more in terms of industry and technology than the rest of China. With its location along the Soviet border, such an area would be the ideal base for the CCP during a long-term struggle for power in China, a base that would provide the Communists with all the advantages they had lacked during the earlier confrontations with the GMD.[80]

Very different from the way he would give orders to other commanders, Mao in the fall of 1946 engaged in a dialogue with Lin Biao, in what almost amounted to a seminar on military strategy. The position of Lin's troops in the Northeast was difficult, but at least they had avoided being routed by the GMD in the manner of CCP forces farther south. Although their eastern and western flanks—along the Korean and Mongolian borders—were gradually being pushed northward by the GMD, their core areas north of the Songhua River were still intact. Mao and Lin agreed that a CCP counterattack in the Northeast would have to be conducted according to principles of conventional warfare, rather than the highly mobile tactics used in the defense of CCP positions in the South. Lin believed that the CCP forces should spend the winter preparing and testing out GMD readiness in small-scale operations across the river to the south. Mao felt that his forces should start a general offensive—albeit with limited aims—as early as November, and establish strongholds south of the Songhua.[81]

Lin's winter campaigns were a compromise between these two approaches, primarily intended to disrupt enemy communications and test out GMD strength. The Communists crossed the frozen Songhua River in four different operations, engaging government units and wrecking parts of the North Manchurian railway system. It is difficult to estimate the losses of each side in these battles; the Communists probably lost more than twelve thousand men and the GMD somewhat fewer. But, as Mao commented in January 1947, the CCP could easily replace these losses from among men recruited locally in Manchuria, while the GMD, Mao thought, would have to bring new forces up from south of the Wall.[82]

Jiang's Challenges: Party Reform and Foreign Policy

While Mao was engaged in conducting war in Manchuria, Jiang Jieshi turned his attention increasingly to political matters. The Generalissimo thought that the end of mediation, the convocation of a national assembly, and the adoption of a new constitution meant that he could concentrate more on the urgent issues of reform of the party and on economic and social issues. Jiang remained dedicated to making the GMD an elite party representing all sections of Chinese society. Although believing that the party and he himself as its leader were predestined to rule China, he still wanted to broaden the party's base and saw a need for party members to improve themselves, getting rid of corruption and other vices.

The party commissions that Jiang set up in early 1947 were all intended to deal with these problems. Unlike many of the committees within the Guomindang in the 1930s, the new commissions included not only old party members from the established factions or groups but also younger people, intellectuals, and representatives of different trades and industries. Even workers' and students' unions were represented. Most important of all, the commissions included a number of local leaders from areas that only recently had fallen under GMD control.[83]

The public's identification of Jiang and his party with the Chinese state was at an all-time high in early 1947. The legitimacy that this identification bestowed on the GMD was substantial, especially at a time when the CCP again seemed headed for the fringes of Chinese politics. But not all of its implications were unproblematic to Jiang's party. The common view of Jiang and the GMD as equaling the state meant that all forms and purposes of public protest were delivered straight to their door. In a society in which protest was gradually becoming legitimate, almost all protest was directed against the state, immediately or by implication. At the same time, many segments of society thought that accepting or even allowing public protests meant a weak state. Just as the political, social, and geographic broadening of the party implied including more groups that would attempt to hold the leadership hostage to their interests, the general identification of the GMD with the state meant new challenges of both an ideological and a practical nature. Although any party that wanted to retain power would have had to overcome such challenges, it can safely be said that these were not the best conditions under which to fight a civil war.

The domestic, social, and economic climate of the immediate postwar years may have made the GMD's dominant position in Chinese politics a curse in disguise for Jiang's regime. For the foreign policy of the nationalist government, however, it looked to be an undisguised blessing. Jiang's government was the one that both of the major foreign powers had to deal with to achieve their aims in China. The Generalissimo, who strongly believed that foreign leaders of whatever nation were primarily interested in their own immediate material advantage, was convinced that he could deal with them to his benefit. With Marshall gone, Jiang saw his freedom of movement as substantially increased. He hoped that increased U.S. global pressure on the Soviet Union could bring Stalin to strike a deal with the Nanjing government. Thus, having defeated the Cold War principles of mutual exclusivity, Jiang could benefit from an alliance with the U.S. in the South and the Soviets in the North—in line with past Chinese rulers' ways of manipulating foreign support.

During the first weeks of 1947, Jiang Jieshi was convinced that both the party and the country were moving in the right direction. At the turn of the year, he had commissioned a review of foreign newspapers' reports on China, and, upon receiving it, had noted with glee that the main papers in London, New York, and Paris agreed with his estimate of the situation.[84] When meeting with his commanders in mid-January, the Generalissimo stressed that the military threats to China from foreign imperialists and their agents, be it the CCP or the Democratic League, were not yet over. While commending his forces on their fighting capabilities, however, he stressed that military expenditures would have to be reduced in the months ahead. Some of his generals, especially those fighting in the Northeast, started worrying that Jiang thought the war against the CCP already won.[85]

But as he repeatedly stressed in his diaries, Jiang knew that more wars are won through political prowess than through battlefront victories. He wanted to strengthen Chinese society, so that it could stand up to the challenges ahead. For Jiang, the war against China's enemies was as much a spiritual battle as a military clash. His main worry, as he stated in letters to his eldest son, Jiang Jingguo, was that the Guomindang could not meet the demands of ruling China.[86] And, as his associates' behavior after the Japanese surrender had shown, he had much to worry about.

3

TAKEOVERS

Resurrecting the Guomindang State

Unknown artist, "Guomindang factory"

One of the distinguishing features of civil wars in the modern era has been the high degree of popular participation in warfare. Relatively speaking, that is not true of the civil war in China; on the contrary, the great majority of the population were passive onlookers, doing their best to stay out of harm's way in the cataclysm that engulfed their country. After the first waves of post–World War II national enthusiasm had been broken, for most Chinese life in the late 1940s became a question of survival—of getting through hunger, social degradation, political oppression, and warfare. It was a time of immense transformation that, above its many disasters, saw a number of new beginnings for China, in political ideas, culture, and daily life.[1]

In order to understand these changes, it is important to view them as connected to two parallel processes of political transformation—the civil war and the GMD takeover of administration in almost all of China. In the summer of 1945, Jiang Jieshi controlled less than 15 percent of China's total territory.[2] A year later, after the Japanese capitulation and the CCP's military defeats, he controlled—more or less effectively—almost 80 percent. The takeover of these territories, some of which were among China's wealthiest and best developed, posed a tremendous challenge to the GMD. The party had to show initiative, strength, and cohesion, while overcoming the corruption and lack of discipline that had spread during the last phase of the anti-Japanese war.[3]

The GMD's failure to meet these challenges is as important a reason for its political and military collapse as the defeats it suffered on the battlefields. The gradual withdrawal of allegiance from the Nationalist government by its urban and rural constituencies followed from the GMD's inability to live up to the people's expectations of what the end of nine years of war would mean. Instead of providing relief, many felt that the government was securing for itself rights and opportunities that had belonged to them or to their communities in the past.

But the withdrawal of allegiance from the Guomindang did not mean an embrace of the authoritarian alternative, the CCP. On the contrary, at least up to the very end of the GMD regime, important parts of Chinese society sought outlets for their activities other than the main parties and their warfare. In spite of misery and human suffering, the Chinese made the late 1940s a period of cultural and organizational growth. In the shadow of civil war, Chinese society began to grow out of political tutelage.

Takeover: The Cities

The 1947 movie *Spring River Flows East*, the most popular of all Chinese films in the late 1940s, depicts a young couple, split by the anti-Japanese war, she with the resistance in the countryside, he in the GMD wartime capital, Chongqing. In 1945 he moves to Shanghai as a high official of the returning government, but, already infected by the vices of corruption and loose living, he sets up a big house for his mistress instead of calling for his wife to return with him. When the faithful wife does come to Shanghai, she ends up finding work as a servant in the house of the husband's mistress.[4]

The movie is an all too obvious allegory of the majority view of what happened in the cities after the GMD's return. The incoming officials were too busy enriching themselves to respond to their countrymen's plight. By comparing the situation in Chongqing before the hero's departure with the situation as he found it in Shanghai, the movie also shows how unprepared the GMD was for the task of ruling all of China. While the coastal cities had continued to develop commercially and culturally under Japanese rule, Chongqing was never more than a makeshift capital for a regime whose largest single source of income in the last year of the war had been U.S. loans. A city like Shanghai, with its bustling commerce and high-energy social life, had always been a tall order to govern for any regime, be it emperors, warlords, or foreign imperialists. For the GMD officials who flew into the city on American planes in the fall of 1945, even if they had the best of intentions, their task seemed daunting.[5]

Jiang Jieshi's orders to the men he sent off to establish GMD rule in the cities were clear: They were to establish a new Chinese administration at all levels, which excluded those who had collaborated with Japan or any agents of foreign influence. They were to confiscate enemy property and prepare for it to be returned to its proper owners or auctioned for the benefit of the state. They were to disarm the Japanese troops and prepare them for repatriation. And they were to do all this while ensuring that there was as little disruption of commerce and public services as possible.[6]

Jiang's instructions were based on his sense of Chinese national pride and on the need he saw for re-establishing order in the cities. In Jiang's view, those parts of China that had suffered from Japanese occupation and other forms of foreign control first and foremost needed to be reintegrated with the rest of the country, to form part of a united China. The unity of all of China was what he had fought for, and what he believed that the majority of those in the occupied areas had fought for as well. Thus, in the first months after the surprising collapse of Japan, Jiang's emphasis was on his government's assumption of formal sovereignty—getting small groups of leading members of the Guomindang into position in all cities and most of the county towns all over China.

In terms of control of the cities, Jiang's success seemed to have been absolute. With the exception of the cities in the Northeast and a few minor cities in the northern borderlands, the GMD controlled all of urban China by early October 1945. In most places, even among perennial skeptics of GMD rule in the metropolitan coastal cities, there was substantial enthusiasm for the setting up of Chinese government. Public participation at rallies held in Shanghai between September and late November 1945 went well beyond the ritual homage that any Chinese city would show its new rulers. Jiang seemed to have interpreted the public mood correctly when he emphasized the formal assumption of power with all its public symbolism.[7]

The public spectacles of welcome were buoyed by the GMD's new efforts at effective propaganda, in which the youth organizations controlled by the party, such as the *Sanqingtuan,* played an important part. Some of Jiang's right-wing advisers had studied how the Hitler and Stalin regimes used propaganda, and how the CCP had used propaganda during the anti-Japanese war.[8] Their knowledge was put to use after the takeover of the cities, as Japanese printing presses all over Central and South China began churning out leaflets extolling the virtues of the Generalissimo and the GMD's version of a united China.[9]

But it was not just Japanese printing equipment that came in handy for the national government. The GMD leaders who had entered the cities in the weeks after Tokyo capitulated found that upholding "order"—not to mention governing—were arduous tasks without the support of the troops, police, and special personnel that they had expected to follow within weeks, if not days. But as Jiang and the Supreme Military Council started deploying their troops to areas threatened by the Communists or local power-holders, the GMD advance teams in the cities found themselves without any organized backup whatsoever. The temptation to continue to make use of the Japanese who had, in effect, been holding the cities for the Guomindang since August 1945, was too great to resist.[10]

In late fall, therefore, the population in many cities, much to their dismay, saw increasing numbers of Japanese soldiers doing guard duty or

Jiang's Instructions for the Sanqingtuan, September 1946

Directions in which the members of the Corps should strive from now on:
The members should emphasize positive reconstruction.

Mentally and psychologically, they must be independent and must seek to strengthen themselves; they must not lose their own self-confidence.

They should respect freedom, but should not tolerate the actions of the Communists designed to undermine national unity, social order, and our desirable national character.

They should devote their attention and energy to social service.

They should awaken youth throughout the country and ask them to be cautious, so that they will not be taken advantage of by others and entrapped.

They should, in accordance with the instructions of the Director-General, call upon youth throughout the country to participate in the task of carrying out the five-point reconstruction program.

Manifesto of the 2d Plenary Session of the *Sanqingtuan*, 12 September 1946, quoted from *Xinwen bao*, 18 September 1946.

even patrolling the streets. In most of these cases, the initiative to use the Japanese came from local GMD cadres. Jiang grudgingly accepted their requests. While he had no qualms about using the Japanese and their former collaborators to deter the CCP or other enemies in those areas where that was necessary, he knew that the political cost of employing the erstwhile occupiers in the cities would be high. Still, the cost of the alternative, which Jiang saw as accepting the rise of public disorder in cities under his formal control, could be much higher. Given this choice, there is some evidence that at least parts of the bourgeoisie agreed with Jiang's decision.[11]

But while the Japanese undoubtedly helped with maintaining one form of order, there was little they could do to keep those with genuine claims of association with the government from exploiting the situation in the cities to their personal advantage. Indeed, one could claim that there was no massive disorder in the cities before trainloads of carpetbaggers from Chongqing descended on them. In the winter of 1945–46, well before any form of effective administration had been established, finance and commerce in the cities came under threat from newcomers who tried to use their government connections to enrich themselves. Although a large number of GMD officials avoided being entrapped by the riches of the cities, the government's inability to deal with corruption tore into its legitimacy.[12]

It could be claimed, with China in the 1980s and 1990s as a prime example, that corruption in and of itself is not necessarily an impediment to economic growth. The problem in the late 1940s, simply put, was that few of the basic incentives for growth were present, and that official corruption prevented some of these incentives from being formed. For instance, national markets could not develop so long as one had to pay a huge premium for getting one's goods transported by the state-controlled railways from one part of the country to another. But even more important, these forms of corruption prevented the state from generating vital income, reducing its ability to decrease the portion of its revenue going to the military, and increasing its dependence on extortion, foreign loans, and inflationary monetary policies.[13]

In terms of public legitimacy, official corruption therefore had a generic negative effect—it presented the state as unjust, and it prompted the regime to take highly unpopular actions to add to its income. Both were important causes for the increasing criticism of the government in 1946. The press highlighted a wide range of cases that were often not merely individual examples of fraud but large-scale plans for swindling businesses or branches. For example, in mid-1946 the head of the GMD party organization in Xiamen, on the southern coast, demanded that all local businesses obtain an affidavit from the party verifying their "patriotic" attitude during the Japanese occupation. Those who did not get a certificate of good behavior had their trading licenses revoked but would receive a small compensation if they transferred the ownership of their businesses to the local authorities. These authorities—meaning the same GMD bosses—then sold the enterprises back to their original owners (now regarded as "new owners" and therefore in no need of an affidavit) for their full worth, pocketing the difference.[14]

By early 1946, the Guomindang government was getting desperately short of cash with which to fund its plans for the civilian and military buildup of postwar China. The money from cheap U.S. wartime loans was running out, and corruption and the lack of an efficient civil service prevented tax money from reaching the central government. It therefore came as no surprise to businessmen in Shanghai, Guangzhou, Tianjin, and other centers of trade and commerce along the coast that the Guomindang reverted to many of the same forms of extortion and confiscations that had been prevalent during the pre-1937 period. Jiang Jieshi, often acting in person, made it plain to the mayors and nonelected officials of the cities that they were responsible for securing the tax income of the

Shanghai Policemen Rue Their Lot, July 1946

Dear Mr Editor,

We are a group of hated policemen. This feeling of hatred and contempt towards us is not due to the fact that we are policemen, but is the result of our being utilized as an instrument to oppress the poor, innocent people. For instance,
we have been ordered to drive away the stall keepers along the streets, to forbid
the peddlers to do business, and what is more heartrending, to confiscate the
goods in the roadside stalls which sell U.S. Army rations. If the U.S. soldiers do
not unlawfully sell their PX rations, how can the stall keepers get hold of them?
Many of these stall keepers, after having had their goods confiscated by the policemen, have begged for the return of the goods through tearful entreaty. They
have borrowed their capital at a high rate of interest and their family members
depend on the money they make for a living. But we are merely carrying out
"instructions."

We love our country just as much as others do. Like others, we do not want
to see the country go on the road to destruction. . . . But for the sake of our
meager salary and because of lack of time, we could not but give up such a
good opportunity to participate in the patriotic movement. . . .

We are, dear Sir,

A Group of Policemen

The publication of this letter in the left-wing newspaper *Wenhui bao* caused the Shanghai
Municipal Police Bureau to order the paper to suspend publication for a week. The phras-
ing of the letter made them suspect that one of the many underground CCP propaganda
groups in the city had had a hand in its publication. *Wenhui bao* (Shanghai), 12 July
1946, trans. by American Consulate General, Shanghai, *Chinese Press Review.*

government. The bill was more often than not presented to businesses or
wealthy citizens, who had to pay up if they did not want licenses revoked,
accidental fires, or even personal threats to themselves or their families.[15]

Guomindang officials extended this form of predatory practice to their
dealings with organized labor. In Tianjin, the second most important industrial center in China, the party leaders allied themselves with the secret societies that had influence among transport workers, in the cotton
mills, and in the matchstick factories. The GMD authorities then forced
the unions that represented those workers to join the official citywide labor union. After they had joined, party bosses made sure that the unions
paid for their membership—often enormous fees, which the unions then
had to collect from their members.[16]

While public opinion in the cities was turning increasingly critical of
the Guomindang's handling of reunited China, the party's leadership
bickered over issues of planning and coordination. Jiang Jieshi, at least

up to the fall of 1946, concentrated primarily on fighting his domestic enemies and negotiating with the Americans, and no other leader within the GMD had the authority to force through even the simplest of decisions. A vital matter such as repairs to the railroads connecting the cities to the interior was held up for months by factional infighting within the government. Even able administrators like Chen Lifu, the much-feared founder of the CC Clique who served as head of the GMD Organizational Department, could not get government ministries to work together in developing plans for the future. Valuable time was lost while ministries, and individual ministers, jockeyed for position within the party.[17]

When Jiang Jieshi started turning his attention to issues of political and economic reform in late 1946, some of these issues were solved and solved quickly, often in a way that had at least a temporarily positive impact on the social and economic situation. Few of these initiatives—in regional administration, tax collection, and transport, to name a few—came from Jiang himself or from his inner circle. In almost every case proposals for reform came from officials in the central government or in the provinces, who had observed firsthand the government's inability to rule. But it was the renewed attention to civil administration by Jiang—prodded by his son Jiang Jingguo, among others—that ended some of the bickering among Guomindang leaders. A few commentators in the cities believed that the new initiatives were signs that Jiang could remake the party the way he had remade it during the Nanjing decade.[18]

Alongside the administrative reforms, Jiang in February 1947 proclaimed an emergency economic reform program particularly intended to offset some of the difficulties in the cities by combating inflation and securing supplies. The government froze all wages at their January levels and introduced price controls for a number of essential goods, including rice, wheat, and oil. It also started supplying government workers in the cities with foodstuffs, fuel, and clothing at fixed prices. For a brief period, these reforms halted the growing disenchantment with Guomindang rule in the cities. But in spite of Jiang's urgings, his government had neither the economic strength nor the political will to follow through on these programs. By April, as will be seen later, inflation and hoarding of goods had returned with a vengeance.[19]

The Guomindang government's inability to stem inflation and secure a minimum of services in the cities naturally brought it into conflict with China's emerging trade unions. The first major strikes took place by the winter of 1945–46, as the effects of the GMD takeover became manifest.

It is quite remarkable how quickly large sections of the working class organized themselves during the first postwar year: In 1946, Shanghai
alone saw more than seventeen hundred strikes and labor disputes, often
run by branches of local unions in a loose, citywide alliance with other
unions.[20]

Even more threatening to the government, these local unions started to
increase their influence within the main GMD-affiliated trade union organization—the Chinese Labor Association (CLA). By August, Jiang had
to call Zhu Xuefan, the CLA head, in to Guling to read him the riot act.
Zhu, an old associate of Jiang's and a former protege of Shanghai gang-
ster-boss Du Yuesheng, found himself caught between the GMD and the
increasing activism of his own members. He tried to explain to Jiang that
using violence to control labor unrest would be counterproductive and
could put the GMD hold on the cities at risk. But by November, Zhu was
out. After a brief exile in Europe, he returned, not to Nanjing, but to
Yan'an.[21]

Jiang Jieshi believed that the GMD could turn labor activism to its advantage by a mixture of infiltration and coercion within the unions, and
by pressure on industrialists to be reasonable in meeting some of labor's
demands. This model had worked well for the Guomindang before the
Japanese attack, when the CLA and similar organizations had been
among the party's main supporters. But in the postwar years, with great
expectations among the working class for better pay and better conditions, and with the regime increasingly dependent on the bourgeoisie for
taxes and political support in the cities, the prewar strategy could not
work. In January 1947, Chen Lifu had to organize a crisis meeting with
GMD labor leaders in Nanjing, at which he concluded that the party's
strategies had failed.[22]

Just as with its economic and supply policies, the party developed a set
of new guidelines for its labor policy in early 1947. Chen Lifu, Wu Kaixian, and other GMD heads organized the setting up of training centers
for labor leaders, local workers' welfare associations, and paramilitary
factory protection units. The aim was to make workers feel a sense of
connection to the government, and to underline the role of the party as
the protector of workers' interests within the state. For a while it seemed
as if many of the local and factory trade unions were attracted by the
protection and prestige that the GMD-sponsored associations could offer. But as the 1947 economic reforms ground to a halt, the local unions'
attraction to the GMD quickly waned.

During 1947, labor unrest in China took on a new meaning, as workers increasingly linked their demands to the political demands of the student movement. The forms of organization, and the types of demands,
varied from factory to factory. In cities such as Shanghai, Tianjin, and
Wuhan, independent local unions, often organizing across different
trades and industries, demanded pay increases, reduction of work hours,
or severance pay, and protested against inflation, unemployment, and
civil war. In smaller cities, and especially in the South, labor actions were
usually confined to single issues, although often with political overtones.

By mid-1947 the GMD turned from co-opting labor's demands to deterring industrial action that could threaten the war effort. In July the
government banned strikes outright and sent units from the Youth Corps
and GMD paramilitary organizations to break up any form of industrial
action that it found threatening. In cities with few independent unions,
such as Beijing, the GMD could still use its workers' organizations to attack student demonstrations. But in most cities, at least by the end of
1947, a sense of solidarity had arisen between students and workers in
their conflicts with the government.[23]

The rapid spread of labor unrest in the latter part of 1947 also provided the CCP with a first-rate opportunity for infiltrating the independent unions. The Communists had had no efficient organization in the
main cities for more than fifteen years. During the anti-Japanese struggle,
when the party expanded its footholds in the countryside, there were no
successes in the big cities—indeed, amid the optimism of the early fall of
1945, it had been a point of contention among the leaders whether their
armies could expect any collaborators from within when attempting to
take the cities. Even during the first two postwar years, the CCP had
problems increasing its membership among the working class in the main
cities. The party was simply too weak to have anything of practical value
to offer the workers—the typical four to six Communists at a large factory or plant could not organize an efficient strike or other forms of industrial action.[24]

To the substantial embarrassment of the heads of the CCP "White
Area" bureaus, even the 1947 wave of strikes did not do much good to
the Communist cells within the labor unions. In industries in which the
Communists already had an efficient organization, such as within the
railway unions in North China, the party did score some successes, notably on actions connected to demands for compensation for accidents.
But the "all-out offensive" of organized labor against capitalist exploita-

The GMD Counterattacks among the Intelligentsia, January 1947

In the last twenty years a great affliction has come to the intelligentsia as the old school of thought was overthrown, and since then no new authoritative thought could establish itself to take its place. Ambitious elements have been able to break the intelligentsia into two camps which carry on an unending pen-battle between them. This is done by presenting the nice title of "progressive elements" to those that follow their lead and labeling those unwilling to do so "out-of-moders" or "diehards." Young people are afraid of being called the latter, as are even those of middle age who have not found a firm standpoint for themselves. Even a cultural organ most renowned in China, the Ta Kung Pao [the newspaper *Da gong bao*] has strayed off to seek the honorable name of "progressives." We pity these people.

There is no positive standard to judge whether thoughts are old or new. Many principles are no less true because they were discovered thousands of years ago. The ambitious elements would call everything that China originally had "poisonous vestiges of feudalism," while imported "progressive thought" of Marx, Lenin, they embellish with flowery propaganda, though it consists of unproved Utopian illusions.

Commentary from the army-controlled Guangzhou paper *Heping ribao*, 17 January 1947, trans. in U.S. Information Service, Canton, *Chinese Press Review*.

tion, inflation, and unemployment and against the GMD government that the CCP had promised in May 1947 did not materialize. Even in Beijing and Tianjin, where urban party cells did start to multiply from early 1947 on, the Communist armies would be almost at the city gates before recruitment started to pick up within the unions.[25]

While the government feared CCP control of the labor unions and, at least in some cities, took effective steps to prevent it, the GMD leaders were much less preoccupied with Communist influence within the bourgeoisie. With the exception of heads of the intelligence units, who knew the situation well, GMD leaders simply refused to believe that by late 1946 a number of the sons and daughters of merchants, mill owners, tradesmen, and teachers had started offering their services to the CCP. In the student movement, at work, or inside their families, these young people became the party's main link to the cities. Their dedication saved the CCP's urban work when the class struggle had let it down; they distributed leaflets, painted slogans, and, often, faced GMD batons or even execution squads with a heroism that added luster to the party and its causes.[26]

Why did these young, middle-class people—extremely privileged in a Chinese setting, even though family fortunes were often flagging—break with their families' traditional views of the CCP as the enemy? Evidence for their motives is as easy to find in the movies and novels of the 1940s as in the memoirs and writings they left behind (often after having been purged or mistreated at least once by the party to which they had dedicated their lives). In a movie made in Shanghai in 1947, *Nothing But a Dream* [*Tiantang chunmeng*], a young Shanghai architect sees his postwar hopes about his own and his country's future crushed. In the city, he finds nothing but misery for just men, while former collaborators are getting richer. After selling his last possessions to survive, the young father has to give away his newborn son to be cared for by someone who has earned much money during the occupation.

Selling one's own son—as powerful a metaphor as there is in Chinese literature—linked up with other symbols to portray members of an elite who were deeply concerned both with political ideals and with personal status. In the chaos that descended on the cities after the GMD takeover, the indigenous middle classes had no immediate role to play. Although it was a minority who were actually impoverished—and almost none reduced to starvation—they were treated as second-class citizens by incoming GMD bigwigs. Their hopes for a modern, efficient, well-organized Chinese state dwindled, as did their families' income or their salaries. Communist propaganda targeted this group with skill and imagination, and made a great harvest.

Takeover: The Provinces

Very different from the situation in the cities, there was little immediate change in the villages and small towns of rural China when the Japanese withdrew to their barracks and the Guomindang moved in. In most places, the local elites that had dominated a county during occupation stayed on, now pledging allegiance to their new masters. In some areas the rich and mighty who had been forced to flee to the far West returned and, in some cases, took revenge on their collaborationist enemies. Such changes were particularly widespread in those provinces that had suffered the most from the final Japanese *Ichigo* offensives. But as a whole, the situation in those many counties that reverted to government control in 1945 stayed remarkably placid in the immediate aftermath of the takeover.

One main reason for this placidity was the lack of effective GMD rule in the provinces. Jiang Jieshi had concentrated his party's efforts in the fall of 1945 on taking over the major cities and securing their supply routes and those of his armies advancing to the North. The instructions that the government sent out for work in rural areas did not emphasize change but stability—the GMD leaders especially wanted party members to work with local elites, educating them and integrating them into the party. As had been the case before 1937, a vital part of Jiang's policy was to invite local leaders to his capital and offer them government services—education, infrastructure, capital—in return for their loyalty to his government. During 1945 and 1946, large numbers of local leaders went to Nanjing, even from areas in which the GMD in a military sense had a tenuous control, to build their links to the national elite.[27]

The pattern seen all over China in the first postwar years was therefore not so much an extension of GMD rule into the provinces as the acceptance by local elites of the legitimacy of Jiang's government. The government promises of support for local projects and protection against alternative elites, bandits, and Communists added to its attraction. Since Jiang, against the belief of many power-holders in occupied China, had in the end won against the Japanese, his promises were well worth holding out for. Unlike the situation in what had been "Free China"—the non-occupied zone—where the GMD had squandered much of its legitimacy through wartime exploitation and misrule, in the rest of the country adherence to the government still meant national cohesion and promise for the future.

The social and economic situation in the countryside, however, did not call for stability, but for change. Since the time of the Japanese attack—and in some areas well before—the always fragile balance between survival and disaster within the agricultural economy had been broken, and, to its inhabitants, parts of rural China seemed headed for a breakdown. The problem, simply put, was that decades of warfare had pulverized the local and regional forms of economic interaction that had emerged during the late imperial and early republican eras. The breakdown of markets made it impossible for farmers with large or midsize land holdings to keep their incomes at the same level as before the war. Day laborers could not find work, and the landowning elites shifted a larger portion of regional and central levies and taxes over onto poor peasants, who already lived at subsistence level. The GMD's need for income therefore accelerated a process of social dislocation that had been in motion at least since the early Republican era.[28]

The effects of war broke social and ideological bonds that had existed for generations. The sudden crushing of the aspirations of the wealthier inhabitants of a community made it easier for them to impoverish others by denying them work, money, credit, or protection. In many cases the physical distance between wealthy and poor in times of war exacerbated this process: After the Japanese attack, many landowners left the war-stricken and chaotic countryside to seek relative safety in the cities. Whether they were in the cities or remained in the countryside, however, most wealthy families increasingly identified with modern, urban elites, consciously or unconsciously breaking with the religious or community-inspired obligations and responsibilities that in the past had tied their forebears to village or district. While this suited the GMD aim of an elite with a "national" consciousness, the ideological shifts may have hurried both the alienation from traditional, mutual bonds of loyalty at the village level and, over the longer term, the elites' affinity to nationalist projects other than the one represented by Jiang Jieshi.[29]

The first postwar years therefore witnessed many elements of a social crisis in the countryside to which the government would have to respond. The records of the GMD show that the heads of the government were aware of some of these problems and tried to formulate solutions. Indeed, as in the cities, GMD attempts at relief in the countryside—rent reductions, public works, antibandit campaigns—joined with the rural elites' affinity with the GMD to provide a grace period for the government, lasting roughly till the fall of 1946. Meanwhile, GMD leaders in the provinces regretted the constant priority that Jiang gave to the cities, while the central GMD leadership despaired over what they saw as corruption and misrule in rural areas.

The sudden wave of peasant resistance frightened the government. But instead of acting to reduce the burdens on the villages, the GMD chose a combination of propaganda and force to deal with the unrest. Coming at a time when the common belief was that Nanjing was winning the war against the CCP, many GMD leaders thought that at least some of the problems in the countryside were caused by Communist agents who stirred up the peasants in an effort to divert the army's offensives. As a result, the GMD spent much money on meetings, leaflets, and the sending of agents to the troubled areas, playing up its military victories and castigating Communist subversion. In some areas the propaganda and the co-optation or arrest of peasant leaders obviously had some effect. But while the Communists in actual fact had been as surprised as the government with the early emergence of peasant activism in nonparty areas, GMD propaganda allowed them to take credit for much of what had happened and prepared the ground for a number of CCP successes after the party's rural offensives in 1947.[31]

Different forms of autonomous peasant resistance continued to plague the GMD and its local representatives for the rest of the war. While the CCP had its own problems with peasant activism, and—as shown in the next chapter—also faced the difficulties created by peasants withholding resources from its armies, the Communists still were far better than the GMD at making use of the anger of the rural underclass for their own purposes. The dissatisfaction in the countryside may not on its own have threatened the survival of the regime. But Jiang Jieshi's inability to stem the declining fortunes of all but the richest rural inhabitants prevented him from drawing on the natural goodwill that his party had had among generally conservative peasants and farmers in the 1920s and 1930s.

Although the resentment at Guomindang attempts at asserting state power was widespread in rural China, there was a distinctive north-south pattern in the degree of peasant unrest. The regions south of the Yangzi River, which had suffered less from the immediate effects of warfare and where the environmental conditions for agriculture were less harsh, generally saw less conflict over resources, taxes, and conscription. In the North, where agricultural conditions were worse and where some areas had seen long periods of warfare going back to the fall of the Qing empire, the clashes between local organizations or communities and the representatives of the government were often intense. In some areas, such as Shandong, parts of Hebei and Shanxi, and Anhui province, the clashes developed into armed confrontations, sometimes—but not always—under the influence of local Communist cadres. However, during the first phase of the civil war, these forms of local armed resistance were usually no match for GMD law enforcement, except in those cases in which PLA units became involved.[32]

GMD takeovers in 1945–46 did not depend solely on the Japanese capitulation and victories over the Communists. Two provinces in which local leaders had used the wartime chaos to achieve de facto autonomy—Yunnan and Xinjiang—were more or less effectively incorporated into GMD China. In the Southwestern province of Yunnan, Jiang Jieshi acted within the first two months after Tokyo's collapse. Ordering the troops of Kunming strongman Long Yun off to Vietnam to accept the Japanese surrender there, Jiang used his own U.S.-trained Fifth Army under Du Yuming to take control of the city, install a new governor, and gradually extended GMD rule to most parts of the province. Yunnan, which had had some form of semiautonomy for most of the Republican era, became a part of the "new" GMD republic.[33]

Takeover: The Northeast

The main challenge to the authority of the GMD government in 1945–46 was in and around Manchuria. Jiang Jieshi rightly believed that the Soviets, through their support for the CCP, had by mid-1946 prevented him from taking over the region. But even after the civil war broke out, and the main CCP armies were pushed up toward the Russian borderlands, the Generalissimo kept his belief that Stalin held the key to developments in the area. The GMD therefore spent much time on secret political and economic talks with the Soviets, attempting to limit Moscow's need to secure their interests through deals with the CCP. Meanwhile, the situation in those large areas of the Northeast that had been taken over by the GMD, including the main cities, started to deteriorate.

The year from mid-1945 to mid-1946 had been a period of successive shocks to the people of the Chinese Northeast. After suffering half a generation of Japanese rule, which brought discrimination and occasional brutality but also relative peace and economic development, the world known to the Northeasterners suddenly collapsed. First came the Soviet-Japanese war, which destroyed Tokyo's Guandong Army. Then came six months of Soviet occupation, characterized by destruction, pillage, and rape. Then came the Communist campaigns against collaborators, landowners, and political enemies. Then came the GMD takeover, which saw the same influx of carpetbaggers and corrupt officials as south of the Wall. And in the midst of all this, banditry increased, as did GMD-CCP warfare. Out of the inferno came those processes that laid the foundation for the first successful CCP counteroffensives in 1947.[34]

Although working against higher odds than they were farther south, the GMD made scant use of those opportunities it did have to increase its support in the Northeast. The administrative structure that Jiang set up in August 1945 at first seemed sound. Determined to keep Dongbei under strict central control, he did not use any of the pre-1932 regional

power-holders in administrative positions, but instead used GMD officials from the South. The main GMD organ in the region, the Northeast
Headquarters of the Central Military Affairs Commission, was headed by
the fifty-three-year-old Southerner Xiong Shihui, with Zhang Jia'ao, the
DL leader Zhang Junmai's brother, in charge of economic affairs, and
Jiang Jieshi's Russian-educated son Jiang Jingguo in charge of foreign affairs. They were all able men who had studied the Northeastern situation
carefully. The strategy that they developed together with the Generalissimo as the Soviets withdrew and the Communists were pushed to the
north emphasized GMD control of the cities and the main lines of communication.[35]

But while a similar strategy had worked in re-establishing some form
of GMD control in the South, it stood much less of a chance of succeeding north of the Wall. In Manchuria the territory was vast, and the regional government simply did not have the personnel to fan out from the
cities to secondary towns and larger villages. Many of the officials who
came in from the south refused to spend time in areas that were chaotic
and dangerous. Instead of going to live in the counties to which they were
assigned, they often limited their visits to occasional "relief expeditions"
to the starving population, handing out supplies and then hurrying back
to the nearest city before nightfall. Xiong repeatedly asked Nanjing for
more personnel, especially professionals—doctors, engineers—who could
start the Northeast on a slow ascent to normal conditions. But in most
cases the capital had few to spare.[36]

The situation in Dongbei was made worse by Jiang's refusal to use the
services of officials from the collaborationist administration or local leaders from before the period of Japanese occupation. Jiang feared that, unlike in the South, the Japanese in Manchuria could still be harboring political ambitions, and therefore he attempted to avoid having to deal with
them or their collaborators in any capacity. Since they probably were the
only people on the spot who could have prevented the slide toward economic and social collapse, Jiang's extraordinary reluctance to make use
of the former enemy prevented the GMD from playing one of their safest
cards in the aftermath of the takeover.[37]

General Du Yuming, appointed head of the army's Northeast Combat
Command fresh from his run-in with regionalism in Kunming, was a
zealous guardian of Jiang's principles against the more pragmatic Xiong.
With thirty thousand Japanese still in Manchuria and dozens of local
"armies" being formed, Du spent much time worrying about how to deal

with what he termed foreigners and traitors as his soldiers fought the Communists along the eastern seaboard and through the mountain passes in the West. General Xiong had recommended using the former Manchuguo armies and Japanese specialists as a part of the GMD attempts to gain full military control of the Northeast. But Du Yuming balked. Although a number of Japanese experts did serve with GMD armies in the region, there is little evidence of any large-scale use of enemy officers in the way that had happened in the South, and the collaborationist troops that did serve in Manchuria were usually brought in from neighboring provinces.[38]

The increasing rivalry between Du and Xiong contributed strongly to the GMD's problems in Manchuria. Du Yuming, a career officer originally from Shaanxi who had fought with and for Jiang Jieshi since the mid-1920s, regarded himself as the Generalissimo's main representative in the Northeast and was constantly on guard against anyone who could play the regional card against the Nanjing leadership. General Du remembered well how regional strongmen had kept these vital provinces out of reach of the central government up to the time of the Japanese takeover. His prime suspect in such a role for the postwar period was Xiong, who as a member of the Political Study group in the 1930s had been critical of some of Jiang's policies.[39]

Xiong's regional government was supposed to function as a kind of "super-administration" for the nine new provinces that Manchuria was divided into. But the headquarters often failed in controlling the provincial administrations, some of which were headed by newcomers who had little sense of what a powerhouse Manchuria could be for the Nationalist cause. General Liang Huasheng, the provincial governor of Jilin, for example, did his best to exploit the remaining industries of what had been the region's most developed area for his own profit, rather than seeing to the repair of the many factories and plants that had been incapacitated by Soviet and Communist looting. The Northeastern headquarters' inability to deal with corrupt officials like Liang hampered recovery efforts and made it difficult for the GMD to put the industrial potential of southern Manchuria behind its military efforts.[40]

The result of the GMD's difficulties in handling the takeover of Manchuria was a steady erosion of popular support for the central government. While never reaching out to potential supporters beyond the cities, the Nationalists failed in their urban policies and thereby destroyed much of the party's legitimacy in the region. By late 1946, both the rural and the urban population in Manchuria, rendered destitute by war, turned to alternative power-holders for protection. As in many areas south of the Wall, the most immediate alternatives to GMD power were local strongmen, bandits, or secret societies. But unlike most provinces in the South, the Northeast also possessed a more comprehensive alternative in the organization of the Communist Party, which was well armed, with support from across the Soviet and North Korean borders and a distinctive regional strategy.

A Troubled Economy

When the war against Japan suddenly ended, most Chinese expected that the economic situation in the country would improve. Many people saw the trouble that the GMD had faced in managing the wartime economy in the Southwest as a product of the war and of the immense efforts it had taken to resist the Japanese onslaughts. But, as in most countries after a war, prosperity did not come easily to postwar China. Jiang Jieshi's determination to fight the Communists—and everyone else who could challenge his domination of China—compounded these general problems of postwar conversion and reform. Combined with the government's bad choices in dealing with macroeconomic issues, the cost of the civil war proved too much for GMD China to bear.

Much of the difficulties of 1945 were the cumulated effects of the anti-Japanese war, and, for some areas of the country, of intermittent military strife ever since the fall of the Qing empire. Warfare and its consequences had put considerable strain on the Chinese economy, up to the point of reversing some of the gains that had been made in the urban capitalist sector during the 1920s and early 1930s. In many provinces overall agricultural production declined, while social and economic inequality increased. While long-term economic, technological, and ecological difficulties may have predisposed China for such a development in the mid-twentieth century, it was war that was the immediate reason for the country's economic troubles.[41]

In terms of government finances, the situation in 1945 was bad, but in no way hopeless. In spite of heavy international debt and its wartime inflationary monetary policies, the GMD regime held substantial gold and currency reserves—the latter amounting to just under U.S. $1 billion at the end of 1945. Backed by Washington, and boosted by its position as one of the victorious powers of World War II, Nanjing met considerable international goodwill in the postwar rescheduling of debts. The United States provided new loans for a total of $132 million in 1945 and 1946, not including transfers of surplus materiel from the U.S. Army and Navy in China or U.S. aid through the UN Relief and Rehabilitation Administration (UNRRA), which together probably amounted to more than $500 million. The UNRRA aid, which began in November 1945, was particularly important for improving the situation in rural areas, providing altogether more than $650 million worth of food, clothing, seeds, and medical supplies to the population, the largest program the organization carried out for any country worldwide. In terms of industrial capacity, most of the factories and plants of the Japanese-held cities had survived the last phase of the war unscathed—unlike, for instance, occupied Europe. In the countryside, for the first time in several years, harvests in 1945 and 1946 were reasonably good.[42]

The first economic issues that the post–World War II GMD regime faced were the lack of government revenue, the need for monetary stabilization, and the wish for state control of industry. As we have seen, the GMD did attempt to reform the tax system in the wake of the war, but with only limited success. Far too little of the taxes driven in at the local level ever reached Nanjing, and glaring loopholes in the tax laws enabled speculators and those with public offices (in some cases the same people) to avoid most forms of taxation. Although total government revenue increased by about 60 percent between 1945 and 1947, it was still too little to cover the government's regular expenses, debt repayment, extraordinary relief costs, and the costs of preparing and fighting a war with the Communists. In addition, some of the new indirect taxes, as well as levies placed on the provinces, could be paid in kind, thereby increasing the rural inhabitants' sense of government plunder.[43]

The GMD's need for revenue also influenced its policies on state control of industries. The GMD had long believed that heavy industry— steel, coal, mining, and the like—should be owned or at least directed by the government. But in the takeover of Japanese or collaborator-owned factories, GMD officials wanted first and foremost a quick buck for the government (and preferably for themselves as well). Many important industrial plants, including heavy industry, were therefore auctioned off to the highest bidder, irrespective of plans for the future of the business. In some cases factories were dismantled and the equipment sold. In others the plants spent many months idle, because the new owners had no idea of how to run their acquisitions or because they had no capital with which to do so. As seen earlier, these procedures held up the process of normalization and imposed some of the same problems of inefficiency and corruption in recovered areas that had been the case in the GMD's Southwestern bases during World War II.[44]

The decline in production led to a sharp rise in prices from late 1945 on. Although the government made many attempts to control price increases between 1946 and 1948, they never came close to dealing efficiently with the problem, primarily because its root cause was the lack of monetary stability. Already in the fall of 1945 the depreciation of the currency of the Japanese-held areas had led to rising prices, in part because of the government's failure to institute a fixed rate of exchange. The GMD's first experiment with fixed prices, in the winter of 1945–46 led predictably to further speculation, hoarding, and closures. Still, against the advice of at least some of his economists, Jiang clung to the idea that he could regulate prices by government fiat. In April 1946, under pressure from, among others, the Chen brothers, he introduced index-regulation of wages, based on the 1936 level multiplied by the current cost-of-living index, and a complete freeze on prices. But the market would not obey.[45]

The February 1947 reforms stood a better chance of at least modest success, because the government this time coupled price controls and a wage freeze with the use of its power against speculators, hoarders, and corrupt officials. Coming at a time of substantial GMD military advances against the Communists, the government's initiatives at stopping the flight of capital and credit were, at least for a while, taken seriously by the market, and both prices and inflation flattened out. The government emergency supply program of food and fuel to the cities also helped restore some urban confidence in the GMD, even though it alienated many of its rural supporters. Had the government made use of this opportunity to introduce serious monetary reform, there could have been a way out of the crisis.[46]

But the problem was that the GMD could not agree on a monetary policy. In the party there were a few Western-trained economists who saw the paradox in devising economic control measures designed to curb a demand that was steadily fueled by the increased issuance of banknotes. But for those few who understood the effects of severe inflation and cautioned against it, there were many others who saw solid political arguments against restricting the money supply: The government needed to pay its expenses; industry and business needed at least a minimum of available credit; and monetary contraction would make production more difficult and increase short-term unemployment.[47]

By not seeking a mandatory reissuance of currency and implementing a stricter financial policy in the spring of 1947, the government lost the last chance it had to stabilize the economy. But Jiang knew that limiting state expenditures meant limiting his war with the Communists, just as his troops were undertaking a general offensive against the rebels. Almost as a declaration of war against conventional economics, Jiang instead issued government bonds, meant to pay for additional military expenses. As could be expected, the bonds found few buyers, since everyone with money well remembered the government's refusal to buy back the bonds issued during the anti-Japanese war.[48]

From the summer of 1947 on, China entered a period of hyperinflation, with all of its social and economic consequences. Local goods could no longer compete with imports in the market because of production difficulties, such as high labor costs and interest rates; increases in the cost of fuel, water, electric power, and shipping; and increased taxes. By mid-1947 10 kg. cost 100,000 yuan; as there was no trust in the new 10,000-yuan bills, people had to carry bundles of notes, and traders had to assume that the packets they received had the correct contents. When, inevitably, some customers or traders gave in to the temptation to remove a few 10,000s of yuan from the bundles and were discovered, it seemed as if the money economy as such was under threat.[49]

Under such circumstances, Chinese capital naturally sought refuge abroad, especially in Hong Kong, among the Chinese in Southeast Asia, or in the United States. In spite of government attempts to legislate against it, by late 1947 the flight of capital had reached alarming proportions. Industrialists refused to invest in their own factories, since there was more money to be earned in Hong Kong or through currency speculation. As a result, increasing numbers of plants worked at reduced capacity or were simply closed down. Unemployment rose further. The plight of the unemployed—and their increasing numbers—testified to China's economic troubles and its government's inability to turn the tide.

Times of Change

Images of war dominate perceptions of China of the late 1940s. But hidden below the surface of battles and proclamations, marches and sieges, was a period of emerging social and cultural changes that would affect China for generations. Many of these changes took place both in the Nationalist-held areas and in the Communist bases; as we shall see in the next chapter, new ideas of modernity and transformation traveled in both directions, often held by people who did not manage to identify completely with either of the parties jostling for power.

The most important changes, even compared with the Communists' land revolution in the countryside, were in the way in which large groups of women saw their role in society. While the 4 May movement of the 1920s had witnessed the first attempts at crushing age-old traditions of oppression and exploitation of women in China, the period up to the mid-1940s in reality saw very little change. In most parts of the country, female babies could still be killed at birth or given away, and girls of ten and younger could be married off or sold as concubines. Bound by the "three obediences"—to her father as a young girl, to her husband as a wife, and to her sons as a widow—women had few opportunities to get an education, to form societies, or to take part in politics. Even in the cities, where traditional ideologies were weakened, the large numbers of young women who escaped rural slavery by becoming industrial workers usually did not escape exploitation as cheap labor.[50]

Still, young women who joined the exodus from the villages to cities and large towns from 1945 on had access to some advantages that women of earlier generations did not have, such as education through evening classes, companionship through welfare associations or unions, and the freedom of having their own wages and access to birth control. Observers writing about Shanghai, Wuhan, and Nanjing in the late 1940s often remarked that the behavior of women had changed the face of the cities. Dressing according to their own choice, rather than tradition, and venturing far outside their traditional confines, these women symbolized change in the midst of economic decay and social upheaval.[51]

Women of course bore a sizable share of the burden that many families were saddled with as a result of the civil war. Both in the countryside and in the cities, women had to increase their responsibility as breadwinners—and as a result, some felt forced into roles that they under other circumstances would not have considered, such as prostitution. But even as the number of prostitutes shot up after the financial debacles of 1946, some of these women kept their agency in ways that would have been impossible a generation earlier. "My mother died recently, my father is old, and we have many debts," a Suzhou woman arrested in 1947 explained to the police. "Forced by the situation, in February of this year I came to

Shanghai, and willingly placed myself at the above address, the home of Shen and Sun, as a prostitute. . . . As soon as I clear my father's debts, I plan to change occupation, either becoming a servant or returning home."[52]

In the workplace, women also took up a more prominent position in the late 1940s. Labor activism among women workers became more widespread, and their organizations more immediately political. As before the war, women workers seemed to prefer joining factorywide "sisterhoods" rather than trade unions. But at least by 1947 several of the sisterhoods had become aggressive political groups rather than the mutual aid societies of earlier decades, and almost as likely to be involved in different forms of industrial action as the male-dominated unions. Many of their leaders had been trained at YWCA night classes or CCP party cells—and to the government's surprise, the militancy of the former was sometimes at least equal to that of the latter.[53]

Among the best known labor conflicts of the civil war era was the 1948 occupation of the Shanghai Shen Xin Number Nine Mill. After the management had repeatedly turned down their demands for distribution of rice and coal rations and for paid maternity leave, six thousand women workers took over the mill for four days. In the end, they were driven out by several hundred policemen aided by three army tanks. Three women were killed in the melee and more than a hundred injured. The brutality of the police prompted solidarity actions from other women's unions and sisterhoods, including the famous Shanghai dance hostesses.[54]

But it was not only in the cities that the GMD government faced a challenge from oppressed groups. In large areas on the outskirts of the empire that the Qing rulers had created in the seventeenth century, ethnic groups such as Tibetans and Xinjiang Muslims were prepared to confront Jiang Jieshi's government. Having had a substantial degree of autonomy since the fall of the Qing, most Tibetans and Central Asian Muslims were not willing to join Jiang's reconstituted Chinese republic unconditionally. Both regions had already set up their own governments. In Tibet the regents of the young Dalai Lama, supported by the British in India, controlled all of its territory. In Xinjiang, Uighur nationalists had set up an East Turkestan Republic (ETR) in the northern and western parts of the province with tacit support from the USSR.[55]

The ETR, which was formed in 1944, sought a compromise solution with the GMD government after the Japanese capitulation. Encouraged by the Soviets, and worried about the power of the GMD armies, Muslim nationalist leaders decided to take up Jiang Jieshi's offer of a coalition government in the province, to be led jointly by GMD General Zhang Zhizhong and Ahmed Jan Kasimi of ETR. The ETR leaders would not, however, allow GMD forces into the territory they controlled in and around the Yili Valley, and they continued to spread nationalist propaganda throughout the province. General Zhang, one of the ablest of Jiang's officers, remained convinced that a military confrontation ought to be avoided, and he took steps to institute reforms that most Muslims welcomed. Local leaders noted that Zhang's determination to use force against corruption and drug smuggling in the province was a substantial change from the attitudes of his Han Chinese predecessors.[56]

Jiang's May 1947 decision to withdraw Zhang Zhizhong from Xinjiang—probably taken because of suspicions of disloyalty—proved a bad mistake. More hard-line local GMD leaders clashed with the heads of the ETR, there were riots in Urumqi and several other cities, and the fragile peace was soon broken. Local groups protested the behavior of Chinese troops, who, it was claimed, violated Muslim women and demanded goods from local merchants, to be paid for "later." Nanjing's appointment to the governorship of Mesut Sabri, a Uighur originally from the North who had long worked with the Chen brothers in the GMD apparatus, did little to allay Muslim fears.[57]

Instead of dealing with local causes of unrest, Jiang believed that the Soviet Union was behind his new troubles in Xinjiang in late 1947 and early 1948. The Generalissimo authorized a series of covert military operations against the ETR regime, in part to show Moscow his willingness to put force behind his accusations. But these actions probably strengthened rather than weakened the ETR, and radicalized its leadership. It also forced the Muslim nationalists to depend more on Soviet support, in spite of the increasing political influence in the region of the Islamic clergy. By mid-1948, as the GMD's hold on China weakened, Nanjing did agree to immediate reforms in Xinjiang, including the issuance of a local currency as a shield against hyperinflation. But the tense situation in the province nevertheless forced Jiang to keep more than ninety thousand troops idle in Xinjiang until the very end of the civil war.[58]

Unlike the peoples of Xinjiang, the Tibetans had both during the Qing and in the republican era had their own autonomous state. The rulers in Lhasa, the Dalai Lamas or their regents, had accepted their country's formal incorporation in China only to the extent that it could keep a high

Struggle for the Motherland, Muslim Rebel Pamphlet from Xinjiang, 1947

This land is our birthright left by our brave ancestors and it is our duty and responsibility to guard this heritage. The Chinese oppressors and usurpers came to this land two hundred years ago, like savages and bandits, seizing our territory, enslaving us, making our land a colony and dishonoring our holy religion. In brief, we became like men who have eyes but are blind, ears but are deaf, tongues but are dumb, and legs but are lame. Such treachery and barbarous treatment. How can they be endured? . . . Why did the Ili uprising occur? It was because we have the right to rise up against oppression for the sake of our liberty, the happiness and prosperity of our sons, and the renaissance of our religion. We also believe that Allah has said to us, "I shall punish all oppressors." We are also fully convinced that the power of the masses is the power of Allah. In this faith we fought, and over-throwing the treacherous Chinese sovereignty in the Three Districts established a free Muslim Eastern Turkestan State.

Translated in Paxton (Consul, Urumqi) to Secretary, January 13, 1947, U.S. Dept. of State, Div. of Chinese Affairs; quoted in Benson, *The Ili Rebellion*, p. 207.

degree of real and practical autonomy. During the early part of the civil war, as before and during World War II, Britain supported and attempted to influence the Lhasa authorities, since the London government wanted to maintain a Tibetan buffer dividing its Indian territory from China. After Indian independence in 1947, Jawaharlal Nehru's new government in Delhi continued much of the British policy, although Nehru was more careful not to wound Chinese feelings over Tibet. Hugh Richardson, the former British Head of Mission in Lhasa, was confirmed in his position as Indian representative by Nehru, who wrote that "we should certainly try to maintain and continue our friendly relations with the Tibetan Government and give them such aid as we have been giving them in the past." "Such aid" included a limited amount of arms, even though Nehru confided that he saw "no chance of any military danger to India arising from any possible change in Tibet."[59]

The Tibetan leadership, ruling on behalf of the 14th Dalai Lama—still a child—was divided on how to best deal with Chinese authorities after 1945. In 1946 there was fighting in Lhasa between forces loyal to the regent, Taktra, and a group supporting the former regent, Reting, who had good relations with the Guomindang. Reting, having lost much support, was later murdered in prison. Still, the regency council decided to send a group of representatives, headed by Thubten Samphel, to Nanjing for the 1948 National Assembly. In order not to give credence to the Chinese

Letter from the Twelve-year-old Dalai Lama to President Truman, 1947

To Mr. Truman, the President of the United States of America.
I am glad that you are enjoying the best of health and doing good service to uplift the happiness and prosperity of the whole world. Here, I am well and doing my best for the religion of Lord Buddha and welfare of all beings. Tsepon Shakabpa, the Financial Secretary of the Tibetan Government, and his assistant Khenchung Changkhimpa are being sent to America to observe trade conditions and to purchase gold and silver for importation into Tibet. Kindly extend your most appreciated assistance to them in purchasing and exporting gold and silver from America. With greeting scarf, a portrait of myself bearing my seal and a silk embroidered Thangka.
Dated 25th of 8th month Fire-Pig Tibetan Year.

Melvyn C. Goldstein, with the help of Gelek Rimpoche, *A History of Modern Tibet, 1913–1951: The Demise of the Lamaist State* (Berkeley: University of California Press, 1989), p. 594.

claim of full sovereignty, Taktra instructed the Tibetan delegates not to vote or even to clap, but to act as observers. Still, when attending the meeting, they accepted election to committees; but then, on Lhasa's instructions, left early so as not to sign the constitution.

Under increasing pressure from Jiang Jieshi, the regent's government was desperately seeking foreign contacts that could keep Chinese influence at bay. With great difficulty it sent trade delegations to London and Washington in 1948, but the Tibetans were unable to meet with President Truman, as they had hoped. Neither the Americans nor the British were much interested in issuing a $2 million loan against repayment in Tibetan products—wool, furs, musk, and yak tails. The Tibetan delegation did get some verbal assurances about the concern of the Western Great Powers with their cause. But when they returned to Lhasa in the fall of 1948, they found that Chinese influence was still on the rise.

For the foreign inhabitants of China, the brief era of Japanese supremacy had changed the scene forever. The century-old system of extraterritoriality, whereby foreign citizens were exempt from Chinese laws and government injunctions, had been ended by agreement between the Western powers and the Guomindang government in 1943. With the Japanese in control of the coastal cities, and with most of their foreign inhabitants interned or driven into exile, the abolishment of the treaty ports was only a limited concession for the West's Chinese allies.

When the war ended, many foreigners hoped to re-establish their communities in China. Those who had made a good living before the war—bankers, businessmen, tradesmen, factory owners, officials, or teachers—hoped that things would return to "normal," even without the protection of the foreign concessions. Even those who came to preach the Gospel—the Christian missionaries—or those who came to escape persecution at home—the Russian and Jewish refugees—hoped for a future in China.

It was the civil war and the economic chaos that accompanied it—and not the 1949 Communist takeover—that destroyed all these hopes and put an end to a century of foreign influence in China. Since it was almost impossible to profit from the financial situation, the foreigners who were in China to do business, and those who depended on such business to make a living, began to leave by 1946. Having to sell their properties to Chinese investors or speculators for a small portion of their prewar worth, many of these foreigners blamed Chinese Communists and radicals for their predicament. When they returned to their countries of origin, some became vocal spokesmen for foreign intervention in the civil war.[60]

For the missionaries who had come to China from a host of different countries and denominations, the late 1940s also became a time of troubles. The 1920s and 1930s had been a good period for the Christian missions, with, for most of them, increasing numbers of conversions and many new parishes. But the missionaries' attempts to continue the work at their stations after the war were often frustrated by administrative chaos in the provinces, military threats, and changing attitudes among the Chinese. Many missions reported that the Chinese nationalist atti-

---

Foreign Business in Wuhan, 1947

We were exactly twelve Europeans in the place, and we used to meet for lunch every day at a grimy Russian restaurant somewhere or other. At the Hankow Race Club the stands were still occupied by Japanese prisoners who had not been repatriated. There was a golf course nearby. . . . That was for those who were keen enough to play golf, which was about six of us. . . . There was no business at all. There was virtually no shipping, there was nothing, the only ships that were moving up and down the river were tank landing craft which were carrying UNRRA supplies to starving Chinese in the interior.

F. C. B. Black, Hongkong and Shanghai Bank manager in Wuhan. Frank H. H. King, *The Hongkong Bank in the Period of Development and Nationalism, 1941–1984*. The History of the Hongkong and Shanghai Banking Corporation, vol. 4 (Cambridge: Cambridge University Press, 1991), p. 158.

tudes that had been born in the war against Japan made conversions more difficult. With declining numbers of converts and an increasing threat from Communist units, ill-disciplined GMD soldiers, and marauding bandits, the numbers of missionaries declined sharply during 1947. Among those who stayed on, some chose to work closely with the Guomindang or with U.S. military missions. As the civil war intensified, and as the number of CCP confrontations with Christian communities increased, these links became both an embarrassment and a danger for numerous Chinese Christians.[61]

As usual, it was those who did not have much money or anywhere else that welcomed them who were the last to leave. Thousands of workers from Western colonies and stateless refugees lined up to get out of China by 1948. At the beginning of that year there were still ten thousand Jews left in Shanghai, mostly people who had fled from persecution in Europe during and prior to World War II. By the end of 1948 they had almost all left—most for Israel, some for the United States. Ten years later, there were fewer than a hundred Jews in Shanghai. As shown by the fate of Shanghai, the most cosmopolitan of Chinese cities, the civil war did more to change the social and ethnic composition of urban China than the Communists managed to do in later years.[62]

The Art of Political Protest

In China, the issue of relating art to society was a central part of the intellectual trends of the twentieth century. Consciously forming worlds apart from daily life, Chinese writers and artists had in the past presented an idealization of antiquity rather than immediate comments on their own time. The post-1911 generation of artists, however, sought their ideals in the present, and wanted to use their work to benefit China in its hour of need.

In many ways, the civil war years saw the culmination of that effort. Writers, playwrights, directors, and—albeit to a lesser degree—painters and sculptors set out to use their gifts to wake their countrymen to action against the country's ills. Chinese art of the late 1940s was realist in tone and critical in attitude—it castigated the government for corruption and ineptitude, and for failing to provide relief to those who were made to suffer for the GMD's mistakes (who, in many tableaus, included artists themselves in a prominent position). In a more effective way than any Communist propaganda, these artists exposed to the middle class the increasing hollowness of the government's claim to represent all of China.

Artistic expression was probably freer during the last part of the 1940s than at any other period of Chinese history up to the 1990s. Although official censorship was reinstituted in 1947, until the very last months of GMD rule their censors did little beyond banning journalism that told the truth from the battlefields or movies that called on the people to rebel. And in an increasing number of cases, the publishing houses and film studios did not care much about the government's wishes. As a result, an amazing series of novels, dramas, and movies commenting in different ways on the last phase of GMD rule were produced.[63]

Throughout the civil war, the direct CCP influence on writers and artists was negligible, in spite of the Center's repeated instructions to its agents in GMD areas to recruit "progressive artists and scholars." The Communist approach to literature and arts seemed to have been too regimented for the tastes of most Chinese writers and artists, too removed from their own experience in the cities. In spite of their failure to recruit, CCP leaders were wise enough to realize that the critical intellectuals were tactical allies against the GMD, although the Communists spent much time worrying about how to deal with their tactical allies after victory was won.[64]

The rich fiction literature of the civil war era influenced the views that the reading classes held of China's fate and of the fighting parties. Often serialized in popular magazines or newspapers prior to publication as books, the most prominent novels reached a wide audience and often formed an important part of the public criticism of the Guomindang regime. Although some of the best novels published between 1945 and 1950 describe events during the anti-Japanese war, the public had few doubts that the society they saw described was contemporary China.

Two of the best-selling novels of the time, Shi Tuo's *Jiehun* (*Marriage*) and Qian Zhongshu's *Weicheng* (*Fortress Besieged*), both from 1947,[65] are satires of middle-class life in the cities during the war of resistance. Shi's book is about deceit, lost fortunes, abandoned love, and murder. The plot centers on the value of medicines on the black market—drugs that could have been used to save soldiers' lives are instead traded as a kind of currency. *Weicheng*, a novel that is so biting in its criticism of unrestrained power that it could not be republished in the PRC before 1980, makes light of the educated class—particularly those trained abroad—and their need to ingratiate themselves with an unpopular regime. In his description of faked diplomas, faked love, and teachers of

ethics who profit from smuggling, Qian presents the need to choose between honesty (and destitution) or dishonesty (and wealth).

Ba Jin's 1947 *Hanye* (*Cold Nights*) is deservedly regarded as a master-
piece of twentieth-century Chinese literature.[66] Also set in Chongqing
during the war, Ba's novel asks whether the sacrifices some intellectuals
were willing to make for the country while fighting the Japanese were
worth the effort. What did they make their sacrifice for? Another author,
Tian Tao, in *Wotu* (*Rich Soil*, 1947) asks the same question on behalf of
a rural family in North China, for whom war meant breakdown and despair.[67] The family's daughters are sold, its men dragged into military service. And the harshness of the climate and the poverty of the soil means
that there is no solution except radical change. Gu Liu's colorful and immensely popular *Xiaqiu zhuan* (*The Tale of Shrimpball*) describes a petty
thief in Hong Kong who ends up robbing his own father and has to run
away to Guangzhou.[68] Joining the South China underworld, Shrimpball
gets involved with corrupt GMD officials and Americans, selling
weapons to both sides during the civil war. But in a somewhat anticli-
mactic ending he repents and joins the PLA in the hills, becoming a hero
of the resistance. The message—vitally important to many Chinese—was
that GMD rule meant destruction of values, and that the Communists
were the only hope for restoring order.

Important as books and magazines were to the Chinese bourgeoisie,
they could in no way compete with the movies for mass popularity. When
1940s urban China—and a great number of small town inhabitants—
wanted to be entertained, they went to watch their favorite film stars per-
form—be it in light comedies, re-enactments of Chinese classics, or more
serious contemporary films. Film studios in GMD China made more than
150 movies during the civil war, and almost twice as many were produced in Hong Kong, most often intended for the Chinese market. The
main film studios, such as Kunlun in Shanghai, were in many periods
dominated by critical left-wing directors, writers, and producers—intellectuals who had trouble with both pre- and post-1949 authorities.[69]

The themes that they chose for their serious films provide useful insights into the self-perception of many urban intellectuals in the 1940s.
Many of the directors and screenwriters saw the inhabitants of the cities
as languid and hesitant; they watched as China moved toward disaster,
unable to act, incapable of preserving what was best in China's traditions
or applying new knowledge to help their country. Even those who tried

to act were kept down by corrupt officials, reactionary parents, or their own numerous obligations in society. In the end, many of these movies seem to suggest, there is no hope for China other than a cataclysm that sweeps away the old and begins to build from scratch.

Apart from *Spring River Flows East* and *Nothing But a Dream*, there were many serious movies that dealt in a direct way with Guomindang China. *Distant Love* [*Yaoyuan de ai*, 1947], a kind of Chinese Pygmalion, depicts a professor's successful attempts to transform a servant girl through education into a modern, liberated woman. When the Japanese attack comes, the girl distances herself from her mentor and becomes a soldier, while the professor remains safely behind the lines. Fei Mu's *Springtime in a Little Town* [*Xiaocheng zhi chun*, 1948] is a beautifully filmed love story, showing that love cannot thrive when the country cannot give opportunities to its best men and women. The magnificent *Ten Thousand Rays of Light* [*Wanjia denghuo*, 1948] portrays a young Shanghai clerk who cannot feed his family because of monetary inflation. The dark mood of the movie—the shots from high up of the city at night, with its ten thousand lights flickering like dying fires, and the narrator's voice prophesying that disaster will come because a few families are privileged but most live in misery—creates an effective condemnation of life in Shanghai under the GMD.

The historical dramas and the comedies also in some cases reflected their directors' views of the state of affairs. *Guohun* [*The Spirit of China*, 1948] shows how the Song dynasty went under because of the emperor's refusal to institute reforms or to resist foreign encroachments. *Secret History of the Qing Court*, a film made in 1948 in Hong Kong but widely popular in China, invited its viewers to see late Qing corruption and decay as a parallel to the demoralization of the GMD regime. *Yanyang tian* [*Brilliant Sun*, 1948] is an irreverent piece of black humor about how black marketeers and former collaborators thrived during the postwar period, while patriots and righteous people were mistreated and impoverished.

One of the distinguishing features of the antiwar student movement was its ability to make use of new forms of protest, closely linked to developments in postwar culture. In turn, the way in which the protest movement spread its message profoundly influenced the character of the movement itself, how it was led, and the political directions it took. Protest tended to be colorful and exciting—bright armbands, bloodied clothing, flags flown at half mast, songs, chants, posters, decorated buses and trains bound for faraway destinations. "Today," wrote an observer of the otherwise drab Shanghai railway station during rallies in June of 1946, "it wore five-colored clothes, with red and green posters and slogans written in multi-colored chalk everywhere on the walls, the posts, the cars and the ground."[70]

From early on, the antiwar movement learned to package its message in different ways for different audiences, using street theater and chants for working-class spectators and petitions and leaflets for officials and the middle class. The leaders became increasingly conscious of the role of their performances. "We have already moved past the old 'Down with such and such' and 'Up with such and such' types [of chants]," said a student leader in 1947. "[Now we] have begun to shout out these lively and specific new slogans: 'Our stomachs are empty!' and 'We are begging food from the mouth of guns!' The style of chanting has also advanced in a new direction: formerly there was always one person leading everybody in chants, and sentences were shouted intermittently. But now people have created linked chants in which sentences are joined together. There are also question and answer refrains, making for livelier chants."[71]

As the confrontations in the streets between police and demonstrators became more intense in 1947, the students developed special techniques to appeal directly to those sent to prevent them from marching. They chanted, "Soldiers, policemen, and students are all part of one family—People don't beat up their own kin—Establish democracy and seek peace." Student activists also sought out students and radical sympathizers who were sons and daughters of the chiefs of police and drilled them in how to plead with their fathers not to attack the demonstrators. They even began appealing to foreign residents, including U.S. soldiers, through leaflets and letters, using biblical language and Western allegories to explain their purpose.[72]

During 1946 and the first half of 1947 the radical student movement had to share the streets with an important but much less noticed GMD loyalist movement. Often but not always organized by the *Sanqingtuan* or other youth movements close to the GMD, the loyalist student marches could attract substantial participation in most cities during the first postwar years. One would often find two demonstrations in the same city on the same day, using similar language and mediums, but with different political content—the loyalists, for instance, changed the radical

---

GMD Proclamation against Student Unrest, March 1947

Those who are short-sighted have steadily succumbed to the lowly pursuit of materialism. As for the better quality youth, they have often become targets of political struggles. This is the time of progress. Yet, our youth who are needed for our national reconstruction are wasting their energies on political activism which is fruitless and inappropriate. National reconstruction needs a firm scholarly foundation, but the majority of today's youth are still neglecting the learning of basic knowledge. It requires various forms of specialized skills, but the majority of today's youth cannot settle down quietly to receive training in practical skills.

Proclamation of the 3d plenum of the 6th GMD Central Executive Committee, 24 March 1947, quoted from Huang Jianli, *The Politics of Depoliticization in Republican China: Guomindang Policy towards Student Political Activism, 1927–1949* (Bern: Peter Lang, 1996), p. 169.

---

slogan *Fan neizhan* ["Oppose civil war"] to *Fan neiluan* ["Oppose chaos in China"]. Their competition with the radicals was sometimes violent but more often carried out through displays or slogans. Up to mid-1947 it seems that the vast majority of students supported neither side, preferring to keep neutral and get on with their studies.[73]

Particularly during its early phase, before the direct influence of the CCP started to grow, the student movement had a distinctly antiforeign tinge. Posters with grotesque caricatures of foreign soldiers and slogans extolling Chinese virtues and condemning foreign treachery were part of many marches and demonstrations. The alleged rape of a Chinese student by U.S. soldiers in Beijing in December 1946 therefore became an immediate cause celebre for the movement. Mass rallies followed all over China, during which the students set up local protest committees consisting of representatives of all the schools in a city. In Shanghai, the GMD—realizing how much genuine public anger the Beijing rape had generated—for the first (and only) time provided police protection for the protest rallies.[74]

The interconnected developments of May and June 1947 constituted a real breakthrough for the radical antiwar movement. The steep decline in living conditions in the cities hit many students hard and removed much of the sympathy that may have existed for the GMD government. In part for that reason, the radical student marches swelled in size and in political importance. Beginning as often before (and later) with rallies on 4

May in the major cities, the antirepression, antihunger demonstrations spread to all urban areas in China. Groups from different areas met in Nanjing on 19 May to create a coordinated, nationwide campaign. The following day, while marching in the capital, the student activists were attacked by police and military units. Fifty student leaders were arrested, and hundreds beaten up.[75]

This showdown in the center of the Nationalist capital was a PR disaster for the GMD, spreading the message of the student movement wide, including to foreign news broadcasters. It also convinced the GMD leadership that it had to prevent similar occurrences in the future. In the heavy-handed repression that followed, the government attempted to arrest radical student leaders and suspended all newspapers that reported favorably on the student movement. Activists were chased off campus by GMD toughs. Some were assassinated. To some extent it could be said that the repression worked. The general strike that the students had called for on 2 June never materialized, and although student unrest continued throughout the GMD period, marches never again reached the size of mid-1947.[76]

Both the government and the students paid a high price for the violent confrontations. The GMD was hit almost immediately by the delegitimizing effect of having to shoot at students in the streets of its own capital. Intellectuals, businessmen, and foreign experts who had served the regime for years began to question its survivability. Even among the GMD military—the regime's staunchest supporter—some high-ranking officers voiced their concern.

But the confrontation also cost the student movement dearly. Most of its leaders were arrested, terrorized into silence, or fled to CCP-held areas. The movement itself was in part forced underground and therefore lost much of its spontaneity, inventiveness, and public support. As a result, it was opened up to CCP infiltration on a much bigger scale than before, and from the late fall of 1947 on the Communists controlled much of the student movement in the cities. As we shall see in Chapter 4, the CCP used this control to limit the aims and the methods of the antiwar movement and steer it away from mass action. Compared with the vitality of the 1946–47 student movement, these meeker tactics go far toward explaining why GMD rule survived in the cities until they were conquered from outside.

For most people in the cities of China, the May 1947 events were the first time since the Japanese occupation that they had encountered large-

scale repression. A poet who witnessed the police beating up students in
Beijing wrote:

> Sons and daughters of the Yellow River!
> Listen! The storm is raging wild and furious
>   over the earth!
> Watch! The sea-spray has wet your brow.
> In our minds an angry wave rises
> high as the peaks of Xiangshan.[77]

4

ADJUSTING HEAVEN

Communist Rule in the Provinces

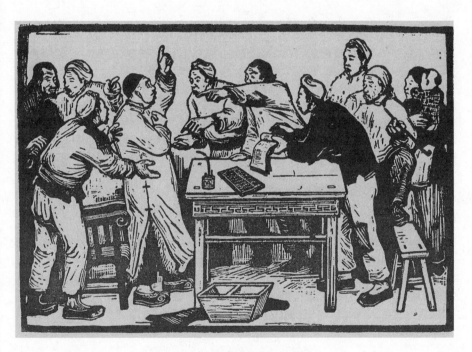

Gu Ruan, "Reducing the Rent"

The war and the lack of government relief had set off a social and eco-nomic crisis in large areas of the Chinese countryside. The Communist leaders were aware of the proportions of the crisis and were eager to ex-ploit it for their own purposes. This story—of how the CCP transformed peasant suffering into military zeal—has been a key motif in writing the history of the civil war. Many historians have seen the transformation as an unavoidable result of the complementarity of Communist policies and peasant demands: The peasants supported the Communists because the CCP gave them what they wanted. More recent literature, however, has modified this picture, stressing the Communists' abilities to manipulate politics at the local level as an important part of their success, especially in those areas in which the party had few or no local roots.

There is little doubt that the CCP by focusing on the land issue had found a cause that many peasants—North and South—thought to be re-lated to their core problem, which was poverty. The party cadres' ability to win an audience in the villages of North China prior to the arrival of the Liberation Army is by itself proof of this.[1] But the change from being a willing audience to providing the minimum of practical and political support that the PLA needed to transform its defeats into offensives was the critical element of change during the late 1940s. It was there that the political abilities of the party cadres played a decisive role, together with the leadership's sometime willingness, at the tactical level, to let its cadres make use of their skills without undue interference.

The story of the Communist base areas during the civil war is there-fore not a story of unyielding expansion based on GMD weakness and the appeal of CCP policies. On the contrary, it is an account of a struggle between the party and its opponents in which thousands of small and large compromises between party cadres and local power-holders played a crucial role. It was the Communists' increasing skills in fitting in locally that gave them the edge in the competition with their enemies, and that saved them when they were squeezed between superior military forces.

The outcome of this struggle was not given until the tide turned at the battlefields in 1948. The Communists made mistakes that made their lo-cal allies lose confidence in them, and some of their compromises failed or they chose the wrong partners, often resulting in the cadres' being hounded from villages they had worked in for months. Sometimes rigid Communist ideas were at the core of the defeat, but as often it was the cadres' willingness to promise all things to all men that got them into trouble. In rural communities that still cherished Confucian ideals of rectitude, the CCP's tactical maneuverability could easily be mistaken for lying and cheating.

In spite of all the campaigns that the Communists conducted in the areas they controlled, only a small part of the peasantry actually participated in the main CCP activities—organizing supplies and fighting the war. In some areas, where villagers viewed exploitation and injustice as having increased sharply during the war years, there was solid peasant support for land confiscations, public denouncements, and the execution of landlords. But in most areas the large majority of peasants remained spectators, treating the Communists no differently than other power-holders who had controlled their villages over the past decades. For the peasants, even more than for the urban dwellers, the late 1940s were first and foremost about survival through troubled times.

Leadership and Military Organization

From mid-1946 on, the Chinese Communist leadership concentrated all their efforts at staving off the GMD military onslaught. It was, as often before, a question of survival, of fighting rear-guard actions and avoiding decisive encounters. But the critical difference between this and the 1920s and early 1930s, or with the anti-Japanese war, was that in 1946–47 the party leadership did not foresee an eventual compromise with the GMD as the outcome of the war. The civil war, they acknowledged, was a fight to the finish—either the Guomindang triumphed, and the Communists were crushed, or the CCP drove the GMD armies on the defensive, undermining Jiang Jieshi's position and becoming the dominant political party in China.

The CCP leaders now believed that the United States and the Soviet Union were headed for confrontation and that Jiang Jieshi had carte blanche within the GMD for war. Out of these perceptions came not only the belief that war was unavoidable but also that the whole party had to be refashioned for the war effort. It is not surprising, therefore, that the party structure itself changed as the war progressed. From using military action as an accompaniment to political maneuvers, as Mao Zedong had often done during the anti-Japanese war, politics from mid-1946 on became dependent on military accomplishments. "A temporary cease-fire is only possible when the enemy's military attacks are repeatedly defeated and their troops are annihilated on a large scale," Mao Zedong told his Northeastern commanders in October 1946.[2]

During the war, Mao stayed in close touch with his commanders in the field; he talked to them and sought their political as well as military advice. There was never any doubt as to who gave the orders—no CCP commander doubted the primacy of the Politburo and its Chairman—but up to the time when Mao made up his mind, there was much discussion and, sometimes, disagreement. Some commanders—especially Lin Biao—got away with a significant amount of tactical insubordination, especially in late 1945 and, again, in early 1947. But at the strategic level, the party's forces could act with remarkable coordination, especially considering the primitive state of their communication systems.

At the operational level—as we have seen in Chapter 2—the party had two main difficulties. One was to secure enough logistical support outside its base areas to expand its military operations. Except in Manchuria, the CCP did not do well in 1945–46 in constructing stable networks of support for its troops outside the districts in which the party had operated during World War II. The other main difficulty was finding a way to shift manpower from one area to another so that the party could transform minor military successes to at least limited offensives. By late 1946, Mao Zedong was desperate to gain at least some victories against the GMD in the field.

The party leadership's response to these difficulties was an almost complete militarization of the CCP-held areas, accompanied by a reorganization of its forces that tied them closer to the political regions they were supposed to represent. The People's Liberation Army, the new form that the Communist forces gradually took during late 1946, symbolized this mass militarization. The party leaders wanted the whole people to take part in the military struggle against Jiang Jieshi—there was to be no division between combatants and noncombatants, and nobody in the CCP-held areas could opt out of the Communist war effort. In the counties, in the villages, and in the families, all should find their place in supporting the PLA.

The militarization of the CCP and the areas it held had antecedents in earlier CCP history and, of course, in international Communism. Lenin and the Soviet party had emphasized the need for regimentation and total mobilization during their civil war between 1917 and 1921. During the last phase of the war against Japan, the party rectification campaign that Mao implemented had as one of its aims to streamline the party ideologically and organizationally in preparation for the postwar power struggle. Many of the elements of that campaign—the chanting of slo-

Protect Chairman Mao, PLA Marching Song, 1947

Green bean rice,
With barley,
Take one bite,
Sweet as honey,
Fills the stomach,
Frees the mind.
Remember the dog food of years past,
Anger wells up in the heart.

Built a house,
Two plots of land,
Now we have a calling,
Never again someone else's donkey,
Never again be treated unfairly.

No longer tenant farmers,
Our bodies content,
Bright prospects today,
due to our Chairman Mao.

Jiang Jieshi,
Puppet emperor,
Seeing people turning over,
Anxiously scratches his head,
Everywhere there is defeat
Scales Yan'an to "attack Chairman Mao,"
"Attack Chairman Mao,"
Our anger swells,
I join the fight at the front,
Capture the old thief,
Shred his skin,
Cull his bones.
My Chairman Mao I shall protect,
My glorious days I will keep!

PLA marching song from Shandong, in Ren Xuexian, ed., *Shandong jiefangqu wenxue yanjiu*, trans. by Sim Chi-yin and the author (Jinan: Shandong renmin, 1983), pp. 429–30.

gans, the collective reading of the party canon, and the search for enemies—were revived in late 1946 and played a role throughout the civil
war.[3]

The increasing militarization also conformed to one of Mao Zedong's
visions of the creation of socialism. Since the early 1920s, Mao had been
preoccupied with the concept of man's regaining his freedom by voluntarily surrendering his will to collective action. To Mao, militarization for
the sake of revolution was the highest stage of such a transformation.
Mobilizing the people as an army was, to Mao, a contribution to the creation of socialism in the future, because many of the qualities and organizational aspects of the army would have to be retained by the socialist
state.

Although the idea of militarization was adopted by the party leaders
as a reasonable response to the GMD threat, some Communists repeatedly warned against giving the PLA political superiority over the party
organs. Ren Bishi, a party leader well versed in Communist theory and
Soviet practice, was one of those who had such concerns. Kang Sheng,
the CCP head of intelligence, was another. But in spite of these concerns,
the PLA became the centerpiece of the party's development between 1946
and 1949.[4]

Mao wanted to make sure, however, that the new army organization
was as closely linked to the political aspects of the party's work as possible. At the central level, he himself headed the Central Committee's Revolutionary Military Committee (Zhongyang geming junshi weiyuanhui),
with Zhu De, Liu Shaoqi, Zhou Enlai, and Peng Dehuai as members, and
Yang Shangkun as secretary. The Military Committee was the nerve center of the war and of CCP decision-making during this period. Its composition did not change until after October 1949.

The Communists divided China into eight military regions, although
one of these, South China, did not have its own army until the reorganization of the PLA in early 1949. The Central Plains army grew in
strength only gradually during 1947. The six others operated out of the
base areas that the CCP had set up during and immediately after the anti-
Japanese war, and they were named after the Chinese abbreviations for
the provinces they operated in. The biggest forces were those of the
Northeast Democratic United Army, commanded by Lin Biao, in
Manchuria. In the Northwest, there was the ShaanGanNing army, and,
closer to Beijing, the JinSui army. The JinChaJi army operated out of the
traditional base areas in North China west of Beijing, while the JinJiLuYu

army covered the northern region toward the seaboard. The New Fourth Army (later renamed the Shandong army and the East China army) under Chen Yi operated farther south along the coast.[5]

The military regions, and the armies, were under the control of the overall army commanders, in spite of the system of political commissars that the CCP had adopted from the Soviet Red Army. Only in a few cases—most notably in the Central Plains army, in which Liu Bocheng had Deng Xiaoping as his "political"—did the commissars have decisive influence over how the region was organized. Other commanders, He Long and Chen Yi especially, were known to routinely disregard the instructions from their political commissars, unless, of course, these were backed up by orders from the Military Committee.[6]

During the first year of the civil war, most of the weapons for the PLA were of Japanese origin. In some cases these weapons had been taken by the CCP forces from the weapons depots of the Imperial Army in North China and Manchuria immediately after Tokyo's capitulation in August 1945. But a very large number of these weapons, and almost all of the Japanese heavy weaponry in the PLA arsenals, were transferred to the CCP by the Soviets in numerous installments from late 1945 to mid-1947. These weapons were of crucial importance for the PLA's survival in the face of the GMD offensives of late 1946 and early 1947.[7]

From 1947 on, the Communist armies relied to an increasing degree on weapons captured from the enemy, especially U.S. weapons transferred to the GMD armies between 1944 and 1946. Of the American weapons that the GMD government received after the United States lifted its ten-month arms embargo in May 1947, a substantial portion fell into enemy hands almost as soon as the GMD High Command had transferred them for use in the field. The Communists became masters at stealing and buying weapons from local GMD units, and they often set up attacks and ambushes especially to capture weapons and equipment. As the major battles of the war commenced, the CCP was therefore reasonably well equipped with modern arms, even though its policy of strict central control of captured weapons and the Center's reluctance to risk heavy weaponry in limited engagements hindered some PLA operations, especially in the spring of 1947.[8]

Up to 1948 the PLA had great difficulty in recruiting soldiers, even from areas that had fallen under their military control. The peasants were, as a rule, no more willing to leave their homes to join the army of the Communists than they were to join with the CCP's enemies. The land redistribution campaigns, which gave many peasants their own land for the very first time, were, ironically enough, counterproductive in terms of supplying manpower for the army: Since they now had land to till, the peasants saw even less of a reason to march off to fight somewhere else. Some, of course, volunteered out of idealism or, more often, out of pressure from the new village authorities. But on the whole, the results of the political campaigns for joining the Liberation Army were disappointing to Yan'an.[9]

Even if, generally speaking, the peasant class were at best unwilling recruits to the PLA, it was not difficult for the Communists to find others to join their armies. As had been the case throughout their military experience, the Communist commanders recruited liberally among the adherents of local strongmen and bandit chiefs, and among people who had been displaced by war. After the GMD started losing battles in the North, a substantial number of the soldiers who were taken prisoner, injured, or left behind by their fleeing officers eventually joined the PLA. Some sources estimate that, by late 1948, almost half of those serving with the regular PLA armies had at some point been fighting on the opposite side. The PLA soldiers, in other words, had far more and far different fighting experience than the term "peasant army" usually denotes.[10]

These recruits were both pulled and pushed into the PLA. Many were attracted by the discipline and dedication of PLA officers, and by their good record of looking out for their men. In many PLA divisions, the recruits would be better clothed and fed than they had ever been before. CCP forces also did considerably better than the GMD in minimizing losses and rescuing injured soldiers—both issues of vital importance to troops in the field. In many cases, however, the push factors were equally important. Deserters feared punishment if they went back to the government side, or the stigma of a defeated soldier if they returned to their villages. Many, before taking up arms, had made enemies in their home areas who might call them to account, as in the case of Gu Liu's antihero in *Shrimpball*. In some cases their villages or families had been displaced or destroyed by war.[11]

The greatest success of the CCP was the organization of supplies and support for its armies. The party had learned much about guerrilla warfare during the 1930s and early 1940s—during the civil war it had to transfer this knowledge to a much more massive form of warfare, whereby whole armies, not only guerilla groups, would have to be supplied. As a by-product of land reform in the villages, the CCP managed

Resisting the Guomindang, 1947

We knew that the Kuomintang officials still wanted to make money from selling the sea salt. They still did not want us to produce the earth salt because the sea salt yielded a tax for them. The CCP, on the other hand, encouraged us to produce anything we could, and purchased many of our items to use in constructing the nation—things like nitrate, for example. We knew that if Chiang Kai-shek returned to power through the civil war, his armed forces would not allow us to make earth salt anymore. They would tax us, or punish us, for making it because the revenue obtained from the salt of the state would be invaded by our earth salt. If Chiang Kai-shek had won, the salt police would have returned and harmed our livelihood. We would have lost the good life we had gotten. By March 1945 the CCP had revoked all taxes imposed by the Kuomintang, including the salt tax. Thus we held a mass meeting in the village, and we told villagers that "when Chiang Kai-shek returns he will bring back all the old land taxes, the miscellaneous taxes, and the salt tax, and we will not have a good life."

Reminiscences by Yao Zhenbian, a peasant salt trader and party leader from Qian Foji, northern Henan. Quoted in Ralph A. Thaxton, Jr., *Salt of the Earth: The Political Origins of Peasant Protest and Communist Revolution in China* (Berkeley: University of California Press, 1997), p. 281.

to set up militia and self-defense units that would assist the PLA during fighting in the area. The village peasant associations and other social organizations, such as the women's associations, agreed with the CCP cadres as to how they could assist the army. At the village level, it was these new associations that supplied the grain, dug the trenches, carried weapons and equipment, and nursed sick and wounded soldiers. They provided the glue that kept the PLA going through the hard times of 1946–47, and the fuel that fired the offensives of 1947–48.[12]

The reason that the CCP could get many peasants to volunteer as labor for the war effort in their area, while the GMD could get similar support only by strong pressure (which lost them political capital), was land reform and the political changes that accompanied it. The peasants knew what happened where the GMD had returned, and they voted with their labor to keep the reforms in place. But, as with recruitment, the development of the civilian war effort showed that the cautious peasants also responded to information from the battlefield. The news about CCP victories in the North did more than anything to fuel peasant enthusiasm for helping the PLA.

CCP Policy-making

According to its party theory, the CCP was a strictly hierarchical organization, based on Leninist principles of centralization. At the apex was the Politburo. Its thirteen members represented the party's Central Committee (CC); full meetings of the CC itself were called only on a few occasions during the civil war.[13] The Politburo directed the work of all party units, including the regional bureaus and the CC committees dealing with military affairs, propaganda, "social affairs" (intelligence), and other areas. The decision-making process at all levels of the party was secret, and information was available to members only on a "need-to-know" basis.

As we have already seen, the party that fought the civil war was different from this ideal, although the ideal was never surrendered and it stayed an important part of the CCP's political framework of reference. In terms of directing the war, the Central Revolutionary Military Committee was the core body, not the Politburo. But even more important, the role of these collectives was gradually being replaced by the authority of the party Chairman, Mao Zedong. Often, when inner party documents during the civil war refer to *zhongyang*—the center—the reference is neither to the Politburo nor the CRMC, but to Mao himself.[14]

Mao's position within the party was based on the construction of party history and party ideology that had taken place during the Yan'an period. Those who had joined the CCP during the anti-Japanese war—which was the great majority of party members—were schooled in stories of the party's creation, its first revolutionary activities, and the Long March that put Mao squarely at the center. He was the one who had saved the party from the political mistakes of the early period, who had led the exodus from southern China to the North, and who had designed the strategy that proved successful in expanding the party's power during the war against Japan. It was Mao's writings that had formed the core of the massive party rectification campaign of 1942–44, during which Mao's line was identified with party policy; all those who at any time had disagreed with the party leader on issues of principle had to carry out self-criticism. Even if political discussions were not uncommon among party leaders and in the Military Committee during the civil war, the party chairman could, if he wanted to, set policy solely by his own authority.

The main strategic issue for CCP decision-making during the civil war was land policy. As the leadership had agreed more than ten years earlier, the party's chances of survival in the countryside depended on how it could shape the political consciousness of the peasants. The key to addressing that question was through deciding who should make use of the land, and how the income derived from the land should be divided. But the party leaders had had a hard time agreeing among themselves as to what was the right land policy.[15]

In early 1946, as the peace process broke down and the CCP came under attack, Mao insisted on radical land reform as the key to the party's survival. The reason, the Chairman thought, why a larger number of peasants tied themselves to the party after land reform than after campaigns for rent reduction or "settling scores" was the political consciousness that redividing the land created. By taking land, the peasants destroyed the political power of landowners and local strongmen as a class in a more fundamental way than by publicly criticizing them or even killing them. But expropriating the property of those who had held power in the village before the arrival of CCP cadres also linked the peasants with the Communist Party by the consequences of their actions. They knew what their fate would be if the GMD returned.[16]

The turn to radical land reform was controversial within the party. As early as the fall of 1946, a number of local cadres complained that the new policies upset the alliances that they had worked out with people or groups of wealth and influence in their villages, alliances on which the security of their bases depended. These complaints were echoed at the central level by leaders who, while supporting the policy in principle, were concerned with the effects it might have on the party's United Front policies. They feared that as reports of the often violent "overthrow" of property owners in CCP-held areas spread, it would be more difficult to penetrate GMD territory—so-called White areas—through local alliances and political bargaining.[17]

A particular difficulty of radical land reform and the political campaigns that accompanied it was the fact that in 1946 and most of 1947, CCP-held areas were mostly restricted to bases that the party had dominated for a very long time. In other words, the campaigns often resulted in the overthrow of local leaders who had worked closely with the CCP or were members of the party. In a report summarizing local experiences in August of 1947, Liu Shaoqi told his colleagues about how "mismanagement" and "leftist excesses" had cost the party dearly. Other party leaders and the Soviets also criticized the campaigns for having gone too far.

Liu Shaoqi on Radical Land Reform, August 1947

When the peasants rose up to depose village cadres, especially when there were excessive leftist actions among the masses—such as calling large meetings to struggle against some village cadres, beating, maligning, or imprisoning them, and incidents such as suicide and flight—they had an enormous impact. The local poor peasants and masses who had been discontent with their village cadres felt elated and sent for work-teams. They informed on their village cadres to the work-teams. On the other hand, the cadres were agitated; some had reasonable views, asking only that they not be struggled against at large meetings and that the seriousness of the justice and injustices [they had committed] and their responsibilities be clarified. Some cadres held views that were fundamentally opposed: They emphasized the merits of the village cadres and the responsibilities of their superiors. They asked whether we wanted to retain the cadres and threatened that if things continued in this way, nobody would dare to become a cadre, and nobody would take responsibility for tasks such as collecting grain for the state, conscription, and military requisitions. It would be like taking off the load and then killing the donkey.

Report to the Central Committee on reports from local areas to the Land Conference on conditions and suggestions for the future, Liu Shaoqi, 4 August 1947, trans. in Tony Saich, *The Rise to Power of the Chinese Communist Party* (Armonk, NY: M. E. Sharpe, 1996), p. 1291.

By late 1947 even Mao had started having serious doubts about the overall effects of radical land reform. As the state of the war hung in the balance, Mao worried that the party was losing too many potential allies because of the confiscation of land. He felt that his warnings throughout 1946 and 1947 about not violating the interests of "middle peasants" and about making use of the GMD apparatus for CCP purposes had not been heeded. The main problem, Mao felt, was that the regional work teams were not good enough at distinguishing between areas with different histories and levels of consciousness and class struggle.[18]

To Mao, land reform had to be geared to the purposes of war. In July 1947, just as the principles of radical land reform were written into law in the CCP-controlled areas, Mao told Liu Bocheng and Deng Xiaoping that

if you want to get out from Dabieshan, you have to work out ways of collecting food and tax. What we did during the Land Revolution [of the early 1930s], confiscating the property of local tyrants, was on the one hand not enough, but on the other [it] destroyed our reputation. Before our administration is set up, we should make use of the existing GMD local tax institutions to collect food for our troops. All the GMD's people, except the extremely bad ones, all can be used.[19]

In late 1947 the party leadership held two important meetings at their new headquarters in southern Hebei, during which the land reform strategy was reviewed. Several leaders—Ren Bishi in particular—called for a relaxation of the class struggle in the countryside, based on the reports that had been coming in to the Center. After some hesitation, Mao agreed to issue new instructions that, while retaining the principle of confiscating land and dividing it among poor peasants, introduced so many exceptions and cautions that local cadres were left in no doubt as to the direction in which the wind was blowing. Ren summed it up in a speech in January 1948: "We [have] treated . . . people as part of the enemy camp. This did not isolate the enemy; it isolated us. What a serious error to have sent people from our own ranks to the enemy's side. . . . [We] must resolutely correct this wrong tendency; otherwise, we will isolate ourselves and lead the revolution to defeat."[20]

Official party historiography insists that the heads of the party revised the land policy because of the new needs created by having to implement reform in the areas the PLA had conquered. But the records show that by late 1947 the Center had concluded that radical land reform was a mixed blessing to the party. It steeled support for the war effort in some vital areas, but it also cost the party dearly through the confusion and conflict it created in areas where the party had already established its power. As with later CCP campaigns, Mao concluded, after counting the costs, that the country was not yet ripe for his visions.[21]

Another issue that the CCP leadership rightly considered essential, but on which they had difficulties making up their minds, was the problem of ethnic minorities. During the 1920s and 1930s, when the Communists were far from establishing their power at a national level, the party had generally been supportive of minorities' rights to secede from China and form their own independent states. The second party congress in 1922 had envisaged socialist China as a federal republic, and the 1931 constitution of the short-lived Chinese Soviet Republic included the full right of secession for all minorities. Taiwan's independence movement had been lauded by the CCP as late as 1941.[22]

During the anti-Japanese war, however, CCP leaders became increasingly skeptical of their previous views on the rights of minority peoples within China to secede from the state. There seem to have been two main reasons for this. On the one hand, the Communists found it difficult to accept the right to secession in a political setting in which their enemies, the Japanese, had a breakup of China as their stated aim. On the other hand, as the war of resistance brought the Communist Party into direct contact with an increasing number of ethnic minorities, its cadres realized—as had the Soviets twenty years before—that at least some minority groups would, if given a choice, opt for full independence, even if the alternative was autonomy within a socialist and egalitarian state. The Tibetans—whom Mao had famously described during the Long March as the only holders of the CCP's "foreign debt . . . for the provisions we were obliged to take from them"—were a particularly troubling example of such independent-mindedness. During the civil war, the CCP Center kept worrying that the population of Tibet and minority areas in Southwest China could be easily manipulated by local reactionaries and foreign imperialists, and could attempt to break away from the new state the Communists were about to create.[23]

How to learn from the Soviet example was an uncertain matter within the CCP of the late 1940s. While all party leaders viewed the Soviet Union as a model for China's future, they tended to emphasize different aspects of the Soviet experience. To Mao, the Leninist concepts of revolution were at the core—it was those concepts he had tried to apply to China, and it was their success in the Soviet Union that had validated the Soviet model. To Liu Shaoqi and Ren Bishi, the state-building functions of high Stalinism dominated their view of the Soviets. To them, as well as an increasing number of party leaders, the Soviet Union was not only the world's first revolutionary state. It also provided concrete blueprints for how the CCP-held areas could start functioning even before socialism was victorious in China—in all aspects of society, from party organization and trade unions to health care and education.[24]

The Sovietization of the CCP in the late 1940s was, alongside its militarization, the most important change to the party during the civil war. The thinking of Liu, Ren, and other leaders about the Soviet Union as a concrete model was boosted by vastly improved contacts with the Soviets after mid-1946. The number of CCP students in Moscow increased sharply, and, from 1947 on, hundreds of Soviet doctors, technical advisers, and military and communications experts served behind the PLA lines in Manchuria. To the Soviets, the contacts through Harbin were not just a way of improving the CCP's war effort, but as much a program of providing training in civilian government for the Chinese Communists.[25]

With Soviet advisers in Manchuria and Soviet military intelligence liaisons in place at Mao's headquarters, the CCP started devoting more space to propagandizing the Soviet example in its publications.[26] Moscow also loomed larger in the party's internal study materials, both through translations of Stalin's writings and speeches and through the increased emphasis that Chinese writers put on studying the Soviet example. Even in military affairs the Soviet influence became more noticeable during 1947. Lin Biao and his commanders in the Northeast kept in close touch with the Soviet advisers in Manchuria and with Soviet Communist Party and Red Army personnel on the other side of the border. Much of what the PLA learned about logistics, battle formations, and armored warfare during the Northeastern campaigns seems to have come from Soviet sources.[27]

At a deeper level, too, the connection with Moscow became central to the party. In his own writings, Mao in the late 1940s increasingly came to draw on Soviet examples and Soviet doctrines when expounding his own views of China's future. It has even been claimed by Chinese scholars that Mao's writing style underwent changes: The free-ranging, discursive style of the 1930s and early 1940s—with frequent allusions to Chinese history and literature—became terser and more doctrinaire in form, more like the proclamations that Stalin and the Soviet leadership liked to put out. Mao frequently asked his colleagues who had seen the "supreme master"—Stalin—in person about his habits and his style, his "methods" and his "formulations."[28] In propaganda terms, both the form and the content of the first wave of the CCP Mao-cult in the late 1940s were directly associated with what Nikita Khrushchev later termed the "personality cult" in the Soviet Union—even if the principle of deifying the leader had deep resonances in the Chinese past.

The policy advice that Stalin gave Mao Zedong and the Chinese Communists always reflected the Soviet leader's basic view that in Marxist terms China was still at the stage of the bourgeois or "national-democratic" revolution, and that the CCP would therefore have to ally itself with the more progressive capitalists and bourgeois in order to gain state power. On several occasions during the late 1940s, Stalin criticized the Chinese leaders for wanting to move too fast in political and military terms, and for forgetting the requirements of United Front policies and the character of the state that the CCP could aspire to set up. In late 1947 the Soviet leader sneered at Mao's optimistic messages declaring the CCP's wish to make China into a one-party dictatorship like the Soviet Union. Stalin made a habit of wondering aloud to his Kremlin associates

Stalin Instructs Mao Zedong on a Coalition Government, 1948

We have doubts about one point in your message where it is said that "In the period of the final victory of the Chinese revolution, following the case of the USSR and Yugoslavia, all political parties, except the CCP, will have to withdraw from the political scene, as this [withdrawal] will consolidate the Chinese revolution substantially."

We do not agree with this. We think that various opposition parties in China, representing the middle strata of the Chinese population and standing against the Guomindang clique, will be viable for a long time ahead, and the Chinese Communist party will [have to] attract them for cooperation [aimed] against the Chinese reaction and imperialist powers, while retaining its hegemony, that is the leading position. Probably, some representatives of these parties will have to be incorporated in the Chinese people's democratic government, and the government as such [will have] to be proclaimed as coalition, so as to expand the basis of the government among the population as well as to isolate the imperialists and their Guomindang agents. It should be kept in mind that after the victory of the people's liberation armies of China—at least, in a postvictory period for which the duration is difficult to define now—the Chinese government, in terms of its policy, will be a national revolutionary-democratic government, rather than a Communist one. This means that nationalization of all lands and cancellation of the private ownership of land, confiscation of properties from the whole, major and petty, industrial and trade bourgeoisie, confiscation of properties from not only large, but middle and small land-owners, who live together with their hired labor, can not be effected yet. It will be necessary to wait for a certain period with these reforms.

Stalin to Mao, 20 April 1948, APRF, f. 39, o. 1, d. 31, p. 28. The message Stalin is referring to was sent 30 November 1947.

what kind of Marxists the Chinese were. CCP attempts at patterning their party on Soviet models—making it more "centralist" and narrowing down the processes of decision-making—did not impress the Boss in the least.

The CCP and the Northeast

Of the CCP-held territory in China in mid-1947, more than half was in the Northeast, where the party had first been able to resist GMD onslaughts. Manchuria had become the main Communist base area, and it was to be the linchpin for the counteroffensives that Mao Zedong and the military leadership planned. From having had the region completely closed to them for almost fifteen years because of the efficiency of Japanese control, the CCP had in two years become the dominant force in Manchurian politics. And it was this domination that enabled the party to rally local support, strengthen its main army, and keep in touch with its Soviet ally across the border.

The CCP's success in the Northeast depended to a large degree on its being able to step into the political vacuum that the GMD's failure to govern Manchuria had created. By the end of 1946, most Northeastern natives seem to have concluded that there was no relief in sight from the government. Power, especially in the countryside, was up for grabs. The CCP leaders—Mao more than anyone—knew that if the PLA could fend off the challenge from Du Yuming's armies, the Communists could establish secure base areas in the Northeast that would be of vital importance in the battles to come.[29]

In appealing for support among peasants in the Northeast, the CCP had four main advantages. First, they were a large, cohesive force that could offer protection in an area where any form of law and order had long disappeared. Second, the government's legitimacy was not established in the Northeast, and the GMD had few local ties. Third, the kind of land reform that the Communists introduced was geared to fit local conditions. And fourth, the party was able to recruit for support among all the nationalities in this hodge-podge of ethnic groups: Han Chinese, Mongols, Muslim and Buddhist minorities, Koreans, and even Japanese.[30]

But the Communists could not have made much use of these advantages if they had not been able to survive militarily in the Northeast. That survival was, as we have seen, dependent on Soviet goodwill and on the tactical abilities of PLA commanders, primarily Lin Biao. In the winter of 1946–47, as the PLA in the Northeast fought for its and the party's existence, the Communists in Manchuria learned much about the interrelatedness of military and political affairs, and about how a marginal advantage in one area can mean the difference between victory and defeat in another.

The Northeast People's Liberation Army was an amalgamated force even by CCP standards. The main part was composed of Communist units from the former Eight Route Army in North China, which had crossed into Manchuria in the fall of 1945. Most of the officers, including nearly all who had served with Lin Biao in staff positions, came from these units. But the presence of these "old" Communists would in no way have been enough to stem the offensives of the best GMD armies. What gave Lin a dramatic advantage was his ability to rapidly integrate a host of other groups into his army: Manchurian exiles returning from the Soviet Union and Mongolia; Korean units; adherents of the former Manchurian warlords; bandits and brigands; and those few Manchurian Communists who had survived underground during Japanese rule. By late 1946, Lin and his advisers were on the brink of developing this motley crew into a modern army, superior to any fighting unit in China.

The means by which Lin was able to accomplish this transformation were rigorous military training, abundant supplies of weapons, and the brutal crushing of all local opposition. While sometimes criticized for neglecting the political training of his troops, Lin placed a strong emphasis on teaching his men the military methods developed in the Soviet Union and in the command areas of North China during the last years of the anti-Japanese war. These methods were mainly "conventional," in the sense that regular formations and positional tactics were preferred over guerrilla-style "people's war." The critical element of the training, however, was speed—the ability to move fast across the great Manchurian Plain, surprise the enemy, and defeat their strategies. Lin's model was the Soviet campaigns through Eastern Europe at the end of World War II, and, with the right kind of training, the ample supplies of Japanese weapons made it, for the first time, possible to contemplate these kinds of operations in China.[31]

Although Lin remained a controversial figure within the PLA establishment, his control of the party's military forces in the Northeast was undisputed after mid-1946. As first secretary of the party's Northeastern Bureau, his voice was also important in politics, although Lin—unlike many PLA commanders—did not consider himself a political as well as a military figure. The party's political leaders in Manchuria resented Lin's direct line to the Chairman but accepted the political implications of his military strategy: the harsh demands put on the people to provide supplies and logistical support for his version of mobile warfare.

Like Lin, all the leaders of the CCP in Manchuria were from south of the Great Wall—they had served the party, and, in most cases, Mao Zedong, for decades. Peng Zhen was the dominant CCP political leader in the Northeast up to the end of 1947, when he was transferred to the CCP-controlled zones of North China. Peng was probably the most efficient top administrator within the party, a man of great organizational skills, who combined outward ruthlessness with dedication to party leaders serving under him at the local level. However, his relationship to Lin

Biao and to the Soviets in Manchuria was never good, and that may have been one of the reasons why he spent the last part of the civil war in Hebei.

The five leaders who formed the core civilian leadership in the region throughout the late 1940s were Chen Yun, Li Fuchun, Zhang Wentian, Gao Gang, and Lin Feng. Chen and Li dealt primarily with administrative and economic matters, as did Lin Feng, whose claim as at least a nominal Northeasterner (he was born in Wangkuei county in eastern Heilongjiang) secured him the position as head of the regional government that the CCP set up in late 1946. Soviet-trained Zhang Wentian had been an opponent of Mao's during the early 1930s, but later in that decade, as titular head of the party, he had willingly made way for the new Chairman. During the civil war, Zhang handled many of the Manchurian party's contacts with the Soviets.[32] Gao Gang, originally a local leader of the CCP in Shaanxi before the Long March, had been rapidly promoted by Mao during the 1940s and was, at least from late 1947, Lin Biao's deputy as head of the party Bureau, and, because of Lin's relative inactivity in political matters, increasingly the one who called the shots.[33]

Under this core leadership, the CCP in Manchuria developed state functions that in many respects became an embryo for later developments farther south. The Northeast Administrative Committee (Dongbei xingzheng weiyuanhui), headed by Lin Feng, was a government in miniature, with departments for administration, finance, construction, education, communications, and nationalities, and with its own Supreme Court and Public Security Bureau. The majority of the members of this government were officially non-Communists, as had been the case in many of the local administrations the CCP set up during the anti-Japanese war. One of its vice chairmen was Zhang Xuesi, son of the warlord who had dominated Manchuria before the Japanese occupation. Gao Chongmin, the other vice chairman, was a noted member of the Democratic League. Both had strong ties to the CCP—Zhang had been a secret member of the party for several years. There was never any doubt as to who were the real power-holders.[34]

The Communist capital in the Northeast, Harbin, was the first big city that the party ever administered, and many of the party leaders from south of the Great Wall went to the task with suspicion and belligerence. There was no love lost between them and the traditional leaders of Harbin society, and, for most well-to-do inhabitants, the first months after the Communist takeover resembled the terror of the Soviet occupation. Soon the administration came under pressure to change its approach; the Soviets and the party Center advised against executions and expropriations, as did some of the heads of the Northeastern Bureau, Chen Yun especially. Slowly, as the military situation stabilized, the local leaders started normalizing the conditions in the city and began to make use of the diverse talents of merchants, engineers, and teachers, including some who had worked closely with the Japanese.[35]

The setting up of local administrations under conditions of civil war was not an easy task for the Communists, especially since the CCP in many areas was not the only contender for power in the vacuum left by the GMD. Local power-holders, whom the CCP invariably referred to as "bandits," were by mid-1946 in command in most of the Manchurian countryside, except where the Communists or the GMD had stationed their armies. Many of these groups originated with the Chinese militia that the Japanese army had set up. Some, especially those that had been displaced by war, preyed upon villages, businesses, and families in ways familiar to the victims of Chinese brigands for many centuries. Others fought to protect the territory of their districts or their clans from "outside" forces. A few had links with former strongmen in the region from before the Japanese occupation. In the Western parts there were traditional religious groups, and in the South secret societies that had spilled over from northern China.[36]

The CCP at first fought a war of ruthless extermination against these groups. In the view of many Communists, the "bandits" symbolized the worst sides of "old society" and were tactical allies of the GMD to boot. Because of the needs created by the war with Jiang's forces, the contest between local power-holders and Communist units was sometimes more even than could be expected. During 1946 and most of 1947, the CCP made only slow advances in fighting these forces, which often had substantial backing in their districts. It was first when the PLA started its offensives against the government's armies and found policies of integrating "bandit" troops in their own ranks that rapid progress was made. But in some areas local fighting continued up to 1950.

Before the cadres going to the Northeast left Yan'an, Mao had instructed them that they should be as flexible as possible when doing political work among the peasants. The Chairman realized that the people of Manchuria had been cut off from the main parts of China for a long time, and that the "class situation" in the countryside was different from that farther south. What neither Mao nor his subordinates knew was

---

A PLA Officer on Bandits and Foreigners in Manchuria, 1947

The residents of Korean origin seemed particularly frightened. The problem was more complicated by their inability to speak Chinese. Nor could the [PLA] detachment find an interpreter among the Han population. Some said, "We moved here only eighteen months ago. We don't understand Korean." Others begged off with the excuse, "Though I've lived here a long time, I've a bad ear for languages. I can't speak a single sentence." And when asked where a Chinese could be found who spoke Korean, they replied evasively: "The plain is big and the people are few and scattered. We really don't know much about the folk in other settlements." As to the local Koreans, the moment they saw so much as a shadow of a PLA man, they ran home and barred their doors, and the whole family huddled together fearfully. . . ." The PLA men found this situation very puzzling. Some were irritated and said the local people were stubborn and backward, that they were all in league with the bandits.

From Qu Bo's novel *Linhai xueyuan* [*Tracks in the Snowy Forest*]. The novel was written in the 1950s, based on the author's experiences as political commissar with the PLA in Manchuria during the late 1940s. Trans. by Sidney Shapiro, 2d ed. (Beijing: Foreign Languages Press, 1965), p. 376.

---

how different the situation was. In many areas of Manchuria, the Japanese collapse had been a disaster that had set off wars and famine. From being the most well ordered (though oppressed) part of China, the Northeast had, by the time of the Communist quest for power, descended into chaos.[37]

Different from that in the South, the role of the CCP in the Manchurian villages was not so much to create social justice as to establish order. Their determined work to create some form of order—Communist order, to be sure—was what gradually provided them with enough support to penetrate the region as a whole. Although Communist power in the Northeast, as in the rest of China, ultimately depended on the fate of the party's military forces, it was the political work in the villages that provided the PLA with enough support to win. The Communist advance teams, a mix of guerrillas and political cadres that operated beyond the military front lines, bore the brunt of this effort and often paid a high price. But in spite of the hostility and suspicion that both the advance teams and the regular work teams met among the villagers, their ability to present themselves as the forces of order often carried the day.[38]

During 1946 and most of 1947, the party therefore practiced a moderate form of land reform in Manchuria, primarily redistributing land expropriated from Japanese owners and prominent collaborators to Communist supporters or the families of PLA soldiers. The party Center knew well that there was, traditionally, more inequality in land holdings in Manchuria than in North China, and large numbers of landless laborers and tenant farmers. But they also knew that a rich soil and a strong agricultural economy (up till the 1945 breakdown) had for generations prevented social unrest in the countryside. A more radical version of Communist policies was unlikely to meet much support among peasants who first and foremost saw the party as the re-establisher of order. Besides, the party Center and its Northeastern Bureau were loath to encourage further dislocation in those very areas upon which they depended for grain, fodder, livestock, tools, and labor for waging the war.[39]

However, in mid-1947, as the military conflict turned more to their advantage, the party leaders started worrying about the long-term effects of putting the revolution on hold in the Northeast. Several major surveys that the party undertook showed little or no effect of political mobilization in the villages. The roughly twenty thousand cadres who had participated in the work teams had not been enough for a region with a population of around forty million. They had rushed from one village to the next, often spending no more than one week in each locality. No wonder, then, the reports complained, that "bad elements and even landlords" had been able to infiltrate the peasant associations and that banditry still was rife, even behind PLA lines.[40]

As Jiang's armies started withdrawing, the CCP therefore relaunched the land reform campaign in the Northeast. Under the slogans "Clean out the cellars" and "Sweep the courtyard," the region started seeing the same so-called struggle meetings, confiscations, and redistribution of land as had been seen farther south about a year earlier. Many people who had served the Communist cause came under attack. In early 1948 the campaigns reached their peak, with a wave of Red terror sweeping the countryside, bringing executions and beatings to real or imagined enemies of the new regime. In Jilin and parts of Liaoning provinces, where many villagers had suffered from the (temporary) return of the GMD in 1946–47, CCP cadres reported that at least some peasants responded "enthusiastically" to the bloodletting. But in the North, where the party had been in control for a long time, it took harder measures to initiate the peasants. In some areas the cadres used mobs from one village to attack "enemies" in the neighboring village, since the party suspected the villagers of sometimes protecting their own kin in spite of class categories.[41]

The campaigns were not abated until regional policies were overtaken by inner-party criticism of radical land reform south of the Wall. In April 1948, Chen Yun conceded that "there were too many deaths," and around the same time the terror was lessened as part of a new campaign to stimulate production for war purposes. The political assessments from the Northeastern Bureau to Mao Zedong and others were, however, very positive. The terror had broken the political hold of the reactionary classes, and the countryside was "pacified," Gao Gang told the Chairman in May of 1948.[42]

The importance of the CCP's foothold in the Northeast to the outcome of the civil war was immense. If the Communists had been defeated in Manchuria, they would have lost any offensive potential against the Guomindang, and their leaders could have been forced either to settle the conflict on their enemies' terms or withdraw into exile in the Soviet Union. In this sense the Northeast truly was, as Steven Levine has put it, the "anvil of victory." But the region was important to the CCP in another sense as well. It provided a laboratory for the setting up of a socialist state and helped to train cadres—under Soviet tutelage—who could take over and successfully run newly conquered territories farther south, particularly in areas in which there previously had been little or no Communist organization. To the CCP, in the long run, such abilities proved as important as military prowess.

Fanshen: Overturning Power in the Villages

In only two years, between mid-1946 and mid-1948, the Chinese Communists managed to build solid political bases for themselves in the countryside on the ruins of war and GMD misrule. The political process by which the Communists entrenched themselves centered on conflicts surrounding the ownership of land, although the party's satisfaction of the peasants' wishes for land was only one level of the story. At another, less explored level, land was a symbol for tradition and cultural hegemony in the villages. By "overturning"—*fanshen*—century-old patterns of life into what the peasants understood to be a new, permanent order, the Communist cadres made room for themselves in the narrow social and political space between the villagers' need for survival and their assertion of beliefs.

As previous studies have underlined, there was of course a continuum between CCP policies in the villages during the civil war and its experiences before and during the anti-Japanese war. The year 1945 does not mark a divide in CCP history when it comes to the matrix for revolution in the countryside. On the contrary, the experiences of radical land reform during the Jiangxi Soviet of the early 1930s and the much more moderate version practiced during the first five years of the war with Japan were—together with Soviet policies—the main points of reference for the discussions within the party during the late 1940s. As we have seen, the policy outcome was highly flexible and oriented toward specific areas. The ideological instincts of most members of the party leadership were for radical policies, but they were held back by the exigencies of war, the faith in studying local conditions, and Soviet pressures for gradualism.[43]

The result was that there were no "typical" base areas for the CCP during the civil war. Even though there was a general pattern to policies south of the Wall—moderate in 1945–46, radical in 1946–47, and piecemeal moderation in 1948–50—the regional variations force us to look at specific areas if we want to understand CCP policies and their outcome in the villages. This flexibility was in part the intended result of instructions from the Center—time and again Mao underlined the need to bend one's specific policies after local conditions. But it also stemmed from differences in views among local cadres, orders that were misunderstood or misimplemented, successful local resistance, and the overall chaos of war.

Before explaining the variations, however, it may be useful to take a closer look at the general aspects of the establishment of Communist control in the villages, in terms of methods, organization, and discourse. Keeping in mind how great were the regional variations in overall approach, we are here talking about instruments that the Communists attempted to fit to their immediate political aims, and that could be employed at different times during the takeover process. Although always modified by the personalities and personal experiences of the cadres, by local politics, and by the needs of the PLA, these instruments provided the core lessons of the cadre schools that the CCP Center set up all over China.[44]

As explained in Chapter 1, during World War II the CCP had developed into what Apter and Saich have called a logo-centric party with a strong emphasis on charismatic leadership. In spite of its outward belief in materialism and constant underlining of practical experience, the party trained its cadres first in the central texts of Mao Zedong, and then in Mao's and his chief lieutenants' outlines of how to recruit support in

A Manchurian CCP County Committee's
Catalog of "Landlord Tricks," 1946

Pretend to be enlightened to lull the masses;
Stir up trouble, cause splits;
Bribe backward persons with money;
Use beautiful women to corrupt cadres and activists;
Infiltrate dog's legs (agents) into peasant associations;
Feign poverty to avoid being struggled;
Act impudently and engage in effrontery;
Encourage factionalism;
Collude with agents and bandits to carry out assassinations.

Changbai County, quoted in Levine, Anvil of Victory, pp. 220–21.

rural areas. These outlines contained step-by-step introductions concerning how the Communists should win over people with influence among the peasants, starting with general moral arguments about inequity and national humiliation, and ending with calls for action against specific targets, landlords, or former GMD officials. They always underlined the patience that a rural cadre had to have, and stressed the dangers for the cadre work teams both in moving too fast and in moving too slow.[45]

Although, as we have seen in Manchuria, the CCP work teams sometimes operated behind enemy lines or in contested territory, most teams moved into villages in areas over which the PLA had already established some form of control. This does not, of course, mean that the CCP cadres were not exposed to physical risks—local power-holders, GMD agents, and peasants enraged at insults to local customs and traditions could often give the Communists a run for their money. But the existence of PLA units at some point within the horizon of the peasants' world did in most cases give the work teams enough time to sow what they termed "the seeds of revolution."

The initial message that the cadres spread in the villages was almost always a message about the party as a force of order and stability. Combining arguments against the GMD for exploiting the countryside and for selling out the country to foreign imperialists, the CCP attempted to appeal to as broad a group of peasants as possible. The first public markers of CCP power—the arrest of collaborators and prominent GMD members (of which most villages had few, if any) and the setting up of peasants' associations—underlined the centrality of power and not of social change. As a rule, more rich peasants and peasants of middle means than poor peasants worked with the party cadres through the first period. The elements of CCP discourse—the texts, the lessons in party history, and the centrality of the Mao figure—appealed to these groups more than it did to destitute and mostly illiterate marginals in peasant society.

The work teams, however, had a different concept of power than did the more well to do peasants in the villages. While the peasants tended to think of the CCP as another power-holder within the mold of earlier rulers (which indeed the CCP propaganda led them to believe), the cadres were preparing a more total grab for power by destroying the old order in the villages, both politically and economically. In order to set off this process, their instructions were to work on winning over and educating selected families of poor peasants in parallel with cozying up to their betters. These poor peasants, the theory went, would then gradually replace those from higher up on the social ladder as leaders of the peasant associations. Although this parallel process of working with different social classes for different purposes went on in almost all CCP-held areas, the degree to which poorer peasants came to the political fore before the onset of radical land reform varied widely. In some areas the cadres tended to be hesitant in upsetting a local order that worked well for the party in terms of labor recruitment, production, and supplies for the front. However conscious they were of the ideological need for a "revolution within the revolution," practical concerns kept them back.[46]

In many areas, the women's associations were vital allies for the CCP cadres. The married and unmarried women who started attending CCP-sponsored meetings signaled to the whole village that they had ceased being the property of their husbands and fathers. By taking this step, they in many cases destroyed their links to their families, and could not easily return to the kind of lives they had led before. Dependent on the Communist Party, and without any easy way back to "old society," these women formed a central part of the shock troops that the cadres used to destroy traditional power in the villages. Because they had already broken with village traditions, they could more easily denounce landlords and rich peasants, and participate in dividing up their lands. Slowly, as the new order took hold, these women could re-enter the family framework in positions of responsibility and power that they had never held before.[47]

The aims of the political campaigns in the villages depended on instructions from the Center. As described above, the first period after the

CCP takeover of any area—except during radical land reform in 1946–47—centered on equaling out the tax burden and reducing the land rent. The CCP cadres viewed these aims as temporary, however, and intended to facilitate the setting up of peasant associations, to conduct political education, and to groom leaders from among the poorer peasants and other formerly disenfranchised groups. According to Communist theory, the demand for land reform and collective forms of ownership would gradually develop from among the peasants themselves. But in reality the party leadership was much too impatient to wait for subtle changes in peasant consciousness. The orders from above to implement radical land reform in most places overturned the long-term battle plan that the cadres had developed, forced them to re-evaluate their methods, and, by so doing, set off revolutionary impulses that ignited intense social conflict and sometimes engulfed the cadres themselves.[48]

Burdened with achieving social transformation in the short term, the work teams had to change their methods radically. Some used forms of popular entertainment—songs, dance, theater—to heighten the peasants' awareness of the change of power in the village. In some cases these shows, which were put on by the Communists and their peasant allies, could lead to direct political action and even violence. Struggle meetings—during which recalcitrant landlords and rich peasants, suspected enemy agents, or anyone else seen as an obstacle to Communist rule, were ritually humiliated before kicking and screaming crowds—were in themselves a form of political theater. Since those in the crowd knew that their fate with the new authorities depended on their eagerness to accuse and to condemn, these meetings frequently ended with severe beatings or murder. Although CCP cadres explained these acts of violence as arising from genuine peasant anger or the wish for revenge, there is little doubt that the Communists often encouraged violent acts as a necessary accompaniment to the confiscation and redistribution of land. The techniques that the Communists used—forcing their victims to bear posters or caps proclaiming their guilt, making them kneel, depriving them of sleep—came straight from the political "rectification" in the CCP areas during World War II.[49]

The point of culmination in the offensives against the old order in the villages was the confiscation and redistribution of land. No village was seen as having properly carried out *fanshen*—"turning over"—before at least some land had changed hands. But both the processes and the results varied widely from one area to another. Some districts limited them-

Expropriating the Landlord, Shanxi, 1946

That evening all the people went to Ching-ho's courtyard to help take over his property. It was very cold that night so we built bonfires and the flames shot up toward the stars. It was very beautiful. We went in to register his grain and altogether found but 200 bags of unmilled millet—only a quarter of what he owed us. Right then and there we decided to call another meeting. People said that he must have a lot of silver dollars—they thought of the wine plant, and the pigs he raised on the distillers' grains, and the North Temple Society, and the Confucius Association. . . . "But this is not enough," shouted the people. So then we began to beat him. Finally he said, "I have 40 silver dollars under the *kang.*" We went in and dug it up. The money stirred up everyone. We beat him again. He told us where to find another hundred after that. But no one believed that this was the end of his hoard. We beat him again and several militiamen began to heat an iron bar in one of the fires.

From William Hinton, *Fanshen: A Documentary of Revolution in a Chinese Village* (Berkeley: University of California Press, 1997 [1966]), pp. 137–38.

selves to redistributing the land and fixed property of collaborators with Japan, or of landowners who had fled to the cities. In other regions, not only was landowners' land confiscated but also large parts of the land of rich and even middle-rank peasants, and the population was organized into work brigades for planting, harvesting, and providing labor for the front. In some districts CCP policies changed radically as one work team left and another moved in. During the period of radical land reform these replacements could be accompanied by rapid changes in village politics and the unleashing of terror from which even Communist Party members were not safe.[50]

Western Shandong was one area in which radical land reform developed into a campaign of terror. After the initial land reform process—the confiscation of land from landlords, accompanied by meetings to criticize landlords, their families, and associates—Shandong cadres in the early summer of 1947 launched a "land reinvestigation" process in many villages. In the increasingly frenzied atmosphere that followed from meetings to classify and reclassify all peasants according to their class origin, rich and middle-rank peasants soon became fair game for all kinds of attacks, including executions. In one county, Sanghe, more than one thousand were beaten to death. As the GMD armies launched their successful counterattacks in the region, the CCP organization in many areas fragmented, with older cadres coming under attack for their "moderation."

Norwegian Missionary Report on Land
Reform in Hunan, Early 1948

We are still in the middle of land reform, and they [the CCP] are busy dealing with the landlords. They are hung by their toes and by their thumbs, they are whipped with thorns, their arms and legs are broken, and there are other tortures. All of this is to make them declare everything they own and where it is hidden. Land, houses, and everything they own are taken from them, and many die as a result of torture. Those who survive are systematically starved to death. They are sent out as beggars, but there is a death penalty for anyone who gives them anything. Many commit suicide. In some cases, even landless laborers are struggled against, while some rich peasants get away. It is often completely random. The people from the peasant association are in command, and they are using land reform to seek revenge on their enemies, whether they are landlords or not.

Bergljot Borgen, who sent this report back to Oslo, was a Norwegian missionary working in Hunan province in the late 1940s. Quoted from Wenche Iversen, "Misjon—Revolusjon: Misjonærer fra Det Norske Misjonsselskap i Kina 1945–1951—Deres holdning til den politiske utvikling [*Mission—Revolution: Missionaries from the Norwegian Missionary Society in China 1945–1951*]," dissertation, University of Bergen, 1971, p. 106.

In some districts, inner-party struggle meetings were followed by suicides or executions. In the ensuing chaos, workers and peasants fled the CCP-held areas in order to get away from the campaigns. Some form of stability first returned to the region when the PLA imposed order after its military victories in mid-1948.[51]

In other regions, local peasant resistance to radical land reform was widespread. Not surprisingly, the resistance was particularly strong in some of the "old" base areas, where the peasants had gotten used to the "moderate" land policies of the anti-Japanese war. In the ShaanGanNing region, for instance, the combined pressures of radical land reform and the general mobilization against Hu Zongnan's GMD troops led to confrontations between village-level and midlevel CCP cadres. A January 1948 report notes that "during mobilization, it was very common that our cadres just portioned out the quotas equally for all families and individuals, leading to gross injustice. Because many village cadres were from middle peasant or even richer families, they did not share our ideas. They always overtly agreed, but covertly opposed, complied in public, but resisted in private, [and] refrained from carrying out our instructions."[52]

Paradoxically, the Communist preoccupation with equaling out land holdings sometimes left other forms of rural production well within a market framework. In the salt-producing areas of northern Henan, across the border from Shandong, peasants made use of CCP rule to take control of the mining, distribution, and sale of their product. These peasants used the flight of landlords and the absence of the feared GMD "Salt Police," which had imposed taxes on production and levies on the transportation of salt, to break into the market themselves. Under cover of the relative wealth that suddenly became common in a traditionally poor region, local cadres concentrated on improving market conditions for the salt-producers, while ignoring the classifications of radical land reform. The killings that took place in 1947 were directed mostly against those landlords who had assisted GMD attempts to retake the area. The immediate GMD threat to the peasants' new-found wealth made a larger percentage of young men join the PLA in the salt-producing region than in surrounding areas, which depended solely on agriculture and where radical land reform had been implemented.[53]

In addition to areas in which traditional agriculture had been overtaken by other forms of production, radical land reform did not take on major significance in the new front-line regions of southern Hebei and southeastern Shanxi. The work teams in those regions, who were recruited mostly from the PLA, did not have the stomach for conducting large-scale land confiscations while establishing CCP control and seeing to the ever-expanding needs of the front. Instead, they generally interpreted the party line as it had been seen a year earlier: In "newly liberated" areas, the emphasis ought to be on rent reduction and tax equalization, not on land reform. When receiving critical reports about the behavior of these cadres, the party Center felt disinclined to impose a more radical line because of the overall success most of them were having in providing for the war effort.[54]

One of the main problems of interpreting CCP policy during the civil war is to ascertain the aims of radical land reform. The radical turn began as a deliberate response to an acute crisis for the party—the GMD offensives during 1946 and 1947. Soon, however, a general radicalization took hold at many levels of the CCP, setting off a series of intense political campaigns and a revolutionary terror in many ways similar to the Great Leap Forward and the Cultural Revolution of later decades. It is likely that the radicalization was, at least in part, a product of changes in the CCP leaders' own thinking, and especially of Mao Zedong's increasing impatience with the slow nature of social change in the liberated areas. Throughout this period, Mao alternated between underlining the basic correctness of radical land reform and warning about the negative effects that the overzealous implementation of this policy could have on the war effort and on the CCP's political alliances. Many party leaders viewed Mao as holding a centrist position on land issues, between party radicals like CC member Rao Shushi and moderates like Ren Bishi.[55]

As Mao often tried to explain to his adherents from the early 1940s onward, his main preoccupation was not with dividing up land as much as with overturning age-old patterns of power in the villages. Only by crushing the symbols of power—of which land ownership was only one—could the Communists prevent the old regime from returning. To Mao, the public humiliation of landlords, the closing of temples and churches, and the prominence of poor peasants and landless laborers in political campaigns were as important to *fanshen* as confiscation of land. The Chairman therefore supported radical land reform as an instrument of revolutionary terror. But he was increasingly skeptical of the splits that the policy had created among the peasantry through its repeated division and redivision of land according to class categories.

By early 1948, the party apparatus worked hard to move CCP policies back to a more flexible and instrumental approach to land reform. Reading the signals coming from the Center as warnings against radical excesses, the cadres attempted to keep the core ideal of land reform intact, while in practice returning to issues of rent, taxes, production, and labor mobilization. In some areas, cadres who had suffered as "moderates" during the preceding months now took revenge on those who had criticized them, including a number of poor peasants who had been recruited as cadres during the early months of radical land reform.

The period of radical land reform, which in most areas ended upon the party's instructions sometime between the fall of 1947 and the late spring of 1948, was a mixed blessing to the overall aims of the CCP. Although there is no doubt about the strong general appeal of tax and rent reductions and the providing of land to landless peasants, the outcome of the CCP's campaigns depended on where and how they were carried out. In areas that had been controlled by the party for years, the first phase of the campaigns may have helped military mobilization against GMD offensives and steeled political support for the CCP. As the campaigns progressed, however, the party lost allies among rich and middle-rank peasants, and the social and political chaos that the Red terror unleashed hindered the war effort. In areas that the party moved into for the first time, the processes of attraction and alienation were more parallel. Rad-

CCP Central Committee Instructions on
Land Reform, February 1948

In the old Liberated Areas set up before the Japanese surrender, and the new Liberated Areas set up after the Japanese surrender, as well as those latest Liberated Areas set up during our counteroffensives, the social situation varies a lot, and [therefore] the content and the adoption of the Law of Land should also vary. The form of organization of the group of poor peasants and the peasant association should differ accordingly . . . In the old Liberated Area, the middle peasants have constituted the bulk of the agricultural population. If we apply the same criteria, [and] make the poor peasants a two-third majority in the peasant association of peasants, then we will risk to break away from the middle peasants . . . Accordingly, in the old Liberated Areas, we don't need to organize a group of poor peasants, or, if we must have such organizations, their function should be limited to the protection of the poor peasant minority, but not to institute the leadership of the poor peasants in the countryside. In the association as well as in the county administration, the poor peasant activists, with the agreement of the middle peasants (a necessary condition) can be elected head of the association or chairmen of the administrations. But it should not necessarily be so, [and] we should mainly encourage fair people among the middle peasants to do these jobs. Ideally, in the associations and the committees in the administrations, the poor peasants should have their own seats, but they must be a minority, namely, one third.

Mao to Li Jingquan et al., 6 February 1948, *Zhonggong zhongyang wenjian xuanji*, vol. 17, pp. 33–34.

ical land reform quickly created a core of CCP support that often held up over time, in part because the party's radical strategies and its use of violence helped to form a gulf between the activists and the village majority that—from either side—would prove hard to bridge.

The CCP and the Cities

The unknown part of the Chinese civil war has been the role played by the Communist underground in the cities. Together with its military strategy and its political work in rural areas, the party's efforts at detaching urban support from the Guomindang and presenting itself as a viable alternative was a main element of its success. In late 1947, when Jiang Jieshi and his generals were planning their main offensives against the Communists, their support in the cities had already eroded to a degree that seriously influenced the GMD's military and political capabilities.

The CCP's minutely planned attempts at influencing the urban middle class—a group that had provided a substantial portion of the GMD's political support—proved an important weapon in the war between the two parties.

As we have already seen, the GMD's mismanagement of the cities it took over from the Japanese provided fertile ground for political alternatives. The early successes of the student movement and of urban labor groups testified to the problems that the Nationalists were facing. In view of these problems, it might seem surprising that the CCP did not have more of an influence in the cities during the initial postwar period. But the Communist urban weakness—going back almost two decades—could not be overcome in a few months. The party had to train new cadres for urban work; set up secret channels for communication; and provide money, cover, and false identities. All of this was done in the training centers in the base areas, organized and controlled by the CC United Front department under the leadership of Zhou Enlai.

The preparations for a new CCP offensive in the cities—the first since the mid-1920s—started in the last years of the war against Japan. Because of the wartime alliance between the GMD and the Americans, CCP leaders believed that after Japan lost or started retreating, their cadres would finally be able to re-enter the cities and to do both legal and illegal work for the Communist cause. Within each base area there were sections of CCP "White area" organizations responsible for urban work. As increasing numbers of city dwellers came to CCP bases, party leaders realized the opportunities this offered for selecting some for training in political work and sabotage before returning them to the cities. The party leaders worked hard to overcome skepticism among base area cadres against the urban newcomers—whom the old-timers termed "guests"— and it was at least mid-1946 before the training centers were established in most base areas.[56]

The other main issue that had to be resolved was how to view the role of the bourgeoisie in the struggle against the GMD. Although the party had adopted the Comintern strategies of the United Front, and had worked hard at establishing a Marxist theoretical framework of how middle-class Chinese could assist the revolution, the bourgeois influx to the base areas and the postwar chance for operating legally in the cities were new phenomena. Many party leaders reacted to the new opportunities for urban work by accentuating the emphasis on the proletariat. Veteran "White area" leaders—such as Liu Shaoqi—kept repeating that the proletariat was the vanguard of the urban revolution, and wanted to increase the party's efforts to influence the trade unions, in spite of the meager results those efforts brought.[57]

These practical and political problems did hamper the CCP's work in the cities during the first postwar period. But with the training centers in place, and with Zhou Enlai in Nanjing, observing the situation firsthand and arguing strongly to Mao and Liu for the need to make use of the goodwill the party had among students, intellectuals, and other middle-class groups, the CCP's urban work started to improve. For the rest of the civil war, the party had sophisticated strategies for recruiting members and sympathizers in the cities, and, more important, for denying such support to the GMD.

Zhou Enlai's main political objective in the cities had to do with the way he understood the class composition of GMD supporters. To the future premier—who has been idolized by generations of Chinese intellectuals—the main purpose of extending the CCP's power into the middle class was to neutralize it as a source of political capital for the Nanjing government. Zhou understood that the weaknesses that often made it difficult for the Communists to win influence among workers—the lack of local roots and trust built over decades—were not major problems with regard to the bourgeoisie. On the contrary, for many young middle-class Chinese—students especially—the exotic qualities of the Communists as outsiders made them increasingly attractive as their own trust in the government waned.

The central cadres who worked with Zhou on developing the CCP's urban work, were, as a rule, young, often foreign educated, and in many cases with family links to the upper echelons of the Chinese bourgeoisie. Most of them were relative newcomers to the CCP, having joined the party in the base areas during the anti-Japanese war. Some had accompanied Zhou to the Chongqing and Nanjing negotiations, while others had stayed in Yan'an, working according to his orders. As a group, they were utterly dedicated to their new cause and to Zhou Enlai as a person.[58]

Their most important task in the first period of the civil war was to preserve and, if possible, extend the network of CCP agents in the cities. Conscious of what had happened the last time Jiang Jieshi turned on his Communist "allies"—the 1927 massacres in Shanghai and elsewhere— the young cadres of the Center United Front department did not want to take any chances. Those who went to work in the cities were trained as secret agents, specializing in how to operate what the CCP referred to as the Underground Party (*dixia dang*). They were instructed in Zhou's dicta about the Three Diligencies (*sanqin*)—in studies, careers, and making friends—and the Three Processes (*sanhua*)—be professional, fit in, and stay legitimate whenever possible. They were trained in how to use and develop networks of classmates, relatives, and hometown acquaintances for their own protection. They studied how to infiltrate independent or GMD organizations. They even took special courses in how to work in alumni associations, amateur theater associations, reading circles, veterans' associations, cooking schools, sports clubs, and the YMCA.[59]

From late 1946 onward, the main focus of the CCP cadres working under cover in the cities was to gain control of the student movement. In spite of the minuscule number of party members among the students in 1946—fewer than twenty at Peking University (BeiDa), for instance—the work that the Communists put into the various activities of the student movement soon marked them for posts of responsibility. Ke Zaishou, a secret CCP member from Fujian, became head of the BeiDa Student Union in early 1947. At the U.S.-funded Yanjing University in Beijing, the Communists controlled the student self-governing association by as early as June of 1946. As a rule, though, in the early phase of the student movement, the Communists could gain posts of influence but were often over-ruled by other students on slogans and strategies for the movement. As long as the movement kept its spontaneous character, organized around a series of "incidents" and special demands, it was not possible for the Communists to gain full control.[60]

The early 1947 movement to protest the rape of a BeiDa student by U.S. Marines was a case in point. As we have already seen, the character of the alleged crime—the violation of a student at China's most prestigious university by foreign soldiers—set off a protest movement that never saw its equal in GMD China. But the local CCP authorities were at first uncertain about what the student response should be. They worried that the issue was too "local" and that it would be difficult to get students from other campuses to participate. They were also concerned about the slogans—would the content of the protest overstep the Center's guidelines on anti-foreignism? Within days, however, the Center decided to create a nationwide movement, but also instructed its cadres to make U.S. troop withdrawal the issue and to avoid general antiforeign sentiments. Still, there is little doubt that the main part of the anti-American protests of early 1947 was organized by students who had affiliations with the CCP.[61]

*CCP Center Instructions to Regional Bureaus on
the Student Movement, January 1947*

The work of our party in Jiang's area should concentrate on making full use of the achievements of the student movement and on increasing patriotic propaganda. . . . Through student activities and newspaper publicity, we should convince workers, shop assistants, housewives, the urban poor, the industrial and commercial entrepreneurs, the unemployed, as well as the overseas Chinese, to engage and to expand the impact of this movement. During the Lunar New Year holidays, we should organize some students to go to the countryside and spread propaganda there.

There have emerged large numbers of activists and enthusiasts in the course of the movement. Our party should help to organize them to become part of the core leadership, [and] thus keep up the movement for long term. In terms of organizational structure, we should both gradually strengthen and expand the core organizations, and, in accordance with the actual situation, improve the political leadership and intensify contacts in those universities where there has been much student activity. In those universities where there is little activity, we must develop and consolidate these activities. In those universities where there is no student organization, we will have to find ways to establish some groups which will fit with the local environment. In general, we should try to organize students by appealing to their patriotism. However, for the purpose of long-term expansion, the activities should be based on groups whose activities are related to the students' daily life.

CCP Center to various party bureaus, 6 January 1947, in *Zhonggong zhongyang wenjian xuanji*, vol. 16, pp. 383–85.

As the student unrest developed into a mass movement in the spring of 1947, the party leaders were concerned with how Communist policies were carried out. In January, Yan'an had warned the Beijing cadres that they "lagged behind the [thinking of] the people. Now, when the movement is developing, leading members of our party in some areas must take care to correct their Right-deviationist thinking. In this specific case they will have to have enough courage and political insight to set the movement on the right track."[62] To the party leadership, that track led to a de-emphasizing of the general political role of the students, and the strengthening of CCP-controlled campus student unions.

After Jiang's crackdown on the student movement in mid-1947—which the CCP had warned about for several months—the party stepped up its pressure on the activists who were still at large to channel their efforts through regular student associations. The Center's reaction was in part determined by its fear of a further decimation of the leadership of the movement, and, worse, of the CCP cadres who had been working with the students. But it was also influenced by Zhou's wish for the CCP to have absolute control of student activities. As long as the movement, in a political sense, fed off the street, taking on new causes and slogans on the spur of the moment, the party could not develop a long-term strategy for the students. And since CCP leaders did not believe in the movement's ever becoming strong enough on its own to challenge the GMD for political power in the cities, it was better to keep its strength controlled and in place for the PLA push from the outside.[63]

The Communists benefited not only from the way the student movement, particularly in 1946 and 1947, stripped political legitimacy from the GMD. They also, through recruitment, acquired important manpower to staff their underground networks for propaganda and education. The secret printing presses that the party established in the main cities—at least three in Beijing, for instance, at the end of 1947—were often manned by recruits from the student movement. From a total of five hundred members in Beijing, Tianjin, and the mining area of Tangshan in August of 1945, there were in the same area in 1948 thirty-four hundred members, almost half of whom were students.[64]

Intelligence was another area in which the CCP excelled through its increasing influence among students. At least from 1947 on, the party had been able to place a number of its young recruits in positions through which they could obtain valuable information, and, in some cases, through their espionage change the course of important military engagements. One such spy was Xiong Xianghui, who had been a secret CCP member for years. In 1946–47 he served as GMD general Hu Zongnan's personal secretary, and gave the Center advance warning about Hu's plans to occupy Yan'an. Another very important CCP agent was Chen Lian, daughter of Jiang Jieshi's main secretary Chen Bulei. In general, Zhou and his regional assistants—of whom the most successful was Liu Ren, the head of the Urban Work Department of the JinChaJi base area—ordered underground members to aim at recruiting influential students, whose families had high social status in the cities.[65]

In spite of its initial lack of success, the Center kept insisting throughout the civil war period that its urban undergrounds not neglect the working class. Contrary to claims by earlier historians, the CCP for obvious ideological reasons spent much effort at increasing its following among workers in the cities. In late 1947 and 1948, they did have some successes, for instance among railway workers in North China or, in the wake of the 1948 strikes, among Shanghai mill workers. But in general the CCP's efforts at winning influence among the urban proletariat were, if not wasted, then a detraction from the party's successes among students and intellectuals.[66]

By 1948 the party Center had arrived at a strategy of using its minimal resources within the labor movement to concentrate on "strategic" industries in which underground Communists could assist the war effort. The CCP underground especially targeted the infrastructure of the White areas, such as public transport, railways, water works, electricity plants, airports, and post and telegraph services. A good part of the infiltration took place at the management level, but at some strategic plants in and around Beijing, Tianjin, and Shanghai, the CCP managed to obtain a limited influence among workers, and therefore a chance to have an impact on their decisions during the final stages of the war.[67]

It was through their work in the cities, and their training of urban youth who left the cities for the CCP bases, that the Communist cadres laid the foundation for what was to become an alternative Chinese state to challenge that of the Guomindang. The young women and men from the cities who came to the party during the first phase of the civil war came to staff many of those crucial functions in which the older CCP cadres had little experience, such as foreign affairs and finance. But most important of all, their presence in the CCP ranks gave the party the ability through propaganda, intelligence, and personal contacts to chip away at the hold that their opponents had traditionally had on the bourgeoisie, state functionaries, and the intelligentsia, and thereby weaken the Guomindang's capacity to govern China.

5

INTO THE CAULDRON

The Guomindang Offensives

Wang Liuqiu, "Revenge for a Dead Man"

In early 1947, while the political vulnerability of the GMD was becoming increasingly obvious, its military strength was still intact. In spite of Jiang Jieshi's disappointment with his commanders' performance in the Northeast and in Shandong, the National Army had lost little of its potential for offensive action. In late February 1947, Jiang's Supreme Military Council met several times to stake out the road ahead. The Generalissimo pressed for military victories that could strengthen his hand in dealing with political problems in the cities. He wanted quick—and if possible spectacular—offensives that could strike at the heart of the CCP's political power.[1]

Within the GMD military leadership, opinions were divided on how best to crush the Communist "rebellion." Several of the top commanders—for instance, Li Zongren and Fu Zuoyi in North China—wanted to use the government's superior forces to isolate the CCP in its core base areas, and to search for a joint political and military strategy to wipe out the Communists in the rest of the country south of the Great Wall. But their advice to Jiang never outlined any concrete proposals for how such an alternative strategy could be built, and the Generalissimo suspected several of them, including Li Zongren and Li's former Guangxi-clique associate Bai Chongxi, of wanting to preserve their own forces to retain some degree of independence from Nanjing.

Other generals argued that the government should lose no time in launching large-scale offensives against the main forces of the PLA in Manchuria and North China. Du Yuming and Hu Zongnan, among others, called for specific operations intended to split the PLA forces and destroy their best fighting units. Du, especially, wanted to use the best trained and best equipped GMD divisions for this strategy. In a letter to Jiang in early March, he warned that keeping the government's crack units in reserve would make victory against the Communists impossible. To General Du, who had observed the growing CCP strength in Manchuria at close hand, the war had already reached a decisive stage.[2]

What was really at stake in the military deliberations among the GMD leaders in the early spring of 1947 was defining the character of their enemy. For some, the CCP was still one rebellion among many that had challenged GMD supremacy since the mid-1920s. To these GMD leaders, the right strategy was the time-tested pattern of isolating the main forces on the periphery, while using a combination of force and compromise to wear down resistance in the central areas. But for others—and Jiang Jieshi increasingly came out in support of this group—the war was now about a massive CCP challenge to the long-term survival of the Guomindang as an integrated national government. If survival was the perspective, the war had to take precedence in all areas of GMD strategy.

GMD Armies, GMD Offensives

In 1946 the armies of the Guomindang government were as motley as they had been during Jiang's other great campaigns—against the Japanese in the 1940s, against the Communists in the 1930s, or against all other contenders for power in China in the 1920s. As then, some units were among the best fighting units that China has ever seen, while others were little more than ragged bands of thieves, scourging the countryside for loot. As then, some commanders owed their allegiance directly to Jiang Jieshi and had an almost religious reverence for the "Savior of China," while others served local power-holders or were themselves heading what in reality were little more than local militias. As then, Jiang distributed commissions, assignments, and supplies both according to overall military needs and according to what would be politically advantageous to him within the Chinese elite.[3]

As in the Guomindang political system, what had changed in military policies were Jiang's pretensions—instead of aiming at a balance of factions, cliques, and provincial elites under his leadership, Jiang wanted to command his armies as armies were commanded by the Japanese or the Soviets. He wanted to be able to send armies from the South to the North without first having to strike political compromises with the Southern commanders. He wanted to have a unified army command, which could serve both his political and military purposes. And he wanted to have the freedom to give absolute priority to the war, without having to look over his shoulder for other civilian power-holders who, for their own reasons, wanted to restrain him.

During the civil war, as in the rest of his career on the mainland, Jiang never achieved those aims. But in 1946 he was probably closer than at any other time. Because of the collapse of Japan, his prestige among army officers was at its peak. In the immediate aftermath of the war, he had crushed or sidelined much of the localist opposition. Jiang was the arbiter of foreign military aid, and in control of the military budget. His attack on the Communists had shown determination, and his approach in terms of commissions had shown that he would reward officers who redirected their primary loyalty to him.

But creating a more efficient army means some form of horizontal integration between units as well as improved vertical lines of command. As the civil war got under way, Guomindang armies were still fighting very much as separate units, and not as an integrated army. Jiang's attempts to move large numbers of soldiers from the South to the North probably exacerbated that tendency, both for cultural and political reasons. Guomindang generals in many cases had an extraordinary distrust of each other, and except in those few cases in which separate armies could fight protracted campaigns without the need for battlefield coordination, this distrust was bound to create immense problems for the GMD offensives. Jiang tried to overcome this handicap by making all generals in a battle zone responsible directly to him for the results—if the campaign failed, they would all risk their commands. But he also contributed to the problem by placing very diverse units in close proximity to each other, thereby, for reasons of political control, inviting exactly the command and coordination problems he sought to avoid.[4]

Within the different units, the situation of the GMD forces was also extremely diverse. All divisions, except those that had been set up during 1944–45 to receive U.S. training and equipment, had been recruited locally, and they would consist of soldiers from one particular region of the country only. While not unusual for large armies and with definite advantages in cohesion and communication, this form of organization exposed the GMD side to mass defections in those cases in which large numbers in a division were captured by the PLA in fighting far from the soldiers' home province. While such units could fight well if properly equipped and deployed not too far from home, their efficiency in other parts of the country was limited at best.

The officer corps was also of mixed quality. Those younger officers who had been trained in the military academies in the prewar years and who had risen through the ranks during the anti-Japanese war were usually the most dependable commanders in Jiang's army. Serving mostly at the regimental level or above, these officers were often the equals of their PLA counterparts in planning, intelligence, and logistics. Some of them succeeded in substantially improving the discipline of their units, and won their soldiers' respect by securing supplies, by successful operations, and by avoiding Communist ambushes. But there were far fewer of these officers than of those GMD commanders who had got their commissions locally, often alongside general recruitment in an area, and who had little or no training in warfare.

For this latter group of officers—in 1946 as during the anti-Japanese war—battle was a form of military activity best avoided, unless the repercussions in the form of sanctions from above for not fighting became too severe. Much like their better-trained colleagues, some of these officers cared about their soldiers' welfare, and some were feared for their brutality. But in the war they were of course much less efficient, often preferring flight or desertion rather than risk an encounter. Units led by such officers tended to be road-bound, if not stationary, and to avoid operating by night or over long distances. They were what PLA marshal Chen Yi dubbed sitting ducks, there to be plucked, quartered, and fried in their own fat.[5]

At the GMD staff level, the situation was also very diverse. The General Staff tended to be totally dependent on the personal authority of the Generalissimo and to have little direct control of the generals in the field. The commanders of the main "zones" or "commands" viewed themselves as having received their posts directly from Jiang and as responsible only to him. Although similar in a way to Mao Zedong's relationship to his generals, the weakness of the GMD organization was particularly visible in terms of the supply system. The rivalry for supplies and manpower was intense between the different commands, and, with no proper mechanism—in the General Staff or the Ministry of Defense—for distribution to those areas where it was most needed, the decisions even at the day-to-day level were left to the Generalissimo's sometimes precarious judgment. In the early phase of the civil war, this inadequate system of decision-making was probably more serious for the GMD war effort than the endemic corruption that linked supply officers to profiteers and black market speculators, and it was directly responsible for the failure of the GMD 1946 winter offensives.[6]

In the late winter of 1946–47, as Jiang raged at the poor performance of his troops in North China and Manchuria, General Hu Zongnan presented the Generalissimo with a strategic plan that in its audacity seemed to satisfy his demands. Hu, the long-time commander of GMD troops in Shaanxi, proposed to conquer Yan'an, the political center of Chinese Communism, and drive the main CCP armies in the province toward the North. The plan was kept secret from the Supreme Military Council and, up to the last minute, from all but a few of the unit commanders who would be involved. Jiang agreed to let Hu have more than 150,000 men and seventy-five aircraft for the operation, which was the biggest the GMD had undertaken thus far in the war. Hu, however, was not satisfied

Guomindang Soldiers during the Anti-Japanese War

China had a conscript army, recruited in the simplest and most cold-blooded fashion. Chinese recruiting had none of the trimmings of number-drawing, physical examination, or legal exemption. Chungking decided how many men it wanted and assigned a certain quota to each province; the quota was subdivided for each county and village, and then the drafting began. In some areas it was relatively honest, but on the whole it was unspeakably corrupt. No one with money need fight; local officials, for a fat profit, sold exemptions to the rich at standard open prices. Any peasant who could scrape the money together bought his way out. The men who were finally seized were often those who could least afford to leave their families. When a district had been stripped of eligible men, passersby were waylaid or recruits bought from organized press gangs at so much a head. Men were killed or mutilated in the process; sometimes they starved to death before they reached a recruiting camp. Men in the Chinese army never had a furlough, never went home, rarely received mail. Going into the army was usually a death sentence—and more men died on their way to the army, through the recruiting process, the barbarous training camps, and long route marches, than after getting into it.

Theodore White and Annalee Jacoby—both left-wing critics of U.S. policy in China—reported for *Time Magazine* on the Sino-Japanese War. White and Jacoby, *Thunder Out of China* (London: Victor Gollancz, 1947 [1946]), p. 129.

with the Generalissimo's response. He wanted troops flown in from South China and the coast, fresh troops who could relieve his forces in the southern and eastern parts of the province. But Jiang, hedging even in what promised to be his greatest triumph in years, would make no further commitment.[7]

After several weeks of discussions, the offensive was set in motion on 12 March. First, several GMD units struck toward the western parts of the province as a diversionary attack for the main force. The local CCP forces put up only light resistance. Two days later the GMD 1st Army and the 29th Army went straight for Yan'an. On 16 March Hu Zongnan's forces were to the immediate south and west of the Communist capital, and Jiang Jieshi received telegrams indicating that the advance units were so close that they could observe through their binoculars the panic that had broken out outside the cave dwellings. Mao turned to the forty-seven-year-old commander Peng Dehuai, who would later lead the Chinese troops in the Korean War, to cover the leadership's retreat. For two days, Peng with about twenty thousand men led a desperate resistance against the attackers just south of the town, providing enough time for the CCP leaders to flee. In the early morning of 19 March, the GMD 1st Army entered Yan'an.[8]

Hu Zongnan had achieved his aim. The Communist capital was taken, together with ten thousand prisoners. Jiang Jieshi, who was never given to euphoria, noted that the capture of Yan'an may have been the beginning of the end of the war. All over China, the GMD propaganda apparatus led by Chen Lifu moved into high gear. Headlines, both in China and abroad, proclaimed that the Communists were defeated, and reporters noted that the next aim for a GMD "lightning offensive" would be North Manchuria. As we have already seen, Hu's offensive led to a noticeable upturn for the GMD political position and even for the government's troubled finances, and both Washington and Moscow took the victory as a sign of the strengthening of Jiang's military hold on China.

If it had not been for the fact that Hu Zongnan's personal secretary was a Communist spy, the GMD's victory might indeed have been decisive. As it was, Mao and the other CCP leaders were kept informed on an almost daily basis of Hu's plans and his discussions with Jiang. Mao faced a dilemma. He did not want to give up Yan'an and the core of the ShaanGanNing base area. But neither did he want to divert much needed forces from North China to defend the Communist capital. For several weeks, while Hu and Jiang were contending over numbers of soldiers and planes, Mao kept hoping that he would not have to make that decision, and that a massive attack could be averted. When the Center was informed of the complete battle plans at the very beginning of March, Mao almost immediately decided to withdraw from Yan'an. He faced opposition from other leaders, most importantly Ren Bishi, who thought that giving up Yan'an would be a disaster for party morale. Ren seems to have been supported by Soviet advice.[9]

But, as usual, Mao prevailed. That the Center had almost two weeks in which to complete the evacuation of Yan'an made it possible not only to save the party leadership but also to move weapons, printing presses, radio equipment, and medicines to the North and East. Speaking to U.S. correspondent Anna Louise Strong the night before she was brought out of Yan'an, Mao told her that "if you ask whether it is better to lose the city or to keep it, of course it is better to keep it. But if we lose it, we are still all right."[10]

For ten days the CCP leaders fled to the North and East. The small bands lost contact with each other, and Mao feared that at least some of them had been captured by Hu's forces. On 29 March the main leaders met again—probably according to a prearranged plan—in Zaolin'gou village in northern Shaanxi. Mao and Zhou Enlai, who had stayed together throughout the flight from Yan'an, presented a plan for how to conduct the work of the Center: Liu Shaoqi, Zhu De, and most members of the central party apparat would continue northeast to the JinChaJi base area. Meanwhile, Mao, Zhou, and Ren Bishi would stay in northern Shaanxi, organizing the battles against the attackers. Liu and his group reached the North China base area on or around 9 April.[11]

After the evacuation of Yan'an, Mao set about constructing a legend of "inviting" Hu Zongnan to occupy the Communist capital in order to expose southern Shaanxi to Communist attacks. The purpose of the myth was threefold. First, Mao realized that the fall of Yan'an had had a negative impact on CCP morale, and he wanted to counter that with some propaganda of his own. Second, the tale contributed to the legend of Mao as all-knowing and ever wise. And third, it motivated the remaining CCP troops in ShaanGanNing to counterattack against the GMD forces. On 9 April, the same day that Liu reached Nie Rongzhen's headquarters, Mao issued a secret statement to the top party cadres from his hideout: "The purpose of [the GMD] military offensives is to settle the Northwest issue, to cut off the right arm of our party and drive the Central Committee of our party and the headquarters of the PLA out of this area. Then they will attack North China. . . . The Central Committee has decided to safeguard ShaanGanNing and the Northwest liberated area . . . [and] that the Central Committee and the headquarters of the PLA must stay in ShaanGanNing."[12] As a result of Mao's deception, for almost a year most CCP members did not know where the real leadership of the party was based. But the Chairman had decided to fight for ShaanGanNing.

Mao's strategy for countering Hu Zongnan's offensive was based on his experience from the 1930s and the Long March. The aim was to isolate parts of the GMD armies—often at the brigade level—and destroy them before the main troops could come to their rescue. The tactics were also taken from Mao's experience as a military commander in the field—ambushes, high mobility, and targets selected to achieve the maximum element of surprise to the enemy. For the Chairman it must have been like returning to his youth. His messages from the two months of 1947 when he himself was directing the battles in Shaanxi were distinctly upbeat. "Our victories," he told Peng Dehuai on 15 April, "have given Hu Zongnan's army a heavy blow and lays the foundation for the complete annihilation of Hu's troops. It has also proved that with our existing troops only, without any outside assistance, we can gradually wipe out Hu's forces."[13]

In Nanjing, while receiving almost daily reports from Hu Zongnan about his hopes to capture Mao and Zhou, Jiang Jieshi spent much time worrying about the situation on Taiwan. The Generalissimo was eager to incorporate Taiwan fully into his Chinese Republic, and he was surprised and angry that some of the Chinese political organizations on the island did not share his vision of Taiwan's future. Among Chinese who had lived on Taiwan under Japanese rule, the respect for the Guomindang was less than total. Many of them considered themselves better educated and more "modern" than their liberators—attitudes that the GMD officials who took over the government of the island found hard to tolerate. As mainlanders gradually squeezed native Taiwanese out of most positions of power and the economy suffered from the broken links with Japan, matters quickly came to a head.[14]

The governor of Taiwan, the GMD General Chen Yi,[15] was a stubborn and grumpy official of the old type. After arriving on the island in 1945, he had consistently refused to speak Japanese—the language of the educated elite on Taiwan—even though he himself was married to a Japanese woman and spoke the language perfectly. Inasmuch as he did not understand MinNan dialect, spoken by most common people on Taiwan, his attempts to communicate directly with his new subjects were somewhat handicapped. His zeal in confiscating Japanese property—in which many Taiwanese also had a stake—and his emphasis on the role of the state in running the economy made much local criticism of him center on economic issues. It was therefore no surprise to observers on Taiwan that the incident that sparked the crisis was economic in character.

What was surprising was the relative insignificance of the tumult that sparked the rebellion. On 27 February 1947 two policemen attempted to confiscate a small amount of contraband, mostly matches and cigarettes, from a widow peddling her wares on the streets in Taibei. Local people protested. In the melee that followed, a bystander was shot dead by the police. By the next morning, thousands of protesters were on the streets. The characters for "China" (*Zhongguo*) had been removed from important buildings and a big banner put up that read, in Japanese: "Down with military tyranny." The protests spread rapidly to other cities. Because of the war against the Communists on the mainland, there were not enough soldiers or military police on Taiwan to keep control. By 1

> ### GMD *General Chen Yi's Radio Speech to the*
> ### *People of Taiwan, 10 March 1947*
>
> Dear countrymen! After the 28 February incident, you hoped to get a solution to the incident during which people were wounded as a result of the confiscation of illegal tobacco. [Then] some of you also wanted improvements in the political system. But a very small number of traitors and rebels used this opportunity to spread irresponsible rumors, to spread confusion, and to lead people astray, and thereby to succeed in their treasonous plots. Over the last ten days the lives of all countrymen of a good heart have been made very painful. Dear countrymen! This suffering is created by traitors and rebels. To end the suffering, the government had no other choice than to declare an emergency, so that the traitors and rebels who have damaged our countrymen's interests can be exterminated. I hope that you have all completely understood this.
>
> From Günter Whittome, *Taiwan 1947: Der Aufstand gegen die Kuomintang* (Hamburg: Institut für Asienkunde, 1991), p. 167. Author's translation from German.

March, Taiwanese-run "Resolution Committees" were in control in many cities, demanding that the military be disarmed, corrupt officials arrested, families of so-called martyrs compensated, and all Taiwanese leaders given amnesty. Some days later, the main Committees also demanded full self-government for the island, democratic elections, and that mainlanders be kept out of positions of power.

Faced with the prospect of a war of independence, Governor Chen Yi was ready to negotiate on all "local matters," as he put it. But Jiang Jieshi had had enough. On 9 March troops began to land in several ports on the island. GMD troops slowly regained control of the cities, in some places after fierce fighting. Around ten thousand people were killed in all, some two thousand of them during the rebellion and the GMD army's retaking of the island. The others were executed by the Nationalist secret police during the months that followed, in what amounted to an offensive of terror to destroy the Japanese-trained elite on the island.

While Mao was busy defending the remaining parts of the ShaanGanNing base and planning attacks in southern Shanxi, he also kept in close touch with Lin Biao in Manchuria. The Chairman wanted Lin to move forces from the North to the South, and to launch a counteroffensive against the Guomindang just north of the Wall in order to take some of the pressure off the CCP defenders in North China. In early May he told his forces that "the next three months are crucial. You have to strike at the enemy inside Shanhaiguan, [and] stop their eastbound movement to

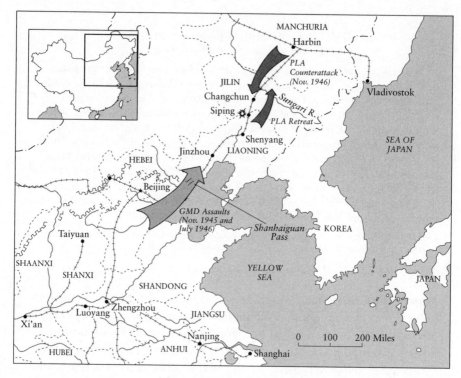

Map 2. Manchuria, 1945–47

ensure the victory in the Northeast."[16] But the cost of his limited winter offensives had taught Lin to be careful. He did not want to risk his core areas in North Manchuria—and his plans for offensives in the West—for the doubtful gain of challenging GMD troop movements to the Northeast.

Hard pressed by the Chairman, Lin proposed a compromise. He would attack Siping—a town crucial to the command of the western route into Manchuria and, since the battles of early 1946, a symbol of power in North China both to Mao and Jiang. The Chairman agreed enthusiastically. The offensive began in mid-May and was, at first, a great success for Lin's forces. The GMD had to evacuate several important towns in western Manchuria; in addition, it lost several thousand men, much new U.S. military equipment, and—at least for a short period—control of the main railway lines. By late May, more than 100,000 PLA soldiers had laid siege to Siping and taken over the valleys leading into the Northeast.[17]

Du Yuming, the GMD general who coordinated the defense of western Manchuria, had two options. He could abandon the city of Siping and contain the PLA forces in the area, while diverting supply routes into Manchuria to other regions of North China. Or he could defend Siping and call on the main GMD forces, which were pushing against the CCP-held areas north of the Sungari to relieve the city. Jiang Jieshi held Du to the last option, in spite of vigorous protests from Xiong Shihui and some of the commanders in north Manchuria. While Lin's soldiers, much to the PLA's surprise, had to fight pitched battles inside Siping, superior GMD forces were approaching from the northeast and east. And as the attackers advanced very slowly, block by block, they were pounded relentlessly by the GMD air force and by GMD artillery. Lin Biao disliked the situation, and told Mao so. On 28 June, with their equipment and morale in tatters, the PLA lifted the siege and withdrew to the north.[18]

The siege of Siping was a tactical blunder by the PLA, brought on by Mao's insistence on some form of revenge for the loss of Yan'an. But although the attempt to take the town cost the CCP dearly in the number of killed and wounded and the loss of precious equipment, the offensive as such had some positive effects for the party as well. First of all, Lin's forces had shown that they were capable of operating throughout Manchuria, and that no GMD-held areas—including the cities—were safe. Secondly, most of the districts that the PLA had taken over on its way to Siping were still held by the party after its retreat, and, in late summer, the Northeast Field Army made use of the weakening of GMD strength along the Sungari to expand eastward. Although Lin Biao in late July offered self-criticism for the failure to capture Siping, he told Mao privately that the overall effects of the operation were not bad, and that his forces would be ready to retake the offensive in the fall.

Although Jiang Jieshi, like Mao, viewed Manchuria as the main theater of war, the Generalissimo in the spring of 1947 also had his mind fixed on driving the CCP out of Shandong. Jiang's preoccupation with Chen Yi's forces stemmed both from the GMD's setbacks in the region the previous winter and from a conviction that the CCP's presence in the province in the long run could enable it to challenge his hold on central Jiangsu and the coast. Jiang had been furious with his commanders that they had not been able to crush Chen's forces when they were on the run in the fall of 1946 and the early part of the winter. His ire reached a peak when Chen almost miraculously was able to strike back at his pursuers during a Lunar New Year counteroffensive in the Yixian-Zaozhuang region, capturing twenty-five tanks and destroying nine brigades. It was the biggest victory the PLA had had in a long while, and Jiang wanted Chen Yi out of Shandong.[19]

The offensives to drive out Chen's army began in February and lasted until late summer 1947. The initial strategy was a two-pronged attack on the CCP-held areas in the mountains in central Shandong. The GMD dedicated some of its best troops to advance both from the north and from the south, and by mid-February they had penetrated deep into the western valleys of the Taishan massif. On 21 February, Chen Yi, in a carefully planned operation, ambushed about half of the troops advancing from the north in a narrow valley east of Tai'an. Some thirty-five thousand GMD soldiers were killed, wounded, or taken prisoner. But the government's offensives continued, with fresh manpower brought in from the south. By early May, the GMD controlled about half of the Shandong Mountains, advancing slowly from the west and southwest.[20]

In spite of Chen Yi's immense bloodletting of Jiang's forces, Mao was convinced that a general counteroffensive in Shandong would be foolhardy. He insisted that Chen not concentrate forces, and that attention be focused away from the battles in the mountains and toward taking over districts in northern Shandong. On 22 May he wrote to Chen congratulating him on his latest victories:

That you destroyed the enemy's 74th Division [near Mengliang'gu] was very good, even if we paid a heavy price in casualties. You have proved that when we are defending ourselves, we can break the enemy's offensives and win decisive victories. . . . Now, on other battlefields all over the country—except in Shandong— our troops are launching offensives. But all of those offensives are for the purpose of helping our troops in Shandong to break the enemy's push there, and the people's campaigns in Jiang's area have the same purpose.[21]

When summer came to the mountains of Shandong, Chen's forces started to feel the pressure. The GMD's Nanma campaign pushed the CCP steadily to the east, and Chen Yi worried about running out of space to operate in. As early as June he had asked Mao to accept his contingency proposals to divide the Shandong forces into four parts and to move them out of the central massif. As PLA casualties increased, Mao kept insisting that substantial losses, up to sixty or seventy thousand, were acceptable in order to keep the government armies busy in central Shandong. By late July, with desertions and supply problems on the increase, Chen finally got the Chairman's permission to rearrange his positions. Five columns, led by Tan Zhenlin and Xu Shiyou, marched eastward to new bases on the Jiaodong peninsula. One column remained in the central mountains to conduct guerrilla operations. A smaller force tried to march past Jinan to the north. The main force moved straight west, toward the plains, where they hoped to link up with Liu Bocheng's army.[22]

Diplomacy and Alliances

While struggling to contain the CCP in what was quickly becoming an all-out military contest for power in China, Jiang Jieshi was also left with a number of diplomatic and political problems to sort out. As the economy deteriorated, Jiang concluded that the only way out in the short run was to obtain increased U.S. support. Based on his previous experience with the Americans, this was not a conclusion that Jiang drew lightly. But his economic advisers told him that such assistance was necessary, and Jiang himself firmly believed that the United States owed a great deal to China for its steadfastness during the anti-Japanese alliance. In the spring of 1947, he therefore readily sanctioned a plan for improving relations with the Americans that his wife, Song Meiling, had worked out together with her brother, the former premier, Song Ziwen, and the Chinese ambassador to Washington, Gu Weijun.[23]

The new GMD diplomatic strategy had three main components. First, the ambassador was to use his considerable local network in Washington, and especially in Congress, to underline the parallel between the situation in China and the situation in Greece and Turkey. The so-called Truman Doctrine—the administration's March 1947 extension of aid to Greece and Turkey because of the alleged Soviet threat to those countries—should also be applied to China, Gu was to argue. Second, the Chinese government was to express, confidentially, its willingness to open the Chinese market to American exports and investments as soon as the civil war was won. And third, Chinese representatives were to target U.S. mass media—for instance, through their extensive contacts within the Luce media empire—to secure a more positive depiction of Jiang's government.[24]

The outcome of this strategy was mixed at best. The Truman administration remained wary of any long-term involvement in China. The president told his cabinet in March that "Chiang Kai-shek will not fight it out. [The] Communists will fight it out—they are fanatical. It would be pouring sand into a rat hole [to give aid] under present conditions."[25]

The new Secretary of State, George Marshall—who had just returned from his futile attempt to force Jiang into line with U.S. policies—was warier than most. After several meetings in which the Chinese ambassador had asked for increased aid, Marshall told Gu in cold anger that Jiang "is faced with a unique problem of logistics. He is losing about 40 percent of his supplies to the enemy. If the percentage should reach 50 percent he will have to decide whether it is wise to supply his own troops."[26]

Marshall's problem, however, was that there was an increasing policy split on China both in Washington and among local U.S. representatives. The Song family was right that the increase in Soviet-American Cold War tension deepened the divide between those Americans who wanted to bolster the GMD and those who insisted on keeping the United States out of the war. During the spring of 1947, Marshall grew increasingly annoyed with suggestions coming from his old colleagues in the military—and especially from War Secretary Patterson—that the United States should increase its involvement in China by supplying more economic aid and more military advisers. In late May, faced with new pressure from the Republicans in Congress, Marshall reluctantly agreed to lift the arms embargo against China and to ask for the release of a $500 million U.S. loan granted in early 1946.[27]

In Nanjing the lifting of the embargo was seen as a major diplomatic victory. Jiang Jieshi, influenced by Song Ziwen and Foreign Minister Wang Shijie, believed that the U.S. decision had been caused in great part by Chinese pressure. The Generalissimo expected such pressure to yield further results as the Cold War intensified and the 1948 U.S. elections approached. That the directors of the U.S. Export-Import Bank, which should provide the loans to China, refused in mid-June to comply with Marshall's request took Jiang completely by surprise. He simply could not understand that the Americans now would not deliver on what he saw as their promises.[28]

Marshall's announcement in late June that he would send a U.S. mission headed by General Albert Wedemeyer to China did little to cheer Jiang. Although the Chinese leader instructed his foreign minister to continue the efforts to get U.S. support, he privately saw the U.S. attitude as opportunistic and racist. In his diary he wrote: "The Americans have developed a plan to assist Greece and Turkey in their struggle against Communism, but will not [help] the Far East. This is evidence of their policy of 'Europe first.' If they do not change [this policy] now, they are sure to regret it in the future."[29] The appointment of Wedemeyer—the only U.S. general from the World War II era in China with whom Jiang had parted on friendly terms—did little to impress the GMD leader. Jiang did not believe that Wedemeyer would have much influence in Washington, whatever his conclusions.

The Wedemeyer Mission, in the end, turned out much worse than even Jiang had anticipated, and was a profound shock for the many within the GMD leadership who had believed that the general's appointment heralded a positive turn in the U.S.-GMD relationship. Before his departure from China in late August, Wedemeyer met with the Chinese State Council and did nothing to hide his exasperation with GMD military incompetence, economic mismanagement, and overall levels of corruption. To hide his embarrassment, Jiang again told his closest associates about his confidence that the forthcoming U.S. election and rising international tension would create the need for a real Sino-U.S. alliance.[30]

This time Jiang Jieshi turned out to be at least half right. As the CCP began its first large-scale offensives in Manchuria in September, pressure mounted on Marshall to increase U.S. military aid. General David Barr and Admiral Oscar Badger, the new heads of the U.S. military mission with the GMD, both called for expanded aid programs. In Congress, the Republican majority headed by Senator Arthur Vandenberg and Speaker of the House Joseph Martin also pushed for more U.S. assistance to Jiang's government. Several Republican congressmen threatened to block U.S. aid to Western Europe unless similar aid was given to China. In November 1947, Marshall proposed to Congress an aid package for China. After much wrangling it was passed in April 1948, providing Jiang with $338 million in economic aid and $125 million in military aid. This aid, together with the more than $1.4 billion that had already been provided to the GMD since the end of World War II, made China into a major U.S. investment in economic terms.[31]

In the early fall of 1947, Jiang accepted suggestions coming from within his own foreign ministry that the GMD should establish better relations with Moscow. Since the break-off of the Sino-Soviet economic talks in the spring of 1946, the GMD's relationship to the only outside power besides the United States that mattered in East Asia had been kept at the lowest levels possible. Although Jiang did not harbor any real expectations for a dramatic change in the Soviet-GMD relationship, he hoped that contacts with the Soviets could be used to pressure Washington into providing further assistance. Chinese foreign ministry officials

---

George Marshall on U.S. Aid to the GMD, February 1948

We must be prepared to face the possibility that the present Chinese government may not be successful in maintaining itself against the Communist forces or other opposition that may arise in China. . . . It can only be concluded that the present government evidently cannot reduce the Chinese Communists to a completely negligible factor in China. To achieve that objective in the immediate future it would be necessary for the United States to underwrite the Chinese government's military effort, on a wide and probably constantly increasing scale, as well as the Chinese economy. The U.S. would have to be prepared virtually to take over the Chinese government and administer its economic, military and governmental affairs. . . . I have struggled and puzzled over the situation continuously since my return. Our trouble has been to find a course which we could reasonably justify before Congress on other than emotional grounds. It has been a long struggle.

Statement to Committees on Foreign Affairs and Foreign Relations, U.S. Congress, 20 February 1948, quoted in *The China White Paper, August 1949* (originally published as *United States Relations with China with Special Reference to the Period 1944–1949* [Stanford, CA: Stanford University Press, 1967], pp. 382–83).

---

read the dispatches coming in from Europe and the United States as saying that another global war was in the making. They hoped that by improving the Sino-Soviet relationship, the GMD regime could keep out of the war and use the opportunity to wipe out the Chinese Communists while Moscow and Washington were battling it out in Europe.[32]

Stalin reacted favorably to the GMD overtures. The Soviet leader had been watching U.S. reluctance to vouch for the GMD regime with great interest, and had nothing against improving the Soviet relationship with Nanjing, at least on the surface. By the early fall of 1947, the Soviet leadership had for the first time started noting in earnest the military capabilities of the PLA, and knew that Soviet influence in China through the CCP would be considerable at least for the foreseeable future—every reason then, Stalin believed, to exploit the U.S. difficulties with the Guomindang and attempt to secure another avenue for Soviet policies. In ideological terms, Stalin still thought of Jiang's regime as a multiclass alliance headed by the national bourgeoisie. At China's stage of development, the national bourgeoisie would not rule out contacts with the socialist Soviet Union, particularly if the Chinese bourgeoisie was jilted by the ruling class of the main imperialist country.[33]

Like U.S. policy, Soviet China policy got its form in part from East Asia specialists who realized the extraordinary importance of the outcome of the civil war, and in part from generalists who often did not give much weight to events outside Europe. But in addition, the carrying out of Moscow's policies was handicapped by the inordinate degree of fear that pervaded Soviet institutions at the end of the Stalin era. Soviet reports could reflect only what the authors believed was the line promoted by the top—that is, by Stalin himself. The second-tier leaders who were supposed to provide expert guidance on special areas—for instance, in the case of China, the heads of the International Department of the CPSU Central Committee, the Far East desk of the Foreign Ministry, military intelligence, the Foreign Intelligence Section of the NKVD, the Nanjing embassy, and the special agents serving with the CCP both in Manchuria and Yan'an—all studied the formal or informal reports from the Boss's inner circle to find out how to angle their reports. The result was often a disjuncted and reactive policy process, in which major initiatives could linger for months before coming to execution, simply because their purposes were not understood by those set to carry them out.[34]

In spite of the coherence that Marxism-Leninism as a formal ideology gave to Soviet policy-making, Soviet officials in China suffered more than most of its representatives abroad from the defects of Moscow's foreign policy practices. The cadres based in China had problems understanding what Soviet goals were, both with regard to the Guomindang and the CCP, and, as a result, they were cautious to the point of inertia in furthering their instructions. This was not least the case in the Nanjing embassy, which only rarely was able to further the Soviet cause with the Chinese government, even on those occasions when Stalin decided to sweeten the relationship.[35]

The Soviet military attache, General Nikolai Roshchin, a former official with the Main Intelligence Directorate of the General Staff,[36] started renewed contacts with the GMD political leadership in September 1947. In his conversations with GMD leaders, Roshchin made two main points. One, that the Soviet Union could influence the CCP to agree to a Soviet-mediated end of the civil war; and two, that any Soviet initiative depended on Jiang Jieshi's agreeing to reopen talks on economic and political cooperation between Moscow and Nanjing. This crude form of diplomatic blackmail did not go over well with the GMD. Although virtually all GMD leaders agreed that Stalin could stop the civil war if he wanted to, they also agreed that it was unlikely that he would, whatever concessions Nanjing came up with. Jiang had gone as far as he could in conceding to Soviet demands in 1945. His nationalist pride prevented him from going further, in spite of the declines in his military fortunes in late 1947.[37]

The Soviet efforts at establishing links with the GMD did, however, provide Jiang with an opportunity to play the Moscow card on the Americans. GMD officials repeatedly mentioned the conversations with Roshchin and other Soviet representatives to American envoys in China, and although no one on the U.S. side believed that Jiang's government would, in Cold War terms, defect full-scale to the other side, the hints about a Soviet "alternative" did worry policy-makers in Washington. GMD intelligence did defeat some of their leader's purpose, however, by feeding the Americans reports of Stalin explaining to the CCP that the Soviet contacts with the GMD were purely tactical in nature.[38]

As U.S. and domestic liberal criticism of Jiang's policies increased in mid-1947, the Generalissimo turned to the right wing within the GMD for support. At a session of the GMD Central Executive Committee in mid-September, Jiang castigated the party membership in general for incompetence and corruption, while holding up some of the rightist leaders associated with the CC-Clique as positive examples of the GMD's "revolutionary tradition." In a major concession to the right, the party leader packed off his more liberal brother-in-law and close collaborator for almost twenty years, Song Ziwen, to be governor of Guangdong province. The fifty-three-year-old Song had served as finance minister, foreign minister, and premier in the Guomindang government, and he had become increasingly impatient with the slowness of the pace of reform. With Song out of the core leadership—at least officially—Jiang became increasingly dependent on hard-line conservative advisers, who saw no chance of accommodation between the GMD and any of the political forces that opposed it in China.[39]

Spurred on by the CC-Clique, Jiang in the fall of 1947 ripped off most of the pluralist façade that his regime had worked hard to build since the start of the Marshall Mission. In November, after failing to split the Democratic League further by offering some of its centrist leaders a place in his government, he abruptly banned all the party's activities. In Jiang's view, he was right to prohibit the League, since his advisers were telling him that the party in some areas collaborated openly with the Communists. But both at home and abroad Jiang's decision was generally seen as a sign of weakness, as was the Generalissimo's proclamation of general mobilization for war and his government's warrant for Mao Zedong's arrest "for treason."[40]

The banning of the Democratic League further reduced the room for maneuver that liberal opponents of the regime had in China. As a political movement the League had not been able to follow up its successes from 1945–46, and throughout 1947 it had been weakened by the defections of some of its most dynamic members to the underground CCP. The main problem of the League during these months had been that it had not been able to link up to the anti-GMD movement in the streets, and, as a result, had not been able to compete with the CCP for the allegiance of antigovernment activists. In late 1947, with its original postwar leadership split into three groups of almost equal size—one dedicated to continue the party in exile, one that had openly or secretly joined the CCP, and one that had at different stages opted for the regime—the Democratic League was no longer an independent political force.[41]

The success that the Chen brothers and their right-wing allies had within the Guomindang was also reflected in the strong position they had in the new National Assembly, which was elected late in the fall of 1947. The elections, which reflected current political trends in the GMD elite rather than any popular sentiment, prompted calls from within the regime for Jiang to disband the "democratic" process altogether and set up a personal dictatorship, thereby creating more efficient and streamlined mechanisms for conducting the war. But Jiang was not happy with these ideas. Over the winter of 1947–48 he told the GMD right wing that they were going too far, and that their ideas would alienate foreign support and make the GMD's situation more difficult in the provinces. As for himself, Jiang wanted to be the "father of his people" and the head of the Guomindang, not some sort of dictator isolated from both the party and the people.[42]

While trying to keep up with the demands of having a "capital on the march" in Northern China, Mao Zedong had diplomatic problems of his own. Although ties between the CCP and the Soviet Union had been gradually expanding since early in the summer of 1946, CCP leaders were disappointed that not more Soviet aid was forthcoming and that Moscow remained pessimistic with regard to the immediate future of the Chinese revolution. In spite of Mao's attempts to tell him otherwise, Stalin kept regarding the retreat from Yan'an as a strategic setback and believed that the CCP would be best served with some form of truce in the fighting.[43]

In 1947, Mao faced a triple problem with regard to the Soviets. His most immediate concern was to secure as much practical Soviet support as possible in the war against Jiang. By the fall of 1947 a fairly stable pattern of support had emerged. The Soviets provided a limited amount of occasional supplies for the war effort in Manchuria for free—blankets, boots, helmets, ammunition. Furthermore, Moscow had already in the spring of 1947 encouraged the CCP leadership to enter into trade agreements, in which raw materials from the CCP-held areas of Manchuria were exchanged for products or hard currency from the Soviet side of the border. By August a number of such agreements were being negotiated. Furthermore, the Soviets had held out prospects of assistance with repairing the Manchurian infrastructure as soon as the military situation had become more settled. Obviously, Soviet support was far below the levels that most Chinese party members had expected from the socialist neighbor. But it was enough for Mao and other leaders to be able to refer to Soviet support when explaining the party's strength to CCP cadres.[44]

Mao was also under pressure to further strengthen the reorganization of the party and CCP-dominated local governments along Leninist lines. This process, which had already started during the anti-Japanese war, aimed at integrating civilian and military administration under party leadership, training cadres in administrative duties, and imposing a more hierarchical structure at the different levels of leadership. Some influential leaders, such as Liu Shaoqi and Ren Bishi, saw this as a process of "Sovietization," learning the structures of socialist practice from the Soviet experience. To some extent Mao shared their perspective. He knew that the only model available for building these socialist practices was the Soviet Union, and he wanted his party to get as much advice and training as possible from Moscow. In order to do so, Mao asked the Soviets to set up training programs for CCP cadres both in the Soviet Union and in Manchuria, and to assist in revising the curricula for party schools and training centers at the local level.[45]

Mao's third Soviet concern was with developing a framework for the relations between his party and Moscow in the future. By late in the summer of 1947, Mao's thinking about the years to come became increasingly concerned with the need to set up a Chinese socialist state on the territory controlled by the CCP. Mao, and virtually all Chinese Communist leaders, believed that the construction and survival of such a state would depend on Soviet support. It was the Soviets whom Mao counted on to provide the technology, the production systems, and the organizational models that would propel socialist China forward. It was Moscow that would extend protection to the new state against immediate attack

---

Stalin Calls off Mao's Visit to Moscow, July 1947

To Terebin [Orlov]:

All your pieces of information with regard to Mao Zedong, as well as on the situation on the fronts are received.

In view of the forthcoming operations and in view of the fact that Mao Zedong's absence might have an adverse effect on the transactions, we consider it appropriate to postpone Mao Zedong's trip temporarily.

F. Kuznetsov

Kuznetsev to Orlov [Stalin to Mao], 1 July 1947, APRF, f. 39, o. 1, d. 31, p. 24.

---

by the imperialists. And it was Stalin's acceptance of the importance of the CCP's revolutionary victories that would enable Chinese Communism to play a key role in the socialist transformation of East Asia—a process on which the security of New China depended.[46]

In order to deal with all of these issues, Mao had decided that he himself would go to see Stalin in Moscow and discuss the main problems of the Chinese and East Asian revolutions with the head of the socialist camp. In the early summer of 1947, Mao thought that the time was right for such a meeting. The military situation in China had stabilized somewhat, and the PLA had shown that it could not easily be wiped out by the government. The CCP leader firmly believed that in a year or, at most, two, the tide of the fighting would start to turn against the GMD. Mao needed Stalin's advice and the Soviet leader's personal commitment to the needs of the Chinese revolution. By agreeing to meet with him, Mao thought that Stalin would signal both Soviet commitment to China's needs and the personal recognition of his leadership role that Mao had craved for more than a decade.[47]

Thus Stalin's decision not to accept Mao's request was a profound disappointment for the Chinese leader, and helped to push his views of international affairs to the left. Mao thought that Stalin refused to receive him in Moscow because the Soviet leaders were afraid of the U.S. reaction to such a meeting. Speaking to his closest comrades when traveling slowly eastward over the winter of 1947–48, Mao on several occasions stressed that Chinese policies had often in the past been more "offensive" than Moscow would allow. He used Stalin's criticism of the "rightist" policies of the French and Italian Communist parties and the more aggressive Communist approach signaled by the founding of the Cominform (to which Chinese Communist leaders were not invited) to frame his critical remarks: The Soviets were, albeit gradually, coming round to his point of view. From his temporary dwellings in loess-brown village huts at the edge of the great North China plain, Mao kept believing that some day the world would give his revolution the respect it deserved.[48]

Death on the Central Plains

The most spectacular military operation of the civil war was Liu Bocheng's 1947 sweep across the Yellow River toward his former base in the Dabie Mountains. This was a new type of offensive for the Communists, penetrating core areas of the Guomindang state, hitting at targets that held the keys to the control of China. By luck and by determination the operation was a startling success that awoke all Chinese to the possibility of the Communists ultimately toppling the government of Jiang Jieshi.[49]

The idea of the campaign was born in the spring, after Liu's forces, on Mao's orders, attacked several GMD strongholds along the Yellow River. The relative ease with which the PLA reached its objectives convinced Mao that the Great Plains area—southwest of GMD operations in Shandong and southeast of Hu Zongnan's campaign in Shanxi—was the "underbelly" of Nationalist military offensives. He also thought that the fifty-five-year-old Liu Bocheng, a former cowherd, miner, and highway robber known for his ruthlessness and for his dedication to the Communist cause, would be the right man to lead such an operation. The chief political officer of Liu's army, Deng Xiaoping, shared the Chairman's thoughts. Like Mao, Deng realized that the CCP needed something flashy, a manifestation of its power, if the political effects of the GMD offensives were to be turned around. The forty-three-year-old Deng, a landlord's son who had studied in Paris and in Moscow, was very conscious of how military power was a currency to be used in battles for the minds and souls of the inhabitants in the GMD areas.[50]

To Mao, flashy victories were also necessary to stem the thoughts of a Soviet-sponsored peace settlement held by some of the political leaders of the CCP after the fall of Yan'an. Liu Shaoqi had told Mao about his short-term pessimism several times after they parted company, and the Chairman had started fearing that his being physically apart from others in the party elite could endanger his ability to lead. In May he gave the go-ahead to Liu Bocheng's and Deng Xiaoping's audacious plan to cross the river and do battle with the GMD on the Central Plains. It was an al-

Famine in Henan

The most superficial observer could see that this was a class famine. In the streets of Loyang, where starving peasant refugees lay dying in the gutters, the restaurants stayed open and a man with money could eat as well as he could afford. Since food was scarce and expensive, many of the poorer city-dwellers began to starve like the villagers, but Kuomintang officials and employees received their full allowance of government wheat throughout the famine. Many corrupt officials handling government wheat made fortunes. While some of the provincial armies disfavored by the central group were put on short rations—and were reduced by desertions—the élite central troops, notably those of Tang En-po, were always kept strong, to "preserve social order."

From Graham Peck's evocative memoir, *Two Kinds of Time*, which describes China's development toward civil war during the early 1940s. Illustrated by the author. Boston: Houghton Mifflin, 1950, p. 393.

most desperate plan—not serving any major strategic objective, except to relieve pressure against Chen Yi's forces in the East and against Peng Dehuai's exhausted soldiers in Shaanxi. It was a plan intended first of all to surprise the enemy and thereby to kill as many of his numbers as possible.[51]

The Central Plains comprise a huge area, stretching from Hebei in the north and the upper reaches of the Yellow River past Loyang in the west to meet the ocean south of Shandong. It was, and is, a very diverse region, including some of China's wealthiest areas in Jiangsu province and some of its poorest in Henan and northern Anhui. For the poorer peasants of the Central Plains, the wars had been disastrous—warfare and its economic curses had robbed them of the precarious incomes they had had earlier, and had left many areas destitute. To make things worse, in March 1947 the Americans had given the government technical assistance to redirect the flow of the Yellow River to its former bed. By a bit of engineering, Jiang had placed half a mile of water between Liu Bocheng's forces and those of Chen Yi. But although the peasants in the area had been forewarned, five hundred villages were submerged and more than 100,000 people were made homeless without compensation. Millions suffered as a result.[52]

If there was a revolutionary situation among the peasantry anywhere in China in 1947, it was in the very area in which Liu's forces landed after having crossed the Yellow River. In a way that surprised many Communist officers who had thought of the Central Plains as enemy territory, many peasants flocked to the PLA and viewed it as a liberator. The Communists knew how to make use of peasant enthusiasm for their purposes—tens of thousands of peasants were drafted into the army, mostly to carry supplies for the soldiers. There is no doubt that the assistance received from the local population was a major reason why Liu's forces could establish themselves south of the river and quickly prepare to move on.

Liu's crossing of the river near Puyang in late June put his and Chen Yi's forces close enough to each other to coordinate their operations. When Liu's main force of about 100,000 men began moving south through the plain, Chen Yi's forward units rushed in from their eastern mountain strongholds to attack the GMD brigades, which suddenly were surrounded by enemies. In three separate battles in July, the GMD 2d and 4th armies suffered severe defeats, losing more than 80,000 men to Chen's and Liu's losses of about 10,500. Their supply lines and communications broken, the GMD armies were easy prey to the highly mobile Communist forces, whom Mao ordered to stay in the area and inflict as much damage as possible. The purpose, Mao said, was killing the enemy and destroying the morale of those who escaped. For the Chairman, the Central Plains battles were, for now, simple and pure propaganda, intended to show that the CCP was a nationwide threat to the regime of Jiang Jieshi.[53]

For the GMD troops who attempted to contain the Communist excursions, these midsummer battles on the plains turned into a hell of carnage and destruction. As whole brigades were annihilated, fear took the best of the regime's forces. After the first two weeks of engagements, the Nationalist units were mostly attempting to stay out of harm's way, sheltering in the main towns, and letting the southward-bound CCP forces pass them. For the GMD commanders in the area, their main preoccupation—if they for some reason had been bypassed by the PLA—was to avoid taking blame for the disasters. Jiang, predictably, was furious. Even though it took some time for him to realize the full and troublesome extent of the GMD defeats, already by August he had sacked every commanding officer who had been involved in the Central Plains debacle, gradually replacing them with men from other commands. In November he appointed the defense minister, General Bai Chongxi—a former leader of the Guangxi clique whom Jiang had distrusted for political reasons—to be the new general commander in the area. Bai, a Muslim who had been a schoolmate of Li Zongren, in Jiang's eyes did have the advantage that the CCP, rightfully, blamed him for having been in charge of the slaughter of Communists in Shanghai in 1927.[54]

In late July, Mao called the military and political leaders in the Northwest to meet with him, Zhou Enlai, and Ren Bishi in the little village of Xiaohe in northern Shaanxi, where the leaders had been staying for some time. The Central Plains battles were the turning point in the civil war, Mao said. From now on, the party's troops would go on the offensive all over China. Mao was triumphant at the meeting, although some of his statements sounded as if they had been prepared to deflect criticism should Liu Bocheng's operation have gone wrong. Now, instead, the Xiaohe meeting marked Mao's ascendance to the role of supreme military genius even within the small circle of party leaders. In the past he had sometimes made crucial military decisions without consultation; after July 1947, Mao made such decisions on his own whenever he felt it necessary. "The war would not last more than five years, before Jiang is defeated," the Chairman prophesied.[55]

It is difficult to say when the idea emerged of making the Dabie Mountains the temporary aim of Liu Bocheng's forces. It is likely that Liu and Deng Xiaoping both were attracted by the option of returning to what had been a CCP base area fifteen years earlier, and where they believed that a strong Communist underground still existed. What was clear was that the PLA forces needed defensible terrain on which to set up a base in central China, and that such terrain could not be found in the lowlands. Mao agreed. "Strike through to Dabieshan," he told Deng Xiaoping in late July, "[and] we establish a stronghold between Wuhan and Nanjing."[56]

With the GMD forces in lackluster pursuit, Liu Bocheng's troops, boosted by enemy defectors and often assisted by local recruits, started on the little Long March back to central China. Liu's main worry was that Jiang would send reinforcements from the east and the south to block their path. But, as it turned out, the CCP's units moved too quickly to be cut off. They did have to fight an unwanted battle with the GMD at the Ru River in late August, but they overcame the resistance and crossed the Huai to reach the Dabie Mountains in early September. They had marched more than five hundred kilometers in less than forty days, and, although they had taken losses, they had reached their objective.[57]

But what they found in the Dabie area shocked even veterans like Deng Xiaoping. Instead of a Communist underground waiting to be "set free," the PLA met a peasantry that had been devastated by years of war and depravation. The new Central Plains Bureau of the Central Committee, of which Deng was the secretary, faced a tough period of rebuilding infrastructure and providing political training in order to secure their base. They had a foretaste of how difficult it would be to transform central and southern China into the Communist image.[58]

Manchurian Pivot

The defeats in Central China forced Jiang Jieshi to take some tough strategic decisions. It was the first time during the war that the GMD had faced an immediate shortage of manpower in any area, and to their surprise the needs were in Central China, considered by many the core of Guomindang power. Jiang faced substantial pressure from Bai Chongxi and other leaders, and from the Americans, to transfer some of the best trained GMD troops from Manchuria to what had become the Central China front. Not surprisingly, Jiang refused such requests, preferring to get forces from the Southern coast and from the Southwest transferred to western Jiangsu and Anhui. Jiang expected the main push from the CCP to come in the Northeast. He wrote:

> If we lose the Northeast, then there will be no protection for North China. The Northeast is our key industrial base; if we lose it to the CCP and the Russians, then they would take advantage of it and sweep through all of China. Also, Liaodong [Eastern Liaoning] and Jiaodong [Eastern Shandong] are the key points for our naval defense. Without Liaoning, Jiaodong would not be able to survive. And if we lost Shandong, then Central China and South China could not survive.[59]

In order to protect Manchuria, Jiang in 1947 transferred there as his main commander General Chen Cheng, the former chief of the General Staff and one of the ablest officers in the GMD army. The forty-seven-year-old Chen, from Jiang's home province of Zhejiang and a former student of the Generalissimo's at the Whampoa Military Academy, would replace both Xiong Shihui and Du Yuming, combining the offices of general commander with being the highest civil authority in the region. Jiang was glad that he had finally found a way to get rid of the endless bickering between Xiong and Du, and he trusted Chen to be Lin Biao's equal in terms of strategic vision. The new commander would have around 500,000 soldiers at his disposal, among whom were most of the American-trained and Western-equipped brigades transferred from the Southwest at the beginning of the civil war. Jiang also promised Chen that he would receive the bulk of whatever new military equipment China would be getting from the United States or Europe.[60]

Chen began his tenure in Manchuria by forcing the warring military and civilian factions in the regional GMD leadership to hold their peace. Those he suspected of not being capable of breaking out of old habits were transferred to posts south of the Wall. He also suspended all of the commanders who had worked with the Japanese and disbanded their units. Chen's strategic plan was to strike at the CCP in October, splitting the PLA forces in the far North from those deployed to the northeast of Siping, and thereby turn around the slow encroachment on the Manchurian cities that the CCP had begun in 1946. Together with GMD forces in North China, Chen's troops would then destroy the southern part of the PLA in Manchuria, before pushing the remaining Communist units toward the Northwest and the Soviet/Mongolian border.[61]

Lin Biao may well have heard at least the broad outlines of this plan from CCP spies at Chen's headquarters. In communicating with Mao in early September, it seemed as if Lin was preparing to preclude just the kind of offensive that Chen was planning. What Lin proposed to Mao was a kind of mirror image of the GMD plan, in which his forces would combine to try to cut the enemy's supply lines to Manchuria from the south. The plan had two main stages. In the first, to begin right before the GMD operation was supposed to get underway, the PLA would attack the Beijing-Liaoning railway as far south as possible. Then, about a week later, the main PLA forces would advance southward, cutting the railways between Shenyang and Siping and between Shenyang and Dalian.[62]

Mao, after some hesitation, agreed to Lin's plan. The Chairman's skepticism was based on his fear that such a large combined operation would risk the main part of the CCP's forces in Manchuria if the enemy proved capable of an effective counterattack. But Mao was also skeptical of the large battlefront operations that Lin had become enamored of, and which the operations planned for the fall seemed logical precursors for. The Soviet battle plans that Lin had studied both during his stays in Moscow and after he came to the Northeast were, to Mao, dangerous aberrations from the principles of people's war.[63]

The main reasons why Mao in the end gave his consent were that the Manchurian operations, if successful, would remake the whole strategic picture in the Northeast and North China, forcing the GMD on the defensive. Coming at the heels of the battles on the Central Plains, such a success could hold the key to the outcome of the war. With increasing Soviet support, and some from North Korea, the Northeastern forces of the PLA were better equipped and better organized than ever. The political preparations for an offensive, which the Manchurian Bureau of the Central Committee had conducted through the summer, suited Mao's tastes in emphasizing land reform and a radical redistribution of power in the villages, alongside recruitment to the PLA. In Mao's view, the chances for success were reasonable.[64]

Throughout the fall and early winter of 1947–48, the content of the Manchurian operations of the PLA was decided by Mao and Lin Biao. From his headquarters south of the Wall, Mao limited his discussions of Manchurian affairs with most other leaders out of fear that they would resist "overextension" of the PLA, including the diversion of attention and support from the fronts in Northern and Central China, and in Shandong. The Chairman may also have suspected that some of the commanders, for instance Peng Dehuai, were jealous of the special relationship that had developed between Mao and Lin. Peng's replacement as acting chief of the General Staff in late August by the somewhat unlikely choice of Zhou Enlai may have been connected to these worries.[65]

What Mao and Lin had in common was first and foremost a propensity for thinking big. After Liu Bocheng's stunning success, Mao had become impatient. "The key to gaining an ultimate triumph in the Guomindang areas is to win as many battles as possible," he wrote in early September.[66] "From now on," Mao wrote in a message to all commanders after reading Lin's descriptions of his preparations for battle in the Northeast, "you must change your habits of relying on supplies from the Liberated Areas. . . . People, food, weapons, clothes—all must come from the enemy troops and the enemy's areas. . . . Whenever you capture enemy soldiers, just fill them into your own forces. . . . Do not take heavy weapons with you, and do not fear being cut off from all connection with the Liberated Areas."[67]

The cold weather came early to the Northeast in 1947. By the time that Lin Biao's men were moving southeast toward their new deployment areas in late September, freezing winds were sweeping the Manchurian plains. The GMD defenders of the railway lines in Jilin and Liaoning were already feeling the impact of the cold, and none more than the newly arrived 49th Army, consisting mostly of men from Jiangsu province. They had the dubious distinction of being the first unit that came under attack, and were almost completely annihilated by Deng Hua's 7th Column of the PLA Northeast Field Army. The Communists pushed on, cutting not only the Beijing-Liaoning line in two places but also generally succeeding with their attacks on the railways in the East. Some units penetrated as far south as the coast, showing that the PLA could now operate all over Manchuria, except in the immediate vicinities of the cities. The Communists made away with large amounts of supplies and grain for the winter before the main forces withdrew in early November.[68]

So successful was Lin's fall offensive that Mao wanted him to continue the operation by further raids toward the towns in Central and Southern Manchuria, killing and taking prisoner as many GMD troops as possible—much in the same way that Liu Bocheng had done south of the Wall. But Lin wanted to consolidate his positions and to rebuild his strength over the winter. The Manchurian commander knew that his losses had been more severe than had been reported to Mao. His one attempt at following Mao's prescription and using his forces in the West to engage Fu Zuoyi's brigades entering from Hebei had ended in failure. Lin, wisely, turned a deaf ear to the Chairman's implorings and sent back his own requests for more men and money.[69]

One of the reasons why Lin initially chose to wait with exploiting the initiative he had gained was that the establishment of a full-fledged trade relationship with the Soviet Union was gradually enabling the Manchurian CCP to get equipment it had not so far had much of. The Communists traded or bartered a great number of products from the Northeast—minerals, grain, furs, and meat—for vehicles, boats, optics, and telephones. The combination of trade and aid had reached a substantial volume by the end of 1947, and Lin hoped that his Soviet links would in a few months remove many of the technical and logistical advantages that the GMD forces still possessed. He was particularly preoccupied with the railway lines from the North to the South: If a general offensive of the kind Lin was contemplating should succeed, he was dependent on using the railways for his own purposes. In his talks with Soviet representatives, one of his main aims was getting Moscow to send more railway technicians and repairmen.[70]

What became known as Lin Biao's Winter Offensive was not initially planned as a broad offensive, nor was it planned to take place in winter. While increasing recruitment and training in November and December, Lin had been discussing with his chief planner, Li Zoupeng, how limited attacks in the GMD areas could be carried out from early spring on. Li and his staff—who usually were well attuned to Lin Biao's rapidly changing moods and ideas—suggested that local guerrillas by January should join PLA units to target areas to the north and west of Shenyang to test GMD defenses and to further isolate the city. In order to placate Mao, Lin then suggested that the operation should be extended to include movements of troops both east and west of Shenyang, if the first attacks were successful. Lin explained his plans to Mao in a general sense, saying that his overall strategy from now on was to put pressure directly against a target, while also committing enough troops to secure the main part of the flanks—a doctrine that Lin later enshrined as One Point, Two Flanks. Mao, jubilant at Lin's change of heart, readily agreed, although he commented to his colleagues that getting Lin to mount a general offensive was harder than forcing a cow to jump a fence. To make certain that the purposes of the offensive were understood, Lin placed Li Zoupeng in charge of the first offensive northwest of Shenyang, which was to begin on January 14.[71]

In Shenyang, GMD commander Chen Cheng had also been discussing starting a winter offensive, but he was dissuaded by his subordinates, who had more local experience, from attempting to challenge the deep frost of the North. Chen Cheng's pride had been badly hurt by the CCP's thwarting of his plans for the fall, and he longed for a chance to show the Generalissimo that he had the situation in Manchuria under control. What finally buried his hopes for major operations in January, however, was the onset of icy winds that would have made air support impossible. Still, Chen was confident that, over winter, his forces would be able to drive the PLA out of several of its strongholds in the East by means of limited operations. To witness the stabilization and the beginning of his counteroffensives, he convinced Jiang Jieshi that the Generalissimo should personally inspect his troops in Shenyang at the beginning of the new year.[72]

Li Zoupeng's troops moved stealthily through the forests and the deep snow north of Shenyang. Probably because of the bad flying conditions, they were not discovered by the GMD until the night before the attack. The GMD 5th Army was routed, and the forces sent from the city arrived too late to interfere. Themselves coming under attack at night by Li's soldiers, the GMD reinforcements fled back to Shenyang. When, on 23 January, Lin Biao got the message about Li's success, he immediately asked Mao's permission to send reinforcements to widen the attack west of

Shenyang to surround the town of Xinlitun, while sending a larger force, commanded by Wu Kehua and Wu Ruilin, east of Shenyang toward the Liaodong peninsula. Mao was enthusiastically in support: "The more battles, the fewer of the enemy's troops are left," he told Lin.[73]

If, in purely military terms, there was one crucial maneuver of the civil war, this was it. Lin's circumvention of Shenyang, pushing the GMD away from the main railway lines and out of the key strategic areas in southeastern Manchuria, was the core of the PLA's military success north of the Wall. Xinlitun fell in late January, with the loss of a full GMD division. With the GMD forces on the run in the East as well, the two Wus captured first Liaoyang and Anshan, and then pushed on southward toward the Bohai Gulf. The port of Yingkou fell in late February, allowing the CCP to send essential supplies and reinforcements across the Bohai to its forces in Shandong. In one stroke, Lin Biao had cut the main railways, isolated Shenyang, and taken control of all the areas between the Korean border and the eastern passes leading into Liaodong and North China. It was a spectacular victory.

From Shenyang, where he had arrived on 12 January, Jiang Jieshi personally witnessed the destruction of some of his best troops, and the hopelessness that spread in GMD ranks as the enemy advanced. After his arrival, Jiang had doubted Chen Cheng's defensive strategy of avoiding moving his main forces so that they should not be cut off and surrounded. In the end, this lack of mobility ensured their complete annihilation. On 27 January, more saddened than angry, Jiang relieved his favorite commander of his position and sent him south "to rest." In his diary, Jiang wrote about difficult times, when "the reports of failure come down just like snowflakes" from the Manchurian sky.[74]

But from south of the Wall, Mao egged Lin on. "Congratulations on your capture of Liaoyang," he wrote on 7 February. "Now, fight on . . . we should trap Jiang's troops in the Northeast and then eliminate them one by one."[75] In order to close the trap and complete the isolation of the Manchurian cities, Lin decided to go again for Siping, the third attempt in two years. But this time the equation of forces was radically changed. Lin, who personally led the attack—perhaps to make up for his earlier failures just here at Siping—this time had more than 100,000 men under his command. The defenders, Peng E's 88th division, had only 19,000, and could not match the heavy artillery that Lin used on the city. Peng's men, many of whom had fought with their commander since he had defended Shanghai from the Japanese ten years earlier, promised each other that they would not give up. But on 12 March, with the PLA in control of most of the city and the valley that surrounds it, Peng and his soldiers spent their last strength on a desperate breakout toward the south. Only a few of them made it back to GMD lines.[76]

By mid-March 1948 the military situation in Manchuria had been completely reversed from where it had been a year before. The GMD held only small pockets of territory, mostly around the main cities of Changchun and Shenyang and on the southern edges of the region. Although a large number of government troops still remained in the Northeast, Lin Biao had seized the military initiative. In many other parts of northern China, CCP forces were slowly turning the tide against the GMD. In the cities, those who had tried to organize a third way, against Jiang's dictatorship but independent of the CCP, had been imprisoned or driven out. All over China people were waiting to see which way the military competition would go. It could be only one way or the other. For the people around Siping, thrice punished by warfare, the main meaning of the city's fall to the Communists was that, at last, there was peace.

6

THE TURN
Battlefields of the North

Li Hua, "Attack"

For some of the men who had been following Jiang Jieshi since the 1920s, when he was a young officer with a mission to rescue China, the spring and summer of 1948 was the first period in which their loyalty to their leader was severely tested. Among these people, civilians and military men alike, there was a growing sense that the Generalissimo had lost interest in them and in their common cause. Without a doubt, Jiang was often on the move, going from one battlefront to another, issuing instructions and firing commanders on the spot if they did not comply with his wishes or failed in carrying them out. But unlike his manner during the war with Japan, the head of the Guomindang seemed to some of his men sometimes to waver in his famed sense of political direction. Perhaps, a few wondered between themselves, their leader was losing his will to fight on.

For Jiang Jieshi himself, two motives of his adult life seemed to come into conflict with each other when defeat heaped upon defeat in the spring of 1948. On the one hand, he saw himself as chosen, almost in a mystical way, to save China from foreign imperialism and domestic subversion. On the other, he believed that he had to take responsibility for the disasters that were again befalling China. But while in earlier times taking responsibility would have meant to Jiang reinforcing his efforts, bolstering all military might and political cunning to defeat the enemy, now his thoughts sometimes turned to the need of sacrifice for the public good or, in his darkest moments, to the fear that his people were deserting him. He still believed that the answer to the Communist challenge was to be found on the battlefield, in one or two giant final battles that the Guomindang would win.[1] But if that strategy should fail, Jiang was already thinking about leaving behind the corrupt and hopeless GMD leadership, withdrawing with his best men to Zhejiang, his home province on the coast, or to Taiwan, and restarting his crusade from there.

The Guomindang, the Cities, and the Economic Collapse

As Jiang Jieshi's inner circle narrowed, increasingly consisting of those who always had been in favor of authoritarian rule and unconditional suppression of the enemies of the Guomindang state, most prominent party members in the civilian administration preferred to carry on with their work while keeping some distance from the Jiang "court." Wang Shijie, the talented but politically weak foreign minister, noted in his diary that it was increasingly difficult to see what kind of regime would come out of the present cataclysm, even if the GMD emerged victorious. Wang's view and the view of many other leading party members was that the Guomindang organization had been weakened during the last stages of the anti-Japanese war and during the civil war, and that the party's resurrection depended not only on winning the war but also on being able to purge its own ranks and regain public trust.[2]

At the other end of the political scale within the Guomindang, among the CC-clique and other right-wingers, there was obvious satisfaction with Jiang Jieshi's political direction, but also worry about the Generalissimo's determination, about the increasing corruption within the party, and about the continued U.S. influence on the Jiang family. Chen Lifu warned in several memoranda that greed, lack of willpower, and pernicious foreign influences were bogging down the party, and that only a strict party rectification based on national and moral values could save it. Jiang Jieshi, having adopted much of the right-wing's agenda, now resented what he saw as the Chen brothers' nagging, and gradually reduced the direct say they had in GMD matters, even though their overall influence remained great.[3]

A more open sign of Jiang's loosening grip on his party was his failure to prevent General Li Zongren from being elected vice president by the National Assembly in April of 1948. The fifty-seven-year-old Li—according to one source the son of a "failed scholar, a tutor and penpusher"—had served under Jiang both against Japan and against the Communists after the war.[4] The problem for the Generalissimo, who was known for his very accurate memory of past challenges, was that Li and his schoolmate Bai Chongxi had, in the early 1930s, headed an autonomous government in their home province of Guangxi that Jiang had had to work hard to get control of. Adding slight to injury, the ambitious but rather unpredictable Li had, while in the National Assembly, associated with remnants of other regionalist and warlord groups, with more liberal members of the Guomindang, and with the representatives of minority parties. It was a coalition of those groupings that succeeded in getting Li elected, but only because Jiang himself had waited too long in fielding an electable candidate of his own.[5]

For all GMD leaders who could lift their vision to encompass more than local issues, the main problem in 1948 was the deterioration of support for the party in the cities, among the bourgeoisie, and even among government officials. The reports that came in to Jiang Jieshi's office and to party headquarters showed these problems in abundance. The question that many—with increasing insolence, according to the reports—asked of party leaders was what the Guomindang was doing to protect them and their interests against the evils of social unrest, official corruption, and economic depression. Business leaders in Shanghai and Wuhan complained that the Guomindang, as the party of social stability and national salvation, did little to prevent soldiers and officials from helping themselves to favors and goods from distraught traders, and that, for legal trade, the margins of profit were so small and the risks so great that many businessmen simply closed down. A wealthy textile merchant from the southern city of Guangzhou, once a Guomindang stronghold, denounced the party in letters to GMD headquarters as "thieves, highway robbers (worse than socialists)."[6]

The economic crisis—in part created by GMD inflationary policies and bad financial management by local and central authorities—reached disastrous proportions in 1948. In the beginning of the year Jiang introduced new taxes to pay for the war effort, and—worse—authorized local authorities to collect "fees" to pay for the defense of towns and cities. He also decreed that army commanders in certain cases had the right to demand supplies directly from the population they were supposed to protect. With the addition of these new taxes, economic activity in some areas came almost to a standstill. In parts of north China, some traders routinely hid their goods in Communist-held areas when Guomindang armies moved through, stating that it was better to pay fees to the CCP than to have half the storage confiscated by GMD officers.[7]

In spite of the contraction of both the economy and its own finances, the government continued to print money well in excess of what had been decreed by the monetary reforms of 1947, and thereby held up the inflationary pressure that tore to the bone of the hard-pressed loyalties of most city dwellers. Gradually, over the first half of 1948, people who had seen most of their family fortunes disappear in 1946 and 1947 faced the prospect of near destitution. With their family businesses collapsed and with official posts paying barely enough to buy rice from one day to the next, those middle-class Chinese who did not have a trade or a craft to fall back on were in serious trouble. Some rescued themselves by joining the booming ranks of black marketeers and speculators. Others directed their rage at the government for not looking out for them. A few even contacted the Communist underground—but they were mostly turned away. The city Communists—themselves generally middle class in origin—had no need for "bad class elements" at this "late stage" of the revolution.[8]

Jiang Jieshi worried increasingly about his government's precarious financial position, but in the first part of 1948 he could not bring himself to make the sacrifices in terms of the war effort that a financially sounder policy would have demanded. During the early summer, in the brief military respite the GMD had after Lin Biao's Manchurian offensives ended, the GMD leader came under mounting pressure to accept some type of financial reform to relieve the crisis in the cities. The pressure came from different angles: The Americans were promoting a total overhaul of the currency system; some representatives of the GMD right wing recommended austerity combined with confiscations; and several of the main generals, joined by Jiang's son, Jiang Jingguo, urged a concerted crackdown on corruption and the misuse of public funds. As was often the case in the GMD, the reform package that was finally announced on 19 August was a mix of all the input in a fairly jumbled form. The core of the reforms was a new currency, the Gold Yuan, with up to two billion issued at a rate of one to three million against the old Yuan. Prices and wages were fixed at their August 1948 levels, and all strikes and public protests prohibited. All precious metals and foreign currencies held by Chinese citizens were to be handed over to the government in exchange for their worth in the new currency.[9]

The main battleground for the emergency measures was Shanghai, where Jiang Jingguo was put in charge of implementing the reforms. His powers, like those of the three other emergency reform commissioners in North, South, and Central China, were at least on paper nearly absolute, including the right to imprison "saboteurs" and opponents of the reforms without trial. The young Jiang went to his new task with determination and substantial public support. More than most GMD leaders, Jingguo realized that the campaign which he was at the helm of might be his party's last chance to stabilize the political and economic situation before the military showdown with the CCP. He used his powers energetically, personally inspecting markets and exchange offices, arresting those suspected of speculation or black marketeering on the spot. By early September more than three thousand suspects were in prison, among them some of Shanghai's best known Chinese businessmen. Although popular with the general public, Jiang junior's actions spread fear among the merchants who remained in Shanghai, reminding them of the predatory policies of the Guomindang when it first took over the city.[10]

Jiang Jingguo—and to a lesser extent his fellow commissioners—succeeded in re-establishing a limited degree of authority for the GMD in urban areas. But their policies helped little with the twin causes of the country's economic ills: depression in the markets and inflationary finance. In Shanghai, after five weeks of steady prices, not only were shops emptying out, since goods could be sold for higher prices in the surrounding provinces, but, in addition, some of the remaining industries had to close because their owners could not keep up with the cost of production. The final nail in the coffin of reform, in 1948 as it had been the year before, was the nonimplementation of limits set for public spending, which, in turn, forced the government to violate its own regulations concerning the issuance of money. By as early as mid-October, Jiang Jingguo had to especially instruct Shanghai movie makers not to lampoon the new currency in their ads.[11]

By the end of October it was clear to everyone that the August reforms had collapsed, and with them the last vestiges of ordinary economic activities in and around the cities. As the Gold Yuan started to depreciate even more rapidly than its predecessor, Jiang Jieshi fired his prime minister and minister of finance. He noted in his diary that he could not afford to concentrate more energy on "political" reform at the moment. What counted now was to stop the CCP's military advance, and to get U.S. support to turn the Communist tide coming in from the North.[12]

The United States and the Guomindang

By early 1948 the Truman administration had become convinced that Jiang Jieshi's government was developing into a liability for the United States in Cold War terms. Not only was Jiang himself incapable of winning the war against the CCP but, in addition, through his political position he prevented any serious alternative from emerging within the Guomindang, making Chinese liberals turn to Communism and the Soviet Union as the lesser of two evils. By as early as the beginning of the year there were suggestions, both in the State Department and within the CIA, that the United States would have to act to get rid of Jiang and increase its own direct influence in China. But John Leighton Stuart, the U.S. ambassador to Nanjing, warned that "there really seems to be no one else who could take [Jiang's] place," and Secretary of State Marshall—who had become increasingly skeptical of any increase in the U.S. commitment in China—remained opposed to direct U.S. interference.[13]

Under pressure from Republicans in Congress, who threatened to hold up American aid to Western Europe if the administration did not do more for China, Truman in February of 1948 had reluctantly asked for a grant for the Jiang government of $570 million. When Congress passed the China Aid Act in April, the sum had come down to $400 million, but with an added $125 million to be "used at China's option for military purposes." Truman had been able to defeat attempts at putting into the bill a call for direct U.S. military assistance "as in Greece," which some representatives had suggested. The aid was held up by disagreements both in Washington and between the United States and China over how the money should be spent and over who on the Guomindang side should be the direct recipients; it was not until 16 November that the first supplies under the China Aid Act began arriving. As early as December 1948, much of the aid was—at Jiang Jieshi's insistence—sent directly to Taiwan.[14]

Some of the delay in getting the aid moving was the result of the U.S. military's insistence that as much of the supplies as possible go to those few GMD generals, such as Fu Zuoyi, who had had some successes against the PLA. Clearly, the purpose was also to strengthen those commanders in their position vis-à-vis Jiang Jieshi.[15] The head of the U.S. military advisory group, General David Barr, underlined the need for such diversion of aid in his messages to Washington. "No battle has been lost since my arrival due to lack of ammunition or equipment," Barr stated. "Their [the GMD's] military debacles in my opinion can all be attributed to the world's worst leadership and many other morale destroying factors that lead to a complete loss of will to fight."[16]

A main reason why the Truman administration found both complete disengagement from China and attempts at removing Jiang difficult to carry out was the increasing political power of those Americans who wanted to keep the Generalissimo in power with U.S. support. Henry Luce, the influential news magnate, used his papers to show how Communism was encroaching on the United States through China, and how Jiang Jieshi was the only man who could stop the menace. As late as December 1948, the Luce-owned *Time* magazine, in its cover story on Jiang, defended the GMD leader and claimed that "the U.S. still had only a partial notion of how big its stake was in the China war."[17] In Congress, these sentiments—that China must be saved for the West—won increasing support as the Cold War took hold, although the number of con-

gressmen and senators who saw themselves as members of an activist
pro-Jiang "China Lobby" was relatively small.

Another reason why cutting loose from the China debacle was so difficult for Washington was the way in which, during the war, U.S. propaganda at home and abroad had lionized Jiang and his wife, Song Meiling,
as true democrats and true Christians. The Guomindang had been able to
use those stereotypes in their attempts at influencing Americans to provide more aid to China after the war. Song, especially, had become a master at playing exactly on those strings that resonated well in the United
States: Christianity, anti-Communism, and loyalty to old allies. Many
U.S. policy-makers saw the war in China in exactly such terms—for John
Foster Dulles, for instance, it was a conflict between Christianity and
Communism that Christianity lost.[18]

A third and powerful reason for Truman's inability to stake out new
ground in his China policy was that 1948 was an election year in the
United States; Truman was pitted against the Republican Thomas Dewey
in a close contest for the presidency. Early on in his campaign Dewey had
picked up on Truman's slowness on China and had cooperated with
those who had threatened to cut U.S. aid to Europe if China were not
benefited along the same lines. Referring often to aid for China in his
election speeches, the Republican candidate said that he did "not know
whether it would be 50 per cent or 80 per cent effective, and I doubt if
anyone knows. Of one thing I am sure, it would be immensely more effective than nothing."[19]

Throughout 1948 the State Department, supported by the White
House, attempted to keep down the number of American military personnel serving in China. Although the Joint Chiefs of Staff saw China as
a major U.S. investment in military and strategic terms and opposed a
complete disengagement, the strategy that underlined an offshore perime-
ter in East Asia as a natural line of American defense against Communism was already beginning to take shape.[20] Even strongholds such as the
navy base at Qingdao on the Shandong peninsula, which the United
States had held since the end of World War II, began to be seen as a liability rather than an asset. The fear that civilian and military advisers to
the president shared was that the continued presence of U.S. Marines in
an area like Shandong could draw the United States deeper into the civil
war than anyone in Washington wanted. There had already been several
minor clashes between the Marines and PLA units in the area. The num-

ber of U.S. Marines in Qingdao was gradually reduced, although the last American unit was not withdrawn until mid-1949.[21]

How much the Guomindang state benefited from U.S. aid that came to China in 1947–48 is difficult to say. The best that can be said about it is that in some areas, where the assistance could be used by officials who cared about the people's welfare, it helped to alleviate the suffering that the civil war brought on. On the other hand, the huge influx of easy money (by Chinese standards) that came into state coffers did its bit to increase inflation by driving up prices on some products. It also further stimulated official corruption: When the financial stakes were raised, it became easier for high-level officials with prior training in corrupt practices to embezzle or ask for bribes, and more difficult for those at the lower levels, with their meager salaries eaten away by inflation, to resist emulating their superiors.

Planning the Offensives

For the CCP leadership, the summer of 1948 was a period of consolidation, regrouping, and preparation for large-scale military campaigns. Surprised by the speed of the Guomindang collapse north of the Wall, Mao Zedong was dramatically revising his estimates of how and when his party could gain complete control of China. Having crossed the Yellow River and set up a new temporary joint headquarters at the little town of Xibaipo—thereby uniting the political and military leadership for the first time since the fall of Yan'an—Mao became increasingly preoccupied with the task of coordinating military planning for the Northeast, for North China, and for the Central Plains area. Based on the advice he had been getting from his military commanders in the field, the Chairman remained deeply uncertain about where the Manchurian units of the PLA ought to engage the enemy in order to break off the Northeast completely from the rest of the country. Mao's initial preference was to circumvent the GMD strongholds along the coast and bypass the cities. The combined forces from Manchuria and North China could then launch an offensive toward the Central Plains sometime in 1949.[22]

Mao's worry with leaving such a great number of GMD troops in place in the Northeast was that, over summer, Jiang could transfer them south of the Wall, where they could fight the PLA under better conditions than they had had in Manchuria. The Chairman complained repeatedly about the quality of Lin Biao's suggestions, as well as those from other military commanders. After getting yet another revised version of Lin's plans in late April, he wrote back, saying:

> The reason why we agree with your suggestion of attacking Changchun first is that it will be good that you attack Changchun, not that it necessarily will be bad if you attack somewhere else, or that [other] operations will create difficulties which cannot be overcome. You think that it is difficult to attack Shenyang, Jinzhou, or to cross south of the Wall to fight. Some of these difficulties are imagined, [and] not real.[23]

Slowly Mao convinced himself, and the others in the leadership, that the main purpose of the fall offensives ought to be to destroy the GMD hold on the areas east of Beijing, cutting off all land routes by which the GMD forces in the Northeast could be rescued and creating a link through which the Communists' Manchurian forces could easily be transferred south. The CCP victories in Shandong and southern Shanxi in early summer were essential for this decision. By mid-May the forces that had remained in these two provinces had, with assistance from the main CCP forces in North China, been able to drive the GMD on the defensive, capturing key parts of central Shandong and advancing through central Shanxi, virtually besieging the provincial capital of Taiyuan. Most of the GMD gains from early 1947—including the former CCP "capital" of Yan'an—had been retaken by the Communists.[24]

Although these victories—especially in the West—had been costly to the CCP in terms of their own losses, Mao saw that at least in theory the party's forces could now operate across Northern China, from the Bohai Gulf to the far side of the mountains of Shanxi. If the Manchurian forces could crush the massive GMD presence in the regions along the coast between Shandong and Liaoning in the East, then Jiang's troops in North China would, in the next round of fighting, have little to fall back on. In June and July, Mao's vision remained a pipe dream. But for every week that went by before Jiang Jieshi pulled back his forces on the southern edge of Manchuria and along the Bohai Gulf, it became more likely that the Chairman's battleground of choice could become a reality. By as early as the end of May, Mao exhorted Lin to get his supply lines ready: "Our troops must have a full food supply—only then is victory possible. The grain [in the area] is not enough for such a big force, so they must get supplies straight from the Northeast."[25]

For the Nanjing government, the main military endeavor in early summer was to prevent a complete collapse in and around Shanxi. Jiang Jieshi was never in doubt that Hu Zongnan's troops had to be reinforced from both western China and from the East after their defeats at the hands of Peng Dehuai. The GMD leader was almost certainly right. With fresh forces available, Hu managed to fight back and trap Peng's advance into the Wei Valley, inflicting a serious defeat on the CCP. After limiting the damage in the West, Jiang was not willing to follow Hu's and Bai Chongxi's advice to withdraw his forces from the Eastern seaboard, combine them with the troops in North China, and, while fighting the CCP in the North, prepare for a later counterattack into Manchuria, possibly from the West. The Generalissimo kept insisting that withdrawing from the East would bring forth a torrent of Communist incursions farther down along the coast, threatening the key areas of GMD political power.[26]

Instead, Jiang wanted to prepare for relief for his besieged forces in the Northeast. His overall plan, sanctioned by the Supreme Military Council, was to use the forces along the Bohai Gulf to assist Wei Lihuang's troops in Manchuria, while transporting in new troops from the south to replenish the armies in North China. With reluctant U.S. support under the new military aid package, the GMD was able to keep up an impressive air-bridge to Shenyang, expanding Wei's total forces up to at least 400,000 by late summer. But with Zheng Dongguo's 1st Army in Changchun completely cut off from the rest of the GMD-held areas, and Fan Hanjie's 6th Army far away in Jinzhou, the actual combined power of the Nationalists in the area was not that impressive. In spite of Wei's suggestions, however, Jiang did not want to attempt to concentrate the forces already in the area before the railway links to Jinzhou had been re-established and Wei's dependence on airlifts reduced.[27]

In order to widen the room for maneuvering that Liu Bocheng's troops had in Central China and create a north-south connection through eastern Henan, the CCP headquarters ordered Chen Yi to cooperate with Liu in an operation centered on the provincial capital of Kaifeng. Chen doubted the wisdom of attacking Kaifeng itself—it was, he argued, useless in a strategic perspective—but he readily agreed to the plan after Mao had explained the main objectives to him in late May. Chen sent some of his forces toward Xuzhou to feign an attack on Jiang Jieshi's precious core area. When the GMD 5th Army began moving from Henan to defend Xuzhou, Liu Bocheng sent six divisions straight north toward Kaifeng, linking up with Chen's forces and isolating the city on 16 June. Seeing the political use of taking the city, albeit temporarily, Mao ordered an immediate attack. Although completely outnumbered, the Nationalist

> ### GMD Air Force Attacks Kaifeng, June 1948
>
> Seconds later the aircraft swooped again. This time I saw from under each wing tiny objects detach themselves. The bombs whistled down, and once again I had that paralysing feeling that so many others have felt, that feeling that the missile is coming right at the watcher's head. The first stick hit the radio station behind the hospital. As they turned again, I raced for the shelter of the south wall. It was machine guns again. I saw bodies rear up from the stretchers, saw the puffs of smoke from the secondary charges as the bullets hit the hospital wall, and then the planes were gone. . . . Our plight was desperate, and I decided to visit Red Army [PLA] headquarters. The East-West road was littered with dead animals and human bodies. The stench was indescribable. Pigs and dogs were feeding on those bodies which had not yet putrefied. Flies and maggots covered the swollen bodies of others. Nobody was in the streets, for the planes were in the habit of machine-gunning anything that moved.
>
> Dr. Ernest Lippa remained in the city of Kaifeng after the CCP took over in mid-1948. Here he describes a GMD air attack in the latter phase of the battle. Lippa, *I Was a Surgeon for the Chinese Reds* (London: George G. Harrap, 1953), pp. 53–55.

defenders under General Li Zhongxin put up stiff resistance, and it took the PLA a week to take the city, with the combined efforts of the Communists and the GMD air force destroying much of it in the process. General Li committed suicide. The CCP withdrew after four days, but in the fighting that followed, the PLA decimated the enemy armies sent to relieve Kaifeng, among them the 5th Army rushing back from Xuzhou.[28]

For the CCP leadership, the success of the Henan campaign was important not least in political terms. The PLA had shown that they could capture provincial capitals south of the Wall. Zhou Enlai reported to the leadership that a number of higher GMD officers had begun having second thoughts after the events in June, and did not want to end up like Li Zhongxin, fighting to the end for a lost cause. Zhou had been in charge of extending the CCP's United Front strategy in mid-1948. Preparations had long been under way to set up a North China People's Government that would administer the CCP-held areas. Mao, in the spring, had wanted to give the new government not just a regional but also a national status, but he had been held back by Soviet advice and by doubts among his main advisers, primarily Zhou and Liu Shaoqi. The government was set up in August with Dong Biwu as president.[29]

Even more important in political terms was the work that Zhou and his colleagues did among the remnants of the Democratic League and disaffected members of the GMD. Through his agents both in the GMD-held cities and in Hong Kong, Zhou attempted to get former DL leaders and those with left-leaning sympathies in the GMD to cooperate with the CCP. By the spring of 1948, the DL had reconstituted its Central Committee in Hong Kong, and a Revolutionary Committee of the Chinese GMD set up in the same place, both controlled by the CCP. As Zhou explained to Mao, these organizations both provided the Communists with valuable intelligence and were vehicles through which GMD defections could be handled. In order to give them a formal place in the embryonic CCP state—and to score a cheap propaganda victory—Mao agreed to let the North China government invite representatives from all "democratic and patriotic" parties and groups to the CCP-held areas, in order to set up a new Political Consultative Conference.[30]

As the military situation improved for the Communists in North China, Chairman Mao increasingly thought in terms of combining operations in southern Manchuria and in the coastal areas of Eastern China south of the Wall. He became increasingly afraid that spending forces on attacking Changchun and Shenyang would hold up the more massive engagements with the enemy farther south, and perhaps even give the GMD time to prepare a counterattack in North China. In late July, Lin Biao had suggested concentrating on the coastal towns of Jinzhou and Tangshan, combining Mao's strategic objective with setting a trap for the remaining GMD forces around Shenyang. Mao readily agreed. As often, in the key battles that were to follow, more depended on the GMD reaction than on CCP capabilities. But now, at least, Mao could tell his associates in Xibaipo that a plan had been agreed upon.[31]

The LiaoShen Campaign:
September to November 1948

The two great military campaigns of the Chinese civil war—the LiaoShen campaign, which was fought in western Liaoning province in the fall of 1948, and the HuaiHai campaign, which took place in the area around Xuzhou in the winter of 1948–49—were closely connected in both strategy and outcome. The first campaign developed out of Mao's impatience with the long-term strategic framework he himself had set up in the spring of 1948 and out of Jiang Jieshi's reluctance to move his troops out of Manchuria without a final showdown with the Communists. The second campaign, HuaiHai—so named after the Huai River and the coastal town of Haizhou, which formed the southern and eastern extremes of the battles—occurred because of the extraordinary results of LiaoShen and Mao's subsequent decision to throw caution to the winds and make one push to take control of all of China north of the Yangzi River. The outcome of these encounters was decisive for the military outcome of the civil war.[32]

The LiaoShen campaign did not get off to a good start for the CCP. Having convinced himself that Lin's Jinzhou plans would be carried out in the fall, the Chairman was shocked to learn that his Manchurian commander was thinking in terms of a more limited winter campaign, as had been discussed before that summer. Mao was furious. He ordered Lin to get going immediately. In a series of telegrams during the first weeks of the campaign, he berated Lin for making serious mistakes:

> On the possibility of the enemy's withdrawing from Northeast, we have told you before you finished your winter operation [that we] hope you can get hold of these troops. If they can transfer from the Northeast to North China on a large scale, it will be very bad for our operations. On the preparation of food supplies for your troops before you move south, we instructed you on this two months ago. However, whether you have cared to do it or not, you never mentioned it in all your telegrams over the past two months. Now, according to your telegram, it seems that you have never even looked into this, so that the troops cannot move because they have no supplies. On the other hand, on the reasons that you cannot decide the date to move, in all your telegrams in recent days you only talked about the enemy's positions and asked whether Yang Chengwu['s PLA forces in North China] can move out earlier. . . . For yourself, you are concerned about the enemy's positions, the food, and even rain gear, but for Yang Chengwu, to the contrary, you do not care about anything. May I ask you: The date for you to move out is uncertain, but at the same time you want Yang's troops to move out. . . . What good will it be to the whole situation? It's quite wrong that you are so reckless with regard to Yang's troops. Also, your judgment on the enemy's positions along the Bei-Ning railway—I read from your telegrams—is also too hasty.[33]

On 3 September, Mao continued his pressure on Lin:

> According to our sources in Nanjing, the Defense Ministry has worked out an operation plan to land in Yingkou. All the troops which will participate in this operation have had full military preparations. . . . After their landing, they plan to push forward to Shenyang and ensure their troops withdrawing from Shenyang. . . . You must prepare to attack those withdrawing troops after you seize Jinzhou, and stop them transferring to Central China.[34]

In late September, as Lin's operation was getting underway, Mao was still angry: "The key to the whole military situation in the Northeast lies in the capture of Yi county, Jinzhou and Jinxi. . . . However, it has been three weeks since your troops moved out [and] you have still not started the attack on Yi. The movement is so unbelievably slow, you should conduct self-criticism."[35]

And then, as Lin had second thoughts in early October, the Chairman ridiculed him:

> Now the enemy in Changchun has not yet moved out, and the enemy in Shenyang dare not aid Jinzhou alone. . . . You should take advantage of this crucial moment, concentrate your main forces and capture Jinzhou. This plan should not be changed. . . . Five months ago, the enemy in Changchun could probably have been easily defeated, but you did not want to do it. Two months ago, the situation remained the same, you still did not want to do it. Now, . . . as the situation has begun to change, you dare not attack Jinzhou, but want to pull back to attack Changchun. We think this is quite wrong.
>
> Where is your command post? It should have been in Jinzhou area before the troops started moving. [I] hope you yourself will move to the front quickly and plan the battle of Jinzhou, thereby ending the fighting as soon as possible. If you delay too long, you will lose the initiative.[36]

To rub it in, and to make sure Lin had a formal order, Mao telegraphed later the same day, 3 October: "We insist that you should not in any way change the planned strategy, leave Jinzhou aside and shift to attack Changchun. . . . [I]nstead, we hold that you should concentrate all your forces and try to seize Jinzhou within about ten days."[37]

And then, on the next day, after Lin signaled his acceptance:

> It is very good that you have made up your mind to attack Jinzhou. . . . Over the past month, we sent you a lot of telegrams, asking you to correct the mistake of preparing to use your troops in both the south and the north, without any focus. However, you have not realized it until now and begin to deploy your main forces around Jinzhou and Jinxi. It will determine the fighting. Anyway, your mistake has been corrected.[38]

Lin's caution was not misplaced. The Guomindang forces in the region were still strong enough to defeat him, if he was not careful in his planning. His fear was obviously that as soon as the enemy realized that Jinzhou was the main target, they would rush their forces both from around the cities and from south of the Wall straight there, leaving him outflanked. Only if some pressure from other CCP forces and some pretense from his own still remained focused on Changchun could he hope that the trap could be successfully set around Jinzhou.[39]

By 24 September most areas in Yi county had been brought under PLA control, thereby cutting off Jinzhou from the north. The main county seat of Yi fell on 1 October, although with considerable Communist losses. These losses, and a slight delay for the PLA troops that were intended to cut Jinzhou off from the south, were probably the reasons why Lin Biao had second thoughts about the operation. Lin—a perfectionist with regard to logistics—this time wanted to make absolutely sure that his quantitative superiority could be made use of. As two circles of CCP units were closing in on Jinzhou, the battle for the city began. It was the beginning of the major offensives that, almost exactly one year later, would allow Mao to proclaim the People's Republic from atop the Gate of Heavenly Peace in Beijing.

Jiang Jieshi and his General Staff had by late September decided that Jinzhou was the immediate aim for Lin's troops. On 26 September, Jiang ordered Wei Lihuang to send some of his own forces from Shenyang to engage the PLA forces, which were about to lay siege to Jinzhou from the north. Wei refused. He still thought that Lin's real objective was Shenyang, and that Jinzhou was a trap. Besides, Wei argued that those parts of Fan Hanjie's 6th Army that were outside the outer PLA encirclement were in a much better position than he was to break any siege of Jinzhou. Jiang threatened to relieve Wei of his command. Wei did not reply to his commander-in-chief's telegram. The head of the General Staff, Gu Zhutong, who went to see Wei at his headquarters, also failed to convince him. Then, on 1 October, Jiang himself returned to Shenyang.[40]

The news that the Generalissimo would be coming had finally made Wei reconsider. As a commander, Wei was not of the imaginative kind, but he had firm ideas and had learned a lot from listening to his more experienced officers after he arrived in Shenyang. His response to Jiang's order was to create two forces, altogether with more than 130,000 men—the core of the remaining GMD troops in Manchuria—which could advance toward Jinzhou from the west and the northeast. He waited for Jiang's arrival to give them their marching orders. The Generalissimo insisted that there was not a moment to lose. In a dramatic meeting with his Northeastern generals, Jiang declared that this was to be the battle for Manchuria. It was win or lose from now on, Jiang said.[41]

When first on their way, the GMD troops moved fast, faster than Lin Biao had calculated. By 11 October they had retaken Yingkou and were advancing along the railway to Jinzhou, threatening to engage the PLA before their attack on the city had started. Lin had to divert some of his forces to stop a more general advance by the GMD from the north, but he still had enough men in place to start the general attack on Jinzhou.

His reports to Mao, however, show that he was aware of the danger he now faced: If the operation could not be completed quickly, the whole idea of using Jinzhou as a bait to get Wei Lihuang to send out his troops could turn against the Communists. Instead of isolating and defeating Wei's troops, Lin's own key forces could be cornered in southeastern Liaoning, far from their base areas, and pushed south to meet battle-ready units of the GMD armies.[42]

The attack on the medieval city walls of Jinzhou began in the early morning of 14 October. Mist was covering the ground and hid some of the PLA units as they moved into position. The shelling was intense—all the training in the use of heavy artillery that Lin's army had undergone over the summer with the help of Soviet instructors was brought to bear on the defenders. As soon as the PLA artillery had breached the walls, the GMD air support became almost useless. It was fighting in the streets from then on, a bloody battle that the GMD could not win. When General Fan finally raised the white flag over the railway station—his last outpost—the PLA had taken more than ninety thousand prisoners. How many GMD soldiers died is difficult to estimate, but a loss of as many as forty thousand during the encirclement and the attack is probable. North of the city other CCP units had stopped the GMD advance, with big losses on both sides.

The tables had turned. The initiative was again with Lin and his commanders. Now the trap could close. Lin immediately swung his main forces that had captured Jinzhou back north, while the other CCP forces in the area closed off the retreat for the GMD troops that had set out from Shenyang. By 26 October the "West-Advancing Army" under Liao Yaoxiang was surrounded by half a million Communist troops. Lin Biao inspected his troops early that morning, telling them that this was the final battle for the Northeast. At dawn the PLA moved in on the enemy, which immediately fell back into the marshland around Heishan. With their communications in disarray and with no hope of being assisted from the outside, the GMD units made easy targets. The carnage was immense. Soon the marshes were literally filled with blood—one CCP officer remembers advancing over the bodies of dead enemy soldiers. Many GMD units were overrun even before they could surrender. The battle lasted two days and one night, and at the end of it the PLA had taken more than sixty thousand prisoners. Liao Yaoxiang was captured, and at least twenty-five thousand of what had been the last big GMD army in Manchuria were killed.[43]

While the core of Wei Lihuang's troops were being massacred at Hei-shan, the keepers of the remaining GMD strongholds in the Northeast had second thoughts about the future. The Communist underground in Changchun had for some time been in touch with the main GMD commander there, Ceng Zesheng. As news of the Jinzhou battles came in, Ceng agreed to talk to some PLA political officers who had been smuggled into the city. He and most of his officers defected to the PLA, and Mao Zedong sent his personal orders to reinstate them with their ranks in the Communist army. They then, on 21 October, proceeded to shell their former comrades, the last loyal GMD troops, who had taken refuge in the Bank of China building, into submission. Twelve days later Shenyang itself fell, after lackluster attempts at defending it. Parts of the remainder of Wei Lihuang's army, which had been stationed there, succeeded in breaking through to Yingkou, from which they were evacuated to the South. Wei had flown out to Huludao the previous week, only to be picked up by Jiang Jieshi's secret police and thrown into prison as payment for his defeat.[44]

The fall of the Northeast had cost Jiang's regime almost 400,000 of its best troops. It had given the Communists full control of one of the richest parts of the country, and provided them with the legitimacy that control implied to most Chinese. In Nanjing, Jiang was aware of what the consequences of this catastrophe could be for his ability to govern China. He wanted to issue immediate orders to counterattack, but his closest advisers convinced him that an order to send more troops beyond the Wall, or to prepare for amphibious landings, could result in defections, or even a rebellion. In the end he decided not even to call a full meeting of the Supreme Military Council, preferring to talk to the head of the General Staff in broad phrases and indicate the need to do everything to stop a Communist advance toward Central China. When he got the message about the fall of Shenyang, Jiang's mind was already on the need to strengthen the GMD troops south of the Yellow River.

In order to support a defense line that would cordon off the key provinces in Central China from Communist attacks from the North, the Generalissimo needed U.S. assistance. For the first time during the civil war, it had become clear to Jiang that the very survival of his regime might, in fact, depend on what kind of help Washington was willing to give him. He had had a rude shock on 12 October, when his Foreign Minister informed him that the United States had decided to evacuate its citizens from Beijing and Tianjin. "We hope," Jiang wrote, "that they will stop the evacuation, or, at least, not make it public. . . . American residents are under the special care of our government. If it becomes necessary, we will be the first to inform [them] about a need to evacuate."[45]

The same day as Shenyang fell to the CCP, Harry Truman was re-elected president of the United States by the narrowest of margins. Like many U.S. news commentators, Jiang Jieshi had been convinced that the Republican, Dewey, would win. For the Generalissimo, the re-election of Truman was a big setback, almost on a par with the military disasters in Manchuria. With the Republicans in power, Jiang had hoped to get back to the kind of close alliance that he felt had existed between China and the United States during World War II. The Republicans, Jiang felt, realized the Communist threat that both China and the United States faced and would have been willing to act to counter it—even at the risk of all-out war. With Truman and the Democrats, there would be little but empty phrases.[46]

On 9 November, Jiang drafted a letter directly to President Truman. He wrote:

> There are many reasons for the deterioration of the military situation in China, but the most important and immediate is the Soviet violation of the [1945] Sino-Soviet Treaty.
> Without Soviet help, the CCP would in no way have been able to sweep through the Northeast. Now the CCP troops are approaching Nanjing and Shanghai—if we fail to stop their advance now, then the democratic countries would lose all of China. We are in great need of American military aid and a firm policy statement of support to China, which would greatly boost our troops' morale. . . . Now the reaction to the urgent situation depends on your sympathy and quick decision.[47]

To underline the seriousness of the situation, Jiang sent his wife, Song Meiling, to Washington on 1 December to plead for a quickening in the pace of U.S. deliveries and for guarantees for more aid in the future. Jiang hoped that Song would help convince her American friends when it mattered most, just as she had done during World War II.

In Xibaipo, Mao Zedong spent much of his time in early October bent over maps. The Chairman studied terrain in Central China that had, over the past twenty years of absence from the region, become unfamiliar to him. He had to make a quick decision on how big an operation the new campaign toward this region—already dubbed the HuaiHai campaign by the CCP leadership—was to become. Over the past months, Mao's status in his party had taken on godlike proportions. The victories in the Northeast, which, with much help from party propaganda, were ascribed to

Mao's military genius, seemed even to people who had known him for a generation to place the Chairman beyond reproach on any issue.[48] His orders on how to conduct HuaiHai would be followed unquestioningly by the party and its military commanders. He only had to make up his mind.

In early September, Mao had still based his political reports on the need to finish GMD rule within five years. In late October, although the five-year period was still used in messages from party headquarters, Mao talked to his closest associates about chasing Jiang out of China in a year's time. The need now, Mao said, was for a continuous offensive, isolating and conquering the cities in North China and advancing toward the cities on the Yangzi River. The HuaiHai campaign fitted well into this perspective, if its aims were widened to defeating all of the Guomindang's core units north and south of the Huai River. The campaign would then become the centerpiece of a general CCP offensive toward the Yangzi. But by the time orders went out for the new campaign in the last week of October, no decision had yet been taken on how many GMD units should be targeted.[49]

It was the news of the spectacular CCP victories in Manchuria that released Mao from the ties that bound his public military strategy—the cautious road toward victory in 1951–52—to the prudent advice on the need to prepare the political conditions that he received from Ren Bishi and Liu Shaoqi, and from the Soviets. Armed with Lin Biao's success, the Chairman could overcome his own doubts and, in early November, order his generals moving toward the Grand Canal to destroy all of the armies under the command of Liu Zhi and Du Yuming at the GMD Xuzhou headquarters. For Mao, this offensive was intended to change the military situation in China forever. But it was also part of his general concern about advancing more quickly toward socialism in China and not being hemmed in by those who were too preoccupied with the country's present backwardness.

HuaiHai: November 1948–January 1949

The HuaiHai campaign—the decisive encounter between the Guomindang and the CCP north of the Yangzi River—was the largest military engagement fought after World War II. At its peak it involved more than 1.8 million soldiers across front lines of about two hundred kilometers. After September 1948, Jiang had strengthened his Xuzhou headquarters with about 150,000 men and had made clear that its task was to stop any

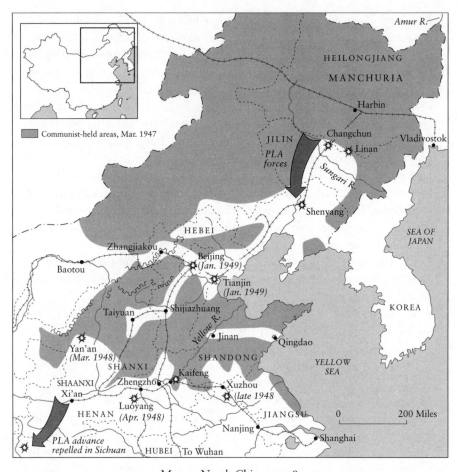

Map 3. North China, 1948

attempt by the CCP to attack toward the south. Up to mid-October, neither Jiang nor his ranking general in Xuzhou, Liu Zhi, believed that the
PLA would direct a major campaign southward before they had transferred the main part of their Northeastern troops to North China,
thereby getting the reserves they needed for a push south. It could also be,
although both Jiang and GMD intelligence doubted it, that the Xibaipo
leadership would give priority to attacking the Northern cities—Beijing
and Tianjin—before moving down toward the Central Plains.[50]

What this planning overlooked when counting months rather than
weeks before an attack was the PLA's possibilities for replenishing its

ranks from among defeated or defecting GMD soldiers during the more limited campaigns that took place in North China parallel to the LiaoShen battles. During the mid-September CCP conquest of Jinan—the provincial capital of Shandong and the first big city south of the Wall to be taken permanently by the Communists—the PLA gained more than 50,000 soldiers. Most of these came over when GMD General Wu Huawen, who guarded the western approaches to the city, defected to the CCP before the battle began. Wu's troops, most of whom had fought on the Japanese side not long ago, were immediately filled into Communist General Su Yu's forces. As a result of the Shandong and Shanxi battles in the fall, Su's and Chen Yi's troop strength had almost doubled. They did not have to wait for reinforcements before moving south.

Although he was aware of the political dangers that this form of "recruitment" entailed to the Communist cause, Mao had been adamant in discussions in Xibaipo that this was the way to proceed. As early as July, in discussions with Liu Bocheng—the CCP commander in East Central China—and his political commissar Deng Xiaoping, Mao had stressed the need to include former GMD troops in the offensives:

This year, in North China, Eastern China, the Northeast and the Northwest—except in a few districts—our troops are not supposed to expand. The population in the countryside has decreased rapidly and in some areas there have broken out uprisings led by landlords. The recruitment of new soldiers (including in Northeast) has gone to extremes. There has emerged a contradiction between the supply to the front and the possibilities in the rear. Without resolving this contradiction, the war cannot be kept going for long. From now on, the standards for recruitment of new soldiers, taxes, provisions, and the proportion between people who are mobilized for production and those who are not in all our areas must be approved by the Central Committee. In the future, there will probably be many more war prisoners [coming from] our capture of the cities. Thus, in every district and every troop, the training of war prisoners must be well organized. In principle, no prisoner will be let go. Most of them will be filled into our troops and some will participate in the production in the rear front. The human resources for our troops to defeat Jiang mainly come from prisoners; this must be brought home to the whole party.[51]

In part because of his successes during the Jinan campaign, Mao chose the young CCP General Su Yu to work out the preliminary strategy of HuaiHai. Su was aware of the difficulties of fighting around Xuzhou when coming in mainly from the North. He had read the imperial annals and knew that Southern dynasties since before the Han had preferred to make battle just here, where rivers and hills abounded, but where the landscape was flat enough for the troops not to be easily cut off from their supply lines in the South. Su also knew that time was scarce—if his and Chen Yi's troops from the North and units from Liu Bocheng's army under Deng Xiaoping from the West failed to move in quickly, Jiang might change his mind and withdraw southward toward the Yangzi, thereby, in his and Mao's estimation, making a decisive victory for the CCP more difficult.[52]

In Nanjing, Jiang Jieshi was discussing the two main strategic alternatives with his General Staff. He now spent almost all his time on military issues; his government, including his prime minister, had trouble getting to see him at all. Worried about the rapid movement of CCP forces toward the Grand Canal, Jiang wanted to withdraw most of his troops in Xuzhou to the Huai River, leaving a smaller force in the city itself. But the GMD commanders in the field demurred. They were fearful of not having enough time to complete such an operation before the PLA arrived in their area. By the end of the first week of November, when the CCP had already moved its advance forces into position east of Xuzhou, the GMD generals had still not made up their minds.[53]

On 5 November, Su and Chen Yi reported to Xibaipo that with some luck, one of the main GMD forces would expose itself to attack first, so that the Communist forces would not have to move close to the city itself to do battle. The next day, the GMD 7th Army Group moved east to protect one of its units that was moving from the coast toward Xuzhou. For Su and Chen, this was the chance they had been waiting for. Mao agreed. He ordered them to rush toward the Canal and cut the 7th Army Group off from Xuzhou itself. Deng's forces should move southwest of the city, feigning an immediate attack.[54]

When the PLA forces two days later suddenly descended on the town of Tai'erzhuang, midway between Xuzhou and the 7th Army Group headquarters at Zhanzhuan, the GMD commanders there decided not to fight. In the middle of the night they made up big fires so that the attackers would be sure to see their white flags. Almost without a shot's being fired, about a third of Jiang's Xuzhou command had been isolated, and the PLA used less than a week to surround it completely. But General Li still insisted that the Communists' immediate aim was Xuzhou. He convinced Jiang to send in more forces from the south and the west. The GMD had still not discovered Deng's forces, which were rapidly advancing with the aim of taking Suxian, cutting off Xuzhou from the south.

When Du Yuming, having escaped from the Manchurian debacle, ar-

rived at Xuzhou to take effective command on 10 November, the GMD
had finally learned of the existence of Deng Xiaoping's forces to their
south. Du had understood one lesson from the Jinzhou battle: Do not allow the enemy to place forces in areas that may be of use as a strategic retreat once the battle has started. He therefore suggested to Jiang that the
Xuzhou forces first attack Deng's troops and force them away from the
railway lines connecting the city with the Huai River. Jiang disagreed. He
insisted that the 7th Army Group should start a major battle now, and
that Du should send forces from Xuzhou to surround the PLA outside
Zhanzhuan.[55]

Du Yuming was almost certainly right. If the GMD had attacked first
toward the south, the whole Communist concept of isolating and defeating the main Nationalist units one by one would probably have failed.
Mao Zedong knew about Du's plans, and he worried that Nanjing would
accept them. If they had, the Chairman's rapidly expanding plans for the
overall significance of the HuaiHai campaign would have been shattered.
The Xibaipo leadership was therefore immensely relieved when, probably on 14 November, they realized that Jiang had ordered Du Yuming to
send the main part of his forces, two army groups, to counterattack at
Zhanzhuan and save the besieged 7th Army group.[56]

On 15 November, Suxian fell to Deng Xiaoping's soldiers. Xuzhou
was, effectively, isolated. Three days later, in some of the most intense
fighting of the civil war, units from Chen Yi's Shandong troops stopped
the armies advancing from Xuzhou among the hills and creeks in the
Nianzhuangxu area east of the city. The tactics the CCP used were similar to those employed in the Northeast: heavy artillery concentrating on
the main units at the center of the GMD formations, and highly mobile
Communist regiments at the outskirts of the battlefield, cutting off the
outer edges of the enemy armies, pushing their flanks into positions increasingly vulnerable to PLA shelling. The GMD advance ground to a
halt. Communications started to break down, and fear spread. On 22
November the rescue troops learned that the remnants of the 7th Army
Group at Zhanzhuan had capitulated. Two days later the rescue troops
made their way back to Xuzhou, carrying their dead with them. In the
GMD camps on the outskirts of the city, in view of the soldiers, bodies
were stacked up, waiting for burial.

At Communist headquarters in southern Hebei, the days during the
HuaiHai campaign started with an almost ecstatic ritual. At dawn, the
top leaders made their way to the farmhouse where Mao Zedong was

The Battle for Xuzhou, November 1948

We piled into a truck and rode out to the front, which bulged to the east and northeast. The dusty, rutted road twisted from village to village. Some of the peasants had remained with their mud huts, their fields, and a pig or two, although shells from [GMD General] Li Mi's 75- and 105-mm guns were screaming overhead towards the Communist-held villages. Abruptly, we were at the front in a village, with Nationalist soldiers, in their winter caps, with earflaps up, padded yellow tunics and leg wrappings, looking at us curiously. Beyond the village there were some trenches and foxholes, but there was no sense of close engagement with the enemy until we walked to a nearby field. The Communists had attacked the village during the night and been repulsed. The bodies of some twenty Communist soldiers lay there. They had been dragged in behind jeeps and ponies from the fields beyond the outer defenses. In dress and appearance, the dead men, their features gray and frozen, looked no different from the Nationalist soldiers about us. Henry F. Lieberman, the *New York Times* correspondent, noticed that some of the dead had secondary wounds, pistol shots in the back of their heads. Angrily, he asked if the men had been executed. A Nationalist officer shrugged. There were no adequate medical facilities for the Nationalist wounded, certainly not for the Communists found on the battlefield. As we drove back from the village to Hsuchow [Xuzhou], we passed the body of a soldier lying beside the road, his head split open like a ripe cantaloupe. No one knew whether he was a Communist or a Nationalist.

Seymour Topping, *Journey between Two Chinas* (New York: Harper and Row, 1972), p. 26. Topping was an Associated Press reporter in China during the late 1940s.

staying. They were met by the Chairman, who had been up most of the night, receiving reports on the fighting and issuing instructions. As they entered, Mao would tell them about the latest victories on the battlefield, usually followed up with predictions about a rapid collapse of the Jiang regime. Although they treated the Chairman with increasing reverence, Mao sometimes mocked his civilian colleagues for their caution. In a commentary for Xinhua, the Communist news agency, on 14 November, he proclaimed that "the military situation in China has reached a new turning point and the balance of forces between the two sides in the war has undergone a fundamental change. The PLA, long superior in quality, has become superior in numbers as well. This is a sign that the victory of the Chinese revolution and the realization of peace in China are at hand."[57]

As the GMD regime seemed to be giving way like a "soft wall," as Mao put it, the CCP as a party became increasingly attuned to the needs of the army. In his directive "On Military Control" from mid-November, the Chairman emphasized that all activities from that point on would depend on the military situation. The party's task was to help the PLA win a complete victory over the enemy. In the rural areas that suddenly had come under party control, this meant that the CCP cadre conscripted peasants to provide and carry supplies for the soldiers almost by the same methods the GMD had used in the past: imposing quotas for each village and threatening severe sanctions in case those quotas were not fulfilled. Important parts of the enormous logistical operation, involving more than two million peasants, that enabled the PLA to win the HuaiHai campaign were carried out by conscript labor from the "new" areas.[58]

In the cities, although the Chairman continued to insist that property be protected, any freedom of expression was severely curtailed. In instructions regarding the press from early November, the Center wrote:

> Newspapers, periodicals and news agencies are means in the struggle between different classes, parties, and social groups—they are not to be regarded as production enterprises. Thus the policy concerning private business cannot be applied to private newspapers and periodicals. Except those very few progressive newspapers that are promoting the people's revolutionary enthusiasm and [therefore] should be assisted in terms of distribution, other private newspapers should not be encouraged. In China especially, most of the so-called nonofficial press has a reactionary political background. If we let these distribute freely, reactionary forces will gain open and legal access to the people, which will be very harmful.[59]

Mao's only remaining uncertainty about the road ahead in November 1948 was how much the militarized CCP could bear in terms of the burdens of war. He worried about the political cost, in terms of relaxing the class struggle in order to emphasize production, and he was afraid that increasing dissatisfaction in the old base areas could create serious political problems. He was also concerned about how the move into the wealthier areas of China—not to mention the cities—would affect his soldiers' morale and revolutionary determination. But all of these concerns, to Mao, became arguments for a great push in order to win the war quickly, before the political concessions that large-scale warfare demanded eroded the ideological content of his revolution.[60]

His conduct of the last phase of the HuaiHai battles confirms this impression. Instead of trying to cut off parts of the failed GMD rescue mission now retreating to Xuzhou, as Su Yu had proposed, Mao ordered his forces to let them get back unhindered. All efforts, Mao said, should be concentrated on defeating the GMD 12th Army Group under Huang Wei, which slowly was making its way from Wuhan to retake Suxian and open communications with Xuzhou from the south. These troops, which had to walk 240 miles to reach their destination, would be tired and demoralized by the time they arrived, Mao thought, and would make an easy target for the PLA, which had had time to rest after the capture of Suxian and the defeat of the 7th Army Group. Should these last rescue forces be beaten, the whole Xuzhou garrison would eventually fall into CCP hands.[61]

The main problem for Liu Bocheng, Chen Yi, and Deng Xiaoping, who were now jointly coordinating operations for the southern front from Suxian, was that they could not use their numerical superiority to trap Huang Wei's forces without risking Du Yuming's breaking out of Xuzhou toward the south. The forces they had available were therefore not much more than Huang's 120,000 troops, most of whom were better trained and better equipped than the CCP forces. The only way, Chen Yi argued, that the mission could be accomplished was by luring the GMD forces into a trap, in which the terrain would assist the PLA in an encirclement. They set such a trap at Shuangduji, southwest of Suxian. Pretending to be in hasty retreat toward Suxian, by late November the CCP forces led Huang's army to the banks of an arm of the Huai River, with hills to the north and east. When Huang Wei realized that a trap had been set, he attempted to withdraw to the southeast, along the only road leading out of the area. But he was blocked by Liu Bocheng's forces. The 12th Army Group, probably the best fighting force left in Jiang's army, was isolated at Shuangduji.[62]

With the 12th Army Group prevented from retaking Suxian, Jiang Jieshi sensed that his strategy was in difficulties. He had Du Yuming flown to Nanjing for a series of meetings in which the other main generals in the field—Fu Zuoyi in Beijing, Bai Chongxi in Wuhan, and Hu Zongnan in Xi'an—also participated. None of them were willing to deploy additional forces of their own to help out the others, and especially to help Du break out of Xuzhou. It was probably too late, Du himself argued, to organize a retreat. The best thing to do would be to stay put and let the PLA waste its forces on Xuzhou's strong defenses. Jiang was furious with his generals. They think only of their own positions and think nothing of the country they are set to defend, he said. At the end of the meetings he ordered Du to begin an immediate withdrawal of his main force out of Xuzhou toward the Huai River, relieving and joining with the 12th Army Group on the way.[63]

On 1 December 1948, before dawn, with cold winds blowing over the plain from the northwest, Du Yuming led his 230,000-strong force out of Xuzhou's South Gate. At least 100,000 civilians, most of them refugees from the north, scrambled to get out of the city with the retreating troops. Soon the southern highway was filled with people, cars, horse carriages, and wheel barrows, clogging up the marching line for the GMD soldiers and making any orderly retreat impossible. Lighting up this carnival of defeat was the burning city of Xuzhou, to which Du's forces had accidentally set fire when exploding some of their heavy equipment.

The Communist attacks began almost immediately. Deng Xiaoping, who had been awake at Communist headquarters when the first message of the retreat came through, had pulled together all the firing power the forward forces of the CCP could muster, and ordered them to start shelling Du Yuming's rear troops. Undoubtedly, a large number of civilians also perished in these attacks. On the morning of the next day, 2 December, all available PLA units rushed to hem in the retreating enemy. By 4 December, Du's withdrawing army was dropping in its tracks. A few days later, Du ordered a temporary halt to the march, at a place called Chenguanzhuang, about three days' journey north of the Huai River.[64]

The sudden exodus from Xuzhou had taken Mao Zedong by surprise. He wanted to attack Du's main force immediately, to prevent it from fleeing south of the river and joining up with the Nanjing forces. But his commanders at the front convinced him that they could both isolate Du's troops and defeat Huang Wei's 12th Army Group. On 6 December, Mao consented. The battle between Huang Wei's crack forces and Liu Bocheng's troops was fierce. Huang several times reported to Jiang that he was on the verge of a breakout. Liu and Deng Xiaoping almost despaired when their attacking soldiers came up against Huang's defense lines of tanks, armored vehicles, and military trucks. The GMD air force flew regular sorties, depleting the unprotected PLA forces. On 13 December, however, the PLA succeeded in splitting the defending troops. In the evening of 15 December, General Huang Wei was captured, and his 120,000 strong army was no more.

With Huang out of the way, Mao asked a joint meeting of Liu Bocheng, Chen Yi, Deng Xiaoping, Su Yu, and Tan Zhenlin to present plans

HuaiHai, the Final Stage, December 1948

A smoke-smudged horizon bent around us and out there somewhere heavy guns thudded and soon we began to pass villages where there had been action. The villages were all small ones, rising like tiny atolls in an ocean of stubble, most of them completely destroyed by flame and shell, their bleak adobe-mud huts tumbled and scattered about. Those villages that were not destroyed were full of troops and around each was a circle of spider holes, dug deep in Japanese fashion. Soldiers standing in these holes up to their chests frequently challenged us, and then passed us along into the hamlet. Late in the day we entered the village of Chiang Chia Hu [Jiangjiahe, in Anhui]. It was crowded with soldiers, some of them busily extending the network of trenches that wound through the thin alleys and under the houses. Every hut was packed with troops, and against the adobe walls rough lean-tos made of kaoliang reeds sheltered more men huddled in the cold. Only a few villagers remained, running at the call of each imperative military voice, their houses commandeered, their heaps of straw being chewed away by the artillery horses, and their rice and vegetables and whatever livestock they had left disappearing into the cooking pots that boiled and simmered wherever rifles were stacked and men squatted by the heat of the smoky fires.

The village had changed hands a couple of times in the course of that strange warfare, and the experience had left its mark on the few survivors we found there. "Who is better?" Li asked one of them, "the Nationalists or the Communists?" "Both are good," the farmer answered quickly. "Only the people are bad."

The photo-journalist Carl Mydans covered the Chinese civil war for *Life* magazine. The same day as Mydans wrote this dispatch, he had to be evacuated south, because the GMD general in charge of the area decided to transfer his loyalties to the CCP. Carl and Shelley Mydans, *The Violent Peace* (New York: Atheneum, 1967), pp. 55–56.

for the capture of Du Yuming and the advance toward the Yangzi River. The five PLA commanders, meeting at the little village of Caiwa, seemed to have emerged from their talks in the village barn almost bewildered at the thought that if the final part of the HuaiHai campaign succeeded, all of China north of the great river would be theirs. There is a photo of them, taken in the wintry light on 18 December: Chen Yi seems to be readying himself to march on the Yangzi immediately; Deng is ashen-faced and unshaven. All of them look exhausted. Su Yu admitted later that he was immensely relieved when Mao ordered them to surround Du's forces, but to delay attacking the main part of the troops until the new campaign the CCP was planning in North China got under way.[65]

For Du Yuming and his soldiers the situation was getting hopeless. A failed breakout attempt on 16 December lost Du almost one-fourth of his troops. On 20 December it started to rain and snow, and the temperature dropped. More than 200,000 men were crowded together in a small area, with insufficient supplies. All attempts at relieving them came to nothing. The airdrops of food and ammunition increasingly failed as the defenders were herded into tiny pockets in the fields around Shuangduji. By New Year's Eve the frozen and hungry soldiers were digging up coffins to burn and slaughtering their horses for food. Du Yuming declined Jiang's offer to rescue him and his staff, but did little to coordinate resistance to the all-out attack that the PLA finally began on 6 January. On 10 January, in the afternoon, Du walked out of his U.S. Army officers' tent and bowed to his Communist captors. One of his officers, after being taken prisoner, admitted that his last meal before capture had been his American sheep-skin gloves.[66]

As the HuaiHai campaign drew to a close, both the political elites and the general population in China were left bewildered at the speed with which military events were unfolding. Overjoyed at the outcome of the battles, Mao Zedong and his companions in Xibaipo were taken aback at the demands put on them and their party by the speedy GMD collapse in North China. For the army, logistics and supplies were in shambles, and the best units were exhausted from covering hundreds of miles on foot. Some of the more cautious PLA commanders, such as Peng Dehuai and Zhu De, worried about a GMD counterattack through Northwest China, which could destroy the exposed and overextended supply lines between the old CCP base areas and the new front zones. Spurred on by Soviet information, Zhou Enlai and his main assistant for intelligence, Li Kenong, would not rule out the possibility of direct U.S. intervention in the South if the Guomindang regime simply collapsed. Such imperialist interventions had taken place before, Zhou argued, both in recent Chinese history and against the Bolshevik revolution in Russia.[67]

Of an even more direct concern for the CCP leaders was how to control and provide food for the almost 100 million people who suddenly were behind their front lines. In areas that had not been much affected by direct warfare, Liu Shaoqi said, food production could easily be restored. But what about those areas, especially in the East and along the coast, where traditional lines of communication and trade had been broken by the war? How could the peasants of the Central Plains be expected to

sow in the spring, when such a large percentage of them had been mobilized for war? And how should the party secure supplies for the big cities
that might soon be taken over, cities such as Beijing and Tianjin? It was
one thing, Liu told the Chairman, to supply the smaller cities that the
party had already taken. Beijing was quite a different matter. And if the
party failed in those tasks after the takeover, the urban proletariat could
turn against the Communists.[68]

For Mao, these practical concerns mattered less than the issue of control. The Chairman had only grudgingly supported the de-emphasizing of
class struggle for the sake of waging war, and one of his main worries in
late 1948 was the subversion of Communist plans and ideals by the enemy in areas that had just been taken over. Mao warned that among the
tens of thousands who flocked to the party there were imperialist agents,
former exploiters, Christians, and all kinds of "bad elements." Such
forces were particularly active in and around the cities. Therefore, Mao
ordered, the takeover of urban areas had to be properly prepared, and
the Communist cadres should understand that they could not trust anyone who had lived through the civil war in the cities.[69]

The cadres who were fighting with the troops to isolate the cities in
North China understood this message. Most of them came from rural areas, and most did not need the Chairman's instructions in order to distrust city folk. But they also knew that the cities were symbols of
power—if their party conquered Beijing or Tianjin, they were closer to
their aim of taking over China. And there was also the fascination with a
kind of life that most of them had never seen: street lights, tall buildings,
elevators. Still, in the winter of 1948–49, the soldiers of the PLA 2d Army
operating along the roads and railway lines outside Beijing were told to
chant:

> Patience we must have, comrades, to wait,
> For raw potatoes make no good food
> Prepare for the campaign well
> Attack we shall when the time comes.[70]

Farther south, along the rims of the populous coastal provinces, news of
the battles on the plains spread rapidly. People who had had no contact
with the Communists before wondered what would happen if the CCP
came to their area. Disenchantment with the government ran high almost
everywhere. But Mao's party was an unknown. The only certainty was
that all was in flux. In the outskirts of the big city by the mouth of the

Yangzi River, the children sang:

> Old Jiang is dead and gone
> Come and hear this song
> Perhaps Shanghai will not be Shanghai
> Come and hear this song.[71]

7

THE CHASE

Crossing the Yangzi

Hang Ren, "Mopping Up"

Even before the last phase of the HuaiHai campaign ended, Jiang Jieshi had decided to carry out the ultimate sacrifice for his cause: He would resign as President of the Republic of China. His statements of resignation, which he had been preparing on and off since late December, were on the surface covered with Confucian humbleness, sincerity, and dedication. But in between, all his followers in China would detect a note of defiance and no regrets. Jiang, proud as ever, seemed to be saying that his country had betrayed him by not living up to the standards he expected. In his declarations, as in his diary, there is also a sense that his retirement was not a final defeat, and that he expected soon to be called back to office to complete the revolution.[1]

In political terms, Jiang attributed the circumstances that forced him to resign to U.S. pressure and the political defection of his vice president, Li Zongren. Li had realized that if Nationalist China were to survive, it would have to bargain for time to put its defenses south of the river in order. The only way such a breathing spell could be had was through some form of negotiations with the Communists. Since Jiang outwardly opposed any form of talks, he would have, at least in formal terms, to resign the presidency. But in spite of his strained personal relationship with Jiang Jieshi, Li was not himself eager to push the Generalissimo out. It took much pressure from Li's old friends in the Guangxi clique—men such as Bai Chongxi, who had come to regard Jiang as anathema to the whole war effort—and from the Americans, for Li to accept the need for Jiang to go.

Li Zongren, Mao, and the Peace Negotiations

On 4 January, in the evening, Jiang Jieshi unexpectedly came to Li Zongren's home in Nanjing to inform him of his resignation. Even though the main commanders and party leaders were informed about Jiang's decision at once, it took several days before Li felt that he had enough backing from Jiang and from the rest of the Guomindang elite to accept the task. Li, of old warlord stock but quite adaptable to 1940s realities, was particularly eager to get U.S. support for his new position, along with promises of increased economic assistance. American representatives, overjoyed to see Jiang go, promised Li full backing and held out the chances for a huge aid program after the new president had taken over. Li feared that it was not enough. Unless he got specific U.S. support now—preferably in the form of a big loan—not only would the GMD armies be pushed farther toward the southern and western fringes of China but, in addition, his own position would remain dependent on Jiang Jieshi, the real power-holder in the party.[2]

Although no concrete plans had been made, there is no doubt that much of the GMD elite expected Li Zongren to be a temporary office-holder, necessary only while negotiations got under way—preferably with some form of superpower involvement—and the Americans came in with more support. With circumstances again put right, Jiang would return to power in whatever remained of the Guomindang state. The plan for negotiations with the Communists, which Jiang and his new prime minister, Sun Fo, had worked out over the New Year without much input from Li, was intended to stop the war and preserve GMD strength. If Washington and Moscow accepted some form of involvement, perhaps even the formality of a change in the presidency would be unnecessary, some of Jiang's supporters thought. Even the GMD right wing, which remained totally opposed to negotiations of any kind, felt that Jiang's was a clever trick—it bought time, while absolving Jiang personally from any blame, whatever the outcome.[3]

News that the GMD would issue a formal offer for renewed negotiations with foreign mediation reached Washington, Moscow, and Xibaipo on 6 January. It was not welcome news. Although he was getting reports about his troops' exhausting their strength, Mao Zedong now had his mind set on the last battles in the North, which soon, he thought, would give the Communists control of Beijing and Tianjin. With the GMD in trouble all over, this was not the time to talk peace. In Washington some leaders, including President Truman, took the offer seriously to start with but were soon talked out of agreeing to any U.S. role by Secretary of State Marshall, who balked at the thought of dragging the administration through another Chinese nightmare of the kind he had experienced firsthand three years earlier. The Soviets, at first, seem to have been as dismissive of the offer as the other addressees. But then, three days later, when Stalin was given a copy of Jiang's letter, the aging Soviet dictator decided to see whether the GMD offer could be turned to his and the CCP's advantage.[4]

Stalin had kept in close personal contact with the Chinese Communist leaders throughout the military campaigns in the fall and winter. On several occasions he had sent his and his generals' advice on how to conduct the military operations. The speed with which the PLA had advanced had taken the Soviet leaders by surprise, and Stalin now believed that the

Communist forces needed to rest and reorganize before pushing farther south. He was concerned that, when crossing the Yangzi River, the CCP would have to confront not only GMD troops but imperialist forces as well. By not ruling out talks, Stalin also hoped to forestall a propaganda victory for the GMD and Washington. In addition, however, it is very likely that the Boss wanted to impress on Mao and the CCP leadership his own status as the master tactician of the world Communist movement—as someone who immediately understood a political situation wherever it came up with more clarity and breadth than "local" leaders. He may have wanted to remind the CCP leaders, in a not too subtle way, of their dependence on Soviet political and diplomatic support notwithstanding the PLA's victories.[5]

In his 10 January telegram to Mao Zedong, Stalin outlined how the CCP should respond to the GMD initiative. In Stalin's draft, Mao did not turn down negotiations, but insisted on talks without the participation of "those war criminals who provoked the civil war in China . . . and without any foreign mediators. The Chinese Communist party especially finds it impossible to accept the mediation by a foreign power which takes part in the civil war against the Chinese popular liberation forces with its armed forces and navy." Touching another sore point in the relationship, Stalin added: "As for your visit to Moscow, we think that in view of the above-mentioned circumstances you should, unfortunately, postpone your trip again for some time, because your visit to Moscow in this situation would be used by the enemies to discredit the Chinese Communist Party as a force allegedly dependent on Moscow, which, certainly, could bring no benefit to the Chinese Communist Party or to the USSR."[6]

The Soviet leader's suggestions came at a moment that inconvenienced and angered Mao Zedong. Having Stalin indicate the possibility of holding talks—even if only for tactical reasons—just as Mao was pushing his commanders to prepare a final military offensive was not welcome among the Communist top leadership in Xibaipo. In his telegram to Stalin of 13 January, Mao not only turned down Moscow's instructions on how his party should respond to the GMD but even had the temerity to suggest to Stalin how he ought to respond to the mediation proposal on behalf of the Soviet Union.

For the leader of a Communist party to respond in such a way to Stalin's instructions was rather unusual in the late 1940s, and it did not endear the CCP to the Soviet leadership. On the Chinese side—even after Moscow basically accepted Mao's reply—there remained a suspicion that

Mao's Letter to Stalin on Negotiations
with the GMD, January 1949

1. We think that the government of the USSR should give the following answer to the note by the Nanjing government proposing that the USSR accepts mediation in the termination of the civil war in China: The government of the USSR has always wished, and still wishes, to see China as a peaceful, democratic and united country. But it is for the people of China itself to choose the way to achieve peace, unity and democracy in China. The government of the USSR, relying on the principle of noninterference in other countries' internal affairs, cannot accept mediation between the two sides in the civil war in China.

2. We think that although the USA, England, and France, and especially the USA, are very willing to take part in mediation to terminate the war in China and thus achieve their goal—to preserve the Guomindang regime—the governments of these countries, especially the U.S. government, have already lost their prestige among the Chinese public, and as the victory of the PLA nationwide and the downfall of the Guomindang regime is already in sight—it seems questionable whether they still wish to continue their assistance to the Nanjing government and thus further offend the PLA. Only the USSR has a very high prestige among the Chinese people, so if the USSR in its reply to the note by the Nanjing government will take the position outlined in your telegram of January 10, it would make the USA, England and France assume that participating in mediation is an appropriate thing, and give the Guomindang a pretext for scolding us as warlike elements. And the broad popular masses, which are displeased with the Guomindang and hope for an early victory of the PLA, would find themselves in despair.

APRF, f. 45, op. 1, d. 330, 102.

Stalin had really wanted to stop the PLA offensives north of the Yangzi River and thereby create a divided China. The visit of Soviet Politburo member Anastas Mikoyan to the CCP headquarters later that winter did not do much to mitigate mutual suspicions; indeed, Mao on several occasions during the decades to come referred to this episode as an example of Soviet duplicity.

On 14 January, after Stalin had given up his initiative, Mao issued his own peace proposal, as had in the meantime been agreed upon with the Soviets. His terms were crude:

Punish the war criminals
Abolish the bogus constitution
Abolish the bogus "constitutional government"
Reorganize all reactionary troops along democratic principles

Confiscate all bureaucratic capital

Reform the land-holding system

Abrogate all treasonous foreign treaties

Convene a Political Consultative Conference without participation of reactionary elements to form a democratic coalition government to take over all the powers of the reactionary Nanjing Guomindang government and of its subordinates at all levels.[7]

In Nanjing, after reading the CCP statement, Jiang had second thoughts about his resignation. He was astonished to learn that some of Li Zongren's advisers seemed ready to accept Mao's blunt terms as an agenda for negotiation. The Generalissimo well knew that he would head the list of "war criminals"—what if Li decided to offer Jiang and his family as part of the payment for a truce? The president started to review his options, hoping that his last-ditch appeals to the Americans—saying that negotiations meant surrender to Mao's and Soviet power—could bring forward a U.S. commitment to save his regime.[8]

But the United States refused to come to Jiang's aid. In the early morning of Friday, 21 January, after having learned from his ambassador in Washington that the appeals had had little effect, Jiang Jieshi brought together the top Guomindang elite—around one hundred people—for a meeting at his residence in Nanjing. They sat in silence, listening to their leader proclaim in a low voice, in parts almost inaudible, that he would withdraw from his office for the best of the country. Many wept. As Jiang rose to leave, some cried out that he was the eternal leader of the party. After signing the declaration, Jiang went to the airport, where an airplane was standing by to take him to his hometown of Fenghua in Zhejiang province. But Jiang had changed his mind—instead of going straight to Fenghua, he left for Hangzhou, where the Chinese air force and several elite units had their main headquarters.[9]

When Li Zongren arrived at the presidential palace that afternoon, he was in for a rude surprise. Jiang's public statement named him "acting president," and it did not include a word about resigning. On the contrary, the statement left the impression that Li was to manage affairs in Jiang Jieshi's absence. Jiang remained head of the party. Jiang had even written and circulated Li's own first statement as president, underlining that "his Excellency [Jiang] has always upheld the interests of the nation and of the people as a guide to his personal activities and to his administration of public affairs." Li Zongren attempted to have both rewritten, but to no avail. The president's staff, acting on Jiang's instructions, refused to take orders from his successor. According to Li, his chief of staff

Li Zongren's Letter to Mao Zedong, 27 January 1949

Honorable Sir,

Since the failure of the earlier political consultations, the civil war has continued for more than three years in addition to the original eight years of the resistance war. The resources of the nation have been greatly depleted and the people have suffered badly. People throughout the country now voice demands for an end to the war and the restoration of peace. . . . You, sir, have repeatedly expressed your willingness to solve the problems by peaceful means. The government has now expressed its sincerity in both words and deeds. . . . [and] has agreed to consider the eight articles that your honorable party has proposed as the basis for future negotiations between us. Once peace negotiations are resumed, all problems will be resolved. . . .

The present crisis is not about honor or humiliation for any individual. It affects the fate of the entire nation and the life of its people. I do not have the slightest prejudice in dealing with any of these matters, nor am I concerned with my own personal gain or loss. My original expectations will be fulfilled and my earnest prayers will be answered if I am relieved of my present responsibility after the present war is ended and a lasting peace is restored.

Your reply will be appreciated. With deepest sincerity, I am,

Your younger brother, Li Zongren

Li Tsung-jen [Li Zongren] and Te-kong Tong, *The Memoirs of Li Tsung-jen* (Boulder, CO: Westview, 1979), pp. 492–94. Slightly amended.

even warned him against pursuing these matters. "You, sir, should realize what kind of environment you are in. Nanking is full of special servicemen; even your own bodyguards are Jiang's men. On what basis do you think you can bargain with him?"[10]

Although his room to maneuver in a city still controlled by Jiang's men was limited, Li refused to be intimidated. He brought to Nanjing a number of his old associates from the Guangxi Clique and gave them impressive-sounding titles and orders to report to him on how the GMD bureaucracy was carrying out its tasks. He kept in close touch with the Americans, and attempted to let Ambassador Stuart feel that he had decisive influence on how the new cabinet was put together. But Li's appeals for massive U.S. aid fell on deaf ears. The $1 billion emergency loan that Li Zongren proposed sounded ridiculous to Stuart, who reported to Washington that in most aspects of GMD policy Jiang, and not Li, was in control.[11]

Li Zongren also thought of reaching out to the Soviets, with whom he had been in contact off and on since the late 1920s. But his meetings with

Ambassador Roshchin were disappointing. In spite of Li's willingness to live up to earlier Soviet demands of a "neutral" foreign policy, and his indication that the U.S. presence in China would end if real negotiations could get going, Roshchin had little to give in return, except a general support for GMD-CCP talks. Obviously under instructions from Moscow to be very cautious, the ambassador avoided giving any sign that Soviet influence with the CCP could be bought by GMD concessions, as he had tried to do with the Jiang government the previous year. The squabble between Stalin and Mao on the mediation issue had obviously had its effect.[12]

Soon after taking office, Li and his closest associates had started working on a personal letter from the new president to Mao Zedong. Against the advice of some of his friends, Li wanted to get negotiations going no matter what. His hope was that, given a three- to four-month extension, the GMD armies south of the Yangzi would be powerful enough to defeat a Communist attempt to cross. But he was also thinking about his home areas, the valleys and gorges of Guangxi, and what would happen there if they were made into a battlefield. He was hoping that managing the negotiations would give him real power—not just the kind of leftover influence that he had so far scavenged from Jiang. But, after the failure of his diplomatic initiatives, Li knew that he had not much time. In the North the PLA was preparing to march into Beijing, and thereby deprive him of the last vestige of national power.

The Fall of Beijing and Tianjin

Since the end of the LiaoShen battles, Mao Zedong had been trying to keep two strategic plans present at the same time. The first, and most important, was the advance toward the Yangzi River through the Central Plains. As that plan—which became the HuaiHai campaign—materialized with a speed and decisiveness that not even Mao himself had thought possible, the Chairman's thinking had turned to the second plan, the attempt to conquer the great Northern cities, Beijing and Tianjin. No one in the CCP leadership had any doubt about the significance of Beijing to Mao—it was there he had first come, as a country boy from Hunan, to learn about Marxism and take part in forming China's future. The Northern Capital had links with China's past that Mao in part cherished and in part resented, but that gave it a symbolic significance in terms of state power that could be denied by no one. To Mao, Beijing as a sym-

bolic city was second to none in China, and on a par perhaps only with
Shanghai, the industrial powerhouse at the mouth of the Yangzi.

The question for the CCP, both from a military and a political point of
view, was how to take over the Northern cities without detracting forces
and energy from the more important battles in Central China. Fu Zuoyi's
armies were still strong and had substantial support from local elites. Lin
Biao was often overheard saying that if he had to fight his way to
Tian'anmen, he could as well forget ever using his forces to drive the
Guomindang from the South. The Chairman had ordered Lin to cross
over the Great Wall to station his troops in the Tianjin-Beijing area, and
together with Nie Rongzhen's local PLA forces gradually isolate the
GMD in and around the big cities. But it was better, Mao thought, to delay any major attacks until it was clear how the HuaiHai battles developed. As long as the CCP Manchurian forces could make sure that Fu's
troops did not intervene in the fighting farther south, and thereby tip the
balance, Mao felt that their strategic strength was not completely
wasted.[13]

The problem with waiting, Mao and Zhou Enlai recognized, was that
the cities could face a rebellion from within—anti-GMD groups, not all
of which were controlled by the CCP, were staging increasingly aggressive
rallies against unemployment and falling wages. The Communist leadership wanted to conquer the cities from outside and did not like the
thought of having to compete with local radical organizations after the
military takeover. The CCP underground in Beijing and Tianjin was
therefore repeatedly ordered to take steps to avoid provoking serious
confrontations with the GMD military police. By early December, with
both cities under martial law, the rallies ceased. Instead, the CCP underground stepped up its propaganda directed toward GMD soldiers. Communist agents, sometimes dressed as wounded government soldiers from
Manchuria, agitated openly against civil war on the streets of Tianjin.[14]

In Beijing, GMD commander Fu Zuoyi could not make up his mind
what to do. He made no secret of his disdain for the "chaos" in Nanjing.
But he still had more than 350,000 soldiers under his command, and he
was uncertain as to CCP intentions. If they decided to bypass the Northern cities and move their troops straight toward the major battles in the
South, he would gain by sitting tight and negotiating based on the outcome of the HuaiHai campaign. In any case, whatever happened, he had
little to gain by attempting to break out and join other GMD forces else-

Refugees in the Temple of Heaven, Beijing, September 1948

This morning we made a trip to the Temple of Heaven. . . . The outer grounds looked much as we remembered them, but inside, what a depressing spectacle! All the buildings . . . are filled with hundreds of young men (also, in certain quarters, girls). They are wartime student refugees from Shanxi, some of whom seem hardly older than twelve or thirteen. Most of the stone terraces outside, as well as the floors of the temple itself, are covered with their thin sleeping pads and meager possessions. . . . The columns of the great temple and adjoining buildings, much faded from their former brilliant red, are covered with ugly written notices, and dust and debris lie everywhere on the once gleaming marble. As one mounts the steps toward places once reserved for the emperor and his followers alone at the most solemn of religious ceremonies, one can but turn from this scene of human misery and degradation. . . . Portions of the courtyard, and even the lower tiers of the Altar of Heaven itself, are littered with half-dried excrement.

The sinologist Derk Bodde, whose diary this extract is from, lived in Beijing throughout 1949. *Peking Diary: A Year of Revolution* (London: Jonathan Cape, 1951), pp. 12–13.

where. Fu decided to attempt to concentrate his forces in and around the big cities and wait out developments.[15]

Under increasing pressure from his military commanders to act against Fu Zuoyi's troops, Mao in early December agreed to let Nie Rongzhen's forces attempt to isolate and possibly defeat the GMD armies that Communist intelligence knew would be withdrawing from Zhangjiakou toward Beijing. In a maneuver reminiscent of the first part of the HuaiHai campaign, Nie's forces, joined by some of Lin Biao's Manchurian units, caught Fu's 11th Army in a trap as they were retreating toward the Northern Capital. When Fu ordered his 35th Army, under Guo Jingyun, to rescue its comrades, those forces were also surrounded at Xinbao'an, a walled town northwest of Beijing. The PLA attacked Xinbao'an with heavy artillery on 22 December. "The city walls," recalls Geng Biao, the PLA commander, "were torn off layer by layer and several V-shaped openings split up." After entering the town, the PLA units used a whole day to wipe out GMD resistance, "fighting by breaking through the walls of the houses along the streets or walking on their roofs."[16] By the end of the day, Guo Jingyun had taken his own life and his remaining troops had surrendered. The Communists buried Guo in the frozen ground outside a railway station platform where he had died. Some weeks later they

> ### The PLA Takes over Yanjing University
> ### outside Beijing, 16 December 1948
>
> That night retreating soldiers streamed past our gates, but we saw no fighting nearby. Next day we heard heavy gunfire to the south of us, but we ourselves spent a quiet day in suspended animation. Then on Thursday morning the victorious army arrived. At intervals through the day Ch'eng-fu village watched Communist troops arriving, well clad in padded clothes, fur-lined coats and huge fur hats. Their shaggy Mongolian ponies looked sleek and well kept, though dusty from hard travel. The soldiers got on to good terms with the villagers straight away. Fu Zuoyi's men had behaved much better than we feared; they had not looted homes or ill-treated people; they had not stolen food. But they had dirtied houses, broken furniture and used up much fuel. The Communists, on the other hand, took neither food nor fuel from the villagers, and would not accept any presents or services. They paid, with their "Great Wall" currency, for all they needed. Whatever furniture they borrowed, they carefully returned, replacing anything damaged or broken. They carried water and swept the courtyards for their hosts. They chatted cheerfully with everyone, and the air was full of stories of their astonishing behavior. Beijing had known many armies through the past fifty years, but never one like this.
>
> Ralph and Nancy Lapwood, *Through the Chinese Revolution* (London: Spalding and Levy, 1954), pp. 44–45.

dug up his corpse and handed it to Fu Zuoyi's troops in Beijing—a warning of what could happen if the Northern Capital was attacked.[17]

The battle of Xinbao'an—and the fall of Zhangjiakou that followed two days later—weakened Fu Zuoyi's will to fight on. At least since late November, Communist agents in Tianjin, where the main part of the GMD forces in the North were located, had been in touch with members of Fu's staff. One of his advisers, and possibly more, were CCP agents, who furnished vital information on the general's military planning. The Communists, assisted by Soviet intelligence in Tianjin, had also been able to recruit Fu Dongju, Fu Zuoyi's daughter, through her fiancé, Zhou Fucheng, a longtime CCP agent. Fu Dongju's reports provided a keen look into her father's worries about the situation in his area and his own predicament. After the fall of Zhangjiakou, General Fu was in contact with the CCP through intermediaries in Beijing, mostly former members of the Democratic League. But the general refused to capitulate. Instead he floated ideas about a "deactivation" of the Beijing-Tianjin theater—a kind of truce while peace negotiations got under way between Nanjing and the CCP.[18]

While planning his next steps, Mao liked to make jokes about the "Northern bourgeoisie" breaking up, and Fu Zuoyi's holding out for some more catties of pork. With most of his attention concentrated on the fighting farther south, the Chairman left the contacts with Fu to the unlikely alliance of Zhou Enlai and Lin Biao, who both were against a military solution in North China. Zhou felt that major battles within the cities would reduce the potential of Beijing and, especially, Tianjin, as manufacturing centers for the Communist war effort. Lin was eager to spare his troops from battles in the North—which he thought to be militarily irrelevant—and quickly move them to Central China, where he felt that the civil war would be decided. In the end, however, Mao's impatience got the better of their concerns. The attack on Tianjin, to be carried out mostly by Lin's troops, was planned for 14 January as an accompanying measure to the stern terms of Mao's conditions for peace, issued from Xibaipo on the same day.[19]

While Lin's forces were preparing to attack Tianjin, the Communist underground in both cities was attempting to prevent the GMD from destroying or removing machines and production plants, and to convince key personnel not to flee to the South. In Beijing, in late December, the CCP underground organized a secret worker inspector corps, whose task was to encourage workers to protect their equipment and to threaten management and owners with severe reprisals if any machines were moved or destroyed. In Tianjin—a major production center for arms and ammunition—the Communist Work Committee set up groups to "protect" arsenals and factories. In both cities the Communists—unsuccessful for so many years in their attempts to organize workers—found both "proletarians" and quite a number of their masters well disposed toward working with the representatives of the power they expected soon would be in control. Only a small fraction of the industrial potential in the Northern cities was destroyed in December and early January.[20]

In Tianjin, in the days before the attack, the streets were deserted. Only at the exits from the city—and particularly around those toward the coast—were people in movement, as thousands tried to flee before the PLA arrived. The GMD commander, Chen Changjie, and most of his officers had heard about the contacts between Fu Zuoyi and the Communists but had not been informed by their boss about the state of the negotiations. At dawn on 14 January, as the PLA started its general attack, Chen ordered his men to resist. At first there was furious fighting at the western and southern approaches to the city. But by the afternoon it was

clear that most Nationalist officers did not have the will to fight on. The
Communist forces advanced toward the city center through the night
against pockets of resistance, mostly concentrated in the south. Chen
Changjie surrendered at 4:00 P.M. on 15 January. The GMD mayor of
Tianjin, who had sworn to fight to the bitter end, was captured with his
concubine in his "secret" downtown apartment. The mayor's wife turned
out to have been a Communist agent.[21]

It is difficult to say whether Mao attacked Tianjin in order to force the
Guomindang to the negotiating table, as he claimed to his Soviet inter-
locutors, or whether the purpose was to prevent real negotiations from
getting going, thereby keeping up the military pressure on the enemy.
There is little doubt that Mao Zedong at this stage preferred a clear-cut
military solution to the civil war, but he was aware that there might be
several ways of achieving that aim—one of which was the disintegration
of the GMD regime through inner conflicts about the conditions for talks
with the Communists. A falling out between Jiang Jieshi and Li Zongren
could even lead to the "Jiang clique" and the "Guangxi feudals and their
bourgeois supporters" having a go at each other with guns and cannons.
Whatever tactics the Chairman was thinking of, his goal was clear: the
complete takeover of China by his party. However unnecessary the Tianjin battle may have been in a strategic sense—and several of his generals
pointed this out to him—within the CCP the Chairman's aim justified his
means.

In Beijing, Communist units were moving into the suburbs. There was
only light resistance. On 16 January, Lin Biao, as commander of the PLA
units besieging Beijing, issued an ultimatum to Fu Zuoyi to begin evacu-
ating his troops from the city, or face an all-out attack. Fu came to two
last meetings with Communist officers and intermediaries, who at this
stage included his own former teacher and several members of his family.
While the final talks went on, life in Beijing continued almost as normal—the city gates stayed open, and the restaurants and cinemas were
filled with people who wanted to use their last Gold Yuan before they became completely worthless. After the main electricity plant was taken
over by the CCP, the Communists sent "their" electricians to cooperate
with those in the city to make sure that the power supplies stayed on. Before dawn on 21 January, after getting a message that Jiang Jieshi would
resign that day, Fu Zuoyi rose and went out of the city to sign a declaration renouncing his allegiance to the Nanjing government. When he

The PLA Marches into Beijing, 3 February 1949

Prominent in the parade were thousands of students and workers from schools and organizations throughout the city. Many of their colored paper banners and Mao Zedong portraits were torn to tatters by the wind. Among the students marched some well known university professors. . . . Of chief interest was, of course, the Liberation Army itself. I missed the first contingents of infantry and cavalry, as well as part of the motorized units. But in what I did see, lasting about an hour, I counted over 250 heavy motor vehicles of all kinds—tanks, armored cars, truckloads of soldiers, trucks mounted with machine guns, trucks towing heavy artillery. Behind them followed innumerable ambulances, jeeps, and other small vehicles. As probably the greatest demonstration of Chinese military might in history, the spectacle was enormously impressive. But what made it especially memorable to Americans was the fact that it was primarily a display of *American* military equipment, virtually all of it captured or obtained by bribe from Guomindang forces. . . . The reaction of the spectators . . . was, like that of most Chinese crowds, less outspoken. Nevertheless they seemed in general quite favorably disposed and obviously deeply impressed by the display of power. As the stream of trucks continued, I heard several exclaim with wonder: "Still more! Still more!"

Derk Bodde, *Peking Diary: A Year of Revolution* (London: Jonathan Cape, 1951), pp. 103–4.

handed it to the PLA representatives, they saw that he was ashen-faced and that his body was stiff as he walked back to his car.[22]

With what they referred to as the "peaceful liberation" of Beijing, the Communist takeover of North China was in most respects complete. Only in the peripheral western regions of the northern half of the country were there enemy forces strong enough to challenge the PLA, and the CCP leaders had no trouble in deciding on meeting that challenge later. The leadership had more difficulty in determining how to deal with the vast territories that suddenly had come under their control. The three major military campaigns of 1948–49—LiaoShen, HuaiHai, and Beijing-Tianjin—had over a period of less than nine months re-created the political map of China. By early 1949, the Communist leaders had to create policies and administrative structures for their newly won areas, or—as Mao Zedong warned—risk "not living up to the revolutionary expectations of the people"—that is, face the same difficulties in taking over as the Guomindang had done in 1945. This fear was particularly deep with regard to the cities—unknown territory for the Communists, and territory whose inhabitants many of them regarded with suspicion and distaste. The jubilant welcome they received when entering Beijing—a city of so many rapturous absorptions of conquerors in the past—filled some Communist cadres with worry about the future even at their moment of victory.

CCP Policies and Diplomacy

Under constant pressure from the military developments, the Communist leaders' discussions on the structure of the New China they were creating was a race against time. The biggest need was in North China, a region in which the CCP had controlled some rural areas since before the anti-Japanese war and where the main areas were gradually coming under full party control. The Northeast had been one early experiment in how the party would manage government and the economy, but it was too different from the main parts of China to serve as an immediate model. The Politburo had decided by as early as May 1948 that North China would be the model for the rest of the country, which the party then hoped to take over in five years' time. Not surprisingly, Mao chose Liu Shaoqi to head the North China Bureau of the Politburo, effectively putting Liu in charge of setting up the new structures of government.

Liu's main political instincts in how to construct the government apparatus were, as always, to organize and to regularize. He wanted a people's government, with the CCP firmly in control, but with some token participation from other "democratic" parties. He designated individual party leaders to deal with specific aspects of administration, from the courts and law-making to the supply of seafood and taxes on luxury clothing. He wrote repeatedly to Mao that there was a disinclination among higher party cadres to take responsibility for anything they had no experience with, and to learn from the experience of others. With "learning from experience" Liu had two things in mind: The CCP's own previous experience (which admittedly was limited, and which Liu and some of his closest associates believed, in terms of civilian government, consisted of as many negative examples as positive ones), and the Soviet experience; the great tradition from the October Revolution to the reconstruction taking place after World War II. Learning from the Soviet Union runs as a theme through most of Liu's inner-party messages from late 1948: To him, and to almost all other party planners, the Soviet experience was the only viable experience to serve as a model for CCP policies under the dramatically changed circumstances, even if Chinese Communist know-how should, ideally, be the medium through which the Soviet model was applied in China.[23]

Concentrated on the war, and with only occasional detours into civilian policy-making, Mao Zedong was much influenced by Liu's thinking about how to set up a new Chinese state. The fact was that the Chairman had given little thought to what his New China should look like, except in quite general terms. Mao's input, which often appeared in private conversations with Liu, Zhou Enlai, and other leaders rather than at meetings or conferences, was connected to a series of core concerns that had remained relatively stable throughout the civil war. He was preoccupied with preserving the unity of the party through what he sometimes described as "the test of victory." He believed that unity at this stage could be achieved only through a higher degree of organizational and ideological centralization. He also believed that the greatest danger to the party—the corruption of its cadres as they "returned" to the cities—could be avoided only through strict and centralized control. It was therefore essential that the CCP had developed specific and uniform urban policies before the takeover of the main cities, and Mao was eager to adopt any comprehensive suggestions within a Marxist framework that could serve this purpose. His praise for Zhang Wentian's August proposals for urban economic policies in Dongbei is an example, even though Zhang's thinking seemed lifted straight from Soviet textbooks on economic affairs, with their emphasis on development of urban heavy industry and the role of the countryside as supplier of raw materials and food for the proletariat.[24]

The extended meeting of the Politburo held in Xibaipo in mid-September 1948 attempted to bring some of these policies together, although most of the meeting ended up dealing with the military situation and the major offensives going on in the Northeast. On future political and administrative structure, the meeting sanctioned Liu Shaoqi's suggestions to make the North China model—a People's Congress and a People's Government under CCP guidance—the centerpiece of the national structure of the future. There was little open disagreement at the meeting, but obvious tension between the majority of the Politburo, led by Liu and Ren Bishi, and some regional political commissars and military commanders on issues concerning reform of the newly conquered areas. Several of them—mostly leaders from the old base areas—objected to the policy of making use of Guomindang administrative structures and even personnel

Mao Zedong on the Lack of Communist Cadres,
September 1948

Because our party and our army grew up isolated by the enemy and the guerrilla war, in the countryside, we allowed a great deal of autonomy to leading regional institutions of our party and army, which ensured initiative and enthusiasm in these party organizations and troops and helped us survive over a long and very difficult time; at the same time, there therefore emerged a situation of anarchy, localism. . . . Now the development of the situation requires our party . . . to concentrate all possible power into the Center or those organs representing the Central Committee. . . .

The task of taking power in the whole country requires our party to rapidly train huge numbers of cadres who will be able to manage military, political, economic, and party affairs, culture and education. In the third year of the war, we will have to prepare well over 30–40,000 cadres at all levels to go with the troops during the fourth year and run the new liberated areas with about 50–100 million people in a proper way. China is a big country and [has] a huge population. With the rapid development of the revolutionary war, we are feeling a great lack of administrative cadres. This is a big difficulty for us. During the third year, even though the preparation of cadres will mostly rely on those old Liberated Areas, we will also need to absorb some from the big cities [now] in GMD areas. . . . The workers and intellectuals in the big cities in GMD areas are better educated than the workers and peasants in the Liberated Areas. Those people who work in GMD economic, financial, cultural and educational institutions, except the reactionaries, should continue to be employed. . . .

Mao Zedong report to leading cadres on discussions in the Politburo, September 1948; in *Mao Zedong junshi wenji,* vol. 5, pp. 54–61.

in areas taken over by the People's Liberation Army, making use of tax systems, duties, and levies set up by the old regime. Liu countered that these temporary policies were needed to sustain the war effort, and that the CCP simply lacked the number of trained cadres needed to carry out reform in the new areas. In general Mao supported Liu and Ren, although, at the meeting or shortly afterward, he voiced concern that the "political takeover" in areas that had been held by the Communists for a while—for instance, in Manchuria—was not progressing fast enough.[25]

There was also tension over land reform, although on that point the course had been set, and the task of the meeting was to criticize those who did not conform. In his comments, Mao complained that not all top level cadres had understood the significance of the antileftist rectification campaign that the party had launched in early 1948. Some of the problems associated with the slogan "Do everything as the masses want it

done"—a slogan from the party's policies on land reform in early 1947—
had not yet been solved, the Chairman stated. The "left extremism" in
some regions held back the productive forces of the peasants and had to
be changed—even if it meant the "overthrow" of local cadres. Although
Mao himself had been squarely behind radical land reform during most
of 1947, in the autumn of 1948, as more moderate policies suited the
party's overall purposes, he was more than willing to point to Liu Shaoqi
as a proponent of an "erroneous" line the previous year.[26]

The meeting passed a number of detailed instructions for party
cadres—for instance, on which issues had to be dealt with by the Center,
and on improving the theoretical level in the party, another of Liu
Shaoqi's pet issues. In this resolution, probably written by Liu, the Politburo criticized its organizations for neglecting Marxist theory. In some
party schools, the resolution states, "people read nothing or almost nothing. This practice is quite wrong. A tendency of ignoring revolutionary
theory has emerged . . . and empiricism has instead become the main danger to our party. The only way to overcome this is through promoting the
study of theory and policy."[27] The Politburo prescribed a number of
books that should be basic reading in the party schools—a mix of Mao's
works and Soviet political and economic theory.

Foreign affairs figured more prominently on the agenda in the mid-
September meetings than at any other previous CCP leadership meeting
since the civil war started. In his opening statement, Mao acknowledged
the inability of the party leadership to understand the international situation fully within a Marxist framework.

> On the current international situation, we had an evaluation in the [Politburo]
> meeting last December [1947]. At that time, we could not reach agreement
> within our party, even inside the Central Committee. Some held that there
> would be either war or peace, whereas others thought that there existed a dan-
> ger of war, but it would not necessarily break out. The reason for the first
> [kind of thinking] was that the power of the world's people was not strong
> enough to stop war, but for the second it was that the Soviet Union and the
> world's people would be able to mobilize necessary forces to stop the war.
> Anyhow, the situation after World War II is different from that after World
> War I, hence the possibility of stopping war is greater.[28]

Quoting a statement by Molotov on the Soviet Union's already being
stronger than the reactionary forces, the Chairman launched an attack on
those within his own party who did not believe in the ability of Soviet
power to prevent a world war. Implicitly, his message was directed
against those who had supported Soviet warnings of caution in launching

PLA offensives over the previous months. Because of Moscow's strength, there was no need to "talk about compromise or a division [of China]," Mao argued. "The Soviet Union can make concessions to America, Britain and France in light of democratic principles—why cannot we make some concessions to the GMD? The centrists think about this. But I do not think so. Soviet policy is noninterference into other countries' domestic affairs; even the Atlantic Charter recognizes the right for all peoples to choose their own political system. And the Chinese people will not choose Jiang Jieshi's system."[29]

In spite of Mao's refusal to heed Soviet hints about caution, the relationship to Moscow grew closer during the latter half of 1948. The exchange of telegrams between Mao and Soviet leaders on the situation in China, tactics and strategy, on military planning, and on foreign affairs became much more frequent. The Chinese leadership sought Soviet advice on most of the problems affecting the party, and Stalin was happy to oblige. During the peak of the HuaiHai campaign, Xibaipo sometimes received several messages per day in the name of "the Great Master," pontificating on issues ranging from troop movements toward Bengbu to the currency situation and trade unions in Guangzhou. Soviet assistance in terms of weapons and ammunition also increased, although Stalin warned against letting the Americans know how much Soviet assistance was coming in.[30]

Mao's big disappointment was that the "Great Master" was still not willing to receive him in Moscow. In July 1948 the Chairman thought that everything had finally been arranged; according to a Soviet intelligence report to Stalin, "Mao Zedong's suitcases were being packed, and leather shoes were bought (like everybody here, he is wearing fabric shoes), and a thick wool coat was tailored. Not only the issue of the trip as such, but its timing, too, had already been decided by him. The only remaining point was by which way to go." On 14 July, Stalin again suddenly decided to postpone the visit, citing the Soviet leadership's preoccupation with the "grain harvest." "Now," Stalin's agent wrote after reading the "Great Master's" message aloud to Mao, "he is quiet in appearance, polite and attentive, amiable in the typically Chinese style. His true soul, however, is difficult to see. By the whole appearance of Ren Bishi it is clearly sensed that he, too, did not expect the postponement of the trip."[31]

It is difficult to know the reason for Stalin's successive postponements of Mao's trip to Moscow (in November 1948, when Stalin did seem to be willing to receive the CCP Chairman, Mao decided that he could not go because of the military situation in China). The Soviet leader did not, relatively speaking, give high priority to events in China, even after the upgrade of Soviet interest in the CCP after mid-1948. We know that by mid-July of 1948, Stalin's staff had started to prepare for the Boss's yearly vacation by the Black Sea, and even Russian or East European Communists who wanted to see him on urgent business had to wait until he returned to Moscow. As Stalin grew older, his need to show everyone in the movement who was in command became, in part, a question of allowing or not allowing Communists access to him personally. Besides, Stalin—famously stingy on most occasions—did not want to give the CCP an occasion to ask him directly for more aid, something that Mao had hinted was high on his agenda. The Soviet leader may also have feared that a Mao visit to Moscow, just at the time when the PLA was taking control of North China, might prove unnecessarily provocative to the United States, and spur a U.S. intervention in the civil war.[32]

Instead of Mao's coming to see him in Moscow, Stalin, after the quarrel over the GMD's mediation proposal, suggested sending "a leading comrade" of the CPSU Politburo to see the Chinese leader in Xibaipo. The man Stalin chose for the not unrisky mission was Anastas Mikoyan, a fifty-four-year-old Armenian Communist veteran who had followed Stalin's line faithfully since the early 1920s and who—alone in the Boss's inner circle—combined a taste for personal adventure with a rigorous Stalinist mindset. Mikoyan arrived in China in late January 1949, and, after crossing through territory still nominally held by the GMD in North China, reached Xibaipo on 30 January. His meetings with Mao and the CCP leadership provided the Chinese with an opportunity to present their viewpoints to Moscow, but also allowed them, with a senior member of the international movement present, to take stock of where the CCP was heading during the next phase of the revolution.[33]

Before turning to bilateral issues, the CCP Politburo gave Mikoyan a broad overview of their thinking on what the future would look like. The civil war would end soon, Mao said, although it could still take up to three years for the PLA to liberate areas like Tibet, Xinjiang, and Taiwan. But taking control of those areas was less important, said the Chairman, than securing the CCP's hold on the main areas north and south of the Yangzi. The Guomindang was already fragmenting—the CCP was "in touch" not only with Fu Zuoyi but also with GMD generals such as Bai Chongxi and Tang Enbo. The "negotiations" with Li Zongren were just for show; after they broke down, the PLA would cross the Yangzi, "probably in April." Even the United States and Britain had realized that Li would not survive, Mao said, adding that an intelligence agent at the U.S. consulate in Tianjin provided the CCP with exact information about American intentions.[34]

Mao, backed by Ren, Liu, and Zhou Enlai, went into considerable detail on the CCP's main worries in intensive meetings that lasted more than a week. Besides correcting "leftist" trends in land reform and administration, the biggest challenges to the party in the "liberated" areas were in terms of finance, supplies, and the lack of trained cadres. According to Ren Bishi, inflation was already becoming an issue in the Communist-held regions, something the party had not expected. The party needed to keep its expenditures under control, which meant that the less the Communists had to spend for military purposes, and the more they could earn from trade with the Soviet Union, the better their position would be as they entered the cities. A complete currency reform was also needed, but at the moment, Ren said, the CCP did not even have paper to print its money on, not to mention all kinds of supplies for major cities like Shanghai or the trained cadres to administer those cities.[35]

On the future construction of a CCP-controlled state in China, Mao claimed that he had learned a lot from Stalin's works and from his recent messages. Although it should not be revealed to the public, Mao agreed with Stalin that China was not at the stage of a "people's democracy" but needed a "dictatorship of workers and peasants" under the leadership of the CCP. In his report to Stalin, Mikoyan wrote: "Mao Zedong said that especially valuable for him had been comrade Stalin's instructions on the Chinese revolution as a part of the world revolution, as well as the criticism of [foreign minister Stanoje] Simic, the Yugoslav nationalist. Mao Zedong emphasized several times that he was comrade Stalin's disciple and that he adhered to the 'pro-Soviet orientation.' "[36] The Chairman did not think that he himself should be president of the new republic but preferred "Song Qingling, the widow of Sun Yixian . . . [who], Mao Zedong said, is totally obedient to us and enjoys a huge authority among the people."[37]

The CCP leadership realized that they had yet to work out a comprehensive policy for the country's ethnic minorities. Mao listened intently when Mikoyan stated that Stalin advised limited autonomy—and not any suggestions of full independence—as the main CCP line toward such groups. Mikoyan commented in his report to Stalin, however, that "it

was evident by his face that he [Mao] was not going to grant independence to anyone." In their discussion on Mongolia, the CCP Chairman
made it clear that he wanted—"in two to three years"—Outer Mongolia
to join Inner Mongolia as an autonomous part of China. Mikoyan, under
orders from Stalin, strongly opposed that view. "If at some time in the future [the Mongolian People's Republic] unites itself with Inner Mongolia,
it certainly will be as an independent Mongolia," Mikoyan said. "In the
end, Mao Zedong burst out laughing and stopped defending his view,"
the Soviet envoy reported to Stalin.[38]

Mao and Zhou Enlai also wanted to discuss how the new Chinese republic was to organize its diplomatic affairs. Fearing that the Western
powers would use diplomatic contacts to subvert the new revolutionary
order, Mao said that he hoped the United States and Britain would not
recognize the new regime, or at least delay their recognition. In Shenyang,
occupied by the CCP in the fall of 1948, the Western powers attempted
to establish de facto diplomatic relations by having their personnel remain after the takeover. "We understand that these consulates stayed
there for [gathering] intelligence against us and the USSR," Zhou said.
"We do not wish to see them in Shenyang, therefore we take measures to
isolate them; [we] create intolerable conditions for them in order to have
them leave . . . [and] drive at having Manchuria covered by the iron curtain against foreign powers except the USSR and people's democracies."[39]

Because Mao as early as mid-1948 had hinted that he wanted major
loans from the Soviet Union as soon as his new republic was set up, he
went out of his way to thank Mikoyan for Moscow's support during the
civil war. "If not for the assistance on the part of the Soviet Union," Mao
Zedong emphasized, "we would hardly be able to win the current victories. This, however, does not mean that we do not have to rely on our
own potentials as well. Nevertheless, one cannot but take account of the
fact that the Soviet Union's military assistance in Manchuria, amounting
to one-fourth of the whole assistance to us, plays quite a substantial
role." The CCP had always followed Soviet instructions to keep Soviet
aid hidden; when entering Beijing, Mao said, "We removed all Soviet
weapons . . . and fully equipped [our forces] with American weapons in
order to emphasize how well Jiang Jieshi supplied us with American
equipment."[40]

When Mikoyan hinted at the need to change the 1945 Sino-Soviet
treaties after a CCP victory, this information was clearly welcome news
to Mao and the Chinese. If so, Mao said, they would have to be replaced

by a new treaty along the lines of the Soviet-Polish treaty of mutual assistance. Mao went out of his way to point out that New China would be
dependent on Soviet protection and assistance. He welcomed Stalin's advice on all matters, praising the detailed instructions Mikoyan brought
on cadre training and on worker, youth, and women issues: "[D]uring
their presentation Mao Zedong and the Politburo members were yes'ing
in chorus," Mikoyan reported to the Boss.[41]

For Mao the Mikoyan visit was the most important development in
the relations to the Soviet Union during the civil war. For the very first
time, he was able to sit down with one of the Soviet top leaders and discuss policy and political theory. The visit also proved, Mao believed, that
the controversies over mediation and military strategies in 1948 and early
1949 had been passed over and a formal alliance between the Soviet
Union and his new Chinese state was in the making. But the talks during
Mikoyan's visit had also reminded him of how many questions concerning the buildup of that new state were still unresolved. Mikoyan agreed.
Although generally positive in terms of the qualities of the CCP leadership, in his report back to Stalin, Mikoyan noted that they had much to
learn: "[A]ll their economic plans are general guidelines without any attempts to be specific, even with regard to what is under their power in the
liberated areas. They are sitting in a tucked away village and are divorced
from realities," Mikoyan noted.[42]

Crossing the Yangzi

The peace negotiations that had started in late January 1949 were
more important to the CCP leadership than they would admit to their Soviet comrades. As seen from Xibaipo, the main point with the negotiations was not to achieve any form of settlement—all the main leaders
thought such a result highly unlikely—but to let the exhausted PLA
troops on the Central Plains have a rest while transferring Lin Biao's
main forces toward the Yangzi in preparation for an attack that, in spite
of Mao's optimistic predictions to Mikoyan, could come as late as July or
August. In the meantime, there were all kinds of political loose ends to tie
up: talks with individual GMD commanders and officials who wanted to
defect, preparations for taking over Nanjing and Shanghai, and making
sure that "democratic leaders" joined the CCP bandwagon and were not
lured by Li Zongren and the Americans to join any form of reformist
coalition government supported by Washington.[43]

In part as a result of information he got from Moscow, Mao's worries about U.S. intentions increased as his armies went south. In his New Year's message to senior party cadres, he emphasized that "[we] have always, when we work out our strategies, taken into consideration the possibility that the United States will send troops to occupy some coastal cites and fight directly against us. This possibility cannot be ruled out now. Otherwise, when it happens, we will all be in a fluster." But his main worry remained with imperialist scheming to subvert the political aspects of the revolutionary victory. In December 1948, he had pointed out to Stalin that the "Americans intend to proceed from active support for the Guomindang to, on the one hand, support for local Guomindang [groups] and local southern Chinese warlords, so that their military forces will resist the People's Liberation Army; and, on the other hand, organize and send their lackeys so that they can infiltrate the Political Consultative Conference and the democratic coalition government and set up an opposition bloc there and undermine the people's liberation front from within, so that the revolution can not be carried out consistently."[44]

In a note to some of the Politburo members, Mao elaborated on his view of a U.S. conspiracy against the new state:

> The main point of the current policy of the American State Department is how to prop up an effective opposition in China to resist the CCP. The American government will give its recognition, in some form, to the new coalition government and resume its trade with China, and [will want to] invest. The American government hopes to split the CCP's united front in this way and [will] spend all its efforts supporting the non-Communists in a coalition government. The preconditions for American recognition of the coalition government will be that the composition of the new government must be acceptable to the United States and recognition of American bases in Shanghai and Qingdao by the coalition government.[45]

Li Zongren's taking over from Jiang Jieshi as "acting president" increased the Chairman's fears. By as early as the fall of 1948 he had predicted that Washington would push Li or He Yingqin to the fore if Jiang was seen to have failed militarily. The current "peace plot" was part of this strategy, Mao thought. His response was to accelerate both the CCP's political maneuvers and the PLA's military preparations to cross the Yangzi as much as possible in order not to give the Americans time to carry out their schemes. "Our main policy," he wrote to Lin Biao in mid-February, "is to rope in Li Zongren, Bai Chongxi, Zhang Zhizhong and Shao Lizi and those capitalists in Shanghai (represented by Yan Huiqing,

*U.S. Intelligence Agencies Discuss the Civil War
in China, December 1948*

Adm. Inglis [Chief of Naval Intelligence]: The gist of it is that [U.S. military advisers in China] think that the situation north of the Yangtze is hopeless and [it] is just a matter of days or weeks before the whole thing folds up. What happens after that, of course, is a matter of terrible concern and conjecture. Do you feel that this Li that is Vice President is going to be successful in forming some kind of coalition government and if so just how much Communist influence will be exerted in that? My people say that they have checked at the working level with Army, State, and the rest and they say that he will be successful and in the beginning the Communists will be in the minor position, but as time goes on [it] will grow as it did in Czechoslovakia. . . .

Director [of Central Intelligence, R. H. Hillenkoetter]: I think our people got the same answer. They said the Communists would come into the government because they would be a recognized government in the United Nations and, as a purely personal thing, that the United States and the West could supply them with articles of trade that they couldn't possibly get from Russia. They would want that for a while. . . .

Adm. Inglis: One thing that puzzles us is the superiority and the strategic direction of the Chinese Communists and their ability to support themselves logistically and in communications. It just doesn't seem Chinese.

Gen. Irwin [Director, General Staff, U.S. Army]: I don't think it is. . . .

Adm. Inglis: And another thing, turning our attention to the situation in Formosa. Does anyone know a strong man in Formosa who we would do well to back instead of carpetbaggers from China or Chiang Kai-shek?

Foreign Relations of the United States, 1945–1950: The Emergence of the Intelligence Establishment (Washington, DC: U.S. Government Printing Office, 1996), pp. 895–96.

Du Yuesheng) and crack down on those hard-liners within the GMD, in order to facilitate our military advance." For this purpose the negotiations would have to continue.[46]

In Nanjing, Li Zongren and his supporters were also vying for time. Li still believed that if he could get a three-month respite from the Communist military offensive, the GMD forces would be able to repel a PLA crossing of the river. If Mao understood the cost of taking the South by force, real negotiations on a formal sharing of power could get going, Li thought. The new president's liberal reforms—the freeing of a large number of political prisoners, the lessening of press censorship, and the lifting of restrictions on public protest—had stabilized the situation somewhat in the areas still under GMD control. But within the party and its core leadership, and within the military, power was still fragmenting. The new

Prime Minister, Sun Yixian's son Sun Fo, had never liked Li Zongren or the Guangxi group, and had upon Li's taking power abruptly removed himself and most of his cabinet to Guangzhou, in spite of the new president's appeals for him to stay in Nanjing. As Li struggled desperately to get the allegiance of local strongmen in the provinces and the commanders of the Nationalist armies, Sun began issuing proclamations from Guangzhou with no or little regard for his president's plans.[47]

Before formal negotiations with the Communists got under way, President Li wanted to explore the intentions of the CCP by sending a group of prominent Shanghai businessmen to Xibaipo for talks. This group arrived in early February and had brief meetings with Mao and Zhou Enlai. On 14 February, Li sent a bigger group, which—although still in theory "independent"—had a mandate from the GMD president to agree to an informal framework for negotiations. Not surprisingly, after Zhou Enlai and his assistants had worked on them for several days, indicating the benefits for them personally in agreeing to CCP terms (and the dangers if they did not), the "intermediaries" signed on to Mao's eight points of 14 January as the basis for talks. When they reported to Li Zongren in late February, the president was understandably horrified that the group, which included several people who had his personal trust, had not been able to wring at least a couple of concessions from the Communist leaders.[48]

In his self-imposed exile at Fenghua, Jiang Jieshi was even more alarmed than Li when he learned about the results of the peace mission. Jiang had been getting reports from GMD intelligence—still fully under his control—of Bai Chongxi's contacts with the Communists, and he began suspecting Bai, and, by implication, Bai's close friend Li Zongren, of planning to defect wholesale to the Communists. Jiang, as he confided to his diary, could pride himself on having been aware of this possibility for some time. He had not been inactive since his "temporary resignation" (as he now termed his late-January departure): Besides making sure that the main GMD armies in the East—those defending the lower reaches of the Yangzi and the city of Shanghai—remained under his personal control, he had also intensified his efforts to build Taiwan into an anti-Communist stronghold, forming the core of a small number of areas—including Fujian and Sichuan—that could still be defended if the CCP successfully crossed the Yangzi. In early February, he had ordered the remainder of the government's gold reserves transferred to Taibei, leaving Li Zongren's government with barely enough to pay its daily expenses.

(When Li in March finally got his courage up to formally ask for the return of the state's gold reserves, Jiang noted his "irritation" in his diary.)[49]

For CCP military planners, the main issue was how and where to cross the river. They assumed that their forces would have to cross under fire, at least in most areas, and that the GMD navy and air force—possibly supported by foreign ships—would attempt to prevent their crossing. Some of the generals, including Su Yu, who had the main responsibility for working out a plan for the attack, were worried about the outcome, and about crossing into southern China, an area most of them knew nothing about. Mao attempted to reassure them by pointing out that there were already secret negotiations going on with elements in the GMD navy, and that if the coming GMD-CCP negotiations in Beijing worked out, the PLA could expect "free passage" to the South; but the generals still reported that any such operation would be dangerous and risky.[50]

On 26 March, the CCP Chairman appointed a group headed by Zhou Enlai and Lin Biao to negotiate with the official representatives of the Nanjing government. On the Nanjing side, Li had selected a broadly composed group to negotiate on his behalf: The team was headed by the former commander in Xinjiang, General Zhang Zhizhong, a GMD veteran, but included members such as the Shanghai businessman Zhang Shizhao, a longtime adversary of Jiang Jieshi, and Shao Lizi, also from Shanghai, and with good personal connections with some of the CCP leaders. Li's task in appointing the delegation had been made simpler by Sun Fo's late-February decision to move the cabinet back to Nanjing, a decision that the ineffectual Prime Minister—described by his colleagues as "having the air of a spoiled son of a prominent family"—took mostly to be able to resign a job he could not handle.[51] His successor, the wartime defense minister He Yingqin, quickly arrived at some form of working relationship with President Li, although General He made it clear that his prime loyalty was to Jiang Jieshi. Agreeing on a peace delegation was, some observers thought, a sign that the new Nanjing administration was beginning to hold its own.

The negotiations began in Beijing on 1 April. The CCP shocked the Nanjing representatives on 6 April by demanding what amounted to full surrender as a precondition for peace: CCP officers in charge of reorganizing the GMD army, the outlawing of the GMD as a party, and the sending of PLA units to southern China. Li Zongren and his government

> ### Western Countries Refuse Aid to Li Zongren, 17 April 1949
>
> British Ambassador [Sir Ralph Stevenson] acted as spokesman. . . . Stevenson said that we all appreciated [the] confidence [the] Acting President had shown by informing [us about the] contents [of] this secret document and expressed our great admiration for the steadfast purpose and calm patience Li Zongren had shown during [the] past several months. [The] British Ambassador continued that he was sure in face of this record that Li would do what was best for [the] Chinese people. As far as [the] British government was concerned he said they stood by [the] Moscow Declaration of 1945 pledging complete non-interference in Chinese internal affairs. Consequently while we had great sympathy with Li and [his] present heavy responsibility and would like to help him, there was in fact nothing his government could do. We all said we agreed with Stevenson. [The] Australian [Ambassador] pointed out [that] it was [a] Chinese problem which must be settled by [the] Chinese themselves. I added that [the] President must not give up hope and [must] do what he thought was right. Li was obviously disheartened, chilled by our reserved, somewhat formal attitudes.
>
> Stuart to the Secretary of State, 18 April 1949, *FRUS*, 1949, vol. 8, p. 246.

would have to accept the demands within two weeks, or the attack on the South would begin. Neither Li Zongren nor any of his close associates wanted to take responsibility for such a "peace." On 17 April, after having made up his mind to refuse the CCP ultimatum, Li made a last attempt to get Western governments to save his regime. But the outcome of the late-night meeting at Ambassador Stuart's residence did not give Li any relief.

The CCP leaders learned of Li's refusal to sign on the morning of 20 April. The Military Committee met at noon to ratify the final plans to cross the river. The operation would start that night, and it would involve three advance groups from the nearly two million–strong army that the Communists had amassed north of the Yangzi. The first group, from Chen Yi's Third Field Army, would cross halfway between Nanjing and Shanghai, forcing the GMD divisions under Tang Enbo's command toward Shanghai and the coast. The second group, from Lin Biao's Fourth Field Army, would aim at Nanjing directly, crossing both east and west of the GMD capital and encircling it. The third group, from Liu Bocheng's Second Field Army, would cross southwest of Nanjing, immediately advancing toward Jiangxi province, splitting the GMD-held areas at the

Crossing the Yangzi, 21 April 1949

No sight or sound betrayed the intense activity on the north bank. In relays, under cover of dark, the boats were carried overland, lowered into the channels, and paddled to the river bank. The troops embarked without lights, lying on the gunwales, their weapons resting on the edge of the boats. They spoke only in whispers, though the enemy was a long way off. Except for the plash of an oar and the creaking of a boat under the weight of embarking men, they said afterwards, the only sound was the drone of mosquitoes. . . .

When they were a hundred yards into the river, the enemy opened up. The boats bobbed like toy ships on a duck pond in the waves aroused by falling shells. Shell splinters damaged several, and one was saved by a soldier, a non-swimmer, who jumped overboard, clung to the craft, and stuffed the hole with his cotton-padded coat while the boat leapt forward. The line of sails advanced, lit up here by flares from enemy planes, here obscured by fog, and by smoke laid down by the little ships themselves.

Peter Townsend, *China Phoenix: The Revolution in China* (London: Jonathan Cape, 1955), pp. 48–49.

coast from those in the interior. It was a plan that made full use of the CCP's numerical superiority, and that aimed straight at the heart of what remained of GMD political power.[52]

In the early morning and throughout the next day, tens of thousands of PLA soldiers walked wearily to the shore of the river and embarked in the vessels that the Communists had carefully assembled for weeks (or, in the case of the less lucky, gripped their buoys of straw or inflated pigskin, and threw themselves into the water). It was a calm night, which was lucky for the eastern group at the river's mouth, which had almost three kilometers of water to cross before getting ashore. In some sectors the arrival of the PLA forces was heralded by intense artillery fire; in other areas, thousands of soldiers just came gliding toward the opposite shore in silence, seemingly unopposed and without effort. For those who watched it was an eerie spectacle, reminiscent of an unnatural flood slowly expanding from riverbank to riverbank.[53]

The defenders would have stood a chance of slowing and perhaps halting the attack had their efforts been in any way coordinated. But since General Tang and his forces in the East refused to obey orders from anyone but Jiang Jieshi, and Jiang wanted him to concentrate on defending Shanghai and the coastal provinces, any possibility of slowing the Communist tide was lost. The treason of the captain at Jiangyin Fort at the mouth of the river ensured Chen Yi's forces a safe landing. Upriver, the whole of the GMD river navy revolted and went over to the PLA, enabling Liu's army to cross easily against light resistance. With the key defenses gone, and with the main GMD armies retreating away from Nanjing, the capital's fate was sealed. Lin Biao's main forces arrived near the city in the morning of 22 April, when Li Zongren was in Hangzhou in an attempt to get Jiang Jieshi to join him in a concerted plan for resistance. With general promises of cooperation from the Generalissimo, Li returned to his capital in the evening, just in time for it to be isolated by the PLA. As Li met with his advisers that night and early morning, Mao ordered his troops to advance toward the city center. Li Zongren fled to the airport in the early morning of 23 April, after learning that all the members of his Beijing negotiating team had defected to the Communists.[54]

The decision to evacuate was taken with such speed that the President at first did not have time to decide where to go. While his plane circled the air above his lost capital, Li first ordered the pilot to go to Guangzhou, where most of the GMD leaders already were. Then he changed his mind. He would go home, to Guilin in Guangxi province, and from there decide how to proceed. After landing, Li went straight to meetings with his advisers and the provincial leaders. Although he knew that some of the strongmen in Guangxi—such as Li Renren, the chairman of the Provincial Assembly—had already joined the GMD Revolutionary Committee, the front organization that the Communists had organized to receive GMD defectors, Li was shocked when a clear majority

---

The Fall of Nanjing, April 1949

For three days prior to liberation, wild yet systematic looting by the people was widespread. Amidst shouting and laughter, the people stripped the residences of top Nationalist officials and army generals, carrying out the contents, ripping out plumbing, electric fixtures, doors, windows, floors, and all wood for kindling. Like vultures, the looters waited patiently until the Nationalists evacuated their homes in panicky flight to escape with as much as possible of their possessions. . . .

At the airport, I witnessed confusion worse confounded. The families of the wealthy had climbed into scores of aircraft with their baggage—in one case, which I saw, with their grand piano. They never got off the ground. The pilots defected or disappeared.

Chester Ronning, *A Memoir of China in Revolution*, pp. 136–37.

at the meetings argued that he should transfer power peacefully to the CCP. Their argument was that by making peace now, the Guangxi troops could be saved from defeat and some of the power of the provincial elite would survive. For a time Li wavered. It was Bai Chongxi and other GMD generals who arrived in Guilin in early May who convinced the president to hold out. They had become convinced that at the moment, at least, the CCP did not have any deal to offer that would suit them. Bai and Li went together to Guangzhou on 8 May.[55]

The PLA used a couple of days to take complete control of the GMD capital. In some areas there were still enemy snipers, and the citizens' committee of intellectuals and industrialists that the CCP had confirmed as the city's temporary civilian power appealed to the PLA commanders to deal with both that problem and the widespread looting as carefully as possible. The Communist troops entered the city quietly, without any of the parades seen in Beijing. The war was still going on farther east, toward Hangzhou, and many of the soldiers were just passing through Nanjing on their way to the front. Some of them could not let the chance pass to have a look at the buildings formerly occupied by their enemies. In the early morning of 25 April, some PLA soldiers decided to have a look at the U.S. ambassador's residence and walked in, waking up Dr. Stuart in his second-story bedroom and, while looking around, telling him "that all this would eventually go to [the] people."[56] Even the PLA commanders could not resist having a go at the GMD relics—Deng Xiaoping remembers how he and Chen Yi took turns sitting in Jiang Jieshi's chair in the reception room at the Presidential Palace.[57]

The CCP leadership, now installed in their new capital, Beijing, waited anxiously for news about how the foreign community in Nanjing had reacted to the Communist takeover. Mao knew already that most foreign embassies would not evacuate their staffs, and he was eager to set up some form of working relationship with them. From communications with Stalin after Mikoyan's visit, Mao knew that the Soviet leader recommended that the new Chinese state not avoid "businesslike" relations with the capitalist powers, including diplomatic contacts and trade. But Mao's concern over how the imperialists would behave toward his regime had been heightened by British attempts to send a naval vessel, the HMS *Amethyst*, to Nanjing just as the PLA was beginning to cross the river. A British gunboat on the Yangzi was too much of a symbol of the "old China" that they were on the verge of defeating to be ignored by the CCP. Having in advance been authorized to resist any foreign interference with the crossing, PLA units shelled the ship and the British frigate *Consort,* which came to its rescue some hours later. The *Amethyst* grounded on a sandbank in the middle of the river. Mao telegraphed General Su Yu, saying that the British were sending two warships to salvage their ship, and that they should not be attacked "unless they interfere with our crossing," even if they proceeded toward Nanjing. But Mao's message came too late. The PLA had already opened fire on the cruiser *London* and another frigate from Shanghai. In total fifty British sailors were killed in the engagements.[58]

The *Amethyst* incident and the reports he was getting about his soldiers' rude awakening of the U.S. ambassador on 25 April further alerted Mao to the dangers of not controlling his party's relations with foreigners. After getting the report on the events in the morning of 25 April, Mao wrote out immediate instructions for the behavior of the PLA toward foreigners in Nanjing, which the CCP Center followed up by more detailed orders two weeks later. "Our people," Mao said, "should be indifferent to the foreign embassies and their diplomatic personnel, and should take absolutely no initiative to contact them." The Center gave its cadres specific orders to protect all foreign institutions, not to enter any foreign-owned buildings, and not to contact foreigners in any way, including arresting them if they broke martial law regulations. Mao even instructed them to let all foreign communications equipment stay in operation, contrary to what had been CCP policy in Manchuria.[59]

With the GMD's southern defenses broken and Nanjing in Communist hands, Mao thought that he could detect a change in the attitude of the imperialist powers to his party. On 28 April, he wrote: "The Americans are asking some people to pass messages to us, asking for establishment of diplomatic relations, and the British are trying hard to engage in business with us. We hold that if the Americans will end diplomatic relations with the GMD, we may consider such a possibility. . . . The American policy of assisting Jiang and opposing Communism has failed, and it seems that it is changing its policy on establishing diplomatic relations with us." Any incidents that would reduce the Center's freedom of choice in diplomatic matters should be avoided. But Mao still could not hide his pride in the outcome of the first major military clash with a foreign power during the civil war. "The incidents with the British warships have shaken the world and become the headlines of all the main newspapers in Britain and America," he told the generals on 28 April.[60]

The Fall of Shanghai

At the end of April, in the city at the mouth of the Yangzi, the barges and tow-boats arrived and departed at the docks in smaller numbers than before. But in spite of the crippling inflation, the closing of the river to commerce, and all the other disasters that had befallen Shanghai over the past several months, the city was still concentrating on commerce and deal-making. Could Shanghai ever change? Could any government ever control this city, created to cater to the greed and desires of the lucky few? In the weeks after Nanjing fell to the Communists, most people in Shanghai were wondering if more than a hundred years of foreign influence were really coming to an end. Most doubted it—the foreigners would not let Shanghai fall without interfering, was the word on the street. But nobody could tell how Shanghai should be preserved as an enclave of commerce, with Communism on the rise all around it.[61]

For most people in Shanghai, including many who had supported the government for years, it mattered less and less who was in control, if only the war and the ills it brought in its wake would come to an end. Several prominent citizens argued that the Communists, too, would need Shanghai to conduct trade, and would not spurn its industrial potential and its contacts with foreign buyers and sellers. "If Communists are welcome even by conservative business interests not to mention populace, it will not be surprising," wrote the U.S. consul-general in Shanghai, John M. Cabot, in mid-May.[62] Those who were not so trusting of the CCP, and especially those who had money or relatives abroad, fled in the first weeks of May. Very few people in Shanghai expected the city's grace period from Communist attack to last long, and most of those who did have a choice did not want to be there when it happened.

As the military situation had deteriorated in February and March, the GMD mayor of Shanghai, Wu Guozhen (K. C. Wu), had attempted to keep the political structure in the city from fragmenting. Although personally close to the Generalissimo for almost two decades, and instrumental in his control of first Shanghai and then Wuhan before the war, Wu had realized that his only hope of avoiding chaos in the city in the short term was to balance the interests of all groups—the Nanjing government, the local military commanders, the traditional Shanghai bourgeoisie, the secret societies, the dwindling foreign communities, and even the Communist sympathizers inside the city. When Jiang's protege, the GMD commander Tang Enbo, tried in February to usurp Wu's mayoral responsibilities by putting parts of the city under direct military control, Wu threatened to resign, forcing Li Zongren to intervene with a compromise. By as early as early February, Wu had handed parts of the mayor's archives, including well selected intelligence files, over to the Americans for "safe-keeping." The mayor knew how to keep some support in all camps. And he knew that that support would be crucial if he was to save the city from destruction.[63]

Saving the city was also the main aim of the city's bourgeoisie. With Li Zongren's blessing, a number of "peace delegations" left Shanghai for Beijing in February and March 1949, in most cases speaking quite openly with CCP leaders about the prospects for a Communist takeover of the city. The leader of the most prominent of the mafia-style gangs in Shanghai, Du Yuesheng—who as leader of the Green Gang had helped Jiang Jieshi massacre thousands of Communists in 1927–28—got in touch with the Communist underground to explain that his motives had always been "sincere" and that he would do whatever was needed to make it "unnecessary" for the PLA to take the city by force. Reading the reports in Beijing, Zhou Enlai—who had been on the receiving end of Du's machinations twenty years before—could almost not believe his eyes, although he understood that even someone like Du could be useful for the Communist cause.[64]

The fragmenting of GMD power in Shanghai and other cities in 1949 is brilliantly satirized by the playwright Qu Baiyin in his *Train to the South*.[65] The play takes place in the first-class dining car of the train to Guangzhou, while it is waiting to depart from Wuhan station. Two wounded soldiers stumble into the car. A GMD general gets up to throw them out, but he is embarrassed when it turns out that the soldiers belong to his own unit, in which before heading for the train he had spread rumors of his heroic death in battle. Outside, on the platform, a young man pleads with his fiancée, a rich girl whose money he wants to use for a ticket south. A GMD official mistakes a rich landlord whose land has been expropriated by the Communists for a Communist agent, and tries to ingratiate himself by praising CCP principles. The old landlord, understandably, has a fainting fit.

Most members of the liberal intelligentsia in Shanghai had already transferred their emotional if not their physical allegiance to the CCP. The former leaders of the Democratic League openly voiced their belief that a Communist takeover of all of China was unavoidable, and that they were ready to cooperate with the new rulers in order to influence

them for the better. To their friends at the U.S. consulate, a group of liberals explained that the CCP's "inexplicable actions [were] due to their
ignorance, provincialism, and suspicion," but that all of this would
change when people like themselves joined the new regime.[66] Although
Mayor Wu had finally resigned in early April—and was replaced by General Chen Liang, who attempted to follow Wu's policies, but did not have
the former mayor's abilities—the situation in Shanghai remained stable.
By late April, many city fathers thought that they had enough influence
in both camps to prevent disaster, and some confidence started returning
to the city in spite of the gradual advances of the PLA.

Then, at the very end of April, disaster struck. After making a defiant
radio-broadcast speech to the nation from his home in Zhejiang, Jiang
Jieshi returned to Shanghai, where he declared that he would fight "to
the end." To the Shanghai intelligentsia and large parts of the bourgeoisie, who keenly remembered how the Generalissimo had brought the
city to heel in the late 1920s, the prospect of having Jiang put up a last-
ditch defense around the beleaguered city filled them with a fear substantially greater than that of a Communist victory. While Jiang and General Tang let the GMD secret police instill fear in "defeatists and traitors"
around the city, prominent Shanghai citizens fled for their lives. Even Du
Yuesheng, the Green Gang chief, was forced to take off for Hong Kong,
head over heels. Yan Huiqing, who had been spearheading the negotiations with the CCP, took refuge in a mental asylum. Hundreds of others
were arrested or forcibly evicted from the city. Suspected Communist
sympathizers of the lower ranks were executed by GMD security chief
Mao Seng's agents, sometimes in the streets of Shanghai. A climate of fear
gripped the city.[67]

As Jiang re-established his rule in Shanghai, what was left of the city's
commercial economy collapsed. The yuan became worthless, and all
transactions had to take place in gold or as barter, since even dollars and
sterling were in short supply. New taxes and levies were written out almost every day, to "support the war effort." In the streets, press gangs
took people away to dig ditches around the city, or to help set up a
wooden stockade that Tang Enbo proclaimed would be the impenetrable
inner defense works for Shanghai (but which most Shanghai people believed was constructed to make a local timber merchant, a friend of the
General's, very rich indeed). By the second week of May, farmers from
the surrounding areas had stopped coming into the city to sell food. The
foreign consuls still left pleaded with General Tang and Mayor Chen to

make Shanghai an "open city" to prevent hunger and massive destruction. But it was to no avail.

By then Jiang had left the city, as suddenly as he had arrived. He had stayed in the harbor on the cruiser *Taikang* until 8 May, when the ship lifted anchor and sailed, slowly, down the coast. The Generalissimo spent another eight days inspecting defense works on the islands outside Fuxing before he headed across to Taiwan. His plan to make that island a fortress against Communism was proceeding well. Few of those who knew Jiang thought that he would really fight for Shanghai; his purpose was to extort as many resources as he could from the city in order to build his island fortress. When he arrived in Taiwan, his governor, General Chen Cheng, reported that the influx to Taiwan of gold, currency, art treasures, advanced machinery, and U.S. aid intended for the provinces was even better than had been planned for. While the Generalissimo got himself set up in the guest villa of the China Sugar Company at Yangmingshan overlooking Taibei, his son, Jiang Jingguo, remained behind on the Yangzi to wring the last possible drops of "support" from the Shanghai capitalists.[68]

Meanwhile, the CCP leaders remained uncertain as to Jiang's real intentions. They did not want to fight their way into Shanghai, but on the other hand they did not want to allow Jiang the propaganda victory of holding the city for long against overwhelming CCP force.[69] While the Military Committee worked out alternatives, the PLA forces, after having overcome the last resistance around Nanjing, slowly approached the city. Hangzhou fell at the beginning of May, and shortly thereafter Shanghai was, for all practical purposes, isolated. The main PLA force moved on the city from the north, and some of the units inadvertently came between the GMD troops and the Jiangsu coast, preventing their evacuation and forcing them to fight. This was a costly tactical mistake, if the real CCP aim was Shanghai. It led to unnecessary fighting, and probably held up the occupation of the city by a couple of weeks, not least by making it more difficult to get in direct touch with the troops guarding the city to convince them to capitulate.[70]

While waiting for a CCP takeover that became increasingly certain, most foreigners remained in the city. As with the Chinese bourgeoisie, those who had had the inclination and the opportunity had already left, the adventurous and those with no place to go staying on. For Shanghai's thousands of stateless Europeans—Russians, East Europeans, Jews—the impending fall of Shanghai meant the end to a place of refuge. Most scrambled to get a passport, any passport, and get out, but few were successful. The lucky few ended up as citizens of the Philippines or Costa Rica, after which they had to pay their lifetime savings for a ticket to their new homeland. On the other hand, quite a number of Western businessmen chose to stay to offer their services to the new government. Their thinking was that a Chinese regime—any Chinese regime—would sooner or later decide that it required their services. The Communists would be no different, the reasoning went.[71]

The opponents of the GMD regime who thought that they could emerge from hiding after the Generalissimo left the city made a dramatic mistake. The terror against the regime's opponents increased during May, with frequent executions, including summary killings in the streets. Even journalists working for the Western news media were not safe; several were arrested, and two Western correspondents were held and threatened with execution for breaking martial law regulations. Still, in spite of the threats, a number of war correspondents made their way to the areas around Shanghai, where they met Guomindang soldiers ready to capitulate—only that there was no one, as yet, to capitulate to. On 18 May, a couple of days after the Shanghai Country Club opened its grass tennis courts for the summer season, Mayor Chen left for Taiwan. By 20 May the PLA had surrounded both Shanghai airports, and looting broke out in some parts of the city. The targets were mostly private houses—Jiang had made certain that little else was left.

On 24 May the remaining GMD authorities in the city arranged a Victory Parade down the main streets of the city. Lots of people came out to celebrate, although few were quite certain what they celebrated. Many came to get a break from the tension of the war, others to show solidarity with the city authorities in a time of crisis. Some came to celebrate the end of old Shanghai. At the stroke of midnight the first advance units of the PLA entered the city. There was no resistance. That night the Communists took over City Hall and the Central Police Station and raided the GMD archives. In the early morning the CCP troops fanned out to take control of all parts of the city. Tying up their horses and mules along the elegant facades of central Shanghai, the Communist soldiers were as much of a sight for the locals as the tall buildings and streetcars were for the invading troops.[72]

Only in a few areas of the city were there significant clashes. The best known of them—termed the Battle of Broadway Mansions by Western residents—went on for two days: GMD soldiers firing from across

Public Executions in Shanghai, Spring 1949

When all the prisoners were ready, they were placed in an open truck. With sirens screaming and firebells clanging, the execution convoy raced through the city's streets to the intersection selected. A hush would fall over the waiting thousands as the execution party arrived. The prisoners were lined up in the middle of the street, each with his executioner behind him. At a signal from an officer, the men were pushed to their knees and shot in the back of the head. As they pitched forward, a roar of applause would come from the crowds. The police then used bamboo sticks, gun butts, and leather belts to restrain the people from rushing forward for a better view of the final death twitchings. Once, the wife of one of the executed men managed to slip through the police cordon. She knelt beside her dead husband and smoothed his blood-soaked hair while she moaned softly. . . . A goose-pimply silence fell over the crowd, suddenly ashamed of its bloodlust. It melted away, quickly.

Harrison Forman, *Blunder in Asia* (New York: Didier, 1950), pp. 53–54.

Suzhou creek made one end of the famous Shanghai waterfront—the Bund—a battle zone, while in the streets behind, most things quickly returned to normal. In Pudong, farther up across the Huangpu River, fighting was fierce as GMD officers and officials tried to fight their way to Wusong on the coast, where Nationalist ships, and U.S. and British warships, were still moored. In the end Mao decided to let them go—the aim of capturing them was not worth the destruction wreaked by the fighting. Besides, Mao's main target at this point had been the city itself, not the GMD troops.[73]

As the fighting died down, the citizens of Shanghai and the soldiers of the People's Liberation Army continued to watch each other in curious amazement. There was almost no contact between the two groups—the soldiers had been forbidden from entering people's houses or even talking to people in the street without permission. Most of the troops were moved out as quickly as possible after the takeover. Among those who remained were many propaganda units, which arranged street meetings and revolutionary theater performances. Shanghai people stopped to watch, repeated the slogans shouted, and then went about their business; the river was again opening to commerce, and there was work to do. The CCP leaders who arrived in the city—among them Chen Yi, who became the new mayor of Shanghai, and Deng Xiaoping—installed themselves anonymously in a hotel in the former French quarter. For some of them it was a return to streets they had not known for twenty years or more.

Avoiding Spiritual Pollution—CCP Instructions on Film Work

On the censorship of movie scripts: Since our movie industry is still in its infancy, our policy should not be too restricted, [because] this will hamper the development of the industry, which in turn will help the old and harmful movies to gain access to the film market. The political censorship of movies should allow films to be made, as long as they are anti-imperialist, anti-feudalist, and against bureaucratic rule, and not anti-Soviet, anti-Communist, or against people's democracy. In terms of movies not openly political, they should be allowed if they are not harmful in propaganda, and at the same time provide some artistic value. . . . But we should also organize correct criticism and organize the directors and actors/actresses to study some basic knowledge of Marxism and bring home to them our party's policy, in order to help them to avoid making political mistakes. Film propaganda in a class society is a means of class struggle, nothing else. . . . We must establish an institution for the censorship of movie scripts. . . . [But] as long as a manuscript has got our permission, [the movie] should be allowed to be produced.

Central Committee instructions, 26 Oct. 1948, *Zhonggong zhongyang wenjian xuanji* vol. 17, pp. 421–23.

Zhou Enlai, alone among the top party leaders, visited the city briefly after it was taken over. During the day he met secretly with local political and business leaders; at night, with a small group of bodyguards, he toured the alleys of Shanghai in which he had risked his life for the cause as a young man.[74]

To the CCP leadership, the takeover of Shanghai was a symbol of their victory. But for some of them it also implied a warning. The party would have to be able to govern the cities properly, while not letting its cadres become contaminated by the ideological and cultural pollution of the urban areas. Message after message from the Center to the small teams that entered the cities warned against enemy agents, imperialist influence, and corruption. They warned that even the people who most welcomed them—student leaders and "democratic" politicians—could be the enemy in disguise. In secret messages to leading cadres in the army, the Center ordered them to keep watch on the representatives of the Communist underground in the cities. They should not be fully trusted before proper investigations had been carried out.

The Communists were surprised that the supply situation in the cities almost solved itself after their takeover. With peace—or at least some form of stability—merchants and peasants alike started putting their goods on the market, and the threat of starvation, which some CCP cadres had talked about, especially for Shanghai, never materialized. The new government did almost immediately introduce forms of rationing and laws against hoarding and speculation, which helped alleviate the situation for the very poor, but more important in the short run was probably the combination of at least limited trust in the new currency and strict physical measures against black marketeers. In Shanghai, for instance, a number of those who had gambled on continuing their trade under CCP rule were proven wrong: They were hauled before "People's Courts" and shot.[75]

In spite of their early successes in the cities, Mao and Liu Shaoqi felt that Soviet assistance was vital in order to get the economy under control. One matter was the loan that Mao hoped to get from Stalin. But he also thought that Soviet advice was needed on how to structure the economy, particularly in the cities. In his letter to Stalin in early May, the Chairman stressed that the CCP did not count on direct Soviet participation in the remaining parts of the civil war. But, Mao said, "in terms of the economy, we need your help. Without economic construction, we cannot realize the revolution. . . . Therefore, please satisfy these requests and send us more Soviet experts to work with."[76]

Mao's fear of foreign intervention also peaked in late May, right after the takeover of Shanghai. In part because of Soviet information, and in part because of CCP intelligence saying that the Americans were reinforcing their naval base at Qingdao, the Chairman thought that the imperialists could attempt to use remaining GMD forces for a counteroffensive through Shandong, using their naval presence to strike behind CCP lines in North China. In spite of the CCP itself having given them no reason to stay, Mao also thought that plans he had become aware of for the evacuation of U.S. and British diplomats from Nanjing fit those suspicions. But in early June, as the U.S. Navy moved out of Qingdao without a fight, his fears abated. He reported to Liu Shaoqi, who was preparing to visit Moscow, that the chances for an open imperialist intervention were now diminishing.[77]

In order to prevent foreign subversion of the party's revolutionary achievements, the CCP Politburo in its report to the Central Committee meeting in March 1949 stressed that foreign diplomats should not under any circumstance receive any form of "legal status" in the CCP-controlled cities. At the meeting—only the second plenum to take place since the last party congress in 1945—Mao also circulated detailed instructions on foreign trade in the new areas that the party controlled. "The basic policy of our foreign trade is: All forms of goods needed by the Soviet Union as well as the new democratic countries in Eastern Europe, we should try our best to export to them; and all those that we can get from them, we should import from them. Only goods that are not needed by them or we cannot get from them, should be exported or imported to and from capitalist countries."[78] The Politburo still stressed, however, that for the time being, local trade administrations could, with the acceptance of the local or regional party bureau, open trade with any foreign company or even companies in GMD-held areas, "as long as this trade is beneficial for us."

In the weeks after the takeover of Shanghai, Mao stressed the need for the PLA to complete the surrounding of the GMD in South China by intensifying its offensive in the Northwest. While the main PLA forces had crossed the Yangzi and conquered Shanghai, Peng Dehuai's soldiers had besieged and captured Taiyuan, the capital of Shanxi province. But it had been a costly victory. The Communist troops, under the command of Xu Xiangqian, had to fight for almost a week to reach the city walls from their trenches, in spite of their total superiority in artillery. It is difficult to estimate PLA losses, but they must have been considerable, and certainly hindered further offensives toward the West. For the PLA, their losses, the destruction wreaked by the fighting, and the determination shown against them by local leaders was a foretaste of the difficulties they were to face in the remainder of their new "long march" toward the West. But for Mao this offensive was essential. As he told his colleagues, capturing the provinces in the West that could be tempted to set up independent regimes was more important to the national unity of China than anything else.[79]

Peng warned Mao that a further offensive could be premature, given that Hu Zongnan's forces in Shaanxi were still more or less intact. But Mao ordered him on. Hu evacuated Xian on 17 May, but he reassembled his forces around Baoji and in the Qinling Mountains to the south. They were joined by five corps—three of them cavalry forces—from the Muslim General Ma Bufang's troops in Gansu province. When Peng's soldiers were marching toward western Shaanxi in early June, they were ambushed, and the retreat that followed could have been catastrophic had not Peng managed to make a stand just to the west of Xian. The PLA lost at least fifteen thousand men. It took another month, and substantial Communist reinforcements, for Peng's troops to recapture lost territory and capture Baoji. Ma's forces retreated, undefeated, back into Gansu, while Hu Zongnan, not trusting his Muslim "allies," retreated toward the south, toward Sichuan province.[80]

In spite of the slow PLA progress in the Northwest, by early summer 1949 the main military confrontations of the civil war were over. Mao's prediction that, if there was no foreign intervention, the CCP would be able to take over the whole country within a year seemed reasonably accurate. On Taiwan, Jiang Jieshi had already in practice established his regime, determined to prevent a CCP takeover. On that island he would make his last stand. The Communists did not expect a quick takeover of Taiwan; Mao believed that he would not be able to attack before July 1950 or thereabouts. The CCP needed a navy and an air force if they were to be certain of success when crossing the Taiwan Straits. Mao also feared an outright U.S. takeover of the island if there was much fighting on and around Taiwan before a PLA victory. An offensive against Taiwan would have to be decisive, as the mainland offensives had been, if it were not to give the imperialists any possibility of intervening. The setting up of a new state, with a formal alliance with the Soviet Union, would make the Communist conquest of China's outlying regions a safer bet, Mao thought.[81]

8

TO TIAN'ANMEN

Constructing New China

"Turning-over Dance"

During the night of 23 March 1949, a small group of men set out from Xibaipo, the village in northern Hebei that had housed the core of the CCP Politburo since late 1947. It was Mao Zedong and his companions Liu Shaoqi, Zhou Enlai, Zhu De, Ren Bishi, and Politburo member Lin Boqu, guarded by a unit from the PLA protection service. The Chairman was leaving for Beijing to set up a new Chinese state. Mao was visibly nervous. He joked that their trip was like going to the capital to sit for the imperial examinations. At Tang county, Ren's jeep broke down, and the party had to spend the night. A special train was waiting for them at Zhuoxian, from which they left at 2:00 A.M. on the 25th under tight security. Mao's group got into Qinghua station just south of the Summer Palace before dawn. They were met by Lin Biao, Nie Rongzhen, Peng Zhen, and the head of CCP security, Li Kenong. Mao drove to the Summer Palace in a bullet-proof Dodge limousine made in Detroit for Jiang Jieshi's personal use in the 1930s. At the Summer Palace, Mao had lunch with the PLA commanders in Beijing. Afterward he reviewed troops at Xiyuan Airport from atop a U.S. jeep. Five hundred shells were fired—the only celebration. In the evening Mao entertained some of the non-Communist political leaders who had come to Beijing. But at midnight he left as stealthily as he had arrived, moving in at a former government guesthouse in the Xiang hills, well outside the city.[1]

The Communists had decided to make Beijing their capital well before their final offensives began. We do not know precisely why—some party leaders argue that they wanted to make a clean break with the Nationalist past and its capital at Nanjing; others emphasize Beijing's being recognized by most Chinese as the capital of the country, since it had served that role for five hundred years under the Ming and Qing dynasties. Mao told the Soviets that it was because of its northern location, and therefore its relative proximity to the Soviet Union. Zhou Enlai pointed out to (presumably disappointed) southern cadres that it was for security reasons: If an imperialist intervention did come, it would come in the South. It was therefore important to locate the capital in the northern part of the country.[2]

But there was another reason, perhaps more meaningful than any of these. Beijing was the only city—except Changsha in his native Hunan—that Mao Zedong knew. For someone famously distrustful of cities, Beijing was the least bad choice for a capital. It formed a natural center for the old PLA base areas in the countryside, where most of the party's core support still was. The task that now awaited the CCP leadership was to transform a rural-based and strongly militarized party into a vanguard in building a socialist state and a socialist economy. In this task the cities would necessarily play key roles. But although the party had prepared for years for taking over cities, very few cadres had any firm idea about how the urban proletariat that they now ruled could be employed in creating socialism, the way Marx and Lenin had foretold. As for Mao, he enjoyed Xiangshan—"Fragrant Hills"—during his stay there. At least, he joked, it was better than places like Little River (Xiaohe) and Yang Family Ditch (Yangjiagou), where he had spent time after the flight from Yan'an only two years before. Mao waited another seven months before moving in at Zhongnanhai, the new leadership compound in Beijing, symbolically located next to the old Forbidden City.

Forming a Government

Mao was at the center of the new state that the Chinese Communists were about to construct. During the civil war, and because of his role as a military leader, he had become identical to the party, not just in the eyes of the rural population—whom cadres in the past had poked fun at for calling the CCP "Mao's party"—but also for many in the party's core membership. The victory had proven Mao right, and even those of his colleagues who had resented his reductionist politics, his quick changes of heart, or his peasant manners now saw him as the personification of the party's success. His likeness was everywhere in the CCP-held territories, and the general reverence in which he was held—as a peasants' substitute for the "good emperor"—contributed significantly to the institution of party rule in the coastal provinces and south of the Yangzi. The resolutions that the Central Committee passed in March prohibiting the celebration of leaders' birthdays were only weak attempts at paying lip service to party norms. In the villages, party cadres were more than willing to encourage the Mao-cult as part of their pattern of control.

But while the posters of the Chairman accompanied the party into the cities, Mao's day-to-day interventions in policy-making fell in number as party concerns began switching from military dispositions to forms of civilian rule. There were many reasons for this. Mao's health was not good; he suffered from a low-grade form of malaria (which was as yet undiagnosed) and severe attacks of bronchitis. His physical well-being was not helped by his doctors, who provided him with sodium amytal—a strong barbiturate—to help him relax.[3] But more important was his exhaustion—for more than ten years Mao had been directing the military struggle, and the last phase of the civil war had been the toughest of them all. Although he remained in overall control, Mao by mid-1949 intervened less in day-to-day political and economic questions than he had up to the start of the Northwestern campaign.

The triumvirate that would be in regular control of the planning of the new state were Liu Shaoqi, Ren Bishi, and Zhou Enlai. At times during the civil war, Mao had criticized each of them for lack of revolutionary "vigor" and political consciousness, but he still regarded them as the ones within the party leadership who best understood the challenges the party faced in the "new" areas. Of the three, Liu was without doubt the most influential, and much of the work in setting up the political and economic institutions of the new regime was done under his leadership. Ren Bishi, the Moscow-educated Chief Secretary of the party organization, introduced a number of key ideas concerning political structures in both rural and urban areas, usually influenced by Soviet practices. In terms of actual position within the party, Ren's stature was in ascendance, although he remained number five in the formal party hierarchy. Zhou Enlai, different from the other two, had clearly defined tasks within his brief. His areas were "united front" issues—relations with nonparty leaders, propaganda, and intelligence—and foreign affairs. His position as Premier-designate reflected those briefs. The government was to deal with the "external," the party with the "internal."

A key problem for the CCP in mid-1949 was economic planning for the period immediately before and immediately after the new state was set up. The big problem was that the Communists had no idea what to expect: What happened when a bourgeois state formation like the Guomindang collapsed, and the Communists controlled the government? Would the capitalists sabotage the new regime by simply ending their economic activities? The Center had had a working group headed by Ren Bishi report on Marxist theory on the matter since mid-1948, but no unified views had emerged. The triumvirate of Ren, Liu, and Zhou tended to think that the capitalists could be goaded into continuing to operate their plants and businesses for the time being (even though by doing so they objectively would be preparing their own destruction by helping the CCP state). Both the Soviet experience and the CCP's own lessons from Manchuria pointed in this direction, Ren thought.[4] The goal of Communist cadres was therefore to convince the capitalists that they would be well treated by the new government. All key cadre units had set up groups to handle "United Front" work with urban industrialists before the takeover of the cities, although few went as far as the Tianjin group, which sent New Year's cards to the city's entrepreneurs, wishing them long life and prosperous business. "If we should take the city in this new year," they declared, "do not be alarmed. We shall restore order quickly and welcome your business."[5]

But not all CCP leaders were that optimistic. Some of the local leaders in Shanghai and Nanjing, in their reports to the Center, pointed to widespread sabotage carried out against factories after the Communist takeover. In Shanghai alone more than three hundred such incidents were said to have occurred during June 1949, and, as a result, fully functional plants had to be closed down. In addition, during June the GMD began bombing the coastal cities, as well as Nanjing and Beijing, from air bases on Taiwan. The bombing raids, although never heavy enough to threaten key functions in the cities, caused fear and uncertainty among the population, and held back some of the vital economic rebuilding. The attempted GMD naval blockade of Shanghai and other ports on the Southern coast served the same objectives, and worried the CCP leaders in ways probably quite out of proportion to its economic impact. Their big fear, however, was that the imperialist powers would join the blockade, and thereby threaten both security and commerce on the South China coast.[6]

The economic problems that already existed, the GMD raids and blockade, and the uncertainties about the immediate future made central CCP cadres promise few immediate social improvements. In March, and again in June, Liu Shaoqi instructed the regional bureaus of the Central Committee to await further orders before committing the party to any major reforms. The caution shown by the Center made many local cadres unhappy and uncertain about the aims of party rule. It also almost certainly lost the party support, both in the cities and in the countryside. But for Liu and his core of experts, prudence in economic and financial matters was essential if the revolution were to survive. In their estimate, the Chinese economy would not even begin to grow until two to three years after the civil war had ended. In the meantime the new Communist government would be extremely vulnerable to domestic counter-revolution and imperialist attack.[7]

The economic uncertainties made support from the Soviet Union and the other "new democratic" countries of Europe essential. In his talks with Mikoyan and in his messages to Stalin in the spring of 1949, Mao made financial assistance one of the centerpieces of the alliance with the Soviet Union that he proposed, and a main point on the agenda for his forthcoming visit to Moscow. In a telegram to Stalin in early May, Mao pointed to the two main tasks of the party in the year to come—economic and military achievements: "With our own experience and power, we ourselves can completely eliminate all our enemies here. But in the economy, we need your help. Without economic construction, we cannot realize the revolution." Mao asked for big loans from the Soviet Union, for Soviet machines and equipment, and—perhaps most important of all—sizable contingents of Soviet experts in areas ranging from education to irrigation to long-range artillery.[8]

As Mao well knew, it was not just a lack of money that would cause problems for the CCP in governing China. The lack of trained personnel to administer and develop the country was perhaps an even greater challenge. As shown, by as early as 1948 Liu Shaoqi had gotten the Politburo's acceptance for using personnel from the old regime as interim administrators if they were not sullied by "crimes against the people." But in some areas, even the combination of old cadres, "new" cadres (people who had joined after the CCP's military victories), and "retained personnel" was not enough to provide essential services—not to mention undertaking reform. In other areas, the percentage of "retained" was so high that the idea of CCP rule was just a thin veneer over a GMD administration. In such areas, Zhou Enlai pointed out, there were often only two groups of former officials—those who had been executed, and those who remained in their posts.[9]

The solution that the party saw to these dilemmas—besides inviting in Soviet experts—was to recruit as many as possible of the Chinese liberal intelligentsia, inside and outside China, to replace Guomindang holdovers, and to serve the party's purposes while gradually being converted to the Communist cause. In many ways, the whole buildup of the new government structure, as it was envisaged in the spring and summer of 1949, was intended to enable temporary alliances with "liberals" while retaining full Communist control. As the United Front Bureau of the CCP in early summer arranged a Preparatory Commission meeting for what was to be another People's Political Consultative Conference (PCC), Zhou instructed them to be vigilant and to make sure that the GMD did not sabotage the meeting by getting its "agents" invited. But he also made sure that on paper the composition of the Preparatory Committee represented as broad a "front" as the CCP could possibly put together. The image of the new regime had to be conducive to the inclusion of "bourgeois liberals" among its servants.[10]

While there is little doubt that the idea of a coalition government reflected the theoretical definition that the CCP leadership had of the current stage of the Chinese revolution—the "national-democracy"—it is also clear that all through the preparations for setting up a government, the top Communist leadership remained concerned with issues of security and control. At times, there was considerable tension between the two concerns. Against the theoretical arguments of Liu, Ren Bishi and others, backed by a steady stream of Soviet input, stood the sense of some military cadres that "counter-revolutionaries should not be let within a mile's sight of the People's Government." Zhou Enlai—as often before and later—was the bridge-builder, with his pragmatic arguments about the revolution's needing the services of bourgeois intellectuals—for the time being.[11]

All through the coalition government talks in the spring of 1949, the Communists went out of their way to get at least a formal acceptance for the formation of the new regime from nonparty leaders. Although most were enough impressed by the CCP's military victories to reformulate their thinking and support the Communist initiative, some proved remarkably stubborn. Even in Beijing, where the peaceful conquest had given the party so much goodwill, it was not always easy to convince the democrats—professors and teachers, writers, journalists—to join up with the new government. Although most of the members of the Preparatory Commission were in place in Beijing by late April, it took almost two months before the first meetings were held, mostly because the CCP needed time to convince prominent nonparty leaders to participate.[12]

The inaugural session of the Preparatory Commission of the PCC, which began on 15 June, was attended by 134 representatives from twenty-two organizations and groups, plus the Communist Party. Most, but not all, of these groups were under de facto CCP control. Most unruly were the representatives of ethnic minorities and religious groups, who on several occasions demanded freedoms that the Communists were not prepared to give, not even in theory. Communist hegemony, however, was safe. The representatives of the Guomindang Revolutionary Committee and the Democratic League had no intention of playing an independent role, and the delegates from the peasant associations, the New Democratic Youth League—which had been formed in April on the pattern of the East European youth organizations—the workers' committees, and the women's movement were under firm party control. The Commission, which met for almost a week, passed the "Organic Rules of the Preparatory Commission"—a form of rudimentary constitution—and elected Mao Zedong Chairman of its Standing Committee, with Zhou Enlai, Li Jishen, Shen Junru, Guo Moruo, and Chen Shutong as vice chairmen.[13]

The setting up of a formal system of government took the CCP much longer than most people inside or outside the party expected. Many observers had thought that the Communists would organize their own national government shortly after their decisive win in the HuaiHai campaign. The reasons why Mao and the Politburo waited until the autumn of 1949 were in part ideological and in part practical. The Communist leaders wanted to get the structures of the new state right according to Marxist theory and Soviet experience—and they needed time to work that out. They also wanted to have Stalin's personal assurances about the correctness of their thinking. On the other hand, a large number of prominent nonparty leaders had to be convinced to take part in the formation of the People's Republic. That also took the Communists longer than they had expected, not least since some of the liberals persisted with ideas that only with difficulty could be molded to fit a Marxist framework.

A People's Republic

A main key to unlocking the gates of the new state was to be found in Moscow. In April 1949, Mao had again proposed to Stalin that the two meet soon, so that the CCP could receive instructions from the Soviet Politburo on how to set up a People's Republic. Finding little enthusiasm for the proposal in Moscow, and probably also themselves realizing that the Chairman's leaving China during the key battles for the South was not such a good idea, the CCP leadership in May decided instead to send the party's number two man, Liu Shaoqi, for meetings with the Soviets. Liu's purpose was to get advice on the construction of the new state, to secure Soviet promises of practical and political support, and to discuss long-term cooperation between the two revolutionary regimes.[14]

The CCP leaders knew that Liu's mission to Moscow was the most important and difficult undertaking ever for their diplomacy. Although the Soviet Union and its policies remained the main sources of inspiration for the Chinese Communists, their practical dealings with Moscow since

1945 had left them uncertain of what to expect from Stalin as their new state was being set up. For Mao it was essential that the Soviet leader give his blessing to the product of the CCP victory—the Chinese people's democratic dictatorship, as the Chairman, in Lenin's terms, called the new Beijing regime. For Mao, as for any midcentury Communist leader, recognition by the Kremlin was part of the essence of political victory. But Mao also knew that Stalin's reaction during the forthcoming meetings with Liu depended to a high degree on the political signals the Chinese sent out before the meeting. That is why Mao, in spite of Moscow's repeated warnings not to publicize the links between the Soviet Union and the CCP's policies, prepared a statement for release during Liu's visit, in which the Chairman for the first time openly described New China's foreign policy as leaning to one side—that of the Soviets.[15]

Liu Shaoqi's delegation—with the head of the Manchurian party, Gao Gang, and ambassador-designate Wang Jiaxiang as the other main members—arrived in Moscow in secret on 26 June. On the day of their arrival, the Chinese were taken to a welcoming banquet at Stalin's dacha, Kuntsevo, where the Soviet leader congratulated them on their victory in the civil war. The following evening, Stalin received the delegation for talks in his Kremlin offices. At the beginning of their conversations, the Soviets informed Liu that they agreed to give the CCP, through the already established Manchurian "People's Government," a loan of $300 million over five years, and that Soviet experts could be sent to China at the request of the CCP. Stalin also promised full Soviet support for the PLA in Xinjiang, and encouraged the Chinese Communists to take control of the province as soon as possible. At the end of the conversation, the Soviet leader noted the difficulties the PLA had faced because it had no navy, and pledged Moscow's support in building and supplying ships, training sailors, and delivering naval artillery. Stalin also baffled the Chinese by agreeing to deliver fighter aircraft to New China and to train Chinese pilots. While leaving, the Chinese were told that the Soviets had agreed to make their visit official, in the form of a Manchurian trade delegation, so that Liu's wish to study the ways in which Soviet state organs function could be more easily accomplished.[16]

Liu Shaoqi, who had known little about what to expect in Moscow, was understandably elated by the reception his delegation received. In his first telegrams to Mao Zedong, Liu underlined the need to get the practical cooperation started immediately, and that his delegation, for that reason, would stay longer in Moscow than originally intended. Mao, on his side, told Liu to explore the conditions for an alliance treaty for the new Chinese state in light of what Stalin had said. He also instructed Liu to make use of his stay in Moscow to present to Stalin and his Politburo a comprehensive overview of CCP policies, and to get the Soviet leadership's sanction for the correctness of Mao's political thinking. In the CCP report, presented to Stalin on 4 July, Liu outlined the Chinese leadership's views on the current stage of the Chinese revolution, its plans for setting up a government, the foreign policy of the new state, and how it saw its relationship to the Soviet Union.[17]

In the report, Liu underlined that the outcome of the civil war had been decided, and that the PLA expected to take over Xinjiang and Taiwan in 1950. The new Political Consultative Conference, which was about to assemble, would be completely under CCP control, and the form of the new state would be a "people's democratic dictatorship" under the guidance of the proletariat. In terms of foreign policy issues, Liu wrote, the imperialists "are trying in every possible way to show that they seek rapprochement with the CCP and, simultaneously, are striving to lure the CCP onto the path of rapprochement with the imperialist states."[18] The possibility of an imperialist intervention against China had been reduced, but it was still present. The CCP expected Soviet and East European recognition right after the proclamation of a People's Republic, but it would prefer to "wait and not hurry" in getting recognition from the imperialists, "purging our domestic front to avoid trouble" first. On the Sino-Soviet Treaty, Liu asked the Soviets to choose between keeping the 1945 treaty, concluding a new treaty after the setup of the PRC, or waiting and negotiating a new treaty later.

Liu Shaoqi's meetings in Moscow, where he stayed until 14 August, marked a watershed in Sino-Soviet relations. Stalin appreciated Liu as a Marxist and as someone who had studied Soviet policies and experiences. The Kremlin boss had realized, well before Liu's arrival, that it was time to deal with the Chinese Communists as a substantial element in the world Communist movement, and that he had to show support for their new state, even if he continued to doubt their ability to advance toward socialism. In several conversations in the spring of 1949, Stalin had emphasized that he viewed the CCP as allied to the more progressive elements of the Chinese bourgeoisie, and that its "national-democratic" revolution was just that (and only that): *national*—against imperialist domination, and *democratic*—against feudal oppression. But in terms of the international class struggle, and the security of the Soviet state, the

---

Liu Shaoqi's Report to Stalin, 4 July 1949

Having for a long time stayed in the countryside waging guerrilla war, we, therefore, have a poor knowledge of external affairs. Today we are to govern such a large state, steer economic construction, and carry on diplomatic activity. We yet have a good deal to learn. Of great significance in this respect are instructions and assistance to us from the Soviet Communist Party. We stand in bad need of these instructions and of this assistance. Besides the sending of Soviet experts to China for assistance to us, we would like to have Soviet teachers sent to China for lecturing and to have delegations sent from China to the USSR for first hand acquaintance and learning. Besides, we would like to send students for a course of education in the USSR. *Yes*

On the question of relations between the Soviet Communist Party and the CCP Comrade Mao Zedong and the CCP Central Committee maintain the following:

> The Soviet Communist Party is the main headquarters of the international Communist movement, while the Communist Party of China is only a single-front headquarters. The interests of a part should be subordinated to international interests and, therefore, the CCP submits to decisions of the Soviet Communist Party, though the Comintern is no longer in existence and the CCP is not within the Information Bureau of European Communist Parties. *No!* If on some questions differences should arise between the CCP and the Soviet Communist Party, the CCP, having outlined its point of view, will submit and will resolutely carry out decisions of the Soviet Communist Party. *No!* We believe it is necessary to establish the closest mutual ties between the two parties, exchange appropriate authorized political representation so as to decide questions of interest to our two parties and, besides, achieve better mutual understanding between our parties. *Yes!*

Excerpt. The inserted comments in italics are Stalin's handwritten remarks on the original report. Liu to Stalin, 4 July 1949, in Odd Arne Westad, ed., *Brothers in Arms: The Rise and Fall of the Sino-Soviet Alliance, 1945–1963* (Washington, DC, and Stanford, CA: Woodrow Wilson Center Press and Stanford University Press, 1998).

---

bourgeois character of the Chinese revolution did not make it less important from Moscow's point of view.[19]

Liu Shaoqi returned to Beijing on 29 August, leaving behind an embryonic embassy that would later be headed by Wang Jiaxiang—a top Chinese Communist who had studied in Moscow in the 1920s and who had, after some wavering, joined Mao's policy line in the late 1930s. Returning to Beijing with Liu went 220 Soviet chief advisers headed by Ivan Kovalev, a party organization expert and former railway vice minister who had assisted Gao Gang and Lin Biao in Manchuria in 1948 and who had served as the Soviet Communist Party's representative to the CCP since early 1949. The Soviet advisers had been selected by Stalin's secretariat to assist the Chinese in all aspects of setting up the new state—central administration, finance, economic policies, transportation, education, law, policing, minority questions, and cultural institutions. In the month leading up to the declaration of the People's Republic—and even more so in the months that followed—Soviet experts came to play key roles in determining how the new state should look, and what its policies should be. In the Finance and Foreign ministries, for instance, the Soviets introduced procedures for information, decision-making, and control that went much beyond the systems that the CCP had developed in the base areas. Needless to say, the men from Moscow also influenced the political decisions themselves to a considerable degree. In the military, which received a new influx of Red Army advisers through Manchuria, the foreign officers contributed much on the use of heavy artillery, air defense, and amphibious operations, although their triumphant PLA counterparts did not always take the advice given.[20]

During Liu's long visit to the Soviet Union, it was other CCP leaders—most notably the two administrative experts from the CCP base areas in the Northeast and North China, Chen Yun and Bo Yibo—who were in charge of the day-to-day planning of the new Chinese state. Zhou Enlai's group dealt with United Front and diplomatic affairs, and, as Premier-designate, Zhou had the overall responsibility for preparing the new government. The deadlines for getting the administration in order put considerable pressure on the CCP leadership, which in itself was not immune to clashes over influence and jurisdiction. In particular, there were tensions between cadres who had served in Manchuria with Gao Gang and Lin Biao, and leaders from Liu Shaoqi's North China center. Personal relations between Liu and Gao had been poor in the past, and they were not improved by Gao's unwillingness to submit to Liu's authority during their Moscow visit. But in spite of Gao's continued primacy in the Northeast after their return, it was people with long associations with Liu Shaoqi who came to form the core of the new government, and, in terms of influence, it was probably Zhou Enlai's position that changed the most—from Mao Zedong's all-round assistant to Premier of the new republic, a position that could give Zhou real power in his own right.[21]

Although the CCP leadership had in reality been executing state power for years within their base areas, the Communist cadres soon found that managing China from Beijing was quite another matter than leading a regional government. Having decided to build their central state administration from scratch, rather than through employing officials from the former regime, the cadres often found that they had little or nothing to go on when setting up their ministries and departments—no records, no contacts, no hands-on experts. The Communists saw themselves as starting—as one of them put it—to rebuild a wasteland. What gave them confidence was faith in their political theories. But even for Chinese Marxists, it often turned out that political theory did not provide much guidance for administrative purposes.

In the months immediately before and after the declaration of the PRC, it was security in the newly conquered regions of Central and Southern China that particularly troubled the CCP leadership. With a lack of cadres to move in and take political control, the party relied on the PLA to keep order and prevent counter-revolutionary uprisings. But both Mao Zedong and Liu Shaoqi felt that this form of military rule was unsatisfactory, and that it might even be dangerous, if the imperialists and reactionaries realized the political weakness of the Communists, especially in the South. For Mao this was the "crisis of victory" that he had talked about in the past, and both to him and to his main assistants the only way of overcoming it was through speeding up the processes of state-building.[22]

In terms of actual CCP power in China and the construction of its state apparatus, 1 October 1949 may seem just an ordinary point on a timeline, a day that was arbitrarily chosen to represent the construction of the People's Republic of China. But for millions of Chinese who had supported the anti-Guomindang cause, the day was symbolic for their victory. Mao had of course thought about symbols when choosing the date—the first day of the month of the Russian October Revolution and the 1911 Wuhan uprising against the Qing. The proximity to these seminal dates gave the day of the declaration of the People's Republic a symbolic quality that the Communists hoped would resonate not only in China but also in the world at large.

For most Communist cadres in Beijing, the weeks preceding 1 October were a period of nervous anticipation. With civil war still raging in the South, and with numerous attacks by GMD military aircraft against targets in North China every week, security was foremost on their minds. Military street patrols were almost doubled, and the number of covert operations against suspected enemies of the new regime was stepped up. The obvious and very visible enthusiasm for the CCP government of most people in the capital-to-be was not enough to calm the apprehension of the cadres at the thought of counter-revolutionary manifestations or even attempts to assassinate their leaders. The security details guarding the leaders were horrified at the idea of their appearing at the Tianan'men— the Gate of Heavenly Peace—"in full view of everyone in Beijing," as one of them put it. Even Mao himself seems to have had some last-minute doubts about the location. But in the end, as often in CCP history, the emblematic defeated the circumspect.[23]

On a cold, windy, autumn day in Beijing, 1 October 1949, Mao Zedong in a high-pitched voice declared a People's Republic of China from atop the Gate of Heavenly Peace.[24] Tens of thousands had converged on the then rather narrow square in front of the gate in order to watch the ceremony. While only official representatives of factories, schools, and organizations were let into the square itself, the parades in the streets, the dancing, and the singing left little doubt that this was a day of celebration for the people of Beijing. Himself unwell and feverish on the great day, the Chairman's own thoughts may have been with the road that had led him to Tian'anmen, through many defeats and many victories. The poet Hu Feng wrote in celebration:

> My comrades at arms,
> My brothers,
> I have seen you
> Dying in a dank and stench-filled prison,
> Starving and freezing in a deserted village.
> You—you and the peasants—have fed lice with your
>   flesh,
> Have drunk bloody water on the battlefield with your
>   friends.
> You have endured repeated hammerings, repeated trials.
> You have conquered pain and death.
> During these
> Many, many years,
> Your hope stayed alive
> And your will stayed alive.
> And today,
> At this very moment that stirs you,
> Forget all the past,
> Except that the past,
> Has purified you, like a newborn child
> Lying in a warm cradle
> His untainted heart overflowing with the blessing of
>   new life.[25]

At the Top of Tian'anmen, 1 October 1949

I was carried away by indescribable emotion. Gazing down, I saw the figures of so many gallant women among the hundreds of thousands of workers, peasants, and soldiers filling the wide square before the Gate of Heavenly Peace. Joyfully, with thumping hearts, they stood before Chairman Mao's inspection. Was this not truly the symbol of the Chinese people and her women having risen up? Did not the wave of red flags, like the sea, and the fireworks that burned in the night sky symbolize new China's brilliant future?

Ono Kazuko, *Chinese Women in a Century of Revolution, 1850–1950*, ed. Joshua A. Fogel (Stanford, CA: Stanford University Press, 1989), p. 176.

The convergence on Tian'anmen in the context of China's past was a key point in the celebrations. From far back in imperial times, it was here, in front of the palaces of the Forbidden City, that people had gathered to protest against the injustices of the state. It was in front of Tian'anmen that students had met on 4 May 1919 to protest imperialist aggression and demand democratic freedoms and social reform, setting off a political movement that gave birth both to the CCP and to the renewal of the Guomindang. Later, groups of the disadvantaged in Chinese society—women, day-laborers, refugees, servants—had met here to attempt their own forms of protest. For many representatives of these groups, it seemed as if 1949 meant that their protests had finally been heard.[26]

Reforming China

While the new CCP regime was slowly finding its way toward the general policies that it wanted to apply to all areas under its control, the practical implementation of these policies had yet to be worked out. In doing so, Communist cadres were caught between the visions of their ideology and the limitations that circumstances and party tactics imposed upon them. Like all successful revolutionary parties, the Chinese Communists found it difficult to transform the country they now controlled in the direction they wanted—at least, difficult in comparison to the relative ease with which they had smashed their way through the final resistance of the old regime. In the cities especially, the Communists found it hard to abolish all the vestiges of "Old China" upon which so much of their hatred of their country's past had been founded. And in addition, being the government meant that the CCP now had to be seen to satisfy the demands of the classes they purported to represent—the peasantry and the working class—while keeping control of both the economy and politics.

The working class in the newly conquered cities represented a particular problem for the CCP. Since there were very few cadres who had any experience with labor organizing, real control of the factories in the period immediately following the Communist takeovers was often held by labor activists from the shop floor. These activists' sympathies were as likely to lie with province or village associations, or with different forms of secret societies, as with the Communist Party. Often, their demands for control of the production process, for benefits, and for wage increases were far ahead of what Communist cadres had been instructed to demand. In the street committees, formed by the Communists in working-class neighborhoods as a kind of parallel to the poor peasant committees in the villages, radicalization was often intense during the first months of CCP rule. The leaders of such committees—be they Communists or not—encouraged poor people to demand immediate social justice, and workers to fight for their interests.[27]

This worker activism—and the fact that much of it was channeled through groups that the party did not recognize—presented a major problem for the Communists. In several reports from mid-1949, the party Center complained that the cadres who were in charge in the cities simply did not understand "urban work," and that they failed to take the needs of the revolution in the whole country into account. Instead of being an asset to the revolution, the cities had become a problem, the Center said—for instance, through cadres' requests to keep more revenue, and their failure to increase production and bring the cost of living under control. At the heart of these mistakes was the cadres' inexperience in organizing and running trade unions, turning the workers' demands into advantages to the party rather than disadvantages.[28]

In the summer and fall of 1949 the party Center sent inspection teams to all the cities to set urban work right. The tone was set by Liu Shaoqi's visit to Tianjin in the spring, during which he berated the local party cadres for getting most of their tasks wrong. Their leftism, Liu told them, was retarding economic recovery and therefore hindering a core party aim. It was wrong, at this stage of the revolution, to mobilize the poor and the working class for action against their class enemies without keeping in mind how such action would affect production. The party should concentrate more on winning over intellectuals and the middle class, and create alliances in factories and schools that would increase party control.

The street committees should be abolished. All factories should hold criticism meetings—not to decide who was politically "correct," but who was a good and productive worker. When Tianjin's most influential businessmen were rounded up and brought in to see the CCP second-in-command, Liu surprised them by promising limited growth in the public sector, no arbitrary limits to profits, and that disputes over wages and working conditions would be "handled" by the party. The baffled Tianjin entrepreneurs wondered whether Liu, who in 1948 had married Wang Guangmei, a woman from a prominent local business family, were after all "one of them."[29]

Liu Shaoqi's political instructions to local party leaders in 1949 centered on control. He defined as a counter-revolutionary anyone who was irrevocably opposed to a major CCP policy and who therefore could be a focus of future resistance. Although imperialist and Guomindang spies, saboteurs, and wreckers figured prominently on the list of enemies, the party's real concern was with organizations that had deep local roots, such as secret societies, religious congregations, hometown associations, or clan hierarchies. The CCP's initial strategy in those cases was to divide the top leadership from ordinary members and break the unwanted organizations up from the inside. To achieve their aims, the Communists often used secret denunciations and selective violence, although the number of executions was quite low, at least at the outset. In general this strategy was quite successful against the bigger organizations, such as the Green Gang and other large semicriminal networks, whose leaders had long experience in feigning adherence to whoever was in power. It was much more difficult to persuade or terrorize smaller local organizations into oblivion, as in the case of Yi Guan Dao, a millenarian Daoist group, in the coastal provinces, or Christian assemblies in the interior.[30]

As in the decades to come, the CCP in 1949 was particularly concerned with independent organizations among workers. The battles to organize the urban proletariat in CCP-controlled trade unions raged well into 1950. In some cases workers were caught between traditional union bosses, often officials in secret societies, who threatened them with death if they "defected," and Communist trade union organizers who recruited in the factories under the protection of policemen from the Public Security Bureau. Elsewhere, the Communists had to confront workers' organizations that had sprung up independently in the wake of the PLA's arrival and that did not wish to conform to party control or party policies. Through propaganda, education, and strong-arm methods, the party did eventually succeed in organizing the proletariat—in Tianjin, for instance, 75 percent was organized by the end of 1949. But problems persisted, not least because many of the former labor bosses, clan chiefs, or local leaders also joined the new unions, and soon emerged as elected officials, applying for party membership.[31]

The economic and financial problems in the newly occupied areas severely limited the CCP's chances of implementing major social reform during its first year in power. In the cities, Communist attempts at collecting taxes led to a number of factories closing, as did the party's initial decrees on stabilizing prices and indexing wages. When the authorities forbade businesses—including foreign-owned companies—to close down without permission, owners simply stopped buying the raw materials necessary for production and stopped paying their workers. Even for those who had the necessary surplus to operate under the new conditions, the GMD blockade and bombing raids created difficult conditions. Over the summer of 1949 the CCP gradually put on hold a number of its social reforms—including mandatory wage increases for the poorest workers—and that did alleviate the situation somewhat, but conditions remained unstable, with the cost of living increasing by 169 percent in Tianjin in August.[32]

By autumn even Mao Zedong was talking about a crisis in the CCP-held cities. The Chairman criticized the party's financial experts for not getting inflation under control, but still, in the end, he ruled out extreme measures, such as Shanghai party secretary Rao Shushi's suggestion of moving the majority of city people to the countryside to get them away from "parasites" and "criminals." Instead the party settled for a system of progressive taxes, mandatory investments in government bonds, and forced savings to take control of the financial situation. A series of natural disasters—plagues in Manchuria, droughts and then floods in Central China—seemed for a time to defeat the government's purpose, making November a very difficult month, with price increases of more than 200 percent in many cities. But during winter the situation began to stabilize—more, it could be argued, as an effect of the absence of warfare than as a result of the government's financial measures. When production began to pick up again in the spring of 1950, many companies found that the centralization of finances through the government's schemes had led to a shortage of liquidity, and that their businesses were thrown straight from an inflationary crisis in the fall of 1949 to an overproduction crisis in the spring and summer of 1950. Still, by late spring most government experts had concluded that at least the most immediate financial problems were taken care of.[33]

As long as the 1949 crisis continued, the party held back from reforms that would bring the urban economy as a whole under socialist control. In the spring of 1950—well helped by the overproduction problems in parts of the economy—the Communists moved to expand the public sector. Some companies were taken over by the government through a state buy-out of their unsold goods. Small firms—transport, services, domestic goods—were required to join up in cooperatives. State trade monopolies were set up after the Soviet pattern, both for foreign and domestic trade—well assisted by the U.S. trade restrictions on more than six hundred products for sale to China in the spring of 1950.[34] At the CCP Central Committee meeting that began in Beijing on 6 June—the first full meeting since the establishment of the PRC—party leaders felt that the country was ready for more fundamental changes, both in the cities and in the countryside.

A main reason why the Communist leaders thought that China was ready for new advances on the road toward socialism was the CCP's success in recruiting students, intellectuals, and other members of the middle class for its cause. Most Communists had expected problems with those groups, especially as the party began "guiding" the press and the universities, but to their surprise the younger "bourgeois" and "petit bourgeois" flocked to the Communist standards in far greater numbers, relatively speaking, than members of any other social group, peasants and proletarians included. With the civil war seemingly at an end, there is little doubt that there was genuine enthusiasm for some of the aims of the revolution among the middle class—much of the Communist rhetoric fitted their nationalism and gave purpose to their urge for action to cure China's ills. The liberal leaders who had expressed a more sustained criticism of Communism—either based on experience or on political outlook—had already left for exile, mostly in Hong Kong or the United States.[35]

The enthusiasm from the middle class toward the new rulers was most directly felt in schools and universities. There, young people whose ancestors had served one or several previous regimes were ready to offer their services to the Communists. The activists—often, but not always, veterans from the student movement—organized study circles for Communist writings, held literacy classes for workers and poor people, and organized fellow students into groups for service along the PLA front

Peking University Students Go to the Countryside, Spring 1949

Later we got a chance to sample the life of peasants in a bigger labor campaign when we were invited to join in "agricultural production." Students from the Department of Economics were the first to volunteer. Because, when they came back, they told us how much they had learned about the life of peasants and how much they had enjoyed the day out in the fresh country air, everybody signed up. We rode out to the fields in trucks, climbed down, and lined up to receive our hoes. Then we went to work on the weeds sprouting under the warm spring sun. A few villagers with shabby clothes and muddy feet hung around staring at the unusual sight of students in uniform working away in their fields. One young peasant plucked up enough courage to speak to a couple of us. . . . "Where are the young masters from?" he asked politely. "We are from Peking University," we told him with a certain pride. "We came out in those trucks there. We came out here to learn the dignity of labor." "Unh," he said. He stared at the truck. "I've never ridden in one of those things."

Maria Yen wrote one of the best-known novels about student life after the revolution. *The Umbrella Garden* (London: Macmillan, 1954), p. 40.

lines in the South. A substantial part of the "new cadres" who joined in the administration of conquered territories came from among the students, and many of them rose to influential positions within the party during the first years of Communist rule. Those who remained as students took the lead in transforming Chinese education according to Communist guidelines, emphasizing technical subjects and political education over traditional learning.[36]

It was often college students who took the lead in implementing social reform in the cities, in some cases pressing well ahead of the official Communist agenda. The mostly unsuccessful campaigns to return refugees in the big cities to their villages was led by students, as were the far more thriving campaigns on public health and on improving the status of women. Re-educating social offenders was also seen by students as falling within their brief, although "old" CCP cadres held tighter reins on those issues. The campaign against prostitution was a case in point: Instead of having the re-education camps overflow with prostitutes as a result of the youthful zeal of the student antivice campaigners, the Communists in Shanghai at the end of 1949 started licensing brothels, much according to the same system the old regime had used. It took another year—and the onset of the next and more radical phase of the revolution—to remove prostitution as a visible social phenomenon in Shanghai.[37]

Rounding up Courtesans in Shanghai, 1950

We loaded them into cars. These people all cried. They didn't get in the cars. They all hung on to the madams, crying, "Mama, Daddy, the Communists are going to murder us, we don't want to go," and so forth. "They're going to sell us again, we want to stay with Mama and Daddy." They cried and carried on. They did not want to accept reform, and by no means did all of them wish to leave the life and marry respectably. Those who did were extremely exceptional—of the ones I encountered, often not even one in one hundred. Very few among those who lived well wished to voluntarily give up the trade. In general, after a prostitute had been in the brothel half a year, her psychology changed. Vagrancy became second nature to them. Like when a pickpocket steals things, becomes habituated to it, finds that there is a profit to be made. Especially for young people, aside from the ruination of one's character and body, the actual life was better than that of factory workers, because the brothels had to bring them up well so that they could be beautiful. They could not enjoy this kind of life if they left the brothels.

Cao Manzhi, head of the CCP Shanghai Civil Administration Bureau after 1949 occupation, in 1986 interview by Gail Hershatter. Gail Hershatter, *Dangerous Pleasures: Prostitution and Modernity in Twentieth Century Shanghai* (Berkeley: University of California Press, 1997) p. 312.

While the Communists in most areas of social policy were inclined to tolerate student activism in spite of its intermittent excesses, the CCP cadres were determined to get exclusive control of the press, publishers, radio, theaters, and movie houses. These, the Communists thought, were the means of production of the bourgeois intelligentsia, through which they would continue to produce bourgeois ideology if not curbed. During the first period of Communist control, the party—as had been decided previously—attempted to control public life through a combination of self-censorship, political pressure, and the influence of Communist agents. For the newspapers and publishing houses this method proved remarkably successful, so that when the authorities in 1950 and 1951 moved in to take direct control of those businesses, very few critical voices were left. In other areas, however, the "political cultural offensives" of the CCP did not work that smoothly. The attempts in 1949 to remove "foreign imperialist" and "decadent" movies from distribution and replace them with Soviet films and films made in the CCP base areas at first failed completely—the theaters in the big cities pleaded with the authorities to release more foreign films and thereby let them regain their customers. It took another year of Communist efforts, and the U.S. trade embargo, to completely remove American movies from Chinese screens.[38]

In rural areas, the CCP's reform efforts depended on their degree of political and military control. In the vast new Communist-held regions in the countryside, in South and Central China, and in the Northwest, the party's priority was to implement the moderate reforms that it had decided on during 1947 and 1948. Meanwhile, in the territories they had held for several years, the Communists were promoting more radical land reform programs. In the "old" areas, party rectification—cleansing the party of undesirable elements—and low-level forms of cooperative agriculture—mutual aid teams—were launched in regions that inspection groups of midranking cadres found ready for such campaigns. But in South China, where the party in most cases was a complete stranger, few cadres could envisage any such rapid moves. Rather, because the Communists had conquered the region militarily, by traditional warfare, the CCP found itself in the unusual situation of controlling the main cities while not yet having much influence in the surrounding areas. In some provinces, the Communists met much resistance, and the cadres were tempted to try land reform as a weapon, as had been the case during the difficult years of 1946 and 1947.

Another weapon, which sometimes turned out to be a double-edged sword, was China's new marriage law, proclaimed on 13 April 1950. For many women the new law was the most revolutionary proclamation of the new regime, abolishing the institution of arranged marriages, giving women the right to divorce and to own land, prohibiting the practice of abandoning wives and children, and giving all children the right to be cared for and to inherit property from their parents. The marriage law, which the Communist cadres observed zealously, could turn important aspects of village life upside down. It gave many women a new sense of freedom and wedded them, if less to their husbands, at least indirectly to the new regime. The party leaders saw the reform as a major step on the road to social justice, but they were also conscious of the effects it had in securing support for the CCP from those who had been among the most downtrodden in traditional Chinese society. It gave the party new allies, but it also created new enemies and secured the impression of the Communists as assailants of local traditions.

The resistance to Communist rule in Southern and Western China was only in very few cases organized by political groups. In most instances, clashes were with clans or families, traditional organizations—such as secret societies—or religious congregations. The Communists were seen as outsiders, who did not speak the local language and who trampled on local customs and creeds. The PLA troops who attempted to secure the areas militarily found themselves in a position remarkably similar to GMD or Japanese units in North China during the wars: A village might be "secured" and hail Communist principles during the day, but as soon as night came and the soldiers went to their camps, the villagers would celebrate their old festivals and honor their traditional leaders. In some areas, for instance in Guangxi and parts of Guangdong, it took several years before the party could pride itself on being fully in control.[39]

In spite of its general skepticism of using radical land reform as a weapon for gaining political control of "new" areas, the party Center did in some cases sanction such measures if local or provincial cadres could prove that only landlords became the immediate targets of the campaigns. But the cadres who spearheaded these campaigns often found that they did not have the same effects as in the North, and they were often resisted by local cadres. Customs and clan allegiances made it more difficult for Southern peasants to denounce their traditional leaders. Even more important, most areas of the fertile South did not have the same level of pent-up economic conflict that the wars had created in the arid North. The Communists found the "consciousness" of the poor peasants far less developed here and in the Western provinces than was the case north of the Yangzi; in reality, most peasants could not see how killing local landlords helped solve their own problems, which were mostly related to weather, pests, or floods. Unless there were commercial markets close by, the peasants even found it difficult to appreciate being given the land that had been divided up.[40]

The party Center still believed that taking over the South, and other new regions, would be far less difficult if it had not been for the extreme lack of cadres to work in those areas. Those who were available were a mix of "old" cadres—a definite minority—and students and urban intellectuals who had joined at the end of the war. But even if the party included people who had worked with the Communists for only months or even weeks, the numbers were so small in comparison with the hundreds of millions who had come under nominal CCP control over the past year that it hardly mattered. In some provinces, for instance in Guangxi, the work teams had to move from one village to another together with PLA units, and they saw very few results of their work during the first two

Communist Reprisals after Peasant Protest, 1950

Ku sat on the bed nervously plucking hairs off his upper lip. Outside in the great hall of the temple they were torturing the men arrested for the riot. "A-yah! Ai-yaw!" came the rhythmic groans. "Uh-ee-ee-yah!" The voice would weaken and trail off, then suddenly turn into a straight, bestial howl, tremendously strong. This could not be true, Ku thought. . . . Scream, and perhaps it would all vanish. In the city it had always been asserted that the Communists never used torture. All the stories of the torture of landlords and suspected spies were lies spread by enemy agents.

But what he found hardest to take was that these men groaning on the "tiger stool" were plain farmers. He knew that [work team head] Wong knew that they could not be tools of spies and saboteurs, as he had told the village. . . . "Don't imagine things," he said to himself. He had a desperate need to believe in Wong and what he stood for. For the thousandth time since the Communists came, Ku told himself, "Believe—for your own good." It had become like opium for the intellectuals, this faith which would enable them to suffer privations cheerfully, deaden all disquieting thoughts and feelings, still the conscience, and generally make life bearable. He was facing a severe test, Ku told himself. He would have to overcome his petty-bourgeois Tender Emotionalism. Of course this riot of hungry peasants was a mere accident, an isolated instance which had no place in the general picture.

Eileen Chang [Zhang Ailing] wrote the novel *The Rice-Sprout Song* in the early 1950s. The story, set in China during the Communist takeover, describes how hunger and pressure to change old ways leads to violence in a CCP-held village (Hong Kong: Dragonfly Books, 1955), pp. 166–67.

years of Communist rule. Indeed, they often ran great personal risks—the work teams were unpopular in many areas because they were seen as receivers of the taxes that the party needed for war and for constructing their new state. More than three thousand cadres were killed during the first year of the Communist regime while trying to collect grain tax from unwilling peasants.[41]

The "shift to cities" that the party announced at the end of the civil war was in part a result of Communist ideology, and in part a consequence of the unexpected wariness with which large groups of peasants outside the old base areas met the victorious CCP. Although Mao Zedong had always pointed to the Soviet experience as the main source of learning for his party—and had, during the late 1940s, increasingly come to underline rapid industrialization as a main part of those lessons—it is still unlikely that the urban, industrial agenda would have come to dominate as completely as it did during the first years of the PRC had it not been for the uncertain welcome for Communism in rural areas. It is indeed ironic that those who welcomed the new Communist state most wholeheartedly were neither peasants nor proletarians, but the urban middle classes, of whom many had ended up seeing the Communist revolution as part of their own modernizing, nationalist agenda.

But both in the countryside and in the cities, those who believed that the Communist state could be adapted to their own agendas were in for rude surprises when, at the end of 1950, the CCP began moving to the second phase of the revolution. In the countryside, land reform became more radical in most parts of the country, with redistribution of land and struggle meetings against "enemies of the people" more prominent. All over China party cadres launched a campaign for the suppression of counter-revolutionaries, among whom were counted numerous people who had some form of sympathy with the CCP state but who also had served the old regime in past. In total, between one and two million Chinese were killed during these campaigns, and millions more saw their futures shattered simply for belonging to the wrong social class. While China's entry into the Korean War in October 1950 undoubtedly heightened the intensity of these campaigns, the war was in no way their cause: The CCP had always intended to move on to more radical policies once its control had been established.

Uniting China: Sichuan, Guangdong, Yunnan, Xinjiang

By mid-1949 the PLA was advancing in the West and in the South, although at a slower pace than in the spring. The Politburo had several times over the summer discussed military strategy and had agreed that the commanders directing the operations—Peng Dehuai in the Northwest, Liu Bocheng in the Southwest, and Lin Biao in Guangxi and Guangdong—should emphasize "peaceful liberation" of these regions if in any way possible. As the takeover of these regions would coincide with the setting up of the new state, it was important that as many as possible of the provincial leaders of the old regime volunteer their support for the CCP government. As Zhou Enlai was fond of pointing out, that would leave the impression that all of China was rallying to support the new state. Measures against "war criminals" would have to wait until the party's power was established in the whole country.[42]

The most difficult task the PLA was up against in military terms was undoubtedly Guangxi. There Bai Chongxi—perhaps the ablest of all the

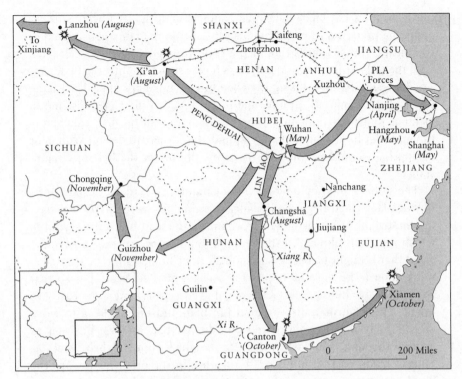

Map 4. South China, 1949

GMD military commanders—was fighting on his home turf. With Nan-jing gone and Li Zongren's government in hopeless disarray, Bai had de-cided to make a last stand for his home province, hoping that the Com-munists could be convinced to let their armies pass by Guangxi, and to leave the provincial elites in charge. Informal negotiations on those issues had taken place since January, but even Zhou Enlai felt that Bai was ask-ing too much. Lin Biao feared that if left alone, Bai and his troops could form a counter-revolutionary "focus" in the heart of South China, over time linking up with the imperialists in Indochina and Jiang Jieshi on Tai-wan.[43]

After the fall of Wuhan on 15 May, Bai had set up a forward line of defense stretching from central Sichuan to northern Jiangxi, a broad front manned by about 250,000 men, most from his own Guangxi forces. As Chen Yi's troops swept down the coast, taking Zhejiang and most of Fujian by early July, Bai's position became increasingly exposed. On 3 July Hunan's governor, Cheng Qian, "transferred his loyalty," as he put it, to the CCP. Since Bai's own contacts with the CCP were still on-going, he preferred to withdraw his forces from the Hunanese capital of Changsha, rather than strike at the traitorous governor. A week later, with the talks still at a standstill, Bai's forces struck against the PLA west of Changsha, badly bruising the CCP forces. But Bai's appeals to Jiang (through Li Zongren), to have the forces loyal to the Generalissimo in Sichuan join his troops in a general offensive, fell on deaf ears. Jiang thought that Bai—who had not responded to orders to defend Wuhan or Changsha—would be an untrustworthy ally under the best of circum-stances.[44]

The setback in Hunan worried the Communist leaders, in spite of its obvious lack of strategic significance. It came just as the party was hav-ing important meetings in Moscow, and in the lead-up to the period in which the establishment of the People's Republic was planned. Mao de-cided that it might be best to circumvent Bai Chongxi's forces after all—not primarily because he hoped for a negotiated solution, but so that Bai's defensive lines could be stretched even farther and so be easier to break. The Chairman also ordered Lin Biao and Liu Bocheng to work more closely together and better coordinate their attacks. In order to achieve this aim, Mao asked them to designate some of their forces as "joint" troops that could operate together in the offensive toward the South. Strategic control of the campaign was left with Lin, and most of the joint troops in reality came under his control.[45]

The summer rains and another round of negotiations with Bai Chongxi delayed the operations. For most of the Communist soldiers, be-ing Northerners, this summer of waiting in the semitropical South was the strangest experience of their lives. Everything there was foreign to them—the food, the buildings, the vegetation, the language. The great majority had little or no contact with the peasants whose villages they were quartered nearby. To a small number of cadres, however, this region was known—they had passed through almost fifteen years before as they were fleeing from the GMD on the first stage of the Long March. But nothing remained of the Communist cells they had set up back then.[46]

In mid-September the PLA struck toward southern Hunan, threatening to cut Bai's communications both with Sichuan and with the coast. Bai Chongxi's core forces fought back furiously, but desertions among his new recruits forced him to withdraw back into Guangxi. After a lightning offensive, Lin's and Liu's forces entered Guangdong on 23 September. The PLA rear troops—more than 300,000 men—pushed down Jiangxi

---

A Southern Cadre Returns Home, 1949

May 12 [1949] (Hangzhou): Went to Political Commissar Tan [Zhenlin]'s place to ask for instructions on several specific questions and, in passing, raised the problem of work for [two comrades]. . . . Tan said that I should not attempt to bring cadres I was familiar with into my own orbit. I felt that this opinion was somewhat harsh. I examined myself and thought that I had indeed searched for more local cadres in order to link with the masses, but I certainly had not thought of creating any kind of clique.

August 10 (Zhuji): In the afternoon, exchanged opinions concerning problems I had discovered with . . . [local officials]. . . . Fourth, some new phenomena have already occurred on the issue of unity, that is, local cadres do not dare speak, and south-bound cadres really have a dominating voice. In the future, [local leaders] should appropriately constrain south-bound cadres and should encourage local cadres.

August 11: After breakfast, continued to listen to situation reports by the military and local organization. While we listened to the report by Political Commissar Zhang on the situation of the troops, I felt that he was somewhat impatient in overly describing and emphasizing the past shortcomings of local cadres and in unwittingly letting these remarks slip in several places, making those opposite feel unhappy. This is no good.

August 27: In the afternoon, returned to the home I hadn't visited for more than ten years to see my mother. I did not recognize many young people. The former young people are now all fathers, and the former middle-aged people have become old men.

December 22 (Linhai): In the evening, had a separate talk with Commissioner Liu. He put forward criticism of several local comrades, principally in relation to their lifestyle and ability, but he did not advance any kind of opinions concerning the south-bound comrades.

These excerpts are from the personal diaries of Yang Siyi, who rose to become one of the top provincial cadres in Zhejiang before being purged in the late 1950s. Keith Forster, trans., "The Diary of Yang Siyi (Excerpts)," *Chinese Law and Government* 33, no. 4 (2000): 21–22.

---

province, with Lin Biao hoping to surround Bai in southern Hunan or eastern Guangxi. But Bai escaped across toward Guilin, although more than half of his army was lost during the retreat.[47]

By September the Guomindang government in Guangzhou was little more than an empty shell. To Li Zongren's horror, Jiang Jieshi had reappeared in Guangzhou from Taiwan on 14 July, and he started calling meetings as head of the Guomindang party. Jiang set up an Extraordinary Committee of the party executive committee, with himself as chairman and Li as his deputy, which had the right to overrule all government decrees. After this coup d'etat against the remnant of the GMD regime, Jiang again left for Taibei, taking with him most of the government archives that had been brought from Nanjing. For a while the hapless Li pondered what to do. When Jiang again returned to Guangzhou, some of the Guangdong and Guangxi generals who advised Li proposed in desperation that he should attempt to assassinate the Generalissimo. But the GMD rump was running out of time for their infighting.[48]

In early October Lin Biao's forces destroyed Guangzhou's weak defenses north of the city in a maneuver similar to his taking of the Manchurian cities the previous year. Lin himself did not even bother to go with his troops to the city—he immediately turned around with his main force in another attempt to encircle Bai Chongxi in Guangxi. Jiang Jieshi had left Guangzhou on 3 October. Li Zongren fled a week later, this time for the wartime capital of Chongqing in Sichuan. The PLA entered Guangzhou, the major city in the Chinese south, on 15 October. Most of the population seemed indifferent to this new change of government. Some thousands fled, by car or on foot, for the Hong Kong border, from which most of them were turned back. In the British colony the defenses were put on highest alert.[49]

British colonial leaders had started preparing for a Communist victory in South China as early as the beginning of 1949. Most Westerners in Hong Kong did not believe that the CCP would attack the colony, but they were preparing for an almost siegelike existence, during which the new authorities could cut off most of the supplies that Hong Kong was getting from the mainland. In London, the Labour government of Clement Atlee—already fighting the Cold War as a staunch U.S. ally— was more alarmist, fearing that Hong Kong might "well become the stage for a trial of strength between Communism and the Western Powers."[50] But for Chairman Mao, Hong Kong was not high up on the list of priorities. He told his supporters that Great Britain did not agree with all U.S. positions on China, and that their colony therefore should be left off the list of CCP targets for the time being. The party might have to reconsider only should a rebellion break out against the British as the PLA approached. Some CCP leaders thought that if China denied them the trade they had come for, the British imperialists might simply give up and go away.[51]

In Chongqing, Li Zongren had stayed for only a couple of weeks when rumors started flying that the Generalissimo was on his way. After their last run-in in Guangzhou, Li had no wish to face Jiang among his loyal soldiers in Chongqing, and he told his few remaining supporters that he planned to fly to Kunming to rally support. On 23 October 1949, Li's government met one final time at Gang Zhuan, a Sichuanese banker's spacious villa that the president had rented. Some ministers wanted to go to Vietnam to seek support from the French. Perhaps Bai's army could escape that way, too. Others were preparing to attempt to make their way to the coast or to Hong Kong. A few wanted to go to Taiwan. As had become usual, no firm decisions were reached. In the evening the meeting had to be adjourned because there was no light. The government had not paid its electricity bill.[52]

On 3 November, Li arrived in Kunming on his way out of Chinese history. After ten days of meetings with Lu Han, the Yunnan provincial governor, the President flew to Guilin to meet his old friend Bai Chongxi. During October and early November the PLA had slowly closed in on Bai's remaining forces in Guangxi. Bai and Li had decided that the situation was hopeless and left for Nanning in China's extreme southwestern corner, leaving their forces under Huang Jie's command. Li was exhausted and depressed. In mid-November the President flew to Hong Kong and ultimately to New York to seek "proper medical treatment."[53] Bai Chongxi, in perhaps the bravest move of his career, flew to Chongqing to offer his services to the Generalissimo.

Jiang Jieshi had arrived in Chongqing on 14 November. His purpose was to show that he was concerned for his troops and officials, more than to direct military operations. Jiang was glad that Li Zongren was out of the way—Li's behavior over the last couple of months, he wrote in his diary, was "shameless and beneath contempt."[54] The Generalissimo told his advisers that what would save China was World War III, which would break out soon. In that war, the Americans would need his help to fight Soviet and Chinese Communists, and the war would give the Guomindang a chance to redeem itself. Jiang's usual travel entourage of several hundred was now reduced to a couple of dozen, and his daily party executive meetings had become increasingly unreal. His right-wing core of advisers, headed by Chen Lifu, was the last group that had stayed loyal. When Bai Chongxi arrived, it was Chen who convinced the Generalissimo that he should be spared, arguing that it would be safer to bring Bai to Taiwan than to set him up as a martyr for the CCP and the Americans.[55] But when the Prime Minister, the defeated Shanxi warlord Yan Xishan, proposed land reform as a key to the GMD's new policies. Chen Lifu angrily responded that "the Communists have not even arrived yet, and we want to persecute the landlords ahead of them?"[56]

In the morning of 30 November, with advance forces from the PLA closing in on the city from the north and northeast, Jiang was awakened early by his security guards. They wanted him to leave straight away. But Jiang refused to be seen to be in a hurry. When his motorcade finally left for the airport, thousands of people clogged the main highway. The PLA was rumored already to be in the city. Caught up in the sea of terrified and fleeing people, Jiang's cars almost did not make it to the airport in time. By next morning the city was in PLA hands. Jiang was in Chengdu, where he continued to hold court and mull over the future. At 2:00 P.M. on 10 December, with Chengdu under threat from the PLA and with the loyalty of local troops in doubt, Jiang Jieshi and his son, Jiang Jingguo, left Chengdu for Taibei. Neither of them would ever again return to the mainland.[57]

While the Guomindang regime was securing Taiwan, the other border areas of China were busy finding ways of dealing with the new Communist government in Beijing. In the Southwest, in Yunnan and western Guangxi, there had been little fighting while Bai's armies were overrun further east. The governor of Yunnan province, Lu Han, who had helped Jiang Jieshi secure a hold on the Southwest in 1945, had already by the summer of 1949 realized that he needed to strike a deal with the CCP to remain in power. On 9 December he defected to the Communists together with several of the commanders of the GMD Southwest Military Region. Those forces that remained loyal to the GMD retreated toward the Burmese border, where they were joined by a few of Hu Zongnan's troops who had escaped the massive PLA attack on Chengdu in late December.[58]

In Xinjiang, the departure of Zhang Zhizhong had led to a renewed de facto division of the province between a Soviet-sponsored Muslim nationalist regime in the West and North and a Chinese administration loyal to the GMD in Urumqi. In early 1949 the GMD had attempted to secure Xinjiang for itself by working out a new agreement with the Soviet Union, in which the Soviets would get mining and trade concessions in return for sacrificing Ahmed Jan Kasimi's secessionist regime and not assisting the CCP in taking over the province. Stalin, as usual, was willing to play along with the GMD, but the Soviet demands during negotiations in Xinjiang and Guangzhou—which would have resulted in making Xinjiang a form of Soviet protectorate—proved too much for Li Zongren to accept. The negotiations dragged on until June, but with no results.[59]

By the end of April, Moscow had assured the CCP that it would help its takeover of Xinjiang as best it could. The Soviets advised Ahmed Jan Kasimi and the other separatist leaders that they would, ultimately, have to come to agreement with the CCP, and that they could not expect Soviet support unless conditions were agreed with Mao Zedong. Meanwhile, in Urumqi, the GMD military commander, Tao Zhiyue, and Burhan Shahidi (Bao Erhan), the Uighur provincial governor, had jointly decided to wait and see how the fighting in the East developed before engaging themselves and the ninety thousand GMD soldiers still in the province. The former governor, Zhang Zhizhong, who had visited Urumqi as head of a GMD delegation before defecting to the CCP in April, seems to have advised them to strive for as much autonomy as they could get. By May, if not before, Burhan was in contact with the local CCP underground. In late July, as Peng Dehuai's troops were ready to cross into Xinjiang after having defeated GMD and local Muslim forces in Gansu and Qinghai, a deal was struck, whereby the provincial government would join the Beijing regime when the Political Consultative Conference met. Until then, the PLA would remain in the Xinjiang border areas. On 14 August the CCP Central Committee member Deng Liqun arrived in Yining via Moscow and Almaty in Soviet Kazakhstan to set up a direct liaison between the Xinjiang leadership and Beijing.[60]

With the Burhan-Beijing agreement, Ahmed Jan Kasimi's regime in Yili had gone from being an asset to being a possible embarrassment for Moscow. On 22 August 1949, Ahmed Jan and his core leadership left Yining for Almaty, ostensibly on their way to Beijing for the PCC meeting. Then nothing more was heard about them. In late October, Beijing announced that all the ETR leaders had died when their plane had crashed near Irkutsk in Siberia. On 26 September, just in time to join the first PCC plenary session, Burhan and Tao announced their "revolt." The PLA entered Xinjiang in October and gradually fanned out—against local resistance—to control most of the province by April 1950.[61] In some areas of the Northwest, however, armed opposition to CCP rule continued at least up to the mid-1950s.

On to Taiwan

When Jiang Jieshi returned to Taibei on 10 December 1949, he found a society that was buckling under the pressure of refugees coming in from the mainland, the lack of services, and the resentment most Taiwanese felt toward the GMD regime. Outside the provincial capital, the situation was nearing chaos, as Taiwanese fled from the cities out of fear for what demoralized and unruly soldiers could do to them and their families. Most observers thought it was a question of months, perhaps weeks, before the GMD regime would collapse in its new location: Even high-ranking GMD members noted what an irony it was that the Nationalists should end up taking refuge on this island, where they had quelled a rebellion only two years earlier.[62]

Generalissimo Jiang himself was exhausted and ill, suffering from ulcers and other ailments. His generals feared that he was getting so mentally depressed that he would commit suicide. But to his inner core of advisers, Jiang kept repeating that Taiwan was a God-send, that the island was their final opportunity to complete the revolution. The next world war would come very soon, Jiang maintained, and with the U.S. victory, the GMD would get its chance to return to the mainland. In the meantime, however, the party had to learn from its mistakes in order to survive on Taiwan.[63]

From late January 1950 on, Jiang Jieshi again began to appear in public on the island. On 1 March he formally "resumed" his presidency of the Republic of China. His new and to many startling message was that the Guomindang had lost the war on the mainland because of its own incompetence, and that the party had to reform completely in order to survive. At his new party school in the Yangming Mountains, called—in true Jiang Jieshi fashion—the Academy for the Study of Carrying Out Revolution, there was surprisingly frank discussion of both the past and the future, including mistakes made by the Jiang family, and how to repair trust between mainlanders and Taiwanese. In his talks with other GMD leaders, Jiang stressed the need to streamline the party organization, weed out corruption, and work among people of all ethnic groups.[64]

But as on the mainland in the past, Jiang's early-1950 exhortations to the party on Taiwan seemed to be to little avail. The social and economic situation continued to deteriorate. Inflation soared in the first months of the year, and there would have been a serious lack of food and other basic supplies if the newly appointed provincial government under Wu Guozhen, the former mayor of Shanghai, had not convinced Jiang that he had to release some of the hoard of U.S. dollars and gold brought from the mainland to import supplies. Worse, refugees kept coming in from islands along the coast as the Communists extended their rule ever closer to Taiwan. Although the GMD generals realized that in military terms their position on the island was, in the spring of 1950, fairly secure, they feared what would happen when their armies began running out of ammunition and weapons, since further U.S. assistance did not seem to be forthcoming.[65]

In Washington, the fall of Southern China and the evacuation of the GMD government to Taiwan had come as no surprise. In most quarters, except with the Republican right wing, opinion tended to favor the view that Jiang Jieshi and the Guomindang had brought their disasters upon themselves by administrative incompetence and military ineffectiveness. Although the United States hesitated to follow Britain's lead and recognize the People's Republic, few policy-makers saw anything to gain from propping up Jiang's regime on Taiwan. On 5 January 1950, President Truman stated that the United States would not use its armed forces to interfere in the ongoing civil war in China or "provide military aid and advice to the Chinese forces on Formosa [Taiwan]."[66] The same day, Secretary of State Dean Acheson, when pressed by journalists, made it clear that Washington was "not going to get involved militarily in any way on the island of Formosa."[67]

As right-wing critics intensified their attacks on the Truman administration's foreign policy in the spring and early summer of 1950—attacks that in part centered on the U.S. "loss of China" to Communism—some members of the administration began having second thoughts on the Taiwan issue. In the State Department, Assistant Secretary Dean Rusk and Head of the Policy Planning Staff Paul Nitze began arguing for a resumption of American aid to the Guomindang on Taiwan, both for domestic political and for strategic reasons. They were joined by the heads of both the Joint Chiefs of Staff and the CIA, who argued that Taiwan would be an invaluable strategic asset in the region in the battle against Communism.[68]

But Truman and Acheson were still not prepared to let the United States be seen as the savior of Jiang Jieshi's rump regime. Neither of the two could be convinced that U.S. interests would be served by assisting a leader whom they regarded as the most unpromising of lapsed allies. Nitze responded in early May by coming up with a scheme to help General Sun Liren, the deputy commander of the Nationalist Army and an American favorite, remove Jiang from power. But both U.S. diplomats and intelligence agents on Taiwan dismissed the plan as unworkable— Sun was no match for the Jiang family, and it would take direct U.S. intervention for a coup d'etat to succeed. By late June 1950, it seemed certain that Washington would let Taiwan suffer whatever fate had in store for it, including a Communist takeover.[69]

Jiang Jieshi awoke on the morning of 25 June 1950 and found that international events had saved him yet again. The North Korean attack on South Korea, and President Truman's immediate decision to oppose the offensive with U.S. forces, were interpreted by Jiang as the start of World War III—and he knew that this would give his regime a new lease on life.[70] The arrival of the U.S. Navy's 7th Fleet in the Taiwan Strait two days later, with orders to stop any attack on the island, was seen in Taibei as the start of the second phase of the U.S.-GMD alliance. Although it was intended from the U.S. side as a strategic measure in the fight against Communism in Asia, Jiang was proven right in seeing the American protection of Taiwan as the beginning of a new U.S. relationship with his party and his government. Spurred by the ongoing conflict in Korea, Congress allocated more than $400 million for military and civilian assistance to Taiwan up to 1952. The CIA-run companies that established themselves on the island for the secret war against the PRC—operations such as Western Enterprises and Civil Air Transport—contributed tens of millions more.[71]

But Taiwan in the 1950s was more than an American client state. In a move that—together with the hard work of the people on the island—was to have massive long-term effects, Jiang Jieshi used his time of grace to institute serious reform to his party, his government, and the "country" he ruled. Jiang's policies for the new GMD were an extraordinary mix of the party's Leninist roots and U.S. influence—a dictatorship that redistributed land and encouraged education and economic growth, while having the party's cells infiltrate and influence all activities on the island. All of this would have been impossible without the American intervention. By saving the rule of the Jiang family on Taiwan, the United States allowed the development of an economic and political experiment with epochal consequences for China and the region. It also made sure that the U.S. hold on the island would remain a constant irritant in its relationship with the PRC.[72]

Jiang Jieshi—the man who had lost China and still been given a second chance—understandably believed that God was controlling his fate and that of the more than two million other refugees who joined him on Taiwan after 1949. His own duty, Jiang thought, was to repay the divine forces and all those who had trusted him with their lives by making his new state a springboard for China's future. In 1944, as the final Japanese offensives had brought his previous regime to the brink of collapse, Jiang had written in his diary:

> Where there is failure, there will be success. Where there is success, there will also be failure. The bad seed of today may bring abundance tomorrow. But also, what we now hold to be disasters may have come from something we originally regarded as beneficial. If we accept this way of viewing the world, we will come to see all things as flowing in eternal contradiction—no final result is absolutely good.[73]

9

TO THE YALU RIVER
New China and the World

Zhao Panbin, "Farewell"

From his rooms by the South Lake at the edge of Beijing's old imperial city, Mao Zedong surveyed the world. In October 1949, as the People's Republic had been set up, the Chairman's visions of what was happening around China were at the core of his views of his new republic's future. As often was the case, however, Mao's views of the outside world took him in two different directions. On the one hand, he believed that the socialist camp, headed by the Soviet Union, was strong enough to deter the imperialist countries from attacking it. On the other hand, he found the new People's Republic to be the weakest link in the chain of "progressive" countries around the Soviet Union, and therefore where an imperialist attack, if it happened, was most likely to come. The first vision prepared him for at least temporary peace, which he knew China needed. The second made him believe in the inevitability of war, since the imperialists would not let China—such a rich prize—be rescued from them without a fight.

It was within this dual perspective that the Chinese leadership prepared New China's place in the world in late 1949. Mao kept reminding his colleagues that the civil war was not over—the two big Chinese islands, Hainan and Taiwan, were not taken yet, and nor was Tibet or parts of the Southwest. The United States and its imperialist allies could attempt to use the PLA's liberation of those areas as an excuse for intervening, as the imperialists had done during previous Chinese regimes. Although Jiang Jieshi was finished, there would be others who could better play the role of imperialism's allies within China. To Mao, the conquest of the South had been almost too smooth and easy. The lack of political preparation had left the old structures there intact, and they could turn against the new regime. Deterring the imperialists from intervening was therefore the best way for New China to survive its infancy.[1]

There were, according to Mao Zedong, three ways of staving off imperialist intervention in the short term during the continuation of the Chinese revolution. The first was through a rapid completion of the military takeover of the country, and through showing determination and strength against foreign attempts at challenging the new regime along its borders. The second was by formalizing a comprehensive military alliance with the Soviet Union, which would dedicate Soviet power to directly defending China against its enemies. Finally, the regime had to root out its domestic opponents: the heads of secret societies, religious sects, independent unions, or tribal and ethnic organizations. By "destroying the bases of domestic reaction," China could, in Mao's view, create a safer world for the Chinese revolution to operate in.[2]

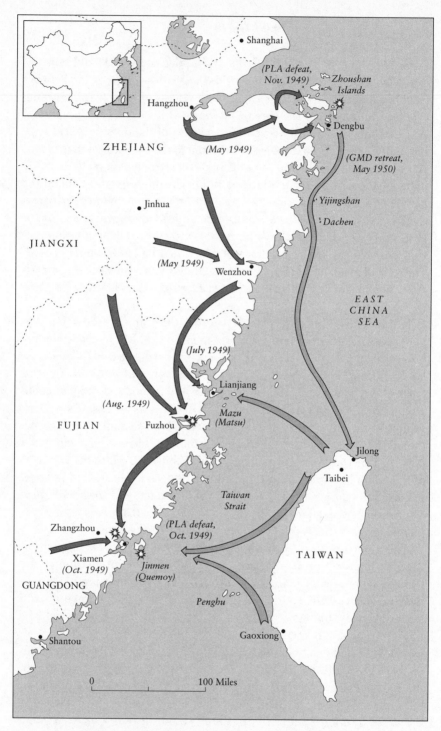

Map 5. Eastern China and the Taiwan Strait, 1949–50

Completing the Takeover

The biggest worry for the Chinese Communists in terms of uniting all of China under their rule was the islands of Hainan and Taiwan. Until a handful of GMD vessels defected in the summer and fall of 1949, the PLA had had no navy, and even with the advice of newly arrived Soviet experts, it would take almost a year to develop army units for full-fledged amphibious operations. Even worse, the Communists had almost no air force, as was painfully demonstrated by GMD planes overflying Shanghai and even Beijing, almost at will. General Su Yu, the PLA commander in charge of planning the seaborne operations against the islands, warned that attacking Hainan, not to mention Taiwan, or even the smaller islands along the Fujian coast, could be very costly. In Beijing, the political leaders worried that a large-scale attack could give the imperialists the very chance they had been waiting for to destroy some of the PLA vanguard.[3]

But Mao pressed on. He had information through the network of CCP agents who had joined the Nationalist leaders on their flight to Taiwan that Jiang was planning to reinforce Jinmen, Mazu, and the other coastal islands. The supply situation in Fujian was bad, with hunger in some areas, and local militias still in control in parts of the interior. The Chairman did not want to wait for Jiang Jieshi, or his successors, to exploit these conditions. Overruling General Su, Mao ordered a surprise attack on Jinmen on 24 October 1949.[4]

The landing went badly wrong for the Communists. The seas were rough, and the PLA soldiers—mostly from the North China plains—suffered from seasickness and fear of the rolling waves. The GMD units near the beach discovered the PLA junks as they approached, and they aimed their tanks and heavy artillery at them. The carnage during the first thirty minutes of the engagements was terrible. The PLA managed to land, but with heavy losses. For a day or so it still seemed as if the Communists would be able to secure a beachhead and protect their supply lines. But then the Nationalist commander, General Gao Kuiyuan, received welcome support from eight thousand to ten thousand GMD reserves and at least twenty tanks that had landed on the outer side of the island. By the morning of 26 October, the exhausted PLA soldiers had started surrendering. In the end, the PLA lost at least ten thousand of its best troops. Not a single one made it back to the mainland.[5]

In spite of all their previous successes—or perhaps just because of them—the CCP leaders were shocked by the news from Jinmen. "This is

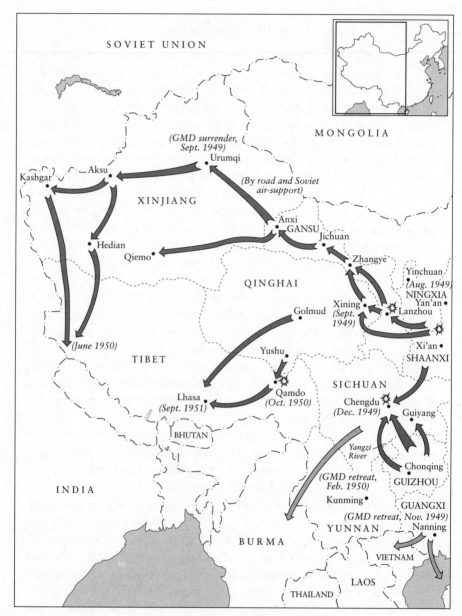

SOVIET UNION

MONGOLIA

(GMD surrender, Sept. 1949)
Urumqi

(By road and Soviet air-support)

Kashgar

Aksu

XINJIANG

Anxi

GANSU

Jichuan

Zhangye

Hedian

Qiemo

QINGHAI

Yinchuan

(Aug. 1949)

NINGXIA

Xining

(Sept. 1949)

Yan'an

Lanzhou

Golmud

(June 1950)

TIBET

Yushu

Xi'an

SHAANXI

Lhasa
(Sept. 1951)

Qamdo
(Oct. 1950)

SICHUAN

Chengdu
(Dec. 1949)

Guiyang

BHUTAN

INDIA

Yangzi River

Chonqing

(GMD retreat, Feb. 1950)

GUIZHOU

Kunming

GUANGXI

(GMD retreat, Nov. 1949)

YUNNAN

Nanning

BURMA

VIETNAM

LAOS

THAILAND

Map 6. Western China, 1949–51

our biggest loss in the war," Mao commented, and, in usual style, chided his local commanders for "carelessness and undue haste."[6] His displeasure increased further a week later, when he got the news that a separate attack on the island of Dengbu—used by the GMD to blockade the mouth of the Yangzi—had also failed. Mao complained that the CCP was losing control of the coast, and that the GMD bases on the islands now could be used for attacks anywhere from the Gulf of Bohai to the Vietnamese border. Although the Chairman exaggerated, the Jinmen and Dengbu battles were important in the sense that the unexpected GMD victories made the CCP postpone its plans for an attack on Taiwan and probably strengthened Jiang's political position there.[7]

But the CCP's worries about the GMD and other resistance to the new regime were not centered solely on the islands. Mao suspected that the area in which there was most room for an imperialist-sponsored counterattack was in the Southwest, where thirty thousand Nationalist soldiers had crossed the border into French-held Vietnam.[8] The Beijing leadership thought that the Americans would enlist French help in their plans to rearm the GMD through a supply line from Taiwan to Hainan and Hanoi. At the same time, the Vietminh, the Vietnamese Communist front led by Ho Chi Minh, had on several occasions appealed for aid from the CCP in its struggle against the French. With the PLA approaching the Vietnamese border, Zhou Enlai, in his meetings with the newly arrived Soviet ambassador, Nikolai Roshchin, asked Moscow to sanction the use of CCP troops inside Vietnam, to assist the Vietminh and prevent the GMD from infiltrating into Guangxi. But the Soviets turned down Beijing's suggestion, probably because of the difficulties that a direct CCP involvement in the war in Vietnam would cause for the French Communists. Soviet intelligence also claimed—correctly, as it turned out—that Paris had already decided to disarm and intern the GMD units rather than letting them operate against the PRC.[9]

The other area in Southeast Asia that the Beijing leadership worried about was its border with Burma. As along the coast near Vietnam, the GMD troops further west gradually ran out of areas in which to operate on the Chinese side of the border. In January they started crossing over into Burma. Unlike in Vietnam, the GMD remnants that arrived in the Shan States of Burma found that their refuge was not tightly controlled by the government. On the contrary, they found anti-Burmese rebels and local Chinese settlers who were sympathetic to their cause, and they could therefore soon set up an area under effective GMD rule. The former commander of the Yunnan-based 8th Army, General Li Mi, was sent from Taiwan through Thailand to command this GMD "army-in-exile." By the summer of 1950, Li Mi's soldiers had defeated Burmese attempts to evict them and had begun recruiting troops from the ethnically mixed villages in the area. Throughout 1950 the GMD on Taiwan struggled to get supplies and military equipment flown into eastern Burma, but with mixed success. In early 1951, however, the CIA began a secret airlift of arms and ammunition that gradually enabled the GMD to extend its positions in Burma and launch small and sporadic operations across the border into Yunnan.[10]

With the takeover of the northwestern province of Xinjiang completed more quickly than Beijing expected—in part thanks to Soviet aid—the CCP turned its attention to Tibet, the most remote of the borderlands the party claimed to be part of Chinese territory. The Communists had hoped that the CCP would be able to incorporate Tibet peacefully, in some form, into their new state. In spite of Mao's fear of foreign imperialists making use of the last phase of the civil war to detach Tibet from China, in the spring of 1949 he had been quite willing to keep the status quo in Lhasa for the time being, since there were so many other unsolved issues on the CCP's agenda. But the Tibetan decision in July 1949 to expel all Chinese from their territory set off jitters in Beijing, confirming to the Communists that they had reason to worry. Their suspicions of Lhasa's motives were further stimulated by the fierce resistance the PLA met when crossing into Tibetan areas of Qinghai and Gansu provinces in September of 1949.[11]

As the PLA advanced, against intense but sporadic opposition, toward the political borders of the Tibetan state in the spring of 1949, the Communists attempted to force the Lhasa government to accept Chinese sovereignty over its territories without having to mount a full-scale invasion. Met with Tibetan refusals to surrender, the PLA moved its core divisions from the armies stationed in Sichuan slowly toward the border, completing their positioning in August of 1950. In October, just as Chinese forces were advancing into Korea, the PLA attacked Tibet. By the end of the month, the Communist troops were about halfway to Lhasa, and Tibetan resistance—inferior in numbers, weapons, and organization—was on the brink of collapse.[12]

While the Communists were applying their mix of negotiations and force on Tibet, the Tibetan leaders were desperately seeking foreign aid for their independence. In spite of increasing U.S. interest in Tibetan in-

---

Tibetan Appeal to the United Nations, 11 November 1950

The armed invasion of Tibet for the incorporation of Tibet in Communist China through sheer physical force is a clear case of aggression. As long as the people of Tibet are compelled by force to become part of China against their will and consent, the present invasion of Tibet will be the grossest instance of violation of the weak by the strong. We therefore appeal through you to the Nations of the world to intercede on our behalf and restrain Chinese aggression. The problem is simple. The Chinese claim Tibet as part of China. Tibetans feel that racially, culturally and geographically, they are far apart from the Chinese. If the Chinese find the reactions of the Tibetans to their unnatural claim not acceptable, there are other civilized methods by which they could ascertain the views of the people of Tibet, or should the issue be purely juridical, they are open to seek redress in an international Court of Law. The conquest of Tibet by China will only enlarge the area of conflict and increase the threat to the independence and stability of other Asian countries.

Cablegram from Tibetan Cabinet (at Indian border) to United Nations, New York, 11 November 1950, in *Tibet in the United Nations* (New Delhi: Bureau of His Holiness the Dalai Lama, n.d.), p. 3.

---

dependence for strategic reasons, the Western powers and India concluded in the spring of 1950 that Lhasa was too insignificant and too weak for any major anti-Chinese covert aid operations to pay off. The appeals from the Dalai Lama fell on deaf ears. After China's intervention in the Korean War, Washington concluded that "every feasible effort should be made to hinder Commie occupation and give [the] case appropriate hearing in [the] UN."[13] But with Beijing's troops advancing on the Tibetan capital, the young Dalai Lama, who had taken refuge close to the Indian border, decided it was time to negotiate. In the winter of 1950–51 the first meetings were held, and in the spring a Tibetan delegation signed a seventeen-point agreement in Beijing, in which the Chinese state promised not to change the political or religious systems in Tibet, and the Tibetans agreed to accept Beijing's sovereignty. In the summer of 1951, the Dalai Lama refused U.S. entreaties for him to go into exile and returned to Lhasa.[14]

Throughout the winter of 1949–50 the CCP leaders had constantly been on the lookout for a way of breaking Jiang Jieshi's island defense. After the Jinmen and Dengbu fiascos, Mao had halted plans for an invasion of Hainan until more favorable conditions could be set up. But in January, after he had arrived in Moscow for his meetings with Stalin, the

---

PLA Appeal to Tibetans, 22 November 1950

With serious concern for the people of Tibet, who have suffered long years of oppression under American and British imperialists and Chiang Kai-shek's [Jiang Jieshi's] reactionary government, Chairman Mao Tse-tung of the Central People's Government and Commander in Chief Chu Te [Zhu De] of the People's Liberation Army ordered the People's Liberation Army troops to enter Tibet for the purpose of assisting the Tibetan people to free themselves from oppression forever. All Tibetan people, including all lamas, should now create a solid unity to give the People's Liberation Army adequate assistance in ridding Tibet of imperialist influence and in establishing a regional self-government for the Tibetan people. They should at the same time build fraternal relations, on the basis of friendship and mutual help, with other nationalities within the country and together construct a new Tibet within New China.

Excerpt from PLA statement, issued in the name of captured Tibetan commander Ngawang Jigme Ngapo, quoted from Warren H. Smith, Jr., *Tibetan Nation: A History of Tibetan Nationalism and Sino-Tibetan Relations* (Boulder, CO: Westview, 1996), pp. 323–41, pp. 287–88.

Chairman changed his mind. Possibly because he wanted a victory to present the Soviet leader with during his visit, Mao reviewed the Hainan situation and found reasons why a military operation against the island should be accelerated. There was already a well-organized Communist guerrilla movement in the mountains on the island. The Americans had not helped Jiang organize supply routes between Taiwan and Hainan. And the eighty thousand GMD soldiers on Hainan seemed to have enough trouble dealing with the unrest created by the influx of refugees from the mainland to be able to deal effectively with a massive PLA crossing of the fifteen-mile strait dividing the island from the coast of Guangdong. In spite of Mao's convictions, however, the operation was postponed for several weeks on Soviet advice, so that the winds would be favorable for a crossing in junks. Moscow did not want to risk the minuscule PRC navy for such a limited purpose. Nor did it want to attract too much U.S. attention to the operation.[15]

The first PLA assault group, trained by Soviet advisers, landed on Hainan's east coast on 5 March. It was followed by several others, most of which managed to land secretly and join up with the Communist guerrillas. On the night of 16 April and in the early morning of 17 April, the PLA landed more than 100,000 soldiers in its main landing force at beachheads already prepared by the Communist guerrillas. The GMD units started crumbling at once. The Nationalist political and military leaders on Hainan had neither the skills nor the will to handle the Communist attack. Plagued by a lack of supplies and ammunition, the GMD leaders on the island soon began squabbling among themselves on how to conduct the "antibandit campaign." The fighting went on for about a week, at the end of which the GMD successfully evacuated almost seventy thousand soldiers and refugees to Taiwan. But Hainan, the last major GMD stronghold close to the Chinese mainland, was lost.[16]

Recognition or Nonrecognition

For the Chinese Communists recognition by the outside world was one of the major motives of their revolution. But Mao Zedong himself drew a sharp distinction between recognition in the sense of foreign countries accepting China's strength and independence, and recognition as diplomatic practice. While looking forward to the former, a recognition created by their own efforts, Mao was uncertain about whether to welcome or fear diplomatic recognition by the imperialist states and their allies. To some of the more pragmatic members of the CCP leadership, such as Zhou Enlai, the advantages of formal intercourse with other states were obvious: trade, hard currency, technology, and easier access to information. But Mao, as he started considering the issue in 1948 and early 1949, was far from convinced. His fear was that diplomatic recognition would be a shield behind which the imperialists could intensify their subversive activities inside China.[17]

In his correspondence with Stalin, Mao had long emphasized this fear, and it does not seem that the Soviet leader's constant underlining of New China's need to trade with capitalist countries did much to dispel it. In December 1948, Mao had told the Soviets that his new state's "trade should be done with the USSR and with the democratic countries. Only what the USSR does not need should be sold to the United States and other countries."[18] In his discussions with Anastas Mikoyan in January 1949, Mao admitted that "there is information that the United States is going to recognize us, and Britain will certainly follow [suit]. For these countries, recognition is necessary for subversive activities against us and for trade with us. What is the use of such recognition? It will open the road for us to other countries and to the UN. This notwithstanding, we are inclined . . . not to haste with establishment of diplomatic relations, but to drag it out while consolidating ourselves."[19]

After the clash with Stalin over Li Zongren's mediation proposal in January of 1949, the Chinese leadership made sure to get Moscow's advice on all steps it took to develop its foreign affairs. Stalin's position was that the new Chinese regime should accept normal diplomatic relations with anybody, as long as they respected China's national integrity and self-determination. Therefore, the contacts that developed with the United States and Britain after the fall of Nanjing were, curiously enough, undertaken by the CCP almost on Stalin's insistence, and with Chairman Mao as a skeptical scrutinizer.[20]

On 5 May, the CCP Center instructed Huang Hua, one of the young Communists in Zhou Enlai's circle who had been trained in underground work, to accept the many appeals for informal contacts that had been secretly transmitted by the Americans since the first months of the year. In his detailed instructions for the meeting, Mao told Huang that when he met with Ambassador Stuart, who had been a virtual Communist prisoner in Nanjing for more than two weeks, Huang should attempt to "detect the American government's intentions and purpose. [Huang] should say as little as possible, [and] just listen to what Stuart has to say. If Stuart is friendly, then [Huang] should be friendly, too, but not too warm. Fu Jingbo [U.S. diplomat Philip Fugh] has said that Stuart would like to continue his position as ambassador to deal with us and change the commercial agreement. We will not reject that."[21]

The contacts with Ambassador Stuart came to nothing, both because of the CCP's insistence that the United States break all relations with the GMD regime and apologize for its former policy, and because of American unwillingness to see the unique in the situation and to stray from diplomatic protocol in order to keep some lines to the CCP leadership open. Ambassador Stuart, aptly described by his Indian colleague as "a minor Mahatma, perpetually surprised at the villainy of the world," felt that the CCP by its propaganda and by its actions had shown that it did not wish normal relations with the United States.[22] Stuart left China on 2 August 1949. Mao was not surprised at the outcome. He wrote: "The war to turn China into a U.S. colony, a war in which the United States of America supplies the money and guns and Jiang Jieshi the men to fight for the United States and slaughter the Chinese people, has been an important component of the U.S. imperialist policy of worldwide aggression since World War II. . . . China, the center of gravity in Asia, is a large country with a population of 475 million; by seizing China, the United States would possess all of Asia. . . . Like Jiang Taigong fishing, they have cast the line for the fish who want to be caught. But he who swallows food handed out in contempt will get a bellyache.[23] . . . What matter if we have to face some difficulties? Let them blockade us! Let them blockade us for eight or ten years! By that time all of China's problems will have been solved."[24]

Mao's attitude toward any form of contacts with the Americans had undoubtedly hardened while the Huang-Stuart meetings went on. One of the reasons for this was the so-called Ward Case—the arrest by the CCP of the U.S. Consul General in Shenyang, Angus Ward, and members of his staff, on charges of espionage. After the fall of Shenyang in 1948, Ward had resisted Communist attempts to force him to leave, and he had stayed on in the city in spite of having no relations with the new authorities. On advice from the Soviets, always sensitive to U.S. intentions in the Northeast, the CCP in November had taken over the consulate, removed its communications equipment, and placed the Consul General under house arrest. Six months later, as the Huang-Stuart meetings were underway, the Communists suddenly charged Ward with spying. There is little doubt that the CIA was running an intelligence operation in the Northeast that had as its main objectives to report on Soviet policy and on the CCP's relations with the Soviets. On the other hand, it seems as if Mao during the Huang-Stuart talks received from the Soviets rather inflated information about the size of this operation, about its aims, and about Ward's personal implication in it. It would not be untypical of Stalin's foreign policy if he, having first goaded Mao into talking to the Americans, later, as he began fearing the consequences of such contacts, took an initiative to sabotage them.[25]

Another reason, ironically, for the CCP leaders' increasing worry about American attempts at meddling in the last stage of the civil war was Washington's release of the *China White Paper,* a lengthy compilation of documents detailing U.S. policy in China since the end of World War II. The Truman administration's purpose in making these materials public, just as Ambassador Stuart was leaving China, was in part to wash its hands of the Guomindang debacle and deflect domestic criticism that the United States had done too little to help Jiang—and also in part to attempt to create a clean slate with the new Chinese government. While being a rude shock to the GMD leadership—"a heavy blow to our people and a great encouragement to the CCP," Jiang called it in his diaries—the publication of the *White Paper* also set off alarm bells in Beijing, where the leaders interpreted it as another devious attempt by Washington to ingratiate itself with those Chinese liberals who had already crossed over to the CCP.[26]

In spite of Mao's reluctance to have formal diplomatic relations with the West and the breakdown of the CCP's contacts with the Americans, the preparations for establishing a foreign policy and a foreign ministry for the new state went into high gear in the summer of 1949. Immediately after the takeover of Tianjin in January 1949, a diplomatic academy had been set up there, with students and staff recruited from among Communist intellectuals (a number of whom had served in CCP intelligence) and from among new converts to the cause from the universities. Their study materials were Soviet manuals hastily translated into Chinese, instructions on diplomatic practice from the Guomindang regime (with notes at the beginning and end underlining their bourgeois nature), and general Chinese and foreign publications on international affairs. In addition, the students learned by heart the Center's instructions on foreign policy from late January 1949 and studied lectures given by Zhou Enlai.[27]

The points that Zhou Enlai made to the students were the same as the foreign policy agenda he had gotten Mikoyan's sanction for in January. All foreign representatives should be subject to strict control by the new authorities. The accounts of foreign-owned businesses should be inspected regularly with a view to taking them over when the opportunity arose. "Former" diplomats would be allowed to stay if they chose to, but they would be given no recognition. Only people with special permission would be allowed to see them. Even foreign military attaches should be allowed to stay, but under strict surveillance, with the view of finding out with whom they cooperated. The only exception to the rule would be Manchuria, which, as Zhou put it to Mikoyan, should be "covered by the iron curtain against foreign powers except the USSR and the People's Democracies."[28] Everywhere foreign missionaries would have to curtail their activities, and foreign schools would have to appoint a Chinese head approved by the authorities and use only government-sanctioned textbooks.[29]

The biggest foreign policy challenge that the new Chinese leadership was up against was how to organize its relations with the Soviet Union. Mao Zedong and everyone in Zhongnanhai thought that Liu Shaoqi's visit to Moscow had been a very big step forward in setting up a pattern of alliance between the People's Republic and the USSR. But in spite of Stalin's benign reception of Liu and the importance of the advice and advisors that Liu brought home with him, Mao still worried about how the

CCP Center Instructions on Foreign Policy, 19 January 1949

We do not have diplomatic relations with any foreign country yet. Many governments of the imperialist countries, especially the American imperialist government, are helping the GMD reactionary government and oppose the liberation of the Chinese people. Thus, we cannot recognize the representatives sent from these countries in China as accredited diplomats. This is reasonable. That we adopt such a stand will let us take the initiative on diplomatic relations, [and] not confine us to the bondage of the humiliating diplomatic traditions of the past. In principle, all privileges enjoyed by the imperialists in China must be abolished and the independence of the Chinese nation must be realized. But in terms of the execution [of these aims], it will be dealt with separately in accordance with the specific situation. The demands that are beneficial to the Chinese people and can easily be settled, we should put forward now; [those that] cannot be settled immediately can wait for a while. Those issues that are not harmful or not very harmful to the Chinese people, even if they could easily be settled, we should not be hurried in dealing with them. All issues that have not been reviewed carefully yet or for which the timing for a solution is not yet right should not be dealt with in a hurry. In a word, in terms of foreign policy, there must be a combination of principle and flexibility.

Zhonggong zhongyang wenjian xuanji, vol. 18.

formal relationship between the two powers should be constructed, both in terms of treaties and diplomatic practice. In Xibaipo, Zhou had asked Mikoyan to explain why the Soviet ambassador had been instructed to go with Li Zongren to Guangzhou when the GMD regime fled from the PLA. The Soviet envoy's rather lame reference to principles of recognition, and his insistence that "this would not at all cause detriment to our common cause, but, on the contrary, would facilitate it," could not have been fully convincing to the CCP leaders.[30] And even Stalin's promise to recognize the PRC as soon as it was set up did not remove Mao's worries that Moscow would not fully consult him on diplomatic initiatives with regard to China.

One of the issues on which the CCP sought Soviet assistance was membership for New China in the United Nations. For the Chinese Communists, the United Nations was in and by itself not of great importance—in February 1949, a CCP spokesman had furiously rejected an Australian proposal for UN mediation in the civil war by pointing to the U.S. dominance in the organization and calling the proposal "absurd" and "a humiliation to the Chinese people."[31] The problem as the Peoples

Republic was being set up was that many of the CCP's nonsocialist allies in the People's Consultative Conference wanted to see tangible and immediate results at the international level from their new state, and since the Communists, for their own reasons, had decided against seeking recognition from the imperialist Great Powers, a seat in the United Nations would be a welcome consolation. By as early as August, Mao had informed Stalin that the PRC would seek representation at the United Nations, and the expulsion from all UN institutions of representatives of the old regime. The Soviets, while noting their own disdain for the United Nations, promised their support, while predicting—correctly, as it turned out—that the United States would block PRC membership until Washington had normalized its own relations with the new state.[32]

The main prize in terms of international recognition, and the only one that really counted for the CCP, was of course recognition by Moscow. Stalin had several times promised that his state would be the first foreign country to recognize New China, but given Soviet behavior toward the CCP in the past, Mao Zedong could never be certain if there would not be some last-minute "tactical" problem that could postpone the setting up of formal state-to-state contacts. During September of 1949, Li Kenong—the CCP head of intelligence who acted as Mao's personal go-between with the Soviets—several times contacted Stalin's representative to the CCP, Ivan Kovalev, and the Soviet Consul General in Beijing, Sergei Tikhvinskii, to make sure that the agreed procedures would be followed. On 2 October—after having quashed a case of Czechoslovak diplomatic overeagerness (which could have led Prague, not Moscow, to be the first Communist regime to recognize the PRC)—Vice Foreign Minister Andrei Gromyko extended the USSR's formal recognition. Tikhvinskii was named charge d'affaires while the question of who was to become Soviet ambassador was decided upon. On the Chinese side, Wang Jiaxiang, who had stayed behind in Moscow from Liu Shaoqi's delegation that summer, was officially appointed as the PRC's first ambassador.[33]

Mao in Moscow

Finding New China's place in the world would, however, depend on more than formal issues of recognition. The new Chairman of the People's Republic, Mao Zedong, was eager to discuss political, strategic, and ideological questions directly with his Soviet allies, and especially with

Stalin himself. Over the longer term, Mao envisaged a division of labor between New China and the Soviet Union in promoting socialist revolution—while Moscow was the center of the world Communist movement, the PRC would have a special responsibility for the East Asian region, including Southeast Asia. Stalin had spoken along similar lines when receiving Liu Shaoqi in Moscow, and Mao expected that he himself would be invited to the Soviet capital soon to discuss these issues. At the same time, Mao hoped that Stalin was ready to sign a new bilateral treaty and enter into specific agreements on Soviet aid in the areas outlined during previous meetings.[34]

Stalin's reappointment of Nikolai Roshchin as Soviet ambassador to China—the same man who had been his last ambassador to the GMD regime, and who had moved to Guangzhou with the GMD after the fall of Nanjing—was an unpleasant surprise for the new Chinese leaders, who had hoped to get a Soviet Communist of some stature as representative in Beijing. In his first conversations with Mao, Roshchin did little to abate the Chinese disappointment, since he had no instructions to prepare a visit to Moscow for the Chairman, and had to throw cold water on the CCP's plans for a military incursion into Vietnam. Zhou Enlai by the end of October had to request that Roshchin inform his superiors of Mao's intention to go to Moscow to pay his respects to Stalin on the Soviet leader's seventieth birthday in December. The *vozhd*—the Kremlin boss—grudgingly gave his consent in mid-November. But when Mao's train finally left Beijing on December 6, the two sides had still not agreed on a framework for what should be discussed in Moscow.[35]

Mao had three matters at the front of his mind as his train wound its way toward the Soviet capital. He wanted security against a U.S. attack. He wanted Soviet assistance in the construction of socialism. And he wanted to remove the stigma that Stalin's and Jiang Jieshi's 1945 treaty had inflicted on Sino-Soviet relations. The best way to achieve all of these aims, Mao concluded, was to sign a new treaty between the two countries, based on Communist solidarity. But the Chinese leader was in no way certain that Stalin would accept such a proposal, and he was prepared to act with great care, so that his wish for a new treaty did not stand in the way of his two other aims, both of which could prove more obtainable.[36]

Stalin, on his side, wanted to test Mao—his commitment to "proletarian internationalism" and his behavior in Moscow. With his unflinchable faith in his own ability to separate friends from enemies, Stalin agreed to a meeting with the new Chinese leader in order to see how Mao would hold up under scrutiny. Stalin had not yet decided on signing a new treaty, nor had he conclusively made up his mind on any major agreements with the new Chinese regime, prior to Mao's arrival in Moscow. Based on what we know of his behavior in other contexts, it is likely that Stalin sought material for his conclusions primarily from the Chinese attitude to the post–World War II territorial arrangements in East Asia and from Mao's attitude to the vozhd personally.

Mao was nervous before his first meeting with Stalin, and still not completely recovered from his recent illness. The Chairman was not enthused by what he considered a low-key reception at the railway station on 16 December, and his first meeting with Stalin in the Kremlin, that same evening, was guarded on both sides. To Mao, it seemed that the Soviet leader now ruled out revising the 1945 treaty, even if the vozhd stood by his promises to assist China militarily and financially. Much of the meeting was taken up by Mao's asking Stalin for general advice, and the Soviet leader, in return, asking the Chairman precise questions about conditions in China—including who controlled the mining of strategic raw materials, and whether "rubber-bearing trees can be grown in southern China." Returning to Blizhniaia, one of Stalin's favorite dachas, which he had been given for his stay, Mao was downcast. He felt that the conversation, which he had looked forward to for so long, had not gone well for him or for China.[37]

Although he saw several of the Soviet Politburo members in the days that followed, Mao received no indication of how or when he would be able to discuss the remaining political questions with Stalin. The Chinese leader must have been somewhat mollified by being invited to sit next to the vozhd himself at the public celebration of Stalin's seventieth birthday in the Bolshoi Theater, and by being given the privilege of speaking before any of the other foreign Communist leaders. But when Stalin again received him, on 24 December, the Soviets were still unwilling to come up with any concrete suggestions for bilateral negotiations. Toward the end of the month, Mao was losing patience. He told Kovalev, who had come to Moscow with him and was visiting at the dacha, that he had come to the Soviet capital to achieve something, and not just to "eat, sleep, and shit." When his hosts invited him to tour Leningrad and other cities, Mao declined and insisted that he was still not well enough to leave Moscow.[38]

Why did Stalin let his guest kill time in Moscow over the New Year holidays? He was clearly aware of Mao's agenda, and that some kind of

Mao meets Stalin in the Kremlin, 16 December 1949

Comrade Mao Zedong: The most important question at the present time is the question of establishing peace. China needs a period of 3–5 years of peace, which would be used to bring the economy back to pre-war levels and to stabilize the country in general. Decisions on the most important questions in China hinge on the prospects for a peaceful future. With this in mind the CC CCP [Central Committee of the Communist Party of China] entrusted me to ascertain from you, comr[ade]. Stalin, in what way and for how long will international peace be preserved.

Comrade Stalin: In China a war for peace, as it were, is taking place. The question of peace greatly preoccupies the Soviet Union as well, though we have already had peace for the past four years. With regards to China, there is no immediate threat at the present time: Japan has yet to stand up on its feet and is thus not ready for war; America, though it screams war, is actually afraid of war more than anything; Europe is afraid of war; in essence, there is no one to fight with China, not unless Kim Il Sung decides to invade China? Peace will depend on our efforts. If we continue to be friendly, peace can last not only 5–10 years, but 20–25 years and perhaps even longer.

Comrade Mao Zedong: Since Liu Shaoqi's return to China, CC CCP has been discussing the treaty of friendship, alliance and mutual assistance between China and the USSR.

Comrade Stalin: This question we can discuss and decide. We must ascertain whether to declare the continuation of the current 1945 treaty of alliance and friendship between the USSR and China, to announce impending changes in the future, or to make these changes right now. As you know, this treaty was concluded between the USSR and China as a result of the Yalta Agreement, which provided for the main points of the treaty (the question of the Kurile Islands, South Sakhalin, Port Arthur, etc.). That is, the given treaty was concluded, so to speak, with the consent of America and England. Keeping in mind this circumstance, we, within our inner circle, have decided not to modify any of the points of this treaty for now, since a change in even one point could give America and England the legal grounds to raise questions about modifying also the treaty's provisions concerning the Kurile Islands, South Sakhalin, etc. This is why we searched to find a way to modify the current treaty in effect while formally maintaining its provisions, in this case by formally maintaining the Soviet Union's right to station its troops at Port Arthur while, at the request of the Chinese government, actually withdrawing the Soviet Armed forces currently stationed there. Such an operation could be carried out upon China's request.

Westad, *Brothers in Arms*, pp. 314–15.

solution must be found. Kovalev reported the content of his conversation directly to the Boss, and he had also supplied Stalin with a very critical memorandum on the views and attitudes of the Chinese leaders, based on his experiences in Beijing. In addition, Blizhniaia was almost certainly bugged by at least one of the Soviet intelligence services. The most likely explanation for Stalin's behavior is that the Soviet leader just could not make up his mind on what the outcome of the Chinese visit should be, and as long as the Boss did not act, his subordinates could not take any initiatives on their own. The exertions of his own seventieth birthday celebrations and the ensuing New Year functions may also have taken their toll on the vozhd and made it inopportune for him to seek out difficult negotiations just at that time.

But in early January the waiting period seemed to come to an end. On 1 January, Stalin wrote up an "interview" with Mao that was published in *Pravda* the next day. In it, the Chinese leader said that "the present . . . treaty" was among the issues that would be discussed during the remaining part of his visit. When Kovalev informed him about the interview, Mao was encouraged. Molotov and Mikoyan visited Stalin in his apartment on the Moscow embankment in the evening of New Year's Day and argued for signing a new comprehensive agreement with the Chinese. On 2 January the two saw Mao at the dacha and signaled Soviet willingness to negotiate on a series of diplomatic, military, and economic issues. Jubilantly, Mao telegraphed the Chinese Premier, Zhou Enlai, to come to Moscow to join in the talks for what he expected to be a new treaty.[39]

Zhou Enlai prepared well on his long train trip across Siberia. From his arrival in Moscow on 20 January, Zhou was the dynamic force in the negotiations, which soon took the form of Chinese proposals and Soviet counterproposals. On almost all issues concerning the alliance treaty, bilateral assistance, trade, and credits and loans, the Chinese drove their agenda forward, while the Soviets argued over details. The Chinese got less, and sometimes much less, than what they bargained for, but they got some form of agreement on all the areas that were important to them.[40]

While the economic negotiations showed the Chinese that Stalin's lieutenants could drive a hard bargain, what really hurt the CCP leaders in a way that none of them ever forgot was the Soviet propensity for introducing territorial issues into their negotiating tactics. The Soviet negotiators made Mao feel as if he was paying with parts of Chinese sovereignty in Manchuria, Xinjiang, and Mongolia to get the assistance he needed.

Excluding all non-Soviet foreigners from Manchuria and Xinjiang and introducing joint Sino-Soviet companies in the Northwest were stipulations not to Chinese liking, and Mao must have felt that he paid a heavy price.

Stalin's tactics, driven by suspicion and rancor, were unnecessary for preventing Sino-American rapprochement and most unhelpful for establishing a lasting Sino-Soviet relationship. Stalin kept his railway and naval concessions in Manchuria (although the leasing period was shortened), and he secured phrasings in the secret additional protocols on Xinjiang and Manchuria that gave him the sense of strategic control of those areas. But Stalin and his associates paid a price for their concessions that was considerably higher than the price Mao paid for signing the agreements that provided him with protection, legitimacy, and aid. By his actions, Stalin helped undermine Chinese faith in the existence of common ideological principles between the two sides.

Creating a Foreign Policy

With the signing of the Sino-Soviet Treaty of Friendship, Alliance, and Mutual Assistance on 14 February 1950, New China entered the Soviet world. Any doubts that the Chinese leaders had about Stalin's behavior were, upon their return to Beijing, kept a secret—questioning Stalin's role, even in private, was considered attacking the very foundations of Communism. Instead, they highlighted the advantages of their achievements in Moscow: The final treaties promised China Soviet military assistance in case of "aggression on the part of Japan or any other state that may collaborate in any way with Japan in acts of aggression"—implicitly providing Beijing with protection in case of a conflict with the United States. In addition, agreements were signed through which the Soviet Union would supply China with credits of around $300 million and expand the programs of military aid in essential areas such as the construction of a PRC air force and development of long-range artillery. In spite of what they knew about the way these agreements had been arrived at, Mao Zedong and the Chinese leaders felt that the treaties in themselves represented the sanction that they had so long sought from "the socialist camp."[41]

After returning to Beijing, Mao had to make sure that this new form of adherence to the Soviet bloc was signaled in all aspects of PRC foreign policy. The British recognition of New China, which London had decided on in early January mainly to protect its commercial interests on the Chinese mainland, was most unwelcome in this respect. As early as his visit to Moscow, Mao had instructed his colleagues in Beijing not to acknowledge the recognition note until the British had fulfilled a list of CCP demands, including the exclusion of all GMD institutions from Hong Kong. The PRC leadership knew that such demands would not be met by the British government, and that the recognition would therefore remain "unconsummated," as Mao put it to Stalin on 22 January. The British abstention on the Soviet proposal to exclude the GMD government from the UN Security Council—the defeat of which led Stalin to order his UN ambassador, Adam Malik, to boycott subsequent meetings—Mao interpreted as a sign that his strategy was working.[42]

Excluded from the United Nations and, by its own strategy, without diplomatic relations even with the foreign powers that had recognized it, New China concentrated on its role as the revolutionary center in East Asia. With the Soviet alliance in place, the CCP leadership could continue its work to promote not only its values but also its organizational style and its military strategies among anti-imperialist forces in the neighboring countries. Although Japan, Korea, Burma, and the Philippines were among the countries in which Mao Zedong saw a role for the new PRC as a guide and patron for national liberation fronts or Communist parties, it was Vietnam that topped his list of worthy candidates for Chinese support. Ho Chi Minh, the leader of the Vietnamese Communists, had spent time with the CCP during the anti-Japanese war, spoke Chinese, and had impressed the Chairman with his willingness to adopt Chinese Communist policies and tactics. To Mao, Ho was the archetypal revolutionary in need of international solidarity, and Vietnam fitted exactly into the mold of a weak Asian country ravaged by imperialism that Mao had described in theory at the outset of his revolutionary career. Mao and the other CCP leaders thought that the PRC, as a new revolutionary state, had to assist Ho and his Vietminh front in their battles with the French colonialists.[43]

At least since early 1948, the CCP had served as a communications center and intermediary for Ho Chi Minh's contacts with Moscow. The first direct aid from the CCP to the Vietminh had come in 1946, after several hundred Vietnamese who had fought with the Chinese Communists returned home. At Ho Chi Minh's request, the CCP Hong Kong Bureau began providing his party with funding sometime in early 1947, and by 1949, in spite of transport difficulties, a regular supply route had been set up between the PLA's temporary bases in Guangxi and Vietminh-held villages in Northeastern Vietnam. By the time the PRC was established, the Chinese Communists were the main foreign supporters and suppliers of the Vietnamese revolutionaries, although the overall assistance—because of the PLA's own needs and transport difficulties—was more limited than the two sides wanted.[44]

During Liu Shaoqi's visit to Moscow, the CCP second-in-command had made it clear that support for the Vietnamese Communists was Beijing's main priority in the region. At that point Stalin had told Liu that China should "do its duty with regard to the revolution in the Far Eastern countries," and had talked about China's "being in charge of" East Asia in the same way as the Soviet Union "took responsibility for" Europe. But when the Chinese leaders in November 1949 had presented him with plans for large-scale PLA assistance to the Vietminh, including the use of Chinese forces across the border into Vietnam, the Soviet leader, as we have seen, soon showed his customary caution. But Mao had in no way given up his plans to assist the Vietnamese. When meeting with Stalin on 24 December, the Chairman, contrary to what the leadership had decided before his departure from Beijing, had again brought the issue up with the Boss. Stalin, in general terms, sanctioned Chinese support for the Vietminh, but he warned against "overconfidence" in confronting the French, since the Americans were bound to support France. Privately, to his colleagues, Stalin made clear that he was not pleased with the way the CCP planned to handle the Vietnam issue.[45]

Mao took Stalin's comments at the 24 December meeting as a go-ahead for the Chinese plans to assist the Vietminh. Liu Shaoqi, in Beijing, immediately cabled Ho Chi Minh to come to Beijing to "discuss all important issues." After a perilous journey, which included a fortnight's trek through the forests of Northeastern Vietnam to the Guangxi border, Ho and his men arrived in Beijing on 30 January. Having made the journey, Ho Chi Minh was not happy just being told about China's decision to support his movement. Wary of China's and the Soviet Union's deciding on Vietnamese problems without his presence, Ho asked the Chinese leaders to help him to travel to Moscow to meet with Stalin and Mao. After having received Stalin's grudging acceptance, Ho arrived in Moscow amid strict secrecy on 9 or 10 February 1950. While the Soviet leaders in most cases cold-shouldered the visiting Vietnamese, Mao and Zhou Enlai promised "to offer all the military assistance Vietnam needs in its struggle against France." Ho Chi Minh returned to Beijing with Mao and Zhou, and held detailed discussions with the Chinese leaders on the Vietminh's strategy and tactics on the way.[46]

Even after it became clear in the spring of 1950 that France would not allow GMD operations from its territory, Mao Zedong and his military planners seem to have believed that the greatest risk for an imperialist intervention against China would be from the south. As Zhou Enlai pointed out in January, it was in Southeast Asia that imperialism was strongest and could draw on most resources. This general view lent particular urgency to the military plans for a forward strategy into Vietnam. In March, Liu Shaoqi instructed General Luo Guibo, who led the PLA advance team with the Vietminh, to prepare for a long-term Chinese involvement in Southeast Asia. On 17 April, the main PLA field armies received orders to prepare military advisers to go to Vietnam immediately, bringing with them their weapons and ammunition. Some PLA officers began arriving in Northern Vietnam in early May to set up what would become the Chinese Military Advisory Group. After Kim Il-sung's forces attacked in Korea on 25 June, Mao decided to speed up—rather than limit, as some military leaders suggested—the Chinese assistance to Vietnam. By August 1950 regular PLA units participated in the fighting in northern Vietnam as part of a Chinese military presence that would last for almost twenty years.[47]

While Vietnam was a top priority for the PRC, Korea was a more limited interest. There were many reasons for this. In spite of there being many North Korean military leaders with close ties to the CCP, Kim Il-sung was not one of them. Mao considered Kim the Soviets' man, and seems to have doubted his leadership qualities. Kim's position was a symbol of Korea as a Soviet domain, in which China had a limited role to play.[48]

Until the summer of 1948, when Korea played a significant role as a base area for PLA operations in Manchuria, the CCP leaders knew that they needed permission from the Soviets, not the Koreans, to move their forces back and forth across the border. Even after the creation of the Democratic People's Republic of Korea under Kim Il-sung's leadership in September 1948, the CCP continued to deal mostly with the Soviets on issues regarding the peninsula or the Koreans in Manchuria. Mao Zedong's chief concern with regard to Korea in 1949 was to prevent its being used as a staging ground for an imperialist attack on China, as had happened in the past. Mao therefore thought that the Soviet presence in

Korea was beneficial for China in security terms, but at the same time he expected China's own role as a protector of Korea to grow after the People's Republic was established.[49]

Before October 1949 the Chinese concern over Korea was centered on the possibilities of an attack by Syngman Rhee's Southern regime, supported by the United States and other imperialist forces, on North Korea. In the summer of 1949, during Liu Shaoqi's Moscow visit, the Soviets had informed the Chinese that such a surprise attack could come soon, and the PLA had, in consequence, sent some units of Lin Biao's forces back to Manchuria to assist the Korean comrades in case of a Southern invasion. After October, however, it was Kim Il-sung's repeated requests to Moscow of support for a pre-emptive offensive against Seoul that most troubled Beijing. Both before and during Mao's visit to Moscow the Chinese leaders had made it clear to the Soviets that they did not think the time was ripe for a reunification of Korea by force.[50]

There were many reasons for the Chinese reluctance to support Kim's bid for Soviet assistance in his quest to reunify his country. Beijing's doubts about Kim's own leadership qualities have already been mentioned. More important, as Mao had told the North Korean leaders by as early as mid-May of 1949, opening a conflict with imperialism in Korea, right on the border of China's most industrially advanced provinces, within striking distance of Beijing, and close to the main routes connecting China to the Soviet Union at a time when the PRC was still fighting a civil war, was simply not good strategy. In addition, the Chinese had their own intelligence from South Korea that contradicted Kim's optimistic reports to the Soviets about spontaneous uprisings among Southern workers and peasants. CCP intelligence, which was well informed about the situation in both parts of Korea, simply did not believe that a Southern offensive would succeed.[51]

Returning from Moscow, Mao thought that the Soviets agreed with his assessment—at least up to a point. Risking the revolutionary achievements in China in order to start an offensive in Korea would be foolhardy. Mao's perception was that the Korean Communists would get the Chinese and Soviet support they asked for, and deserved, some time in 1951, after the Chinese civil war had ended. Although Mao during his visit had agreed with Stalin's proposal to tell Kim Il-sung that they would assist in his plans for reunification by force, the Chinese leader was therefore surprised and dismayed when Kim came to Beijing on 13 May 1950, fresh from a visit to Moscow, to inform the Chinese leaders that he had already secured Soviet consent to an offensive against the South. Mao sent Zhou Enlai to see Ambassador Roshchin that night, demanding an immediate personal confirmation from Stalin. The Boss replied the next morning:

> In their conversation with Korean comrades, Filippov [Stalin] and his friends expressed an opinion that because of the changed international situation they agreed with a proposal of the Koreans to begin unification. At the same time, they made it clear that this question must be finally decided by the Chinese and Korean comrades jointly. In the event that the Chinese comrades disagree, the resolution of the question must be postponed until new consideration. The Korean comrades can tell you the details of the conversation.[52]

Put on the spot by Stalin, Mao Zedong had no alternative but to confirm his support for the North Korean plans. Doing otherwise would not only have been in disregard of the Soviet leader's instructions but also would have contradicted Mao's and the CCP's profound belief in solidarity with the revolutionary forces of other Asian countries. In the wake of the late April PLA takeover of Hainan, which the CCP had hailed as a major step on the road to the unification of China under its regime, how could Mao refuse a representative of the revolutionary forces in a smaller country, Korea, the attempt to reunify his nation? The Chairman told Kim Il-sung that he had expected that a military offensive in Korea would have come after a PLA attack on Taiwan, and he warned that U.S. and possibly Japanese involvement in the fighting could not be completely excluded. But he did agree to the plans, and did promise Chinese support, although not explicitly the support of PLA troops.[53]

The leaders in Beijing in 1950 had as much difficulty as historians have today in deciding why Stalin had thrown overboard his earlier caution and agreed to Kim's planned offensive. Some of the PLA military leaders, especially, seem to have believed that Stalin's OK was a feeble one, and that the Soviets would change their mind eventually, as had happened so often in the past. But by the first weeks of June it became clear to the Chinese, in spite of their lack of official information from Pyongyang and Moscow, that the North Korean and Soviet preparations for an attack on South Korea were being sped up and that the offensive could be expected to begin by that summer. Evidently, Soviet military planners had concluded that the North would maximize its chances for success if the attack took place sooner rather than later, since the South's own military preparedness seemed to catch up quickly with the North's capabilities.[54]

Fighting Imperialism—Making Revolution

In spite of the preparations that went on in North Korea, there was no war fever in Beijing in the early summer of 1950. The CCP leadership concentrated on completing its own offensives against the GMD-held islands and against Tibet, and on intensifying the pace of reform in the PRC. At the Central Committee plenum in early June, almost all of the discussion centered on reform proposals, both to establish firmer control in the cities and to advance social changes in the countryside. Issues of how far to extend land reform and how much to advance public ownership in industry were at the core of these debates, with Liu Shaoqi's and Ren Bishi's gradualist line being pushed further to the left by members of the Central Committee (now headed by Gao Gang), who were impatient with the slow pace of reform. At the June plenum the opposition to Liu and Ren had some encouragement from Mao Zedong, who himself felt that the ideals of a quick socialist transformation were being unnecessarily held up by the caution of his chief lieutenants.[55]

Beijing got only a few days' warning that the North Korean attack was to take place on 25 June. Immediately after the war broke out, the Chinese, Soviets, and North Koreans held several meetings in Beijing on how China could contribute to the success of the North Korean offensive, at which the PLA and Chinese intelligence suggested a number of options, ranging from freighting Korean forces across from the Shandong peninsula to land behind enemy lines to using CCP agents to sabotage U.S. supplies for South Korea in California or at naval ports in the Pacific. Because of Stalin's immense prestige as the main Marxist interpreter of the international situation, the Chinese leadership continued to believe until late August that the United States would not launch massive counterattacks in Korea with its own forces. They therefore expected that China would not need to use its own troops to fight in Korea. Although the deployments of Chinese forces to the border areas that had started in the spring intensified after the outbreak of war, there was little sense through July and early August that these PLA units were being prepared for an intervention. In his 18 August telegram to Gao Gang, head of the CCP in the Northeast, Mao did however warn Gao that the Northeast Border Defense Army should be ready for military operations in Korea by the end of September, if the military situation demanded it.[56]

All of Mao's suspicions of Kim Il-sung's lack of leadership ability came to the fore in Beijing after U.S. troops landed at Inchon on 15 September and in a spectacular fashion turned fortunes on the battlefield. Together with the obvious Soviet misinterpretation of American will and capabilities, it was Kim's throwing all caution to the winds after the initial victories that had led to the disaster, Mao thought. With North Korean forces in full retreat toward the Yalu River and the Chinese border, pursued by well-equipped U.S. troops, Beijing had to make up its mind quickly on how to respond. The Chinese leaders were prodded by Stalin, who on 1 October informed them that the situation in Korea was grave and that without a Chinese intervention the Korean Communist regime would collapse.[57]

Mao Zedong seems to have been in little doubt that the PRC would have to intervene for the sake of the Korean revolution and revolutionary movements elsewhere in East Asia. But the majority in the Politburo and among the PLA leadership had serious reservations about sending Chinese troops to Korea. Civilian leaders such as Liu Shaoqi and Ren Bishi feared that a new war would throw up immense difficulties for a gradual and well-organized reform process in China. Many military leaders, including Lin Biao, thought that a Chinese offensive in Korea would be logistically and tactically difficult, and could endanger Chinese security in Manchuria and in areas along the coast. For both groups the prospect of an all-out war with the United States must have loomed large: Just as the Chinese revolution was being completed in spite of the constant danger of imperialist intervention, Kim and Stalin were asking the CCP to go to war by their own will with the most powerful imperialist nation in the world.[58]

At the extended Politburo meeting on 2 October no clear-cut decision could be arrived at, and it took at least three more days of intense discussion before Mao's line won out. The three core arguments that the Chairman put forward in favor of intervention were the CCP's debt to the Koreans who had fought with them during the Chinese civil war, the U.S. threat to Chinese security, and the availability of Soviet support for the war effort. But beyond the persuasiveness of each of these points, it was Mao's immense prestige in military and political affairs that won the day. Mao was the leader who had brought the party victory in the civil war. Even when they disagreed with him, as the majority did in the crucial case of intervention in Korea, his colleagues in the CCP leadership were willing to defer to his wishes, since Mao alone was seen to have the strategic vision that could make the party achieve its political aims. In diplomacy, as in domestic politics, the successes of the civil war meant that few were willing to consider differences in what those aims were, and Mao could invariably have his way when he took a distinct political position.

But even if the Chinese leadership by 8 October had already, at Mao's insistence, decided to intervene, Beijing wanted to make sure that they knew exactly what kind of Soviet support would be forthcoming. While Mao ordered the transformation of the Northeast Border Defense Army into the "Chinese People's Volunteers" under the command of the civil war General Peng Dehuai, Zhou Enlai traveled to the Crimea to meet with Stalin. Twice, while Zhou attempted to wrest military concessions from a cautious Stalin in return for doing his bidding on Korea, Mao had to stop Peng's preparations to consider how the news from Crimea could be built into the plans for the offensive. The Soviet leader's refusal to honor his earlier promise of air cover for the advancing Chinese troops was particularly difficult for Mao, since the assistance of the Soviet air force had been one of his key military arguments in favor of an intervention. But on 18 October, the day after Zhou Enlai returned to tell of minimal Soviet commitments, the order still went out from Beijing for "the Volunteers" to join in the fighting on the Korean side of the Yalu River. Mao had made up his mind: He would fight over Korea, even at the risk of new challenges to his own revolution.[59]

For the Chinese people there was to be no interruption to warfare. With the civil war still underway outside the core provinces, many of the PLA's best troops were transported straight from battle zones in the South or West to the Korean front. The peasants of the Siping area, like those of other areas in North and Northeast China who had seen warfare so often that century and who had hoped that Communist victory meant stability, saw their sons once again marched off to war. More than two million Chinese served in Korea; at least 152,000 died there, and around 230,000 were wounded, in a war in which the result, after three years of carnage, was the re-establishment of the prewar division line between the two parts of the country.[60] The 6.2 billion yuan that the PRC spent in total on the war was probably, in annual terms, about 20 to 25 percent of the total Chinese central government's budget under the first five-year plan. The war crippled the new state's economy, and made it increasingly dependent on Soviet credits and assistance.

For Mao Zedong, it was not the human or economic cost of the war in Korea that mattered.[61] For the Chairman, the main point of the war was to show that revolutionary New China could take on the most powerful imperialist nation in the world and hold its own. To him, and to most of his colleagues, the initial Chinese victories in the war—in spite of the tremendous price that their country and their countrymen paid—meant that the PRC had proven itself on the international scene. Their state had done what no other Chinese government had managed to do over the past 150 years: It had stood up to imperialism, and it had not lost the war. For the new regime, and most of all for Mao himself, the Korean War was a triumph that gave the People's Republic international credibility and increased its domestic legitimacy.

The Beijing leadership clung to this sense of victory, even if they understood that it was the Korean War that had deprived them of Taiwan, the main prize in the ongoing battle for Chinese unification. To Mao, this seems to have been a conscious choice: In terms of his overall agenda, fighting imperialism in Vietnam and Korea was probably more important in the short run than doing away with the last stronghold of the GMD regime. He also seems to have realized that there was a high probability that the United States would intervene to protect Jiang's regime if the CCP sent its forces to fight outside its own borders. When, immediately after the North Korean attack, President Truman sent units from the U.S. Navy's 7th Fleet into the Taiwan Strait to block off the island from PLA landings, the attitude among the top PRC leadership was therefore more one of outrage than of shock.

With the Korean War, the CCP leaders had finally gotten the direct military encounter with imperialism that their political theory had told them to expect. In spite of Stalin's and Kim's having played topsy-turvy with the Marxist position on the origins of war—it was, after all, the imperialists who were supposed to attack, and not the other way around—the conflict confirmed to the party leaders the lasting enmity of imperialism, and the need to take action, domestically, to counter it. Even though, as we have seen, the political decisions to radicalize the reform campaigns in the PRC had been taken well before the outbreak of war, there is no doubt that the sense of emergency brought on by events in Korea intensified the implementation of the campaigns. Making the link between landlordism in the countryside, bourgeois behavior in the cities, and treason to the Chinese cause in Korea enabled party cadres to exploit nationalist sentiment in mobilizing people to criticize, dispossess, or murder alleged opponents of the regime. While the violent political campaigns of the early 1950s were completely within the framework that party leaders had envisaged for their revolution, there is little doubt that without the Korean War, many leaders—both at the Center and locally—would have preferred a slower and more careful implementation of the party's policies.

Other events also contributed to the radicalization of the Chinese revolution and the renewed turn to mass campaigns. On 27 October 1950, Ren Bishi died in Beijing at the age of forty-six. Ren had been a member of the party leadership since the mid-1930s and was perhaps its main Marxist theoretician. During the latter stage of the civil war, Ren had increasingly come to ally himself with Liu Shaoqi's Soviet-inspired gradualist approach to reform. His death deprived Liu of crucial support, and made it easier for other leaders, such as Gao Gang, to challenge Liu's positions. With Ren gone, the constraints on Mao Zedong in requesting more radical policies were also reduced. In early 1951, as Mao was beginning to think of the "new-democratic" phase of the revolution as ending with the completion of land reform—and not beginning with it, as Liu had claimed—a clash was unavoidable. When Liu in July 1951 criticized Gao's policies in the Northeast as "an erroneous, dangerous, and utopian notion of agrarian socialism," Mao sided with Gao, telling Liu and his associates that he could not "side with them" but was "with the minority that holds the truth."[62] As with the Korean War, the majority caved in because the Chairman held other views. Liu Shaoqi's political turn enabled him to outmaneuver Gao Gang and keep his position as Mao's chief lieutenant, but it defeated his political purpose. Instead of a gradual transition to socialism, China got a series of campaigns intended to catapult the country into the kind of modernity that Mao envisaged.

POSTSCRIPT
The Chinese Civil War Today

China's entry into the Korean War was the first of many unexpected twists in the history of the People's Republic. With each of these political turns—most of which were well beyond the horizon in 1950—the Communist state came to shatter the expectations of another group of its citizens. The Campaign to Suppress Counter-Revolutionary Activities—implemented during the Korean War, but planned well before its outbreak—defined more than two million people as "local tyrants, enemy agents, backbone members of reactionary parties and groups, or heads of reactionary secret societies." A million and a half were killed, and the others—most of whom had never actively opposed the new regime—saw their lives destroyed. In 1955 the peasants, including those who had first received land through land reform, were forced to join farming collectives. In 1958, as Mao Zedong's utopianism and impatience grew stronger, the party launched a Great Leap Forward to catch up with production levels in the imperialist states. At least twenty million people died as a result of ignorance, mismanagement, and blind faith, mostly from starvation in the countryside.

Some prominent historians of China find that in spite of these policies the CCP regime's successes outweigh its failures. They point to the attainment of national integration and independence under Communist rule, and to the dramatic increases in levels of education and health-care over the past fifty years. Most of all they underline the economic advances under socialism, which saw an extraordinary 30 percent increase in industry's share of national income during Mao Zedong's rule (1949–76). The foundation for these successes, it is claimed, lay in land reform, which broke the rule of reactionary landlords, increased social equity, and, through collectivization, provided the agrarian surplus needed to finance state-sponsored industrialization. Without these reforms, the high growth rates in the post-1976 era would not have been possible.[1]

Seen in this light, both the successes and the failures of the People's Republic are in some measure connected to the civil war. The late 1940s decided not only the outcome of the struggle for political power in China. It also influenced—sometimes decisively—the victorious party's aims and methods during the last half of the twentieth century. Much of what went wrong in Chinese history over the past fifty years—and in my opinion there was more wrong than right—was based on the experiences of the civil war by the generation who fought it. The militarization of society, the deification of the supreme leader, and the extreme faith in the power of human will and of short, total campaigns—all came out of the lessons the Chinese Communists believed to have learned from the late 1940s.[2] So too did their obsession with the control of intellectuals, labor leaders, and national minorities, their enmity with the United States, and their application of Soviet models. At crucial moments during the history of the PRC, when the fate of millions was decided upon, the experiences of the civil war often contributed to the wrong decisions being taken.

Why was that so? Why did the leaders of the CCP take out of their great victory lessons that in so many later cases would lead to defeat? For them, as for all other political leaders, managing war (or even managing society at war) is very different from leading a normal society. Even for a party with revolutionary aims, the continuation of policies of mass mobilization and regimentalization after a country is at peace must lead to unnecessary exacerbation of conflict and to resistance from society at large. Chinese history, not least of all, has plenty of such examples, from the Qin emperor twenty-two hundred years ago to Mao Zedong and his revolution. Marxism-Leninism, the authoritarian political theory that Mao and his supporters adhered to, stimulated their fascination with the use of military methods to achieve revolutionary aims. But it was still basically their choices that made the difference. And, as most of us do, the CCP elite acted on lessons: They believed that the methods of war were the party's best choice in promoting reform, even in peacetime, because these methods were what the party was good at and what had brought it its victories in the revolutionary struggle.

This book shows the assumption that militarization brought victory to be only partially true, even for the civil war period. While emphasizing the decisive impact of military encounters on the outcome of the Chinese civil war, the present volume also underlines contingency—the crucial battles might have turned out differently if only slightly different dispositions had been made. During the decisive encounters—the Manchurian battles, LiaoShen, and HuaiHai—both the CCP and the GMD military leaderships made mistakes that could have cost them the victory, but the Guomindang made the most, as its state came under pressure from within. The military history of the civil war is therefore not a unilinear story, in which the PLA went from strength to strength, but a much more complex and uncertain tale in which the outcome was not given until very late in 1948.

But the encounters on the battlefield show only one part of the overall story of the civil war and the CCP victory. The account presented here has stressed the late 1940s as a period of decisive encounters between Chinese and foreigners, between ethnic groups within China, and between social classes. It has also emphasized changing relations within Chinese families, between generations and between men and women. Finally, the book has underlined the post-1945 frictions between the GMD state and local groups. It is in these sets of encounters, we have claimed, that the other main reason for the Guomindang collapse must be sought. Within a rapidly changing society, Jiang Jieshi's regime failed at creating the alliances that would have been necessary to uphold its rule. On the contrary, the attempts by a war-weary and enfeebled government to extend its rule and powers of taxation to new areas met with often successful local resistance. These clashes benefited the CCP and enabled the party to manipulate local politics in order to create the minimum of support needed to sustain its military campaigns.

In spite of their capacity for helping us to understand the conditions under which the civil war was fought, structural explanations—be they based on observations of society or of military affairs—are therefore not sufficient to explain the outcome of the war. Human decisions—often referred to by social scientists, with an unfortunate choice of terms, as agency—are at the center of this story. But an understanding of the structures of Chinese society should tell us that it is not just decisions at the top level of politics or military affairs that count. Often during the civil war, decisions made by individuals or communities far away from central politics were what mattered most—people who, for the most part, voted with their feet against the GMD regime and therefore helped the CCP defeat it. That a CCP victory, in a narrow sense, was not the outcome many of these people sought is another matter. Unforeseen consequences seem to be even more prevalent in the history of revolutions than in general political history.

One of the basic "structures" of the study of the Chinese civil war must be the history of the Chinese revolution. Before the 1945–50 conflict lie thirty years of revolutionary struggle by the CCP—a history that had taken the party through an amazing number of ups and downs (mostly downs) before the victories in the civil war. For the CCP leaders, this history of war, executions, and narrow escapes formed the matrix on which their decisions rested. Whether this knowledge of the personal background and experience of Mao and his comrades should predispose us to judge their long-term actions more leniently, I do not know. What is crucial for grasping their historical roles—and those of their GMD opponents—is to attempt to understand where they came from and what their ambitions were, and how their aims and experience fed into the decisions they made.

The version of the civil war that is presented in this volume also burrs into the ideological claims that present-day CCP leaders often present. Their belief that the outcome of the war somehow still legitimizes their rule is hard to defend if the 1945–50 period for most Chinese was about escaping warfare and other effects of authoritarian centralism. For the CCP regime, it is obviously of crucial importance that the heroic image of the civil war persist—for instance, through the way the war is presented in history textbooks. As I experienced during my stay in China in 1989— when the battle for legitimacy was fought on the streets—the Communist victory in the civil war is still, for many Chinese, a viable argument to use in the defense of CCP rule. For a great number of those who lived through the chaos of the 1940s, and for some of their descendants, 1949 "chose" Mao and his successors to rule China.

This background of historical memory and legitimization—however constructed it might be for today's generations—is what complicates some of the most important questions that China faces today. The environmental crisis, the challenges of under- and unemployment, of official corruption, and exploitation of workers, could all have been dealt with more efficiently if the state had not based part of its legitimacy on military conquest. Even more important, the challenges that face China on its periphery—Taiwan, Tibet, and Xinjiang—are in part direct legacies of the civil war and can be met in the long run only by a revaluation and deheroization of the conflict locally and among most Chinese. The way forward in these difficult conflicts will have to be illuminated by the new light on the past that historians in China are now creating.

Sooner or later the CCP dictatorship in the People's Republic of China will have to give way to a more pluralist form of government, just as the Guomindang dictatorship on Taiwan in the 1980s was replaced by a more inclusive political system. When that happens, the saddest legacies of the civil war—authoritarian rule and the suppression of individual rights—will have been overcome. It is my guess that on the Chinese road to democracy many of the political and intellectual debates of the late 1940s will be resumed with only few variations. The discussions about how to bridge the urban-rural divide and how to end the exploitation of workers and peasants are already re-emerging in forms very similar to those of fifty years ago, as are examinations of good education and artistic freedom. Minority rights and political representation will be hotly debated in the decades to come. It is up to the next generation of Chinese to form their own positions in these debates. It is to be hoped that they will create answers that will lead to a better life for a larger number of people than resulted from the civil war. As a new century opens, the wish is that it may be more peaceful, happy, and prosperous for the people of China than was the past century.

Notes

Introduction

1. Anna Louise Strong, *The Chinese Conquer China* (Garden City, NY: Doubleday, 1949); Jack Belden, *China Shakes the World* (New York: Harper, 1949); Annalee Jacoby and Theodore White, *Thunder Out of China* (New York: William Sloane, 1946); Harrison Forman, *Blunder in Asia* (New York: Didier, 1950); Freda Utley, *The China Story: How We Lost 400,000,000 Allies* (Chicago: Henry Regnery, 1951). The classic report on the earlier stages of the GMD-CCP conflict from a pro-CCP viewpoint is Edgar Snow's *Red Star over China* (London: Victor Gollancz, 1968 [1937]).

2. Tang Tsou, *America's Failure in China, 1941–50* (Chicago: University of Chicago Press, 1963); Lionel Chassin, *La conquête de la Chine par Mao Tse-Tung, 1945–1949* (Paris: Payot, 1952), in English as *The Communist Conquest of China: A History of the Civil War, 1945–1949*, trans. Timothy Osato and Louis Gelas (Cambridge, MA: Harvard University Press, 1965).

3. Lucien Bianco, *Origins of the Chinese Revolution, 1915–1949*, trans. Muriel Bell (Stanford, CA: Stanford University Press, 1971).

4. Chalmers Johnson's *Peasant Nationalism and Communist Power: The Emergence of Revolutionary China, 1937–1945* (Stanford, CA: Stanford University Press, 1962) had emphasized nationalism as the key to the rise of the CCP. Johnson's 1970s critics, on the other hand, underlined socioeconomic causes for the Communist advances during the anti-Japanese war; see Mark Selden, *The Yenan Way in Revolutionary China* (Cambridge, MA: Harvard University Press, 1971) and Tetsuya Kataoka, *Resistance and Revolution in China* (Berkeley: University of California Press, 1974). For an overview of the debate, see Kathleen Hartford and Steven M. Goldstein, "Introduction: Perspectives on the Chinese Communist Revolution," in Hartford and Goldstein, eds., *Single Sparks: China's Rural Revolution* (Armonk, NY: Sharpe, 1989); Lloyd Eastman, *The Abortive Revolution: China under Nationalist Rule, 1927–1937* (Cambridge, MA: Harvard University Press, 1974) and *Seeds of Destruction: China in War and Revolution, 1937–1949* (Stanford, CA: Stanford University Press, 1984); Suzanne Pepper, *Civil War in China: The Political Struggle, 1945–1949* (Berkeley: University of California Press, 1978; rev. ed. Lanham, MD: Rowan and Littlefield, 1999).

5. For an overview, see Tony Saich and Hans van de Ven, eds. *New Perspectives on the Chinese Revolution* (Armonk, NY: M. E. Sharpe, 1994). Particularly important studies in English are Yung-fa Chen [Chen Yongfa], *Making Revolution: The Communist Movement in East and Central China, 1937–1945* (Berkeley: University of California Press, 1986); Odoric Y. K. Wou, *Mobilizing the Masses: Building Revolution in Henan* (Stanford, CA: Stanford University Press, 1994); and Ralph A. Thaxton, Jr., *Salt of the Earth: The Political Origins of Peasant Protest and Communist Revolution in China* (Berkeley: University of California Press, 1997). Two influential studies that take a broader view of the period are Elizabeth J. Perry, *Rebels and Revolutionaries in North China, 1845–1945* (Stanford, CA: Stanford University Press, 1980); and Prasenjit Duara, *Culture, Power, and the State: Rural North China, 1900–1942* (Stanford, CA: Stanford University Press, 1988). For a survey of some of the work that has been undertaken in China since the early 1980s, see *Dang de wenxian mulu suoyin* [An Index Catalog to *Dang de wenxian*] (Beijing: Zhongyang wenxian, 1998). *Dang de wenxian* [*Party Documents*] is one of the main Chinese journals for the study of CCP history; for a more comprehensive survey of such journals, see the bibliographical essay.

6. See note 4 for examples of these trends. This joining of the debate is, as yet, more evident in Chinese language journals, such as, in the PRC, *Dang de wenxian*, *Zhonggong dangshi yanjiu*, and *Jindaishi yanjiu*, or, in Taiwan, *Jindaishi yanjiu tongxun*, than in the main English-language journals.

7. The theorists' turn toward explanations that emphasize individual agency and specific cultural influences in the wake of the regime changes in South Africa, Latin America, and Eastern Europe in the late 1980s has done little to challenge the usefulness of overall structural approaches (although it has made debates about theory more palatable to many historians); see John Foran, ed., *Theorizing Revolutions* (London: Routledge, 1997) and Fred Halliday, *Revolution and World Politics: The Rise and Fall of the Sixth Great Power* (London: Macmillan, 1999).

8. See the work of Chen Yongfa and Ralph Thaxton. See also Mark Selden's discussion in *China in Revolution: The Yenan Way Revisited* (Armonk, NY: M. E. Sharpe, 1995); and, for a text-centered approach, David E. Apter and Tony Saich, *Revolutionary Discourse in Mao's Republic* (Cambridge, MA: Harvard University Press, 1994). For two of the CCP's main constituencies, women and youth, see Christina K. Gilmartin et al., eds., *Engendering China: Women, Culture, and the State*, Harvard Contemporary China Series 10 (Cambridge, MA: Harvard University Press, 1994); and Jeffrey Wasserstrom, *Student Protests in Twentieth Century China: The View from Shanghai* (Stanford, CA: Stanford University Press, 1991).

9. See Yongfa Chen's work, and James C. Hsiung and Steven I. Levine, *China's Bitter Victory: The War with Japan, 1937–1945* (Armonk, NY: Eastgate, 1992).

10. Frederick C. Teiwes with Warren Sun, "From a Leninist to a Charismatic Party: The CCP's Changing Leadership, 1937–1945," in Tony Saich and Hans van de Ven, eds., *New Perspectives on the Chinese Communist Revolution* (Armonk, NY: M. E. Sharpe, 1995).

11. See Apter and Saich, *Revolutionary Discourse in Mao's Republic*; see also

David Apter, "Discourse as Power: Yan'an and the Chinese Revolution," in Saich and van de Ven, *New Perspectives on the Chinese Communist Revolution*.

12. See Hsiung and Levine, *China's Bitter Victory*.

13. For this argument, see Eastman, *Seeds of Destruction*.

14. See Odd Arne Westad, *Cold War and Revolution: Soviet-American Rivalry and the Origins of the Chinese Civil War, 1944–1946* (New York: Columbia University Press, 1993).

15. Ibid.

16. For an attempt at putting these tendencies into a larger historical perspective, see Lucien Bianco, "Conflict and Resistance in Twentieth Century China," *Chinese Studies in History* 33, no. 2 (2000): 1–91.

17. For studies of CCP policies that survey these trends in the longer term in key base areas, see the work by Chen Yongfa and Odoric Wou cited above. See also Gregory Benton's two important volumes, *Mountain Fires: The Red Army's Three-Year War in South China, 1934–1938* (Berkeley: University of California Press, 1992), and *New Fourth Army: Communist Resistance along the Yangtze and the Huai, 1938–1941* (Berkeley: University of California Press, 1999); Steven I. Levine, *Anvil of Victory: The Communist Revolution in Manchuria, 1945–1948* (New York: Columbia University Press, 1987); Pauline B. Keating, *Two Revolutions: Village Reconstruction and the Cooperative Movement in Northern Shaanxi, 1934–1945* (Stanford, CA: Stanford University Press, 1997); Kathleen J. Hartford, "Step by Step: Reform, Resistance, and Revolution in Chin-Ch'a-Chi Border Region, 1937–1945," Ph.D. dissertation, Stanford University, 1980; David Mark Paulson, "War and Revolution in North China: The Shandong Base Area, 1937–1945," Ph.D. dissertation, Stanford University, 1982.

Chapter 1. East Asian Cockpit

1. My interest in the civil war as a research field was first stimulated by listening to old people in the villages of the Siping area tell their histories during a visit in the spring of 1984. I am grateful to them for their hospitality and for their candor.

2. Lloyd E. Eastman, *Family, Fields, and Ancestors: Constancy and Change in China's Social and Economic History, 1550–1949* (New York: Oxford University Press, 1988); Stein Tønnesson and Hans Antlöv, eds., *Asian Forms of the Nation* (Richmond, UK: Curzon Press, 1996); James C. Scott, *The Moral Economy of the Peasant: Rebellion and Subsistence in Southeast Asia* (New Haven: Yale University Press, 1976).

3. See, for instance, Heather Sutherland, *The Making of a Bureaucratic Elite: The Colonial Transformation of the Javanese Priyayi* (Singapore: Heinemann, 1979); and the overview in Rudolf V. Albertini, with Albert Wirz, *European Colonial Rule, 1880–1940: The Impact of the West on India, Southeast Asia, and Africa*, trans. John G. Williamson (Westport, CO: Greenwood Press, 1982).

4. See the essays in Hans Antlöv and Stein Tønnesson, eds., *Imperial Policy and Southeast Asian Nationalism, 1930–1957* (Richmond: Curzon Press, 1995); for a general discussion, see Jürgen Osterhammel, *Colonialism: A Theoretical Overview*, trans. Shelley L. Frisch (Princeton, NJ: M. Wiener, 1997).

5. For the challenges that 1945 created in the region, see, on Indonesia, Bene-

dict R. O'G. Anderson, *Java in a Time of Revolution: Occupation and Resistance, 1944–1946* (Ithaca, NY: Cornell University Press, 1972); on Malaya, Cheah Boon Kheng, "The Erosion of Ideological Hegemony and Royal Power and the Rise of Post-War Malay Nationalism, 1945–1946," *Journal of Southeast Asian Studies* 19, no. 1 (1988): 1–26; on the Philippines, Benedict J. Kerkvliet, *The Huk Rebellion: A Study of Peasant Revolt in the Philippines* (Berkeley: University of California Press, 1977); on Vietnam, David G. Marr, *Vietnam 1945: The Quest for Power* (Berkeley: University of California Press, 1995); and Stein Tønnesson, *The Vietnamese Revolution of 1945: Roosevelt, Ho Chi Minh, and De Gaulle in a World at War* (London: Sage, 1991); and on Korea, Bruce Cumings, *The Origins of the Korean War*. Vol. 1: *Liberation and the Emergence of Separate Regimes, 1945–1947* (Princeton, NJ: Princeton University Press, 1981). For a general overview, see Robert Holland, ed., "Emergencies and Disorder in European Empires after 1945," *Journal of Imperial and Commonwealth History* 21, no. 3 (special issue, 1993).

6. For key differences, see Joshua A. Fogel, "Issues in the Evolution of Modern China in East Asian Comparative Perspective," *History Teacher* 29 (1996): 4, 425–48. The best overview is Jürgen Osterhammel, *China und die Weltgesellschaft: Vom 18. Jahrhundert bis in unsere Zeit* [*China and World Society: From the 18th Century to Our Time*] (Munich: C. H. Beck, 1989); see also Michael H. Hunt, "Chinese Foreign Relations in Historical Perspective," in Kenneth Lieberthal et al., eds. *Perspectives on Modern China: Four Anniversaries* (Armonk, NY: M. E. Sharpe, 1991).

7. For a summary of developments, see Edward Dreyer, *China at War, 1901–1949* (London: Longman, 1995); and E. R. Hooton, *The Greatest Tumult: The Chinese Civil War, 1936–49* (London: Brassey's, 1991). See also Edward A. McCord, *The Power of the Gun: The Emergence of Modern Chinese Warlordism* (Berkeley: University of California Press, 1993).

8. For the general effects of the war, see the essays in James C. Hsiung and Steven I. Levine, *China's Bitter Victory: The War with Japan, 1937–1945* (Armonk, NY: Eastgate, 1992); for politics in the occupied areas, see Poshek Fu, *Passivity, Resistance, and Collaboration: Intellectual Choices in Occupied Shanghai, 1937–1945* (Stanford, CA: Stanford University Press, 1993); on the economy, see Arthur N. Young, *China's Wartime Finance and Inflation, 1937–1945* (Cambridge, MA: Harvard University Press, 1965); and Li Xuetong, ed., *Guomin zhengfu yu dahoufang jingji* [*The Republican Government and the Economy of the Rear Areas*], vol. 5 in the series *Kangri zhanzheng* [*The Anti-Japanese Struggle*] (Chengdu: Sichuan daxue, 1997). Some of the key GMD reports on the costs of the war are in Zhongguo Guomindang zhongyang weiyuanhui dangshi weiyuanhui, comp., *Zhonghua minguo zhongyao shiliao chubian—dui Ri kangzhan shiqi* [*Preliminary Compilation of Important Historical Materials on the Republic of China—The Period of the War of Resistance against Japan*] vols. 3 and 6 (Taibei: Zhongguo Guomindang zhongyang weiyuanhui dangshi weiyuanhui, 1981).

9. Elizabeth J. Perry, *Rebels and Revolutionaries in North China, 1845–1945* (Stanford, CA: Stanford University Press, 1980).

10. As Lucien Bianco points out, such practices varied from area to area, and were rather exceptional for the country as a whole (Lucien Bianco, personal communication to author, Apr. 2001).

11. See Thaxton for case study; for the effects of the wars, see Prasenjit Duara, *Culture, Power, and the State: Rural North China, 1900–1942* (Stanford, CA: Stanford University Press, 1988), esp. pp. 217–18.

12. On the role of women, see Kazuko Ono, *Chinese Women in a Century of Revolution, 1850–1950* (Stanford, CA: Stanford University Press, 1989).

13. Letter to the Propaganda and Action Council of the Peoples of the East, Dec. 1921, V. I. Lenin, *Polnoe sobranie sochinenii* [*Complete Collected Works*], 5th ed. (Moscow: Gos. idz-vo polit. lit-ry, 1969), vol. 44, p. 282. For the European influence, see Marilyn A. Levine, *The Found Generation: Chinese Communists in Europe during the Twenties* (Seattle: University of Washington Press, 1993).

14. On the political effects of 4 May, see Edward X. Gu, "Populist Themes in May Fourth Radical Thinking: A Reappraisal of the Intellectual Origins of Chinese Marxism (1917–1922)," *East Asian History* 10 (1995): 99–126. See also Arif Dirlik, *The Origins of Chinese Communism* (Oxford: Oxford University Press, 1989); Hans J. van de Ven, *From Friend to Comrade: The Founding of the Chinese Communist Party, 1920–1927* (Berkeley: University of California Press, 1991); Wen-hsin Yeh, *Provincial Passages: Culture, Space, and the Origins of Chinese Communism* (Berkeley: University of California Press, 1996). For one later CCP leader, see Chae-Jin Lee, *Zhou Enlai: The Early Years* (Stanford, CA: Stanford University Press, 1994).

15. Marie-Claire Bergère, *Sun Yat-sen*, trans. Janet Lloyd (Stanford, CA: Stanford University Press, 1998). For the Soviet role, see Martin Wilbur and Julie How, *Missionaries of Revolution: Soviet Advisers and Nationalist China, 1920–1927* (Cambridge, MA: Harvard University Press, 1989); and, for a more critical overview based on recently available sources, see Bruce A. Elleman, *Diplomacy and Deception: The Secret History of Sino-Soviet Relations, 1917–1927* (Armonk, NY: M. E. Sharpe, 1997).

16. Wai-Chor So, *The Kuomintang Left in the National Revolution, 1924–1931* (Oxford: Oxford University Press, 1991); Arthur Waldron, *From War to Nationalism: China's Turning Point, 1924–25* (Cambridge: Cambridge University Press, 1995).

17. Remarkably enough, there is no good full-scale biography of Jiang Jieshi in English. For his early years, see Ch'en Chieh-ju, *Chiang Kai-shek's Secret Past: The Memoir of His Second Wife, Ch'en Chieh-ju*, ed. Lloyd E. Eastman (Boulder: Westview Press, 1993). A good recent biography in Chinese is Wang Rongzu and Li Ao, *Jiang Jieshi pingzhuan* [*A Critical Biography of Jiang Jieshi*], 2 vols. (Taibei: Shangzhou wenhua, 1995). See also Zhang Xianwen and Fang Qingjiu, *Jiang Jieshi quanzhuan* [*A Complete Biography of Jiang Jieshi*], 2 vols. (Zhengzhou: Henan renmin, 1996, 1997).

18. K. M. Panikkar, *In Two Chinas: Memoirs of a Diplomat* (London: Allen and Unwin, 1955), p. 25.

19. Jiang's published diaries are our best primary source to his thinking. Ex-

cerpts from the diaries were first published by the Japanese newspaper *Sankei shinbun* in 1974; in Chinese as Koya Keizi, ed., *Jiang zongtong milu: Zhong-Ri guanxi bashinian zhi zhengyan* [*The Secret Records of President Jiang: The Lessons of Eighty Years of Sino-Japanese Relations*] (Taibei: Zhongyang ribao, 1974–78). The most comprehensive version of the diaries—though still abridged and edited—is in *Zongtong Jiang gong dashi changbian chugao* [*A Draft Extensive Chronology of President Jiang*], 8 vols. (n.p.: n.p., 1978; hereafter *Jiang chugao*). Although the authenticity of the diaries is beyond doubt, questions have been raised about omissions in the published editions, particularly since scholars so far do not have access to the original documents. See Huang Renyu [Ray Huang], *Cong da lishi de jiaodu du Jiang Jieshi riji* [*Reading Jiang Jieshi's Diary from a Broader Historical Perspective*] (Taibei: Shibao wenhua, 1994). For a selection of Jiang's writings, see Zhongguo Guomindang Zhongyang weiyuanhui dangshi weiyuanhui, ed. and comp., *Zongtong Jiang gong sixiang yanlun zongji* [*A General Collection of President Jiang's Thought and Opinions*] (Taibei: n.p., 1984—hereafter *Jiang sixiang yanlun*). The Taiwan Academia Historica (*Guoshiguan*) began the opening of some of Jiang's private and official papers to scholars in the late 1990s.

20. The classic account of the 1927 events is Harold Isaacs, *The Tragedy of the Chinese Revolution* (Stanford, CA: Stanford University Press, 1961); see also Wilbur and How, *Missionaries of Revolution*. The Comintern documents on the First United Front are now available; see Go Kheniui [Guo Hengyü] and M. L. Titarenko, chief eds., *VKP(b), Komintern i natsionalno-revoliutsionnoe dvizhenie v Kitae: dokumenty* [*VKP(b), Comintern, and the National-Revolutionary Struggle in China: Documents*], 3 vols. (Moscow: Buklet, 1994–). See also *Gongchan guoji, Liangong (bu) yu Zhongguo geming wenxian ziliao xuanji, 1926–1927* [*Selected Documents and Materials on the Comintern, the VKP(b), and the Chinese Revolution, 1926–1927*], 2 vols. (Beijing: Beijing tushuguan, 1998); N. L. Mamaeva, *Komintern i Gomindan, 1919–1929* [*The Comintern and the Guomindang, 1919–1929*] (Moscow: ROSSPEN, 1999).

21. For overviews of the Nanjing decade, see Lloyd Eastman, *The Abortive Revolution: China under Nationalist Rule, 1927–1937* (Cambridge, MA: Harvard University Press, 1974); and Frederic Wakeman, Jr., and Richard Louis Edmonds, eds., *Reappraising Republican China* (Oxford: Oxford University Press, 1999).

22. Mao Zedong's group reached northern Shaanxi in October 1935, but it took another year before all the surviving CCP units had reached the area; Yan'an did not become the center until January 1937. See Benjamin Yang, *From Revolution to Politics: Chinese Communists on the Long March* (Boulder, CO: Westview, 1990); Harrison Salisbury, *The Long March: The Untold Story* (New York: Harper and Row, 1985).

23. There are now a number of Mao Zedong biographies available in English; by far the best is by Jung Chang and Jon Halliday (forthcoming, 2003); see also Ross Terrill, *Mao: A Biography*, 2d ed. (Stanford, CA: Stanford University Press, 1999); and Philip Short, *Mao: A Life* (New York: Henry Holt, 2000). For a penetrating study of Mao's mind, see Stuart Schram, *The Thought of Mao Zedong*

(Cambridge: Cambridge University Press, 1989). Schram has also edited an excellent edition of Mao's writings for the early period; *Mao's Road to Power: Revolutionary Writings, 1912–1949*, 5 vols. (Armonk, NY: M. E. Sharpe, 1994–).

24. Parks M. Coble, *Facing Japan: Chinese Politics and Japanese Imperialism, 1931–1937* (Cambridge, MA: Harvard University, Council on East Asian Studies, 1991); Peter Duus, *The Japanese Informal Empire in China, 1895–1937* (Princeton, NJ: Princeton University Press, 1989).

25. Zhonggong zhongyang wenxian yanjiushi, comp., *Mao Zedong nianpu (1893–1949)* [*Mao Zedong Chronology (1893–1949)*] (Beijing: Renmin, 1993), vol. 1, pp. 620–30; see also Yang Kuisong, *Xian shibian xin tan: Zhang Xueliang yu Zhong Gong guanxi zhi yanjiu* [*A New Investigation of the Xian Incident: A Study of the Relations between Zhang Xueliang and the CCP*] (Taibei: Dongda, 1995).

26. The best recent overview is Hsiung and Levine, *China's Bitter Victory*. For the origins of the war, see Youli Sun, *China and the Origins of the Pacific War, 1931–1941* (Macmillan, 1993).

27. William C. Kirby, "The Chinese War Economy," in Hsiung and Levine, *China's Bitter Victory*, pp. 185–87.

28. Chen Yongfa [Chen Yung-fa] has an excellent analysis of this process in his *Making Revolution* and in *Zhongguo gongchan geming qishinian* [*Seventy Years of Chinese Communist Revolution*] (Taibei: Lianjing, 1998).

29. See David E. Apter and Tony Saich, *Revolutionary Discourse in Mao's Republic* (Cambridge, MA: Harvard University Press, 1994); for political and cultural repression in Yan'an, see Dai Qing, *Wild Lilies*, ed. David E. Apter and Timothy Cheek; trans. Nancy Liu and Lawrence R. Sullivan (Armonk, NY: M. E. Sharpe, 1994).

30. Odd Arne Westad, *Cold War and Revolution: Soviet-American Rivalry and the Origins of the Chinese Civil War, 1944–1946* (New York: Columbia University Press, 1993).

31. Stalin to Molotov, Beria, Malenkov, and Mikoyan, 10 Nov. 1945, Rossiiski Gosudarstvenni Arkhiv Sozialno-Politicheskoi Istorii (RGASPI), Moscow, f. 558, o. 11, d. 98, p. 81.

32. On the Marshall Mission, see Larry I. Bland, ed., with Roger B. Jeans and Mark F. Wilkinson, *George C. Marshall's Mediation Mission to China, December 1945–January 1947* (Lexington, VA: George C. Marshall Foundation, 1998).

33. Entries for 5–9 May 1946, *Wang Shijie riji* [*Wang Shijie Diary*] (Taibei: Zhongyang yanjiuyuan jindaishi yanjiusuo, 1990), vol. 5, pp. 314–17.

Chapter 2. Two Bridges

1. Odd Arne Westad, *Cold War and Revolution: Soviet-American Rivalry and the Origins of the Chinese Civil War, 1944–1946* (New York: Columbia University Press, 1993); for a comprehensive view of the Soviet understanding of China in 1945–46, see the Soviet Foreign Ministry report, written by T. Okvortsov and A. Savelev, "Vnutrennee polozhenie v Kitae i grazhdanskaia voina" ["Internal Affairs in China and the Civil War"], 4 Dec. 1945, Foreign Policy Archive of the Russian Federation, Moscow [hereafter AVPRF], f. 129, op. 29, pa. 167, d. 17, pp. 3–30.

2. Jiang diaries, 22 Apr. to 28 Apr. 1946, *Jiang chugao*, pp. 114–24.

3. Mao Zedong to Lin Biao and Peng Zhen, 21 Apr. 1946, quoted in Ding Xiaochun et al., eds. *Dongbei jiefang zhanzheng dashiji* [*Chronology of the Liberation War in the Northeast*] (Beijing: Zhonggong dangshi ziliao, 1987), p. 20.

4. Michael Lindsey, *China and the Cold War* (Melbourne: Melbourne University Press, 1955), p. 88.

5. For Mao's strategy, see his telegrams to Lin Biao, 6 and 8 Apr., *Mao Zedong junshi wenji*, 6 vols. (Beijing: Junshi kexue and Zhonggong wenxian, 1993), vol. 3, pp. 159–62.

6. See for instance Mao's telegram to Lin Biao, 15 May 1946, ibid., pp. 218–19.

7. There is still no good full-scale biography of Lin Biao; between the hagiographies of the Cultural Revolution and the demonographies following Lin's death fleeing Mao in 1971, the best publication in Chinese is Lin Qingshan, *Lin Biao zhuan*, 2 vols. (Beijing: Zhishi, 1988). For an up-to-date summary in English, see Jin Qiu, *The Culture of Power: The Lin Biao Incident in the Cultural Revolution* (Stanford, CA: Stanford University Press, 1999), esp. pp. 62–70.

8. Jin Chongji, ed., *Mao Zedong zhuan, 1893–1949* [*Mao Zedong Biography, 1893–1949*] (Beijing: Zhongyang wenxian, 1996), pp. 764–69.

9. *Ren Bishi zhuan* [*Ren Bishi Biography*] (Beijing: Zhongyang wenxian, 1994), pp. 584–92; *Zhongguo tudi gaige shi (1921–1949)* [*A History of Chinese Land Reform (1921–1949)*] (Beijing: Renmin, 1990); *Jiefang zhanzheng shiqi tudi gaige wenjian xuanji* [*A Selection of Documents on Land Reform during the War of Liberation Period*] (Zhonggong dangshi ziliao congshu 4; Beijing: Zhonggong dangshi ziliao, 1988).

10. For a full translation, see Saich, *The Rise to Power*, pp. 1280–85.

11. The CCP terms *landlords, rich peasants, middle peasants, poor peasants,* and *landless peasants* are—in spite of their obvious oversimplification of the situation in any one area—quite useful for understanding social divisions in the Chinese countryside, and will be used throughout this book. According to the CCP vocabulary, landlords are those who possess much land, who do not themselves work but exploit peasants through land rent, usury, taxes, and fees. At the opposite end of the scale, landless peasants are those who do not own land or any form of tools, and have to sell all their labor. The best definition of the other "classes" are Ren Bishi's: "Those who own large tracts of land, animals, and tools, who work themselves and exploit the work of other peasants, these are rich peasants. Those who own land, animals, and tools, who work themselves and generally do not exploit others, these are middle peasants. Those who have small plots of land, and some animals and tools, who work their land themselves, but also have to sell their labor, these are poor peasants"; Ren Bishi speech, 12 Jan. 1948, in *Ren Bishi xuanji* (*Ren Bishi Selected Works*) (Beijing: Renmin, 1987), p. 417.

12. 4 May directive, in *Liu Shaoqi xuanji* [*Liu Shaoqi Selected Works*], 2 vols. (Beijing: Renmin, 1985), vol. 2, pp. 377–83. The May Fourth Directive is obviously a composite text written up by different authors and granted authoritative status by the CCP Politburo. Most party historians would now agree, however, that Ren was a more important contributor to the final version than Liu Shaoqi.

13. See Central Committee instructions to all bureau and district party committees, 28 Mar. 1946, Zhongyang tongzhanbu and Zhongyang dang'anguan, eds., *Zhonggong zhongyang jiefang zhanzheng shiqi tongyi zhanxian wenxian xuanbian* [Selected CCP Central Committee Documents on the United Front during the War of Liberation] (Beijing: Dang'an, 1988).

14. Zhonggong zhongyang wenxian yanjiushi, comp., *Liu Shaoqi nianpu* [*Liu Shaoqi Chronology*], 2 vols. (Beijing: Zhongyang wenxian, 1996), vol. 2, pp. 55–56; Ren Bishi's views can be found in his speech to party intellectuals, 26 Aug. 1946, in *Ren Bishi xuanji*, pp. 402–5.

15. Chen Lian, *Juzhan de licheng* [*The Course of the Decisive Battle*] (Hefei: Anhui renmin, 1991).

16. Notes of conversation, Jiang-Marshall, 22 May 1946, *Foreign Relations of the United States* (hereafter *FRUS*) 1946, vol. 9, p. 880.

17. Ibid., p. 881.

18. *Zhou Enlai zhuan, 1898–1949* [*Zhou Enlai Biography, 1898–1949*] (Beijing: Zhonggong zhongyang wenxian, 1989), p. 628; for context, see also Zhonggong zhongyang wenxian yanjiushi, comp., *Zhou Enlai nianpu, 1898–1949* [*Chronological Biography of Zhou Enlai, 1898–1949*] (Beijing: Zhongyang wenxian, 1989), pp. 667–68, and *Zhou Enlai junshi huodong jishi, 1918–1975* [*A Record of Zhou Enlai's Military Activities, 1918–1975*] (Beijing: Zhongyang wenxian, 2000), vol. 1, pp. 671–72.

19. Although there is still room for a critical biography of Zhou Enlai both in English and Chinese, the official *Zhou Enlai zhuan* is very detailed and informative; for Zhou's formative years, see Xiong Xianghui, *Dixia shiernian yu Zhou Enlai* [*Zhou Enlai's Twelve Underground Years*] (Beijing: Zhonggong zhongyang dangxiao, 1991). Han Suyin, *Eldest Son: Zhou Enlai and the Making of Modern China, 1898–1976* (New York: Hill and Wang, 1994) is a comprehensive but panegyric and error-ridden overview.

20. Marshall to Song Ziwen, 29 May 1946, *FRUS*, 1946, vol. 9, p. 912.

21. See for instance entry for 6 May 1946, *Jiang chugao*, vol. 6, book 1, p. 133.

22. See Wang Rongzu and Li Ao, *Jiang Jieshi pingzhuan* [*A Critical Biography of Jiang Jieshi*], 2 vols. (Taibei: Shangzhou wenhua, 1995), vol. 2. For another view of Jiang, emphasizing his nontraditional behavior, see Lloyd Eastman, *The Abortive Revolution: China under Nationalist Rule, 1927–1937* (Cambridge, MA: Harvard University Press, 1974).

23. Niu Jun, "Guomindang and CCP Policies toward the United States during the Marshall Mission," in Larry I. Bland, ed., with Roger B. Jeans and Mark F. Wilkinson, *George C. Marshall's Mediation Mission to China, December 1945–January 1947* (Lexington, VA: George C. Marshall Foundation, 1998); entry for 3 June 1946, *Jiang chugao*, vol. 6, book 1, pp. 168–70.

24. Entry for 4 June 1946, *Jiang chugao*, vol. 6, book 1, p. 170. See also Sun Zhaiwei, *Jiang Jieshi de chong jiang Chen Cheng* [*Jiang Jieshi's Favorite General Chen Cheng*] (Zhengzhou: Henan renmin, 1990).

25. Forrest C. Pogue, *George C. Marshall. Vol. 4: Statesman, 1945–1949* (New York: Viking, 1987), p. 115.

26. See Zhonggong zhongyang wenxian yanjiushi, comp., *Mao Zedong nian-*

pu (1893–1949) [*Mao Zedong Chronology (1893–1949)*] (Beijing: Renmin, 1993), vol. 3, pp. 89–90; *Zhou Enlai nianpu*, pp. 670–72. See also He Long's report concerning the meetings at a cadre conference of the CCP CC Shaanxi-Suiyuan sub-bureau at Xing county, 19 June 1946, *He Long junshi wenxuan* (Beijing: Jiefangjun, 1989), pp. 229–54.

27. *Zhou Enlai zhuan*, pp. 628–29.

28. Record of conversation, Marshall and Zhou Enlai, 10 June 1946, *FRUS*, 1946, vol. 9, p. 1012.

29. Record of conversation, Marshall and Zhou Enlai, 20 June 1946, *FRUS*, 1946, vol. 9, p. 1105; record of conversation, Marshall–Zhou Enlai, 26 June 1946, ibid., p. 1215; *Zhou Enlai nianpu*, pp. 277–78.

30. Entry for 4 July 1946, *Jiang chugao*, vol. 6, book 1, p. 208.

31. Entry for 26 June 1946, ibid., vol. 6, book 1, p. 191; Moscow embassy to Foreign Minister Wang Shijie, 24 July 1946, "SuE dui wo guo zhengzhi dongxiang," ["Trends in Soviet Policy towards Our Country"], ROC Foreign Ministry Archives, Taibei, Taiwan (hereafter ROC-Waijiaobu), 197.1 310.53.

32. Yueh-hung Chen Ting, "The Intellectuals and the Chinese Revolution: A Study of the Chinese Democratic League and Its Components, 1939–1949," Ph.D. dissertation, New York University, 1978, pp. 186–87.

33. *Mao Zedong nianpu*, vol. 3, pp. 92–93.

34. Junshi kexueyuan junshi lishi yanjiubu, ed., *Zhongguo renmin jiefangjun zhanshi. Disanben: Quangguo jiefang zhanzheng shiqi* [*A Battle History of the Chinese People's Liberation Army. Volume Three: The War for the Liberation of the Whole Country*—hereafter *Zhongguo renmin jiefangjun zhanshi*] (Beijing: Junshi kexue, 1987), pp. 69–72.

35. Entry for 14 July 1946, *Jiang chugao*, vol. 6, book 1, p. 217.

36. *Zhongguo renmin jiefangjun zhanshi*, pp. 50–58; E. R. Hooton, *The Greatest Tumult: The Chinese Civil War, 1936–49* (London: Brassey's, 1991), pp. 128–29.

37. *Chen Yi nianpu* [*Chen Yi Chronology*] (Beijing: Zhonggong wenxian, 1995), vol. 1, pp. 469–71.

38. Ibid.

39. Mao to Nie, 10 Oct. 1946, *Mao Zedong junshi wenji*, vol. 3, pp. 517–18.

40. Raymond J. de Jaegher and Irene Corbally Kuhn, *The Enemy Within: An Eyewitness Account of the Communist Conquest of China* (Garden City, NY: Doubleday, 1953), p. 292.

41. Wenshi ziliao yanjiu weiyuanhui, ed. *Fu Zuoyi shengping* [*The Life of Fu Zuoyi*] (Beijing: Wenshi ziliao, 1985), esp. pp. 263–70.

42. Mao to Zhou Enlai et al., 28 Oct. 1946, *Mao Zedong junshi wenji*, vol. 3, p. 530; see also *Zhongguo renmin jiefangjun disi yezhanjun zhanshi* [*A Battle History of the Chinese People's Liberation Army's Fourth Field Army*] (Beijing: Jiefangjun, 1998), pp. 152–59.

43. The *Times*, lead article, 12 Sept. 1946.

44. William Stueck, *The Wedemeyer Mission: American Politics and Foreign Policy during the Cold War* (Athens: University of Georgia Press, 1984), pp. 29–45.

45. Mikhail Kapitsa, author's interview, Moscow, 7 Sept. 1992; Nikolai Fedorenko, "Stalin i Mao Tsedun," *Novaiia i noveishaia istoriia*, nos. 5 and 6
(1992): 98–113; 83–95; A. Petrov to Vyshinskii and Stalin, Report on developments in China October–December 1946, AVPRF, f. 07, op. 12, pa. 24, d. 313,
1–31. Mikhail Kapitsa had been stationed in China up to early 1947, and served
later as a China specialist with the International Department of the Soviet Communist Party Central Committee; Apollon Aleksandrovich Petrov (1907–49) was
Soviet ambassador in China to 1947.

46. Record of conversation, Marshall and Jiang Jieshi, 8 Aug. 1946, *FRUS*,
1946, vol. 9, p. 1469.

47. Entry for 30 Aug. 1946, *Jiang chugao*, vol. 6, book 1, p. 244. For Jiang's
reaction to the U.S. reluctance to sell arms, see entry for 18 Aug. 1946, *Jiang
chugao*, vol. 6, book 1, p. 238.

48. Entry for 30 Aug. 1946, *Jiang chugao*, vol. 6, book 1, p. 244; *The China
White Paper, August 1949* (originally published as *United States Relations with
China with Special Reference to the Period 1944–1949* [Stanford, CA: Stanford
University Press, 1967]), p. 180.

49. Entry for 27 Oct. 1946, *Jiang chugao*, vol. 6, book 1, p. 290; Ren Donglai,
"Bupingmeng de tongmeng: Mei yuan yu ZhongMei waijiao yanjiu, 1937–1946"
["Unequal Alliance: U.S. Aid and Sino-American Diplomatic Discussions,
1937–1946"], Ph.D. dissertation, Nankai University, 1988; C. X. George Wei,
Sino-American Economic Relations, 1944–1949 (Westport, CT: Greenwood,
1997), pp. 85–109. For the CCP reaction, see Mao Zedong's remarks to an extended Politburo meeting, 1 Feb. 1947, *Mao Zedong wenji [Mao Zedong Works]*
(Beijing: Renmin, 1996), vol. 4, pp. 219–23. A different version appears in *Mao
Zedong xuanji* and its English-language translation, *Selected Works of Mao Zedong* (Beijing: Foreign Languages Press, 1961), where it is published under the title "Greet the New High Tide of the Chinese Revolution," vol. 4, p. 121.

50. See Zhongyang dang'anguan, comp., *Zhonggong zhongyang wenjian
xuanji [Selected Documents of the CCP Center]* (Beijing: Zhonggong zhongyang
dangxiao, 1992), vol. 16, pp. 232–40, for the text of the 7 July declaration. In his
commentary on the text to leading CCP members, Mao stressed: "We have to
strengthen relations with the American people . . . [and] try to draw the Americans over to our side. We should not comment in any way on Marshall's own behavior, because we need the mediation to go on. We should avoid conflict with
the American army in all areas. . . . Some middle-of-the-roaders may think that
the declaration is too tough. We will have to explain it to them" (Mao to all CC
bureaus, 6 July 1946, ibid., pp. 230–31).

51. Mao to Zhou, 21 June 1946, *Mao Zedong nianpu*, vol. 3, pp. 94–95.

52. For Mao's hopes, see Mao to Lin Biao, 25 June 1946, ibid., pp. 94–95; for
the Soviet position, see Malik to Vyshinski, 15 Jan. 1947, AVPRF, f. 07, op 12,
pa. 24, d. 317, pp. 12–14; see also Niu Jun, *Cong Yan'an zouxiang shijie: Zhongguo Gongchandang duiwai guanxi de qiyuan [From Yan'an to the World: The
Origins of the Chinese Communist Party's Foreign Relations]* (Fuzhou: Fujian
renmin, 1992), esp. pp. 244–50.

53. Westad, *Cold War and Revolution*, p. 137.

54. See, for instance, *Minzhu bao* (Chongqing), 1 Apr. 1946, for such reports.

55. See the initial chapters of Zhang Yufa, ed., *Xuechao yu zhanhou Zhong-guo zhengzhi (1945–1949)* [*Student Strikes and Postwar Chinese Politics*] (Taibei: Dongda, 1994) for a good summary.

56. See, for instance, Jiang's speech to Guomindang activists, 8 Aug. 1946, in *Jiang sixiang yanlun*, vol. 21, pp. 370–88. This speech was widely reported in the newspapers at the time.

57. *Zhongguo xuesheng yundongshi, 1945–1949* [*A History of the Chinese Student Movement, 1945–1949*] (Shanghai: Shanghai renmin, 1992); *Jiefang zhanzheng shiqi diertiao zhanxian: Xuesheng yundong juan* [*The Second Front during the War of Liberation: Volumes on the Student Movement*], ed. Zhong-gong Beijing shiwei dangshi yanjiushi (Beijing: Zhonggong dangshi, 1997), vol. 1; Zhonggong Yunnan shengwei dangshi ziliao zhengzhi weiyuanhui and Zhong-Gong Yunnan shifan daxue weiyuanhui, eds. *Yieryi yundong* [*The 21 January Movement*] (Beijing: ZhongGong dangshi ziliao, 1988).

58. Ting, "The Intellectuals and the Chinese Revolution," pp. 158–68; see also *Minmeng shi hua, 1941–1949* [*On the History of the Democratic League, 1941–1949*] (Beijing: Zhongguo shehui kexue, 1992), pp. 300–419.

59. Zhang, *Xuechao yu zhanhou Zhongguo zhengzhi*, pp. 59–75.

60. See, for instance, Zhou Enlai's instructions to the Beijing and Tianjin CCP city committees, 27 Feb. 1947, quoted in *Zhou Enlai zhuan*, p. 668.

61. On Zhou, see ibid., pp. 667–69; on Ren, see *Ren Bishi zhuan*, pp. 600–613.

62. Zhou Enlai's instructions to the Beijing and Tianjin CCP city committees, 27 Feb. 1947, quoted in *Zhou Enlai zhuan*, p. 668.

63. *Ren Bishi zhuan*, pp. 609–612; see also *Mao Zedong nianpu*, vol. 3, pp. 162–63.

64. *Mao Zedong nianpu*, vol. 3, pp. 140–42; Yang Kuisong, *Zhonggong yu Mosike de guanxi, 1920–1960* [*The CCP and Moscow, 1920–1960*] (Taibei: San-min shudian, 1997), pp. 568–70; see also *Liu Shaoqi nianpu*, vol. 2, p. 53.

65. *Mao Zedong nianpu*, vol. 3, p. 125.

66. Entry for 6 Nov. 1946, *Jiang chugao*, vol. 6, book 1, p. 296.

67. Ting, "The Intellectuals and the Chinese Revolution," p. 173.

68. Jiang's speeches at the opening of the National Assembly in *Jiang sixiang yanlun*, 21, pp. 435–48; see also entries for 15 Nov. 1946, *Jiang chugao*, vol. 6, book 1, pp. 303–9.

69. Entry for 26 Oct. 1946, *Jiang chugao*, vol. 6, book 1, p. 290.

70. For the recall to Yan'an, see *Zhou Enlai nianpu*, p. 705; for Zhou's per-sonal contacts in Nanjing, see Zhang Baijia, "Zhou Enlai and the Marshall Mis-sion," in Bland, *George C. Marshall's Mediation Mission to China*.

71. *Mao Zedong nianpu*, vol. 3, pp. 150–51.

72. Ibid.; see also Mao's speech to a Central Committee meeting 21 Nov. 1946, *Mao Zedong wenji*, vol. 4, pp. 196–200.

73. For Marshall's departure, see Pogue, *George C. Marshall*, pp. 128–30.

74. Entry for 12 Dec. 1946, *Jiang chugao*, vol. 6, book 1, p. 325.

75. *Zhongguo renmin jiefangjun diyi yezhanjun zhanshi zhanshi* [*A Battle His-tory of the Chinese People's Liberation Army's First Field Army*] (Beijing:

Jiefangjun, 1975), pp. 20–34; *Kanluan zhanshi* [*A Battle History of Rebel Suppression*], vol. 3 (Taibei: Guofangbu shizhengbianyiju, 1980–81). For a summary, see Hooton, *The Greatest Tumult*, p. 70.

76. Ren's speech to the plenary meeting of the Military Affairs Commission's Second Department, 13 Jan. 1947, *Ren Bishi xuanji* (Beijing: Renmin, 1987), pp. 408–10. On the difficulties the CCP faced, see also Nie Rongzhen's 15 Sept. 1946 report at the cadre conference of the JinChaJi CC Bureau, *Nie Rongzhen junshi wenxuan* (Beijing: Jiefangjun, 1992), pp. 250–53.

77. Mao notes, 5 Jan. 1947, in *Mao Zedong junshi wenji*, vol. 3, pp. 603–4.

78. *Mao Zedong zhuan*, pp. 786–92; see also Zhonggong zhongyang wenxian yanjiushi, comp., *Liu Shaoqi zhuan* [*Liu Shaoqi Biography*] (Beijing: Zhongyang wenxian, 1998), vol. 1, pp. 559–61.

79. For Liu's background, see *Liu Shaoqi zhuan*, vol. 1.

80. Mao to the CC Northeast Bureau, 25 Oct. 1946, *Mao Zedong junshi wenji*, vol. 3, p. 529; also in *Zhonggong zhongyang wenjian xuanji*, vol. 16, p. 321.

81. *Mao Zedong nianpu*, vol. 3, p. 143 (entry for 22 Oct. 1946) and p. 145 (entry for 1 Nov. 1946); *Zhongguo renmin jiefangjun disi yezhanjun zhanshi*, pp. 162–84.

82. Mao to Lin Biao, 11 Jan. 1947, *Mao Zedong junshi wenji*, vol. 3, pp. 612–13.

83. See the discussion at the 3d Plenum of the 6th GMD Central Committee, 15–24 Mar. 1947, *Zhonghua minguo shi dang'an ziliao huibian* [*A Collection of Archival Materials on the History of the Republic of China*] 5th series, 3d collection: Politics 1945–1949 (Nanjing: Jiangsu guji, 1999) (hereafter *Zhonghua minguo shi dang'an ziliao huibian*, 5, 3) book 1, pp. 377–493.

84. Entry for 28 Dec. 1946, *Jiang chugao*, vol. 6, book 1, pp. 346–47.

85. Zhang Yufa and Shen Songqiao, interviewers and eds., *Dong Wenqi xiansheng fangwen jilu* [*Record of an Interview with Mr. Dong Wenqi*] (Taibei: Zhongyang yanjiuyuan jindaishi yanjiusuo, 1986), pp. 113–65.

86. *Jiang Jingguo quanzhuan* [*A Complete Biography of Jiang Jingguo*], vol. 1, pp. 108–9; see also Chen Pengren, *Jiang Jingguo xiansheng zhuan* [*A Biography of Mr. Jiang Jingguo*] (Taibei: Zhongyang ribao, 1990).

Chapter 3. Takeovers

1. Jack Goldstone et al., eds., *Revolutions of the Late 20th Century* (Boulder, CO: Westview, 1991); Stephen Walt, *Revolution and War* (Ithaca, NY: Cornell University Press, 1996); and Theda Skocpol, "Social Revolutions and Mass Military Mobilization," *World Politics* 40, no. 2 (Jan. 1988): 147–68. For comparative perspectives, see Peter Feldbauer and Hans-Jürgen Puhle, eds., *Bauern im Widerstand: Agrarrebellionen und Revolutionen in Ländern der Dritten Welt und im vorindustriellen Europa*, Beiträge zur historischen Sozialkunde. Beiheft, 1/1992 (Vienna: Böhlau, 1992); Gil Carl AlRoy, *The Involvement of Peasants in Internal Wars* (Princeton, NJ: Center for International Studies, Woodrow Wilson School of Public and International Affairs, 1966); and Eric Wolf's classic *Peasant Wars of the Twentieth Century* (New York: Harper and Row, 1969).

2. Meaning territory in Sichuan, Yunnan, Guizhou, Shaanxi, and Gansu.

Whether Xinjiang, Qinghai, and Tibet, though not under Japanese control, had enough central GMD influence to qualify is doubtful.

3. For an overview, see Suzanne Pepper, *Civil War in China: The Political Struggle, 1945–1949* (Berkeley: University of California Press, 1978; rev. ed. Lanham, MD: Rowan and Littlefield, 1999), pp. 95–96; or Li Huade, *GuoGong junzheng da bodou* [*The Great Military and Political Struggle between the GMD and the CCP*] (Hong Kong: Zhongyuan, 1993), esp. pp. 35–99.

4. *Spring River Flows East* [*Yijiang chunshui xiang dong liu*] was directed by Cai Chusheng and Zheng Junli and produced in two parts at the Kunlun Studio in Shanghai. When the second part was screened in 1948, it was seen by more than 700,000 people in three months. See Marie-Claire Quiquemelle and Jean-Loup Passek, *Le cinema chinois* (Paris: Centre Georges Pompidou, 1985), pp. 182–83.

5. For background, see Wen-hsin Yeh, *Wartime Shanghai* (London: Routledge, 1998).

6. See Jiang's speech on 24 August 1945 and his instructions to military officers, 11 and 14 Nov. 1945, in *Jiang sixiang yanlun*, vol. 21, pp. 170–75, 176–85.

7. Huang Yulan, ed. *Zhengqu heping minzhu, 1945–1946* [Fighting for Peace and Democracy, 1945–46] (Shanghai: Shanghai renmin, 1995); see also General Albert Wedemeyer's report from Shanghai, 20 Nov. 1945, FRUS, 1945, vol. 7, pp. 650–56.

8. *Sanqingtuan* is an abbreviation for *Sanminzhuyi qingnian tuan*, or Three Principles of the People Youth Corps, set up by Jiang Jieshi as a paramilitary youth brigade of the GMD. See Lloyd Eastman, *Seeds of Destruction: China in War and Revolution, 1937–1949* (Stanford, CA: Stanford University Press, 1984).

9. See Jiang's messages to youth groups in August–September 1946, in *Jiang sixiang yanlun*, vol. 21, pp. 394–430.

10. See, for instance, the GMD Central Office documents from Nov. 1945 in Zhongguo Guomindang zhongyang weiyuanhui dangshi weiyuanhui, comp., *Zhonghua Minguo zhongyao shiliao chubian—dui Ri kangzhan shiqi* [*Preliminary Compilation of Important Historical Materials on the Republic of China— The Period of the War of Resistance against Japan*], 7 vols. (Taibei: Zhongyang wenwu gongying, 1981–), vol. 1, pp. 11–21; Zhongguo dier lishi dang'anguan, comp. *Zhonghua minguoshi shiliao changbian* [*An Extensive Collection of Historical Materials on the History of the Republic of China*], 70 vols. (Nanjing: Nanjing daxue, 1993), vol. 69, pp. 305–7. See also Myrl S. Myers (U.S. Consul General, Tianjin) to Secretary of State, 25 Nov. 1945, FRUS, 1945, vol. 7, p. 669.

11. On the protests, see the documents from January to February 1946 in *Zhonghua minguo shi dang'an ziliao huibian*, 5, 3, book 4, pp. 239–61; for support for GMD policy, see Smyth to Secretary of State, 6 Apr. 1946, FRUS, 1946, vol. 10, pp. 891–92.

12. Pepper, *Civil War in China*, pp. 155–60.

13. For general aspects, see Arvind K. Jain, ed., *Economics of Corruption* (Boston: Kluwer Academic, 1998).

14. Zhang Wenzhen, *Buxi de langtao: Xiamen daxue jiefang geming douzheng*

fengmao [*Spare No Effort: The Characteristics of Xiamen University's Struggle for Liberation and Revolution*] (Xiamen: Xiamen daxue, 1986); see also *Xiamen gongren yundong shi* (Xiamen: Xiamen daxue, 1991), pp. 270–79.

15. Lu Yangyuan and Fang Qingqiu, chief eds., *Minguo shehui jingji shi* [*A Social and Economic History of the Republic*] (Beijing: Zhongguo jingji, 1991), pp. 794–802.

16. Joseph K. S. Yick, *Making Urban Revolution in China: The CCP-GMD Struggle for Beiping-Tianjin, 1945–1949* (Armonk, NY: M. E. Sharpe, 1995), p. 73; see also Fu Tao and Zhao Zuchang, *Tianjin gongye sanshiwu nian* [*Thirty-five Years of Tianjin Industry*] (Tianjin: Tianjin shehui kexue bianjibu, 1985), pp. 10–36.

17. See Ch'en Li-fu, *The Storm Clouds Clear over China: The Memoir of Ch'en Li-fu*, ed. and comp. Sidney H. Chang and Ramon H. Myers (Stanford, CA: Hoover Institution Press, 1994). Nobody seems certain what the initials "CC" stood for in the appellation of one of the GMD's best known factions or groups. As the group centered on the Chen brothers, Chen Guofu and Chen Lifu, it may have been the initials of their surnames, or it may, as some claimed, stand for "Central Corps"—under any circumstance, it is a curious Westernized name for a faction that was traditionalist and nativist in its policies. For Jiang Jieshi's relationship with the Chen brothers, see Wang Xueqing, *Jiang Jieshi he Chen Lifu Chen Guofu* [*Jiang Jieshi and Chen Lifu and Chen Guofu*] (Changchun: Jilin wenshi, 1994).

18. See, for instance, the entries for January 1947, *Wang Shijie riji*, vol. 6, pp. 1–17; editorial comment, *Da gong bao*, 11 Dec. 1946.

19. Lu and Fang, *Minguo shehui jingji shi*, pp. 810–21.

20. For an overview, see *Dangdai Zhongguo gongren jieji he gonghui yundong* [*Contemporary Chinese Working Class and Trade Union Movement*] (Beijing: Dangdai Zhongguo, 1997), pp. 43–59.

21. For an outline of GMD policies with regard to labor organizations in 1946–47, see *Zhonghua minguo shi dang'an ziliao huibian*, 5, 3, book 4, pp. 28–91; see also Zou Bei, chief ed., *Zhongguo gongren yundong shi hua* [*The Brilliant History of the Chinese Workers' Movement*] (Beijing: Gongren, 1993), vol. 5, pp. 10–47.

22. Kai Jun, ed., *Zhongguo gongren yundong shi jiaocai, 1919–1949* [*Teaching Materials on the History of the Chinese Labor Movement, 1919–1949*] (Shanghai: Huadong shifan daxue, 1988), pp. 289–320.

23. For a local example, see *Zhejiang gongren yundong shi* [*History of the Zhejiang Workers' Movement*] (Hangzhou: Zhejiang renmin, 1988), pp. 211–51. For CCP perceptions, see Liu Shaoqi's speech on 14 Dec. 1947, *Liu Shaoqi lun gongren yundong* [*Liu Shaoqi on the Workers' Movement*] (Beijing: Zhonggong zhongyang wenxian, 1988).

24. CCP CC to party districts in GMD-held areas, 28 February 1947, Zhonghua quanguo zonggonghui, comp. *Zhonggong Zhongyang guanyu gongren yundong wenxian xuanbian* [*A Selection of the CCP Central Committee's Documents on the Workers Movement*], vol. 3 (Beijing: Dang'an, 1986), pp. 195–96.

25. Yick, *Making Urban Revolution in China*, pp. 144–52.

26. The two best overviews are *Zhongguo xuesheng yundongshi, 1945–1949* (Shanghai: Shanghai renmin, 1992); and, from a more critical perspective, Zhang Yufa, ed., *Xuechao yu zhanhou Zhongguo zhengzhi (1945–1949)* [*Student Strikes and Postwar Chinese Politics*] (Taibei: Dongda, 1994). See also Jeffrey Wasserstrom's excellent *Student Protests in Twentieth Century China: The View from Shanghai* (Stanford, CA: Stanford University Press, 1991), esp. pp. 240–76.

27. See, for instance, the report dated 16 Oct. 1946, *Zhanhou Zhongguo*, vol. 4, pp. 425–27.

28. For an overview, see Yu Zhimin, "Shinian neizhan qijian Zhongguo nong-cun jingrong zhuangkuang" ["The Economic Situation in China's Rural Areas during the Ten Year Civil War"], *Minguo dang'an* 2 (1992): 77–84; Lin Meili, "Shinian lai Taiwan you guan kangzhan shiqi jingjishi shehuishi zhi yanjiu" ["Research in Taiwan over the Past Decade on Economic and Social History during the War of Resistance"], *Jindai Zhongguoshi yanjiu tongxun* 26 (1998): 108–18. For the wider context, see Loren Brandt, "Reflections on China's Late 19th and Early 20th Century Economy," *China Quarterly* 150 (1997): 282–308.

29. For insights into these processes in different provinces, see Ralph A. Thaxton, Jr., *Salt of the Earth: The Political Origins of Peasant Protest and Communist Revolution in China* (Berkeley: University of California Press, 1997), pp. 279–315; Odoric Y. K. Wou, *Mobilizing the Masses: Building Revolution in Henan* (Stanford, CA: Stanford University Press, 1994), pp. 333–36; and Elise Anne DeVido, "The Making of the Communist Party-State in Shandong Province, 1927–1952," Ph.D. dissertation, Harvard University, 1995, pp. 67–72.

30. See, for instance, Huimin diwei dangshi ziliao zhengweihui, "Jiefang zhanzheng shiqi Bohai qu de tudi gaige yundong" ["The Land Reform Movement in the Bohai Area during the War of Liberation"], *Shandong dangshi ziliao* 2 (1985): 1–124. See also Shaanxi sheng junqu zhengzhibu, comp. *Guomindang budui jiyi douzheng shiliao xuanbian* [*A Collection of Historical Materials on the Guomindang's Incorrect Principles for Struggle*] (N.p.: N.p., n.d.).

31. The documents on GMD "pacification campaigns" in rural areas in 1946–47 in *Zhonghua minguo shi dang'an ziliao huibian*, 5, 3, book 2, pp. 103–291, are very useful for Nanjing's perceptions of what went on outside the main centers. For CCP views of the autonomous peasant movements, see Mao's speech at a 21 November 1946 meeting, *Mao Zedong wenji* [*Mao Zedong Works*] (Beijing: Renmin, 1996), vol. 5, pp. 196–200.

32. *Zhonggong Shandong dangshi dashiji, 1921–1949* [*CCP Shandong Party History Chronology, 1921–1949*] (Jinan: Shandong renmin, 1986), pp. 249–64.

33. There are two good biographies of the eccentric warlord Long Yun, who belonged to the Lulu nationality of Southwestern China: Jiang Nan, *Long Yun zhuan* [*Long Yun Biography*] (Taibei: Tianyuan, 1987); and Xie Benshu, *Long Yun zhuan* [*Long Yun Biography*] (Chengdu: Sichuan renmin, 1988).

34. The best overview is Steven I. Levine, *Anvil of Victory: The Communist Revolution in Manchuria, 1945–1948* (New York: Columbia University Press, 1987).

35. On Zhang, see Donald Gillin and Ramon H. Myers, eds., *Lost Chance in China: The Diary of Chang Kia-ngau* (Stanford, CA: Hoover Institution Press,

1989); on Jiang, see Han Shanbi, *Jiang Jingguo pingzhuan* [*A Critical Biography of Jiang Jingguo*] (Hong Kong: Dong xi wenhua shiye, 1988), esp. pp. 183–90.

36. Xiong Shihui to GMD Central Office, 20 Feb. 1946, *Zhanhou Zhongguo*, vol. 1, pp. 637–39; see also Zhang Xianwen and Fang Qingjiu, *Jiang Jieshi quanzhuan* [*A Complete Biography of Jiang Jieshi*], 2 vols. (Zhengzhou: Henan renmin, 1996, 1997), vol. 2, pp. 588–93.

37. Entry for 8 Apr. 1946, *Jiang chugao*, vol. 6, book 1, pp. 103–4; see also Zhang Yufa and Shen Songqiao, interviewers and eds., *Dong Wenqi xiansheng fangwen jilu* [*Record of an Interview with Mr. Dong Wenqi*] (Taibei: Zhongyang yanjiuyuan jindaishi yanjiusuo, 1986), pp. 112–15.

38. See record of meeting, Supreme National Defense Council, 29 May 1946. *Guofang zuigao weiyuanhui changwuhui yijilu* [*Records of the Discussions at the Ordinary Meetings of the Supreme National Defense Council*] (Taibei: Zhongguo guomindang zhongyang weiyuanhui dangshi weiyuanhui, 1996).

39. On Du, see Zheng Dongguo et al., *Du Yuming jiangjun* (Beijing: Zhongguo wenshi, 1986).

40. Pepper, *Civil War in China*, p. 169.

41. An overview of the economic effects of the anti-Japanese war can be found in *Shi nian lai zhi Zhongguo jingji, 1938–1947* [*The Chinese Economy during Ten Years, 1938–1947*], 2 vols. (Nanjing: Nanjing gu jiu shudian, 1990 [1948]); see also William C. Kirby, "The Chinese War Economy," in James C. Hsiung and Steven I. Levine, *China's Bitter Victory: The War with Japan, 1937–1945* (Armonk, NY: Eastgate, 1992); and the excellent essays in Li Xuetong, ed. *Guomin zhengfu yu dahoufang jingji* [*The Republican Government and the Economy of the Rear Areas*], Kangri zhanzheng 5 (Chengdu: Sichuan daxue, 1997).

42. *The China White Paper, August 1949* (originally published as *United States Relations with China with Special Reference to the Period 1944–1949* [Stanford, CA: Stanford University Press, 1967]), pp. 225–27, 1046–47; Dong Changzhi and Li Fan, *Zhongguo xiandai jingjishi (1919–1949 nian)* [*An Economic History of Modern China (1919–1949)*] (Changchun: Dongbei shifan daxue, 1988), pp. 230–31; Kuang Haolin, *Jianming Zhongguo jindai jingjishi* [*A Concise Economic History of Contemporary China*] (Beijing: Zhongyang minzu, 1989), pp. 362–64.

43. Dong and Li, *Zhongguo xiandai jingjishi*, pp. 232–36.

44. Ibid.; see also Lu and Fang, *Minguo shehui jingji shi*, pp. 845–50.

45. Lu and Fang, *Minguo shehui jingji shi*, pp. 776–81.

46. Pepper, *Civil War in China*, pp. 109–12; Lu and Fang, *Minguo shehui jingji shi*, pp. 770–74.

47. On GMD monetary policies, see *Zhonghua minguoshi shiliao changbian*, vol. 70, pp. 40–43.

48. Entry for 23 May 1947, *Jiang chugao*, vol. 7, book 2, p. 458. For the causes, see Munir Quddus et al., "Money, Prices, and Causality: The Chinese Hyperinflation, 1946–1949 Reexamined," *Journal of Macroeconomics* 11, no. 3 (1989): 447–53.

49. Lu and Fang, *Minguo shehui jingji shi*, pp. 806–20; see also Pepper, *Civil War in China*, pp. 118–21; Chou Shou-hsin, *The Chinese Inflation, 1937–1949*

(New York: Columbia University Press, 1963); and Arthur N. Young, *China's Wartime Finance and Inflation* (Cambridge, MA: Harvard University Press, 1965).

50. For an overview, see Kazuko Ono, *Chinese Women in a Century of Revolution, 1850–1950* (Stanford, CA: Stanford University Press, 1989). See also *Jindai Zhongguo funü shi yanjiu* [*Studies in Contemporary Chinese Women's History*], esp. recent articles by Xu Huiqi and Zang Jian.

51. See, for instance, articles in *Zhongguo xinwen*, vol. 2 (1948), issues 8 and 9 on women's role in Chinese society. For the Communist-held areas, see the documents in Zhonghua quanguo funü lianhewei funü yundong lishi yanjiushi, comp., *Zhongguo funü yundong lishi ziliao, 1945–1949* [*Materials on the History of the Chinese Women's Movement*] (Beijing: Zhongguo funü, 1991), esp. pp. 158–255.

52. Gail Hershatter, "Modernizing Sex, Sexing Modernity: Prostitution in Early Twentieth-Century Shanghai," in Christina K. Gilmartin et al., eds., *Engendering China: Women, Culture, and the State*, Harvard Contemporary China Series 10 (Cambridge, MA: Harvard University Press, 1994), pp. 167–68.

53. Emily Honig, *Sisters and Strangers: Women in the Shanghai Cotton Mills, 1919–1949* (Stanford, CA: Stanford University Press, 1986).

54. Ibid., pp. 234–49.

55. Liu Xiaoyuan, "The Kuomintang and the 'Mongolian Question' in the Chinese Civil War, 1945–1949," *Inner Asia* 1 (1999):169–94.

56. On Zhang's policies, see David D. Wang, "An Oasis for Peace: Zhang Zhihong's Policy in Xinjiang, 1945–1947," *Central Asian Survey* 15, nos. 3–4 (1996): 413–29. Some key documents on GMD policies are in *Zhonghua minguo shi dang'an ziliao huibian*, 5, 3, book 5, pp. 480–516. See also diaries of Wu Zhongxin, GMD governor of Xinjiang 1944–46, ibid., pp. 235–480.

57. David D. Wang, *Under the Soviet Shadow: The Yining Incident: Ethnic Conflicts and International Rivalry in Xinjiang 1944–1949* (Hong Kong: Chinese University Press, 1999).

58. See, for instance, entry for 12 January 1948, *Jiang chugao*, vol. 7, book 1. See also Linda Benson, *The Ili Rebellion: The Moslem Challenge to Chinese Authority in Xinjiang 1944–1949* (Armonk, NY: M. E. Sharpe, 1990).

59. Nehru to Secretary-General, Ministry of External Affairs, 9 July 1949, in *Selected Works of Jawaharlal Nehru*, 2d series (New Delhi: Jawaharlal Nehru Memorial Fund, 1991), vol. 12, p. 410.

60. For two insightful descriptions of these sentiments, see the accounts of two non-European residents in China in the late 1940s—the Indian Kumara Menon, *Twilight in China* (Bombay: Bharatiya Vidya Bhavan, 1972); and the Filipino Mariano Ezpeleta, *Red Shadows over Shanghai* (Quezon City: Zita, 1972).

61. For two different approaches among Western missionaries, see Raymond J. de Jaegher and Irene Corbally Kuhn, *The Enemy Within: An Eyewitness Account of the Communist Conquest of China* (Garden City, NY: Doubleday, 1953); and Lawrence D. Kessler, *The Jiangyin Mission Station: An American Missionary Community in China, 1895–1951* (Chapel Hill: University of North Carolina Press, 1996).

62. David Kranzler, *Japanese, Nazis, and Jews: The Jewish Refugee Commu-*

nity in Shanghai, 1938–1945 (Hoboken, NJ: Ktav, 1986), p. 581; see also Marcia Reyndus Ristaino, *Port of Last Resort: Diaspora Communities in Shanghai* (Stanford, CA: Stanford University Press, 2002).

63. See Jiang Pei, "Nanjing guomin zhengfu yishi xingtai guanli nanxi" ["Analysis of Ideological Control by the Nationalist Government in Nanjing"], *Minguo dang'an* 3 (1993): 71–79. On the GMD's earlier attempts at political censorship of movies, see Xiao Zhiwei, "Film Censorship in China, 1927–1937," Ph.D. dissertation, University of California, San Diego, 1994.

64. See, for instance, CC instructions on mass work, 23 May 1947, Zhongyang tongzhanbu and Zhongyang dang'anguan, eds., *Zhonggong zhongyang jiefang zhanzheng shiqi tongyi zhanxian wenxian xuanbian* [Selected CCP Central Committee Documents on the United Front during the War of Liberation] (Beijing: Dang'an, 1988), pp. 157–59 (there is some doubt about when these instructions were issued; see Zhongyang dang'anguan, comp., *Zhonggong zhongyang wenjian xuanji* [*Selected Documents of the CCP Center*] (Beijing: Zhonggong zhongyang dangxiao, 1992), vol. 16, p. 454).

65. Both published in Shanghai by Chenguang chuban gongsi.

66. Shanghai: Chenguang chuban gongsi, 1947.

67. Shanghai: Wenhua shenghuo chubanshe, 1947.

68. Hong Kong: Xin minzhu, 1948.

69. For an overview, see Zhang Yingjin and Xiao Zhiwei, *Encyclopedia of Chinese Film* (New York: Routledge, 1998).

70. Wasserstrom, *Student Protest*, p. 211.

71. Ibid., p. 212.

72. For examples of these activities in Beijing, see Gongqingtuan Beijing shiwei qingnian yundong shi yanjiushi, comp., *Beijing qingnian yundong shi, 1919–1949* [*History of the Beijing Youth Movement, 1919–1949*] (Beijing: Beijing, 1989).

73. Wasserstrom, *Student Protest*; see also examples in Guangzhou qingnian yundong shi yanjiu weiyuanhui, eds., *Jiefang zhanzheng shiqi Guangzhou qingnian yundong ziliao xuanbian* [*Selected Materials on the Guangzhou Youth Movement during the War of Liberation Period*] (Guangzhou: n.p., 1984).

74. Gongqingtuan zhongyang qingyunshi yanjiushi et al., eds., *Jiefang zhanzheng shiqi xuesheng yundong lunwenji* [*Selected Essays on the Student Movement during the War of Liberation Period*] (Shanghai: Dongji daxue, 1988).

75. Hua Binqing, *Wuerling yundong shi: 1947 nian wei dadi xuesheng yundong* [*A History of the 20 May Movement: The 1947 Student Anti-imperialist Movement*] (Nanjing: Nanjing daxue, 1990).

76. *Jiefang zhanzheng shiqi diertiao zhanxian: Xuesheng yundong juan* (Beijing: Zhonggong dangshi, 1997), vol. 2.

77. From a poem that circulated under the pseudonym Wang Ming, printed in Zhonggong Beijing shiwei xuanchuanbu; Zhonggong Beijing shiwei dangshi yanjiushi; Beijing shi wenhuajuan, comps., *Jiefang zhanzheng shiqi Beiping diertuan zhanzheng de wenhua douzheng* [*The Cultural Struggle of the Second Front in Beijing during the War of Liberation Period*] (Beijing: Beijing, 1998), p. 86 (trans. by the author).

Chapter 4. Adjusting Heaven

1. See, for instance, Feng Chongyi and David S. G. Goodman, eds., *North China at War: The Social Ecology of Revolution, 1937–1945* (Lanham, MD: Rowan and Littlefield, 2000); and David S. G. Goodman, *Social and Political Change in Revolutionary China: The Taihang Base Area in the War of Resistance to Japan, 1937–1945* (Lanham, MD: Rowan and Littlefield, 2000).

2. Politburo to Northeast Bureau, 25 Oct. 1946, Zhongyang dang'anguan, comp., *Zhonggong zhongyang wenjian xuanji [Selected Documents of the CCP Center]* (Beijing: Zhonggong zhongyang dangxiao, 1992), vol. 16, p. 321.

3. See Jing Huang, *Factionalism in Chinese Communist Politics* (Cambridge: Cambridge University Press, 2000), pp. 143–51.

4. See *Ren Bishi zhuan [Ren Bishi Biography]* (Beijing: Zhongyang wenxian, 1994), pp. 612–14; and *Zhou Enlai junshi huodong jishi*, vol. 1, pp. 730–32.

5. The ShaanGanNing army and the JinSui army merged in early 1947 to form the Northwest field army, later the PLA 1st Field Army, under Peng Dehuai. A part of these units, under He Long's command, was moved to Southwest China later during the civil war. The JinJiLuYu army became the core of the 2d Field Army under Liu Bocheng; the New Fourth Army became the 3d Field Army under Chen Yi; and the CCP forces in the Northeast became the 4th Field Army under Lin Biao.

6. On the relationship between Liu and Deng, see Ren Tao, *Deng Xiaoping cai Zhongyuan [Deng Xiaoping at the Central Plains]* (Beijing: Zhongyang wenxian, 1993). For He Long's attitudes, see his report dated 19 June 1946 in *He Long junshi wenxuan* (Beijing: Jiefangjun, 1989).

7. We still do not have a detailed overview of which weapons were transferred, and when, from the Soviets to the CCP. The Soviet military archives are still closed, and the provincial archives in Manchuria, which are gradually opening to scholars, do not as a rule allow access to military records. We do, however, have the records of the Soviet Foreign Ministry and its Harbin consulate, through which many of the CCP requests for weapons and supplies were made.

8. *Zhongguo renmin jiefangjun disan yezhanjun zhanshi*, pp. 105–26.

9. See, for instance, the reports in Shaanxi sheng dang'anguan and Shaanxi sheng shehui kexueyuan, comps., *Shaan-Gan-Ning bianqu zhengfu wenjian xuanbian [Selected Documents from the Shaan-Gan-Ning Border Area Government]* (Beijing: Dang'an, 1986–91), vol. 11, especially the report dated 4 July 1947, p. 79.

10. Mao's instructions of 3 Sept. 1947, *Mao Zedong junshi wenji*, vol. 4, p. 236; see also Chen Yongfa, *Zhongguo gongchan geming qishinian [Seventy Years of Chinese Communist Revolution]* (Taibei: Lianjing, 1998), pp. 721–22.

11. Statement on the treatment of deserters, 25 June 1948, in *Shaan-Gan-Ning bianqu zhengfu wenjian xuanbian*, vol. 12, p. 134.

12. See, for instance, *Zhongguo renmin jiefangjun disan yezhanjun zhanshi*, pp. 154–69.

13. The members were Mao Zedong, Zhu De, Liu Shaoqi, Zhou Enlai, Ren Bishi, Chen Yun, Kang Sheng, Gao Gang, Peng Zhen, Dong Biwu, Lin Boqu, Zhang Wentian, and Peng Dehuai. Mao, Zhu, Liu, Zhou, and Ren constituted the Secretariat.

14. For the organization of the CCP Center during the civil war, see Fei Yundong and Yu Guihua, "A Brief History of the Work of Secretaries in the Chinese Communist Party (1921–1949)," *Chinese Studies in Law and Government* 30, no. 4 (1997).

15. On the origins of the debates over land policy, see *Zhongguo tudi gaige shi (1921–1949)* [*A History of Chinese Land Reform (1921–1949)*] (Beijing: Renmin, 1990); and Zhongyang dang'anguan, comp., *Jiefang zhanzheng shiqi tudi gaige wenxian xuanbian (1945–1949 nian)* (Beijing: Zhonggong zhongyang dangxiao, 1981).

16. Mao's report to an enlarged Central Committee meeting in Xiaohe, 21 July 1947, in *Mao Zedong wenji* [*Mao Zedong Works*] (Beijing: Renmin, 1996), vol. 4, pp. 266–71.

17. See Mao Zedong's comments on instructions from Liu Shaoqi to He Long concerning land reform, 25 July 1947, *Zhonggong zhongyang wenjian xuanji*, vol. 16, pp. 486–93. For practical examples of these excesses, see William Hinton, *Fanshen: A Documentary of Revolution in a Chinese Village* (Berkeley: University of California Press, 1997 [1966]), pp. 232–40.

18. Jin Chongji, ed., *Mao Zedong zhuan, 1893–1949* [*Mao Zedong Biography, 1893–1949*] (Beijing: Zhongyang wenxian, 1996), pp. 816–17.

19. Mao Zedong to Liu Bocheng and Deng Xiaoping, 30 July 1947, *Mao Zedong junshi wenji*, vol. 4, p. 162.

20. Tony Saich with Benjamin Yang, eds., *The Rise to Power of the Chinese Communist Party: Documents and Analysis* (Armonk, NY: M. E. Sharpe, 1996), pp. 1300, 1305; Ren's 12 January 1948 speech in Zhongyang tongzhanbu and Zhongyang dang'anguan, eds., *Zhonggong zhongyang jiefang zhanzheng shiqi tongyi zhanxian wenxian xuanbian* [*Selected CCP Central Committee Documents on the United Front during the War of Liberation*] (Beijing: Dang'an, 1988), pp. 163–83.

21. Center's working committee to Northeast bureau et al., 31 Dec. 1947, *Zhonggong zhongyang wenjian xuanji*, vol. 16, pp. 602–4; and Mao to Li Jingquan et al., 6 Feb. 1948, ibid., vol. 17, pp. 33–34. See also Liu Shaoqi's speech attacking "leftism" in February 1948 in Zhongguo renmin jiefangjun Guofang daxue dangshi dangjian zhenggong jiaoyanshi, comp., *Zhonggong dangshi jiaoxue cankao ziliao* [*Reference Materials for Teaching Party History*] (Beijing?: n.p., 1986), vol. 14, pp. 346–49.

22. See Christopher Hughes, *Taiwan and Chinese Nationalism: National Identity and Status in International Society* (London: Routledge, 1997), pp. 10–16, and Chen Yongfa's discussion of the development of CCP Taiwan policies in *Zhongguo gongchan geming qishinian*.

23. On the CCP's nationality policies up to 1945, see Warren H. Smith, Jr., *Tibetan Nation: A History of Tibetan Nationalism and Sino-Tibetan Relations* (Boulder, CO: Westview, 1996), pp. 323–41. See also Edgar Snow, *Red Star over China* (London: Victor Gollancz, 1968 [1937]), p. 203.

24. Record of Mao's conversation with Liu Shaoqi and Zhou Enlai in Yan'an, 21 Nov. 1946, Zhonggong zhongyang wenxian yanjiushi, comp., *Mao Zedong nianpu (1893–1949)* [*Mao Zedong Chronology (1893–1949)*] (Beijing: Renmin, 1993), vol. 3, pp. 15–152; Mao, 8 Sept. 1948, in Zhonghua renmin gongheguo

waijiaobu and Zhonggong zhongyang wenxian yanjiushi, eds., *Mao Zedong wai-jiao wenxuan* [*Mao Zedong Selected Works on Foreign Affairs*] (Beijing: Zhong-yang wenxian, 1994); Liu Shaoqi speech, 1 July 1948, *Zhonggong dangshi jiao-xue cankao ziliao*, vol. 18, pp. 438–48; Ren Bishi's two telegrams on behalf of the Central Committee, 8 May 1948 and 28 June 1948, *Ren Bishi xuanji*, pp. 438–56.

25. See, for instance, Soviet Ambassador Roshchin's quarterly report to For-eign Minister Molotov for Oct.–Dec. 1948, AVPRF, f. 07, op. 22, pa. 36, d. 229, pp.1–29.

26. Patricia Stranahan, *Molding the Medium: The Chinese Communist Party and the Liberation Daily*, pp. 140–51.

27. See, for instance, instructions on propaganda work from the Center, 9 Nov. 1947, *Zhonggong zhongyang wenjian xuanji*, vol. 16, pp. 580–81; *Zhong-guo renmin jiefangjun disi yezhanjun zhanshi*, pp. 279–85; see also Mao's com-ments in 4 Feb. 1949 talk with Mikoyan, Archiv Prezidenta Rossiiskoi Federatsii [Archive of the President of the Russian Federation, hereafter APRF], f. 39, o. 1, d. 39.

28. Mao usually referred to Stalin (the temporal Stalin, as opposed to Stalin the Marxist theorist) as the "Supreme Master" (*zuigao dashi*) or "Main Master" (*zhuyao dashi*).

29. Mao to Lin Biao, 11 July 1946, *Mao Zedong nianpu*, vol. 3, pp. 106–7.

30. This and the following paragraphs on the situation in Dongbei are based on Ding Xiaochun et al., eds., *Dongbei jiefang zhanzheng dashiji* [*Chronology of the Liberation War in the Northeast*] (Beijing: Zhonggong dangshi ziliao, 1987), esp. pp. 48–55.

31. *Zhongguo renmin jiefangjun disi yezhanjun zhanshi*, pp. 192–97.

32. On Zhang's role in the late 1940s, see Liu Ying, *Wo de Zhang Wentian mingyun yu gong de licheng* [*My and Zhang Wentian's Destiny and Joint Course*] (Beijing: Zhonggong dangshi, 1997), pp. 131–65; and Frederick C. Teiwes with Warren Sun, "From a Leninist to a Charismatic Party: The CCP's Changing Lead-ership, 1937–1945," in Tony Saich and Hans van de Ven, eds., *New Perspectives on the Chinese Communist Revolution* (Armonk, NY: M. E. Sharpe, 1995), pp. 348–49.

33. On Gao Gang, see Jing Huang, *Factionalism in Chinese Communist Poli-tics*, pp. 143–45.

34. Steven I. Levine, *Anvil of Victory: The Communist Revolution in Man-churia, 1945–1948* (New York: Columbia University Press, 1987), pp. 87–121.

35. Ibid., pp. 146–48; Malik to Molotov, 23 Feb. 1947, AVPRF, f. 07, o. 12, pa. 24, d. 315, pp. 15–17; Zhonggong zhongyang dangshi ziliao zhengji weiyuan-hui and Zhonguo renmin jiefangjun dang'anguan, comp. and ed., *Dongbei ren-min jiefangjun silingbu zhen zhong riji, 1946.11–1947.12* [*The Battle Diary of the Headquarters of the Northeast People's Liberation Army, Nov. 1946 to Dec. 1947*], 2 vols. (Beijing: Zhonggong dangshi ziliao, 1987).

36. Wang Yuannian et al., *Dongbei jiefang zhanzheng chu jian jiao fei shi* [*A History of Eliminating Traitors and Suppressing Bandits during the War of Lib-eration in the Northeast*] (Changchun: Heilongjiang jiaoyu, 1990), pp. 46–89.

37. Levine, *Anvil of Victory*, pp. 45–49.

38. *Zhongguo renmin jiefangjun disi yezhanjun zhanshi*, pp. 293–98.

39. Levine, *Anvil of Victory*, pp. 197–235.

40. Wang Yuannian, *Dongbei jiefang zhanzheng chu jian jiao fei shi*, pp. 230–37.

41. Levine, *Anvil of Victory*, pp. 224–28.

42. *Mao Zedong nianpu*, vol. 3, p. 312.

43. Odoric Y. K. Wou, *Mobilizing the Masses: Building Revolution in Henan* (Stanford, CA: Stanford University Press, 1994), pp. 342–54.

44. Mao to Li Jingquan et al., 6 Feb. 1948, *Zhonggong zhongyang wenjian xuanji*, vol. 17, pp. 33–34.

45. See the documents in *Jiefang zhanzheng shiqi tudi gaige wenxian xuanbian* for prototypes of this kind.

46. Examples of these difficulties may be found in *Shaan-Gan-Ning bianqu zhengfu wenjian xuanbian*, such as the 18 Jan. 1948 report on labor mobilization, vol. 12, pp. 6–8.

47. See the documents collected in Zhonghua quanguo funü lianhewei funü yundong lishi yanjiushi, comp., *Zhongguo funü yundong lishi ziliao, 1945–1949* (Beijing: Zhongguo funü, 1991) for the roles of women in the CCP areas.

48. Zhonggong Liaoning shengwei dangshi yanjiushi, comp., *Jiefang zhanzheng zhong de LiaoJi genjudi* [*The Base Areas in Hebei and Liaoning during the War of Liberation*] (Beijing: Zhonggong dangshi, 1991), pp. 415–56, on difficulties in mobilizing.

49. Elise Anne DeVido, "The Making of the Communist Party-State in Shandong Province, 1927–1952," Ph.D. dissertation, Harvard University, 1995, pp. 168–82.

50. Wou, *Mobilizing the Masses*, pp. 348–49.

51. In early 1948, the Center sent Kang Sheng as head of a Central Investigation Group to put an end to the chaos in Shandong. Kang, who himself had been accused of "radical excesses" in Yan'an during party rectification, seems a poor choice for the job, and there is no evidence that his arrival did anything to abate the situation (see DeVido, "The Making of the Communist Party-State in Shandong Province, 1927–1952"). See also *Zhonggong Shandong dangshi dashiji, 1921–1949* [*CCP Shandong Party History Chronology, 1921–1949*] (Jinan: Shandong renmin, 1986), pp. 297–99.

52. Document dated 18 Jan. 1948, *Shaan-Gan-Ning bianqu zhengfu wenjian xuanbian*, vol. 12, p. 6.

53. Ralph A. Thaxton, Jr., *Salt of the Earth: The Political Origins of Peasant Protest and Communist Revolution in China* (Berkeley: University of California Press, 1997), pp. 297–303.

54. Zhonggong zhongyang wenxian yanjiushi, comp., *Liu Shaoqi nianpu* [*Liu Shaoqi Chronology*], 2 vols. (Beijing: Zhongyang wenxian, 1996), vol. 2, pp. 125–27.

55. For an interesting example of Mao's position, see his comments on Ren's January 1948 report on land reform, *Mao Zedong nianpu*, vol. 3, pp. 265–66.

56. Zhonggong Shanghai shiwei dangshi ziliao zhengji weiyuanhui, comp.,

Jiefang zhanzheng shiqi Shanghai xuesheng yundong shi [*A History of the Shanghai Student Movement during the War of Liberation*] (Shanghai: Shanghai fanyi, 1991), pp. 83–95; Zhonggong zhongyang wenxian yanjiushi, comp., *Zhou Enlai junshi huodong jishi, 1918–1975* [*A Record of Zhou Enlai's Military Activities, 1918–1975*] (Beijing: Zhongyang wenxian, 2000), vol. 1, pp. 675–710.

57. 28 Apr. 1948 speech, *Liu Shaoqi lun gongren yundong* [*Liu Shaoqi on the Workers' Movement*] (Beijing: Zhonggong zhongyang wenxian, 1988).

58. For the story of one of Zhou's young assistants, see Yang Gongsu, *Cangsang jiunian: Yige waijiao teshi de huiyi* [*Ninety Years' Experience of Life: The Reminiscences of a Diplomatic Special Envoy*] (Haikou: Hainan, 1999).

60. Mo Wenhua, *Huiyi jiefang Beiping qianhou* [Remembering Beiping before and after Liberation] (Beijing: Beijing, 1982); see also Zhou Enlai to Dong Biwu, 6 Jan. 1947, in Zhonggong zhongyang wenxian yanjiushi, comp., *Zhou Enlai nianpu, 1898–1949* [*Chronological Biography of Zhou Enlai, 1898–1949*] (Beijing: Zhongyang wenxian, 1989), pp. 714–15.

61. The alleged rape of BeiDa student Shen Chong on Christmas Eve of 1946 has taken on symbolic meanings that still make it difficult to disentangle what really happened that night. Of the two U.S. Marines involved, one was court-martialed and found guilty, but six months later the verdict was set aside by higher authorities in Washington who found the charges "not proven." The facts of the story are not made easier to get at in view of the information, which the party revealed in 1950, that Shen Chong was already a secret CCP member when the incident took place. It has never been proven that Shen had listened too closely to the instructions of the Beijing CCP Urban Work Committee, issued in July 1946, that its members should "inform" the masses of the "atrocities" of the U.S. soldiers, such as traffic accidents, sexual assaults, and suppression of the people. For the CCP version, see *Wuerling yundong ziliao* [*Materials on the 20th May Movement*] (Beijing: Renmin, 1985), esp. pp. 24–26; and Zhonggong Beijing shiwei dangshi yanjiushi, comp., *Kangyi Meijun Zhu Hua Baoxing Yundong Ziliao Huibian* [*A Collection of Materials on the Movement to Protest Atrocities by the American Army Stationed in China*] (Beijing: Beijing daxue, 1989).

62. Ibid.

63. *Zhou Enlai nianpu*, p. 737; see also *Jiefang zhanzheng shiqi diertiao zhanxian: Xuesheng yundong juan* (Beijing: Zhonggong dangshi, 1997), vol. 3.

64. Joseph K. S. Yick, *Making Urban Revolution in China: The CCP-GMD Struggle for Beiping-Tianjin, 1945–1949* (Armonk, NY: M. E. Sharpe, 1995), pp. 80–126; Zhonggong Beijing shiwei xuanchuanbu; Zhonggong Beijing shiwei dangshi yanjiushi; Beijing shi wenhuajuan, comps., *Jiefang zhanzheng shiqi Beiping diertuan zhanzheng de wenhua douzheng* [*The Cultural Struggle of the Second Front in Beijing during the War of Liberation Period*] (Beijing: Beijing, 1998), pp. 464–92.

65. Han Suyin, *Eldest Son: Zhou Enlai and the Making of Modern China, 1898–1976* (New York: Hill and Wang, 1994), pp. 198–99; Yick, *Making Urban Revolution in China*, p. 113. For the memoirs of two of these successful CCP spies, see Xiong Xianghui, *Wo de qingbao yu waijiao shengya* [*My Life in Intelligence and Diplomacy*] (Beijing: Zhonggong dangshi, 1999); and Cai Huilin, *"Chonggao de shiming": Hui zhandou zai Guomindang yinglei de suiyue* [*"Lofty*

Mission": Remembering Years of Fighting in the Guomindang Camp], 2 vols. (Beijing: Junshi jiaoxue, 1990).

66. See Zhonghua quanguo zonggonghui, comp., *Zhonggong zhongyang guanyu gongren yundong wenxian xuanbian* [*A Selection of the CCP Central Committee's Documents on the Workers Movement*], 3 vols. (Beijing: Dang'an, 1984–86), vol. 3, pp. 170–301. For the development in one large factory, see *Shanghai disanshiyi mianfangzhichang gongren yundong shi, 1914–1949* [*A History of the Worker's Movement at the Shanghai Number 31 Textile Mill, 1914–1949*] (Beijing: Zhonggong dangshi, 1991).

67. The Center's instructions on underground work in Beijing and Tianjin, 13 Dec. 1948, *Zhonggong zhongyang guanyu gongren yundong wenxian xuanbian*, 3, pp. 272–76. See also Zou Bei, ed., *Zhongguo gongren yundong shi hua* [*The Brilliant History of the Chinese Workers' Movement*] (Beijing: Gongren, 1993), vol. 5, pp. 10–47; and *Xiamen gongren yundong shi* [*A History of the Worker's Movement in Xiamen*] (Xiamen: Xiamen daxue, 1991).

Chapter 5. Into the Cauldron

1. Jiang's speech to the joint session of the GMD Central Bureau and the National Government, 13 Jan. 1947, *Jiang sixiang yanlun*, vol. 22, pp. 1–7.

2. Du Yuming et al., *GuoGong neizhan milu* [*The Secret History of the GMD-CCP Civil War*] (Taibei: Papilun, 1991).

3. See Diana Lary, *Warlord Soldiers: Chinese Common Soldiers, 1911–1937* (Cambridge: Cambridge University Press, 1985); Lloyd Eastman, *The Abortive Revolution: China under Nationalist Rule, 1927–1937* (Cambridge, MA: Harvard University Press, 1974); Hsi-sheng Ch'i, *Nationalist China at War: Military Defeats and Political Collapse, 1937–45* (Ann Arbor: University of Michigan Press, 1982).

4. Speech to military commanders, 10 July 1947, *Jiang sixiang yanlun*, vol. 22, pp. 216–20; see also entry for 23 May 1947, in *Jiang chugao*, p. 458.

5. *Chen Yi zhuan* (Beijing: Dangdai Zhongguo, 1991), p. 384.

6. See, for instance, the record of the meeting of the Supreme National Defense Council, 9 Oct. 1946, *Guofang zuigao weiyuanhui changwuhui yijilu* [*Records of the Discussions at the Ordinary Meetings of the Supreme National Defense Council*] (Taibei: Zhongguo guomindang zhongyang weiyuanhui dangshi weiyuanhui, 1996), vol. 8, pp. 514–39.

7. Li Yanxing, *Huang tudi, hong tudi: Zhuanzhan Shaanbei juan* [*Yellow Earth, Red Earth: A Book on the Shifting Battles in Northern Shaanxi*] (Beijing: Jiefangjun, 1992), pp. 18–26.

8. Ibid.; *Zhongguo renmin jiefangjun diyi yezhanjun zhanshi*, pp. 41–66; Zhonggong zhongyang wenxian yanjiushi, comp., *Mao Zedong nianpu (1893–1949)* [*Mao Zedong Chronology (1893–1949)*] (Beijing: Renmin, 1993), vol. 3, pp. 174–77.

9. Jiao Beiguo, *Zhuanzhan Shanbei diyinian* [*The First Year of Military Change in Northern Shaanxi*] (Hohhot: Nei Menggu xinhua shudian, 1985).

10. Anna Louise Strong, *The Chinese Conquer China* (Garden City, NY: Doubleday, 1949), p. 230.

11. *Ren Bishi zhuan* [*Ren Bishi Biography*] (Beijing: Zhongyang wenxian, 1994), pp. 615–31.

12. *Mao Zedong junshi wenji*, vol. 4, pp. 35–36.

13. Mao to Peng Dehuai and the Northwest Front Committee, 15 Apr. 1947, *Mao Zedong junshi wenji*, vol. 4, p. 37.

14. Entries for 28 Feb. and 1 Mar. 1947, *Jiang chugao*, vol. 6, book 2, pp. 396–97. The account of the 1947 Taiwan uprising in this and ensuing paragraphs is based on Lai Tse-han, Ramon T. Myers, and Wei Wou, *A Tragic Beginning: The Taiwan Uprising of February 28, 1947* (Stanford, CA: Stanford University Press, 1991); and Günter Whittome, *Taiwan 1947: Der Aufstand gegen die Kuomintang* (Hamburg: Institut für Asienkunde, 1991).

15. Not to be confused with the PLA general whose name has an identical spelling in transcription.

16. Mao to ShaanGanNing army commanders, 8 May 1947, *Mao Zedong junshi wenji*, vol. 4, p. 66.

17. *Zhongguo renmin jiefangjun disi yezhanjun zhanshi*, pp. 91–99.

18. Mao to army commanders in North China, 22 June 1947, *Mao Zedong junshi wenji*, vol. 4, p. 111.

19. *Zhonggong Shandong dangshi dashiji, 1921–1949* [*CCP Shandong Party History Chronology, 1921–1949*] (Jinan: Shandong renmin, 1986), pp. 278–91.

20. *Zhongguo renmin jiefangjun disan yezhanjun zhanshi*, pp. 111–54.

21. Mao to Chen Yi, 22 May 1947, *Mao Zedong junshi wenji*, vol. 4, pp. 81–82.

22. *Chen Su da jun zhengzhan jisubian* [*Records of the Battles of the Chen Su Great Army*] (Beijing: Xinhua, 1991), pp. 338–52.

23. Entry for 11 Mar. 1947, *Jiang chugao*, vol. 6, book 2, pp. 401–2.

24. *Gu Weijun huiyilu* [*Gu Weijun (Wellington Kuo) Memoirs*] (Beijing: Zhonghua shudian, 1988), vol. 6, pp. 87–100.

25. Douglas J. Macdonald, *American Intervention for Reform in the Third World* (Cambridge, MA: Harvard University Press, 1992), pp. 107–8.

26. Ibid., p. 110.

27. For Marshall's position, see Marshall to Carter, 22 July 1946, FRUS, 1946, vol. 10, p. 753.

28. Entry for 30 June 1947, *Jiang chugao*, vol. 6, book 2, p. 488. It did not help Marshall's request that one of the board members was Clarence E. Gauss, a former U.S. ambassador to China whom Jiang had succeeded in having recalled in 1944; see Macdonald, *Adventures in Chaos*, p. 111.

29. Ibid.

30. William Stueck, *The Wedemeyer Mission: American Politics and Foreign Policy during the Cold War* (Athens: University of Georgia Press, 1984), pp. 35–40; entry for 25 Aug. 1947, *Jiang chugao*, vol., 6, book 2, p. 553.

31. *The China White Paper, August 1949* (originally published as *United States Relations with China with Special Reference to the Period 1944–1949* [Stanford, CA: Stanford University Press, 1967]), pp. 387–90.

32. Entries for 15 and 16 Sept. 1947, *Jiang chugao*, vol. 6, book 2, pp. 558–59; Jiang's 10 July 1947 speech to military commanders, *Jiang sixiang yan-*

lun, vol. 22, pp. 216–20; Xu Zupu, Foreign Ministry First Research Section, "Shicha LüDa jishi ji shanhou duice" [The Facts about the Inspection Tour of Lüshun and Dalian and a Plan for the Future], 4 July 1947, ROC-Waijiobu, Taibei, 119.13/320.25, quoted in Brian Murray, "Western versus Chinese Realism: Soviet-American Diplomacy and the Chinese Civil War, 1945–1950," Ph.D. dissertation, Columbia University, 1995, pp. 278–80.

33. Andrei M. Ledovskii, "Na diplomaticheskoi rabote v kitae v 1942–1952 gg" ["On Diplomatic Service in China, 1942–52"], *Novaia i noveishaia istoriia* 6 (1993): 102–32; Mikhail Kapitsa, author's interview, Moscow, 7 Sept. 1992; Yakov Malik to Vice Minister of Internal Affairs, M. A. Serov, 13 Sept. 1947, AVPRF, f. 0100, op. 40a, pa. 268, d. 57, pp. 19–20; V. Vasiukevich (consul in Manchuria) to Malik, 8 Oct. 1947, ibid., d. 67, pp. 10–11.

34. Ivan V. Kovalev, "Dialog Stalina s Mao Tsedunom" ["The Stalin-Mao Zedong Talks"], *Problemu dalnego vostoka* 6 (1991): 83–93, esp. 84–85; Nikolai Fedorenko, "Stalin i Mao Tsedun" ["Stalin and Mao Zedong"], *Novaiia i noveishaia istoriia* 5 (1992): 98–113, and vol. 6: 83–95.

35. Mikhail Kapitsa, author's interview, Moscow, 7 Sept. 1992; Sergei L. Tikhvinskii, "Kitai v moei zhisni" ["China in My Life"], *Problemu dalnego vostoka* 4 (1990): 103–12. A telling example of these difficulties is Ambassador Apollon Petrov's report to Stalin and Molotov on developments in China Oct.–Dec. 1946, dated 19 Jan. 1947, AVPRF, f. 07, op. 12, pa. 24, d. 313, pp. 1–31.

36. Later known as the Soviet General Staff's Main Intelligence Directorate, *Glavnoe razvedyvatelnoe upravlenie* (GRU).

37. See, for instance, Jiang's summing up of the relationship to the Soviets in a conversation with his son, Jiang Jingguo, after the latter's meeting with Roshchin, entry for 12 Dec. 1947, *Jiang chugao*, vol. 6, book 2, pp. 589–90. See also Murray, "Western versus Chinese Realism," pp. 313–34.

38. Rice to Butterworth, 18 Dec. 1947, "Factors Presently Working for and against a Sino-Soviet Rapprochement," FRUS, 1947, vol. 8, pp. 404–10.

39. Entry for 14 and 16 Sept. 1947, *Jiang chugao*, vol. 6, book 2, pp. 558–59; Zhang Xianwen and Fang Qingjiu, *Jiang Jieshi quanzhuan* [A Complete Biography of Jiang Jieshi], 2 vols. (Zhengzhou: Henan renmin, 1996, 1997), vol. 2, pp. 660–63.

40. See Jiang's 6 Oct. 1947 speech to military commanders in Beijing, *Jiang sixiang yanlun*, vol. 22, pp. 266–76.

41. Yueh-hung Chen Ting, "The Intellectuals and the Chinese Revolution: A Study of the Chinese Democratic League and Its Components, 1939–1949," Ph.D. dissertation, New York University, 1978, p. 228; see also *Minmeng shi hua, 1941–1949* [On the History of the Democratic League, 1941–1949] (Beijing: Zhongguo shehui kexue, 1992), pp. 360–89.

42. 12 Nov. 1947 speech to newspaper editors, *Jiang sixiang yanlun*, vol. 22, pp. 344–51.

43. Stalin to Mao Zedong [Kuznetsov to Terebin], 1 July 1947, APRF, f. 39, o. 1, d. 31, p. 24. As late as February 1948, Stalin was uncertain about the CCP's long-term potential; see his conversation with Georgi Dimitrov and other Balkan

Communist leaders, 10 Feb. 1948, Georgi Dimitrov, *Dnevnik: 9 mart 1933–6 fevruari 1949* [*Diary: 9 Mar. 1933–6 Feb. 1949*] (Sofia: Sv. Kliment Okhridski, 1997).

44. For an overview of Soviet-CCP trade, see Kosichenko et al. to Molotov, Mikoyan, Kaganovich, and Vyshinskii, "On Trade with the People's Republic of China," 12 Feb. 1950, AVPRF, f. 07, o. 23a, p. 237, d. 18, pp. 1–47.

45. For an overview of these activities, see Kovalev to Stalin, 5 Jan. 1949, AVPRF, f. 07, o. 11, p. 231, d. 5, pp. 3–6; see also Zhonggong zhongyang wen-xian yanjiushi, comp., *Liu Shaoqi nianpu* [*Liu Shaoqi Chronology*], 2 vols. (Beijing: Zhongyang wenxian, 1996), vol. 1, pp. 77–78.

46. See Mao's remarks to a CCP Center meeting in Xiaohe, 21 July 1947, *Mao Zedong wenji* [*Mao Zedong Works*] (Beijing: Renmin, 1996), vol. 4, pp. 266–71. A series of newly available documents from later in 1947 confirms this orientation; see Mao's speech to a CCP Center meeting in Yangjiagou, 21, 25, and 28 Dec. 1947, ibid., pp. 324–36. See also Yang Kuisong, *Zhonggong yu Mosike de guanxi, 1920–1960* [*The Relationship between the CCP and Moscow, 1920–1960*] (Taibei: Sanmin shudian, 1997), pp. 567–70, and his *Mao Zedong yu Mosike de enen-yuanyuan* [*The Love-hate Relationship between Mao Zedong and Moscow*] (Nanchang: Jiangxi renmin, 1999).

47. *Mao Zedong nianpu*, vol. 3; see also Kuznetsev to Orlov [Stalin to Mao], 17 June 1947, APRF, f. 39, o. 1, d. 31, p. 23. Major General Fedor Kuznetsev was head of the Soviet General Staff intelligence division's Third Department, the department in charge of communicating Stalin's messages; Andrei Orlov (code name *Terebin*) was the military intelligence officer who headed the Soviet mission to the CCP leadership.

48. Handwritten notes on Mao's meetings with local commanders, 17 Oct. and 28 Oct. 1947, Chinese Central Archives; copies in author's possession.

49. The following paragraphs are based on *LiuDeng dajun jiangdu Huanghe ziliao xuan* [*Selected Materials on the Liu-Deng Army's Crossing of the Huanghe*] (Jinan: Shandong daxue, 1987); *Liu Bocheng huiyilu* [*Liu Bocheng Recollections*] (Shanghai: Shanghai wenzhi, 1987), esp. vol. 3; and Ren Tao, *Deng Xiaoping cai Zhongyuan* [*Deng Xiaoping at the Central Plains*] (Beijing: Zhongyang wenxian, 1993).

50. See *LiuDeng dajun jiangdu Huanghe ziliao xuan*; Ren, *Deng Xiaoping cai Zhongyuan*.

51. Mao to Li Xiannian et al., 28 May 1947, *Mao Zedong junshi wenji*, vol. 4, pp. 87. Mao wrote that the operation had to be carried out "even under the most problematic circumstances . . . when we are facing difficult times because of Jiang's offensives" (ibid.).

52. Ren, *Deng Xiaoping cai Zhongyuan*, pp. 145–63.

53. *Zhongguo renmin jiefangjun disan yezhanjun zhanshi*, pp. 146–51; Zhonggong Shandong shengwei dangshi ziliao zhengzhi yanjiu weiyuanhui et al., *Quanguo jiefang zhanzheng shi ji Shandong zhongyao zhanyi ziliao congshu* [*A Collection of Materials on the Main Battles in Shandong during the War of Liberation*] (Jinan: n.p., 1988). Some historians claim that Mao's intention was to make use of the resources available in enemy territory; I have found no evidence for this in the sources.

54. Entry for 30 Nov. 1947, *Jiang chugao*, vol. 6, book 2, pp. 586; Chen Lian, *Juzhan de licheng* [*The Course of the Decisive Battle*] (Hefei: Anhui renmin, 1991).

55. Li, *Huang tudi, hong tudi*, p. 211; Zhonggong zhongyang wenxian yanjiushi, comp., *Zhou Enlai junshi huodong jishi, 1918–1975* (Beijing: Zhongyang wenxian, 2000), vol. 1, p. 750; Jin Chongji, ed., *Mao Zedong zhuan, 1893–1949* [*Mao Zedong Biography, 1893–1949*] (Beijing: Zhongyang wenxian, 1996), pp. 812–15; *Ren Bishi zhuan*, p. 636. There is some disagreement among Chinese scholars as to the exact dates for the Xiaohe meeting, but the most likely period is 21 to 23 July 1947.

56. *Mao Zedong junshi wenji*, 30 July 1947.

57. Ren, *Deng Xiaoping cai Zhongyuan*, p. 185.

58. Ibid., p. 180.

59. Entry for 5 Aug. 1947, *Jiang chugao*, vol. 6, book 2, p. 529.

60. On the relationship between Jiang and Chen, see Sun Zhaiwei, *Jiang Jieshi de chong jiang Chen Cheng* [*Jiang Jieshi's Favorite General Chen Cheng*] (Zhengzhou: Henan renmin, 1990).

61. Ibid., pp. 190–92.

62. *Zhongguo renmin jiefangjun disi yezhanjun zhanshi*, pp. 167–75.

63. Ibid.

64. *Mao Zedong nianpu*, vol. 3, pp. 244–45.

65. *Zhongguo renmin jiefangjun diyi yezhanjun zhanshi*, pp. 79–84; see also Wang Yanzhu, ed., *Peng Dehuai nianpu* [*Peng Dehuai Chronology*] (Beijing: Renmin, 1998) pp. 350–52.

66. Instructions for the second year of the War of Liberation, 1 Sept. 1947, *Mao Zedong junshi wenji*, vol. 4, p. 227.

67. Mao to Chen Yi et al., 3 Sept. 1947, ibid., p. 236.

68. Ding Xiaochun et al., eds., *Dongbei jiefang zhanzheng dashiji* [*Chronology of the Liberation War in the Northeast*] (Beijing: Zhonggong dangshi ziliao, 1987), pp. 141–45. See also vol. 2, pp. 310–17 of *Renmin Jiefangjun Dongbei silingbu zhen zhong riji, 1946.11–1947.12* [*The Battle Diary of the Headquarters of the Northeast People's Liberation Army, Nov. 1946 to Dec. 1947*] (Beijing: Zhonggong dangshi ziliao, 1987).

69. Mao to Lin Biao, 13 Oct. 1947, *Mao Zedong junshi wenji*, vol. 4, pp. 305–6.

70. On Lin's requests for aid, see Lin Biao to Molotov, 1 Sept. 1948, RGASPI, f. 17, o. 128, d. 614, p. 64; Gromyko to Stalin and Molotov, 17 Dec. 1948, AVPRF, f. 07, op. 21, pa. 21, d. 308, pp. 2–4, and the summary in Gromyko to Molotov, 16 Dec. 1948, ibid., pp. 5–8.

71. *Renmin Jiefangjun Dongbei silingbu*; *Zhongguo renmin jiefangjun disi yezhanjun zhanshi*, pp. 258–70.

72. Sun, *Jiang Jieshi de chong jiang*, pp. 145–60.

73. Mao to Lin Biao, 8 Jan. 1948, *Mao Zedong junshi wenji*, vol. 4, p. 366.

74. Entry for 31 Dec. 1947, *Jiang chugao*, vol. 6, book 2.

75. Mao to Lin Biao, 7 Feb. 1947, *Mao Zedong junshi wenji*, vol. 4, pp. 390–91.

76. Zhou Jiefu, *Sipingjie gongjian zhan* [*The Assault on the Siping Fortress*] (Hong Kong: n.p., 1985).

Chapter 6. The Turn

1. Speech at a military training session, 1 Jan. 1948, *Jiang sixiang yanlun* 22, pp. 383–93.

2. Entry for 10 Feb. 1948, Wang Shijie diary, vol. 6, pp. 173–75.

3. *Er Chen he CC* [*The Two Chens and CC*] (Zhengzhou: Henan renmin, 1993).

4. Diana Lary, *Region and Nation: The Kwangsi Clique in Chinese Politics* (Cambridge: Cambridge University Press, 1974), pp. 35–36.

5. On Sun Fo's role in getting Li elected, see Lai She-hang. "A Study of a Faltering Democrat: The Life of Sun Fo, 1891–1949." Ph.D. dissertation, University of Illinois at Urbana-Champaign, 1976, pp. 224–44.

6. Zhongguo dier lishi dang'anguan, comp. *Zhonghua minguoshi shiliao changbian* [*An Extensive Collection of Historical Materials on the History of the Republic of China*], 70 vols. (Nanjing: Nanjing daxue, 1993), vol. 70, pp. 179–80. See also Premier Zhang Qun's report on the political and military situation, 18 Oct. 1947, in *Zhonghua minguo shi dang'an ziliao huibian* [*A Collection of Archival Materials on the History of the Republic of China*], 5th series, 3d collection: Politics (1945–1949) (Nanjing: Jiangsu guji, 1999), book 1, pp. 182–94.

7. Lu Yangyuan and Fang Qingqiu, eds. *Minguo shehui jingji shi* [*A Social and Economic History of the Republic*] (Beijing: Zhongguo jingji, 1991), pp. 803–6.

8. See, for instance, CCP Center to CC Northeast Bureau, 6 Feb. 1948, Zhongyang dang'anguan, comp., *Zhonggong zhongyang wenjian xuanji* (internal ed., 14 vols.) vol. 14 (Beijing: Zhonggong zhongyang dangxiao, 1987), pp. 19–20.

9. Dong Changzhi and Li Fan, *Zhongguo xiandai jingjishi (1919–1949 nian)* [*An Economic History of Modern China (1919–1949)*] (Changchun: Dongbei shifan daxue, 1988), pp. 237–39; C. X. George Wei, *Sino-American Economic Relations, 1944–1949* (Westport, CT: Greenwood, 1997), pp. 131–38.

10. A good account of Jiang Jingguo's activities in Shanghai is in Thomas Marks, *Counterrevolution in China: Wang Sheng and the Kuomintang* (London: Frank Cass, 1998), pp. 97–117. See also Chen Pengren, *Jiang Jingguo xiansheng zhuan* [*A Biography of Mr. Jiang Jingguo*] (Taibei: Zhongyang ribao, 1990); and Wang Zhangling, *Jiang Jingguo Shanghai da hu ji: Shanghai jing ji guan zhi shi mo* [*Jiang Jingguo's Great Tiger Hunt in Shanghai: A Full Record of the Shanghai Economic Developments*] (Taibei: Zhizhong, 1999).

11. See Jiang's speech, 12 Sept. 1948, in which he summarizes his program for Shanghai, and his response to his critics in a speech of 6 Oct. 1948, in *Jiang Jingguo xiansheng quanji* [*Complete Works of Mr. Jiang Jingguo*] (Taibei: Xingzhengyuan xinwenju, 1991), vol. 3. See also Suzanne Pepper, *Civil War in China: The Political Struggle, 1945–1949* (Berkeley: University of California Press, 1978; rev. ed. Lanham, MD: Rowan and Littlefield, 1999), p. 125.

12. Entry for 25 and 28 Oct. 1948, *Jiang chugao*, vol. 7, book 1, pp. 158–60.

13. Stuart to Marshall, 23 Apr. 1948, *The China White Paper, August 1949* (originally published as *United States Relations with China with Special Reference to the Period 1944–1949* [Stanford, CA: Stanford University Press, 1967]), p. 851. The Soviets, interestingly, got detailed intelligence on these debates through the

United States; see Aleksandr S. Paniushkin (Soviet ambassador in Washington) to Vyshinskii, 6 Jan. 1948, AVPRF, f. 0129, op. 32, pa. 207, d. 21, pp. 6–13.

14. *The China White Paper*, pp. 390–94.

15. Director of Office of Far Eastern Affairs, W. Walton Butterworth to Sec., 27 July 1948, FRUS, 1948, vol. 7, pp. 379–81.

16. *The China White Paper*, p. 358.

17. *Time*, 6 Dec. 1948, p. 28.

18. T. Christopher Jespersen, *American Images of China, 1931–1949* (Stanford, CA: Stanford University Press, 1976), pp. 162–65.

19. Tang Tsou, *America's Failure in China, 1941–50* (Chicago: University of Chicago Press, 1963), p. 471; *New York Times*, 25 Nov. 1947.

20. Marshall to Stuart, 7 May 1948, FRUS, 1948, vol. 8, pp. 513–14.

21. The Soviets were worried about U.S. long-term intentions all the way up to the final withdrawal of U.S. troops; see Fedorenko to Vyshinskii, Nov. 1948, AVPRF, f. 07, op. 22, pa. 36, d. 221, pp. 1–3.

22. Shanghai bureau 23 Sept. 1948 instructions, Zhonggong Shandong shengwei dangshi ziliao zhengji yanjiu weiyuanhui et al., eds., *Jiefang zhanzheng shiqi de Zhonggong zhongyang Shanghai ju* [*The CCP CC Shanghai Bureau during the War of Liberation Period*] (Shanghai: Xuelin, 1989), pp. 389–91.

23. Mao to Lin Biao, 22 Apr. 1948, *Mao Zedong junshi wenji*, vol. 4, p. 455.

24. Cheng Xiulong, *Jiefang Taiyuan zhi zhan* [*The Battle for the Liberation of Taiyuan*] (Taiyuan: Shanxi renmin, 1982).

25. Mao to Lin Biao, 31 May 1948, *Mao Zedong junshi wenji*, vol. 4, p. 470.

26. See entry for 22 May 1948, *Jiang chugao*, vol. 7, book 1, pp. 92–93; see also *Zhongguo renmin jiefangjun diyi yezhanjun zhanshi*, pp. 137–48.

27. Jiang Kefu, *Guo Gong liang jun de erci guonei zhanzheng* [*The Second Civil War between the GMD and CCP Armies*] (Beijing: Zhonghua shudian, 1995), vol. 2.

28. *Kaifeng zhanyi ziliao xuanbian* [*Selected Materials on the Battle of Kaifeng*] (Kaifeng: Henan renmin, 1980); see also Zhonggong Kaifeng shiwei dangshi bangongshi, comp., *Youdong zhanyi* [*The Battle for Youdong*] (Zhengzhou: Henan renmin, 1988).

29. Zhonggong zhongyang wenxian yanjiushi, comp., *Liu Shaoqi nianpu* [*Liu Shaoqi Chronology*], 2 vols. (Beijing: Zhongyang wenxian, 1996), vol. 2, pp. 161–63. For the Soviet advice, see Stalin to Mao Zedong, 20 Apr. 1948, APRF, f. 39, o. 1, d. 31, pp. 28–29.

30. Zhonggong zhongyang wenxian yanjiushi, comp., *Zhou Enlai nianpu, 1898–1949* [*Chronological Biography of Zhou Enlai, 1898–1949*] (Beijing: Zhongyang wenxian, 1989), pp. 771–72; Zhonggong zhongyang wenxian yanjiushi, comp., *Mao Zedong nianpu (1893–1949)* [*Mao Zedong Chronology (1893–1949)*] (Beijing: Renmin, 1993), vol. 3, pp. 329–30; Yueh-hung Chen Ting, "The Intellectuals and the Chinese Revolution: A Study of the Chinese Democratic League and Its Components, 1939–1949," Ph.D. dissertation, New York University, 1978, pp. 206–28.

31. Mao to Lin Biao, 22 July 1948, *Mao Zedong junshi wenji*, vol. 4, pp. 541–42.

32. Mainland historians usually refer to the three big campaigns of the civil war, adding the Beijing-Tianjin campaign. That campaign—fought, mostly, in parallel with HuaiHai—did not, however, have the same level of troop engagement or the same strategic significance as the battles in Manchuria and north of the Yangzi River.

33. Mao to Lin Biao, 12 Aug. 1948, *Mao Zedong junshi wenji*, vol. 4, pp. 563–64; see also Mao's criticism of Lin's strategy in telegrams sent 30 July, 7 Aug., and 9 Aug. 1948, ibid., pp. 548, 552–53, and 556–57.

34. Mao to Lin Biao, 3 Sept. 1948, ibid., p. 590.

35. Mao to Lin Biao, 29 Sept. 1948, ibid., vol. 5, pp. 28–29.

36. Mao to Lin Biao, 3 Oct. 1948, ibid., pp. 37.

37. Ibid.

38. Mao to Lin Biao, 4 Oct. 1948, ibid., vol. 5, pp. 39–40.

39. This and the following paragraphs on the LiaoShen battles are based on *Liaoshen Juezhan: Xuji* [*The Decisive Battle for Liaoning and Shenyang: Sequel*] (Beijing: Renmin, 1992).

40. Du Yuming et al., *GuoGong neizhan milu* [*The Secret History of the GMD-CCP Civil War*] (Taibei: Papilun, 1991).

41. Entries for 1–7 Oct. 1948, *Jiang chugao*, vol. 7, book 1, pp. 143–44. See also Jiang's speech, 11 Oct. 1948, in *Jiang sixiang yanlun*, vol. 22, pp. 494–501.

42. Lin's reports, summarized in *Mao Zedong junshi wenji*, vol. 5, pp. 71, 87.

43. *Zhongguo renmin jiefangjun disi yezhanjun zhanshi*, pp. 315–26.

44. Zhao Jinxuan, *Shenyang, 1948: Jiefang Shenyang zhi shi* [*Shenyang, 1948: The History of the Liberation of Shenyang*] (Beijing: Junshi kexue, 1997).

45. Entry for 12 Oct. 1948, *Jiang chugao*, vol. 7, book 1, pp. 148–50.

46. Entry for 9 Nov. 1948, ibid., pp. 173–74.

47. Entry for 9 Nov. 1948, ibid.

48. As far as I know, the first time the CCP press used the term *genius* to describe Mao was in *Jiefang ribao*, 12 Sept. 1948.

49. Jin Chongji, ed., *Mao Zedong zhuan, 1893–1949* [*Mao Zedong Biography, 1893–1949*] (Beijing: Zhongyang wenxian, 1996), pp. 880–85.

50. The outline of the HuaiHai battles is presented on the basis of Zhonggong zhongyang dangshi ziliao zhengji weiyuanhui, comp. *HuaiHai zhanyi* [*The Battle of HuaiHai*], 3 vols. (Beijing: Zhonggong dangshi ziliao, 1988); Zhongguo renmin jiefangjun lishi ziliao congshu bianshen weiyuanhui, ed., *HuaiHai zhanyi huiyi shiliao* [*Memoirs and Historical Materials on the HuaiHai Battle*] (Beijing: Jiefangjun, 1988); and, especially, Jiang Shen, *HuaiHai zhi zhan* [*The HuaiHai Battle*] (Beijing: Jiefangjun, 1992). See also Liu Hsiang Wang, "The Fall and Rise of the Nationalist Chinese: The Chinese Civil War from HuaiHai to the Taiwan Strait, 1948–1950." Ph.D. dissertation, Pennsylvania State University, 1997.

51. Mao to Liu and Deng, 17 July 1948, *Mao Zedong junshi wenji*, vol. 4, pp. 529–30.

52. Su Yu, *Su Yu junshi wenji* [*Su Yu's Military Works*] (Beijing: Jiefangjun, 1989).

53. Du Yuming et al., *GuoGong neizhan milu*.

54. Mao to Su Yu et al., 7 Nov. 1948, *Mao Zedong junshi wenji*, vol. 5, pp. 177–78.

55. Jiang, *HuaiHai zhi zhan*, pp. 62–74.

56. See Mao's two messages to Liu Bocheng and Chen Yi on 14 Nov. 1948, *Mao Zedong junshi wenji*, vol. 5, pp. 213–17.

57. Xinhua press statement, 14 Nov. 1948, ibid., pp. 218–19; for Mao's internal summing up, see his letter to Lin Biao, 11 Nov. 1948, *Mao Zedong wenji* [*Mao Zedong Works*] (Beijing: Renmin, 1996), vol. 5, pp. 193–94.

58. *Mao Zedong nianpu*, vol. 3, p. 391.

59. The Center's instructions on handling Chinese and foreign press and news agencies in the newly liberated cities, 8 Nov. 1948, Zhongyang dang'anguan, comp., *Zhonggong zhongyang wenjian xuanji* [*Selected Documents of the CCP Center*] (Beijing: Zhonggong zhongyang dangxiao, 1992), vol. 17, pp. 465–70.

60. See Mao to Lin Biao et al., 11 Nov. 1948, ibid., vol. 17, pp. 473–74.

61. See Mao's messages to Liu Bocheng, Chen Yi, and Deng Xiaoping, 23 and 26 Nov. 1948, *Mao Zedong junshi wenji*, vol. 5, pp. 267, 278.

62. *Liu Bocheng huiyilu* [*Liu Bocheng Recollections*] (Shanghai: Shanghai wenzhi, 1987), vol. 2, pp. 376–92.

63. Zhang Xianwen and Fang Qingjiu, *Jiang Jieshi quanzhuan* [*A Complete Biography of Jiang Jieshi*], 2 vols. (Zhengzhou: Henan renmin, 1996, 1997), vol. 2, pp. 666–69.

64. A good eyewitness account, from the CCP perspective, of this stage of the battle is in Zhi Xia, *Zhanyi riji: HuaiHai zhanyi jianwenlu* [*Battle Diary: An Eyewitness Account of the HuaiHai Battle*] (Shanghai: Shanghai wenyi, 1993). On Deng's role, see Deng Maomao, *Deng Xiaoping: My Father* (New York: Basic Books, 1995), pp. 430–43.

65. Su Yu, *Zhanzheng huiyilu* [*War Memoirs*] (Beijing: Jiefangjun, 1989), p. 606.

66. Jiang, *HuaiHai zhi zhan*, pp. 346–52; see also Liu Ruilong, *Wo de riji* [*My Diaries*] (Beijing: Jiefangjun, 1985), pp. 123–24.

67. *Zhou Enlai nianpu*, pp. 781–82; on Li Kenong, see Qiao Jun, *Li Kenong jiangjun zhuan* [*A Biography of General Li Kenong*] (Chengdu: Chengdu, 1996), pp. 230–70. See also *Zhongguo renmin jiefangjun diyi yezhanjun zhanshi*, pp. 201–4.

68. *Liu Shaoqi nianpu*, vol. 2, pp. 162–63.

69. See, for instance, the Center's instructions on political work in newly occupied cities, 30 Nov. 1948, in *Zhonggong zhongyang wenjian xuanji* (internal ed.), vol. 14, pp. 431–34.

70. *Reminiscences of Geng Biao* (Beijing: China Today Press, 1994), p. 436.

71. Recollection of Yang Yuanliang, who in 1949 lived on the outskirts of Shanghai. Author's interview, Aug. 1994.

Chapter 7. The Chase

1. Temporary resignation was a tactic that Jiang had used twice before as a method of confounding his enemies and showing his allies his indispensability; see Zhang Xianwen and Fang Qingjiu, *Jiang Jieshi quanzhuan* [*A Complete Bi-*

ography of Jiang Jieshi], 2 vols. (Zhengzhou: Henan renmin, 1996, 1997), vol. 1, pp. 240–63.

2. Li Tsung-jen [Li Zongren] and Te-kong Tong, *The Memoirs of Li Tsung-jen* (Boulder, CO: Westview, 1979), pp. 481–82; see also Stuart to Secretary of State, 5 Feb. 1949, FRUS, 1949, vol. 8, pp. 108–10.

3. Lai She-hang. "A Study of a Faltering Democrat: The Life of Sun Fo, 1891–1949." Ph.D. dissertation, University of Illinois at Urbana-Champaign, 1976, pp. 249–50; on the plan for negotiations, see also Chinese Foreign Ministry to French Ambassador, 8 Jan. 1949, ROC-Waijiaobu, 405.4 158.16.

4. Zhonggong zhongyang wenxian yanjiushi, comp., *Mao Zedong nianpu (1893–1949)* [*Mao Zedong Chronology (1893–1949)*] (Beijing: Renmin, 1993), vol. 3, p. 430; Lovett to Stuart, 12 Jan. 1949, FRUS, 1949, 8, pp. 41–42; Mikhail Kapitsa, author's interview, Moscow, 8 Sept. 1992.

5. Andrei Ledovskii, "Sekretnaia missiia A. I. Mikoyana v Kitai (janvar–fevral 1949 g.)," *Problemu dalnego vostoka* 2 (1995): 96–111. See also Ivan V. Kovalev's extensive manuscript memoirs, which the author has been able to consult, but not to cite or quote. For Soviet attempts at exploring the GMD's position, see record of conversation, Molotov and Fu Bingchang, 12 Jan. 1949, AVPRF, f. 06, o. 11, pa. 15, d. 225, pp. 1–3; for the level of detail of Stalin's involvement, see Stalin to Mao Zedong, 20 Apr. 1948, APRF, f. 39, o. 1, d. 31, pp. 28–29.

6. APRF, f. 45, op. 1, d. 330, pp. 97–99.

7. *History of the Chinese Communist Party: A Chronology of Events (1919–1990)* (Beijing: Foreign Languages Press, 1991), footnote to p. 204.

8. Stuart to Secretary of State, 21 Jan. 1949, FRUS, 1949, vol. 8, pp. 67–69; entry for 22 Jan. 1949, *Jiang chugao*, vol. 7, book 2, pp. 241–42.

9. Zhang and Fang, *Jiang Jieshi quanzhuan*, vol. 2, pp. 686–88.

10. *The Memoirs of Li Tsung-jen*, p. 489.

11. Stuart to Secretary of State, 6 Mar. 1949, FRUS, 1949, vol. 8, pp. 163–64.

12. Brian Murray, "Western versus Chinese Realism: Soviet-American Diplomacy and the Chinese Civil War, 1945–1950," Ph.D. dissertation, Columbia University, 1995, pp. 380–83.

13. See, for instance, Mao's letter to Lin Biao, 18 Dec. 1949, *Mao Zedong junshi wenji*, vol. 5, pp. 420–21.

14. Zhonggong zhongyang wenxian yanjiushi, comp., *Zhou Enlai junshi huodong jishi, 1918–1975* (Beijing: Zhongyang wenxian, 2000), vol. 2, pp. 52–53; *Tianjin jieguan shilu* [*A Historical Record of the Takeover of Tianjin*] (Beijing: Zhonggong dangshi, 1991); see also Shu Yun, *Tian'anmen xia de wo shou: Beiping heping jiefang neimu* [*On Guard Below Tian'anmen: The Inner Story of the Peaceful Liberation of Beiping*] (Jinan: Jinan, 1992).

15. Wenshi ziliao yanjiu weiyuanhui, ed. *Fu Zuoyi shengping* [*The Life of Fu Zuoyi*] (Beijing: Wenshi ziliao, 1985), pp. 263–394; Wang Zongren and Shi Jingran, *Fu Zuoyi jiangjun yu Beiping hetan* [*General Fu Zuoyi and the Beiping Peace Talks*] (Beijing: Huayi, 1991).

16. *Reminiscences of Geng Biao* (Beijing: China Today Press, 1994), pp. 449–52.

17. Liu Guangji, *PingJin zhanyi shi* [*History of the Beiping-Tianjin Battle*] (Kaifeng: Henan daxue, 1994).

18. Dong Shigui and Zhang Yanzhi, *Beiping hetan ji shi* [*Some Facts about the Beijing Peace Talks*] (Beijing: Xinhua, 1991), esp. pp. 136–68; He Dong and Chen Mingxian, *Beiping heping jiefang shi-mo* [*The Full Story of the Beiping Peace Talks and Liberation*] (Beijing: Jiefangjun, 1985); Joseph K. S. Yick, *Making Urban Revolution in China: The CCP-GMD Struggle for Beiping-Tianjin, 1945–1949* (Armonk, NY: M. E. Sharpe, 1995), pp. 162–64; Sergei Tikhvinskii, author's interview, Oslo, Sept., 1996.

19. Mao to Lin Biao, 10 and 12 Jan. 1949, *Mao Zedong junshi wenji*, vol. 5, pp. 479–82; see also *Mao Zedong nianpu*, vol. 3, pp. 432–33.

20. The Center's instructions on work in Beijing, 20 Jan. 1949, Zhonghua quanguo zonggonghui, comp., *Zhonggong zhongyang guanyu gongren yundong wenxian xuanbian* [*A Selection of the CCP Central Committee's Documents on the Workers Movement*] (Beijing: Dang'an, 1986), vol. 3, pp. 283–84.

21. Liu, *PingJin zhanyi shi*, pp. 182–99; see also Yick, *Making Urban Revolution in China*, p. 174. For the PLA military reports, see Nie Rongzhen to CCP Center, 8–16 Jan. 1949, *Nie Rongzhen junshi wenxuan* [*Nie Rongzhen's Military Works*] (Beijing: Jiefangjun, 1992), pp. 309–11.

22. Wen Jian et al., *Ping Jin juezhan zhong de Fu Zuoyi jiangjun* [*General Fu Zuoyi in the Battle of Beijing and Tianjin*] (Beijing: Zhongguo wenshi, 1993), esp. pp. 79–86; Wang and Shi, *Fu Tsuoyi jiangjun yu Beiping hetan*. Fu must have been further downcast when he discovered soon afterward that his daughter Fu Ju had been a secret CCP member for at least a year.

23. Zhonggong zhongyang wenxian yanjiushi, comp., *Liu Shaoqi zhuan* [*Liu Shaoqi Biography*] (Beijing: Zhongyang wenxian, 1998), vol. 2, pp. 620–31.

24. Mao's comments at the extended Politburo meeting in Xibaipo in early September 1948 are crucial to understanding his views; see extracts from his remarks, 8 and 13 Sept., *Mao Zedong wenji* [*Mao Zedong Works*] (Beijing: Renmin, 1996), vol. 5, pp. 131–45; Jing Huang, *Factionalism in Chinese Communist Politics* (Cambridge: Cambridge University Press, 2000), p. 166.

25. For the resolutions from the September meeting, see *Zhonggong zhongyang wenjian xuanji* [internal ed.], vol. 14, pp. 344–53.

26. See Frederick Teiwes, *Politics and Purges*, 2d ed. (Armonk, NY: M. E. Sharpe, 1993), pp. 62–77.

27. The Center's instructions on party school teaching materials, 15 Sept. 1948; see also Liu's remarks to the meeting, Zhonggong zhongyang wenxian yanjiushi, comp., *Liu Shaoqi nianpu* [*Liu Shaoqi Chronology*], 2 vols. (Beijing: Zhongyang wenxian, 1996), vol. 2, pp. 161–62.

28. 8 Sept. 1948, Zhonghua renmin gongheguo and Zhonggong zhongyang wenxian yanjiushi, eds., *Mao Zedong waijiao wenxuan* [*Mao Zedong Selected Works on Foreign Affairs*] (Beijing: Zhongyang wenxian, 1994), pp. 68–70.

29. Ibid.

30. Parts of this correspondence are in APRF, f. 39, op. 1, d. 31, although only a part has been declassified in Russian archives; see, for instance, Mao to Stalin, 30 Dec. 1948, pp. 49–52.

31. Terebin to Kuznetsev, 17 July 1948, APRF, f. 39, o. 1, d. 31, pp. 39–40.

32. Dmitri Volkogonov, *Autopsy for an Empire: The Seven Leaders Who Built the Soviet Regime* (New York: Free Press, 1998), pp. 135–36.

33. Mikoyan's 1960 reports to the Soviet Communist party leaders on his 1949 visit to China were published in part in *Problemu dalnego vostoka* 2 (1995): 96–111 and 3: 94–105. His extensive daily reports to Stalin are in APRF, f. 39, o. 1, d. 39. These verbatim records (referred to below as "Mikoyan report," followed by date and page number) provide fascinating insights into Mao's and other CCP leaders' thinking about domestic and international issues in the final phase of the civil war.

34. Mikoyan report, 31 Jan. 1949, pp. 17–24.

35. Ibid., 5 Feb., pp. 74–77.

36. Ibid., 30 Jan., pp. 1–6.

37. Ibid., 6 Feb., p. 81.

38. Ibid., 6 Feb., pp. 78–88.

39. Ibid., 1 Feb., pp. 17–24.

40. Ibid., 5 Feb., pp. 64–73.

41. Ibid., 5 Feb., p. 76.

42. Ibid., (n.d.—presumably 7) Feb., pp. 89–95.

43. Mao to Stalin, 10 Jan. 1949, APRF, f. 39, op. 1, d. 31, pp. 54–58.

44. Mao to Stalin, 30 Dec. 1948, ibid., pp. 49–52. For fears of a U.S. attack as the HuaiHai campaign ended, see He Long's report on CCP Politburo discussions, 19 Dec. 1948, *He Long junshi wenxuan* (Beijing: Jiefangjun, 1989), pp. 406–25.

45. He Long's report on CCP Politburo discussions, 19 Dec. 1948, *He Long junshi wenxuan*, pp. 410–411.

46. *Mao Zedong nianpu*, vol. 3, pp. 329–30, 459; see also *Jiefang zhanzheng shiqi de Zhonggong zhongyang Shanghai ju* [*The CCP CC Shanghai Bureau during the War of Liberation Period*] (Shanghai: Xuelin, 1989), pp. 408–19.

47. Lai, "A Study of a Faltering Democrat," pp. 250–52; Li and Te-kong, *The Memoirs of Li Tsung-jen*, pp. 496–97.

48. Dong and Zhang, *Beiping hetan ji shi*, pp. 239–63. The most prominent members of the delegations were Yan Huiqing, Shao Lizi, Zhang Shizhao, and Jiang Yong. See also Zhonggong zhongyang wenxian yanjiushi, comp., *Zhou Enlai nianpu, 1898–1949* [*Chronological Biography of Zhou Enlai, 1898–1949*] (Beijing: Zhongyang wenxian, 1989), pp. 813–14.

49. Entries for 7, 11 Feb. and 21 Mar. 1949, *Jiang chugao*, vol. 7, book 2, pp. 250, 252, 263.

50. Su Yu, *Zhanzheng huiyilu* [*War Memoirs*] (Beijing: Jiefangjun, 1989), p. 608.

51. Ch'en Li-fu, *The Storm Clouds Clear over China: The Memoir of Ch'en Li-fu*, ed. and comp. Sidney H. Chang and Ramon H. Myers (Stanford, CA: Hoover Institution Press, 1994), p. 201.

52. *Zhongguo renmin jiefangjun zhanshi*, vol. 3, pp. 326–27.

53. *Du jiang he jiefang Nanjing* [*Crossing the River and Liberating Nanjing*] (Shanghai: Shanghai renmin, 1979), esp. pp. 45–68.

54. Ibid., pp. 85–104; Li and Te-kong, *The Memoirs of Li Tsung-jen*, p. 516. According to some sources, Zhang Zhizhong could not make up his mind on whether to stay in Beijing or return south to face the wrath of his superiors. Zhou Enlai talked him into staying by quoting a precedent of what could happen to

those who acted against Jiang Jieshi: "After the Xian Incident [of 1936], we did a disservice to a friend by the name of Zhang [Xueliang]. Today we should not make the same mistake again." *Zhou Enlai zhuan, 1898–1949* [*Zhou Enlai Biography, 1898–1949*] (Beijing: Zhonggong zhongyang wenxian, 1989), p. 761.

55. Li and Te-kong, *The Memoirs of Li Tsung-jen,* pp. 522–23; Jia Dingshi et al., *Bai Chongxi xiansheng fangwen jilu* [*Record of an Interview with Mr. Bai Chongxi*], 2 vols. (Taibei: Zhongyang yanjiuyuan jindaishi yanjiusuo, 1984), vol. 2, pp. 860–72.

56. Stuart to Secretary of State, 25 Apr. 1949, FRUS, 1949, vol. 8, p. 723.

57. Deng Maomao, *Deng Xiaoping: My Father* (New York: Basic Books, 1995), p. 449.

58. Malcolm H. Murfett, "A Pyrrhic Victory: HMS Amethyst and the Damage to Anglo-Chinese Relations in 1949," *War & Society* 9, no. 1 (1991): 121–40; Noel Barber, *The Fall of Shanghai: The Communist Take-over in 1949* (London: Macmillan, 1979), pp. 84–92; *Mao Zedong nianpu,* vol. 3, pp. 485–86.

59. The Center's instructions on diplomatic issues, 25 April 1949, and the Center's instructions on the handling of foreign residents by the Nanjing garrison troops, 7 May 1949, in Zhongyang dang'anguan, comp., *Zhonggong zhongyang wenjian xuanji* [*Selected Documents of the CCP Center*] (Beijing: Zhonggong zhongyang dangxiao, 1992), vol. 18, pp. 233–34, 267–69.

60. Record of Mao Zedong's conversations, 28 Apr. 1949, *Mao Zedong waijiao wenxuan,* p. 83.

61. The description of the takeover of Shanghai is based mostly on Yu Jin, *Shanghai: 1949 da pengkui* [*Shanghai: The Great Collapse of 1949*] (Beijing: Jiefangjun, 1993); and Shanghai shi dang'anguan, eds., *Shanghai jiefang* [*Liberating Shanghai*] (Beijing: Dang'an, 1989); see also Li Wei, *1949: JingHu baodong ji shi neimu* [*1949: Some True Inner Stories about the Insurrections in Beijing and Shanghai*] (Chengdu: Sichuan wenyi, 1993), which is an evocative but somewhat unreliable account.

62. Cabot to Secretary of State, 16 May 1949, FRUS, 1949, vol. 8, p. 323.

63. Cabot to Secretary of State, 28 Jan. 1949, FRUS, 1949, vol. 8, p. 91; Huang Zhuoqun, *Wu Guozhen zhuan* [*Wu Guozhen Biography*] (Taibei: Ziyu shibao, 1995).

64. *Zhou Enlai nianpu,* p. 772.

65. *Nanxia lieche* (Shanghai: Yezhang, 1950).

66. Cabot to Secretary of State, 23 Mar. 1949, FRUS, 1949, vol. 8, p. 196.

67. Entries for 30 Apr. and 3 May 1949, *Jiang chugao,* vol. 7, book 2, pp. 291–93; Liu Caifu, *Tong tian jiao zhu: Du Yuesheng yu Guomindang zhengquan* [*Living Together: The Full Story of Du Yuesheng and the Guomindang*] (Nanjing: Jiangsu renmin, 1998), pp. 261–68.

68. Han Shanbi, *Jiang Jingguo pingzhuan* [*A Critical Biography of Jiang Jingguo*] (Hong Kong: Dong xi wenhua shiye, 1988), pp. 263–70; for the "evacuation" of art to Taiwan, see P. Van de Meerssche, *A Life to Treasure: The Authorized Biography of Han Lih-wu* (London: Sherwood Press, 1987), pp. 74–83.

69. Instructions from the CCP Shanghai city committee, 8 Apr. 1949, *Jiefang zhanzheng shiqi de Zhonggong zhongyang Shanghai ju,* pp. 420–25.

70. *Zhongguo renmin jiefangjun zhanshi*, vol. 3, pp. 330–33; *Shanghai jiefang*, pp. 336–50.

71. Mariano Ezpeleta, *Red Shadows over Shanghai* (Quezon City: Zita, 1972), pp. 157–65.

72. Yu, *Shanghai: 1949 da pengkui*, vol. 2, pp. 866–86.

73. Harrison Forman, *Blunder in Asia* (New York: Didier, 1950), pp. 65–66.

74. It is uncertain exactly when Zhou's secret visit to Shanghai took place, but it is assumed by party historians that it was on 3–4 June 1949. See also Yu, *Shanghai: 1949 da pengkui*, vol. 2, pp. 921–26.

75. Ibid., pp. 962–67.

76. *Mao Zedong nianpu*, vol. 3, p. 496.

77. Military Affairs Commission to Peng Zhen et al., 28 May 1949, *Zhonggong zhongyang wenjian xuanji*, vol. 18, pp. 308–9.

78. Center to North China Bureau, 16 Feb. 1949, ibid., vol. 18, pp. 136–37.

79. *Mao Zedong nianpu*, vol. 3, p. 515; Cheng Xiulong, *Jiefang Taiyuan zhi zhan* [*The Battle for the Liberation of Taiyuan*] (Taiyuan: Shanxi renmin, 1982); see also *Zhongguo renmin jiefangjun diyi yezhanjun zhanshi*, pp. 212–25. For the losing side, see Shanxi sheng wenshi ziliao yanjiu weiyuanhui, eds., *Yan Xishan tongzhi Shanxi shishi* [*Historical Facts on Yan Xishan's Rule in Shanxi*] (Taiyuan: Shanxi renmin, 1984), pp. 393–434.

80. *Peng Dehuai zhuan* [*Peng Dehuai Biography*] (Beijing: Dangdai Zhongguo, 1993), pp. 372–74. For an overview, see Liu Qi et al., *Jiefang zhangzheng zhong de Xibei zhanchang* [*Battlefields of the Northwest in the War of Liberation*] (Beijing: Zhongguo wenshi, 1992).

81. *Mao Zedong nianpu*, vol. 3, pp. 519–20.

Chapter 8. To Tian'anmen

1. Interviews with Chinese party historians; Harrison Salisbury, *The New Emperors: China in the Era of Mao and Deng* (Boston: Little, Brown, 1992); articles by Li Yinqiao and Wang Guangmei in Zhonggong Beijing shi Haidian quwei dangshi yanjiushi, ed., *Zhonggong zhongyang zai Xiangshan* [*The CCP CC at Xiangshan*] (Beijing: Zhongyang dangshi, 1993). See also Guo Wentao and Guo Chen, *Kaiguo zangsang* [*The Experience of Founding the State*] (Beijing: Jiefangjun, 1993), pp. 268–74.

2. Interviews with Chinese party historians; see also Pang Song and Lin Yunhui, *Liguo xinbang: 1945–1956 nian de Mao Zedong* [*Founding New China: Mao Zedong in 1945–1956*] (Beijing: Zhongguo qingnian, 1993), pp. 111–13.

3. Li Zhisui, *The Private Life of Chairman Mao*, trans. Tai Hung-chaa (New York: Random House, 1974), pp. 72–73, 107–8.

4. For Ren Bishi's views, see his speech to the inaugural congress of the All-China New Democratic Youth Association, 12 Apr. 1949, in *Zhonggong zhongyang zai Xiangshan*.

5. Suzanne Pepper, *Civil War in China: The Political Struggle, 1945–1949* (Berkeley: University of California Press, 1978; rev. ed. Lanham, MD: Rowan and Littlefield, 1999), p. 368.

6. Shanghai shi dang'anguan, eds., *Shanghai jiefang* [*Liberating Shanghai*] (Beijing: Dang'an, 1989), pp. 360–70.

7. Zhonggong zhongyang wenxian yanjiushi, comp., *Liu Shaoqi nianpu* [*Liu Shaoqi Chronology*], 2 vols. (Beijing: Zhongyang wenxian, 1996), vol. 2, p. 213; see also Liu's speech, 3 Feb. 1949, in *Liu Shaoqi lun gongren yundong* [*Liu Shaoqi on the Workers' Movement*] (Beijing: Zhonggong zhongyang wenxian, 1988); Jing Huang, *Factionalism in Chinese Communist Politics* (Cambridge: Cambridge University Press, 2000), pp. 156–57.

8. Zhonggong zhongyang wenxian yanjiushi, comp., *Mao Zedong nianpu (1893–1949)* [*Mao Zedong Chronology (1893–1949)*] (Beijing: Renmin, 1993), vol. 3, p. 496.

9. *Zhou Enlai zhuan, 1898–1949* [*Zhou Enlai Biography, 1898–1949*] (Beijing: Zhonggong zhongyang wenxian, 1989), p. 700.

10. See the memoirs of Zhou's assistants Cen Yuangong and Tong Xiaopeng in *Zhonggong zhongyang zai Qiangshan.*

11. *Chen Yi nianpu* [*Chen Yi Chronology*] (Beijing: Renmin, 1995), vol. 1, p. 571; Zhonggong zhongyang wenxian yanjiushi, comp., *Zhou Enlai nianpu, 1898–1949* [*Chronological Biography of Zhou Enlai, 1898–1949*] (Beijing: Zhongyang wenxian, 1989), pp. 828–29.

12. *Jiefang zhanzheng shiqi diertiao zhanxian: Xuesheng yundong juan* (Beijing: Zhonggong dangshi, 1997) vol. 3.

13. See *Zhou Enlai nianpu*, pp. 829–31.

14. Niu Jun, "The Origins of the Sino-Soviet Alliance," in Odd Arne Westad, ed., *Brothers in Arms: The Rise and Fall of the Sino-Soviet Alliance, 1945–1963* (Washington, DC, and Stanford, CA: Woodrow Wilson Center Press and Stanford University Press, 1998).

15. This is Mao's article, "On the People's Democratic Dictatorship," *Mao Zedong xuanji* (Beijing: Renmin, 1977), vol. 4, pp. 1473–86. For its origins, see *Mao Zedong nianpu*, vol. 3, pp. 523–24.

16. An excellent overview of Liu's trip to Moscow is Dieter Heinzig, *Die Sowjetunion und das kommunistische China* [*The Soviet Union and Communist China, 1945–1950*] (Baden-Baden: Nomos, 1998), pp. 285–373; see also Andrei M. Ledovskii, "Vizit v Moskvu delegatsii Kommunisticheskoi Partii Kitaia v iiune-avguste 1949 g" ["The Visit to Moscow of a Chinese Communist Party Delegation, June–August 1949"], *Problemu dalnego vostoka* 4 (1996): 66–83, and vol. 5, pp. 84–94.

17. *Liu Shaoqi nianpu*, vol. 2, pp. 215–17; Liu Shaoqi's report to Stalin and Soviet Politburo, 4 July 1949, in Westad, *Brothers in Arms*, p. 313.

18. Liu to Stalin, 4 July 1949, in Westad, *Brothers in Arms.*

19. See, for instance, record of conversation, Stalin and Enver Hoxha, 23 Mar. 1949, APRF, f. 45, o. 1, d. 249, pp. 55–74.

20. Shi Changuang, *Wang Jiaxiang zhuan* [*Wang Jiaxiang Biography*] (Hefei: Anhui renmin, 1978); Shi Zhe, *Zai lishi jüren shenbian: Shi Zhe huiyilu* [*At the Side of Historical Giants: Shi Zhe's Memoirs*] (Beijing: Zhongyang wenxian, 1991), p. 425; for military assistance, see Lü Liping, "Fu Su can yu tanpan yuan jian kongyun de huiyi" ["Remembering Going to the Soviet Union and Negotiating Assistance for the Founding of the Air Force"], *Junshi shilin* 1 (1994). For CCP reactions to the outcome of the Moscow talks, see He Long's report to a mil-

itary commanders' conference of the PLA Northwest Region, 26 Aug. 1948, *He Long junshi wenxuan* (Beijing: Jiefangjun, 1989), pp. 451–58.

21. See Fredrik Teiwes, *Politics and Purges*, 2d ed. (Armonk, NY: M. E. Sharpe, 1993); see also Pang and Lin, *Liguo xingbang*, pp. 175–81; and Guo and Guo, *Kaiguo zangsang*. For Liu's and Zhou's summing up of the case against Gao after his purge in late 1953, see the records of their conversations with Soviet ambassador Iudin, 2 and 13 Feb. 1954, AVPRF, f. 0100, op. 47, pa. 379, d. 7, pp. 25–35, 36–40.

22. *Mao Zedong nianpu*, vol. 3, pp. 566–67.

23. See final ch. in *Zhonggong zhongyang zai Xiangshan*.

24. According to popular lore, this is when Mao uttered the famous words "China has stood up." In fact, the Chairman said nothing of the sort. His speech was a rather drab declaration of the coming into existence of the new People's Republic (see Michael Schoenhals, " 'Non-People' in the People's Republic of China: A Chronicle of Terminological Ambiguity," Indiana Working Papers Series on Language and Politics in China [summer 1994], www. indiana.edu/~easc/pages/working-papers). The term comes from Mao's opening address to the first plenary session of the Political Consultative Conference, 21 Sept. 1949: "Fellow delegates, we are all convinced that our work will go down in the history of mankind: [It will] demonstrate that the Chinese people, comprising one quarter of humanity, have now stood up. The Chinese have always been a great, courageous, and industrious nation; it is only in modern times that they have fallen behind. And that was due entirely to oppression and exploitation by foreign imperialism and domestic reactionary governments"—*Mao Zedong wenji* [*Mao Zedong Works*] (Beijing: Renmin, 1996), vol. 5, pp. 343–44.

25. Hsu Kai-yu, *Twentieth Century Chinese Poetry: An Anthology* (Ithaca, NY: Cornell University Press, 1970), pp. 380–81. In the early 1950s, Hu Feng was criticized by the new government for continuing to harbor bourgeois ideas. In 1955 he was arrested and jailed for being a counter-revolutionary, a Guomindang agent, and the leader of an anti-Communist underground network; see Jonathan P. Spence, *The Gate of Heavenly Peace: The Chinese and Their Revolution, 1895–1980* (New York: Viking, 1981), p. 330.

26. Linda Hershkovitz, "Tiananmen Square and the Politics of Place," *Political Geography Quarterly* 12, no. 5 (1993): 395–420.

27. For one such group, see *Zhongguo meikuang gongren yundong shi* [*History of the Chinese Coal-mining Workers' Movement*] (Changsha: Hunan renmin, 1986), pp. 580–83. For an overview of labor activism in 1949–50, see *Dangdai Zhongguo gongren jieji he gonghui yundong* [*Contemporary Chinese Working Class and Trade Union Movement*] (Beijing: Dangdai Zhongguo, 1997), pp. 43–145.

28. Zhonggong zhongyang wenxian yanjiushi, comp., *Liu Shaoqi zhuan* [*Liu Shaoqi Biography*] (Beijing: Zhongyang wenxian, 1998), vol. 2, pp. 626–31.

29. Liu arrived in Tianjin on 10 April and stayed for almost a month. For his speeches, see *Liu Shaoqi nianpu*, vol. 2, pp. 192–202. See also Kenneth G. Lieberthal, *Revolution and Tradition in Tientsin, 1949–1952* (Stanford, CA: Stanford University Press, 1980), pp. 40–51. There is disagreement about whether Liu was

sent to Tianjin by Mao and whether Mao agreed with Liu's viewpoints at the time; see Jing, *Factionalism in Chinese Communist Politics*, pp. 161–65.

30. For these kinds of obstacles to CCP rule, see Zhonggong Zhejiang sheng-wei dangshi ziliao zhengzhi yanjiu weiyuanhui and Zhongguo renmin jiefangjun Zhejiang shengjunqu weiyuanhui, eds., *Zhejiang jiefang* [*Liberating Zhejiang*] (Hangzhou: Zhejiang renmin, 1989); and Sichuan sheng wenshi yanjiuguan, eds., *Jiefang zhanzheng shiqi Sichuan dashiji* [*A Chronology of the War of Liberation Period in Sichuan*] (Chengdu: Sichuan renmin, 1990), esp. pp. 197–231.

31. See *Zhejiang gongren yundong shi* [*History of the Zhejiang Workers' Movement*] (Hangzhou: Zhejiang renmin, 1988), pp. 211–51; 279–80; Center's instructions on the workers' movement in the cities, 10 Jan. 1949, and Center's instructions on work in Beijing, 20 Jan. 1949, Zhonghua quanguo zonggonghui, comp., *Zhonggong zhongyang guanyu gongren yundong wenxian xuanbian* [*A Selection of the CCP Central Committee's Documents on the Workers' Movement*] (Beijing: Dang'an, 1984–86), vol. 3, pp. 283–84. Lieberthal's account of the battle for control of the transport sector in Tianjin is instructive; see *Revolution and Tradition in Tientsin*, pp. 60–77. In this case the party had to set up a municipal freight company to get workers under control.

32. *Shanghai jiefang*, pp. 360–62.

33. Mao Zedong to all CC bureaus and all military districts, 5 Dec. 1949, *Mao Zedong junshi wenji*, vol. 6, pp. 52–53; Richard Gaulton, "Political Mobilization in Shanghai, 1949–1951," in Christopher Howe, ed., *Shanghai: Revolution and Development in an Asian Metropolis* (Cambridge: Cambridge University Press, 1981), pp. 35–65. For the financial aspects, see also Richard Burdekin and Fang Wang, "A Novel End to the Big Inflation in China, 1950," *Economics of Planning* 32 (1999): 211–29.

34. For the overall political directions, see Chen Yun's 3 March 1950 speech, Zhonggong zhongyang wenxian yanjiushi, eds., *Jiangguo yilai zhongyao wenxian xuanbian* [*A Selection of Important Documents since the Founding of the PRC*] (Beijing: Zhongyang wenxian, 1991), vol. 1, pp. 130–36.

35. See, for instance, the final chapters in Zhonggong Zhejiang shengwei dangshi yanjiushi and Zhonggong Hangzhou shiwei dangshi yanjiushi, eds., *Jiefang zhanzheng shiqi diertiao zhanxian: Xuesheng yundong juan* (Beijing: Zhonggong dangshi, 1997), vol. 3.

36. Suzanne Pepper, *Radicalism and Education Reform in 20th-Century China: The Search for an Ideal Development Model* (Cambridge: Cambridge University Press, 1996), pp. 157–211; see also Ezra F. Vogel, *Canton under Communism: Programs and Politics in a Provincial Capital, 1949–1968* (Cambridge, MA: Harvard University Press, 1980 [1969]), pp. 55–60.

37. See Gail Hershatter, *Dangerous Pleasures: Prostitution and Modernity in Twentieth Century Shanghai* (Berkeley: University of California Press, 1997), pp. 304–24.

38. Wang Chaoguang, "Haolaiwu de chenfu: Minguo nianjian Meiguo dianying zai Hua jingyu yanjiu" [Hollywood's Enchantments: Researching the Circumstances of American Movies in China during the Republican Era], *Meiguo yanjiu* 2 (1998): 113–39.

39. See, for instance, Chen Shengnian and Hu Ronggui, *Jiefang Yunnan zhi zhan* [*The Battle for the Liberation of Yunnan*], 2d ed. (Kunming: Yunnan renmin, 1984), pp. 3–43.

40. In villages in the northwestern Gansu province, the PLA had to use military tactics to overcome peasant resistance as late as December of 1950. The villagers interpreted the new government's beheading of three clan elders and leaders of the Big Sword Society as apocalyptic warnings, and rose in rebellion (Jun Jing, *The Temple of Memories: History, Power, and Morality in a Chinese Village* (Stanford, CA: Stanford University Press, 1996), pp. 46–49).

41. For some of these difficulties, see Zhou Enlai's speeches in May 1950, *Jiangguo yilai zhongyao wenxian xuanbian*, vol. 1, pp. 220–27; Teiwes, *Politics and Purges*, 2d ed., p. 34.

42. *Zhou Enlai junshi huadong jishi* [*A Record of Zhou Enlai's Military Activities*] (Beijing: Zhongyang wenxian, 2000), vol. 2, pp. 110–11.

43. *Zhongguo renmin jiefangjun zhanshi*, vol. 3, pp. 343–49.

44. Lao Jia et al., *Nan Zhongguo: San da zhanyi zhihou de Zhongguo zhanzhang* [*South China: The Three Great Battles at the End of the Struggle for China*] (Beijing: Tuanjie, 1993), esp. pp. 182–92.

45. Mao to Lin Biao et al., 24 July 1949, *Mao Zedong junshi wenji*, vol. 5, pp. 647–48.

46. *Zhongguo renmin jiefangjun disi yezhanjun zhanshi*, pp. 493–98.

47. Ibid.

48. Te-kong Tong and Li Tsung-jen, *The Memoirs of Li Tsung-jen* (Boulder, CO: Westview, 1979), pp. 531–32.

49. Lao et al., *Nan Zhongguo*; for the CCP underground in Guangzhou, see Zhonggong Guangdong shengwei dangshi ziliao zhengji weiyuanhui and Zhonggong Guangdong shengwei dangshi yanjiu weiyuanhui, eds., *Te zhi shi nian* [*Ten Special Years*] (Guangzhou: Guangdong renmin, 1988), pp. 249–64.

50. Cabinet Papers 129/35, CP (49) 118, 24 May 1949; cited in Steve Yui-sang Tsang, *Democracy Shelved: Great Britain, China, and Attempts at Constitutional Reform in Hong Kong, 1945–1952* (Hong Kong: Oxford University Press, 1988), p. 105.

51. *Mao Zedong nianpu*, vol. 3, p. 535.

52. T. G. Li, with Roman Rome, *A China Past: Military and Diplomatic Memoirs* (Lanham, MD: University Press of America, 1989), p. 283. See also Tong and Li, *The Memoirs of Li Tsung-jen*, pp. 544–46.

53. Li, *A China Past*, p. 545. For the CCP advance into Sichuan, see Sichuan sheng wenshi yanjiuguan, eds. *Jiefang zhanzheng shiqi Sichuan dashiji* [*A Chronology of Sichuan during the Liberation War*] (Chengdu: Sichuan renmin, 1990), pp. 259–90.

54. Entry for 21 Nov. 1949, *Jiang chugao*, vol. 7, book 2, p. 420.

55. Ch'en Li-fu, *The Storm Clouds Clear over China: The Memoir of Ch'en Li-fu*, ed. and comp. Sidney H. Chang and Ramon H. Myers (Stanford, CA: Hoover Institution Press, 1994), p. 211.

56. Ibid.

57. Keiji Furuya, *Chiang Kai-shek: His Life and Times* (New York: St. Johns University, 1981), p. 909.

58. Chen Shengnian and Hu Ronggui, *Jiefang Yunnan zhi zhan* [*The Battle for the Liberation of Yunnan*], 2d ed. (Kunming: Yunnan renmin, 1984); for political developments in Yunnan, see also Zhonggong Kunming shiwei dangshiban and Yunnan sheng dang'anguan, comps., *1948 Kunming 'Fan MeifuRi' yundong* [*The 1948 "Oppose US Support for Japan" Movement in Kunming*] (Kunming: Yunnan renmin, 1989).

59. See *Zhonghua minguo shi dang'an ziliao huibian* [*A Collection of Archival Materials on the History of the Republic of China*], 5th series, 3d collection: Politics (1945–1949) (Nanjing: Jiangsu guji, 1999), book 5, pp. 480–516, for details; see also the diaries of the former GMD governor of Xinjiang, Wu Zhongxin, ibid., pp. 235–480.

60. For situation in Xinjiang in late 1948, see Barnett, *China on the Eve of the Communist Takeover* (New York: Praeger, 1963), pp. 236–81; for Burhan's own version of his role, see "Xinjiang heping jiefang de huiyi," *Wenshi ziliao xuanji* 69:152–59. For CCP policies, see David D. Wang, *Under the Soviet Shadow: The Yining Incident: Ethnic Conflicts and International Rivalry in Xinjiang 1944–1949* (Hong Kong: Chinese University Press, 1999), pp. 362–86. The so-called Liqun Station in Yining was one of the most sophisticated CCP takeover missions. It integrated diplomatic work, intelligence, and long-term planning, and was crucial in the successful Communist occupation of Xinjiang.

61. Andrew D. W. Forbes, *Warlords and Muslims in Chinese Central Asia: A Political History of Republican Sinkiang 1911–1949* (Cambridge: Cambridge University Press, 1986), pp. 219–25. See also ibid., pp. 225–28, on PLA campaigns against Muslim separatists in 1950–51, as well as Zheng Weishan, *Cong Huabei dao Xibei: Yi jiefang zhangzheng* [*From North China to the Northwest: Remembering the War of Liberation*] (Lanzhou: Jiefangjun, 1985).

62. See Xu Jidun, *Taiwan jindai fazhan shi* [*A History of Modern Developments on Taiwan*] (Taibei: Jianwei, 1996), pp. 543–52.

63. Entries for 24 and 25 Dec. 1949, *Jiang chugao*, vol. 7, book 2, pp. 509–10.

64. See, for instance, Jiang's first message to the Academy, 23 Jan. 1950, in *Jiang sixiang yanlun*, vol. 23, pp. 98–110; see also Bruce J. Dickson, "The Lessons of Defeat: The Reorganization of the Kuomintang on Taiwan, 1950–1952," *China Quarterly* 133 (Mar. 1993).

65. David Michael Finkelstein, "From Abandonment to Salvation: The Evolution of United States Policy toward Taiwan, 1949–1950," Ph.D. dissertation, Princeton University, 1990; for a Soviet view of U.S. policies with regard to Taiwan, see Fedorenko to Vyshinskii, 17 June 1949, AVPRF, f. 07, op. 22, pa. 36, d. 219; and Boris Trofimovich Kulik, "SShA i Taivan' protiv KNR. 1949–1952 gg.: Novye arkhivnye materialy" ["The United States and Taiwan against the People's Republic of China, 1949–52: new archival documents"], *Novaia i noveishaia istoriia* 5 (1995): 19–40. On the economic conditions, see Liu Jinqing, *Taiwan zhanhou jingji* [*The Taiwan Economy after the War*] (Taibei: n.p., 1992).

66. *Public Papers of the Presidents: Harry S. Truman, 1950* (Washington, DC: U.S. Government Printing Office, 1965), pp. 11–17.

67. Remarks by Secretary Acheson, 5 Jan. 1950, *Department of State Bulletin* 12 (16 Jan. 1950).

68. Rusk to Secretary of State, 30 May 1950, FRUS, 1950, vol. 6, pp. 349–51;

see also Nancy Bernkopf Tucker, *Taiwan, Hong Kong, and the United States: Uncertain Friendships* (New York: Twayne, 1994), pp. 26–32; and Robert Accinelli, *Crisis and Commitment: United States Policy toward Taiwan, 1950–1955* (Chapel Hill: University of North Carolina Press, 1996), pp. 3–27.

69. Howe to Armstrong, 31 May 1950, FRUS, 1950, vol. 6, pp. 347–49. On Sun, see *Sun Liren jiangjun Fengshan lianjun shilu* [*Historical Records of General Sun Liren and the Fengshan Army*] (Taibei: n.p., 1993).

70. Entry for 28 June 1950, *Jiang chugao*, vol. 8, p. 8.

71. A useful overview of the GMD's leaders' expectations of U.S. support, as compared with what they had received in 1948–49, is in an undated (Nov. 1950?) report in the ROC-Waijiaobu, 443.7 III c.5. For the cooperation between GMD and U.S. intelligence during the first years on Taiwan, see Jay Taylor, *The Generalissimo's Son: Chiang Ching-kuo and the Revolutions in China and Taiwan* (Cambridge, MA: Harvard University Press, 2000), pp. 206–20.

72. Dickson, "The Lessons of Defeat: The Reorganization of the Kuomintang on Taiwan, 1950–1952."

73. Entry for 31 May 1944, *Jiang chugao*, vol. 5, book 2, pp. 529–30.

Chapter 9. To the Yalu River

1. See, for instance, Mao's message to Lin Biao and others, 11 Oct. 1949, *Mao Zedong junshi wenji*, vol. 6, pp. 35–36; and Mao's telegram to the CCP South China Bureau, 27 Nov. 1949, ibid., pp. 167–68.

2. Ibid., and Mao's message to Lin Biao, 5 Oct. 1949, *Jianguo yilai Mao Zedong wengao* [*Mao Zedong's Writings since the Founding of the Country*] (Beijing: Zhongyang wenxian, 1987), vol. 1, pp. 19–21.

3. Su Yu, *Zhanzheng huiyilu* [*War Memoirs*] (Beijing: Jiefangjun, 1989); memorandum of conversation, Soviet Ambassador Roshchin and Zhou Enlai, 31 Oct. 1949, AVPRF, f. 0100, op. 42, pa. 288, d. 19, p. 75.

4. Xu Yan, *Jinmen zhi zhan, 1949–1959* [*The Battles for Jinmen, 1949–1959*] (Beijing: Zhongguo dianshi guangbo, 1992), pp. 11–23.

5. On the PLA side, see General Ye Fei's two accounts, *Zhengzhan jishi* [*Records of War*] (Shanghai: Shanghai renmin, 1988) and *Ye Fei huiyilu* [*Ye Fei Memoirs*] (Beijing: Jiefangjun, 1988); on the GMD side, see General Gao Guiyuan's account in *Jinmen Guningtou Zhoushan Dengbudao zhi zhan shiliao* [*Historical Materials on the Jinmen, Guningtou, Zhoushan, Dengbu Battles*] (Taibei: Guoshiguan, 1979), vol. 1. See also Liu Hsiang-wang, "The Fall and Rise of the Nationalist Chinese: The Chinese Civil War from HuaiHai to the Taiwan Strait, 1948–1950." Ph.D. dissertation, Pennsylvania State University, 1997, pp. 116–47; and Xu, *Jinmen zhi zhan*.

6. Mao to the Jinmen army front committee, 29 Oct. 1949, *Jianguo yilai Mao Zedong wengao*, vol. 1, pp. 100–101.

7. For the GMD side, see *Dengbu zhanyi* [*The Battle of Dengbu*] (Taibei: Military History and Translation Bureau, 1957). See also Mao to Su Yu, 14 Nov. 1949, *Jianguo yilai*, vol. 1, p. 137.

8. King C. Chen, *Vietnam and China, 1938–1954* (Princeton: Princeton University Press, 1969), pp. 201–11.

9. Record of conversation, Roshchin and Zhou Enlai, 10 Nov. 1949, AVPRF,

f. 07, op. 22, pa. 36, d. 220, pp. 54–55; record of conversation, Roshchin and Li Ruchen (former GMD general, Vice President of Guomindang Revolutionary Committee), 26 Oct. 1949, AVPRF, f. 0100, op. 43, pa. 302, d. 10, pp. 50–51. See also record of conversation, L. Shibaev (NKVD station chief, Soviet embassy, Beijing) and Li Kenong, 28 Dec. 1949, AVPRF, f. 0100 0. 43 d. 10 pa. 302, pp. 53–56. Li had served as head of intelligence for the CCP CC, and was appointed PRC Vice Foreign Minister in 1949. In 1949–50, Li served as a secret liaison between Mao Zedong and the Soviet embassy in Beijing.

    10. Bertil Lintner, *Burma in Revolt: Opium and Insurgency since 1948* (Boulder, CO: Westview, 1994), pp. 92–102. For CCP concerns, see record of conversation, Roshchin and Mao Zedong, 1 Jan. 1950 (Moscow), AVPRF, f. 0100, op. 43, pa. 302, d. 10, pp. 1–4.

    11. For a summary of the negative CCP views on Tibet, see record of conversation, Roshchin and Zhou Enlai, 15 Nov. 1949, AVPRF, f. 07, op. 22, pa. 36, d. 220, pp. 57–66; see also Warren H. Smith, Jr., *Tibetan Nation: A History of Tibetan Nationalism and Sino-Tibetan Relations* (Boulder, CO: Westview, 1996), pp. 257–63; Melvyn C. Goldstein, with the help of Gelek Rimpoche, *A History of Modern Tibet, 1913–1951* (Berkeley: University of California Press, 1989), pp. 611–27; and Tsering Shakya, *Dragon in the Lands of Snow: A History of Modern Tibet since 1947* (London: Pimlico, 1999).

    12. *Zhongguo renmin jiefangjun zhanshi*, vol. 3, pp. 391–94; see also Liao Zugui, *Xizang de heping jiefang* (Beijing: Zhongguo Zangxue, 1991); and Smith, *Tibetan Nation*, pp. 265–85.

    13. Secretary of State to New Delhi embassy, 6 Jan. 1951, *FRUS*, 1950, vol. 6, p. 618.

    14. Dalai Lama, *Freedom in Exile: The Autobiography of His Holiness The Dalai Lama of Tibet* (London: Hodder and Staughton, 1990), pp. 65–77; Smith, *Tibetan Nation*, pp. 309–13.

    15. Mao (in Moscow) to Lin Biao, 10 Jan. 1950, *Mao Zedong junshi wenji*, vol. 6, p. 74; record of conversation, Shibaev and Li Kenong, 16 Jan. 1950, AVPRF 0100, 0. 43, pa. 302, d. 10, pp. 38–44. For an excellent overview, see Liu Zhenhua, ed., *Hainan zhi zhan* [*The Battle of Hainan*], 2d ed. (Shenyang: Liaoning renmin, 1994).

    16. Liu, *Hainan zhi zhan*, pp. 170–211.

    17. For an informative discussion, see Niu Jun, *Cong Yan'an zouxiang Shijie: Zhongguo Gongchandang duiwai guanxi de qiyuan* [*From Yan'an to the World: The Origins of the Chinese Communist Party's Foreign Relations*] (Fuzhou: Fujian renmin, 1992).

    18. Orlov to Kuznetsev, 10 Jan. 1949, relaying record of conversation with Mao Zedong, 7 Jan. 1949, APRF, f. 39, 0. 1, d. 31, pp. 54–58. Orlov complained in his report about the CCP center's lack of understanding of Soviet policies, about being excluded from key meetings, and about having to listen to the "Queen's" (Jiang Qing's) "various complaints about various illnesses" (ibid.).

    19. Record of conversation, 31 Jan. 1949, Mikoyan and Mao Zedong, APRF, f. 39, 0. 1, d. 39, pp. 7–16.

    20. See Sergei L. Tikhvinskii, "O 'Sekretnom demarshe' Chzhou Enlaia i neof-

fitsialnykh peregovorakh KPK s amerikantsami v iune 1949g" ["On Zhou Enlai's 'Secret Demarche' and the CCP's Unofficial Talks with the Americans in June 1949"], *Problemu dalnego vostoka* 3 (1994): 133–38.

21. Mao Zedong to CCP Nanjing Party Committee, 10 May 1949, Zhonghua renmin gongheguo and Zhonggong zhongyang wenxian yanjiushi, eds., *Mao Zedong waijiao wenxuan [Mao Zedong Selected Works on Foreign Affairs]* (Beijing: Zhongyang wenxian, 1994), p. 87.

22. K. M. Panikkar, *In Two Chinas: Memoirs of a Diplomat* (London: Allen and Unwin, 1955), p. 48.

23. Jiang Taigong lived in the Zhou Dynasty. According to legend, he once fished in the Weishui River, holding a rod without hook or bait three feet above the water, and saying, "The fish that is destined to be caught will come up."

24. *Selected Works of Mao Tse-tung*, vol. 4 (Beijing: Foreign Languages Press, 1969), pp. 433–40.

25. For the Ward incident, see Chen Jian, "The Ward Case and the Emergence of Sino-American Confrontation," *Australian Journal of Chinese Affairs* 30 (1993): 149–70; and Michael M. Sheng, *Battling Western Imperialism: Mao, Stalin, and the United States* (Princeton: Princeton University Press, 1997), pp. 164–77. In his conversation with Mikoyan on 1 February 1949, "Zhou Enlai stated that a new problem had emerged in relations with Americans when our [the CCP's] troops had occupied Mukden [Shenyang] last year. Stationed there, the foreign consulates (American, British, and French) hinted to us that they were not going to evacuate and would like to establish de facto relations with us. We understood that these consulates stayed there for intelligence against us and the USSR. We don't wish to see them in Mukden, therefore we take measures to isolate them, [we] create intolerable conditions for them in order to have them leave Mukden. In the future, we shall raise the question of consular networks on the basis of parity. In general," said Zhou Enlai, "we shall act toughly against the Americans, because 'we are at war with them and we are not with other powers.' The Americans undermine our regime and we should isolate the United States in our country" (record of conversation, Mikoyan and Zhou Enlai, APRF, f. 39, o. 1, d. 39, pp. 17–24).

26. Zhonggong zhongyang wenxian yanjiushi, comp., *Mao Zedong nianpu (1893–1949) [Mao Zedong Chronology (1893–1949)]* (Beijing: Renmin, 1993), vol. 3, p. 336.

27. On the diplomatic academy, see Yang Gongsu, *Cangsang jiushinian: Yige waijiao teshi de huiyi* [90 Years' Experience of Life: The Reminiscences of a Diplomatic Special Envoy] (Haikou: Hainan, 1999).

28. Record of conversation, Mikoyan and Zhou Enlai, APRF, f. 39, o. 1, d. 39, p. 19.

29. See Zhou's speech at the founding of the PRC Foreign Ministry, 8 Nov. 1949, Zhongguo renmin jiefangjun Guofang daxue dangshi dangjian zhenggong jiaoyanshi, comp., *Zhonggong dangshi jiaoxue cankao ziliao* (Beijing?: n.p., 1986), vol. 18, pp. 590–92.

30. Record of conversation, Mikoyan and Zhou Enlai, APRF, f. 39, o. 1, d. 39, pp. 17–24.

31. Statement by CCP spokesman, 13 Feb. 1949, in Zhongyang dang'anguan,

comp., *Zhonggong zhongyang wenjian xuanji* [*Selected Documents of the CCP Center*] (Beijing: Zhonggong zhongyang dangxiao, 1992), vol. 18, pp. 129–30.

32. *Mao Zedong nianpu*, vol. 3, p. 579.

33. Sergei L. Tikhvinskii, author's interview, Oslo, 23 Sept. 1996; Gromyko to Stalin, 2 and 3 Oct. 1950, AVPRF, f. 07, o. 22a, pa. 13, d. 198, pp. 1–5.

34. Record of conversation, Ambassador Roshchin and Mao Zedong, 16 Oct. 1949, AVPRF, f. 0100, op. 42, pa. 288, d. 19, pp. 28–31; see also record of conversation, Roshchin and Zhou Enlai, 31 Oct. 1949, AVPRF, f. 0100, op. 42, pa. 288, d. 19, pp. 74–77.

35. Record of conversation, Ambassador Roshchin and Zhou Enlai, 10 Nov. 1949, AVPRF, f. 07, op. 22, pa. 36, d. 220, pp. 52–56; record of conversation, Ambassador Roshchin and Li Kenong, 17 Nov. 1949, AVPRF, f. 07, op. 22, p. 36, d. 220, pp. 67–73; Gromyko to Stalin, 26 Nov. 1949, AVPRF, f. 07, op. 23d, pa. 30b, d. 19, pp. 32–36. Li Kenong, in a not too subtle message, informed the Soviets that imperialist agents were busy portraying Sino-Soviet trade as "robbery of food and natural resources from China and attack the Sino-Soviet treaty of 1945, characterizing it as an unequal, imperialist treaty, as a result of which China lost Guandong peninsula and all industrial equipment in Manchuria."

36. Sergei Tikhvinskii, author's interview (Tikhvinskii accompanied Mao on the trip to Moscow).

37. Shi Zhe, *Zai lishi jüren shenbian: Shi Zhe huiyilu* [*At the Side of Historical Giants: Shi Zhe's Memoirs*] (Beijing: Zhongyang wenxian, 1991), pp. 418–73; Sergei Tikhvinskii, author's interview.

38. Ivan V. Kovalev, "Dialog Stalina s Mao Tsedunom," *Problemu dalnego vostoka* 1 (1991): 83-93 and *ibid.* 1-3 (1992): 77-91; Heinzig, *Die Sowjetunion und das kommunistische Kina*, pp. 469–74; Odd Arne Westad, "Fighting for Friendship: Mao, Stalin, and the Sino-Soviet Treaty of 1950," *Cold War International History Project* [CWIHP] *Bulletin* 8/9 (1998).

39. *Pravda* 2 Jan. 1950; Mikhail Kapitsa, author's interview; Mao Zedong to CCP Center, 2 Jan. 1950, *Jianguo yilai Mao Zedong wengao*, vol. 1, pp. 211–12.

40. *Zhou Enlai nianpu*, vol. 1, pp. 22–26; Vyshinskii to Stalin, 2 Feb. 1950, AVPRF, f. 07, op. 23a, pa. 18, d. 234; summary of conv., Zhou Enlai-Mikoyan, 12 Feb. 1950, AVPRF, f. 07 op. 23a, pa. 18, d. 234, esp. pp. 29–34.

41. Records of conversation, Stalin and Mao, 16 Dec. 1949 and 22 Jan. 1950, APRF, f. 45, op. 1, d. 329, pp. 9–17 and 29–38; see also Sergei Goncharov et al., *Uncertain Partners: Stalin, Mao, and the Korean War* (Stanford, CA: Stanford University Press, 1993), pp. 121–29; and Chen Jian, *China's Road to the Korean War: The Making of the Sino-American Confrontation* (New York: Columbia University Press, 1994).

42. Mao to Stalin, 2 Jan. 1950, APRF, f. 45, op. 1, d. 334; Kovalev to Stalin, 7 Jan. 1950, APRF, f. 3, op. 65, d. 533; Mao to Zhou Enlai, 29 Jan. 1950, *Jianguo yilai Mao Zedong wengao*, vol. 1, p. 253; see also Vyshinskii to Stalin, 12 Feb. 1950, AVPRF, f. 07, op. 23a, pa. 18, d. 234, pp. 64–68.

43. Guo Ming et al., *ZhongYue guanxi yanbian sishinian* [*40 Years Development of Sino-Vietnamese Relations*] (Nanning: Guangxi renmin, 1992), pp. 15–20; Wu Xiuquan, *Huiyi yu huainian* [*Memories and Memorials*] (Beijing: Zhonggong zhongyang dangxiao, 1991), pp. 242–44; see also the excellent over-

view in Chen Jian, *Mao's China and the Cold War*, pp. 118–127, and Zhai Qiang, *China and the Vietnam Wars, 1950–1975* (Chapel Hill, NC: University of North Carolina Press, 2000), pp. 20–26.

44. Mikhail Kapitsa, author's interview; Chen Jian, *Mao's China and the Cold War*, pp. 119–120; Christopher E. Goscha, "L'aide militaire chinoise au Viêt-minh (1949–1954), *Revue historique des armées* 3 (2000): 15–24; Zhai Qiang, *China and the Vietnam Wars*, pp 13–16; see also Mari Olsen's forthcoming University of Oslo PhD thesis.

45. Qiu Jing, "Mao Zedong yu Sidalin de huiwu," *Dang de wenxian* 2 (1996); Pei Jianzhang, ed., *Zhonghua renmin gongheguo waijiaoshi, 1949–1956* (Beijing: Shijie zhishi, 1993), p. 18. The author has been allowed to see a Russian summary of the 24 December conversation, but, unfortunately, a full record is not yet available.

46. Liu Shaoqi to Ho Chi Minh, 25 Dec. 1949, quoted by Luo Guibo in Fu Hao and Li Tongchen, eds., *Kaiqi guomen: Waijiao guang de fengcai* [*Opening the Country's Gate: The Achievements of Diplomats*] (Beijing: Huaqiao, 1995), pp. 153–54. It is possible that the Chinese did not expect Ho himself to turn up on their border; see ibid., p. 160. For Liu's trip, see Zhonggong zhongyang wenxian yanjiushi, comp., *Liu Shaoqi nianpu* [*Liu Shaoqi Chronology*], 2 vols. (Beijing: Zhongyang wenxian, 1996), vol. 2, p. 241; Wu Xiuquan, *Huiyi yu huainian* [*Recollections and Memories*] (Beijing: Zhongyang dangxiao, 1991), pp. 242–43. According to Kapitsa (author's interview), Stalin said after giving his assent that Mao could then as well invite all of the revolutionary leaders from the Far East to Moscow, and then one of them would bring a bomb and blow everyone up. Zhou quoted in Han Huanzhi et al., eds., *Dangdai Zhongguo jundui de junshi gongzuo* [*The Military Affairs of the Contemporary Chinese Army*] (Beijing: Zhongguo shehui kexueyuan, 1988) p. 576.

47. Lu Guibo in Fu and Tong, *Kaiqi guomen*; record of conversation, Roshchin-Zhou Dapeng, 4 July 1950, AVPRF, f. 0100, op. 43, pa. 302, d. 10; Yang Kuisong, *Changes in Mao Zedong's Attitudes toward the Indochina War, 1949–1973* (CWIHP Working Paper; Washington, DC: Woodrow Wilson Center, 2002).

48. See Alexandre Y. Mansourov, "Communist War Coalition Formation and the Origins of the Korean War," PhD dissertation, Columbia University, 1997.

49. See Chen Jian, *China's Road to the Korean War*, esp. pp. 24–27.

50. See Mansourov, "Communist War Coalition Formation and the Origins of the Korean War," esp. pp. 139–211; Kathryn Weathersby, "To Attck or Not to Attack: Stalin, Kim Il Sung, and the Prelude to War," *CWIHP Bulletin* 5 (1995).

51. See Xu Yan, *Diyici jiaoliang: kangMei yuanChao zhanzheng de lishi huigu yu fansi* [*The First Test of Strength: A Historical Review and Evaluation of the War to Resist America and Assist Korea*] (Beijing: Zhongguo dianying, 1990).

52. Vyshinskii to Roshchin, containing a telegram from Filippov (Stalin) to Mao Zedong, 14 May 1950, APRF, f. 45, o. 1, d. 331, p. 55, quoted in Alexandre Y. Mansourov, "Communist War Coalition Formation and the Origins of the Korean War," Ph.D. dissertation, Columbia University, 1997, p. 315.

53. Summaries of the key Mao-Kim conversations on 13 and 15 May are in

the Soviet Foreign Ministry's chronology of events surrounding the outbreak of the Korean War, AVPRF, f. 05, op. 58, pa. 34, d. 266.

54. Chen Jian, *China's Road to the Korean War*, pp. 109–13; see also Niu Jun, "The Origins of the Sino-Soviet Alliance," in Westad, ed., *Brothers in Arms*, p. 74.

55. Bo Yibo, *Ruogan zhongda juece yu shijian de huigu* [*Review of Several Important Decisions and Events*] (Beijing: Zhonggong zhongyang dangxiao, 1991), vol. 1, pp. 120–33.

56. Record of conversation, Roshchin-Zhou Dapeng, and annexed documents, 4 July 1950, AVPRF, f. 0100, op. 43, pa. 302, d. 10; Mao to Nie Rongzhen, 7 July 1950, *Jianguo yilai Mao Zedong wengao*, vol. 1, p. 428; Mao to Gao Gang, 18 Aug. 1950, *ibid.*, vol. 1, p. 469.

57. Shen Zhihua, "Sino-Soviet Relations and the Origins of the Korean War: Stalin's Strategic Goals in the Far East," http://www.fas.harvard.edu/~hpcws/shen.pdf; Stalin to Mao, 1 Oct. 1950, *CWIHP Bulletin* 6–7 (1995–96).

58. Information from Chinese party historians. The records of CCP Politburo deliberations are not yet available, but see the insightful discussion in Chen Jian, *China's Road to the Korean War*, ch. 5, and Zhang Xi, "Peng Dehuai and China's Entry into the Korean War," *Chinese Historians* 6 (1993): 8–16.

59. Chen Jian, *China's Road to the Korean War*, pp. 190–209.

60. Chen Jian, "Chinese Policy and the Korean War," in Lester H. Brune, ed., *The Korean War: Handbook of the Literature and Research* (Westport, CT: Greenwood, 1996), p. 202.

61. That is the case in spite of the fact that Mao's son, Mao Anying, was killed in Korea. According to a 1967 Red Guard publication, Mao's comment was: "In war there must be sacrifice. Without sacrifices there will be no victory. To sacrifice my son or other people's sons is just the same" (http://www.maoism.org/msw/vol7/mswv7_143.htm).

62. Jing Huang, *Factionalism in Chinese Communist Politics* (Cambridge: Cambridge University Press, 2000), pp. 179–80.

Postscript

1. Maurice Meisner, *The Significance of the Chinese Revolution in World History*, Working paper 1 (London: LSE Asia Research Centre, 1999).

2. While seeing immediate connections to decisions taken during the civil war, it is, of course, impossible to deny that many of these traits have deeper roots in Chinese history than those leading back a mere fifty years. The control of intellectuals, for instance, was of crucial importance to previous dynasties; see Jonathan Spence's vivid image of the early-eighteenth-century Yongzheng emperor's concerns in *Treason by the Book* (New York: Viking, 2001).

Studying the Chinese Civil War:
A Brief Bibliography

There are, unfortunately, few manuals, aids, and bibliographies available to the student of Chinese domestic or international history. The purpose of this section is therefore to present some suggestions as to where one may begin to look for further information on the different topics dealt with in this volume. I have included works primarily in English and Chinese, the two languages that most students of the war may be expected to know. For the benefit of the general reader, the emphasis in the thematic sections is on materials available in the West as well as in China, and books are given preference over articles. Some of the works cited are in the genre called "historical reportage"—generally (and often correctly) spurned by Chinese historians as inaccurate; the best of these books are often based on extensive interviews with participants and may be enlightening if used with caution. In addition to this bibliography, readers should consult the notes to each chapter for further suggestions.

I. Overviews, Bibliographies, and Maps

The best general overview of research and sources on Republican China is William C. Kirby et al., eds., *State and Economy in Republican China: A Handbook for Scholars* (Cambridge, MA: Harvard University Press, 2000), but see also Endymion Wilkinson, *Chinese History: A Manual* (Cambridge, MA: Harvard University Asia Center, 2000). Ye Wa and Joseph W. Esherick, eds., *Chinese Archives: An Introductory Guide,* China Research Monographs 45 (Berkeley: University of California Press, 1996), is an excellent presentation of the main archives in the PRC and on Taiwan. For CCP research materials, see Fernando Orlandi, *New Sources and Opportunities for Research into the History of Contemporary China, the International Communist Movement, and the Cold War* (Levico Terme: Centro studi sulla storia dell'Europa orientale, 2000).

The best general bibliography for the Republican period is Beijing tushuguan, ed., *Minguo shiqi zong shumu* [*Comprehensive Catalog of Republican Era Books*], 21 vols. (Beijing: Shumu wenxian, 1991–97), for works published in China between 1911 and 1949. For historical studies published later, see Hu Pingsheng, ed., *Zhongguo xiandaishi shuji lunwen ziliao juyao* [*Enumeration of Books, Essays, and Materials on Modern Chinese History*], 2 vols. (Taibei:

Xuesheng, 1999), and, for studies of the CCP, the annual or biannual biblio-graphical surveys in the journals *Zhonggong dangshi yanjiu* and *Zhongguo lishi nianjian.* For newspapers and magazines from the 1940s, see Wang Huilin and Zhu Hanguo, chief eds., *Zhongguo baokan cidian [Chinese Press Dictionary]* (Taiyuan: Shuhai, 1991).

Wu Yuexing, chief ed., *Zhongguo xiandaishi dituji [Collection of Maps on the History of Modern China]* (Beijing: Zhongguo ditu, 1999), is the most compre-hensive overview of maps. For military maps, see Junshi kexueyuan junshi lishi yanjiubu, ed., *Zhongguo renmin jiefangjun zhanshi. Disanben: Quangguo jiefang zhanzheng shiqi [A Battle History of the Chinese People's Liberation Army.* Vol-ume Three: *The War for the Liberation of the Whole Country]* (Beijing: Junshi kexue, 1987); and *Atlas for the Arab-Israeli Wars, the Chinese Civil War, and the Korean War* (Wayne, NJ: Avery Publishing Group, 1986).

II. Historiography

For the historiography of the civil war, the Introduction to this volume may be the best place to begin. Suzanne Pepper, *Civil War in China: The Political Strug-gle, 1945–1949* (Lanham, MD: Rowan and Littlefield, 1999 [1978]), and two volumes in the series *Zhonghua minguo shi [History of the Republic of China]*, Wang Chaoguang, *Cong kangzhan shengli dao neizhan baofa qianhou [From the Victory in the War of Resistance to the Outbreak of Civil War]* and Zhu Zong-zhen and Tao Wenzhao, *Guomindang zhengquan de zong bengkui he Zhonghua minguo shiqi de jieshu [The Total Breakdown of Guomindang Political Power and the End of the Chinese Republican Era]*, vols. 5 and 6, series 3 (Beijing: Zhonghua shuju, 2000), are the benchmark studies of Chinese politics during the civil war. "Reappraising Republican China," a special issue of *China Quarterly* (vol. 150, 1997) is an excellent overview of the state of the art for the whole Re-publican era, but see also William C. Kirby and Stephen C. Averill, "More States of the Field," *Republican China* 18, no. 1 (1992): 206–24. For a more critical view, see Prasenjit Duara, "The Regime of Authenticity: Timelessness, Gender, and National History in Modern China," *History and Theory* 37, no. 3 (1998): 287–308.

III. Biographic Aids

Howard L. Boorman, ed., *Biographical Dictionary of Republican China,* 5 vols. (New York: Columbia University Press, 1967–79), is unsurpassed in any language for its accuracy. The most comprehensive Chinese overview is Wang Ji-xiang, chief ed., *Zhongguo jinxiandai renwu zhuanji ziliao suoyin [Index to Bio-graphical Materials on Individuals of the Modern and Contemporary Periods]* (Changchun: Dongbei shifan daxue tushuguan, 1988). For Guomindang leaders, see the series *Geming renwuzhi [Materials on Revolutionary Personalities]*, 23 vols. (Taibei: Dangshihui, 1964–). For the CCP, see Donald W. Clark and Anne B. Clark, eds., *Biographical Dictionary of Chinese Communism, 1921–1965,* 2 vols. (Harvard University Press, 1971), and the very extensive *Zhongguo gongchandang mingren lu [Record of Famous CCP Personalities]* (Chengdu: Sichuan renmin, 1997), and *Zhonggong dangshi renwu zhuan [Biographies of*

CCP Personalities] (Xi'an: Shaanxi renmin, and Beijing: Zhongyang wenxian, 1980–).

For aliases, pseudonyms, and false identities, see Xu Weimin, chief ed., *Zhongguo jinxiandai renwu bieming cidian* [*Dictionary of Alternative Names of Personalities from the Modern Period in China*] (Shenyang: Shenyang, 1993), and Chen Yutang, ed., *Zhonggong dangshi renwu bieming lu* [*Record of Alternative Names of Personalities in Party History*] (Beijing: Hongqi, 1985).

IV. Published Documents and Other Sources

Since the early 1980s there have appeared a number of extremely useful and extensive series of document collections on Chinese modern history. For the Guomindang and the Republican government, the ones I have found most useful are Zhongguo Guomindang zhongyang weiyuanhui dangshi weiyuanhui, comp., *Zhonghua Minguo zhongyao shiliao chubian—dui Ri kangzhan shiqi* [*Preliminary Compilation of Important Historical Materials on the Republic of China— The Period of the War of Resistance against Japan*], 7 vols. (Taibei: Zhongyang wenwu gongying, 1981–), and the very extensive *Zhonghua minguo shi dang'an ziliao huibian* [*A Collection of Archival Materials on the History of the Republic of China*] (Nanjing: Jiangsu guji, 1991–), compiled by the Republican Era (Number II) Archives in Nanjing; its Fifth Series, Third Collection, covers the years 1945–49. The *Zhonghua minguoshi shiliao changbian* [*An Extensive Collection of Historical Materials on the History of the Republic of China*] compiled by the same archive in seventy volumes (Nanjing: Nanjing daxue, 1993) is less good on the post-1945 years. The same can be said for the serial *Geming wenxian* [*Documents on the Revolution*], compiled by the Guomindang Central Executive Committee.

On the CCP, the key collection is the eighteen-volume *Zhonggong zhongyang wenjian xuanji* [*Selected Documents of the CCP Center*] (Beijing: Zhonggong zhongyang dangxiao, 1989–1992), compiled by the Central Archives. There is also a fourteen-volume internal edition of this title, published by the same publisher in 1982–1987. These should be supplemented, however, by older collections, such as the two series *Zhonggong dangshi jiaoxue cankao ziliao* [*Teaching Materials on the History of the Party Center*] (Beijing: n.p., n.d. [1979–86?]), compiled by the Party History and Party Education Collection and Study Office of the National Defense University, and special collections of Party Center documents published by the Central Archives or the CCP Central Committee's Office for the Study of the Center's Documents [Zhongyang wenxian yanjiushi] on individual topics, some of which are mentioned below.

At the local and provincial level in China, almost every town and valley now has its own serials of historical documents or reminiscences. These can be gold mines for the historian who knows where to look. I have found many of them useful for this volume—especially *Shaan-Gan-Ning bianqu zhengfu wenjian xuanbian* [*Selected Documents from the Shaan-Gan-Ning Border Area Government*], 13 vols. (Beijing: Dang'an, 1986–1991), compiled by the Shaanxi Provincial Archives and the Shaanxi Provincial Academy of Social Science; and the ongoing serials *Zhonggong Shanghai dangshi ziliao* [*Shanghai CCP History*

Materials]; *Fujian dangshi ziliao* [*Fujian Party History Materials*]; *Guangdong dangshi ziliao* [*Guangdong Party History Materials*]; and *Hebei geming huiyilu* [*Hebei Revolutionary Reminiscences*].

Reprints, such as Zhou Gucheng, chief ed., *Mingguo congshu* [*Republican Era Book Series*] (Shanghai: Shanghai shudian, 1989–; at least five hundred volumes published so far); and Shen Yunlong, chief ed., *Jindai Zhongguo shiliao congkan* [*Collection of Historical Materials on Modern China*] (Taibei: Wenhai, 1966–86; more than three thousand volumes in three series), are very useful for locating publications from the period that are out of print or hard to find in the original in libraries.

V. Journals

The main Chinese historical journals that regularly publish articles on the civil war era are, in the PRC, *Jindaishi yanjiu* [*Modern History Studies*]; *Zhonggong dangshi yanjiu* [*CCP Party History Studies*]; *Zhonggong dangshi ziliao* [*CCP History Materials*]; and *Dangde wenxian* [*Party Documents*]. On Taiwan, the main journal is *Jindaishi yanjiu tongxun* [*Modern History Studies Bulletin*]. In addition, there are of course numerous journals dealing with different aspects of the history of the Republican period or CCP history at the local or specialized level. Outside China, the best journals that cover the Chinese civil war are *China Quarterly*; *Modern China*; *The China Journal*; *20th Century China* (formerly *Republican China*); and *Modern Asian Studies*. For international aspects, see *Cold War History*; *Journal of Cold War Studies*; and the on-line Cold War International History Project: www.cwihp.si.edu.

VI. Political Background

For a general overview, see Lloyd E. Eastman et al., *The Nationalist Era in China, 1927–1949* (Cambridge: Cambridge University Press, 1991). Eastman's *Seeds of Destruction: Nationalist China in War and Revolution, 1937–1949* (Stanford, CA: Stanford University Press, 1984) is probably still the best single volume on the demise of the GMD state, but see also Ch'i Hsi-cheng, *Nationalist China at War: Military Defeats and Political Collapse, 1937–1945* (Ann Arbor: University of Michigan Press, 1982); and James C. Hsiung and Steven I. Levine, *China's Bitter Victory: The War with Japan, 1937–1945* (Armonk, NY: Eastgate, 1992). Zhang Yufa, *Zhonghua minguo shigao* [*A Survey History of the Republic of China*] (Taibei: Lianjing, 1998), gives a good overview of the political history of the 1911–49 period.

VII. The Economy

For overviews of recent research, see Loren Brandt, "Reflections on China's Late 19th and Early 20th Century Economy," *China Quarterly* 150 (1997): 282–308; and Philip C. C. Huang, "The Study of Rural China's Economic History," *Republican China* 18, no. 1 (1992): 164–76. See also Mi Rucheng, ed., *Zhongguo jindai jingjishi yanjiu zongshu* [*Outline of Research on Modern Chinese Economic History*] (Tianjian: Tianjin jiaoyu, 1987).

Good survey texts are Dong Changzhi and Li Fan, *Zhongguo xiandai jingjishi (1919–1949 nian)* [*An Economic History of Modern China (1919–1949)*] (Changchun: Dongbei shifan daxue, 1988); and Kuang Haolin, *Jianming Zhongguo jindai jingjishi* [*A Concise Economic History of Contemporary China*] (Beijing: Zhongyang minzu, 1989).

For the World War II period, see *KangRi zhanzheng shiqi Xinan jingji fazhan gaishu* [*A Survey Volume on the Economic Development in the Southwest during the War of Resistance against Japan*] (Chongqing: Xinan shifan daxue, 1988); Li Xuetong, ed., *Guomin zhengfu yu dahoufang jingji* [*The Republican Government and the Economy of the Rear Areas*], vol. 5 in series *Kangri zhanzheng* [*The Anti-Japanese Struggle*] (Chengdu: Sichuan daxue, 1997).

For the CCP areas, see *Huabei jiefangqu caizheng jingji shi ziliao xuanbian* [*A Selection of Materials on the Financial and Economic History of the Liberated Areas in North China*], 2 vols. on the 1945–49 period (Beijing: Xinhua, 1996).

Monetary and agricultural aspects of the economy are covered in Zhongguo renmin yinhang canshi shi, ed., *Zhonghua minguo huobishi ziliao* [*Materials on Republican Era Monetary History*], 2 vols. (Shanghai renmin, 1991); and Zhonghua renmin gongheguo caizhengbu, ed., *Zhongguo nongmin fudan shi, 1927–1949* [*A History of the Burden of the Chinese Peasants*] (Beijing: Xinhua, 1990).

For a case study of China's foreign economic relations during the civil war years, see C. X. George Wei, *Sino-American Economic Relations, 1944–1949* (New York: Greenwood, 1997).

VIII. Social Conditions and Movements

a. The Cities

We still lack good studies of the GMD 1945 takeover of the main Chinese cities, although Joseph K. S. Yick, *Making Urban Revolution in China: The CCP-GMD Struggle for Beiping-Tianjin, 1945–1949* (Armonk, NY: M. E. Sharpe, 1995), is an excellent start. From the CCP perspective, see Zhonggong Beijing shiwei xuanchuanbu, Zhonggong Beijing shiwei dangshi yanjiushi, and Beijing shi wenhuaju, comps., *Jiefang zhanzheng shiqi Beiping diertuan zhanzheng de wenhua douzheng* [*The Cultural Struggle of the Second Front in Beijing during the War of Liberation Period*] (Beijing: Beijing, 1998); and for insights into United Front policy-making, Zhonggong Jiangsu shengwei dangshi gongzuo weiyuanhui et al., comp., *Zhonggong Zhongyang Nanjing Ju* [*The CCP Central Committee's Nanjing Bureau*] (Beijing: Zhonggong dangshi, 1990); Zhonggong Shandong shengwei dangshi ziliao zhengji yanjiu weiyuanhui et al., *Jiefang zhanzheng shiqi de Zhonggong zhongyang Shanghai ju* [*The CCP CC Shanghai Bureau during the War of Liberation Period*] (Shanghai: Xuelin, 1989); and Nanfangju dangshi ziliao zhengji xiaozu, comp., *Nanfangju dangshi ziliao* [*Party Southern Bureau History Materials*], 6 vols. (Chongqing: Chongqing, 1990).

The CCP takeover of the cities is covered in, among others, Zhao Jinxuan, *Shenyang, 1948: Jiefang Shenyang ji shi* [*Shenyang, 1948: The History of the Liberation of Shenyang*] (Beijing: Junshi kexue, 1997); Zhonggong Dalian shiwei dangshi ziliao zhengji bangongshi, comp., *Jiefang chuqi de Dalian* [*The Early Pe-*

riod in the Liberation of Dalian] (N.p.: n.p., 1985); Dong Shigui and Zhang Yanzhi, *Beiping hetan ji shi* [*Some Facts about the Beiping Peace Talks*] (Beijing: Xinhua, 1991); He Dong and Chen Mingxian, *Beiping heping jiefang shi-mo* [*The Full Story of the Beiping Peace Talks and Liberation*] (Beijing: Jiefangjun, 1985); Zhonggong Beijing shiwei dangshi yanjiu shi and Beijing shi dangan guan, comps., *Beiping de heping jiguan* [*The Peaceful Takeover of Beiping*] (Beijing: Beijing, 1993); *Du jiang he jiefang Nanjing* [*Crossing the River and Liberating Nanjing*] (Shanghai: Shanghai renmin, 1979); Shanghai dang'anguan, comp., *Shanghai jiefang* [*Liberating Shanghai*] (Beijing: Dangan, 1989); Zhonggong Shanghai dangshi yanjiushi, comp., *Jieguan Shanghai* [*Taking over Shanghai*] (Beijing: Zhongyang guangbo dianshi, 1993); Chengdu shiwei dangshi yanjiushi, ed., *Jieguan Chengdu* [*Taking over Chengdu*] (Chengdu: Chengdu, 1991); Li Wei, *1949: JingHu baodong ji shi neimu* [*1949: Some True Inner Stories about the Insurrections in Beijing and Shanghai*] (Chengdu: Sichuan wenyi, 1993).

b. The Youth and Student Movement

There is a substantial literature on protest movements in the cities; see Jeffrey Wasserstrom, *Student Protests in Twentieth Century China: The View from Shanghai* (Stanford, CA: Stanford University Press, 1991), for a long-term overview; and Zhang Yufa, ed., *Xuechao yu zhanhou Zhongguo zhengzhi (1945–1949)* [*Student Strikes and Postwar Chinese Politics*] (Taibei: Dongda, 1994); *Zhongguo xuesheng yundongshi, 1945–1949* [*A History of the Chinese Student Movement, 1945–1949*] (Shanghai: Shanghai renmin, 1992); and Gongqingtuan zhongyang qingyunshi yanjiushi et al., eds., *Jiefang zhanzheng shiqi xuesheng yundong lunwenji* [*Selected Essays on the Student Movement during the War of Liberation Period*] (Shanghai: Dongji daxue, 1988), for the civil war years.

For individual cities, see Gongqingtuan Shanghai shiwei, ed., *Shanghai xuesheng yundong shi, 1945–1949* [*A History of the Shanghai Student Movement, 1945–1949*] (Shanghai: Shanghai renmin, 1983); Zhonggong Shanghai shiwei dangshi ziliao zhengji weiyuanhui, comp., *Jiefang zhanzheng shiqi Shanghai xuesheng yundong shi* [*A History of the Shanghai Student Movement during the War of Liberation*] (Shanghai: Shanghai fanyi, 1991); Gongqingtuan Beijing shiwei qingnian yundong shi yanjiushi, comp., *Beijing qingnian yundong shi, 1919–1949* [*History of the Beijing Youth Movement, 1919–1949*] (Beijing: Beijing, 1989); Guangzhou qingnian yundong shi yanjiu weiyuanhui, eds., *Jiefang zhanzheng shiqi Guangzhou qingnian yundong ziliao xuanbian* [*Selected Materials on the Guangzhou Youth Movement during the War of Liberation Period*] (Guangzhou: n.p., 1984); and Zhonggong Kunming shiwei dangshiban and Yunnan sheng dang'anguan, comps., *1948 Kunming 'Fan MeifuRi' yundong* [*The 1948 "Resist US Support for Japan" Movement in Kunming*] (Kunming: Yunnan renmin, 1989).

For an overview of individual protest movements during the civil war, see the three-volume *Jiefang zhanzheng shiqi diertiao zhanxian: Xuesheng yundong juan* [*The Second Front during the War of Liberation: Volumes on the Student Movement*]—the first volume, edited by Zhonggong Beijing shiwei dangshi yanjiushi, covers 1945–46; the second, edited by Zhonggong Nanjing shiwei dangshi bangongshi, covers the spring and summer of 1947; and the third, jointly edited by Zhonggong Zhejiang shengwei dangshi yanjiushi and Zhonggong Hangzhou shiwei dangshi yanjiushi, covers the final period up to 1949 (Beijing: Zhonggong dangshi, 1997); see also Hua Binqing, *Wuerling yundong shi: 1947 nian wei dadi xuesheng yundong* [*A History of the 20 May Movement: The 1947 Student Antiimperialist Movement*] (Nanjing: Nanjing daxue, 1990); Zhonggong Beijing shiwei dangshi yanjiushi, comp., *Kangyi Meijun zhu Hua baoxing yundong ziliao huibian* [*A Collection of Materials on the Movement to Protest Atrocities by the American Army Stationed in China*] (Beijing: Beijing daxue, 1989), and their *Fan ji'e fan neizhan yundong ziliao huibian* [*Collected Materials on the Movement against Hunger and Civil War*] (Beijing: Beijing daxue, 1992); Zhonggong Yunnan shengwei dangshi ziliao zhengzhi weiyuanhui and ZhongGong Yunnan shifan daxue weiyuanhui, eds., *Yieryi yundong* [*The 21 January Movement*] (Beijing: Zhonggong dangshi ziliao, 1988).

c. The Labor Movement

The labor movement during the 1945–49 era is another under-researched field. Emily Honig, *Sisters and Strangers: Women in the Shanghai Cotton Mills, 1919–1949* (Stanford, CA: Stanford University Press, 1986); and Elizabeth Perry, *Shanghai on Strike: The Politics of Chinese Labor* (Stanford, CA: Stanford University Press, 1993) give a good overview of Shanghai. The three Chinese volumes I have found most useful are *Dangdai Zhongguo gongren jieji he gonghui yundong* [*Contemporary Chinese Working Class and Trade Union Movement*] (Beijing: Dangdai Zhongguo, 1997); Kai Jun, ed., *Zhongguo gongren yundong shi jiaocai, 1919–1949* [*Teaching Materials on the History of the Chinese Labor Movement, 1919–1949*] (Shanghai: Huadong shifan daxue, 1988); and volume 5 in Zou Bei, chief ed., *Zhongguo gongren yundong shi hua* [*The Brilliant History of the Chinese Workers' Movement*] (Beijing: Gongren, 1993).

A literature on other cities and individual unions is slowly emerging; see, for example, *Zhongguo meikuang gongren yundong shi* [*History of the Chinese Coal Miners' Movement*] (Changsha: Hunan renmin, 1986); and *Zhejiang gongren yundong shi* [*History of the Zhejiang Workers' Movement*] (Hangzhou: Zhejiang renmin, 1988).

For CCP policies, see Zhonghua quanguo zonggonghui, comp., *Zhonggong zhongyang guanyu gongren yundong wenxian xuanbian* [*A Selection of the CCP Central Committee's Documents on the Workers Movement*], 3 vols. (Beijing: Dang'an, 1984–86); and *Zhongguo gongyun lishi wenxian* [*Documents on the History of the Chinese Workers' Movement*] (Beijing: Gongren, 1959).

For individual labor leaders, good starting points are Lucien Bianco, ed., *Dictionnaire biographique du mouvement ouvrier international: La Chine* (Paris: Éditions ouvrières, 1985); and the serial *Zhongguo gongren yundong de xianqu* [*Pioneers of the Chinese Workers' Movement*] (Beijing: Gongren, 1984–).

d. Women

For an overview of gender studies with regard to China, see Christina K. Gilmartin et al., eds., *Engendering China: Women, Culture, and the State,* Harvard Contemporary China Series 10 (Cambridge, MA: Harvard University Press, 1994). For an historical overview, see Kazuko Ono, *Chinese Women in a Century of Revolution, 1850–1950* (Stanford, CA: Stanford University Press, 1989); and the excellent journal *Jindai Zhongguo funü shi yanjiu* [*Studies in Contemporary Chinese Women's History*], published in Taiwan. CCP policies are covered in Zhonghua quanguo funü lianhewei funü yundong lishi yanjiushi, comp., *Zhongguo funü yundong lishi ziliao, 1945–1949* [*Materials on the History of the Chinese Women's Movement, 1945–1949*] (Beijing: Zhongguo funü, 1991). See also Shanghai shi hulian, comp., *Shanghai funü yundong shi, 1919–1949* [*A History of Women's Movement in Shanghai, 1919–1949*] (Shanghai: Shanghai renmin, 1990).

e. Land Reform

Strangely enough, considering the emphasis given to the land issue by most historians, there is still no monograph in English on land-reform during the civil war. Two contemporary accounts, sympathetic to the CCP, are William Hinton, *Fanshen: A Documentary of Revolution in a Chinese Village* (Berkeley: University of California Press, 1997 [1966]); and Isabel and David Crook, *Revolution in a Chinese Village: Ten Mile Inn* (London: Routledge and Kegan Paul, 1959). The historical background is well covered in Kathleen Hartford and Steven M. Goldstein, *Single Sparks: China's Rural Revolutions* (Armonk, NY: M. E. Sharpe, 1989); and *Zhongguo tudi gaige shi (1921–1949)* [*A History of Chinese Land Reform (1921–1949)*] (Beijing: Renmin, 1990). The classic study of land reform in a CCP base area during the war against Japan is Yung-fa Chen, *Making Revolution: The Communist Movement in East and Central China, 1937–1945* (Berkeley: University of California Press, 1986), but see also Zhonggong Liaoning shengwei dangshi yanjiushi, comp., *Jiefang zhanzheng zhong de LiaoJi genjudi* [*The Base Areas in Hebei and Liaoning during the War of Liberation*] (Beijing: Zhonggong dangshi, 1991). For CCP policies during the civil war, see *Jiefang zhanzheng shiqi tudi gaige wenjian xuanji* [*A Selection of Documents on Land Reform during the War of Liberation Period*] (Beijing: Zhonggong dangshi ziliao, 1988); and Zhongyang dang'anguan, comp., *Jiefang zhanzheng shiqi tudi gaige wenxian xuanbian (1945–1949 nian)* [*Selected Documents on Land Reform during the War of Liberation Period, 1945–1949*] (Beijing: Zhonggong zhongyang dangxiao, 1981).

f. Literature and Arts

There is very little specifically on literature and the arts during the civil war; for general overviews of fiction and film, see Ellen Widmer and David Der-wei Wang, *From May Fourth to June Fourth: Fiction and Film in Twentieth Century China* (Cambridge, MA: Harvard University Press, 1993); and, for literature, Bonnie S. McDougall and Kam Louie, *The Literature of China in the Twentieth Century* (New York: Columbia University Press, 1997). For painting, see the multivolume *Modern Chinese Painting, 1911–1949* (Taibei: Guoli lishi bowuguan, 1998). For film, see Regis Bergeron, *Le cinema chinois. I: 1905–1949* (Lausanne: Alfred Eibel, 1977); and Cheng Jihua's magisterial *Zhongguo dianying fazhan shi* [*A*

History of the Development of Chinese Film], 2 vols. (Beijing: Zhongguo dian-ying, 1980). For foreign influences in film, see Wang Chaoguang, "Haolaiwu de chenfu: Minguo nianjian Meiguo dianying zai Hua jingyu yanjiu" ["Hollywood's Enchantments: Researching the Circumstances of American Movies in China during the Republican Era"], *Meiguo yanjiu* 2 (1998): 113–39. For woodcuts, see Hung Chang-tai, "Two Images of Socialism: Woodcuts in Chinese Communist Politics," *Comparative Studies in Society and History* 39 (1997): 34–60; and for cartoons, see Hung's excellent "The Fuming Image: Cartoons and Public Opinion in Late Republican China, 1945 to 1949," ibid. 36 (1994): 122–45.

IX. Political Parties and Leaders

a. The Guomindang

The literature on the Guomindang and its leaders during the civil war is expanding, although there is still not a good history of the party during this period written from the now open GMD archives; Chen Xiaowei, *Wei shenme shiqu dalu* [*Why the Mainland Was Lost*] (Taibei: Yuesheng wenhua, 1988); Liu Jian-qing et al., *Zhongguo Guomindang shi* [*A History of the Chinese Guomindang*] (Nanjing: Jiangsu guji, 1992); and Li Songlin et al., *Jiang Jieshi bingbai dalu* [*Jiang Jieshi's Defeat on the Mainland*] (Shijiazhuang: Hebei renmin, 1993), are merely a beginning. There are a number of good studies and memoirs of individual leaders, such as; Ch'en Li-fu, *The Storm Clouds Clear over China: The Memoir of Chen Li-fu, 1900–1993,* ed. Sidney H. Chang and Ramon H. Myers (Stanford, CA: Stanford University Press, 1994); *Er Chen he CC* [*The Two Chens and CC*] (Zhengzhou: Henan renmin, 1993); *Last Chance in China: The Diary of Chang Kia-ngau,* ed. Donald Gillin and Ramon Myers (Stanford, CA: Hoover Institution Press, 1989); *Zhang Zhizhong huiyilu* [*Zhang Zhizhong Memoirs*] (Beijing: Wenshi ziliao, 1985); Gu Weijun, *Gu Weijun huiyilu* (13 + 2 vols. (Beijing: Zhonghua, 1984–93, 1997); *Chen Cheng ping zhuan* [*A Critical Biography of Chen Cheng*], Fengyun Shuxi, no. 12 (Taibei: Qunlun, 1986); and Zheng Dong-guo et al., *Du Yuming jiangjun* [*General Du Yuming*] (Beijing: Zhongguo wenshi, 1986). On the rivalry between Jiang Jieshi and his vice president, Li Zongren, see Huang Jishu, *Da duikang: Jiang Li enyuan, GuoGong douzheng* [*The Great Rivalry: The Jiang-Li Relationship and the GMD-CCP Struggle*] (Taibei: Zhong-yuan, 1991); and Liang Shengjun, *JiangLi douzheng neimu* [*The Inner History of the Jiang-Li Struggle*] (Taibei: Xinxin wenwen, 1992).

The oral history program at the Institute for Modern History at Academia Sinica in Taibei has produced a number of useful records, such as Jia Dingshi et al., *Bai Chongxi xiansheng fangwen jilu* [*Record of an Interview with Mr. Bai Chongxi*], 2 vols. (Taibei: Zhongyang yanjiuyuan jindaishi yanjiusuo, 1984). The best study of the GMD's youth and student policies is Huang Jianli, *The Politics of Depoliticization in Republican China: Guomindang Policy towards Student Political Activism, 1927–1949* (Bern: Peter Lang, 1996).

There are now some useful studies of Jiang Jieshi and his son and successor, Jiang Jingguo, although both still await full and researched biographies. For the elder Jiang, see Wang Rongzu and Li Ao, *Jiang Jieshi pingzhuan* [*A Critical Bi-*

ography of Jiang Jieshi], 2 vols. (Taibei: Shangzhou wenhua, 1995); Yang Shu-biao, *Jiang Jieshi zhuan* [*A Biography of Jiang Jieshi*] (Beijing: Tuanjie, 1989); and Zhang Xianwen and Fang Qingjiu, *Jiang Jieshi quanzhuan* [*A Complete Biography of Jiang Jieshi*], 2 vols. (Zhengzhou: Henan renmin, 1996, 1997); and in English, Keiji Furuya, *Chiang Kai-shek: His Life and Times* (New York: St. Johns University, 1981). The most complete collection of Jiang Jieshi's speeches and documents is Zhongguo Guomindang Zhongyang weiyuanhui dangshi weiyuan-hui, ed. and comp., *Zongtong Jiang gong sixiang yanlun zongji* [*A General Collection of President Jiang's Thought and Opinions*], 40 vols. (Taibei: n.p., 1984–).

For Jiang Jingguo, see Jay Taylor, *The Generalissimo's Son: Chiang Ching-kuo and the Revolutions in China and Taiwan* (Cambridge, MA: Harvard University Press, 2000); and the reminiscences by Jiang's main CIA contact, Ray S. Cline, *Chiang Ching-kuo Remembered: The Man and His Political Legacy* (Washington, DC: U.S. Global Strategy Council, 1989). See also Jiang Nan, *Jiang Jingguo zhuan* [*A Biography of Jiang Jingguo*] (Beijing: Zhongguo youyi, 1984); Chen Pengren, *Jiang Jingguo xiansheng zhuan* [*A Biography of Mr. Jiang Jingguo*] (Taibei: Zhongyang ribao, 1990); Han Shanbi, *Jiang Jingguo pingzhuan* [*Critical Biography of Jiang Jingguo*] (Hong Kong: Dongxi wenhua shiye gongsi, 1988). *Jiang Jingguo xiansheng quanji* [*Complete Works of Mr Jiang Jingguo*], multiple vols. (Taibei: Xingzhengyuan xinwenju, 1991), is a far from complete collection of Jiang Jingguo's works.

b. The CCP

The party history industry has become a big business in mainland China; there are at least four large and a multitude of smaller publishers that specialize in more or less trustworthy accounts of the party and its leaders. It is ironic, then, that the best general CCP party history is written by a Taiwan scholar—Chen Yongfa, *Zhongguo gongchan geming qishinian* [*Seventy Years of Chinese Communist Revolution*] (Taibei: Lianjing, 1998). For the Yan'an period, see David E. Apter and Tony Saich, *Revolutionary Discourse in Mao's Republic* (Cambridge, MA: Harvard University Press, 1994). *History of the Chinese Communist Party: A Chronology of Events* (Beijing: Foreign Languages Press, 1991), is a useful overview, and Fei Yundong and Yu Guihua, "A Brief History of the Work of Secretaries in the Chinese Communist Party (1921–1949)," *Chinese Studies in Law and Government* 30 no. 4 (1997) shows some of the organizational development of the party. Huang Jing, *Factionalism in Chinese Communist Politics* (New York: Cambridge University Press, 2000), deals with some of the same issues from a more critical perspective. The most comprehensive published collection of party documents is the previously mentioned "open" edition of *Zhonggong zhongyang wenjian xuanji*. There are, of course, numerous collections of party documents on specific topics; one of the most useful is Zhongyang tongzhanbu and Zhongyang dang'anguan, eds., *Zhonggong zhongyang jiefang zhanzheng shiqi tongyi zhanxian wenxian xuanbian* [*Selected CCP Central Committee Documents on the United Front during the War of Liberation*] (Beijing: Dang'an, 1988). In English there is the thirteen-hundred-page collection edited by Tony

Saich, with a contribution by Benjamin Yang, eds., *The Rise to Power of the Chinese Communist Party: Documents and Analysis* (Armonk, NY: M. E. Sharpe, 1996). See also Zhongyang dang'anguan, comp., *Zhonggong zhongyang zai Xibaipo* [*The CCP Center at Xibaipo*] (Beijing: Haitian, 1998).

The biographies, document collections, chronologies, and recollections dealing with Mao Zedong are almost as numerous as the rest of the party history publications put together. These materials range in quality from the highly useful to the downright silly. The official biography, with party history supremo Jin Chongji as chief editor, *Mao Zedong zhuan, 1893–1949* [*Mao Zedong Biography, 1893–1949*] (Beijing: Zhongyang wenxian, 1996), and the three-volume Zhonggong zhongyang wenxian yanjiushi, comp., *Mao Zedong nianpu (1893–1949)* [*Mao Zedong Chronology (1893–1949)*] (Beijing: Renmin, 1993), are very informative. The most comprehensive collections of Mao's work for the pre-1949 period are *Mao Zedong wenji* [*Mao Zedong Works*], 5 vols. (Beijing: Renmin, 1996), *Mao Zedong ji* [*Mao Zedong Works*], 2d ed., 10 vols. (Tokyo: Sososha, 1983), and *Mao Zedong ji: Bujuan*, 10 vols. (Tokyo: Sososha, 1985), compiled and edited by the Japanese scholar Takeushi Minoru. See also Zhonghua renmin gongheguo and Zhonggong zhongyang wenxian yanjiushi, eds., [*Mao Zedong's Selected Works on Foreign Affairs*] (Beijing: Zhongyang wenxian, 1994); and *Mao Zedong junshi wenji* [*Mao Zedong's Works on Military Affairs*], 6 vols. (Beijing: Junshi kexue, 1993). The best English edition is Stuart Schram, ed., *Mao's Road to Power: Revolutionary Writings 1912–1949*, 5 vols. thus far (Armonk, NY: M. E. Sharpe, 1992–).

There are a number of useful official works on other leading CCP members. For Zhou Enlai, see *Selected Works of Zhou Enlai*, vol. 1 (Beijing: Foreign Languages Press, 1989); Zhonggong zhongyang wenxian yanjiushi, comp., *Zhou Enlai nianpu, 1898–1949* [*Chronological Biography of Zhou Enlai, 1898–1949*], and their *Zhou Enlai zhuan, 1898–1949* [*Zhou Enlai Biography, 1898–1949*], both published in Beijing by Zhongyang wenxian in 1989, with revised editions in 1997. They also compiled *Zhou Enlai zhuan, 1949–1976* [*Zhou Enlai Biography, 1949–1976*] in two volumes, and *Zhou Enlai junshi huadong jishi, 1918–1975* [*A Record of Zhou Enlai's Military Activities, 1918–1975*], 2 vols., published by the same press in 1998 and 2000, respectively. Together with Zhongguo renmin jiefangjun junshi kexueyuan, they compiled *Zhou Enlai junshi wenxuan* [*Zhou Enlai Military Works*] in four volumes, published by Renmin in 1997. There are a number of works on Zhou's role in foreign affairs; see Zhonghua renmin gongheguo waijiaobu and Zhonggong zhongyang wenxian yanjiushi, comps., *Zhou Enlai waijiao wenxuan* (Beijing: Zhongyang wenxian, 1990); and Zhonghua renmin gongeheguo waijiaobu waijiaoshi yanjiushi, comp., *Zhou Enlai waijiao huodong dashiji, 1949–1975* [*A Chronology of Zhou Enlai's Foreign Policy Activities, 1949–1975*] (Beijing: Shijie zhishi, 1993).

For Liu Shaoqi, see *Selected Works of Liu Shaoqi*, vol. 1 (Beijing: Foreign Languages Press, 1984), *Jianguo yilai Liu Shaoqi wengao* [*Liu Shaoqi Manuscripts since the Founding of the Country*] (Beijing: Zhongyang wenxian, 1998–), *Liu Shaoqi zhuan* [*Liu Shaoqi biography*], 2 vols., ed. Jin Chongji (Beijing: Zhongyang wenxian, 1998), and *Liu Shaoqi nianpu* [*Liu Shaoqi Chronology*], 2 vols., ed. Chen Shaochou and Liu Chouyuan (Beijing: Zhongyang wenxian, 1996), all compiled by Zhonggong zhongyang wenxian yanjiushi. For Ren Bishi, see the very useful *Ren Bishi zhuan* [*Ren Bishi Biography*] (Beijing: Zhongyang wenxian, 1994), perhaps the best of the official biographies. Cheng Zhongyuan, *Zhang Wentian zhuan* [*A Biography of Zhang Wentian*] (Beijing: Dangdai Zhongguo, 1993); and *He Long junshi wenxuan* [*He Long Selected Military Writings*] (Beijing: Jiefangjun, 1989) have proven very useful from the civilian/diplomatic and military sides, respectively. Also informative are the biographies of Zhu De, Peng Dehuai, Chen Yi, He Long, Luo Ronghuai, Nie Rongzhen, Xu Xiangqian, Ye Jianying, Luo Ruiqing, and Su Yu, all published by Dangdai Zhongguo in Beijing in the 1990s. While there are numerous series and individual volumes of reminiscences and biographies of PLA commanders (some of which are referred to in the notes), the long disgraced Lin Biao—perhaps the foremost CCP general of the civil war era—still lacks proper biographical attention.

c. Democratic Parties

Not surprisingly, there is much less available on the democratic and liberal parties and groups than on the two main parties. Dou Aizhi, *Zhongguo minzhu dang pai shi* [*A History of the Democratic Parties and Groups in China*] (Tianjin: Nankai daxue, 1992), provides a good overview, and Wang Chaoguang's volume on 1945–46 (see section II) is an excellent balanced treatment. Edmund S. K. Fung, *In Search of Chinese Democracy: Civil Opposition in Nationalist China, 1929–1949* (Cambridge: Cambridge University Press, 2000), puts the civil war period into a wider perspective.

Zhongguo qingnian dang [*The China Youth Party*] (Beijing: Dang'an, 1988), is a fair but brief introduction to one of the democratic parties.

X. Negotiations

The place to begin is with the records of the negotiations themselves, many of which are included in Chongqing shi zhengxie wenshi ziliao yanjiu weiyuanhui and Zhonggong Chongqing shiwei dangxiao, comps., *Zhengzhi xieshang huiyi ji shi* [*History and Records of the Political Consultative Conference*], 2 vols. (Chongqing: Chongqing, 1989); and *Chongqing tanpan ziliao* [*Materials on the Chongqing Negotiations*], 2d ed. (Chengdu: Sichuan renmin, 1982). The best historical overview is still Niu Jun, *Cong Hu'erli dao Maxie'er: Meiguo tiaochu GuoGong maodun shimo* [*From Hurley to Marshall: The Full Story of American Mediation of the GMD-CCP Conflict*] (Fuzhou: Fujian renmin, 1989). For the CCP's records of the Marshall mission, see Zhongyang wenxian yanjiu shi, comp., *Zhou Enlai 1946 nian tanpan wenxuan* [*Selected Negotiation Documents of Zhou Enlai in 1946*] (Beijing: Zhongyang wenxian, 1996). See also Liang Jingtun, *Maxie'er shihua baogao shu jian chu* [*Marshall's Mission to China: A Commentary on the Report*] (Taibei: Zhongyang yanjiuyuan jindaishi yanjiusuo, 1994); and Chongqing shiwei dangshi gongzuo wenyuanhui et al., eds., *Chongqing tanpan jishi, 1945 nian 8–10 yue* [*A Record of the Chongqing Nego-*

tiations] (Chongqing: Chongqing, 1983). Huang Youlan et al., *Zhengqu heping minzhu, 1945–1946* [*Fighting for Peace and Democracy, 1945–1946*] (Shanghai: Shanghai renmin, 1995), discusses the period up to the outbreak of civil war in a broader perspective. Larry I. Bland, ed., *George C. Marshall's Mediation Mission to China* (Lexington, VA: George C. Marshall Foundation, 1998), includes contributions by American and Chinese scholars.

XI. The Military

While the literature in Chinese on the military aspects of the civil war is prodigious, especially on the Communist side, there are very few informed treatments available in English. Lionel Max Chassin, *The Communist Conquest of China: A History of the Civil War,* trans. Timothy Osato and Louis Gelas (Cambridge, MA: Harvard University Press, 1965), is probably still the best overall discussion. The most comprehensive Chinese account is Junshi kexueyuan junshi lishi yanjiubu, comp., *Zhongguo renmin jiefangjun quanguo jiefang zhanzhengshi* [*A History of PLA's War to Liberate the Whole Country*], 5 vols. (Beijing: Junshi kexue, 1997), and the best detailed overview in Chinese is the four volumes entitled battle histories of the First, Second, Third, and Fourth PLA Field Armies: *Zhongguo renmin jiefangjun diyi yezhanjun zhanshi* (1995); *Zhongguo renmin jiefangjun dier yezhanjun zhanshi* (1991); *Zhongguo renmin jiefangjun disan yezhanjun zhanshi* (1996); and *Zhongguo renmin jiefangjun disi yezhanjun zhanshi* (1998). Chen Lian, *Juzhan de licheng* [*The Course of the Decisive Battle*] (Hefei: Anhui renmin, 1991), attempts to cover both the GMD and CCP perspectives.

Li Huade, *GuoGong jun-zheng da bodou* [*The Great Military and Political Struggle between the GMD and the CCP*] (Hong Kong: Zhongyuan, 1993), shows the connections between political and military decisions. Du Yuming et al., *GuoGong neizhan milu* [*The Secret History of the GMD-CCP Civil War*] (Taibei: Papilun, 1991), is a summing up from the GMD perspective.

Huang Youlan, *Zhongguo renmin jiefang zhanzheng shi* [*A History of the Chinese People's Liberation War*] (Beijing: Dang'an, 1992); Ji Haijie, *Xiong ba tian xia: Kangzhan hou Guo Gong liang dang da jiaofeng jishi* [*A History of the Great Clash between the GMD and the CCP after the War against Japan*] (Beijing: Zhongyang bianyi, 1994); and Jiang Kefu, *Guo Gong liang jun de erci guonei zhanzheng* [*The Second Civil War between the GMD and CCP Armies*], 2 vols. (Beijing: Zhonghua shudian, 1995), are all good general treatments. Jiang Siyi and Sun Jingyun, chief eds., *Zai jiefang zhangzheng zhong fengfu fazhan* [*The Rich Development during the War of Liberation*] (Beijing: Jiefangjun, 1991), concentrates on the political work in the PLA during the civil war.

XII. Battles

No aspect of war fascinates as much as battles, and nothing is more difficult to portray in writing. Of the major battles of the Chinese civil war, HuaiHai is best covered so far, through Jiang Shen, *HuaiHai zhi zhan* [*The HuaiHai Battle*] (Beijing: Jiefangjun, 1992); Huai Bing, *Xubang huizhan* [*The Terrible Battle of Xu-*

bang] (Taibei: Yaosheng wenhua, 1993); and the extensive Zhonggong zhong-yang dangshi ziliao zhengji weiyuanhui, comp., *HuaiHai zhanyi* [*The Battle of HuaiHai*], 3 vols. (Beijing: Zhonggong dangshi ziliao, 1988). Zhongguo renmin jiefangjun lishi ziliao congshu bianshen weiyuanhui, ed., *HuaiHai zhanyi huiyi shiliao* [*Memoirs and Historical Materials on the HuaiHai Battle*] (Beijing: Jie-fangjun, 1988), has some eyewitness accounts by common PLA soldiers; see also section XVII.

The battles in North China are dealt with in Chou Jianxin et al., *PingJin zhanyi shilu* [*A Historical Record of the Beijing-Tianjin Battle*] (Shijiazhuang: Hebei ren-min, 1997), and those in the Shandong area in Jinan shi bowuguan, *Jinan zhanyi ziliaoxuan* [*Selected Documents and Materials on the Battle for Jinan*] (Jinan: n.p., 1979); Zhonggong Shandong shengwei dangshi ziliao zhengji yanjiu weiyuanhui et al., comps., *Jinan zhanyi* [*The Battle of Jinan*] (Jinan: n.p., 1988); and *Quanguo jiefang zhanzheng shi ji Shandong zhongyao zhanyi ziliao congshu* [*A Collection of Materials on the Main Battles in Shandong during the War of Liberation*] (Jinan: n.p., 1988). The main clashes in Central China are presented in Zhonggong Kaifeng shiwei dangshi bangongshi, comp., *Yudong zhanyi* [*The Battle for Yudong*] (Zhengzhou: Henan renmin, 1988); and *Kaifeng zhanyi ziliao xuanbian* [*Selected Materials on the Battle of Kaifeng*] (Kaifeng: Henan renmin, 1980). For the PLA's campaign to cross the Yangzi River, see Zhongguo renmin jiefangjun lishi ziliao bianshen weiyuanhui, comp., *Dujiang zhanyi* [*The Cam-paign to Cross the Yangzi River*] (Beijing: Jiefangjun, 1995). The campaigns in the Northwest—from Shanxi to Xinjiang—are discussed in Jiao Beiguo, *Zhuanzhan Shanbei diyinian* [*The First Year of Military Change in Northern Shaanxi*] (Hoh-hot: Nei Menggu xinhua shudian, 1985); Cheng Xiulong, *Jiefang Taiyuan zhi zhan* [*The Battle for the Liberation of Taiyuan*] (Taiyuan: Shanxi renmin, 1982); Li Yanxing, *Huang tudi, hong tudi: zhuanzhan Shaanbei juan* [*Yellow Earth, Red Earth: A Book on the Shifting Battles in Northern Shaanxi*] (Beijing: Jiefangjun, 1992); Zhang Zhunbiao, *Ao bing Xibei* [*Hard Battle for the Northwest*] (Beijing: Jiefangjun, 1989); Zheng Weishan, *Cong Huabei dao Xibei: Yi jiefang zhang-zheng* [*From North China to the Northwest: Remembering the War of Libera-tion*] (Lanzhou: Jiefangjun, 1985); and Zhonggong Qinghai shengwei dangshi zi-liao zhengji weiyuanhui and Zhongguo renmin jiefangjun Qinghai shengjunqu zhengzhibu, eds., *Jiefang Qinghai huace* [*The Brilliant Strategy to Liberate Qing-hai*] (Xining: Qinghai renmin, 1989). The final battles in Southwest China are covered in Chen Shengnian and Hu Ronggui, *Jiefang Yunnan zhi zhan* [*The Bat-tle for the Liberation of Yunnan*], 2d ed. (Kunming: Yunnan renmin, 1984).

XIII. The Northeast (Manchuria)

By far the best volume on the civil war period in the Northeast is Steven I. Levine, *Anvil of Victory: The Communist Revolution in Manchuria, 1945–1948* (New York: Columbia University Press, 1987). Ding Xiaochun et al., eds., *Dong-bei jiefang zhanzheng dashiji* [*Chronology of the Liberation War in the North-east*] (Beijing: Zhonggong dangshi ziliao, 1987); as well as Liu Tong, *Dongbei jiefangzhanzheng jishi* [A Factorial Record of the War of Liberation in the Northeast] (Beijing: Dongfang, 1997), provides a useful overview, while Chong-sik Lee, *Revolutionary Struggle in Manchuria: Chinese Communism and Soviet Interest, 1922–1945* (Berkeley: University of California Press, 1983), gives some of the historical background. For LiaoShen, see the two-volume *LiaoShen juezhan* and *LiaoShen juezhan: xuji* [*The Decisive Battle for Liaoning and Shenyang: Sequel*] (Beijing: Renmin, 1988, 1992), both edited by Zhonggong zhongyang dangshi ziliao zhengji weiyuanhui et al.; and Zhongguo renmin jiefangjun lishi ziliao congshu bianshen weiyuanhui, ed., *LiaoShen zhanyi* (Beijing: Jifangjun, 1993). Zhang Zhenglong, *Xuebai xuehong: Liaoning zhanyi juan* [*White Snow, Red Blood: A Book about the Liaoning Campaign*] (Beijing: Jiefangjun, 1989), is a dramatic but well-written account of the LiaoShen campaign in reportage form.

XIV. The South

The civil war in the South is still a relatively unexplored topic. Lao Jia et al., *Nan Zhongguo: San da zhanyi zhihou de Zhongguo zhanchang* [*South China: The Three Great Battles at the End of the Struggle for China*] (Beijing: Tuanjie, 1993), gives a general overview, while *Hunan heping jiefang zhuanji* [*The Quick and Peaceful Liberation of Hunan*] (Changsha: Hunan wenshi, 1989); and Zhonggong Zhejiang shengwei dangshi ziliao zhengzhi yanjiu weiyuanhui and Zhongguo renmin jiefangjun Zhejiang shengjunqu weiyuanhui, eds., *Zhejiang jiefang* [*Liberating Zhejiang*] (Hangzhou: Zhejiang renmin, 1989), show developments in these two provinces, respectively.

XV. Espionage

In addition to the individual accounts mentioned in the notes, Fu Qianwen, *Da daoge: Zhonggong cefan shilu* [*Great Defections: A Record of the CCP's Incitement to Rebel*] (Hong Kong: Liwen, 1995); and Ge Jun, *Zhongguo gongchandang baiqu douzheng shi* [*The Chinese Communist Party's Struggle in the White Areas*] (Beijing: Renmin, 1996), give fair overviews of both CCP and GMD strategies. For an informative (though not always accurate) survey of the CCP's espionage activities, see Xu Wenlong, *Zhonggong tegong: Dixia douzheng de yingxiong* [*CCP Special Agents: Heroes in Underground Struggles*] (Xining: Qinghai renmin, 1996). For a memoir by a top CCP spy within the Guomindang, see Xiong Xianghui, *Dixia shiernian he Zhou Enlai* [*Twelve-year Underground Activities and Zhou Enlai*] (Beijing: Zhongyang dangxiao, 1991).

XVI. Minorities

There are almost no separate studies of Chinese ethnic minorities during the civil war. For Tibet, see Melvyn C. Goldstein, with the help of Gelek Rimpoche, *A History of Modern Tibet, 1913–1951* (Berkeley: University of California Press, 1989); or, from a Chinese point of view, Ji Yuquan, *Bai xue: Jiefang Xizang jishi* [*White Blood: The History of Liberating Tibet*] (Beijing: Zhongguo wuzi, 1993); on Mongolia, see Liu Xiaoyuan, "The Kuomintang and the 'Mongolian Question' in the Chinese Civil War, 1945–1949," *Inner Asia*, 1 (1999):169–94; on

Xinjiang, see David D. Wang, *Under the Soviet Shadow: The Yining Incident: Ethnic Conflicts and International Rivalry in Xinjiang 1944–1949* (Hong Kong: Chinese University Press, 1999).

XVII. Foreign Affairs

a. General

While foreign affairs are perhaps the best researched of all aspects of the civil war, there are still lacunae in our knowledge. The place to begin for the Sino-U.S. relationship is Dorothy Borg and Waldo Heinrichs, eds., *Uncertain Years: Chinese-American Relations, 1947–1950* (New York: Columbia University Press, 1980); and, from a Chinese perspective, Zi Zhongyun, *Meiguo duiHua zhengce de yuanqi he fazhan* [*The Origins and Development of American China Policy, 1945–1950*] (Chongqing: Chongqing, 1987). The memoirs of U.S. diplomats—John Service, John Melby, and others—who served in China at the time are also useful, as are Nancy Tucker, *Patterns in the Dust: Chinese-American Relations and the Recognition Controversy, 1949–1950* (New York: Columbia University Press, 1983); Harry Harding and Yuan Ming, eds., *Sino-American Relations, 1945–1955: A Joint Reassessment of a Critical Decade* (Wilmington, DE: Scholarly Resources, 1989); and Lanxin Xiang, *Recasting the Imperial Far East: Britain and America in China, 1945–1950* (Armonk, NY: M. E. Sharpe, 1995).

With increased access to primary sources beginning in the late 1980s, scholarly interest focused on the mindsets and motivations behind the CCP-U.S. conflict. Some of the best work has been done by historians working in China. Niu Jun's two books, *Cong He'erli dao Maxie'er* and *Cong Yan'an zouxiang shijie: Zhongguo gongchandang duiwai guanxi de qiyuan* [*From Yan'an to the World: The Origins of the Chinese Communist Party's Foreign Relations*] (Fuzhou: Fujian renmin, 1992), are outstanding. Tao Wenzhao's *ZhongMei guanxi shi: 1911–1950* (Chongqing: Chongqing, 1993), and *KangRi zhanzheng shiqi Zhongguo duiwai guanxi* [*Chinese Foreign Relations during the Anti-Japanese War*] (Beijing: Zhonggong dangshi, 1995), are useful background, as is Zhang Jishun, *Zhongguo zhishifenzi de Meiguo guan, 1943–1953* [*Chinese Intellectuals View the United States*] (Shanghai: Fudan daxue, 1999). Odd Arne Westad, *Cold War and Revolution: Soviet-American Rivalry and the Origins of the Chinese Civil War, 1944–1946* (New York: Columbia University Press, 1993), explores the interaction between domestic and international factors in the outbreak of civil war. Michael H. Hunt, *The Genesis of Chinese Communist Foreign Policy* (New York: Columbia University Press, 1996), is an expert analysis of the historical origins of CCP foreign affairs. Michael M. Sheng's *Battling Western Imperialism: Mao, Stalin, and the United States* (Princeton: Princeton University Press, 1997), emphasizes the ideological perspectives. See also the contributions by Warren I. Cohen, Chen Jian, Michael Sheng, John Garver, and Odd Arne Westad in the symposium "Rethinking the Lost Chance in China," *Diplomatic History* 21 (1997): 71–115; and Thomas J. Christensen, "A 'Lost Chance' for What? Rethinking the Origins of U.S.-PRC Confrontation," *Journal of American-East Asian Relations* 4, no. 3 (1995): 249–78.

For Sino-Soviet relations during the civil war, the older literature is of less relevance, and the best starting point is Dieter Heinzig's exhaustive *Die Sowjetunion und das kommunistische China, 1945–1950* [*The Soviet Union and Communist China, 1945–1950*] (Baden-Baden: Nomos, 1998). Odd Arne Westad, ed., *Brothers in Arms: The Rise and Fall of the Sino-Soviet Alliance, 1945–1963* (Washington, DC, and Stanford, CA: Woodrow Wilson Center Press and Stanford University Press, 1998), provides an overview of the alliance, and John Garver, *Chinese-Soviet Relations, 1937–1945: The Diplomacy of Chinese Nationalism* (New York: Oxford University Press, 1988), analyzes the historical background. Yang Kuisong's two books *Zhonggong yu Mosike de guanxi, 1920–1960* [*The Relationship between the CCP and Moscow, 1920–1960*] (Taibei: Dongda, 1997), and *Mao Zedong yu Mosike de enen-yuanyuan* [*The Love-Hate Relationship between Mao Zedong and Moscow*] (Nanchang: Jiangxi renmin, 1999), are the best accounts in Chinese.

Chen Jian's magisterial *Mao's China and the Cold War* (Chapel Hill: University of North Carolina Press, 2001), places the civil war period into a wider context, and has an excellent bibliographical essay at the end.

b. Korea, Vietnam, and Southeast Asia

Chen Jian, *China's Road to the Korean War: The Making of the Sino-American Confrontation* (New York: Columbia University Press, 1994), is the best overview of China's entry into the war. Sergei N. Goncharov, John Wilson Lewis, and Xue Litai, *Uncertain Partners: Stalin, Mao, and the Korean War* (Stanford, CA: Stanford University Press, 1993), is an early view based on Russian sources, and should be complemented by forthcoming work by Kathryn Weathersby and Alexandre Mansourov. For China's role in the Korean War, see Shu Guang Zhang, *Mao's Military Romanticism: China and the Korean War 1950–1953* (Lawrence: University of Kentucky Press, 1995), is the best overview, but see also Chen Jian, "China's Changing Aims during the Korean War, 1950–1951," *Journal of American-East Asian Relations* 1, no. 1 (1992): 8–41. For representative Chinese language studies, see Xu Yan, *Diyici jiaoliang* [*The First Test of Strength*] (Beijing: Zhongguo guangbo dianshi, 1991); Shen Zhihua, *Mao Zedong, Sidalin yu hanzhan* [*Mao Zedong, Stalin and the Korean War*] (Hong Kong: Tiandi, 1998); and Junshi kexueyuan junshi lishi yanjiubu, comp., *Kangmei yuanchao zhanzheng shi* [*A History of the War to Resist America and Assist Korea*], 3 vols. (Beijing: Junshi kexue, 2000). The connection between the Korean War and Chinese domestic developments still awaits proper historical treatment.

For Vietnam, Zhai Qiang's comprehensive study *China and the Vietnam Wars, 1950–1975* (Chapel Hill: University of North Carolina Press, 2000), is the new starting point, but Chen Jian, "China and the First Indo-China War, 1950–1954," *China Quarterly* 133 (1993): 85–110, is also useful. *Zhongguo junshi guwentuan yuanyue kangfa douzheng shishi* [*A Factual Account of the Participation of the Chinese Military Advisory Group in the Struggle to Assist Vietnam and Resist France*] (Beijing: Jiefangjun, 1990), provides much important information, as do the diaries of the head of the Advisory Group, *Chen Geng riji* [*Chen Geng Diaries*] (Beijing: Jiefangjun, 1984). See also Huang Zhen, *Hu Zhiming yu Zhongguo* [*Ho Chi Minh and China*] (Beijing: n.p., 1987).

There is very little literature on the interactions between the Chinese revolution and the countries of Southeast Asia. Kwei-chiang Chui, *The Response of the Malayan Chinese to Political and Military Developments in China, 1945–1949* (Singapore: Institute of Humanities and Social Sciences, College of Graduate Studies, Nanyang University, 1977), is a starting point for Malaya, but much more needs to be done.

XVIII. Taiwan

The best study of the Taiwan uprising against the Guomindang is Lai Tse-han, Ramon T. Myers, and Wei Wou, *A Tragic Beginning: The Taiwan Uprising of February 28, 1947* (Stanford, CA: Stanford University Press, 1991), but it should be supplemented by Günter Whittome, *Taiwan 1947: Der Aufstand gegen die Kuomintang* (Hamburg: Institut für Asienkunde, 1991). Social and economic conditions are well covered in Liu Jinqing, *Taiwan zhanhou jingji* [*The Taiwan Economy after the War*] (Taibei: n.p., 1992). There are far too few studies of the reorganization of the Guomindang on Taiwan, but a starting point is Bruce J. Dickson, "The Lessons of Defeat: The Reorganization of the Kuomintang on Taiwan, 1950–1952," *China Quarterly* 133 (March 1993): pp. 56–84. For U.S. policies, see David Michael Finkelstein, *Washington's Taiwan Policy, 1949–1950: From Abandonment to Salvation* (Fairfax, VA: George Mason University Press, 1993), and Robert Accinelli, *Crisis and Commitment: United States Policy toward Taiwan, 1950–1955* (Chapel Hill: University of North Carolina Press, 1996). The CCP's strategy is covered in Xu Yan, *Jinmen zhi zhan, 1949–1959* [*The battles for Jinmen, 1949–1959*] (Beijing: Zhongguo dianshi guangbo, 1992); and He Di, "The Last Campaign to Unify China: The CCP's Unmaterialized Plan to Liberate Taiwan, 1949–1950," *Chinese Historians* 5 (1992): 1–16. Pei Kequan, *Taigong panluan ji fuwang jingguo jishi* [*Record of the Rebellion and Defeat of the Taiwanese Communists*] (Taibei: Shangwu yinshuguan, 1986), provides some useful information on the crushing of the Taiwanese Communist movement.

XIX. First Years of the PRC

We still lack good, comprehensive studies of the first years of the PRC. Frederick Teiwes, *Politics at Mao's Court: Gao Gang and Party Factionalism in the Early 1950s* (Armonk, NY: M. E. Sharpe, 1990), is a good beginning for CCP politics; Li Zhancai and Zhang Lifu, *Zhongguo xinminzhuzhuyi jingji shi* [*An Economic History of Chinese New People's Democracy*] (Hefei: Anhui jiaoyue, 1990), gives an overview of economic developments during the first years; and Zhongguo shehui kexueyuan and Zhongyang dang'anguan, comps., *Zhonghua renmin gongheguo jingji dang'an ziliao xuanbian, 1949–1952* [*Selected Archival Materials on the Economy of the People's Republic of China, 1949–1952*] (Beijing: Zhongguo wusi, 1990–), is an ongoing document series with volumes on individual industries. Zhongyang wenxian yanjiushi, comp., *Jianguo yilai zhongyao wenxian huibian* [*A Collection of Important Documents since the Founding of the People's Republic*] (Beijing: Zhongyang wenxian, 1992–), is the best published collection of PRC policy documents.

XX. Eyewitness Accounts

In writing this history, I have found contemporary eyewitness accounts to be both helpful and entertaining. Some of the best are: Knight Biggerstaff, *Nanking Letters, 1949* (Ithaca, NY: China-Japan Program, Cornell University, 1979), which deals with the situation in Nanjing before and after the CCP takeover; Derk Bodde, *Peking Diary: A Year of Revolution* (London: Jonathan Cape, 1951); and Mariano Ezpeleta, *Red Shadows over Shanghai* (Quezon City: Zita, 1972), a Philippine diplomat's colorful account of the fall of Shanghai. William Hinton's *Fanshen* is unsurpassed in telling the history of land-reform at the village level, while Raymond J. de Jaegher and Irene Corbally Kuhn, *The Enemy Within: An Eyewitness Account of the Communist Conquest of China* (Garden City, NY: Doubleday, 1953), is written from the perspective of an anti-Communist missionary. Fritz Jensen, *China siegt [China Victorious]* (Berlin: Dietz, 1950), is perhaps the best overall view by a foreign Communist. There are some excellent Chinese battle accounts available—Feng Yilu, *Xubang zhanyi jianwenlu [Eyewitness Accounts of the Xubang Battle]* (Hong Kong: Xiandai, 1970); and Zhi Xia, *Zhanyi riji: HuaiHai zhanyi jianwenlu [Battle Diary: An Eyewitness Account of the HuaiHai Battle]* (Shanghai: Shanghai wenyi, 1993), give insights into those horrors of war that no history will be able to capture.

Index

In this index an "f" after a number indicates a separate reference on the next page, and an "ff" indicates separate references on the next two pages. A continuous discussion over two or more pages is indicated by a span of page numbers, e.g., "57–59."

Academy for the Study of Carrying Out Revolution (GMD), 290
Acheson, Dean, 291
Administration: GMD, 70–72, 74–75; in rural areas, 80–83; CCP, 229–30, 263–64, 269–70
Aid, 241; U.S., 161f, 186, 188, 190; Soviet, 165f, 235, 263, 266
Alliances, 9–10, 116, 255, 329; with United States, 159–61
Amethyst, HMS, 244–45
Anhui province, 47, 82, 172
Anshan, 177
Anti-American protests, 140
Anti-communism: U.S., 186f, 291
Antiforeign movement, 101
Anti-Japanese war, 151, 333n4
Antiwar movement, 99–100
Armies, 17; supplying, 4–5, 113–14; in Manchuria, 84f; GMD, 148–51, 155f, 157–58, 290–91. *See also* National Army; People's Liberation Army; *various subdivisions by name*
Arms embargo: U.S., 49, 160
Art, artists: and GMD, 96–97
Atlee, Clement, 286
Australia, 309

Ba Jin: *Hanye*, 98
Badger, Oscar, 161
Bai Chongxi, 147, 170–71, 172, 182, 190, 206, 215, 233, 237, 239, 244, 287; defense of Guangxi, 282–85, 286
Bandit chiefs, 113
Bandits, banditry, 125ff
Bao Erhan (Burhan Shahidi), 289
Baoji, 254f
Barr, David, 161, 186

Beijing, 77, 101, 103, 197, 200, 210, 223, 244, 299, 364n32; student movement in, 140–41; CCP, 142f, 216, 228; PLA attack on, 226–27; Mao Zedong and, 221–22; as CCP capital, 259–60
Beijing-Liaoning railway, 173
Belden, Jack, 2
Bianco, Lucien, 2
Black market, 183, 253
Blockades, 262, 307
Bo Yibo, 269
Bohai Gulf, 177, 189
Bourgeoisie, 182, 247; and CCP, 78–79, 138–39, 278; international class struggle and, 267–68
Brilliant Sun (Yanyang tian) (film), 99
Bund (Shanghai), 251
Burhan Shahidi (Bao Erhan), 289
Burma: GMD in, 301–2
Businesses, 95; GMD and, 73–74, 183f; CCP and, 239, 262

Cadres, 5, 107, 127, 229, 277; defections of, 61–62; land reform and, 116f, 136; CCP and, 130–31, 134f, 277; urban, 139–40; government organization and, 230f, 261–62, 269–70; in rural areas, 280–81; in South China, 284f; nationalism and, 324–25
Caiwa, 208
Campaign to Suppress Counter-Revolutionary Activities, 327
Cao Manzhi, 278
Capital flight, 89
CC, *see* Central Committee
CC-Clique, 52, 75, 164, 182, 347n17
CCP, *see* Chinese Communist Party
Ceng Zesheng, 197

Censorship, 97, 205, 252
Central China, 46, 190, 197–98, 270, 279
Central Committee (CC), CCP, 38–39, 115, 137
Central Committee (DL), 192
Central Plains: and PLA, 111f; CCP offensive in, 168–72, 188; food supply in, 209–10
Central Revolutionary Military Committee (CRMC), 115
Changchun, 35, 41, 178, 189, 192, 194, 197
Changsha, 284
Charismatic movement: CCP as, 5–6, 13, 30
Chassin, Lionel, 2
Chen Bulei, 142
Chen Changjie, 225–26
Chen Cheng, 172–73, 176, 249
Chen Guofu, 347n17
Chen Lian, 142
Chen Liang, 248, 250
Chen Lifu, 52, 75f, 152, 182, 287, 347n17
Chen Shutong, 265
Chen Yi (CCP army commander), 46, 150, 169, 244, 251, 283, 352n5; in Shandong, 157–59; Central Plains offensive and, 170, 190; HuaiHai offensive, 201ff, 206, 207–8; and Yangzi offensive, 241, 243
Chen Yi (GMD Taiwan governor), 154f, 358n15
Chen Yun, 124f, 128, 269, 352n13
Cheng Qian, 283–84
Chengdu, 288
Chenguanzhuang, 207
China Aid Act, 186
China Lobby, 187
China Sugar Company, 249
China White Paper, 307–8
Chinese Communist Party (CCP), 2, 7f, 17, 23, 28, 31, 91, 115, 255, 330f; as charismatic movement, 5–6; alliance-building by, 9–10; and land reform, 10–11, 38–40, 113–14, 116–18, 135–37, 230–31; and political power, 12–13; Jiang Jieshi and, 25, 32, 41–43; leadership of, 26–27, 38, 129–30, 269–70; growth of, 29–30; and Manchuria, 35–36, 53, 83, 85f, 121–28, 173–76; strategies of, 39–40; Zhou Enlai and, 44–45; defeats of, 47–48, 61–62; and Soviet Union, 49–50, 119–21, 165–67, 216–18, 231–33, 235–36, 262–63, 265–69, 318–19, 359n43; and United States, 51–52, 237, 306–8; National Assembly and, 57–58; propaganda by,

60–61; military strategies of, 63–64, 153–54, 188–89, 190–91, 204–5, 241–42; GMD and, 72, 299, 301; and labor unions, 77–78; bourgeoisie and, 78–79; rural peasants and, 82, 107–8, 169–70; student movement and, 102, 140–41; militarization of, 109, 111–12, 328–29; ethnic minorities and, 118–19, 234–35; village policies and, 128–32; in cities, 137–43, 183–84; working class and, 142–43, 273–74; retreat from Yan'an by, 152–53; and siege of Siping, 156–57; and Shandong, 157–58; Central Plains offensive of, 168–72; Winter Offensive of, 175–77; and regional politics, 191–92; military campaigns of, 192–93, 216–17; LiaoShen campaign of, 193–99; HuaiHai campaign of, 205–11; Tianjin and, 225–26; and North China, 227–28; government organization by, 228–20, 233–34, 260–65, 272–73; negotiations with, 240–41, 243–44; gunboat Amethyst and, 244–45; and Shanghai, 247, 249–53; and foreign diplomats, 253–54; in Beijing, 259–60; economic planning and, 261–62; security for, 270–71; financial system and, 275–76; middle class and, 276–77; mass media and, 278–79; in rural areas, 279–82; and Xinjiang, 288–89; and Vietnam, 301, 316–18; in Tibet, 302–3; foreign policy and, 308–9; and Korean War, 321–23; political strategies of, 324–25; governance of, 327–28
Chinese Labor Association (CLA), 76
Chinese Military Advisory Group, 318
Chinese People's Volunteers, 323
Chinese Soviet Republic, 118
Chongqing, 28, 70, 98, 139; GMD in, 286–88
Christians, Christianity, 96, 187, 274
CIA, 292, 302, 307
Cities, 56, 77, 273; GMD and, 70f; CCP in, 78–79, 137–43, 321; women in, 90–91; student movement in, 140–41; economic crisis in, 183–84; GMD authority in, 184–85
Civil Air Transport, 292
CLA, see Chinese Labor Association
Clans, 274, 280
Class struggle, 118, 127, 267–68
Cold War, 4, 286; GMD and, 9, 42, 65, 164, 185; U.S.-Soviet rivalry and, 52, 160; and China, 186–87
Collaboration, collaborators, 7, 83, 127, 133
Colonialism: in East Asia, 18–19

Comintern (Third International), 22
Concessions: foreign, 94
Confucianism, 56, 107–8
Consort, HMS, 245
Corruption, 169, 229; GMD, 11, 29, 72–74, 85, 182ff; crackdown on, 184–85
Costa Rica, 250
CRMC, *see* Central Revolutionary Military Committee
Currency: reforming, 184f
Currency speculation, 89

Da gong bao (newspaper), 78
Dabie Mountains, 46–47, 171–72
Dalai Lama, 91f, 93f, 303
Dalian (Port Arthur), 173
Daoists, 274
Defections: GMD, 192, 197, 200–201, 243, 288
Democratic League (DL), 45, 55–56, 58f, 124, 191f, 224, 264; banning of, 164–65; in Shanghai, 247–48
Deng Hua, 175
Deng Liqun, 289
Deng Xiaoping, 46, 112, 117, 168, 201, 244, 251; and Dabie Mountains, 171–72; and HuaiHai campaign, 202f, 206, 207–8
Dengbu, 301
Dewey, Thomas, 187, 198
Distant Love (Yaoyuan de ai; film), 99
DL, *see* Democratic League
Dong Biwu, 191, 352n13
Dongbei, *see* Manchuria
Du Yuesheng, 76, 247f
Du Yuming, 48, 83, 147, 157, 199; in Manchuria, 84–85, 122, 172; HuaiHai campaign and, 202–3, 206–7, 208–9

East Asia: colonialism in, 18–19; nationalism in, 22–23
East China army, 112
East Europeans, 249
East Turkestan Republic (ETR), 91–92
Eastern China, 192
Eastern Europe, 267
Eastman, Lloyd, 2
Economy, 29, 73, 188, 253; under GMD, 11, 26, 76–77, 88–89, 183–84; rural, 80–81; post-war, 86–88; women in, 90–91; CCP and, 253, 261–62, 275–76
Eighth Route Army, 122
88th division, 177
11th Army, 223
Elites, 56, 79; GMD, 8, 80, 165; land re-

form and, 11, 116. *See also* Intelligentsia; Landlords
Embargos: U.S. arms, 49, 160
Espionage, 142, 152, 173, 307
Ethnic minorities: rural areas, 17–18; nationalism of, 91–94; CCP and, 118–19, 264, 297; and government organization, 234–35
ETR, *see* East Turkestan Republic
Executions, 251

Factories, 262, 273f
Families, 280
Famine, 169
Fan Hanjie, 190, 195f
Fenghua, 219
5th Army (GMD), 176, 190
Films, 79, 98–99, 252; CCP control of, 278–79
Financial policy: GMD, 88–89, 183–84; CCP, 275–76
Financial reform, 184
Food supply: for armies, 4–5; for peasants, 209–10
Forbidden City, 260; symbolism of, 271f
Foreign policy, 65; PRC, 308–9, 315–16
Foreign relations: CCP, 244–45
Foreigners, 94–96, 101, 126; PLA and, 244–45; in Shanghai, 246, 248–50; CCP and, 253–54
Forman, Harrison, 2
Fourth Field Army, 241, 352n5
49th Army, 174–75
France, 18f, 301, 316, 317–18
Fu Dongju, 224
Fu Jingbo (Philip Fugh), 306
Fu Zuoyi (Fu Tso-i), 48, 147, 175, 186, 206, 224f, 233; and defense of Beijing, 222–23, 226–27
Fujian province, 26

Gang Zhuan, 287
Gangs, 247, 274
Gansu, 302, 374n40
Gao Chongmin, 124
Gao Gang, 124, 266, 268f, 321, 325, 352n13
GATT, *see* General Agreement on Tariffs and Trade
Gauss, Clarence E., 358n28
General Agreement on Tariffs and Trade (GATT), 51
Geng Biao, 223
Germany, 18, 23
GMD, *see* Guomindang
GMD loyalist movement, 100–101
GMD Revolutionary Committee, 243

GMD Southwest Military Region, 288
Gold reserves: GMD, 239–40
Gold Yuan, 184f
Government: GMD, 11–12, 70–72
Grand Canal, 47
Great Britain, 251, 253, 286; imperialism of, 18f; and Tibet, 91, 93; gunboat *Amethyst* and, 244–45; and PRC, 305f, 315–16
Great Leap Forward, 327
Green Gang, 248, 274
Gromyko, Andrei, 310
Gu Liu: *Xiaqiu zhuan*, 98
Gu Weijun, 159f
Gu Zhutong, 195
Guandong Army, 83
Guangdong, 280, 282, 284
Guangxi, 221, 243, 280–81, 288; Bai Chongxi's defense of, 282–85; Vietnam and, 316–17
Guangxi Clique, 220
Guangzhou, 21; GMD in, 23, 73, 183, 239, 285–86; Li Zongren in, 243f
Guerrillas: Communist, 30, 47f, 176
Guilin, 244, 285, 287
Guo Jingyun, 223–24
Guo Moruo, 265
Guohun (*The Spirit of China*) (film), 99
Guomindang (GMD), 2, 13, 53, 58, 61, 78, 112f, 249, 262, 299, 316; after World War II, 7–8; and CCP, 8–9, 108, 143, 233–34, 321; government, 11–12; regional control by, 23–24, 25–26, 69, 82–83; and Japanese invasion, 24–25, 29; and United States, 31–32, 42, 43–45, 49, 50–51, 159–61, 185–88, 197–98, 216, 291–92, 307–8; and Manchuria, 35–36, 63, 83–86, 172–73, 177–78; and Siping, 40–41, 156–57; war strategies of, 46–47; murder and intimidation by, 54–55; legitimacy of, 64–65; Jiang Jieshi's leadership of, 65–66, 74–75, 181–82; administration by, 70–72; corruption in, 72–74, 184–85; labor unrest and, 75–77; rural administration, 79–81; peasant resistance and, 81–82, 114; economic assistance to, 86–87; industrial policies, 87–88; and monetary policy, 88–89; ethnic nationalism and, 91–92; art and, 96–99; student movement and, 101–2; military strategies of, 147–48, 329; armies, 148–51; and Taiwan, 154f, 289–91; and Shandong, 157–59; and Soviet Union, 161–64; offensives against, 168, 170–71, 188–89; railway defense by, 174–75; and Winter Offensive, 176–77; leadership of, 182–83, 215–16; economic crisis of, 183–84; defense of Shanxi by, 189–90; defense of Kaifeng of, 190–91; defections from, 192, 197, 200–201, 243; defense of Jinzhou by, 195–96; HuaiHai campaign and, 201–11; Li Zongren and, 219–21, 238–39; defensive positions of, 222–24; defense of Tianjin by, 225–26; CCP administration and, 229–30; negotiations by, 240–41, 243–44; and Shanghai, 246–47, 248–49, 250–51; control of, 285–86; in Southeast Asia, 301–2; defense of Hainan, 304–5
Guomindang Revolutionary Committee, 264

Hainan, 299, 303, 304–5, 320
Haizhou, 193
Hangzhou, 219, 244, 249
Hanye (*Cold Nights*) (Ba Jin), 98
Harbin, 36, 124–25
He Long, 46, 112, 352n5
He Yingqin, 237, 240
Hebei, 82, 124, 135, 175, 203–4
Heishan, 196
Henan province, 48, 135, 169
Hillenkoetter, R. H., 238
Histories: revolutionary, 2–3
Ho Chi Minh, 301, 316, 317–18
Hometown associations, 274
Hong Kong, 89, 98f, 192, 248, 286f
Hong Kong Bureau (CCP), 316–17
Houhua, 61
Hu Feng, 271
Hu Zongnan (Hu Tsung-nan), 134, 142, 147, 206, 254f, 288; and Yan'an offensive, 150–52, 153–54; in Shanxhi, 189–90
Huai'an, 47
HuaiHai campaign, 9f, 192–93, 198f, 205–11, 224, 227, 232, 329; planning, 201–2; and Mao Zedong, 203–4, 221; defense of Beijing and, 222–23
Huai River, 192–93, 199, 206f
Huang Hua, 306
Huang Jie, 287
Huang Wei, 206f
Huangpu, 24
Huangpu River, 251
Hunan, 26, 134, 283–84
Hundred Regiments Offensive, 30
Hyperinflation, 89

Ichigo, 29f
Identity: ethnic, 17–18

Imperialism, 18–19, 324
Inchon, 321–22
India, 91, 93, 303
Indochina, 283
Industry: GMD policies on, 87–88
Inflation, 11, 88f, 188
Inglis, Admiral, 238
Inner Mongolia, 235
Intelligence, 142, 247; CCP, 192, 209, 321; U.S., 238, 307
Intelligentsia, 78, 381n2; in Shanghai, 247–48; CCP and, 273, 278
Intimidation: by GMD, 54–55
Italy, 18

Jacoby, Annalee, 2
Jaeger, Raymond de, 48
Japan, Japanese, 17, 94f, 129, 154; and China, 7, 70–71, 119; imperialism of, 18–19; attack on North China, 28–30; collapse of, 30–31; GMD use of, 71–72; and Manchuria, 83ff, 127; weapons, 112, 123
Jews, 95f, 249
Jiang Jieshi (Chiang Kai-shek), 7, 9, 12, 28, 31, 49, 69, 76, 114, 141, 147, 243; leadership of, 23f, 25f, 29, 30–31, 74–75, 181–82, 329; and United States, 31f, 42–45, 50–51, 53–54, 159–61, 186–88, 197–98, 291–92, 358n28; and Manchuria, 35, 83–84, 172–73, 176f; and Siping, 40–41; war strategy of, 46–47; National Assembly and, 57f, 165; and Taiwan, 58–59, 154f, 249, 255, 289–90, 292–93; and George Marshall, 60–61; government legitimacy and, 64–65, 73; and civil war, 65–66; administration by, 70–71, 74–75; rural administration and, 80, 82–83; military strategies of, 148f, 150–51, 189–90, 195, 197–98, 202, 206–7, 242; and Soviet Union, 161–62, 163–64; and Liu Bocheng's offensive, 170–71; financial reform, 184f; and Xuzhou, 199–200, 203; resignation of, 215–16, 365n1; and Li Zongren, 219–20, 226; in exile, 239–40; and Shanghai, 246, 248; and Bao Chongxi, 283f; in Guangzhou, 285–86; in Chongqing, 287–88
Jiang Jingguo (Chiang Ching-kuo), 75, 84, 184–85, 249, 288
Jiangsu, 46f, 172, 174–75, 249
Jiangxi, 284–85
Jiangxi Soviet, 129
Jiangyin Fort, 242–43
Jiaodong peninsula, 159

Jiehun (Marriage) (Shi Tuo), 97
Jilin, 41, 85, 127, 174
Jinan, 201
JinChaJi army, 111, 142, 153
JinJiLuYu army, 111–12, 352n5
Jinmen, 299, 301
JinSui army, 111, 352n5
Jinzhou, 192; CCP capture of, 193–94, 195–96

Kaifeng, 190–91
Kalgan, see Zhangjiakou
Kang Sheng, 111, 352n13, 355n51
Kasimi, Ahmed Jan, 92, 288f
Ke Zaishou, 140
Kim Il-sung, 313, 318, 319–20, 321–22
Korea, 19, 318–19
Korean War, 17, 282, 292, 318–19, 320; CCP and, 321–22, 327; Mao Zedong and, 322–24, 381n61; nationalism and, 324–25
Koreans, 126
Kovalev, Ivan, 268–69, 310, 312, 314
Kunming, 45, 54–55, 287
Kurile Islands, 313

Labor policy: GMD, 76–77
Labor unions, 91; GMD and, 74, 75–77; CCP and, 77–78, 138f, 142–43, 273, 274–75, 297
Land: redistribution of, 132–33
Land reform, 129, 132–33; CCP, 10–11, 29, 38–40, 107f, 116–18, 135–37, 230–31, 234, 280, 282, 327–38; and PLA recruitment, 112–13; militias and, 113–14; in Manchuria, 122, 126–28; terrorism, 133–34
Landlords, landowners, 20, 81, 108, 136, 340n11; and land reform, 38, 39–40, 133
Leadership: CCP, 5–6, 9, 11, 37f, 44, 129–30, 260–61, 265, 269–70; Jiang Jieshi's, 24ff, 29, 30–31, 64–65, 74–75, 148–49, 181–82; Mao Zedong's, 26–27, 115; land reform and, 116–17; GMD armies, 149–51; GMD, 182–83, 215–16; Li Zongren's, 219–21
Legitimacy: of GMD government, 64–65, 72–74, 85
Lenin, V. I., 22f
Leninism, 119
Li Fuchun, 124
Li Gongpu, 45, 54
Li Jishen, 265
Li Kenong, 209, 259, 310, 379n35
Li Mi, 47, 204, 302

Li Renren, 243
Li Xiannian, 47
Li Zhongxin, 191
Li Zongren (Li Tsung-jen), 147, 171, 182, 237, 247, 309; GMD leadership of, 215–16, 219–21, 243f, 286–87; and Jiang Jieshi, 226, 239–40, 285–86; CCP negotiations with, 233–34, 236, 240–41; GMD reform and, 238–39
Li Zoupeng, 175–77
Liang Huasheng, 85
Liang Shuming, 55
Liao Yaoxiang, 196
Liaodong peninsula, 177
Liaoning, 127, 174
LiaoShen campaign, 192, 193–97, 227, 329
Liaoxi-Shenyang campaign, 10
Liaoyang, 177
Liberated Areas, 137
Lieberman, Henry F., 204
Lin Biao, 35–36, 46, 48, 226, 237, 240, 259, 269, 319, 352n5; military strategies of, 63–64, 109, 155f, 172f, 174, 188–89, 192, 222, 225, 241; and Soviet Union, 120, 268; in Manchuria, 122–24; and Peng Zhen, 123–24; siege of Siping, 156–57; Winter Offensive, 175–77; LiaoShen campaign and, 193–96; in South China, 282ff, 285f
Lin Boqu, 259, 352n13
Lin Feng, 124
Lindsey, Michael, 35–36
Lippa, Ernest, 191
Literature: civil war, 97–98
Liu Bocheng, 46, 112, 117, 159, 174, 201, 241, 282, 284, 352n5; Central Plains offensive, 168f, 170f; and Kaifeng, 190–91; and HuaiHai campaign, 202, 206, 207–8
Liu Ren, 142
Liu Shaoqi, 11, 38, 40f, 44, 153, 191, 199, 259, 262, 270, 318, 321f, 325, 340n12, 352n13; and CCP politics, 60, 62, 111; on land reform, 116f; and Soviet Union, 119, 166, 253, 265–67, 268, 308, 311, 317; White area strategies, 138–39; and military strategies, 168, 243; on food production, 209–10; and government organization, 228–29, 230f, 234, 261, 263, 269; on working class, 273–74
Liu Zhi, 199f
Loans, 86, 94, 235, 253
London, HMS, 245
Long March, 27, 36
Long Yun, 83

Loyalist movement: GMD, 100–101
Lu Han, 287f
Luce, Henry, 186
Luo Guibo, 318

Ma Bufang, 254f
Malik, Adam, 316
Manchuria, 28, 32; GMD and, 8, 25, 43, 83–86, 147, 172–73, 189, 190, 319; CCP in, 9f, 31, 45, 53, 121–28, 192, 279; Soviet Union and, 31, 56, 119f, 166, 266, 314f; control of, 35–36, 42, 47–48, 63; CCP and, 36, 44; PLA in, 111, 188; military strategies in, 155–57, 174–75; Lin Biao's offensives in, 175–77, 193–99; Mao's victories in, 198–99
Manchurian Bureau of the Central Committee, 174
Mao Anying, 381n61
Mao Zedong, 8, 32, 40, 239, 270, 286, 325, 352n13; personality cult of, 5–6; leadership of, 9, 11, 26–27, 30, 115; and Jiang Jieshi, 31, 58; and Manchuria, 35f, 63, 125–26; and Lin Biao, 37, 193–94; and land reform, 38, 117–18, 135–36, 230–31; CCP strategy and, 44, 62, 129–30, 152; military strategies, 45–46, 63–64, 151f, 153–54, 155–56, 157f, 168–69, 171, 173–74, 175, 188–89, 190, 192, 198–99, 204–5, 221–22, 223, 226, 240, 251, 284, 338n22, 360n53; and United States, 51–52, 237–38, 306–7, 343n50; political strategies of, 58ff, 228ff, 233–34, 244–45, 297, 321, 327; and warfare, 108–9; rectification campaign of, 109–11; Soviet Union and, 119, 120–21, 165–67, 235–36, 255, 266–67, 310–11, 317–19; and Stalin, 167–68, 216–18, 232–33, 236, 262–63, 266, 311–15, 354n28, 380n46; and Winter Offensive, 176–77; LiaoShen campaign and, 193–94, 197; HuaiHai campaign, 198, 201, 203–4, 205–6, 207–8, 209f; peace proposals, 218–19; and Beijing, 221–22; and Marxism, 231–32; on ethnic minorities, 234–35, 289; on foreign relations, 245, 253–54; and Beijing, 259–60; government organization and, 260–61, 265; PRC and, 271, 305, 310, 372n24; GMD resistance and, 299, 301; and Hainan, 303–4; foreign policy, 308–9; and Korean War, 319–24, 381n61
Market production, 134–35, 253
Marriage law: CCP, 279

Marshall, George C., 31–32, 52, 60, 160ff, 185, 216; and Jiang Jieshi, 41–42, 43–44, 50–51, 53, 358n28
Martin, Joseph, 161
Marxism, 11, 22f, 231–32, 265, 328
Mass media, 159, 250; CCP control of, 278–79
May Fourth Directive, 38–39, 340n12
May Fourth movement, 90
Mediation, 41–42, 43, 45
Middle class: CCP and, 78–79, 138–39, 183–84, 273, 276–77, 282; art and, 96–99
Mikoyan, Anastas, 218, 233, 234–36, 262–63, 305, 309, 314, 378n25
Militarization: of CCP, 109, 111–12, 328–29
Military: GMD, 9f, 36, 71, 120, 147–48, 161; Soviet, 31, 35; U.S., 49f, 186, 187–88, 291f, 321–22; CCP, 108–9; Lin Biao's strategies, 122–23. See also People's Liberation Army
Military Committee (CCP), 241, 249
Military intelligence, 120, 238
Militias: CCP, 114
Mill workers, 143
MinNan dialect, 154
Minorities: CCP and, 118–19, 264, 297; government organization and, 234–35
Missionaries, 95–96, 134
Molotov, Vyacheslav, 314
Monetary policy: GMD, 88–89
Mongolia, 235
Moscow Declaration, 241
Most-favored-nation status, 51
Movies, see Films
Murders: by GMD, 45, 54–55
Muslims, 91–92, 93, 289

Nanjing, 28, 50, 90, 139, 154, 240, 253; GMD control of, 24, 41; student protests in, 56, 102; CCP control of, 243–44, 262
Nanjing decade, 25–26
Nanma campaign, 158
Nanning, 287
National Army, 48, 147; in Southeast Asia, 301–2
National Assembly, 165; politics of, 57–60; Tibetans and, 93–94
National consciousness, 56
Nationalism, 333n4; urban areas and, 21–22; East Asian, 22–23; ethnic, 91–94; Chinese, 95–96; CCP, 324–25
Nationalists, see Guomindang
Navy: British, 244–45

Nehru, Jawaharlal, 93
Netherlands, 19
New China, 297, 311; organization of, 228–36; recognition of, 305, 315–16
New Democratic Youth League, 264
New Fourth Army, 112, 352n5. See also East China army; Shandong army
Nie Rongzhen, 48, 153, 222f, 259
Nitze, Paul, 291
North China, 10, 20, 28, 111; GMD and, 25, 49; CCP in, 29, 45f, 48, 142, 152, 188, 227–28; military in, 122f; HuaiHai campaign in, 199, 200–211; government organization in, 229–30; United Nations and, 309–10
North China Bureau (CCP), 228
North China People's Government, 191
Northeast Administrative Committee, 124
Northeast Border Defense Army, 321, 323
Northeast China, see Manchuria
Northeast Democratic United Army, 111
Northeast Field Army, 157, 175
Northeast Headquarters of the Central Military Affairs Commission, 84
Northeast People's Liberation Army, 122–23
Northern Expedition, 24
North Korea, 48, 319f, 321f
North Manchurian railway, 64
Northwest China: PLA in, 254–55, 282; CCP control of, 288–89
Nothing But a Dream (movie), 79
Novels, 97–98

October Revolution (Russia), 270
Officers: GMD, 149–50
One Point, Two Flanks doctrine, 176
Opium Wars, 19
Organization Department (GMD), 75
Outer Mongolia, 235

Patterson, Robert P. (US Secretary of War), 160
PCC, see Political Consultative Conference
Peace delegations, 247
Peace negotiations, 217, 218–19, 224, 236, 238f; Li Zongren and, 240–41
Peasant associations, 130–31
Peasants, 17, 19, 80, 151, 340n11; food supply and, 4–5, 209–10; CCP land reform and, 10–11, 116ff; rural poverty and, 20–21; resistance by, 81–82, 374n40; CCP and, 107–8, 130–32, 279–82; PLA and, 112–13, 114, 169–70; in Manchuria, 122, 125–26;

market production, 135–36; in Dabie Mountains, 171–72
Peking (Beijing) University (BeiDa), 140, 227; BeiDa Student Union, 140
Peng Dehuai, 111, 151–52, 153, 174, 190, 209, 323, 352–53nn5, 13; in Northwest China, 254–55, 282, 289
Peng E, 177–78
Peng Zhen, 123–24, 259, 352n13
People's Courts (Shanghai), 253
People's Liberation Army (PLA), 10, 120, 135, 149, 187, 191, 233f, 237, 249, 266f, 270, 302, 318–19, 321, 352n5, 374n40; and land reform, 11, 118; in rural areas, 82, 107, 280; CCP militarization and, 109, 111–12; recruitment by, 112–13; supply and support of, 113–14; in Manchuria, 122–23, 126, 156–57, 175; siege of Siping, 156–57; in Shandong, 157–59; Central Plains offensive, 169–72; Winter Offensive of, 175–77; military strategies and, 188–89, 222, 329; LiaoShen campaign and, 193–99; defections to, 200–201; Huai-Hai campaign and, 202–11, 223–24; and Stalin, 216–18; in Beijing, 221, 226–27; and Tianjin, 225–26; Yangzi crossing by, 241–43; in Nanjing, 243–44; gunboat Amethyst and, 244–45; in Shanghai, 250–51; in Northwest China, 254–55, 288–89; students in, 276–77; in South China, 282–83, 284–85, 288; and Jinmin, 299, 301; and Hainan, 304–5. See also various armies; subdivisions by name
People's Republic of China (PRC), 2, 282, 292, 331; organization of, 265–70; security for, 270–71; declaration of, 271–72, 372n24; recognition of, 291, 305, 309–10, 315–16; and Soviet Union, 306, 311–17; and foreign policy, 308–9; and Vietnam, 317–18; and Korean War, 321, 323–24; governance by, 327–28
Pepper, Suzanne, 2
Personality cult: Mao Zedong's, 5–6
Philippines, 250
PLA, see People's Liberation Army
Playwrights, 96
Police: Shanghai, 74
Politburo, 115, 231; government organization and, 228, 229–30, 233–34
Political Consultative Conference (PCC), 192, 237, 263, 264–65, 267
Politics, 1, 107; Communist party control of, 12–13; CCP, 30, 108–9, 191–92; Manchurian, 122, 124–26; village, 128–29

Port Arthur, 313
Poverty, 20–21, 107
PRC, see People's Republic of China
Preparatory Commission (CCP), 263–65
Price regulation, 88, 184
Production: industrial, 87–88
Propaganda, 5, 81, 120; CCP, 10, 37, 45, 60–61, 79, 153, 251; Mao Zedong and, 26, 30, 198–99; anti-U.S., 51–52; GMD, 71, 152, 187
Protests, 55; anti-state, 65, 272; student movement, 99–100, 101–3
Prostitution, 90–91, 277f
"Protect Chairman Mao" (song), 110
Public sector, 276
Pudong (Shanghai), 251

Qian Zhongshu: Weicheng, 97–98
Qing dynasty, 91f, 99, 270
Qingdao: U.S. base at, 187–88, 253
Qinghai, 302
Qinling Mountains, 254
Qu Baiyin: Train to the South, 247

Railway workers, 142
Railways, 173, 174–75, 177
Rao Shushi, 136, 275
Rape: by U.S. Marine, 101, 140, 356n61
Rebellion: on Taiwan, 154–55
Recruitment, 142, 149; PLA, 112–13, 276
Rectification campaign, 109, 111, 132
Red Army, 53, 112, 120, 269
Refugees, 53, 22, 290; foreign, 95f; in Shanghai, 249–50
Regency: of Dalai Lama, 93–94
Religious groups, 125, 264, 274, 297
Ren Bishi, 11, 38, 40f, 44, 57, 111, 118, 136, 199, 259, 321f, 325, 340nn11, 12, 352n13; CCP role, 62f; and Soviet Union, 119, 166; on military strategy, 152f, 171; and government organization, 229, 234, 261
Republic of China, 215, 290
Resolution Committees (Taiwan), 155
Reting, 93
Revenues: GMD, 87–88
Revolution, 5, 330; foreign influences on, 21–22
Revolutionary Committee of the Chinese GMD, 192
Revolutionary Military Committee, 111
Richardson, Hugh, 93
Roshchin, Nikolai, 163f, 221, 301, 311
Ru River, 171
Rural areas, 20, 277; ethnicity in, 17–18; CCP defections in, 61–62; GMD in, 79–81, 82–83; peasant resistance in,

81–82; in Manchuria, 84, 125; CCP and, 107–8, 130–31, 279–81, 321; market production, 134–35. *See also* Land reform; Villages
Rusk, Dean, 291
Russians, 95, 249

Sabotage, 262
Sabri, Mesut, 92
Sakhalin Islands, 313
Salt production, 12, 114, 135
Samphel, Thubten, 93
Sanqingtuan (GMD youth corps), 71f, 100
Savings: forced, 275
Secessionism: of ethnic minorities, 118–19, 288f
Second Field Army, 241
Secret History of the Qing Court (film), 99
Secret societies, 125, 274, 297
Security: CCP government, 270–71
7th Army Group (GMD), 202, 206
ShaanGan Ning army, 111, 134, 152f, 352n5
Shaanxi province, 5, 29, 153, 254, 338n22
Shan States, 301–2
Shandong, 12, 23, 43, 47, 177, 189; battles in, 46, 157–59; peasant resistance in, 82, 355n51; land reform in, 133–34
Shandong army, 112
Shandong Mountains, 158
Shangduji, 209
Shanghai, 21, 36, 76f, 96, 99, 143, 242, 299; GMD control of, 24–25, 70f, 73f, 183, 246–47, 250–51; Japanese attack on, 28f; student protests in, 56, 100; CCP in, 62, 143, 247–48, 249–50, 251–53, 262; women in, 90f; GMD reform in, 184–85; U.S. influence on, 237–38; Jiang Jieshi and, 239, 248–49; prostitution in, 277f
Shanghai Country Club, 250
Shanghai Shen Xin Number Nine Mill, 91
Shanhaiguan, 155
Shanxhi province, 39, 46, 82, 135
Shanxi, 133, 189–90, 254
Shao Lizi, 237, 240
Shen Dong, 356n61
Shen Junru, 265
Shenyang (Mukden), 173, 176ff, 190, 192, 197, 235
Shi Tuo: *Jiehun*, 97
Shuangduji, 206
Sichuan province, 255, 284, 286
Simic, Stanoje, 234
Sino-Soviet Treaty of Friendship, Alliance and Mutual Assistance, 315
Siping, 156–57, 173, 177–78, 323

Siping County, 17, 32; battles in, 36, 40–41
Sisterhoods, 91
Socialism, 23, 111
Song Meiling (Soong Mei-ling, Mme. Chiang Kai-shek), 24f, 159, 187, 198
Song Qingling (Soong Ch'ing-ling), 24, 234
Song Ziwen (T.V. Soong), 159f, 164
Songhua River, 64
South China: CCP in, 46, 111, 270, 277, 279–80, 282–85, 288
South Korea, 319, 321
Southeast Asia, 301–2
Southwest China, 8, 119, 282, 288, 352n5
Soviet Communist Party, 268f
Soviet-Japanese War, 83
Soviet Union, 18, 22, 28, 35, 57, 60, 123, 160, 259, 352n7; and CCP, 8, 10, 23, 26, 31, 38, 49–50, 53, 57, 119–20, 175, 216–18, 228–29, 231–34, 253ff, 262–63, 265–69; and Manchuria, 36, 56, 63, 83, 124–25, 173f; Lin Biao in, 36–37; and United States, 52, 108, 362n13; and GMD, 65, 161–64; Muslim nationalists and, 91–92; and Mao Zedong, 165–67, 244, 310–11, 318–19; Li Zongren and, 220–21; and government organization, 235–36; and Xinjiang, 288–89; and PRC, 305, 308–9, 310, 311–17; and Korea, 318–19, 320f
Spring River Flows East (film), 70, 346n4
Springtime in a Little Town (*Xiaocheng zhi chun*) (film), 99
Stalin, Joseph, 23, 35, 120–21, 163, 288, 306; and CCP, 26, 31, 216–17, 265f, 269, 359n43; and China, 49f, 234–35; and Mao Zedong, 52, 167–68, 232–33, 234, 236, 253, 262–63, 305, 311–14, 317–18, 354n28, 380n46; and GMD, 65, 162; and Liu Shaoqi, 267f; and Korean War, 320f, 322f
Stalinism, 119
State, 3–4, 18
Stevenson, Ralph, 241
Street committees, 274
Strikes, 75–76, 77, 143
Strong, Anna Louise, 2, 152
Strongmen, 113, 125, 239
Struggle sessions, 132
Stuart, John Leighton, 50, 185, 220, 241, 306
Student movement, 55f, 77, 99–100, 138; CCP and, 78, 140–42; protests, 101–3
Students: CCP and, 276–77
Su Yu, 240, 245, 299; HuaiHai campaign, 201–2, 205, 207–8

Summer Palace, 259
Sun Fo, 216, 239f
Sun Liren, 291
Sun Yixian (Sun Yat-sen), 23f, 234, 239
Sungari, 157
Supplies, 160, 186; army, 4–5, 51; for
    PLA, 113–14, 166; for Shanghai,
    252–53; to Vietminh, 316–17
Supreme Military Council (GMD), 71, 147
Surplus property: U.S. transfers of, 51, 87
Suxian, 203, 206
Suzhou Creek, 251
Syngman Rhee, 319

Tai'erzhuang, 202
Taikang, 249
Taiping rebellion, 19
Taiwan, 2, 118, 186, 262, 267, 330; Jiang
    Jieshi and, 58–59, 154f, 181, 239, 249,
    255, 288, 289–90, 291–93, 303; GMD
    on, 289–91; CCP and, 299, 324
Taiwan Strait: U.S. protection of, 292, 324
Taiyuan, 189, 254
Taktra, 93f
Tan Zhenlin, 158–59, 207–8, 285
Tang Enbo, 233, 241f, 246–47, 248
Tang Tsou, 2
Tangshan, 142, 192
Tao Zhiyue, 289
Taxation, 114, 117, 183, 275; GMD and,
    73–74, 87
Temple of Heaven, 223
Ten Thousand Rays of Light (*Wanjia
    denghuo*) (film), 99
Terrorism, 127–28, 133–34, 136, 250
Third Field Army, 241, 352n5
Third International (Comintern), 22
Three Diligencies, 140
Three Processes, 140
Tian Tao: *Wotu*, 98
Tianan'men, 271–72
Tianjin, 21, 77, 197, 200, 210, 221f, 224;
    GMD in, 73f; CCP, 142f, 216, 262,
    302–3, 308; PLA attack on, 225–26,
    227, 364n32; working class activism in,
    273–74, 275
Tibet, Tibetans, 91, 92–94, 119, 330; CCP
    in, 302–3, 304, 321
Tikhvinskii, Sergei, 310
Time (magazine), 186
Topping, Seymour, 204
Torture, 134
Trade: foreign, 254, 305, 379n35
Train to the South (Qu Baiyin), 247
Treaties: Sino-Soviet, 235–36, 313, 315,
    379n35

Treaty of Friendship, Commerce, and Nav-
    igation (U.S.-China), 51
Treaty ports, 94
Truman, Harry S., 31, 43, 94, 291f, 324;
    on U.S.-Chinese relations, 49f, 60, 159,
    185–88, 198, 216, 307
Truman Doctrine, 159, 160–61
12th Army Group, 206f

Uighur, 91, 289
Underground party, 140
Unions, *see* Labor unions
United Front, 23, 26, 28, 31, 40, 57, 116,
    120, 262; Mao Zedong and, 29f; Zhou
    Enlai and, 138, 191
United Front Bureau, 263–64
United Nations, 303, 305, 309–10, 316
United Nations Relief and Rehabilitation
    Administration (UNRRA), 87
United States, 7, 18, 35, 94, 169, 279, 303;
    GMD and, 8f, 31–32, 50–51, 86–87,
    159–61, 162, 164, 185–88, 190,
    197–98, 216, 291–92; Jiang Jieshi and,
    41–42, 43–45, 53–54, 182; and China,
    49, 50–51, 60, 237–38; Mao Zedong
    and, 51–52, 343n50; and Soviet Union,
    65, 108, 362n13; Beijing rape and, 101,
    140; and CCP, 234, 237, 245, 253,
    306–8, 315, 378n25; and Shanghai, 247,
    251; and Taiwan, 291–92, 324; and
    PRC, 305f, 310, 317; Korean War and,
    321–22
U.S. Congress, 186–87
U.S. Export-Import Bank, 160
U.S. Marines, 187–88, 356n61
UNRRA, *see* United Nations Relief and
    Rehabilitation Administration
Urban areas, 21, 71, 229; films and,
    98–99; CCP in, 137–38. *See also various
    cities by name*
Urban Work Department, 142
Urumqi, 92, 289
Utley, Freda, 2

Vandenberg, Arthur, 161
Versailles Treaty, 23
Vietminh, 301; CCP aid to, 316–17
Vietnam, 22, 83, 287, 301; CCP and,
    316–18, 324
Villages, 126; and land reform, 10–11,
    136; CCP policies in, 128–32

Wang Guangmei, 274
Wang Jiaxiang, 268, 310
Wang Shijie (Wang Shih-chieh), 160,
    181–82

Ward, Angus, 307
Ward Case, 307
Warlords, 124, 237
Weapons: PLA, 112, 123, 175, 232; Soviet, 235, 352n7
Wedemeyer, Albert, 160f
Wedemeyer Mission, 161
Wei Lihuang, 190, 195ff
Wei Valley, 190f
Weicheng (Fortress Besieged) (*Qian Zhongshu*), 97
Wen Yiduo, 45, 54
West-Advancing Army, 196
Western China, 279–80
Western Enterprises, 292
White, Theodore, 2
"White areas": CCP strategies in, 138–39
Winter Offensive, 175–77
Women: societal role of, 90–91, 279
Women's associations, 131
Women's movement, 265
Workers' committees, 264–65
Working class: labor unrest and, 75–77; CCP and, 142–43, 273–75
World War II, 7; impacts of, 28–30
Wotu (Rich Soil) (Tian Tao), 98
Writers, 96f
Wu Guozhen (K. C. Wu), 246–47, 248, 290
Wu Kaixian, 76
Wu Kehua, 177
Wu Ruilin, 177
Wuhan, 21, 77, 90, 95, 270; and GMD, 24, 183; CCP and, 47, 62
Wusong, 251

Xiamen, 73
Xi'an, 28, 254
Xiang Hills (Xiangshan), 259f
Xiaohe, 171
Xiaqiu Zhuan (The Tale of Shrimpball) (Gu Liu), 98
Xibaipo, 188, 198–99, 203, 209, 217, 225, 239, 309
Xinbao'an, 223–24
Xinhua, 204
Xinjiang, 93, 315, 330; GMD in, 8, 82, 91–92; PLA in, 266f; CCP in, 288–89
Xinlitun, 177
Xiong Shihui (Hsiung Shih-hui), 84f, 157, 172
Xiong Xianghui, 142
Xiyuan Airport, 259
Xu Shiyou, 158–59
Xu Xiangqian, 254
Xuzhou, 190, 207; CCP campaign and,

192, 206; GMD defense of, 199–200, 202–3, 204

Yalta Agreement, 313
Yan Huiqing, 237, 248
Yan Xishan, 287
Yan'an: GMD capture of, 151–52
Yan'an period, 5–6, 30, 58, 115; regional control, 45–49; internal politics of, 59–60
Yang Shangkun, 111
Yangmingshan, 249, 290
Yangzi River, 242, 246; as strategic goal, 199, 202, 221; Soviet Union and, 217f
Yanjing University, 140, 224
Yellow River: PLA offensive across, 168ff
Yi County: CCP offensive in, 194–95
Yi Guan Dao, 274
Yili Valley, 92, 289
Yingkou, 177, 195
Yixian-Zaozhuang region, 157–58
Youth Corps, 77
Youth organizations, 264; GMD, 71f, 100
Yunnan province, 82f, 288–89, 302
YWCA, 91

Zaolin'gou, 153
Zhang Dingcheng, 47
Zhang Jia'ao, 84
Zhang Junmai, 55, 84
Zhang Shizhao, 240
Zhang Wentian, 124, 229, 352–53n13
Zhang Xuesi, 124
Zhang Zhizhong (Chang Chih-chung), 92, 237, 240, 289, 368–69n54
Zhangjiakou (Kalgan), 48, 223f
Zhanzhuan, 203
Zhejiang, 181
Zheng Dongguo, 190
Zhongnanhai, 260, 308
Zhou Enlai, 35, 41–42, 57, 59–60, 111, 142, 174, 209, 259, 305, 352n13, 368–69n54; CCP strategy and, 44–45, 139–40; and United States, 52, 378n25; and United Front, 138, 191; military strategies of, 153, 171, 222, 225, 282; political work of, 191–92; and government organization, 229, 234f, 261, 263–64, 265, 269; GMD negotiations and, 239f; and Shanghai, 247, 252; and Vietnam, 301, 317–18; and foreign policy, 308f; and Soviet Union, 311, 314, 323
Zhou Fucheng, 224
Zhu De, 111, 153, 209, 259, 352n13
Zhu Xuefan, 76